Theologia Cambrensis

Protestant Religion and Theology in Wales,
Volume 1: 1588-1760

From Reformation to Revival

D. DENSIL MORGAN

D1452803

UNIVERSITY OF WALES PRESS

2018

www.uwp.co.uk

British Library CIP Data
A catalogue record for this book is available from the British Library.

ISBN: 978-1-78683-237-5 (hardback)
978-1-78683-238-2 (paperback)
e-ISBN: 978-1-78683-239-9

The University of Wales Press acknowledges the financial support of the University of Wales Trinity Saint David.

Typeset by Marie Doherty
Printed by CPI Antony Rowe, Melksham

Er cof am
Blodwen Mair Rees (1928–2011)
Edgar Rees (1931–2014)

Contents

Preface

Theologia Cambrensis is a two-volume survey of Protestant theology and religion in Wales from 1588, the year of the publication of the Bible in Welsh, to the dawn of the twentieth century. The present volume, *1588–1760: From Reformation to Revival*, covers the period between the reign of Elizabeth I to the Civil Wars, the impact of Puritan theology and the development of Welsh Anglicanism, the emergence of the Dissenting tradition and, despite mutual tensions, the way in which Churchmen and Dissenters made common cause where possible on the basis of a shared Protestant faith. The narrative proceeds to analyse the way in which High Church teaching and its accompanying sacramentalism impacted popular piety, delineates the growing influence of continental Pietism through the work of the Society for the Promotion of Christian Knowledge (the SPCK), and portrays the immense significance of Griffith Jones, rector of Llanddowror. This included not only his well-known educational exertions through the circulating schools, but the dissemination of an explicitly Reformed theology through the immense popularity of his catechisms and expository publications. The eighteenth century witnessed doctrinal rifts between High Calvinists and Arminians within Protestant Dissent, though an evangelistically vibrant moderate Calvinism came to enshrine a norm which would contribute richly to the post-1735 Evangelical Revival. The volume concludes with an assessment of the initial phase of the Revival, the emergence of the Methodist movement, and evaluates both the continuity and the change which had occurred in the century and three-quarters since the publication of William Morgan's Bible in 1588.

This is the first assessment to concentrate explicitly on theology since 1900, when the Calvinistic Methodist scholar William Evans published his *An Outline of the History of Welsh Theology*. Although social historians have never been oblivious to theological concerns, while historians of religion have been obliged to take doctrinal matters seriously, it is surprising that a full-scale history of Protestant theology *per se* has not been attempted for well over a century. Some, though by no mean all, of the texts analysed in the following narrative have been studied by scholars of Welsh literature, but their interest has been more in style, rhetoric and linguistic expression than in their theological content. Readers will readily perceive the enormity of my debt to generations of social, religious and literary scholars who have written in both Welsh and English, but the focus of the work is on theology or the way in which Welsh Protestants understood, contemplated and conveyed the truths of the Christian revelation to their contemporaries.

In his superb *Essay on the Development of Christian Doctrine* (1878), the great nineteenth-century Catholic theologian John Henry Newman claimed, notoriously, that '[t]o be deep in history is to cease to be a Protestant'. Apart from such radical innovators as William Erbury and Morgan Llwyd who were convinced that the end of history was at hand, this view would not have endeared itself to the bulk of those whose work will be evaluated in the following chapters. They all believed that the God who had caused Holy Scripture to be translated into Welsh and sent forth the gospel message of justification by faith alone, was uniquely active in the story of the people that they had been called to serve. For them, to be Protestant *was* to be steeped in the historical process. As well as providing an appraisal of the way in which their convictions and formulations developed in Wales between the Reformation and the Evangelical Revival, I hope that the exposition of these numerous, and for the most part little-known texts, will serve as a contribution to a contemporary *ressourcement* theology, inspiring fresh reflection on the riches of the past along with their creative application to the challenges of the present. As well as being an exercise in historical theology, it aims at providing a modest contribution to practical theology as well.

A preface always affords an author the pleasure of listing his indebtedness to others. Professor David Bebbington of the University of Stirling convinced me that this was a project worth undertaking and one in which readers beyond Wales would be interested; this is only one of the many kindnesses that he has shown me over the years. Professor John Coffey of the University of Leicester and Dr R. Brinley Jones, president of the University of Wales Trinity Saint David, gave me the benefit of their wide erudition in their specific fields of expertise, English

Puritanism and the Civil Wars in the one case and Renaissance thought in Wales in the other, while Dr Eryn Mant White of Aberystwyth University undertook the onerous task of reading the typescript in its entirety. Her comments have been invaluable, many of which have been incorporated into the finished text. I am also indebted to the very positive account supplied by the University of Wales Press's anonymous reader. Although I have benefitted enormously by all suggestions made by these scholars, it goes without saying that the interpretation which follows, and all accompanying mistakes and weaknesses, are wholly my own.

My gratitude to the University of Wales Press for undertaking the publication of *Theologia Cambrensis* is considerable. Initial support by Helgard Krause, then director of the Press, was invaluable, while Llion Wigley and his colleagues, Dafydd Jones, Siân Chapman, Elin Nesta Lewis and Elin Williams, have shown unfailing skill, kindness and professionalism throughout all stages of the process. Publication would not have been possible without the generous financial support of the University of Wales Trinity Saint David, for which I am sincerely appreciative. A warm thanks to all who have supported the venture.

Unless otherwise noted, all translations from Welsh are my own. For the English sources, spelling, punctuation and capitalization have been modernized throughout, but not in the titles of early printed books.

D. Densil Morgan
January 2018

Abbreviations

BQ	*The Baptist Quarterly*
BBCS	*Bulletin of the Board of Celtic Studies*
CA	*Carmarthenshire Antiquary*
CH	*Cylchgrawn Hanes. Journal of the Historical Society of the Presbyterian Church of Wales*
CCH	*Cylchgrawn Cymdeithas Hanes y Methodistiaid Calfinaidd*
DWB	*Dictionary of Welsh Biography*
JBS	*Journal of British Studies*
JEH	*Journal of Ecclesiastical History*
JHSCW	*Journal of the Historical Society of the Church in Wales*
JMHRS	*Journal of the Merioneth Historical and Record Society*
JWBS	*Journal of the Welsh Bibliographical Society*
JWEH	*Journal of Welsh Ecclesiastical History*
JWRH	*Journal of Welsh Religious History*
JTS	*Journal of Theological Studies*
NLW	National Library of Wales
NLWJ	*National Library of Wales Journal*
ODNB	*Oxford Dictionary of National Biography*
PRJ	*Puritan Reformed Journal*
TCAS	*Transactions of the Carmarthenshire Antiquary Society and Field Club*
TCHB	*Trafodion Cymdeithas Hanes y Bedyddwyr*
TCHS	*Transactions of the Caernarfonshire Historical Society*
THSC	*Transactions of the Honourable Society of Cymmrodorion*
TRHS	*Transactions of the Royal Historical Society*
WHR	*Welsh History Review*

Introduction:
The Bible in Welsh

In a text which has been described as the 'manifesto of the Renaissance and Welsh Protestant humanism',[1] the scholar William Salesbury (*c.*1520–*c.*1584) called his compatriots to do everything within their power to secure the Word of God in their own tongue:

> Insist on having learning in your own language ... Insist on having the Holy Scriptures in your own tongue ... Make barefoot pilgrimage to his Grace the King and his Council and ask leave to have the Holy Scriptures in your own language.[2]

A young man from Denbighshire's Vale of Clwyd, he had been inspired by the twin ideals of Protestant Biblicism and humanist reform while at Oxford and subsequently at the Inns of Court.[3] Clearly Salesbury was exceptionally talented. He was said, during his academic training, to have mastered Latin, Greek and Hebrew as well as French and German. Certainly Hebrew, an essential tool for biblical scholarship, had been taught at Oxford by Robert Wakefield, canon of Christ Church and King's lecturer in Hebrew, since 1530, and following his death in 1537, by John Shepreve of Corpus Christi and Thomas Harding, fellow of New College.[4] Whatever the detail of his scholarly formation, Salesbury's remarkable publishing programme of the late 1540s and early 1550s included the first Welsh translation of the epistles and gospels of the Book of Common Prayer entitled *Kynniver Llith a Ban* ('So many Lessons and Verses') (1551). With the gradual transition from Latin in the liturgy during the latter years of Henry VIII and in 1549, under the reforms of Edward VI, the required use in all parish churches of the English Book of Common Prayer, no provision had been made for a version in Welsh.[5] As the vast majority of the Welsh populace had no English, an English version would have been as unintelligible as the former liturgy in Latin. Salesbury took it upon himself to translate the designated scriptural passages and appeal to the bishops of the four Welsh sees and the diocese of Hereford, which included at the time many Welsh-speaking parishes, to encourage its use 'so that the Word of God be allowed to go forth freely throughout our localities'.[6] Consequently, during the reign of Edward VI and before the reversal of Protestant fortunes with the accession to the throne of the Catholic Mary in 1553, substantial parts of the New Testament were available in the vernacular in order for the mission of God, as Salesbury would have it, to succeed among the people of Wales.

It was one thing to have the scriptural portions of the liturgy in Welsh. It was quite another to have the whole Bible, along with a complete Book of Common Prayer, in the common tongue. However, with the accession of Elizabeth as a Protestant monarch following Mary's death in 1558, the Privy Council was petitioned, probably by Salesbury, to make such a provision, and by April 1563 an act of parliament had been passed stipulating that the four Welsh bishops and the bishop of Hereford take responsibility for the translation of the Bible and Prayer Book into Welsh by 1 March 1567.[7] The single Welsh bishop who was academically best equipped and theologically most committed to take the task forward was Richard Davies (?1501–81), a native of the Conwy Valley, Caernarfonshire, a graduate of New Inn Hall, Oxford, and during the Marian persecution an exile for the Protestant cause in Frankfurt.[8] He had been appointed by Queen Elizabeth to the diocese of St Asaph early in 1560 and translated to the see of St David's by September of the following year. It was he, along with a few like-minded colleagues, including the humanist antiquary Humphrey Lhuyd, MP for Denbigh, who had facilitated the act's passage through parliament, and now was engaged himself in the work of translation. Having contacted William Salesbury, the two men worked out a schedule with Davies turning his hand to I Timothy, Hebrews, James and I and II Peter, and Salesbury translating the rest of the New Testament apart from the Book of Revelation which was delegated to a Breconshire clergyman, Thomas Huet, a graduate of Corpus Christi College, Oxford, and canon precentor of St David's Cathedral. Even to have completed the New Testament by the assigned date would have been quite a feat, but by the end of

1566 Salesbury was in London overseeing the printing of the Book of Common Prayer replete with the Book of Psalms, all of which he had put into Welsh himself. Publication occurred in May 1567 and it has been estimated that soon over a thousand copies had been printed and distributed.[9] If the text of the Prayer Book was translated directly from Thomas Cranmer's English version, the scriptural portions (and the Psalter)[10] bear the marks of Salesbury's meticulous scholarship having been rendered into Welsh not only from Erasmus's pioneering versions of the modern Greek texts published between 1516 and 1522 but the more recent editions collated by the Paris scholar Robert Estienne and Geneva's Theodore Beza.[11]

Whereas the Prayer Book and Psalter were issued in May, the New Testament appeared in October. It was prefaced by the celebrated *Epistol E[sgob] M[ynyw] at y Cembru*, Bishop Richard Davies's 'Epistle to the Welsh',[12] his great apologia in favour of the reformed faith as being not only scripturally pure and theologically sound but as representing the historic creed of the Welsh people. In what would become a massively influential theory, he claimed that the faith of the Elizabethan establishment was the true Catholicism, a renewal of the old Celtic Church which had been instituted in the apostolic age through the missionary endeavours of Joseph of Arimathea, a disciple of Christ. This church had remained evangelistically vibrant and scripturally pure until the seventh century when it was corrupted by Augustine of Canterbury, the apostle to the English, who represented the corrosive influence of Rome. Despite pretensions to the contrary, this Romanized religion was neither genuine nor chaste; neither was it authentically Welsh. It was, in fact, *ffydd y Sayson* ('the faith of the English'),[13] while the creed of the forefathers, the original inhabitants of the Isle of Britain, had been 'an unadulterated religion, pure Christianity, a fruitful and purposeful faith'.[14] It was this original Christianity, biblically informed and purged of Roman corruption, which was being restored to the realm by Elizabeth, the sovereign queen. An 'audacious rewriting of history'[15] this may have been; it was also 'a *tour de force* of Protestant propaganda'[16] which created perhaps the most potent religious myth in modern Welsh history, that Welsh Protestantism was in direct continuity with the ancient Celtic past and that the very identity of the Welsh nation was bound up with the reformed, biblical faith.[17] 'Implicit in the whole tone and approach of this "Letter" was the conception that it was the Reformation, and the translation of the scriptures, which constituted the great purpose for which God had been preserving the Welsh people and their language.'[18] It was a theme that would resonate in the Welsh consciousness for centuries to come.

Despite the remarkable feat of producing both the New Testament and the Prayer Book within the short span of four years, the directive to produce the whole Bible in the vernacular remained unfulfilled. There were also glaring problems with the version of each of the texts that had been produced. On the basis of scholarship, Salesbury's translation of the New Testament was superb. Nevertheless, as a means of making the Word of God understood by the people, it would prove deeply problematic.[19] Although there is evidence that the new Welsh version of the Scriptures was used in worship, not everyone was happy with the result. The radical Puritan John Penry, writing in 1588, described the typical worship service with which he had been acquainted as a youth:

> A few psalms, a few prayers, with one chapter of the New Testament in Welsh (for the Old never spake Welsh in our days) … most pitiably evil read of the reader, and not understood of one among ten of the hearers.[20]

Even a less jaundiced critic, the loyal churchman Maurice Kyffin, complained: 'There was such a broad accent and many strange and alien words in the printed version that the ear of any true Welshman could not bear to listen to it.'[21] The problem was, that as a humanist scholar, Salesbury was determined to show how the Welsh words used in the text derived from Greek or Latin roots. Rather than writing words phonetically, or, indeed, according to the standard orthography that was employed by the bards, he retained forms which approximated most closely their classical originals. For instance, rather than using the normal Welsh word for 'church', *eglwys*, he would write *eccles* following the Greek. Similarly, for 'disciple' he would use *discupl*, echoing the Latin *discipulus* rather than the everyday Welsh word *disgybl*. 'God', for Salesbury, was always *Deo*, the Latin form, rather than the word that everybody used, *Duw*. 'The notion that a word should be spelt as it was pronounced struck Salesbury as incredibly stupid.'[22] Also, according to humanist usage, he would supply as many alternatives to individual words as was possible, if not in the text in the copious notes that were printed in the margins. If this provided the listener with a rich variety of different readings, it placed a heavy burden on those whose responsibility it was to read the text aloud, namely the often ill-educated parish clergy. And if this were not enough, Salesbury was seriously averse to including mutated forms of words which widened the gulf between his text and the language of the common people even farther: in everyday Welsh mutations were and are universal. To be fair, it is inconceivable that he intended the text to be spoken as it was written. He almost inevitably expected the clergy to express the words according to normal everyday use. Also, beneath these orthographical quirks, the translation, on the whole, reads very well. Salesbury obviously had a feel for the rhythms of the spoken language as well as a profound scholarly knowledge of the literary forms; once one becomes used to the strangeness of the text, its qualities, even now, shine forth. Nevertheless on the lips of a largely ill-trained clergy who had not been purposefully instructed, it was the eccentricities of the translation rather than its virtues that were most obvious. By the 1570s, however, the New Testament and the Prayer Book liturgy were available in Welsh which means that one of the prime ideals of the Protestant Reformation had been partially fulfilled. There was, alas, much more that needed to be done.

Initially Richard Davies and William Salesbury persevered with the task of translating the rest of the Bible, the Apocrypha as well as the Old Testament, but around 1575 irreconcilable differences of approach – according to Sir John Wynn of Gwydir a dispute over the right translation of a single word – caused a rift between them: 'Davies, if less a scholar than Salesbury was also less of a pedant, and ... as a shepherd of souls was much more closely attuned to the practical needs of the parish priest and his parishioners'.[23] In fact, his contributions to the New Testament had been much plainer and easy to read than those of his colleague's. Not only did the partnership end but the prospects of completing the task were in danger of being jeopardized. The bishop, already in his seventies and still the administrative and spiritual head of a large and needy diocese, died in 1581 while Salesbury, a much younger man, published nothing else of a religious nature and died, it is thought, sometime after 1584.[24] Fortunately, however, there was a third figure waiting in the wings whose contribution to the project of translating the Bible into Welsh would be even more significant. His name was William Morgan.

More will be written of Morgan's contribution to the forging of a theological consensus in the late Elizabethan church in Chapter One. Suffice it to state here that since 1578 he had been the incumbent of the parish of Llanrhaedr-ym-Mochnant in the northern part of mid Wales and had already begun completing the work that Davies and Salesbury had commenced.[25] A graduate of St John's College, Cambridge, and soon to be awarded the DD degree from his university, it is supposed that he had already been sounded out as a possible successor in the task of translation by Richard Davies who had appointed him to the sinecure living of Llanbadarn Fawr in the diocese of St David's in 1572. Following Davies's death, he had submitted a draft of his work to the two north Wales bishops, his present diocesan at St Asaph (and Cambridge contemporary) William Hughes, and Nicholas Robinson of Bangor, both of whom were competent Welsh scholars, and gaining their approval carried on with the work.[26] It was the Welsh bishops after all, and their associate in Hereford, who had been tasked with producing the whole Welsh Bible nearly two decades before. Being informed of this development, John Whitgift, Archbishop of Canterbury, provided considerable practical and financial support: it is possible that they had known one another in Cambridge or during Whitgift's time as vice-president of the Council of the Marches between 1577 and 1583 when he served as bishop of Worcester.[27] For the archbishop, the need to finish the task was given added impetus following the publication of the *Aequity* (1587), John Penry's scathing attack on the hierarchy's failure to provide preaching and the Bible in Welsh.[28]

By then, perhaps unbeknown to Penry, the Bible was ready to go to press. It had been completed in the summer of 1587 and Morgan had spent virtually the following year in London overseeing its publication. The result was 1,222 folio pages in black print on fine French paper along with an ornate and beautiful title page. It had been produced by Christopher Barker, the Queen's printer, and handsomely bound in leather. A thousand copies were produced to be sold at a pound each. The product would prove remarkable. Like Salesbury's New Testament, its scholarship was impeccable. Morgan had worked with the 1524–5 Venice edition of the Hebrew text complemented by the Antwerp edition of 1572,[29] completing the task single handed in a remote country rectory far from Oxford colleges or Cambridge libraries. Not only that, but he had 'revised the New Testament purging it of its inaccuracies, of which there were many' as he had explained in the introduction to his work.[30] In short, he provided the whole of the Bible in the most exquisite, noble yet accessible Welsh prose. A magisterial expertise in Hebrew and Greek and an encyclopaedic knowledge of the ancient bardic tradition were blended with sensitivity to the rhythms of pure, spoken Welsh to create a masterpiece:

At a fateful juncture for the language, when the bards, hitherto the guardians and exponents of its classical strengths and purity, had entered into a period of irreversible and accelerating decline, Morgan embodied in his translation all that was best and finest in that tradition.[31]

As scholarly as Salesbury's volume, it possessed a clarity and eloquence of its own: 'Whereas Salesbury's translations seemed like a verdant jungle through which the reader had to hack his way, Morgan's work was more like a formal garden whose very order gave an added pleasure to its beauty, symmetry and scent.'[32] On 22 September 1588 the Privy Council, directed by Whitgift, ordered that the bishops of Hereford and Wales be informed 'that the translation of the Bible into the Welsh or British tongue, which by act of parliament should long since have been done, is now performed by a Doctor Morgan and set forth in print'.[33] A copy was to be purchased by every Welsh-speaking parish and used in worship forthwith.

The significance of having the Bible in virile, readable Welsh cannot be overemphasized. Although the pace of reform would be slow, it would help secure the acceptance of the Protestant Reformation in a conservatively inclined, formerly steadfastly Catholic part of the realm. Henry VIII's constitutional changes had been only tepidly received, Edward VI's renovations had hardly registered and there was danger that Wales would revert wholly to the Old Faith even after the death of Mary Tudor.[34] For Protestantism to be embraced rather than resented and despised, Elizabeth's ecclesiastical policies needed to win the people over. The appointment of pastorally effective, native-born bishops who would be resident in their sees had been essential, while Richard Davies's brilliant *coup* in convincing Welsh Christians that the new establishment was in continuity with the ancient Celtic Church – in his introduction to the New Testament, William Salesbury had referred to Davies as 'a second St David' (*ail Dewi Menew*)[35] – assisted in securing those gains. Now having the whole Bible in Welsh, and by 1599 Morgan's revised translation of the Book of Common Prayer in equally impressive prose,[36] instituted a biblicized faith which, in the fullness of time, won the allegiance of the people.[37] The foundations had been laid for a Protestant culture which would become even more influential following the educational exertions of Griffith Jones in the early eighteenth century and the ensuing Evangelical Revival, while by the nineteenth

century Protestant Nonconformity with its biblical norms would seem
to embody the identity of the Welsh nation.[38] Not only would Welsh
be preserved as a viable language even into the present century, but for
three centuries theological discourse would be a mainstay of the nation's
intellectual life. Our task in the following narrative will be to assess the
nature of this discourse and gauge its significance.

Notes

[1]   Saunders Lewis, 'Damcaniaeth eglwysig Brotestannaidd', in *idem, Meistri'r
       Canrifoedd: Ysgrifau ar Hanes Llenyddiaeth Gymraeg*, ed. R. Geraint Gruffydd
       (Caerdydd: Gwasg Prifysgol Cymru, 1973), pp. 116–39 (127).

[2]   William Salesbury, *Oll Synnwyr pen Kembero ygyd* (1547), ed. J. Gwenogvryn
       Evans (Bangor: Jarvis and Foster, 1902), A. iv; the foreword (Sig. A. ii–v)
       is reproduced in Garfield H. Hughes (ed.), *Rhagymadroddion 1547–1659*
       (Caerdydd: Gwasg Prifysgol Cymru, 1967), pp. 9–16.

[3]   James Pierce, *The Life and Work of William Salesbury, A Rare Scholar*
       (Tal-y-bont: Y Lolfa, 2016); Glanmor Williams, 'The achievement of William
       Salesbury', in *Welsh Reformation Essays* (Cardiff: University of Wales Press,
       1967), pp. 191–205.

[4]   Gareth Lloyd Jones, *The Discovery of Hebrew in Tudor England: A Third
       Language* (Manchester: Manchester University Press, 1983), pp. 182–7,
       199–200; for Wakefield (d.1537), Shepreve (1509–42) and Harding (1516–
       72), see *ODNB*.

[5]   Diarmaid MacCulloch, *Tudor Church Militant: Edward VI and the Protestant
       Reformation* (London: Allen Lane, 1999), p. 81.

[6]   William Salesbury, *Kynniver Llith a Ban* (1551), ed. John Fisher (Cardiff:
       University of Wales Press, 1931), Introduction; for a Welsh version of
       the Latin introduction see Ceri Davies (ed. and trans.), *Rhagymadroddion
       a Chyflwyniadau Lladin, 1551–1632* (Caerdydd: Gwasg Prifysgol Cymru,
       1980), pp. 18–21.

[7]   Glanmor Williams, *Wales and the Reformation* (Cardiff: University of Wales
       Press, 1997), pp. 236–9; Eryn M. White, *The Welsh Bible* (Stroud: Tempus,
       2007), pp. 23–6; the text of the Act is reproduced in Pierce, *A Rare Scholar*,
       Appendix, pp. 372–4.

[8]   Williams, 'Bishop Richard Davies (?1501–81)', in *Welsh Reformation Essays*,
       pp. 155–90.

[9]   R. Geraint Gruffydd, 'The Welsh Book of Common Prayer', *JHSCW*, 17
       (1967), 43–55.

[10]   Gwilym H. Jones, 'The Welsh Psalter of 1567', *JHSCW*, 17 (1967),
       56–61; Isaac Thomas, *Yr Hen Destament Cymraeg* (Aberystwyth: Llyfrgell
       Genedlaethol Cymru, 1988), pp. 83–133.

[11]   Isaac Thomas, *Y Testament Newydd Cymraeg, 1551–1620* (Caerdydd: Gwasg
       Prifysgol Cymru, 1976), pp. 151–205.

12 Richard Davies, 'Richard ... Episcob Menew ... ir Cembru oll', Hughes (ed.), *Rhagymadroddion 1547–1659*, pp. 17–43.

13 Davies, 'Richard ... Episcob Menew ... ir Cembru oll', p. 23.

14 Davies, 'Richard ... Episcob Menew ... ir Cembru oll', p. 18.

15 White, *The Welsh Bible*, p. 28.

16 White, *The Welsh Bible*, p. 29.

17 See Lewis, 'Damcaniaeth eglwysig Brotestannaidd'; Glanmor Williams, *Reformation Views of Church History* (London: Lutterworth Press, 1970), pp. 63–5; Lloyd Bowen, 'The Battle of Britain: History and Reformation in Early Modern Wales', in Tadhg Ó hAnnracháin and Robert Armstrong (eds), *Christianities in the Early Modern Celtic World* (Basingstoke: Palgrave Macmillan, 2014), pp. 135–50.

18 Williams, *Wales and the Reformation*, p. 246.

19 For a spirited and systematic defence of Salesbury's methods of translation, see Pierce, *A Rare Scholar*, *passim*.

20 *An Exhortation unto the Governors and people of Her Majesty's Country of Wales* (1588), in John Penry, *John Penry: Three Treatises Concerning Wales*, ed. and intro. David Williams (Cardiff: University of Wales Press, 1960), pp. 49–98 (56).

21 Maurice Kyffin, foreword to *Deffynniad Ffydd Eglwys Loegr* (1595) in Hughes (ed.), *Rhagymadroddion 1547–1659*, pp. 89–96 (92).

22 R. Geraint Gruffydd, *The Translation of the Bible into the Welsh Tongue* (London: BBC, 1988), pp. 14–15.

23 Williams, 'Bishop Richard Davies (?1501–81)', p. 186.

24 Pierce, *A Rare Scholar*, pp. 276–8.

25 For an excellent précis, see Glanmor Williams, 'Bishop William Morgan and the first Welsh Bible', in *idem*, *The Welsh and their Religion: Historical Essays* (Cardiff: University of Wales Press, 1991), pp. 173–229.

26 Isaac Thomas, *William Morgan and his Bible* (Cardiff: University of Wales Press, 1988), pp. 42–6; for Hughes (d.1600) and Robinson (*c*.1530–85), see *ODNB*.

27 Glanmor Williams, 'William Morgan's Bible and the Cambridge connection', *WHR*, 14 (1989), 363–79.

28 *The Aequity of an Humble Supplication ... unto Her Majesty and this High Court of Parliament in the behalf of the Country of Wales* (1587), in Penry, *Three Treatises Concerning Wales*, pp. 1–45.

29 Thomas, *Yr Hen Destament Cymraeg*, pp. 174–254.

30 '*Y Beibl Cyssegr-lan* (1588): cyflwyniad i'r Frenhines Elisabeth I', in Davies (ed. and trans.), *Rhagymadroddion a Chyflwyniadau Lladin, 1551–1632*, pp. 64–70 (67).

31 Williams, *Wales and the Reformation*, p. 353.

32 Gruffydd, *The Translation of the Bible into the Welsh Tongue*, p. 26.

33 Quoted by Williams, *Wales and the Reformation*, p. 351.

34 See Katherine K. Olson, '"Slow and cold in the true service of God": Popular beliefs and practice, conformity and reformation in Wales, c. 1530–c. 1600',

in Ó hAnnracháin and Armstrong (eds), *Christianities in the Early Modern Celtic World*, pp. 92–110.

[35]   William Salesbury, 'At yr oll Cembru', Hughes (ed.), *Rhagymadroddion 1547–1659*, pp. 44–5 [44].

[36]   Williams, *Wales and the Reformation*, pp. 384–5; *idem*, 'Bishop William Morgan and the first Welsh Bible', pp. 217–22.

[37]   See Peter R. Roberts, 'The union with England and the identity of "Anglican" Wales', *TRHS*, 5th series, 22 (1972), 49–70.

[38]   See White, *The Welsh Bible*, pp. 73–122; Glanmor Williams, 'Language, literacy and nationality in Wales', in *idem*, *Religion, Language and Nationality in Wales* (Cardiff: University of Wales Press, 1979), pp. 127–47.

1

1588–1642

Theology in Wales and the late Elizabethan Church, c.1588–c.1603

The first significant contribution to the dissemination of reformed theology in Wales was the work of Maurice Kyffin (c.1555–98). The eldest child of a distinguished family from Oswestry, Shropshire, Kyffin was steeped in the Welsh bardic tradition. Following bardic training at the hand of the master poet Wiliam Llŷn, he migrated to London and by 1578 was employed as tutor to the household of Thomas Sackville, Lord Buckhurst, the first earl of Dorset. His first published work, *The Blessedness of Britain* (1587), was a thirty-three stanza poem celebrating the virtues of Queen Elizabeth, not least her championing of the true faith according to the Scriptures and, in Wales, the preaching of the gospel in the vernacular. It was written in the wake of the Babington Plot which sought to assassinate Elizabeth and transfer the throne to her cousin, the Catholic Mary Queen of Scots. A year later Kyffin published an English prose translation of the comedy *Andria* by the Latin dramatist Terence. By then he was no longer in the employ of Buckhurst but in the civil service and abroad, first as surveyor of the muster rolls and then, in 1591, in Normandy as vice-treasurer to the forces. It was during this period that he began his most ambitious literary project to date, the translation into sonorous Welsh of the *Apologia Ecclesiae Anglicanae* (1562), Bishop John Jewel's classic defence of the reformed, biblical and catholic nature of the established church of the realm.

The translation was published in London, the dedication being dated October 1594. 'Here', he claimed, 'for the good of your soul, in this book, is the essence or summary of the true catholic faith, to train and perfect you in the path of God's service and humankind's salvation'.[1] Kyffin, a layman, explains how he took it upon himself both to share the rudiments of the Protestant faith with his compatriots for their spiritual benefit, and to ensure that Wales, and the Welsh language, be afforded the same honour as was taken for granted among the cultured peoples of Europe. This renaissance ideal, typical of that nurtured by Welsh humanists of his generation, fused a fervent patriotism with a zealous Protestant commitment in which Kyffin strove to take forward the Christian mission which had been so ably served by the publication of William Morgan's magnificent translation of the Welsh Bible six years earlier. It was, he claimed, 'a necessary, masterly, pious and learned work for which Wales can never repay that which he deserves' (p. ix).[2] Unlike Lady Anne Bacon's English translation of the *Apologia* issued in 1685 in which she inserted convenient chapter divisions and numbered paragraphs, Kyffin's translation reproduced faithfully Jewel's unbroken Latin text. Although this makes it more difficult to follow, the quality of the translation is excellent and modern literary scholars have acclaimed the work as a classic.[3]

In Anne Bacon's version, the volume consists of six sections of between seventeen to thirty numbered paragraphs of which only section two, namely the doctrines held by the reformed English Church, need concern us. Jewel, in Kyffin's translation, begins with an affirmation of the trinitarian nature of God and proceeds to delineate the reality of the incarnation which occurs in order, through God's gracious decree, to accomplish human salvation. He affirms the sacrificial nature of Christ's death, his bodily resurrection, ascension and session along with the expectation of his coming again in glory to judge the world. The Holy Spirit, which proceeds from both the Father and Son, is shed abroad in order 'to soften the hardheartedness of men … either through the sound preaching of the gospel or through any other means' (p. 26), leading to newness of life and the eternal hope of salvation. The emphasis, however, is on the reality of the church. God's holy church possesses unity and catholicity; Christ is her only prince and head whose people are served by a diverse order of ministers including deacons, presbyters and bishops. Quoting the authority of Cyprian, Jerome and Augustine, Kyffin claims that unlike the bishop of Rome, the bishops share jurisdiction rather than have it centralized in a single person who 'has turned his back on the faith and is the forerunner of Antichrist' (p. 29).

All ministers, he claims, should be lawfully called, and on fulfilling their calling are granted the power of the keys to bind and loosen sin solely through the preaching of the gospel. Auricular confession, 'these

whispering murmurs as the popish priests everywhere do' (p. 31), is forbidden, priestly celibacy is rejected and the honour of marriage upheld
not only for lay people but for those ordained as well. The supreme
authority in all religious matters is the canonical scriptures of the Old
Testament and the New:

> These scriptures, we claim, are the very voice and speech of heaven
> through which God has made known to us his will, in which alone the
> human heart can safely find rest, in which fully and sufficiently all things
> needful for our salvation have been provided. (p. 35)

The patristic authorities here quoted are Origen, Augustine, Chrysostom
and Cyril. As well as through the Word, Christ makes himself known
among his people through the two sacraments of baptism and the Lord's
Supper, 'both being kinds of visible words, the seals of righteousness
and the symbols of grace' (p. 36). The doctrine set forth here is not
memorialist but participatory, signifying a deep spiritual union while
communion should be available in both kinds, in bread and in wine.
Through 'the enlivening flesh of the Son of God, the communion of the
body and blood of Christ' claims Kyffin, we are 'quickened, strengthened
and fed to immortality and conjoined with, united to and incorporated
in Christ that we may remain with him and He with us' (p. 37). Baptism,
for its part, signifies the washing away of sin in the blood of Christ and
is open to infants as they too belong to the covenant people of God.

For Bishop Jewel, like all the principal Continental reformers, this
high sacramental doctrine was in full accord with biblical teaching, especially that of the Apostle Paul. Union with Christ was not mystical but
through faith, a lively apprehension of God's forgiving grace through the
gospel. Christ is certainly present through the Spirit in the sacrament,
but in no way did this imply a change in the elements. Adoration of the
elements was idolatrous and a blasphemy. The change occurred, rather,
in those who partook of the sacraments in true and simple faith. 'By saying this we do not scorn the Lord's Supper nor teach that the sacrament
is merely a cold unbeneficial ceremony as many believe' (p. 41). Rather in
baptism we are clothed in Christ and in the Supper, through faith, we can
feast on him. The difference between the faith of the reformed English
Church and that of Rome was total: 'They have turned the sacraments
of Christ into pageantry and pomp', he claimed, while 'purgatory is a
late invention and an old wives' tale' (p. 44). Similarly Christ, not Mary,

was the sole mediator between humankind and God. Although it had rejected the superstitious idolatry of Rome, nevertheless the English Church remained hierarchical, governed by its bishops, and liturgical possessing its own forms of public worship:

> Prayer should be offered, as is proper, in the tongue the people can understand, so that the people are edified, as St Paul stated, through common prayer, this being the universal practice of the ancient fathers and the catholic bishops in the Old and New Testaments. (pp. 46–7)

Although *Deffynniad Ffydd Eglwys Loegr* is more a treatise on ecclesiology and church polity than on personal religion, Jewel, in Kyffin's translation, does not neglect the importance of the individual's appropriation of the gospel. In full accord with Reformed theology,[*] he holds to the radical sinfulness of humankind through the Fall, the impotence of good works as a means of being justified before God, and the supreme necessity of turning to Christ alone for salvation. That salvation was wrought through the cross, the fount of the divine forgiveness, Christ's sacrifice being wholly sufficient for our redemption: 'Thus, when he gave up his spirit and said "It is finished", in that hour he fully paid the price and ransom for the sins of all the world' (pp. 48–9). Our responsibility is to make this redemption our own through faith and costly repentance, and thereafter live lives of obedience to God's command:

> True faith is living and fruitful, and we cannot be idle. See how we teach the people, that God has called us not to debauchery or licentiousness as St Paul says, but to good works that we can walk in them, as He has called us out of darkness to serve the living God. (pp. 49–50)

Kyffin's work was a masterpiece of Welsh prose which partook of the humanist ideal of wedding the Word of God to the treasures of antiquity according to the best in European culture of the day. He set out his scholarly principles in the book's introduction, namely to follow the practice used in English, French, Italian and Spanish literature of augmenting the ordinary speech of the people with technical words which accorded best with ancient Greek or Latin. His contempt towards those who saw no purpose in providing literary instruction in Welsh as this impeded the people from quickly learning English, was withering: 'Could not the devil himself say anything better!' (p. xiv). In September 1596, a year after *Deffynniad Ffydd Eglwys Loegr* was issued, Kyffin was appointed

Comptroller of the Musters in Ireland where he died, in his early forties, on 2 January 1598, and was buried in Dublin's Christ Church Cathedral. There is no evidence that he ever returned to Wales.

Huw Lewys (1562–1634) was a Caernarfonshire man who matriculated at All Souls College, Oxford, aged twenty in 1582, graduated BA from Hart Hall in 1587 and proceeded to take his MA from St Edmund Hall four years later. Since 1579 the Oxford curriculum had included compulsory instruction in the Calvinist Alexander Nowell's catechism, the Heidelberg Catechism and that of John Calvin himself, with optional reading of the Geneva reformer's *Institutio*, Jewel's *Apologia* and the works of the Zürich reformer Heinrich Bullinger. This reflected the highly Reformed tone of Oxford divinity at the time and there is every reason to believe that Lewys affirmed this teaching wholeheartedly. He would have been encouraged to pay especial heed to the university's preachers: 'Throughout the 1590s the Calvinist message rang loudly and clearly from the Oxford pulpits.'[5] His only published work, *Perl Mewn Adfyd* (1595) ('A Pearl in Adversity'), a skilled translation of Miles Coverdale's *A Spiritual and most Precious Pearl* (1550) which was itself a translation of the Zürich pastor Otto Werdmüller's 1548 treatise on self-discipline and Christian fortitude, was written during his time at Oxford, presumably after 1591. It was the first Welsh book to be printed by Joseph Barnes whose publishing house, next door to the university church of St Mary's, issued a wealth of Protestant literature during these years.

The *Perl*, a close translation of the work of Coverdale, doctrinally a Lutheran, and the Zwinglian Werdmüller, was more an exercise in pastoral theology than dogmatic theology as such. Its content was uncontroversial. Its three sections include thirty-one chapters counselling believers to draw close to Christ in adversity, to practise evangelical repentance and to have faith in the merciful God. Lewys's preface reflects a young clergyman's reforming zeal. The Reformed ideal was for the inculcation of practical godliness through the preaching and application of the Word. 'Many prelates and churchmen are neglectful of their calling', he complained, 'and do not preach or apply the mystery of God's Word to the people, but are dumb and speechless, like dogs with no bark, a bell with no chime or lights hidden under a bushel.'[6] Consequently, he claimed, there were too many white-haired men, well beyond their sixties, who were no more able to provide an account of true faith as any newborn child. The pressing need was for the inculcation of practical godliness through sound literature and the preaching of the Word.

Lewys was instituted to the benefice of Llanddeiniolen, a few miles from his Bontnewydd home, in 1598, was appointed canon chancellor of Bangor Cathedral in 1608 and became executor to the will of Henry Rowland, bishop of Bangor, 'one of the best bishops of the age'.[7] He personified the values of the so-called 'moderate puritans' of the Elizabethan and early Jacobean church,[8] conformist in liturgy and ceremonial but Reformed in doctrine and primarily concerned with the peaceable advance of godliness amongst their flocks. When in 1623 the visitation of Lewis Bayly, Rowland's successor in the see, recorded non-residency as blighting the adjoining parish of Llandygái and a dearth of preaching in Llanllechid ('But three sermons the last year') and Llanbeblig ('No quarterly sermons'), the parishioners of neighbouring Llanddeiniolen were admirably served.[9] Lewys's ministry reflected his Oxford training: 'The ministers trained in this school were not normally rigid or extreme in outlook, but rather were concerned with high standards of education, pastoral care, and evangelism.'[10] He died, aged seventy-one, in 1634.

If Maurice Kyffin was a layman whose formative years were spent in London and abroad, and Huw Lewys had been confirmed in his moderate Puritanism while at Oxford, Robert Holland (1557–1622), who also contributed to the consolidation of Protestant divinity in Wales, was a Cambridge man. The son of Hugh Holland of Conwy and Jane, his wife, he matriculated from Clare Hall in 1577, graduated BA from Magdalene College and took his MA at Jesus College in 1581. He was ordained deacon in his home diocese of Bangor, apparently in 1579, and priested in the diocese of Ely in April 1580. Despite the increasingly Puritan atmosphere in Cambridge during the middle years of Queen Elizabeth's reign, neither Clare Hall, Magdalene nor Jesus were regarded as bastions of the Puritan faith and little tainted with nonconformity to say nothing of the incipient Presbyterianism so feared by some of the leaders of the Established Church. It would have been inconceivable, however, were the young Welshman not to have been affected by developments in the university at the time.

The year Holland matriculated saw John Whitgift's elevation from the mastership of Trinity College to the see of Worcester and thence, in 1583, his appointment as Archbishop of Canterbury. Many of the younger fellows, especially in Christ's College and St John's, were still aggrieved at the treatment meted out by Whitgift five years earlier to Thomas Cartwright, the then Lady Margaret Professor of divinity, when he had been deprived of his chair and stripped of his fellowship. Cartwright's misdemeanour had been to challenge the prevailing episcopacy in the name of a Presbyterian church order as practised in Geneva under Calvin's successor, Theodore Beza. If Cartwright had been deposed, many other Puritans, not necessarily doctrinaire Presbyterians, remained to exert considerable and growing influence over undergraduates both in the individual colleges and throughout the university as a whole. In 1584 Laurence Chaderton, 'the pope of Cambridge Puritanism',[11] was drawn from his position as fellow of Christ's to become the first master of the new Emmanuel College, virtually a seminary to train Puritan ministers for the national church. Chaderton's Sunday afternoon sermons at St Clement's, where he would remain preacher for over fifty years, attracted throngs of students and one imagines that Holland would have been among them. Neither is it fanciful to believe that he would have taken part in the 'conferences', modelled on the ministers' meetings in Zürich and other centres of continental Protestantism, where Chaderton trained generations of zealous students in the art of preaching, pastoral application and practical divinity.[12]

As Holland spent his first decade of ministry in the diocese of Ely, as curate of Weston Colville and schoolmaster at neighbouring Dullingham some ten miles to the east of Cambridge, he may well also have been drawn into the pastoral fellowship that flourished during these decades in those environs and within easy reach of the town.[13] At the centre of this group was Richard Greenham who was especially skilled as a 'doctor of souls': 'The most attractive "godly pastor" was Richard Greenham of Pembroke [College], rector from 1571 to 1591 of Dry Drayton, five miles from Cambridge.'[14] Eschewing controversy and polemics, his principal concern was to care for his village flock through simple gospel preaching, catechetical instruction and pastoral attention. He died of the plague in London in 1594, and his works were published five years later by Henry, Robert Holland's brother.[15] Henry had graduated from Magdalene in 1579 and served as vicar of Orwell, within close distance to both Dry Drayton and Weston Colville. Doctrinally a Calvinist with a pronounced belief in predestination, the perseverance of the saints and the workings of providence in people's lives, he typified the resolute Puritanism that had become something of a Cambridge norm. A staunch conformist however, it can be assumed that his younger brother was of the same stamp.

Robert Holland returned to Wales in 1591 when he was appointed incumbent of the parish of Prendergast, Pembrokeshire, in the diocese of St David's. He would become rector of Llanddowror, Carmarthenshire, in 1600, Walwyn's Castle in Pembrokeshire once more in 1607 and Robeson West in 1612. It is not clear how a north Walian found his way to the expansive if poor south Wales diocese of St David's, nor who instituted him there. His diocesan, Marmaduke Middleton, 'the ultimate black sheep of the whole Elizabethan bench',[16] spent virtually all of 1590 until his ignominious removal from office in 1593 in London, either at the Court of the High Commission or the Court of the Star Chamber, parrying accusations of fraud, embezzlement, marital impropriety, forgery and deceit. His attestations of innocence were in vain and he became the sole Elizabethan prelate to be stripped of both Episcopal and priestly status.[17] Ironically it had been Middleton who, in 1583, had issued 'the most severely critical sets of injunctions to its clergy and people ever to have come from the pen of an Elizabethan bishop'.[18] Despite having been overseen for two decades by Richard Davies, Marian exile, translator of the New Testament into Welsh in 1567 and the most distinguished of the early Reformation bishops, the work of restoration had hardly begun.[19] Superstition was rife, pilgrimages and holy days were kept assiduously, prayers for the dead were commonplace, images, altars and rood lofts were still prevalent in parish churches, candles were used in worship, worshippers knelt when taking the sacrament and in all 'the people doth retain a memory of the idolatrous mass'. In a report to the Privy Council of the same year, Middleton complained of the rank ignorance of his non-preaching clergy: 'The gospel was hindered through such ignorant persons, the people perish through want of food'.[20] If a Cambridge Puritan needed a challenge, he need hardly have come to a better place.

Holland's principal contribution to the development of theology in Wales was as a translator of the practical divinity of the Puritan William Perkins. They had been contemporaries at Cambridge, Perkins matriculating from Christ's College in 1577, graduating BA in 1581 and MA three years later. A pupil of Laurence Chaderton, he was appointed fellow of his college in 1584 and lecturer or regular preacher at the church of Great St Andrews. Unlike Chaderton, however, he refused to undermine ecclesiastical authority and sought to conform, as far as possible, to the stipulations and practices of the Book of Common Prayer. This was not due to an exaggerated deference to official polity but simply because he held that ceremonial, if shorn of papist symbolism, was part of the *adiaphora* or 'things indifferent', not pertaining to salvation. It was reasonable, he believed, to observe the minimal ceremonial that the Established Church required of its clergy.[21] As tensions mounted within the establishment after 1588 and hope for more radical church reform abated,[22] many leading Puritans saw the wisdom of emphasizing not polity or the purification of liturgy but to inculcate in the baptized if nominal members of the church a more sincere and effective personal religion. The emphasis of the 1590s would be not church order, the propriety of using the sign of the cross at baptism, the use of the ring in marriage or whether the laity should kneel when receiving the sacrament, but what it meant to be truly converted. The challenge now was to make real the experiential aspect of the doctrinal Calvinism enshrined in the 39 Articles of Religion and held conscientiously by virtually all the senior clergy of the Established Church and a great part of its most influential lay governors as well.[23]

Perkins began his literary career in 1584, and by the time of his premature death, aged forty-four, in 1602, he had become the most prolific published theologian of his generation. His reputation spread rapidly through the Reformed churches of Europe and by the end of the seventeenth century as many as 372 editions of his writings had appeared in a score of different languages: 'If contemporary influence be the criterion, Perkins was easily the most preeminent English churchman and theologian of his remarkable generation.'[24] Whereas an earlier generation including John Calvin in Geneva, Heinrich Bullinger in Zürich, Thomas Cranmer in Lambeth and Richard Davies in Wales had set forth a specifically biblical theology in order to subvert Catholic dogma and create a Reformed ecclesiastical establishment, Perkins's aim, decades later, was to apply this theology to the workings of the individual soul.[25] It was he more than anyone else who developed a morphology of conversion in which conviction of sin through the preaching of the divine law became a presupposition for the application of the gospel which, in turn, would release the soul to experience salvation. 'Perkins' system', according to Richard A. Muller, 'is characterized by continual application of doctrine to inward piety.'[26] What is implicit in the earlier theology now becomes explicit and certain themes such as predestination, reprobation and the need to comfort the afflicted conscience, now become much more central to the scheme. In fact, Perkins was 'the theological giant of English predestinarianism and [became] the virtual inventor of conscience-literature'.[27] The prime elements in this system are set forward most clearly in such works as *A Treatise Tending unto a Declaration whether a Man be in the Estate of Damnation or Salvation* (1588) and *A Golden*

Chaine … Containing the Order of the Causes of Salvation and Damnation according to God's Word (1591).[28]

The first of Holland's translations was neither of these but Perkins's 1592 tract on the Lord's Prayer which appeared in 1599 as *Agoriad byrr ar Weddi'r Arglwydd* ('A Short Exposition on the Lord's Prayer'). There are no extant copies of this edition but it was reissued after the Restoration in the composite volume *Cyfarwydd-deb i'r Anghyfarwydd* ('A Guide for the Unfamiliar') (1677). At around the same time he issued an original work (not a translation) of exceptional literary merit called *Ymddiddan Tudur a Gronw* ('A Conversation between Tudur and Gronw'). Aimed at the ordinary people among whom he had been labouring, it was in the form of a lively dialogue between two friends, Tudur, a plain countryman, and Gronw who is more biblically informed, on the subject of witchcraft. Henry Holland, Robert's brother had published his learned and substantial *Treatise on Witchcraft* (1590) dedicated to Robert Devereaux, the earl of Essex, while Perkins had released *A Discourse on the Damned Art of Witchcraft* (1593) a few years later. Robert Holland's pamphlet, although serious minded, is written with a marvellous lightness of touch and imaginative creativity. The two friends discuss the meaning of the common proverb *bwrw cath i gythraul* ('throwing a cat to the devil'), and whereas Tudur sees little wrong with the white magic which was commonly practised among rural people, Gronw is implacably opposed to any form of magic as being inspired by the devil and contravening God's Word: 'This is how God allows the devil to blind the reprobates, as the devil can neither help nor hinder anyone, only to the extent that God permits.'[29] Whereas this is not a work of theology as such, it does reflect the new piety in referring to the irredeemably wicked as reprobates and in its talk of predestination, 'those who are foreordained to be saved' (p. 170). Yet God's salvation was being made available to all: 'There are good Christians to be had wherever God's Word is preached fluently and the gospel is held in respect' (pp. 171–2), while Gronw encourages Tudur to make sure his calling: 'Listen to God's Word, read God's Word and pray faithfully and fruitfully' (p. 172). The clergy, complains Tudur, are neglecting their task and sermons were not being preached in the parish churches, and as for the Scriptures, 'The Bible is too expensive for a poor man to buy and keep at home. God knows how dire is the condition of we, the ordinary folk' (p. 172).

Although this tract was, in fact, published and printed sometime before 1600, it has only survived in MS form[30] and represents the sole example we have of Holland's skill as an original author. In 1604, following the accession of James I and the year of the Hampton Court Conference in which the new monarch sought to respond to the concerns of the Puritans in matters of liturgy and ceremonial, Holland published his translation of James's own work, the *Basilikon Doron* (1599), a treatise which had been written by the king to his son setting out the responsibilities of a Christian prince. Holland's aim was to assure the king that the Welsh, 'a nation of great antiquity keeping their country and continuing their language so long a time inviolate without change or mixture', were loyal subjects faithful to the policy of uniting the two kingdoms of England and Scotland under a single crown, especially as this reflected the unity of the ancient island of Britain when it was ruled by Cadwaladr, James's forebear and last king of the Britons. In fact, Holland urged the monarch to learn the language of his Welsh subjects and thus be 'able both to speak unto his people, and also to understand them speaking unto him, without interpreters'.[31] Apart from its politico-cultural purpose, there is no doubt that Holland was drawn to the work due to the fact that James urges his son to be faithful to the Word of God in scripture, and to fulfil his duties in fear of the Lord. According to J. Gwynfor Jones, the Welsh text of the *Basilikon Doron* (of which only a fragment survives) 'is not really political propaganda at all but fatherly advice to a young prince'.[32] All the evidence points to the fact that Holland's programme of evangelization through literature was well advanced during these years, with two more of Perkins's works, the *Two Treatises: Of the Nature and Practice of Repentance, and Of the Combat of the Flesh and Spirit* (1593) as well as *A Direction for the Government of the Tongue* (1593) already in the hands of the printer, the London Welshman Thomas Salisbury,[33] when a fire destroyed the MSS during an outbreak of the plague.[34]

We know little of the nature of Holland's labours during the following decades until he published, late in his career, a translation of Perkins's catechetical work *The Foundation of Christian Religion* (1590). This was a work of simple instruction in six succinct parts expounding the reality of God; the fact of human sinfulness; the means of salvation through Christ's sacrificial death; the call to repentance and faith; the central importance of preaching, the sacraments and prayer; and the inevitability of judgement. This was published in 1622 when Holland was sixty-five years old having served his west Wales parishes for over three decades. His former diocesan, Anthony Rudd, having taken the place of the disgraced Marmaduke Middleton as bishop of St David's in 1594, had shown his sympathy for a more thoroughgoing reform of the Established Church along Puritan lines during the Hampton Court Conference in 1604.[35] Ominously, however, Holland's final tract was issued just as the anti-Calvinist William Laud was appointed to oversee the diocese.[36] Like his other works, Holland's translation only survives in later editions, one issued in 1649 by the Puritan author Evan Roberts and another entitled *Catechism Mr Perkins* ('Mr Perkins's Catechism'), brought out by the Congregationalist Stephen Hughes in 1672. It provides an excellent example of the sort of didactic literature which would remain a mainstay of Protestant divinity in Wales for the next two centuries and more.

Following a short exposition of the six principles listed above, Perkins provides a more detailed treatment of each in turn. Beginning with the doctrine of God, he states that God is known both through scripture and reason, there being sufficient evidence within creation to witness to his existence while conscience points not only to the fact that God is but that he is the judge of sin. The author warns against the propensity of the human mind to create God in one's own image, 'as the foolish and the ignorant do, who think of him like an old man sitting in heaven' (p. 22; p. 254).[37] Rather, God is wise, holy, eternal and infinite, the creator and sustainer of all things and distinguished as Father, Son and Holy Spirit: 'The Father is he who has begotten the Son, the Son being he who is begotten of the Father, the Holy Spirit having proceeded from both Father and Son' (pp. 23–4; pp. 255–6). In the second section, he paints the human predicament in sombre colours: 'Every man in his own nature is dead in sin like an obnoxious corpse or a dead body rotting and stinking in the grave' (p. 24; p. 256). Having elaborated on the nature and extent of sin and the bondage of the will, he puts the blame squarely on Adam's fall and its effect on his posterity. All of humanity is implicated in this catastrophe, each individual having made Adam's sinfulness their own. Perkins mentions neither reprobation nor election, only that each sinner's plight is 'eternal damnation and the fire of hell of which every man is guilty and in as much danger as an apprehended traitor of being hung, drawn and quartered' (p. 28; p. 260). His only hope, therefore, is Jesus Christ, the subject of the third section, who, as prophet, priest and king, is unique in both deity and humanity, born of the Virgin, sanctified through the Holy Spirit, whose sacrificial death quenches the divine wrath and whose resurrection pronounces victory over death. To the question 'With whom does this glorious king share the means of salvation?' the answer is: 'With all, and these means are wholly sufficient to keep all, though not all will be saved as not all receive them through faith' (pp. 32–3; pp. 264–5). The doctrine of predestination is not foregrounded in this treatise while the idea of reprobation, or God having actively chosen some for destruction, is barely mentioned at all.

The fourth sections explain how individuals are encouraged to apply this salvation to themselves through faith. Although faith is simply the means by which people take hold of Christ, it is prepared for by the working of the Holy Spirit on the human heart, 'by bruising them as though man's hard heart is crushed to powder, this in order to make him humble' (pp. 33–4; pp. 265–6). This occurs through the application of the divine law to the conscience as revealed in the Ten Commandments. When this process of conviction is complete, the seed of faith is ready to be sown, the person prays for deliverance and is lead to an assurance of the divine mercy in Christ: 'It is this assurance which constitutes a living faith' (p. 37; p. 269). As the assurance of faith was such a contentious matter in Puritan theology and would be equally controversial in eighteenth-century Welsh Methodism, it is instructive to see how Perkins responds to his catechist's question: 'Are there different degrees and measures in true faith?' Weak faith, even though genuine, is often bereft of constant assurance of the divine forgiveness though the believer knows that his sins are pardonable so he strives for a clearer perception of God's mercy. The full assurance of faith is not granted immediately 'but after many days of self-discipline and practised repentance' the experience of God's love will be granted (pp. 37–8; pp. 269–70). The emphasis is first on introspection and only then on looking to Christ for justification, sanctification and release from the guilt and penalty of sin. In order to know that he is justified a man need 'not ascend to heaven to seek God's secret counsels, but to descend into his own heart and there ask whether he has been sanctified or not' (p. 30; p. 272). Although a godly person may lose this assurance through yielding to sin, if genuine, salvation can never finally be forfeited.

The final two sections have to do with the means of grace and the last judgement. Salvation comes through the preaching of the Word, planting and increasing the seed of faith in the elect while at the same time condemning the impenitent on the basis of their own sins. It is necessary for listeners to hear the preached Word in order to be awakened to faith and thereafter partake of the sacraments. Perkins's sacramental doctrine is fairly minimal. Baptism and the Lord's Supper, although called 'sacraments', are more signs of the covenant than the means through which the believer is grafted into Christ and partakes of his body and blood. This is a less exalted doctrine than that expounded in Calvin's *Institutio* or Bishop Jewel's *Apologia Ecclesiae Anglicanae*. The physicality of sacraments is an indulgence to human weakness, sealing God's mercy to our senses 'because we are dull to consider or remember them' (p. 46; p. 278). Baptism, though partaken by children within a Christian realm, becomes valid only through faith, 'though that may be many years afterwards, when the power of regeneration is felt, making active that which had been promised previously' (p. 48; p. 281). The Supper, for its part, is the seal which the Lord himself applies to his covenant. The concept of both baptismal regeneration and Eucharistic presence is avoided while the wording of Cranmer's Prayer Book: 'Take and eat in remembrance that Christ died for thee, and feed on him in thy heart by faith with thanksgiving', is replaced with: 'Christ has received [the believer] through faith, and nourishes and upholds the body and soul of the communicant to everlasting life' (p. 49; p. 281). It is noteworthy that neither Perkins[38] nor Holland mentions the way in which the church should be governed. The oversight of bishops is taken for granted. We know that Perkins was a conformist and there is no evidence that the Welshman was anything other than wholly loyal to the ecclesiastical establishment of the day. The book's final section underlines the inevitability of death with Christ returning in order to inaugurate the final reckoning: 'He will grant salvation to the elect and the godly but will announce and exercise the condemnation against the unfaithful and reprobate' (p. 53; p. 285), sending them to eternal perdition. And with that William Perkins, in the lucid Welsh prose of Robert Holland, concludes his instruction in the Christian faith.

A decade and a half after Holland had arrived in the diocese of St David's, a clergyman from the diocese of Llandaff published a work aimed at further establishing basic Protestant divinity among the Welsh people. Edward James (1570–*c*.1610), a native of Glamorgan, had gone up to Oxford in 1586 as a lad of sixteen, matriculated at St Edmund Hall, graduated BA from Jesus College in June 1589 before taking his MA in July 1592. The Reformed nature of Oxford theology at the time has already been mentioned,[39] while the establishment of Jesus College in 1571, the first specifically Protestant college in the university, was in order to provide learned clergy who would promote the Elizabethan religious settlement in Wales.[40] James was appointed fellow of his college around 1589–90 and remained resident until 1596 when he was drawn back to Wales almost certainly at the behest of William Morgan, translator of the Bible and newly elected bishop of Llandaff, in order to assist with the deeper entrenchment of Elizabethan Protestantism within the see. Under Morgan's patronage, James advanced rapidly. He was appointed vicar of Caerleon in February 1596, rector of Shirenewton near Chepstow in August 1597, rector of Llangatwg-juxta-Usk near Raglan in April 1598 and vicar of Llangatwg-feibion-Afel a year later, parishes that were within easy reach of the bishop's palace at Mathern. In keeping with the tradition of bardic hospitality, Morgan combined his ecclesiastical role with that of patron of poets and men of letters, while Edward James and John Davies, later of Mallwyd, shared this fellowship as prose writers and contributors to reform. Although Morgan was translated to the diocese of St Asaph in 1601 (and took John Davies with him), work on James's signal contribution to the theological task had probably already begun. His 'Welsh translation of the *Book of Homilies* in 1606 [was] a text on which the influence of William Morgan was writ plain and large'.[41]

The first Book of Homilies, *Certaine Sermons or Homilies Appointed to be Read in Churches*, had been published in 1547 during the reign of Edward VI in order to inculcate basic Protestant doctrine among a populace that was still overwhelmingly Catholic in faith and sympathy. Its principal author was Thomas Cranmer, Archbishop of Canterbury between 1532 and his execution under Mary Tudor in 1556. Having already provided a vernacular liturgy in the Book of Common Prayer, he strove to explain to the faithful the prime convictions of the Reformation as it was now understood by the church of the realm. The first book included twelve homilies or sermons, four on morality and Christian ethics, four on aspects of practical piety including good works, and four on the church's doctrines. Cranmer himself was the author of sermons I, III, IV and V, on the reading of scripture, the salvation of humankind, on true and living faith, and on good works:

> The Archbishop's twin concerns in the homilies was to establish the nature of salvation as God's free gift of grace by faith, while demonstrating to the person in the pew that this did not result in the collapse of morality and that good works were still an essential part of the Christian life.[42]

The core Protestant convictions of *sola scriptura, sola fide* and good works as a result rather than a precondition of faith, are stated clearly and resolutely in order to confound absolutely papist error.

The second Book of Homilies (1571), written mostly by John Jewel, bishop of Salisbury and author of the *Apologia Ecclesiae Anglicanae*, contains twenty-one sermons. These are, on the whole, of a more practical bent than those in the earlier volume but they also include homilies on the right use of church buildings, on the importance of the liturgy, common prayer and the sacraments, on the major festivals including the Nativity, Good Friday, Easter and Whitsun, and on the church as a valid and scripturally based religious establishment. Although there was no fundamental difference between Jewel's doctrinal, ecclesiological and Eucharistic views and those of Cranmer, the Homilies, along with the Prayer Book, presupposed the hierarchical nature of the reformed English Church replete with its threefold ministry of bishop, presbyter and deacon flourishing under the protection of a Christian sovereign. Although preserving full fellowship with the best Reformed churches of the continent, by the 1560s the English Church was steadily developing a character of its own. Critics would soon complain that the Elizabethan establishment was 'but halfly reformed'.[43]

Apart from the witness of the London-based separatist John Penry (1559–93),[44] radical criticism of the Established Church never materialized in sixteenth-century Wales. During his exile in Frankfurt in Mary Tudor's reign, Richard Davies, the doyen of early Welsh Protestants, had sided not with the Geneva-inspired John Knox but with the conformist Richard Cox who remained faithful to the Prayer Book worship of the Edwardian years.[45] For the Welshman, the Edwardian Prayer Book embodied the quintessence of reformed Christianity. There was no disconnect between the pure Word of God and the norms of an episcopally sanctioned and responsible liturgical worship. Indeed, it was through the Prayer Book that the church manifested its continuity, duly purged, with the living tradition of the Christian past. This was the norm that Davies established during his two-decade tenure as bishop of St David's, and it was into this legacy that William Morgan was initiated.

Morgan (1545–1604) had been born in Penmachno, Caernarfonshire, and educated initially under the auspices of the Wynn family, substantial landowners at Gwydir in the Conwy Valley. In the spring of 1565 along with his friend Edmund Prys, latterly archdeacon of Merioneth and translator of the Psalter into metrical Welsh, he had entered St John's

College, Cambridge, at a time of considerable religious discontent. A substantial minority of the college's 240 students and forty-seven fellows had given up wearing the surplice to daily chapel, urging that the Elizabethan Church should be more thoroughly reformed. As well as being a centre of Puritan discontent, St John's was renowned for the quality of its biblical scholarship and expertise in Hebrew and New Testament Greek.[46] If the two young north Walians held aloof from the college's strong Puritan faction and conformed to the ceremonial norms of the Prayer Book liturgy, they took full advantage of the academic benefits that were available. Morgan took his BA in 1568, his MA in 1571 and proceeded to the advanced degree of BD through which his knowledge of Hebrew would be perfected, in 1578. He would take his DD in 1583. Prys also graduated BA in 1568 and MA in 1571 by which time he had been appointed fellow and would soon be chosen college preacher (1574) and chaplain (1575).[47] Although both men would play a vital part in the progressive reformation of the Welsh Church, Prys as a senior ecclesiastic in the Bangor diocese between the mid-1570s and his death in 1623, neither could be said to have been outright Puritans.[48] They were, rather, solidly Reformed and biblically enlightened Church of England men. Morgan had been ordained deacon by Richard Cox, bishop of Ely, in April 1568 and proceeded to the order of presbyter in December of the same year. Appointed non-resident vicar of Llanbadarn Fawr in the St David's diocese in December 1572 almost certainly through the good offices of Richard Davies, he transferred to Welshpool in the St Asaph diocese in August 1575 where his St John's contemporary William Hughes had recently been installed bishop.[49] It was at Llanrhaeadr-ym-Mochnant, however, on the border between Denbighshire and Montgomeryshire, where he served as rector between 1578 and 1594, that he would undertake and complete the herculean task of translating the Bible into Welsh.

As a conscientious minister of the reformed (and Reformed) church of the realm, Morgan did his best to inculcate biblical discipline among his somewhat recalcitrant parishioners.[50] An active preacher as well as a pastor and resident among his flock, he strove for reformation within the structures of the establishment. The nature of his churchmanship is clearly displayed in the Latin preface of the 1588 Welsh Bible. He praises Queen Elizabeth, to whom the preface was addressed, not only for championing reformed religion throughout the land, not least through the Welsh language among her subjects in Wales, but for providing a Prayer Book as well as the Scriptures, 'that volume which determines the form of public prayer and the order of administrating the sacraments'.[51] His warmest appreciation is reserved for John Whitgift, Archbishop of Canterbury, 'that most zealous defender of the truth and ever wise custodian of order and propriety', while he refers to his compatriot Gabriel Goodman, dean of Westminster, as 'a most excellent man in practice as well as in reputation, wholly devoted to piety'.[52] Whitgift had lent his steadfast support throughout the translation project while Goodman, a native of Denbigh, had provided lodgings in the deanery for a whole year as Morgan had undertaken the laborious task of seeing the volume through the press.

Whitgift, of course, was the *bête noire* of the Puritans: 'I know that prelate to be a great enemy of God', claimed John Penry, 'his saints and [of] truth'.[53] Early in life he had become a fervent reformer and throughout his career he remained wholeheartedly a Calvinist. In 1565, however, as a young fellow of Peterhouse, Cambridge, he had decided to uphold the principles of conformity. Already Lady Margaret Professor of divinity, he found favour with the sovereign and advanced rapidly to the Regius chair, the mastership of Pembroke Hall in 1567 and that of Trinity three years later. As Regius Professor he took the lead in refuting Thomas Cartwright's espousal of Presbyterianism as a pattern of government within the Established Church. This would have instigated parity among the clergy, the abandonment of episcopacy and the threefold ministry, the introduction of an element of lay control and the discontinuance of liturgical worship. Promoted to the see of Worcester in 1577 he vigorously enforced conformity among the clergy. Greatly admired by Queen Elizabeth, she appointed him Archbishop of Canterbury and primate five years later. Whitgift fully shared the Calvinistic consensus which characterized the Elizabethan Church, indeed the Lambeth Articles which he had promulgated in 1595 were strongly predestinarian in nature.[54] In matters of liturgy and ceremonial however and the need for absolute obedience to ordained authority, he would brook no opposition. It was this and not doctrine as such that lay at the root of his condemnation and execution of John Penry, for sedition, in 1593.[55]

Gabriel Goodman, with whom Morgan conferred regularly during his stay at the deanery of Westminster, was equally suspect amongst those who strove for more radical reform within the Church. 'Goodman, Dean for forty years from 1561, was marked out as the very opposite of a Puritan in his churchmanship: a most unusual figure among senior English Protestant clergy, as was his successor Lancelot Andrewes.'[56]

The abbey with its choir, organ, elaborate ceremonial and studied down-playing of the accepted doctrinal norms represented a strand within the English church that would become dominant three decades later during the archepiscopate of William Laud. Morgan must have realized that the ethos of his own piety was subtly different from that of these mentors, but his core convictions, like theirs, remained staunch. All Protestants were one in their view that the scriptures, and they alone, were essential for salvation, and that the Bible should be available in the common tongue. 'It is through faith', he declared, 'that all must live, and faith comes through hearing, and hearing by the Word of God, a word which heretofore has been virtually inaudible to the ears of our compatriots as it has been buried in a foreign tongue'.[57] The salvation of the people could only occur through a studied listening to and effective preaching of the Word of God. Having the Bible in Welsh was crucial for the mission of God within the realm.

William Morgan was elected bishop of Llandaff in July 1595. Whitgift had recommended him to William Cecil, the first Lord Burghley, Elizabeth's principal advisor, some months earlier. Both he and his Cambridge contemporary, Richard Vaughan of Nyffryn on the Llŷn Peninsula, currently archdeacon of Middlesex and soon to be appointed bishop of Bangor, were described as 'two very worthy men', while Morgan was later cited in Whitgift's correspondence as being exceptional for 'integrity, gravity and great learning'.[58] During his first Episcopal visitation in the October following his installation he insisted that the clergy should preach regularly within their parishes, though the dire poverty of the diocese and a serious lack of able graduates made this an aspiration rather than a reality.[59] During his six years at Llandaff and even more so following his move to St Asaph in 1601, he endeavoured strenuously to instigate a viable preaching ministry in the dioceses over which he presided.

The move to instruct the Welsh people in the mainstream theology of the Edwardian and early Elizabethan Church nearly half a century after that had been done in England shows the difference in pace between the spread of Reformation principles among the two nations. Politically Wales had long been absorbed into the English state. The so-called 'Acts of Union' of 1536–43 represented only the final stage of an integration that had begun as early as 1282 with the death of the last native prince and accelerated following the failure of the rebellion of Owain Glyndŵr, 1400–15.[60] By the late sixteenth century it was not incongruous for the Welsh to refer to their established church as *Eglwys Loegr*, 'The Church of England'. If ecclesiastically the four Welsh dioceses remained under the jurisdiction of Canterbury, culturally they were very different indeed. It has been estimated that well over 90 per cent of the people were monoglot Welsh, and if the Reformation were to succeed it would have to express itself in the only language that the people knew. The massive difference between the success of the Reformation in Wales and its abject failure in Gaelic-speaking Ireland was that the Elizabethan government treated Welsh cultural identity not with contempt and antagonism but with sensitivity and tact.[61] Elizabeth's policy had been to appoint Welsh-speaking bishops who took pride both in their cultural distinctiveness and in the truth of the Protestant faith. Rather than being alienated, the bardic classes who represented learning and high culture were drawn into the Tudor endeavour. If the spread of reform was slow it was due not to open rejection of the message (notwithstanding the partial persistence of recusancy),[62] but to the unwieldy structures of administration, a still medieval system of ecclesiastical government and the conservative nature of Welsh society as a whole.

By the time *Pregethau a osodwyd allan ... i'w darllein ymhob Eglwys blwyf* ('Sermons appointed ... to be read in each parish church') appeared in 1606, Edward James was serving as the vicar of Cadoxton near Neath in the western part of the diocese, and had been appointed by Francis Godwin, Morgan's successor, as canon chancellor of Llandaff.[63] Like Maurice Kyffin's translation of *Apologia Ecclesiae Anglicanae*, such is the quality of its prose style that James's version of the Book of Homilies has been hailed as a classic of early modern Welsh literature.[64] Its immediate importance, however, was in attempting to ground the Protestant faith more deeply in the minds and hearts of the Welsh people. According to Homily III in Book One, 'On the Redemption of Humankind', justification occurred not by works but solely by faith on the basis of the finished work of Christ: 'This justice or righteousness which we receive by God's mercy through the merits of Christ and embrace by faith, God accepts and takes and deems perfect and full righteousness on our behalf.'[65] Referring to the Epistle to the Romans, the Apostle Paul mentions the necessity of three things:

> On God's part, his great mercy and grace; on Christ's part, righteousness, namely that justice be satisfied or the price of our redemption paid through the offering of his body and the shedding of his blood, all of

which fulfils the law in its perfection and entirety; and on our part, true
and lively faith in the merits of Jesus Christ. (p. 26)

Such faith is not a human virtue which contributes to this salvation;
rather it is a gift of God's sheer unmerited goodness: 'This faith is not
our own but the result of God's work in us' (p. 28). Although this is not
a matter of synergy between man and God, nevertheless the believer is
involved in the process: 'God's grace does not exclude the divine righteousness in our justification; it only excludes human righteousness, that
is the righteousness of our own works as the basis of our acceptance
before God' (p. 28). Nevertheless, the only contribution that we can make
is to accept the gift in humility and thanksgiving.

Justification, therefore, is by faith alone, the gift of faith which we
are called upon to affirm. All repentance, love and fear of God, namely
the virtues linked to faith, are the fruit of faith rather than its presupposition. Faith is wholly and entirely God's free gift:

All the good works that we can do are imperfect and as such cannot
earn justification for us; but our justification comes freely, through God's
mercy alone, and so great is this mercy that the whole world could not
contribute the slightest part towards it. Yet it pleased our heavenly
Father from his infinite mercy, with nothing of our own deserts, to provide for us the most valuable jewels of Christ's Body and Blood through
which our ransom could be paid to the full, the law fulfilled and his
righteousness wholly satisfied. (p. 28)

Salvation is totally of God: 'The greatest presumption that Antichrist
could invent would be to claim that man through his own works purges
himself of his sins and therefore justifies himself before God' (p. 32).
Whereas Cranmer had in his sights the errors of mid-sixteenth century popery, not the least of the challenges faced by Edward James, in
Llandaff especially, fifty years later was the persistence of recusancy.[66]
Yet it was not just a residual Catholicism that was the main problem, but
an ingrained religiosity which thought of salvation in terms of 'doing
good' in order to earn one's way to heaven. For conventional Christians,
the truths of evangelical religion were novel and potentially offensive.

Such faith, however, was not just notional. According to Homily IV,
'On True, Living and Christian Faith': 'This is not a general belief of
the truths of our faith, but a real trust and confidence in God's mercy

through our Lord Jesus Christ and a sure hope that we will receive all good things through his hand' (p. 41). The three elements of faith which are held forth are: 'Firstly, it is not notional or dead but active, creating good works; secondly, that without faith good works, acceptable to God, are impossible; thirdly, that true faith is not offered to assuage God or in fear of his judgement or wrath, but is accepted humbly, as a gift' (p. 42). Whereas the homily on faith introduces the necessity of good works as the evidence of justification: 'A true faith cannot be kept secret but will break out and show itself by good works' (p. 46), this is expanded upon in Homily V, 'On Good Works Connected to Faith', which is, in fact, an introduction to the doctrine of sanctification. The correct order is insisted upon once more: 'Let me repeat; no one should depend upon their good works before they have faith. Where faith is lacking, there can be no good works' (p. 58). Quoting extensively from Augustine, Ambrose and John Chrysostom, he hammers home the point once again: 'When faith in Christ is not our foundation, there are no good works however we attempt to build' (p. 59). Yet in order for people to live the true Christian life, justification must issue forth in true holiness. This occurs through an active obedience to the law of God contained in the Ten Commandments and the precepts of Jesus: 'You should accept this as the most wholesome doctrine from the lips of Christ himself, that the works of God's moral law are the works of faith, which lead us into the blessed life of the world to come' (p. 63).

Despite the initial emphasis on justification by faith, at least three of the homilies in Book One, 'Against the Swearing of Oaths and Perjury', 'Against Whoring and Adultery' and 'Against Strife and Contention', as well as four in Book Two, 'On Good Works and Fasting', 'Against Gluttony and Drunkenness', 'Against Wearing Fine Clothes' and 'On Almsgiving', are on specific ethical matters in which the general appeal to obey is made concrete. The accent is on avoiding blatant or public sins, on deference to authority and on following the ethical stipulations of the New Testament:

> Oppress no-one, kill no-one, neither hurt, slander nor despise anyone but love all, speak well of all, help those who you can, yes even your enemies and those who hate you and say all things ill of you and seek your harm … As you do this you will not fail, according to Christ's promise, to enter the life eternal where you will live in glory and joy with God forever. (p. 79)

In good Augustinian fashion, the Christian populace is not expected to be perfect. The fact that swearing, perjury, whoring, adultery, strife, contention, gluttony and drunkenness are warned against is sufficient evidence of their prevalence among the baptized faithful. It is also noteworthy that Homily X in Book One is entitled 'An Exhortation to Obedience' while despite its title, the final homily in Book Two, 'A Homily against Disobedience and Rebellion', is not a sermon at all but an extended treatise on the need for wholesale submission to the powers of the state. The ideal here is of a Christianized civic society, acutely conscious of the spiritual perils of popery at home and the political threat of Catholic enemies abroad, nourished by the Word of God and loyal to the sovereign, its Christian prince.

Despite being published early during the reign of James I, the vision enshrined in Edward James's translation is typical of the Elizabethan Church of Bishops Richard Davies and William Morgan. Theologically it is strongly Reformed. The doctrine of predestination, though not blatant, is presupposed clearly as a concomitant to the principle of justification by faith alone and salvation wholly of grace. Episcopal oversight was not a matter of prelacy, however strenuously John Penry had argued to the contrary,[67] but of pastoral effectiveness in continuity with revered historical precedent. Parochial ministry was not sacerdotal in character but existed in order to bring the people to the knowledge of the Word. Justification, though by faith, needed to issue forth in righteous behaviour. Following the Zürich model of Reformation, the church was not independent of the state as in Beza's Geneva, but was subject, under Christ, to the royal supremacy. Although enjoying fellowship with the best European Reformed churches, this church possessed a character of its own.[68] Parochial boundaries and arch-diaconal structures had been retained and the medieval ecclesiastical system had been preserved intact. Unlike the continental churches where the clergy were allowed to conduct worship either *ex tempore* or according to a loose directory, close adherence to the Book of Common Prayer was prescribed. Although Bible-centred, worship was liturgical while the clergy were expected to wear surplice and cope. If the calendar had been simplified, the great feasts of Christmas (Book Two, Homily XII), Good Friday (Homily XIII), Easter Sunday (Homily XIV) and Whitsun (Homily XVI) had been retained. Worship was to be celebrated nowhere else but in the buildings dedicated to the purpose:

> The church, as a temple wrought by human hands, has been appointed,
> according to the use and constant example of the Old Testament and
> the New, for the coming together of the people of God for the purpose of
> hearing the holy Word of God, of calling upon his holy name, of thank-
> ing him for his manifold blessings and of partaking duly and diligently
> of his holy sacraments. (Book Two, Homily I, 'On the Correct use of the
> Church as God's Temple,' p. 2)

By 'listening intently to these godly, learned sermons' wrote James in
his Introduction, the devout would 'learn in time to believe in God
truly and faithfully, to call upon him seriously and worthily, and fulfil
their responsibilities to God and to their neighbours, and in this knowledge enjoy eternal life in the world to come through our Saviour Jesus
Christ'.[69] This vision was wholly in keeping with the strongly Reformed
Calvinism of the Elizabethan Church and had much in common with
the pastoral concerns of such moderate and conformist Puritans as Huw
Lewys in the Bangor diocese and Robert Holland in St David's and their
respective bishops. Also, it was in full accord with the policies of his own
diocesan, Francis Godwin, who followed William Morgan in 1601.[70]
Despite the comparative dearth of preachers in the different dioceses
– a point made pointedly by Edward James in the Introduction of his
volume – by the beginning of the seventeenth century, an unobtrusive
zeal for effective preaching, for pastoral care in the biblical mode and
for the spread of practical godliness had become a characteristic of the
reformed Welsh Church.

Theology in Wales during the Jacobean era, 1603–25

The cordiality of the Welsh people's reception of James I is illustrated
by Robert Holland's effusive introductory comments to his translation
of *Basilikon Doron* (1604) which was issued within a short time of the
sovereign's accession to the throne.[71] The king reciprocated readily
by affirming their traditional loyalty to Henry Tudor and his dynasty,
from whom James was descended, and their more recent adherence to
the Protestant succession. Moreover, he commended the older union
between Wales and England as a model for his proposed reconciliation
between the English and Scottish crowns, and rewarded influential
members of the indigenous gentry class by issuing state honours of
knighthoods and lands.[72] Always jealous for the strengthening of royal

prerogatives including, as it would transpire, his divine right to rule, he sponsored those who showed the readiest support for the new *status quo*. The position of the reformed Established Church, which was already securing the adherence of the Welsh people through its liturgy, worship and vernacular biblical instruction, was strengthened even further in 1606 by the publication of the Book of Homilies in Welsh. Although he was opposed implacably to Presbyterianism with its potentially levelling implications, and was equally inimical to the more intemperate manifestations of Puritanism, the new king was totally committed to the Calvinistic creed of the church of the realm.[73] The fusion of moderate, conformist Puritanism with the sturdy Reformed doctrine so characteristic of the Welsh church of the day would provide the context for the development of theology in Wales for the two decades to come.

The basic continuity between this and the late Elizabethan period is illustrated by the publication in 1612 of the *Llyfer Plygain*, a translation of the English Primer or devotional handbook which became a popular means of inculcating Protestantism among the laity during the Virgin Queen's reign.[74] The book included an exposition of the Ten Commandments, the Apostle's Creed, the Lord's Prayer and the two dominical sacraments along with the Church Catechism, in this case Alexander Nowell's shorter catechism, *Catechismus … Primum Latinae* (1572).[75] Nowell, sometime dean of St Paul's and principal of Brasenose College, Oxford, had, along with Richard Davies, been a refugee in Frankfurt during the Marian persecution. He had returned to help forge the Calvinistic character of the Elizabethan Church while his writings became staple fare in Oxford's theological schools.[76] The work was translated by Daniel Powel, son of David Powel, who had been mentioned by William Morgan in the Introduction to the Bible of 1588 as 'David Powel, Doctor in Divinity', who had afforded him 'not inconsiderable help' in his labours.[77] Powel (1522–98), a native of Wrexham and one of the earliest graduates of Jesus College, Oxford, had returned as incumbent of Rhiwabon in his home locality and was noted as being one of the few preachers operative in the St Asaph diocese. He had returned to Oxford in 1583 to take his DD. The author of the *Historie of Cambria* (1584) and compiler of a Latin compendium including Geoffrey of Monmouth's *Britanniae Historiae* and Giraldus Cambrensis's medieval *Itinerarium …* *et Descriptio Cambriae* (1585), like his fellow Protestant humanists, he blended a regard for the classical past with a zeal for religious reform.[78] Though begun by him, the primer had been completed by his son, Daniel

Powel (?–1620?), brother of the better known Gabriel Powel (*c.*1567–
1611),[79] domestic chaplain to Richard Vaughan, the Welshman and
'evangelical' whom James had appointed bishop of London in 1605.[80]

In requiring the catechumen to recite the principal themes of
Christianity, the Holy Spirit is referred to as 'he who sanctifies me and
all of the elect people of God'.[81] Although Nowell does not shy away from
the language of baptismal regeneration, 'through baptism we are born
again' (p. 82), this is made conditional on the exercise of personal faith:
'Through baptism we are brought into the church and become indubita-
bly children of God, having been grafted into the Body of Christ' (p. 78).
Despite being administered to children, that which has been promised
in baptism must be acted upon in order to be made effective: 'When
they come of age, they themselves must understand, believe and confess
and thereafter show forth Christian responsibilities in their lives' (p. 80).
Nowhere does the catechism countenance the idea of the sacrament being
effective *ex opere operato*. In the Lord's Supper, which signifies a spiritual
participation in Christ's body and blood, the elements remain wholly
unchanged, while the communion points to the finished work of the
cross: '[Christ] offered himself up once and for all to abolish sin, the one,
only, perfect and eternal sacrifice, accepted by God the Father' (p. 86). As
well as explaining simply and succinctly the sacramental teaching of the
Reformed establishment, the catechism places much emphasis on obedience to instituted authority, both temporal and ecclesiastical, while the
primer itself includes the litany as well as forms of prayer designed to
be used in personal and family devotion. In his preface, Daniel Powel not
only pays homage to his late father, 'Dr Powel, who yearned for the good
of all of God's church' (p. 3), but appeals to his readers to take its contents
to heart: 'Although this book appears small, its substance is immense,
being medicine for the soul. Any man desiring eternal salvation must,
of necessity, learn from it and act according to its stipulations' (p. 4).

It was one thing to issue theological literature in Welsh; to ensure
that it was read and acted upon was quite another. Literacy was confined
to the gentry, the professions and the higher clergy who had access to
the English language and had been educated in the classical languages
as well. Whereas the Welsh population has been estimated at some
320,000,[82] a larger group (perhaps a quarter of the population), including
the minor gentry, freeholders and yeoman farmers, the more substantial
tenant farmers and the generality of the clergy, would be literate in their
own language though not in English, and it was to these that much of

the edifying literature was aimed.[83] A third group, and by far the largest, would have been illiterate. It included tenant farmers, craftsmen, cottagers, labourers and paupers for whom instruction would have to be given aurally through catechizing and the patient application of the preached Word. Moreover, despite the reforming zeal of the more conscientious bishops and churchmen, there remained an alarming level of scriptural ignorance and religious apathy among the populace as a whole. A generation earlier John Penry had bewailed the fact that there was

> not one in some score of our parishes, that have a saving knowledge. Thousands there be ... that know Jesus Christ to be neither God nor man, king, priest nor prophet ... The rest of our people ... never think of any religion true or false, plainly mere atheists or stark blinded with superstition.[84]

Even if this view reflected Puritan partisanship of an extravagant kind, more centrist figures realized that the mission of the Reformation was yet incomplete and that extensive evangelization remained to be done. The besetting problem of the Welsh dioceses was their poverty. Following Henry VIII's dissolution of the monasteries, monastic properties including parish lands had, for the most part, fallen into the rapacious hands of many of the local gentry thus preventing the church in its proto-Protestant guise from establishing itself as an effective body.[85] The clergy had been paid by the raising of revenue through their lands. Although the post-Reformation clergy were still entitled to the tithe, this, first, had to be collected, and secondly, was frequently insufficient to provide a realistic living for the incumbent. Many of the clergy would farm their glebe in order to augment their income while the higher clergy, including the bishops, would multiply livings sometimes scandalously, in order to collect tithe funds from the individual parishes, employing minor clergy for the cure of souls. This, of course, was hardly conducive to maintaining an effective preaching ministry let alone fulfilling the Puritan ideal of sustaining a single, well-supported, godly and learned ministry in each parish.[86]

There is little doubt, however, that the standard of pastoral care was improving and that the principles of reformed churchmanship were gaining ground.[87] Even after the demise of William Morgan in 1604, the leaders of the four Welsh sees were men of quality. Anthony Rudd, who would remain in St David's until 1615, had shown sympathy to

Puritanism by defending nonconformist clergy in convocation on more than one occasion,[88] while George Carleton, who had succeeded Francis Goodwin to Llandaff in 1617, was one of the four British delegates to the Synod of Dort, the council of theologians that had defined the Reformed faith in response to the free-will theology of the Dutchman Jacob Arminius (1560–1609).[89] Held in the city of Dordtrecht in the Netherlands between November 1618 and May 1619, the synod bequeathed to the world the 'five points' of Calvinism which would become pivotal in Welsh theology for the next two centuries: total depravity, unconditional election, limited atonement, irresistible grace and the perseverance of the saints.[90] The profound difference between these men, however, and their Elizabethan predecessors was that by birth, language and cultural affiliation, they were English. Apart from at Bangor, where Henry Rowland presided until 1616 to be succeeded by Carmarthen-born Lewis Bayly, and at St Asaph where, until 1624, Richard Parry perpetuated the tradition of Welsh biblical scholarship previously exemplified so splendidly by William Morgan, the Jacobean bishops had little natural empathy with the people whom they had been called to serve. Carleton, who, following his translation to Chichester in 1619 was replaced by the distinctly lacklustre Theophilus Field in 1619 (who, in turn, replaced William Laud at St David's in 1627), was sufficiently candid to admit that his ignorance of Welsh prevented him from being an effective spiritual leader to his flock.[91] For all that, they were, on the whole, able and conscientious administrators who brought credit to the Established Church in Wales.

Because Welsh churchmen were well disposed to King James's ideal of being 'a reforming Christian prince invested with a divine authority to govern the Church, supported by the apostolic order of bishops',[92] the Hampton Court Conference of January 1604 did not affect Wales unduly.[93] The farthest James went in responding to English Puritan demands for radical reform was to agree that pluralism, where possible, should be curtailed, that parish-based preaching ministries should be strengthened, that minor changes in the Prayer Book liturgy should be instigated and that a new translation of the Bible should be published. In exchange, the king required from his clergy a wholehearted accept-ance of Prayer Book worship including the wearing of surplice and cope, their affirmation of the threefold ministry of bishop, presbyter and dea-con, and a ready obedience to Episcopal rule.[94] As there is no evidence that nonconformity or a conscientious refusal to practise extra-biblical rites stipulated by the Church had ever been prevalent in Wales, these conditions were accepted without demur. The one result of the conference that would have the most profound, albeit indirect, effect on the Welsh Church was the publication of a new translation of the Bible, the so-called 'Authorized Version', in 1611.

The one person who had been spurred on by 'the King James Bible' of 1611 to provide an updated version of the scriptures in Welsh was Richard Parry (1560–1623), bishop of St Asaph. A native of Flintshire, he had been educated at Westminster School and Christ Church, Oxford, where he had graduated BA in 1584, MA two years later, BD in 1594 and DD in 1597. He had been ordained in the Bangor diocese during the year of his graduation, had served as headmaster of Ruthin School, a school established by Gabriel Goodman, dean of Westminster, in order to educate boys from his home locality,[95] and as chancellor of Bangor Cathedral before following William Morgan in 1604 as leader of the see of St Asaph. He was, in fact, 'one of the ablest and most learned churchmen of the period',[96] whose contribution to the history of the Welsh Bible has been eclipsed by Morgan and by his undoubtedly brilliant brother-in-law and assistant, Dr John Davies of Mallwyd.[97] In the Latin Introduction addressed to James I in his 1620 revision of the Welsh Bible, he stated that the best way that he could serve his God, sovereign and countrymen was 'by exercising my complete energies in producing a Welsh version of the Bible as has been done so successfully with the English version'.[98] Rather than having been commissioned to do the task, he had undertaken it of his own volition:

> Now, when the Bibles in most of our churches have either gone missing or have been worn out, and no-one, as far as I had heard, had intended to print a new edition … I took it upon myself, my sovereign, following your instruction to the English and after the pious example of my reverend predecessors, Richard Davies, bishop of St David's who, with the assistance of William Salesbury, translated the New Testament, and William Morgan, the late bishop of St Asaph, who gave to the world the Holy Bible in the Welsh language.[99]

Parry's was not to be a new translation; certainly it was not a Welsh translation from the English of the Authorised Version. It was, rather, a scholarly revision of Morgan's work, rewritten in the light of the latest textual scholarship in Hebrew and Greek, with an eye to the practical needs of the general worshipper in their parish church. 'In the light of these amendments', he claimed, 'it will be difficult to judge whether it is my version or that of [Bishop] Morgan.'[100]

Although his name did not appear in the Introduction, Parry had been assisted by a younger clergyman, John Davies (*c*.1567–1644), who was destined to become 'the greatest scholar of the later Renaissance period' that Wales would ever produce.[101] Born in Llanferres, Denbighshire, he 'belonged to that first generation of Welsh men and women who, from early childhood, were able to hear the liturgy, the Psalms and the New Testament read in their mother tongue'.[102] Educated at Ruthin School, he spent some years at the rectory at Llanrhaeadr-ym-Mochnant being tutored in Hebrew by William Morgan when the translator was work-ing on his *magnum opus*. When he went up to Jesus College in 1589, Anthony à Wood noted that he was already steeped in the biblical lan-guages having been 'bred up at the feet of William Morgan, afterwards Bishop of St Asaph'.[103] As well as having been immersed in Hebrew, he would have been instructed in the skills of translation and initi-ated into his mentor's mastery of the Welsh bardic tradition. No date can be given for his ordination, but there is evidence that he served as bishop's personal secretary and chaplain, first at the palace at Mathern, Monmouthshire, following Morgan's appointment to Llandaff in 1595, and then in St Asaph from 1601. Consequently he assisted with the revision of the New Testament and compilation of the 1599 Book of Common Prayer. A fortnight after Davies's appointment to the recto-ral benefice of Mallwyd, Merionethshire, in 1604, Morgan died. It was from Mallwyd that John Davies would make his signal contribution to scholarship in Wales for the next forty years.

In 1607 Davies married Jane, the sister of Gwen Parry, wife of his new diocesan. Having already recognized his superior qualities, John Parry appointed his brother-in-law chaplain and then canon chancellor of St Asaph Cathedral. Encouraged also to proceed with his scholarly career, Davies returned to Oxford, to Lincoln College this time, taking his BD in 1608 and his DD in 1615. He remained, however, assiduous in his parochial responsibilities in rural Merionethshire. Along with his pastoral duties he was busy preparing for the publication of his renowned grammar, *Antiquae Linguae Britannicae ... Rudimenta* (1621) and collaborating with Parry on the new version of the Bible. Although the level of his contribution to the project has always been a matter of conjecture, the consensus view is that Davies, with his superior training in Hebrew and his long experience as William Morgan's amanuensis, provided the basis for the work though Parry was far from being a negligible biblical scholar in his own right. What the 1620 Bible did was to correct the typographical errors in the 1588 version, mostly in the Apocrypha, to bring the text into a closer harmony with what the translators deemed to be the more correct rendering of the Hebrew and Greek, and to eradicate some of Morgan's more colloquial terms. Echoes from the Welsh poetic tradition, in which Davies, like Morgan, had considerable expertise, resonate throughout the work. In all, about a third of William Morgan's text was revised.[104] Like the earlier version, the 1620 Bible has also been hailed as a masterpiece:

> Translation of the Bible into Welsh in the Renaissance period reached its zenith with the 1620 revision … Davies had the necessary background in Welsh literature with a grasp on Welsh vocabulary and syntax, to produce a version that established itself as the official and accepted Welsh Bible for centuries.[105]

Nevertheless its foundation was the Bible of 1588: 'The result could be regarded as a culmination and completion of Morgan's work.'[106] Despite the scholarly input of Richard Parry and John Davies, '[p]osterity has judged it to be William Morgan's Bible still and that is by no means an unjust conclusion'.[107] It would be the basis upon which all Welsh theology would be done for the next three and a half centuries.

The one other text to be published during King James's reign which would also have an enormous effect on the worship of the Welsh people and to enhance even further their biblical literacy was *Llyfr y Psalmau, wedi eu cyfieithu, a'i cyfansoddi ar fesur cerdd, yn Gymraeg* (1621) ('The Book of Psalms, translated and composed in the metre of song, in Welsh'), or the *Salmau Cân*, Edmund Prys's massively popular edition of the metrical psalms. The friendship of Edmund Prys (1544–1623) with William Morgan, his exact contemporary at St John's College, Cambridge, has already been mentioned.[108] They shared the same reformed (if conformist) churchmanship, an identical cultural background and common vision for the spread of disciplined biblical piety through the structures of the Established Church. A native of Llanrwst in the Conwy Valley, his St John's career had seen him elected fellow and chaplain of his college as well as university preacher. He had been ordained deacon in Ely Cathedral by Richard Cox in 1567 and priest a year later. Like Morgan he had sided

with John Whitgift, Regius Professor of divinity, against Puritan innovation and would remain unbending in his loyalty to the Prayer Book
norms. Appointed rector of Ffestiniog and Maentwrog in the diocese of
Bangor in 1573, he became archdeacon of Merioneth three years later,
positions that he would retain for the rest of his life. As well as having
extensive administrative responsibilities within the diocese, he served
for decades as a Justice of the Peace. As a member of the gentry class, his
social standing was high. In cultural circles he was best known as a poet,
the most accomplished of his generation outside the professional guild.[109]
His marathon bardic contest with Wiliam Cynwal, a professional poet
from Denbighshire, which lasted between 1580 and 1587, shone a vivid
light on the growing rift between the obscurantism of the traditional
bards and the freshness and innovation of the new learning. Like David
Powel and Richard Vaughan, he was commended in the Introduction of
the Bible of 1588 for having assisted William Morgan in his labours,[110]
while a generation later, in the preface to his grammar, John Davies was
effusive in his praise: 'Edmund Prys, Archdeacon of Merioneth: outstanding elder due to the range of his scholarship, revered greatly for numerous
reasons, at all times my dearest friend.'[111] He too was one of the exceptionally gifted scholars and ecclesiastical figures of his day.

Attempts at putting the Psalms into verse had been made since
the end of the sixteenth century, culminating in Wiliam Midleton's
Psalmae y Brenhinol Brophwyd Dafydd ('The Psalms of the Royal Prophet
David'), a version of the complete Psalter in strict metre poetry, in
1603. These, however, had been a contribution to literature rather than
worship, though James Parry, a squire from the Welsh-speaking part
of Herefordshire, and his son George Rhys Parry, had translated the
Psalms into free verse, more suited to congregational use, though their
fine translation was to remain in MS form. In 1603 Edward Kyffin, a
London clergyman and brother of Maurice Kyffin, translator of Bishop
Jewel's *Apologia Ecclesiae Anglicanae*, had issued his *Rhann o Psalmae
Dafydd Brophwyd* ('A Section of the Psalms of King David'), though they
made little impact at the time.[112] It was Prys's 1621 version, which was
issued alongside the revised version of the Book of Common Prayer, also
fashioned by Richard Parry and John Davies, which revolutionized congregational praise in the parish churches. Prys's 'undoubted masterpiece
and the crown of his literary career' had an immense impact almost from
the beginning.[113] Realizing that the translation needed to be simple, easy
to sing and retentive, he produced a *tour de force*: 'His judgement was

vindicated by the immediate, immense, and enduring success of his own version of the Psalms in simple metre and plain language, no fewer than ninety-nine versions of which were published between 1621 and 1865.'[114] Prys was seventy-eight years old at the time and still in harness. 'With the publication of the Metrical Psalms', states Gruffydd Aled Williams, 'the process of giving the new Protestant Church the necessary means to ensure the loyalty of the Welsh people was now complete.'[115] Prys passed away in September 1623 having reached his eightieth year.

The latter years of James I's reign would mark a sea change in the religious complexion of the kingdom. A reaction against the Calvinistic nature of the Established Church had already registered during the 1590s, with individual academics at both Oxford and Cambridge emphasizing the differences rather than the similarities between the Church of England and the Reformed churches of continental Europe. By the second decade of the seventeenth century what has been termed 'Anti-Calvinism' had become emboldened with powerful clerics intent on creating an establishment which was radically different from that championed by the reformed bishops of Elizabeth's reign. They included Lancelot Andrewes, since 1609 bishop of Ely who would proceed to Winchester in 1619; John Overall at Coventry and Litchfield; Richard Neile, the party's leader, bishop of Durham since 1617 who would later become archbishop of York; and most markedly, William Laud, formerly president of St John's College, Oxford, from 1621 to 1626 bishop of St David's, thereafter Bath and Wells, London, and ultimately Archbishop of Canterbury.[116] Initially their interest was in the externals of religion: order, seemliness and a stricter adherence to liturgical worship, the vital importance of the sacraments at the expense of preaching and exaggerated claims for Episcopal authority, but soon their antipathy to the Reformed doctrines of election and salvation by grace alone would come to the fore. The Arminian themes of free will, co-operation with divine grace and moral striving as an aspect of salvation would supersede predestination, the application of Christ's atoning sacrifice to the elect and the perseverance of the saints as the characteristic themes of theological discourse.[117] Although this would not really impact Wales for some time, the changes were ominous. According to one authority: 'The rise of the Arminians soon destabilized the English Church and brought it crashing down in ruin.'[118]

Not that anyone would have foreseen this, especially not in Wales. King James, by now ill and enfeebled, had forfeited the affection of many of his subjects by refusing to stand by Friedrich V, elector of the

Palatinate who had married James's daughter, Elizabeth, in expanding Protestant rule into Bohemia at the beginning of what would become the Thirty Years War.[119] His residual Calvinism was being diluted by the growing influence in court of Andrewes, Laud and George Villiers, duke of Buckingham. His son, Charles, prince of Wales, whose marriage to a Spanish Catholic princess was being arranged, had already embraced Arminianism and ceremonial religion of an advanced kind. Much of this was hidden from the king's Welsh subjects whose main concern in the 1620s was whether profits from cloth, butter and cattle would be sufficient to ensure a buoyant economy.[120] What was nearest the hearts of Welsh churchmen was the need to further entrench the truths of biblical reformation in the lives of the people. Lewis Bayly's 1623 diocesan visitation in Bangor showed how much more work needed to be done. The depressing litany of 'two sermons in ... the last twelve-month' (Llanfairpwll); 'No sermon preached there this five or six years past' (Penmon); 'No quarterly sermon' (Llanddyfnan); 'No sermons at all' (Llangwyllog); 'But two sermons there' (Llanegryn) and many more, was complemented by the too frequent complaints of non-residency, neglect or the scandalous lives of the clergy: 'The parson there is presented for not relieving the poor, being non-resident, and for no sermons' (Llanfechell); 'The curate is presented for the haunting of alehouses, and for often being overseen in drink ... also for quarrelling and brawling with his parishioners and others' (Llanddeusant).[121] Reformed and practical Christianity was still more an ideal than a fact. During the same year, Maurice Wynn, an apprentice merchant in the German city of Hamburg, suggested that his father, Sir John Wynn of Wydir, should use his great wealth to sponsor an effective preaching ministry in his home town of Llanrwst as well as providing temporal support for the people. If there was famine in Europe there was another kind of dearth in Wales,

> that is the want of God's Word preached ... by reason of which diverse souls perish for want of knowledge. None can be saved without faith and how is it wrought in men's hearts but by hearing the Word. Where the Word is not heard there can be no faith, and without faith it is impossible to please God.[122]

The challenge to make the Reformed faith a practical reality among the people would still dominate the mission of the Established Church in Wales during the early part of the reign of Charles I.

Welsh theology between the accession of Charles I and the First Civil War, 1625–42

Just as there had been much continuity between the reign of Queen Elizabeth and James I, there was little sign that the kingship of Charles I would instigate any marked change in the fortunes of the land. The trend towards appointing English bishops continued, with William Laud succeeding Richard Milbourne at St David's in 1621 before proceeding to Bath and Wells in 1626 to be replaced by Llandaff's Theophilus Field, while he in turn was replaced by the Scot William Murray who would embody the anti-Calvinist liturgical disciplinarianism which came to characterize the latter years of Charles's reign. At St Asaph John Hanmer, a Welshman native to the diocese, had succeeded Richard Parry in 1624 to be followed five years later by John Owen who, despite his Welsh roots was from Northamptonshire. Both Hanmer and Owen were conscientious diocesans strongly supportive of the need to strengthen preaching ministries at parish level.[123] The same had been true of Lewis Bayly, a cantankerous figure, who would remain at Bangor between 1616 and 1631. His 'pugnacious temperament and violent tongue' had got him into trouble more than once.[124] He was indicted by the Privy Council in 1612 and in 1621, following a sharp exchange with the king, and was even incarcerated briefly in the Fleet. In his diocese he had clashed with powerful magnate Sir John Wynn and even more spectacularly with another landed family, the Griffiths of Cefnamwlch on the Llŷn Peninsula, which included Edmund Griffith, his own dean (and Episcopal successor).[125] Despite everything he remained a diligent Reformed bishop, zealous for the Protestant legacy of the Established Church. In his correspondence with King Charles in April 1630, he claimed to have insisted that his clergy affirm publicly their full adherence to the 39 Articles and the Book of Common Prayer, that they should be good scholars and live blameless lives. He had instigated a regular preaching ministry in the cathedral since 1617, had taken care over confirmations and had held 'synods', or regular meetings in which the clergy reported on matters within their parishes:[126] 'I have planted grave and learned preachers all over my diocese, three or four for one preaching minister that I found there; that I took care that catechizing be duly observed in all parishes, and suffer none to preach that are [not] conformable.'[127]

Whatever Bayly's contribution was to the welfare of his diocese, his prime distinction in the history of theology in Wales was through the vernacular version of his devotional classic *The Practice of Piety* (1611). Translated by Rowland Vaughan (*c.*1590–1667), the squire of Caer-gai, Merionethshire, *Yr Ymarfer o Dduwioldeb* (1630) helped spread the influence of the practical divinity that was so characteristic of the Puritan way.[128] Bayly, who was born in Carmarthen, had graduated from Exeter College, Oxford, in the 1590s returning to take his BD in 1611 and DD two years later. Sponsored by the Johns family of Abermarlais, he had been ordained in the diocese of Worcester, being appointed vicar of Evesham in 1600. *The Practice of Piety* grew from his regular preaching ministry in the Evesham parish church, while the strong emphasis on rigorous self-discipline, practical godliness, the keeping of the Sabbath and the centrality of the sermon all within the context of strict Prayer Book conformity, placed the author squarely in the moderate Puritan camp. Bayly soon drew the attention of King James who appointed him royal chaplain in 1607, and despite his sometimes intemperate indiscretions, he always retained the sovereign's favour.

The *Ymarfer o Dduwioldeb* ('The Practice of Piety') has been described as 'the first book in Wales which contains anything like an approach to a systematic treatment of theological and ethical truths'.[129] Its opening section of thirty-three pages includes a treatment of the being of God, followed by some hundred pages on the corrupt nature of humankind after the Fall which prevents men and women from practising the life of piety. Thereafter the volume proceeds to instruct its readers on prayer, public and private worship including the singing of psalms, the keeping of the Sabbath, Bible reading, sacramental religion and discipline in the face of adversity, illness and death. As an exercise in practical theology, linking moral theology with devotional practice, the original version was phenomenally successful, reaching 164 known editions in eleven different languages, affording its author an international reputation in Reformed or Puritan circles;[130] for Protestants in Reformation Britain it became '[t]he most successful devotional handbook of all [and] ... the uncontested champion of early modern British Protestant devotional writing'.[131] It is as an introduction to Reformed Church of England theology in a winsome and elegant Welsh guise that it will concern us here.

For Bayly God exists as a triune being of Father, Son and Holy Spirit. He begins his treatise by emphasizing this trinitarian nature of the one eternal God: 'These three persons are not three separate beings or three aspects of the one divine being but three distinct persons sharing the divine essence, that one eternal essence existing of itself and being upheld by no other.'[132] If the unity of the godhead is basic to his doctrine, the divine trinity is derivative of the fact. Although co-equal, there exists a definite order among the persons. God the unbegotten Father is the root or the source of the Trinity; God the Son is eternally begotten of the Father while the Holy Spirit proceeds from both Father and Son. The incarnation occurred when God the eternal Son conjoined himself fully with humankind in the person of Jesus of Nazareth and by so doing took impersonal or general human nature in order to show solidarity with the whole race and effect its salvation. Consequently as the incarnate Son, Christ possesses two unchanged, unconfused and undivided natures: 'Just as a soul and a body constitute a man's being, so deity and humanity constitute the one Person of Christ' (p. 8). Having laid out his trinitarian presuppositions, Bayly proceeds to instruct his readers concerning the attributes of God, his essential attributes being simplicity, immensity, immutability and eternity, while listing as his communicable attributes: life, understanding, will, strength and authority. Under the subheading of will he includes love, righteousness, mercy, goodness (which encompasses grace), truth, long suffering, holiness and wrath. Each of these attributes is rooted in God's triune nature and characterizes Father, Son and Spirit. This knowledge is not speculative but practical: 'This, therefore, is the correct portrayal of God as he has revealed himself to us in his Word. This doctrine, more than any other, is necessary for the true practice of piety' (p. 28).

The next hundred pages constitute a typically Reformed assessment of the human condition blighted by sin. Although the subject matter is grim, the prose is arresting and aimed at driving the reader to Christ and redemption. Yet even this should not be presumed upon or taken for granted. God's grace is sovereign and limited to the elect: 'It is true that whenever a sinner repents God will forgive, but scripture never says that a sinner can repent at will, only when God grants him grace' (p. 96). Salvation, according to the Reformed scheme, is totally of God: 'To repent and believe is to come to Christ. No one can do this without having been drawn by their heavenly Father' (p. 96). Whereas the official creed of the Elizabethan Church had been Reformed, the more pronounced Puritans had leaned towards so-called 'experimental predestinarianism' while the bishops, following the lead of John Whitgift, had adhered to 'creedal predestinarianism', believing that the elect and the reprobate could not necessarily be told apart. God's hidden decree would be made active through the regular worship of the faithful according to the Book of Common Prayer and attendance at the preaching of the Word. As pastoral leaders of a national church including intractable sinners as well as prospective saints, the bishops were content to allow edification to be regulated by conformity to external order.[133] The more definite Puritans, on the other hand, exhorted the faithful to make their election sure by *experiencing* the reality of the new birth. Bayly's work stood somewhere between these two points. If it was frequently impossible to differentiate between reprobate and elect, nevertheless the baptized should strive to make their calling a reality. He warned constantly against the danger of an insincere profession: 'Do not deceive yourself with the mere name of Christian; whoever persists in some accustomed sin is not in a state of grace' (p. 98). Grace is not universal. If one thief on the cross repented and was saved, the other was denied the grace of repentance and was damned. Similarly, justification by faith, though a sacred truth, can never excuse presumption, and all who would feign to reach heaven must strive to enter in. Following the Fall, the human will is hopelessly marred: 'Man is in a state of corruption whose free will only chooses evil and not virtue' (p. 102). Election, therefore, can only be made good by partaking of the means of grace, principally the preaching of the Word: 'The preaching of the gospel is the chief means ordained by God to save souls, those of whom he has chosen to redeem' (p. 107). The next three hundred or so pages describe Bayly's ideal for those who would deign live the life of practical godliness.

This was not the only work of practical divinity to appear in a Welsh guise in 1630. In his preface to *Llwybr Hyffordd … i'r Nefoedd*, his translation of the English Puritan Arthur Dent's *The Plain Man's Pathway to Heaven* (1601) dated September 1629, Robert Llwyd (or Lloyd) noted that the Welsh version of *The Practice of Piety* was already in the hands of the printers and would appear 'before the winter'.[134] All that the godly would need in order to live the Christian life would be found 'in that magnificent book' (Sig. A6v; p. 130). For his part, Rowland Vaughan, Bayly's translator, also mentioned the appearance of 'that excellent book entitled *A Pathway to Heaven* translated by that learned man of letters, my dear teacher Mr R[obert] Lloyd, the vicar of Chirk' (p. xxii). It appears that both Vaughan's translation of Bayly, and Llwyd's translation of Dent, were at the printer's at the same time and appeared simultaneously, early in 1630.

Robert Llwyd (1565–1655) was a Caernarfonshire man who had graduated BA at Christ Church, Oxford, in 1588 and had taken his MA in 1591. His clerical career was spent in the diocese of St Asaph where

he served as rector of Halkyn and vicar of Wrexham while simultaneously holding the benefice of Chirk (1595–1650). It was as 'the Vicar
of Chirk' that he would make his literary reputation, while remaining
an influential diocesan figure and treasurer of the cathedral. He had
already issued Arthur Dent's *Sermon on Repentance* (1582) as *Pregeth
dduwiol yn traethu am … edifeirwch* (1629) ('A godly sermon concerning … repentance'), while his reforming credentials are apparent not
only in the sermon but in the preface to the *Llwybr Hyffordd*: 'Learn this
from the outset, appreciate your present condition, experience the true
regeneration as a child of God and by so doing gain eternal treasure in
heaven' (Sig. A2v). The author of the original, a Cambridge Puritan who
had graduated from Christ's College in 1575, had been rector of South
Shoebury, Essex, where he had fallen foul of the authorities on account
of his refusal to wear the surplice, to baptize with the sign of the cross
and generally to follow the rubrics of the Book of Common Prayer.
His pugnacious nonconformity was more typical of mid-Elizabethan
English Puritanism than the less abrasive Welsh variety, though it was
as an author (who had died in 1603) that he had aroused the interest of
Llwyd's bishop, John Hanmer. Like his Bangor colleague, Lewis Bayly,
Hanmer (1575–1629) had been a chaplain to James I and shared the
Jacobean Church's Calvinistic consensus and a desire to facilitate godly
living within his diocese. It was he who had encouraged Llwyd, in 1627,
to begin translating Dent's exceptionally popular work.[135]

Although as didactic as Bayly's *Practice of Piety*, the *Pathway to Heaven*
was a work of creative literature cast in the form of a lively dialogue
between four characters: Theologus, 'a preacher'; Philagathus, 'a good
man'; Asunetus, whom Llwyd calls 'an unskilled man'; and Antilegon or
'a quarrelsome man', 'a contentious man' or 'a brawler'. Despite being
stereotypes, each character represents the range of attitudes to biblical
Christianity which the Elizabethan Church, and the early seventeenth-
century Welsh Church, held as their norm. The six points regarded as
axiomatic were: the plight of man in his unregenerate state; the unrighteousness of the present times; 'the marks of the children of God and
those of the reprobates, or plain signs of both salvation or damnation';
the difficulty of reaching heaven and that only few will arrive there; the
ignorance of the world and 'the delectable promises of the gospel'
(Sig. A7v). Theologus is the main character while Philagathus, the godly
layman, provides the questions through which the author, in the guise
of the preacher, seeks to enlighten his readers. Asunetus, the unlettered

peasant, shows that ignorance of the saving truths of the gospel was still rife, while Antilegon represents stubborn unbelief which, despite pretentions to religiosity, marks the seared conscience of a reprobate mind:

> If a man says his prayers and recites his Creed and Ten Commandments, says nothing bad against anyone and does no one harm … if he has good faith towards God and has an honest religion, surely there is no doubt that he will be saved without gadding about after sermons and this constant, ridiculous palaver about the scriptures. (p. 27)

Like him, Asunetus sees little virtue in listening to sermons which were, for the most part beyond his capacity anyway, but believed that if he said his prayers and did harm to no one, surely God would be merciful towards him. Theologus's response is to press home the need for spiritual enlightenment and to warn him that good works, however sincere, were insufficient to earn him redemption.

In the next section, Dent, in Llwyd's prose, lists the besetting sins of the age: pride, sexual impropriety, miserliness, disdain, mendaciousness, drunkenness, sloth and the oppression of the poor. Whereas Asunetus, with due humility, affirms the truth of the preacher's analysis, Antilegon justifies himself constantly, asserting that these so-called sins were nothing but peccadilloes and the result of normal human frailty. Philagathus, like Theologus, will have none of it:

> There is none so blind as those who believe that if they only come to church, listen to the common prayer or the occasional sermon, then they are free of sin despite taking no trouble to turn from unrighteousness. They think that by so doing they have repaid their debt to God and can carry on sinning with impunity. (p. 140)

In the following section, in which the author sets out his doctrine of redemption, he warns against presuming on God's mercy: 'It is true that Christ died for all in as much as his death is sufficient for all, but it is not fruitful for all. It is only the elect who will be saved' (p. 297). The doctrinal basis for the preacher's exhortations is humankind's complete incapacity to extricate itself from inherited guilt following the fall of Adam, God's righteous anger against sin expressed in the decree of reprobation, and his gracious election as the only means of escaping damnation: 'Our salvation has its foundation in the eternal decree of God, and as such it is firm and unshakeable' (p. 268). Listeners of the gospel are urged to apply the promises to themselves and give evidence of repentance: 'If we do not discover these notes or signs of election being active within us, we can have no assurance in this salvation' (p. 328). Whereas this provokes Antilegon's fury: 'You should realize that repentance is God's exceedingly precious gift, and is only granted to some' (p. 312). Asunetus, whose function in the narrative is to show that the Reformed message of the Established Church was effective in creating vital godliness, is ultimately saved. However undemonstrative, his newfound piety is patently real: 'Now I can begin to believe that God's promises have been granted to me, that my sins have been forgiven, and that I am among those who will be saved' (p. 444). Far from disputing either the outcome or the content of the narrative, Robert Llwyd implores his readers to do their utmost to take the story to heart. Both the vicar of Chirk and his bishop were keen to see many more ordinary Welsh people following Asunetus's lead in living a life of true piety and righteousness.

As well as seeing the publication of these two key works of devotion, 1630 was also notable for being the year when the first modestly priced Welsh Bible, *Y Beibl Bach*, 'The Little Bible' or *Y Bibl Cyssegr-Lan* appeared. Its significance cannot be overstated. A quarto edition costing 5s., the price of a sheep, its publication was subsidized by two wealthy London-Welsh merchants who had been touched by a deep strain of Puritan humanitarianism, Sir Thomas Myddleton (1550–1631), a former lord mayor of London, and his colleague Rowland Heylyn (1562–1631).[136] Whereas William Morgan's Bible of 1588 and its successor, Richard Parry's version of 1620, were bulky and expensive tomes for liturgical use within the parish churches, this Bible was not only relatively inexpensive but modestly sized. 'It will serve you not to leave it in church, like a stranger', read the Introduction,

> but it must accompany you into your chamber and under your roof. It is not for you to greet it once a week or once a month, depending how often you attend church, but it must accompany you everywhere like an old friend, and eat of your bread, like a dear acquaintance and best companion.[137]

Its appearance was greeted warmly by both clergy and laymen who were keen to see the extension of godliness within the land. Rhys Prichard, the vicar of Llandovery, was ecstatic in his praise:

Mae'r Beibl Bach yn awr yn gyson
Yn iaith dy fam, i'w gael er coron;
Gwerth dy grys cyn bod heb hwnnw,
Mae'n well na thref dy dad i'th gadw.

Gwell nag aur a gwell nag arian,
Gwell na'r badell fawr na'r crochan;
Gwell dodrefnyn yn dy lety
Yw'r Beibl Bach na dim a feddi.[138]

[The Little Bible is now to be had in your mother tongue for a crown; sell your shirt rather than being without a copy, it's far more valuable than even a father's inheritance. Better than gold, better than silver, better than a cauldron pot; your home will never have a better fixture than the Little Bible for you to cherish.]

Prichard's home-spun verses would become hugely popular and infinitely more effective than the prose works that we have already discussed in spreading basic religious knowledge among the illiterate and semi-literate and did more than anything, sermons included, to popularize the Reformed convictions which had become a norm within the early seventeenth-century Welsh Church. One of his verses provided his rationale for his missionary method:

Abergofi pur bregethiad,
Dyfal gofio ofer ganiad;
A wnaeth im droi hyn o wersi
I chwi'r Cymry yn ganiadau.[139]

('Sound preaching is soon forgotten, vain songs are well remembered; it's this that has caused me to turn these lessons into verse for my fellow Welshmen.')

Rhys Prichard (*c.*1579–1644/5) was born to a middle-status gentry family in Llandovery, Carmarthenshire, and educated at the Carmarthen Grammar School before proceeding to Jesus College, Oxford, in 1597. He graduated BA in 1602 having been ordained to a curacy in Wytham, Essex (probably through the influence of Sir George Devereaux of Llwyn-y-brain, Llandovery, brother of the earl of Essex), and returned, in the same year, to be priested in the diocese of St David's. Despite receiving substantial preferments within the diocese – the sinecure rectory of Llanedi in 1613, prebendary of the collegiate church at Brecon in 1614 and canon chancellorship of St David's Cathedral in 1626 – Llandovery would remain his home and the base for a vigorous parochial ministry for the rest of his career. The 250 or so poems incorporating thousands of catchy, easy-to-remember verses, only came to be published after his death.[140] They represent the same strain of doctrine that has been described above: the innate sinfulness of the human condition; the bondage of the will and God's gracious elective decree; redemption through Christ's unique sacrifice on the cross; the call to faith and costly repentance; the centrality of preaching, perseverance of the saints and the inevitability of judgement. The context, once more, is incontrovertibly 'Anglican'.[141] Liturgical forms are taken for granted as is the threefold ministry of deacon, presbyter and bishop; Prichard has no qualms about referring to the parish clergy as 'priests' (*offeiriaid*) nor of urging the people to avail themselves of the service of even unworthy clergy as it was they who had been validly ordained. (His critique of disreputable or corrupt clergy, nonetheless, could be scathing). The Prayer Book Catechism replete with its sacramental teaching concerning baptism and the Eucharist is the basis for parochial teaching. The great festivals of the church year, Christmas, Easter and Whitsun, are to be celebrated. The piety is of a piece with the practical divinity of Reformed Anglicanism or moderate Puritanism: sabbatarian, strict and morally bracing. Many of Prichard's stanzas are verse equivalents of Vaughan's Welsh version of Bayly's *Practice of Piety*.[142] By the 1620s the vicar of Llandovery's reputation as an effective reformer was complete. 'I bless God for his goodness', wrote Marmaduke Lloyd, the Brecon advocate, in 1626, 'and heartily wish that our church now, when the light of the gospel is grown dim, may shine gloriously with such lights as yourself who are, to the people of those parts, a lantern to their feet and a light to their paths'.[143]

Unlike the situation in some parts of England, London, the Midlands and East Anglia especially, the blend of Reformed churchmanship and parish-based, clerically controlled, Prayer Book Puritanism which characterized Welsh religion at its best during the pre-Laudian years owed little to the more populist, nonconformist strand that was prevalent within some sections of the English Puritan movement.[144] It is true, however, that in some pockets of Wales a more pointed Puritanism, less deferential to ecclesiastical authority, had begun to take root. These were

invariably in the towns, where English was understood, where literacy
had become more widespread and clerical pretentions were being challenged by a more confident laity of the middling sorts. Lectureships,
funded by local boroughs and little amenable to Episcopal control, were
established in order to supplement what was deemed to be inadequate
provision for the effective preaching of God's Word. As early as 1603
Sir William Meredith had bequeathed a legacy in order to sponsor a
gospel lecture in Wrexham; in 1615 Sir William Jones had done the
same for the town of Monmouth and in 1623 one Lewis Owen contributed £7 per annum to pay for a monthly lecture in Caernarfon. A
similar pattern was replicated in the towns of Swansea, Carmarthen
and Haverfordwest.[145] Oliver Thomas's handbook of Bible instruction,
Car-wr y Cymru, yn annog ei genedl anwyl ... i chwilio yr Ysgrythurau (1631)
('The Welshman's Kinsman, urging his dear compatriots ... to search
the Scriptures') was aimed, like the verse of Rhys Prichard, to maximize
the effectiveness of the 'Little Bible' of the previous year, yet unlike the
vicar of Llandovery, Thomas was the first Stuart author in Wales to
emerge from the more nonconformist wing of the Puritan movement.

Oliver Thomas (*c*.1598–1652), the scion of a gentry family from
Montgomeryshire, proceeded from Shrewsbury School to Hart Hall,
Oxford, matriculating in 1616 and graduating BA in 1620. His marriage record of February 1620, at the parish of St Mary's, Shrewsbury,
lists him as a 'minister' while he refers to himself in the *Car-wr* as a
'cleric' (*eglwyswr*), though where he was ordained, and by whom, has
never emerged. By 1628, when he took his MA, he had made his home
at West Felton, Shropshire, where, despite much travelling during the
next two decades, he would remain for the rest of his life. Being drawn
into the vigorous proto-Presbyterian sub-structure which characterized Puritan witness in parts of Shropshire and Cheshire at the time, he
seems to have taken a more radical stance than was usual among Welsh
Puritans: he would later fall foul of the authorities by claiming, in 1639,
that 'all subordinate magistrates had their authority only from the devil,
and that he and you with others of that congregation had endured the
yoke' for too long, and 'were in a fair way to being freed'.[146] In the 1620s
he had been a regular supply at the Wrexham lectureship while during
the Interregnum he would become an active member to the Second
Shropshire Classis.[147]

The tone of the *Car-wr*, however, is irenic and conciliatory. The fact
that Thomas had obtained the imprimatur of Robert Llwyd, author of

the *Llwybr Hyffordd*, diocesan dignitary in St Asaph and vicar of Chirk, is noteworthy: 'After having read and considered it', wrote Llwyd, 'I rejoiced greatly on seeing his willingness and desire to do good towards his countrymen, especially in the matter of their salvation' (p. 119; p. 151).[148] Thomas's complaint, 'forty or sixty churches with no preaching throughout the long summer Sundays' (p. 13; p. 43) was made more in sorrow than in anger, while his criticism of his fellow clergy for neglecting a pulpit ministry, 'Woe to those who will not arouse themselves from the sleep of apathy and feed the flock entrusted to their care by God' (p. 14; p. 44) was much more temperate than that of the conformist vicar of Llandovery:

> Gwae pob bugail mud, anghynnil,
> Na phregetha Grist a'i 'fengyl;
> Gwaed eneidiau mil ofynnir,
> Ar law hwnnw pan ei bernir.[149]

('Woe to every dumb shepherd who preaches neither Christ nor the gospel; the blood of many thousand souls will be required of him in the judgement'). Condemnation is not the forte of the *Car-wr*, rather a desire, common to all reformist churchmen of the time, to spread piety and biblical knowledge throughout the land.

Along with the epistle dedicatory in English and two introductory chapters, one addressed to the clergy and another to his lay readers, the volume is set out in the form of a dialogue between *Car-wr* ('Kinsman') and his compatriot *Cymro* or 'Welshman'. They discuss the virtue of having, for the first time, the scriptures in a readily available form, something that had long been taken for granted in England: 'Among the English there is virtually no-one who cannot read, and even lads and lasses of the lowest degree, tinkers and coopers and the like, own their Bibles and are familiar with their contents' (p. 23; p. 53). Responding to 'Welshman's' question, 'Kinsman' explains that now the Bible was readily available in the language of the people, not only the clergy and the learned but all manner of people could profit from its contents:

> the labourer, the craftsman, the carpenter, the weaver, the cobbler, the miller, the blacksmith, the tailor, the shopkeeper, the goldsmith, yes, all manner of men ... for the souls of the base and the lowly are as much valued by God as the souls of the powerful. (pp. 34–5; pp. 64–5)

In urging all types of people to read the Bible, they should do so, said 'Kinsman', not only for interest's sake but in order to find redemption. The Holy Scriptures were not only a compendium of sacred history and wisdom but a revelation of God's saving purpose for his people: 'Whoever is not conversant with the scriptures will have no knowledge of Christ, and without Christ there is no salvation' (pp. 44–5; pp. 74–5). In order to know Christ, however, God himself would have to touch the reader's, or the listener's, heart. 'But how will Christ give them eyes to see, and hearts to understand the scriptures?', 'Welshman' asks. 'Through the preaching of the Word', is the reply:

> That is why the preaching of the gospel is called the ministry of the Spirit, through which God works in his chosen people the ability to comprehend the Spirit and the Word, and a desire to seek out the deep and mysterious things of God. (pp. 57–8; pp. 87–8)

The doctrinal basis of the *Car-wr* is, once more, Calvinistic or Reformed. The twin truths of predestination and election are taken for granted. Such a doctrine had always been contentious. How, asks 'Welshman', can anyone possibly know whether they are among the elect? The answer, of course, was in the scriptures: 'This is the indestructible golden chain linking heaven to earth, reaching into the hearts of the elect on earth and back again' (p. 62; p. 92). All should endeavour to know whether they were among God's chosen ones by responding positively to the gospel message, by striving to enter through the straight gate and by experiencing the grace of justification and sanctification for themselves. But was this not a formula for loose living and immorality? Not so, responded 'Kinsman', for those who had experienced God's undeserved kindness would necessarily display a spirit of unfeigned thankfulness and deep and sincere humility (pp. 63–4; pp. 93–4).

The whole tone of Thomas's handbook is practical and functional. Predestination apart, it contains no polemical divinity or doctrinal complexity. Matters of church government are studiously avoided as are baptismal theology and Eucharistic practice. The festivals of the church year, the Nativity, Easter and Whitsun, garner no mention at all. The author goes out of his way not to give offence. He includes forms of prayer that heads of family can use for home devotions. There was nothing untoward in this: '[T]his was an age when almost all Protestants, puritan and conformist alike, accepted the legitimacy of the use of set prayers in both private and public devotions.'[150] Far from being an exercise in Puritan ideology, the *Car-wr* is a contribution to the mission of the reformed church broadly understood. There was no wonder that Robert Llwyd's commendation was so fulsome: 'Accept, therefore, cordially this small and useful book and whatever benefit you glean from it, give God, the giver of all good gifts, the glory and pray heartily for its author' (p. 121; p. 153).

The final publication to be mentioned before tracing the development of Welsh theology in the latter years of Charles I's reign is *Llyfr y Resolution* (1632), John Davies's magnificent translation of *A Book of Christian Exercise, appertaining to Resolution* (1584), Edmund Bunny's Protestantized version of the Jesuit Robert Parson's book of the same name. Davies's share in the production of the Bible, William Morgan's version of 1588 and John Parry's edition of 1620, has already been elucidated.[151] As well as his work in biblical scholarship, the rector of Mallwyd is recognized as being Wales's premier grammarian and lexicographer of the early modern period.[152] The year which saw the publication of his landmark Welsh-Latin/Latin-Welsh dictionary, the *Dictionarium Duplex* (1632), perhaps the climax of his scholarly career, also witnessed the appearance of his version of Bunny's volume. By then he was sixty-five years old, having laboured in his mountainous parish for a quarter of a century. 'Although I have been absent from you but seldom', he wrote in his address to his parishioners, 'and that more often than not on affairs relating to your salvation and that of others of God's people', in order to make good that neglect he had decided to translate what he considered was 'one of the best books for teaching men to renounce their evil way of life and to turn to God'.[153]

Edmund Bunny (1540–1619), fellow of Merton College, Oxford, and chaplain to Edmund Grindal, the Elizabethan archbishop of York, had adapted the Roman Catholic Robert Parsons's powerful evangelistic treatise for Protestant consumption in 1584, two years after the publication of the original, and in this guise it had become a popular work of godly instruction.[154] The 'resolution' to which Parsons referred was the individual's resolve to turn in penitence to God and embrace the salvation wrought by Christ which had been safeguarded by the Catholic Church. The emphasis, however, was not on the sacramental system as such but on the need to turn from sin and be reconciled to God. Consequently the changes made by Bunny were minimal, though all references to the idea of infused grace and other specifically Romanist doctrine were

expunged, with the unique nature of Christ's sacrifice being brought to
the fore. Good works were in no way meritorious, rather the sinner's
grateful response to having been justified by faith alone. Bunny's version was reprinted numerous times during the Elizabethan and Jacobean
period, and its evangelistic effectiveness was well known. A year or two
before Davies's translation had appeared, the young Richard Baxter
had been given a copy of 'an old torn book … which was called *Bunny's
Resolution*, being written by Parsons the Jesuit and corrected by Edmund
Bunny … And in reading of this book, when I was about fifteen years of
age, it pleased God to awaken my soul.'[155] It was to that end that John
Davies had issued his version of the same text.

Davies's version was a quarto volume of 363 pages in two parts,
Part One including ten chapters explaining why a person should resolve
to live a life of piety with six chapters in Part Two emphasizing the
difficulties to be overcome: 'The aim of this book is to urge the one
who professes to be a Christian in name to become a Christian in truth,
following the aspiration of his own heart' (p. 2). The opening chapters
advocate sober self-assessment, a realization of having been created by
God in order to live a life of obedience, an understanding of the reality
of God's demands and that we will be accountable to him in the last day.
Sin is not something to be trifled with: 'Should we be surprised that God
is so fierce and severe towards evildoers in the next world when they
are so contemptuous of him in this one?' (p. 51). The harsh and bitter
scriptural warnings about the fate of the ungodly arise from the divine
holiness on the one hand and the seriousness of sin on the other:

> Who, therefore, with a modicum of sense would not fear to be found in
> such a state? Who could not eat, drink or sleep soundly until, in true
> repentance, he would feign purge his conscience of all sin? Who, therefore,
> has no fear? Who would not tremble? Who would not be in dread? (p. 68)

Among the reasons listed in Part Two why many neglect turning to
God was that they presume on God's mercy. Surely God in his mercy
would save all well-disposed people in the end?

> But you say, is not God merciful? Yes my brother, God is very merciful,
> most merciful, merciful beyond measure, in fact he is mercy itself; his
> nature and essence are such that he cannot not be merciful any more than
> he cannot not be God. But, as the prophet has it, he is holy and righteous

as well. As the godly St Bernard once said: 'The Lord walks on two feet, namely mercy and truth, with which he walks towards those who walk towards him'. Every sinner who turns sincerely to the Lord must grasp these two truths. Were he only to grasp after justice without mercy, he would be lost and without hope. So, if ever he is to be saved, he must bow in humility and kiss both these feet. Fearing God in his righteousness, he will have confidence in God and in his compassion. (p. 298)

The year that John Davies published *Llyfr y Resolution* saw the appointment of Richard Neile as archbishop of York while a year later William Laud was elected to the see of Canterbury. Already Calvinism was being proscribed within the Established Church and the draconian policies of the two archbishops marked an end to the Reformed consensus that had characterized Church of England theology since the reign of Elizabeth I. The doctrines enshrined in the 39 Articles and incorporated into the liturgy of Cranmer's Prayer Book would now yield to a novel 'Arminianism' in which an infused sacramental grace displaced the centrality of the preached Word, the capacity of the individual will to accept or reject salvation rendered the biblical truth of election redundant while the possibility that justification could be forfeited would replace the traditional emphasis on the perseverance of the saints.[156] Doctrine apart, 'the English Arminian mode, as it emerged during the 1630s, was that of a communal and ritualized worship rather than an individual response to preaching or Bible reading'.[157] In practice, the distinction between true and nominal believers was systematically blurred. What was required of those who made a Christian profession was outward conformity and obedience to constituted authority. For those who yearned for a deeper spirituality, an exacting discipline which rooted moral improvement in Eucharistic piety and 'High Church' ceremonial took the place of Puritan precisionism, but this tradition of 'holiness', characterized by the work of such divines as George Herbert, the poet of *The Temple* (1633), and Jeremy Taylor, author of *Holy Living* (1650) and *Holy Dying* (1651), represented a much more elitist strand of piety than Reformed 'godliness', and would, in fact, have less appeal for ordinary church members.[158]

But even more conspicuous were the changes in externals. Communal communion cups were now exchanged for ornate chalices, communion tables were to be treated as 'altars' and removed from the nave where the congregation would sit to the east wall of church chancels – a move apparently resisted by John Davies in Mallwyd[159] – communicants were told that they were to receive the elements by kneeling rather than sitting or standing, while a more punctilious keeping of liturgical minutiae, feasts and festivals and extra-biblical forms was expected of the clergy. The ministerial ideal was transformed from the prophetic to the priestly, less preacher of the Word than priest sacrificing at the altar. Whereas the Welsh bishops almost immediately tightened their control over the parishes in response to pressure applied by Laud, all new Episcopal appointments after 1633 went to so-called 'formalists' who were either acolytes of the archbishop or in full sympathy with his views: this was true of Roger Mainwaring appointed to St David's in 1635, William Roberts at Bangor in 1637 and Morgan Owen at Llandaff in 1639.[160] Radical change within the universities also impacted upon the Welsh Church. Just as Cambridge had become a Puritan bastion in the 1570s, Oxford underwent its own 'Laudian revolution' in the 1630s, with the colleges at All Souls and Magdalen becoming centres of pronounced High Church ecclesiasticism and ultra-royalist fidelity. The appointment of Francis Mansell of Cydweli as principal in 1630 brought Jesus College into the Laudian mainstream. Jesus-trained laymen from gentry families in the Vale of Glamorgan, the Aubreys of Llantrithyd and the Stradlings of St Donats among others, returned to become zealous proponents of High Church mores within the diocese of Llandaff,[161] while during and beyond the Interregnum clergy trained at Jesus in the 1630s would become the backbone of anti-Puritan loyalism, mostly in Llandaff but in the other dioceses as well.[162] It was a remarkable *volte-face* that few would have anticipated. One of its unintended consequences was to create a nonconformist reaction that prepared the ground for a Dissenting witness which would become hugely influential in the ultimate development of theology in Wales.

Between 1633 and the outbreak of the civil war little theology was published in Wales, nevertheless the religious situation became increasingly fraught. Since 1629 Charles had ruled his domain without the support of his parliament, while the monarch's patent disdain for the Protestant landowning class and its representative institutions found a religious echo in the High Churchmen's championing of the novel and (in traditional Church of England terms) wholly erroneous idea of *jure divino* episcopacy or the divine right of bishops. Long convinced that the Reformed faith was inherently un-Anglican, and that Puritanism, even in its mildest form, was an insidious threat to the integrity and authority of the establishment, Laud revived the Court of High Commission as

a means of disciplining refractory clergymen. Along with this, he persuaded a more-than-willing king that ecclesiastical uniformity should be
enforced with punctilious zeal. In Wales the bishop who responded with
most alacrity to these instructions was William Murray of Llandaff. In
his triennial visitation in January 1634, he was disconcerted to find signs
of an incipient Puritan movement gaining ground in his diocese linked
with the names of William Wroth, the long-time rector of Llanfaches,
Monmouthshire, William Erbury, the recently established vicar of the
parish of St Mary's in Cardiff, and his curate Walter Cradock, whom he
referred to as 'a bold ignorant young fellow'. Murray reported to Laud
and the archbishop in turn reported to the king. Erbury and Cradock
'had been very disobedient to your majesty's instruction and have
preached very schismatically and dangerously to the people', wrote Laud,
while a year later, in January 1635, Wroth and Erbury were reported as
'having wilfully persisted in their schismatic course' and had 'led away
many simple people after them'.[163] For the new regime, zealous exhor-
tative preaching which made an impact on its hearers was 'dangerous'
while any teaching not in accord with the heavy ceremonialism and
strident anti-Puritanism of the Arminian prelates was 'schismatic'. Not
surprisingly, considerable contention would ensue.

Long recognized as the 'father' of Protestant Dissent in Wales,
William Wroth's (?1576–1641) contribution to the Welsh theological
discourse would be in the realm of ecclesiology. A native of Abergavenny,
he had graduated from Christ Church, Oxford, in 1596 though he took
his MA from Jesus College nearly ten years later. He was not instituted
to a parish until 1613 when he became rector of Llanfihangel Roggiet
near Chepstow, adding neighbouring Llanfaches to his charge in 1617.
Following a dramatic conversion experience in 1625 both his life and
his ministry were transformed, after which Llanfaches (he resigned
Llanfihangel in 1626) became a model reformed parish and magnet
for the godly from further afield. Later dissenting lore would describe
Wroth as 'a foundation stone in the great building of God in Wales',
while his reputation was laid well before he found himself at odds with
the ecclesiastical authorities.[164] 'For the powerfulness and efficaciousness
of his preaching', it was said, 'with the exemplary holiness of his life,
was called the Apostle of Wales, for the papists, and all sorts almost,
honoured him for a holy man'.[165] What brought him to the attention
of his diocesan was his failure to wear the surplice and refusal to read
The King's Majesty's declaration to his subjects concerning lawful sports, the

so-called 'Book of Sports', issued by Charles in October 1633. Knowing that this declaration concerning the lawfulness of partaking of recreations and revelries on Sundays would offend the sabbatarian sensibilities of the Puritan clergy, the monarch's plan, abetted by Laud, was to force the Puritans to show their hand and face discipline and dismissal. Along with that of Erbury, his case was forwarded to the Court of High Commission, but whereas the younger man resigned his Cardiff living, Wroth, now aged sixty-two, conformed.

This, however, was by no means the end of the story. In November 1639, Henry Jessey, Congregational minister in London, was sent by his church

> for the assisting of old Mr Wroth, Mr Cradock and others in their gathering and constituting the church of Llanfaches in Monmouthshire in South Wales, which afterwards, like Antioch, the mother church in that gentile country, being very famous for her officers, members, orders and gifts; for the furtherance of which this worthy servant of God was instrumental, and ever afterwards acknowledged so by them.[166]

This gathering, which was called together 'according to the New England way', was more of a voluntary fellowship of covenanted believers than a reformed Church of England parish, and as such represented a radically new departure in the development of ecclesiology in Wales. Since 1629, emigrants to the newly populated colonies of Massachusetts, New Haven, Connecticut and Rhode Island, had formed themselves into gathered, self-governing congregations where they could worship free of the restrictions which they had found progressively more irksome since Charles I's accession to the throne. Unlike 'the Pilgrim Fathers', the separatists who in 1620 had established the first New England colony of Plymouth, these more recent emigrants professed themselves loyal to the Church of England but, as Puritans, they chafed against the stifling clericalism and lack of spiritual discipline which prevailed in the parish system that they had left behind. Although nominally under the jurisdiction of the bishop of London, they were in fact free to experiment with structures which better reflected their ideal of what a church should be, namely a gathering of committed believers, not only sound in the faith but having felt the power of godliness through personal conversion, replete with its own chosen ministers, elders and deacons. Although all members of the community being baptized would be expected to attend congregational worship, only those who could subscribe to the covenant and give a credible account of conversion would be allowed to partake of communion and elect church officers.[167] The church leader most connected with this ideal was John Cotton, formerly incumbent of St Botolph's, Boston, Lincolnshire, but since 1633 minister in Boston, Massachusetts, while the detail of the polity would be set out in detail in *The Cambridge Platform* (1646).[168]

Like the New England Puritans, the Llanfaches grouping were in no way wholehearted separatists severing all contact with the Established Church, but a covenanted community sharing worship with the older parish congregation and happy to endorse tithes and other aspects of the establishment, but having submitted themselves to a binding covenant and specific church discipline: 'To some degree, therefore, they represented a godly community of saints whose worship supplemented rather than undermined the parochial system'.[169] Whereas Wroth retained his status as vicar of the parish, he was also elected minister of the gathered church. By the early 1640s its fame had become widespread. 'What light and labour in the Spirit was there!', rhapsodized William Erbury in 1652, 'what holy language among them!, what prayers night and day, in the way they went, in the work they did at their plough!' Such was the attractiveness of the community that people from the adjacent counties of Glamorgan, Radnorshire and Herefordshire and as far off as Gloucestershire and Somerset 'came in multitudes with delight to Llanfaches'.[170] Wroth died, aged sixty-five, early in 1641, before the outbreak of the civil war. His will was proved in April of that year.

Although the contribution of Erbury and Cradock to the theological discourse in Wales will be considered in Chapter Two, their experiences between being summoned by the Court of High Commission and the beginning of the civil war in 1642 call to be outlined.

Erbury (1604–54), a merchant's son from Roath, Cardiff, had graduated from Brasenose College, Oxford, in 1623 before proceeding to the Queens' College Cambridge where he graduated again in 1626. Ordained in the diocese of Bristol during that year, he became curate at St Woolos, Newport, Monmouthshire, in 1630, and vicar of St Mary's parish, Cardiff, in August 1633. His sponsor there was Sir Thomas Lewis, the squire of Pen-marc, son of the powerful landowner Sir Edward Lewis of the Fan, Caerphilly, a long-term benefactor of William Wroth. Due to the slow progress of his case before the Court of High Commission, he did not resign his living until 1638. Among his converts during these years was the young Christopher Love (1618–51), subsequently a Presbyterian zealot who would pay with his life for supporting the Scots' attempt to restore Charles II to the throne.[171] Erbury's first publication was *The Great Mystery of Godliness* (1639) of which more anon. Although the evidence is sketchy, he was instrumental in forming a church on the Llanfaches model in Cardiff at around the same time, though his status as a clergyman was no longer recognized by the diocesan authorities.

The convening of the Long Parliament, however, in November 1640, which put paid effectively to the prelatical reign of the Arminian bishops, opened the way for Erbury and his by now emboldened colleagues, to petition the House of Commons for fundamental religious change. The tone and content of his first petition, *The Humble Petition of Mr Erbury and the whole Principality of Wales* of December 1640, was reminiscent of that of John Penry fifty years earlier, complaining that through the lack of effective preaching, the ordinary people were facing damnation. Of the thousand or so parishes in the thirteen counties of Wales, there were no more than thirteen preachers who would preach twice on a Sunday and expound the catechism in Welsh during the afternoons. Of the 115 Glamorgan parishes, there were only five preachers who could do the same. As for the generality of the clergy, they were either pluralists, non-resident, idlers or scandalous. The result of 'the people being led by blind guides and the sheep having dumb dogs to be their shepherds' was that superstition, gross ignorance, idolatry and 'all manner of sins abound everywhere'. The fault, claimed Erbury, was squarely with the bishops, especially their propensity to licence unqualified candidates: 'Every silly reader ordered to by a bishop may in a surplice and with a service book take the cure of souls.' Whereas conformist quasi-Puritans like Rhys Prichard could be unflinching in their criticism of clerical vice, they were fully supportive of the ecclesiastical system *per se*. They would have found this abrasive strand of nonconformist radicalism unsettling in the extreme. For Erbury, however, only root and branch reform would suffice: 'If the bishop and the [prayer] book be but removed, then all our blind curates will be also dumb in a day.'[172] In the meantime, he and his fellow signatories – Walter Cradock, Ambrose Mostyn, Henry Walter and Richard Symonds[173] – urged parliament to allow worshippers the freedom to forsake their own parish churches and seek nourishment wherever the true Word of God was being expounded. The fact that the petition was granted so readily on 12 January 1641 illustrates the momentous changes which were already underway.[174]

A month later a second petition was forwarded, much in the same vein and with the same signatories though with the addition this time of the name of William Wroth. The style, tone and temper, however, is that of Erbury (and perhaps Cradock), and it is possible that Wroth was entreated to endorse the document in the manner of an elder statesman whose imprimatur would have added weight to the appeal. Again the parish clergy are censured bitterly for greed, immorality, non-residency and when they did preach, an aversion to doing so in Welsh, the only language that many of the people knew. As for the curates, they 'are for the most part dumb, drunken fellows and the very scum and refuse of the country'. Whereas the clergy excused or even condoned wickedness, godliness, it seems, was being actively punished:

> Those that desire to live honestly in a religious course are in diverse places excommunicated … and many driven out of the land for hearing of sermons out of their parishes, godly meetings which are only for the good of their souls, and indeed there is more safety and quietness by far for Papists than earnest and faithful Protestants.

The real villains of the piece are the Laudian bishops,

> who … by suppressing all godliness as far as they be able by suspensions, excommunications, delivery to the terrible Court of High Commission, so banishing out of the land both ministers and people which sought the welfare of the country and the salvation of their own and other souls.

Added to their tyranny was the colour of their churchmanship and profligate nature of their ceremonies, 'multiplying their popish canons and articles so making void the commandments of God'.[175] The appeal this time was more general, that the high court of parliament would systematically redress these grievances and allow able and zealous gospel preachers to exhort freely and at will. This petition was delivered on 16 February 1641.

Beneath the likely exaggeration of polemic, these petitions suggest that there existed in the diocese of Llandaff and possibly beyond vigorous, perhaps multiple groups of godly lay folk who were responding increasingly to pointed gospel preaching, and that the vision for religious renewal which had been broached since the Elizabethan era was gradually being fulfilled. The third person linked with both Wroth and Erbury was Walter Cradock (?1610–59), the son of a prosperous family from Llangwm, Monmouthshire, who had been educated at Oxford, probably at Jesus College, before being ordained to a curacy at Peterston-super-Ely in the Vale of Glamorgan. His activities at St Mary's in Cardiff, where he became Erbury's curate in 1633, have already been mentioned.[176] After having his preaching licence revoked by Bishop Murray, by October 1634 he had found refuge in Wrexham, Denbighshire, in the diocese of St Asaph, as curate to the staunchly conformist Robert Llwyd, translator of Dent's *The Plain Man's Pathway to Heaven* and literary supporter of the Presbyterian Oliver Thomas.[177] According to later Dissenting tradition, 'By both his preaching and expounding, a great reformation followed, which had not followed upon the reading of the Common Prayer, and many sinners were turned to the Lord.'[178] Within a year or so, tensions between Cradock and more staid townspeople saw him head south, this time for the border areas between Shropshire and Montgomeryshire where he greatly impressed the youthful Richard Baxter: 'At about twenty years of age [1635], I became acquainted with Mr Symonds, Mr Cradock and other very zealous godly nonconformists in Shrewsbury and the adjoining parts, whose fervent prayers and savoury conference and holy lives did profit me much.'[179] Then, like many fervent Puritans, Cradock found sanctuary in Brampton Bryan, Herefordshire, under the protection of the squire Sir Robert Harley who, in 1637–8, procured for him the living of Llanfair Waterdine in the Valley of the Teme, over the river from Radnorshire.[180] Although still nominally a cleric in the Established Church, his by now settled radical ideas, along with his association with a separatist conventicle within the parish, attracted the disapproval of Sir Robert's formidable wife, Brilliana: 'Mr Cradock is a worthy man, but sometimes he does not judge clearly of things.'[181] When Richard Symonds, Cradock's colleague who had been appointed tutor to the Harley children, refused to share worship with the faithful in the reformed Church of England parish at Brampton Bryan, Lady Brilliana was appalled. The Brownists (or separatists), she wrote, 'would have the church nowhere but in their parlour in Amsterdam'.[182] The sectarian tendency implicit in the more radical nonconformity was already being felt, and Cradock, like Symonds, was deeply involved. Although the ecclesiology of Llanfaches, where Walter Cradock found himself late in 1639, was a deal more temperate, a mood of militancy had now been unleashed which would prove difficult ultimately to keep in check.

But to return to the situation under Archbishop Laud: just as William Murray was disciplining errant clergy in Llandaff, Theophilus Field was doing the same in St David's. In January 1634 an unnamed lecturer, possibly in Haverfordwest or Tenby, was discharged for 'inconformity', and others who had 'with their giddiness offered to distemper the people' were driven from the diocese.[183] A year later, in January 1635, Field had dismissed 'one Roberts, a Welsh lecturer, for inconformity'.[184] In all probability this was Evan Roberts (c.1567–1650), a native of Denbighshire who had graduated from St Edmund Hall, Oxford, in 1608, and would publish, along with Oliver Thomas, the catechism *Sail Crefydd Ghristinogol* ('A Foundation of the Christian Faith') in 1640. During the commonwealth he would be presented with the Cardiganshire living of Llanbadarn Fawr.[185] In January 1637, two years after Roberts's dismissal, Field's successor, Roger Mainwaring, reported that Marmaduke Matthews, vicar of Pen-maen on the Gower peninsula, 'preaches against the keeping of holy days ... as fond profane convictions', and forwarded his case to the Court of High Commission.[186] Rather than facing the court's discipline, Matthews (1606–83), a native of Llangyfelach, Swansea, and graduate of All Souls College, Oxford, resigned his charge, emigrated to New England and in 1638 was appointed minister at Yarmouth, Massachusetts. He would spend the next sixteen years in the colonies, returning to Wales in 1654 as incumbent of the parish of St John's, Swansea, during the commonwealth regime.[187]

In Wrexham, where Cradock had not only provoked opposition through his fiery preaching in the parish church in 1634–5 but had drawn a spirited following as well (including a youthful Morgan Llwyd) and where Oliver Thomas had been a regular preaching supply under the lectureship system, by January 1641 bishop John Owen reported the presence of 'a conventicle of mean persons' within his diocese, almost certainly converts of Cradock and Thomas, who had been apprehended and reported to the Council of the Marches.[188] By then, alas, it was too late. With the advent of the Long Parliament two months earlier, the accumulated grievances of the previous decade reached a crescendo and a ferocious reaction against the political hubris of the monarch and the religious oppression of the ritualist clerics manifested itself. After eleven years of the so-called 'personal rule', Charles had been forced to recall parliament. The revenues which had for nearly a decade been raised by 'ship money', the tax levied on coastal areas in order to replenish the exchequer, had now run dry, and with the threat of a Scottish rebellion following the king's foolhardy attempt to foist an Episcopalian Book of Common Prayer on a resolutely Presbyterian northern kingdom, Charles needed parliament in order to raise taxes once more.[189] The soldiers he had taken to fight the Scottish rebels needed to be paid, and only parliament, through sanctioning the raising of funds, could provide him with the means to do so. When it met on 13 April 1640 for the first time in eleven years, even its most loyalist members were exasperated at the sovereign's disregard for the people's rights. They were also very wary of the exaggerated ritualism of the leading ecclesiastics who seemed to be undermining the Protestant nature of the Established Church. Richard Baxter identified two main factions in this new parliament and its successor: those 'good commonwealth men' who opposed arbitrary government and abhorred the fact that the king seemed to be subjecting the law to his personal whim, and 'the more religious men' who agreed with their more secular colleagues but were even more aggrieved at the policies of the prelates:

> These most inveighed against the innovations in the Church, the bowing to altars, the Book of Sports on Sundays, the casting out of ministers, the troubling of the people by the High Commission Court, the pillorying and cutting off of men's ears for speaking against the bishops [a reference to the fate of the Puritans William Prynne, Henry Burton and John Bastwick at the behest of the Star Chamber in June 1637], the putting down of lectures and afternoon sermons and expositions on the Lord's days, with such other things that they thought of greater weight than ship money.[190]

For over a decade all authority had resided in the royal court. Parliament was not only offended by this usurpation of power but deeply distrustful of the queen, the French Catholic Henrietta Maria, and the malign influence of her Roman Catholic courtiers, especially in foreign policy. They were fearful that Charles, aided by William Laud, was preparing to take both the church and the realm back into the papal fold. In order to gain parliament's support, the king would have to agree to radical change within his domains.

Charles's first parliament, the Short Parliament, only lasted until 5 May. Convocation, the ruling body of the Church of England, usually met at the same time as parliament but this time it remained in session after the Short Parliament had been dissolved. Far from moderating its zeal for ceremonial reform or tempering its absolute loyalty to the king, the canons issued by convocation in late May upheld the changes of the previous decade and emphasized the fact that they should be unquestioningly obeyed. They included a renewal of the conviction that the sovereign ruled by divine right, that he was entitled to call and dismiss parliament as he chose, that all should pay taxes to him as required and to take up arms against the king was a sin for which offenders would be damned. All clergy would be obliged, by a date set for six months hence, to swear an oath never to 'consent to alter the government of this church by archbishops, bishops, deans and archdeacons *et cetera*, as it stands now established'.[191] The 'et cetera oath', in effect, demanded that all clergy endorse unequivocally and in detail the Arminian *status quo*.

While these demands were being made, the political situation was only getting worse. Charles's move to check the Scottish army which by now had crossed the Tweed failed ignominiously. In August his weak force, which was only half-hearted in its support of his cause, was routed at the battle of Newburn near Newcastle upon Tyne. Desperate to raise funds and rally the country behind him, he summoned parliament for a second time. This parliament, the Long Parliament convened on 3 November 1640, which would outlive Charles by eleven years, had profound consequences for the future. Before heeding the king's requests, it demanded fundamental religious change.[192] Within a week it had impeached the earl of Strafford, the king's principal enforcer, 'as a subverter of fundamental law and an introducer of tyranny'.[193] Six months later he would be executed – Charles, who signed the death warrant, having yielded to parliament's demands rather than come to his supporter's defence. Then, in February 1641, just as Erbury's second petition gained the Commons' approval and after the bishop of St Asaph's complaint about the Wrexham sectaries had reached Lambeth Palace, Laud himself was accused of treason and imprisoned in the Tower. He too would be executed in 1645: 'At the end of the personal rule complaints against clerics centred on bishops who were seen as epitomizing all that was wrong with the church.'[194] Soon each of his Welsh bishops would fall foul of the new regime.

The longest serving bishop, John Owen, who had been at St Asaph since 1629, was one of the eleven prelates who, along with Morgan Owen of Llandaff and William Roberts of Bangor, was impeached for high treason after petitioning parliament in December 1640 from being prevented from taking their place in the Lords. After a short incarceration in the

Tower of London, he was released though his bishopric was sequestered in April 1642 when he was allowed £500 compensation. According to Walker's *Sufferings of the Clergy*, 'he retired into Wales and died there, 15 October 1651'.[195] Morgan Owen, bishop of Llandaff since 1639, had been a protégé of Laud from the time when the primate had served at St David's two decades earlier. Owen had scandalized Protestant sensibilities in 1637 by commissioning the statue of the Virgin and Child above the porch of St Mary's, the university church in Oxford.[196] He too was imprisoned: first in December 1640 and, following his release, again in August 1641 for his part in promulgating convocation's canons of the previous year. After having being freed from the Tower and deprived of his see in May 1642, he returned to his family estate in Myddfai, Carmarthenshire, where he was befriended by Rhys Prichard, the puritanically inclined vicar of Llandovery.[197] Both had been young clergymen linked to the cathedral church at St David's decades before. Like Morgan Owen, Roger Mainwaring had been eager in his support for Laud for many years before being appointed to the see of St David's in 1635. He too had been accused of treason and deprived of his diocese in February 1642. 'Afterwards', recorded the diocesan history, 'the Rebellion breaking out, he was imprisoned, violently persecuted from place to place, lost all his temporalities and had only some small temporal estate to maintain him and his family'.[198] He died in 1653. Finally William Roberts, another fervent Laudian and bishop of Bangor since 1637, had also been impeached, imprisoned and released, though he would not be deprived until 1646. He was the only Welsh bishop to survive the civil wars and commonwealth, and would be restored to his charge in 1660.

With such disruptive change it is hardly surprising that little theology was being published at the time. Yet Glanmor Williams has observed that 'by 1640 Welsh Protestant prose had reached a high pitch of mastery'.[199] William Erbury's first book, *The Great Mystery of Godliness*, appeared in 1639 and was reissued a year later, while 1640 also saw the publication of *Sail Crefydd Ghristinogol* ('A Foundation of Christian Religion'), a catechism jointly composed by the Presbyterian Oliver Thomas and Evan Roberts, latterly the commonwealth incumbent of Llanbadarn Fawr. Although Puritan in emphasis, both works exhibited the Reformed didacticism that had characterized Welsh theology since the late Elizabethan period. Nothing representing Laudian Arminianism appeared in print either in Welsh or from a Welsh author during these years.

Both the *Mystery* and the *Sail* were catechetical works apparently
original to their authors. Erbury's forty-page catechism had been written
by 1637 and although published in London, was aimed partially at a south
Wales readership, probably among those who were being increasingly
brought under his radical sway.[200] The readership of the *Sail*, also published in London and forty pages long, was among those who were yet
to embrace Puritan convictions but as conventional Christians were in
need of instruction. As such the informative element is more to the fore
while Erbury's emphasis is on the experiential. The *Sail* is divided into
four parts. Part One explains the biblical doctrine of God, his holiness
and threefold nature as Father, Son and Spirit, his works including the
eternal decree and creative and redemptive design, the fact of human corruption and inherited guilt measured by all people's inability to fulfil the
Ten Commandments. Each commandment is expounded and clarified,
with a typically Puritan emphasis on the Sabbath. Sunday is to be a day
of worship and not an excuse for riotous games. Having expounded the
Decalogue, Part Two leads on the Work of Christ. As sinless mediator,
Christ's life is put forth as a sacrifice to God's holiness and the means of
human redemption, a redemption that is accessed through faith. Though
it is a sovereign gift, faith nevertheless can be prepared for by a concerted
striving after inward righteousness: 'God moves the heart to grief and
anguish for sin, by causing men to realize that they deserve the divine
wrath and condemnation for ever' (p. 20; p. 190).[201] This, in turn, prepares
the heart to accept the gospel, while Part Three lists the evidences of
faith and true repentance and Part Four describes the means by which
salvation is attained and the Christian life is lived. These include prayer,
including an exposition of the Lord's Prayer, and partaking of the sacraments which are described as 'a sign to signify, a seal to assure, and a
means whereby Jesus Christ and all his gifts are brought, as they were
not before, into the heart of the true Christian' (p. 31; p. 201).

Erbury's *Mystery* for its part accentuates the concept of election and
eschatology to a greater extent than the work of Thomas and Roberts,
and the need for believers to examine themselves constantly to see
whether their conversion was sincere. It is in full accord with the expe-
rientialism of the Reformed tradition: 'O how miserable and wretched
is the man or woman that lives and dies in this corrupt and cursed
condition without Christ!' (p. 6; p. 48).[202] What is most striking is the
strand of mysticism which would become more pronounced as Erbury
diverged spectacularly from orthodox Calvinism during the succeeding

decade. Although the believer is justified by faith which leads to union with Christ, that union was 'mystical':

> Christ has so taken my flesh as never to be divided from it ... I am betrothed and married to him forever, and not only betrothed but I am of his body, of his flesh and of his bones, nay by faith I eat his flesh and drink his blood. What nearer union can be? (p. 10; p. 49)

At this juncture, however, 'Erbury teaches a traditional Puritan approach to the Christian life. It reflects orthodox Calvinism and emphasises the place of Word and sacraments.'[203] The work remained within the broad consensus of Protestant theology as had been promulgated in Wales since the Elizabethan era.

The dismissal of the bishops boded ominously for the future. Although Wales, far from the centre of power and staunchly loyal, in the main, to the king, was shielded from the worst excesses of the civil wars, the next decades would be decisive for the progress of Protestant theology for two centuries to come. The upheavals of 1641–2 – the Irish rebellion of October 1641, the Grand Remonstrance listing 150 of the sovereign's misdeeds and passed by the Commons in November, Charles's entering the house in January 1642 to accuse five of its leaders of treason, the establishment of 'the Oxford Parliament' of loyalist MPs in March and the Commons decreeing the validity of laws without the royal consent – impacted, for the most part, the ruling class or those with commercial links with London.[204] There were, however, religious leaders, both radical and loyalist, who would contribute both to the wider discourse and bring official policy to bear within Wales itself, or alternatively would oppose it vigorously, during the next two momentous decades. If a very small minority pressed for sweeping religious change, many more were faithful to what the more conscientious clergy believed was a hard-won theological legacy.

By 1640 the Reformed Church of England had been slowly winning the loyalty, even the affection, of the Welsh people. The sonorous cadences of William Morgan's noble translation of the Bible, the exquisite quality of Cranmer's liturgy in Richard Davies's resonant Welsh accompanied by the music of Edmund Prys's metrical psalms were rooting themselves in the psyche of innumerable worshippers.[205] Unlike the situation in England, no Welsh county petitioned in favour of either the abolition of episcopacy or the banning of the Prayer Book. Although cautiously supportive of biblical reform at the parish level, none of the Welsh MPs were drawn to the radical views which were fomenting in London and the south-east that the ecclesiastical establishment should be dismantled root and branch. In Wales even to contemplate the abolition of the Prayer Book filled the faithful with foreboding. After 'so many years in the practice thereof', stated the north Wales petition to parliament of 1642, '[we] cannot without some trembling entertain the thought of change'.[206] The call to real rather than notional faith as urged by diocesan clergy of calibre such as Robert Holland and Rhys Prichard in St David's, Huw Lewys and John Davies in Bangor, Edward James in Llandaff and Robert Llwyd in St Asaph, showed that, however slowly, reform was beginning to be achieved. Certainly these men represented only a minority of the clergy and grave weaknesses remained, but within the span of two generations the situation was being gradually transformed. On the eve of the civil wars neither Arminian formalism nor radical innovation represented the best of Welsh Protestant Christianity. By 22 August 1642, however, with the raising of the royal standard at Nottingham, all was about to change.

Notes

[1]   Maurice Kyffin, *Deffynniad Ffydd Eglwys Loegr* (1595), ed. W. Pritchard Jones (Bangor: Jarvis and Foster, 1908), p. vi; page numbers which follow are in the text.

[2]   Cf. Ceri Davies, 'The 1588 translation of the Bible and the world of Renaissance learning', *Ceredigion*, 11 (1988–9), 1–18.

[3]   The first to do so was R. Ambrose Jones (Emrys ap Iwan) in his essay 'Y Clasuron Cymraeg' in 1893; see D. Myrddin Lloyd (ed.), *Erthyglau Emrys ap Iwan*, vol. 2 (Llundain: Y Clwb Llyfrau Cymraeg, 1939), pp. 1–44.

[4]   'Reformed' in upper case will be used to refer to the predestinarian theology of the principal Continental churches including Geneva, while 'reformed' refers to the implementation of the Protestant Reformation in England and Wales more generally.

[5]   C. M. Dent, *Protestant Reformers in Elizabethan Oxford* (Oxford: Oxford University Press, 1983), p. 222; for the Reformed content of the curriculum, see pp. 87–93.

[6]   Huw Lewys, *Perl Mewn Adfyd* (1595), ed. W. J. Gruffydd (Caerdydd: Gwasg Prifysgol Cymru, 1929), p. xxi.

[7]   Glanmor Williams, 'The early Stuart church', in *idem*, William Jacob, Nigel Yates and Frances Knight, *The Welsh Church from Reformation to Disestablishment, 1603–1920* (Cardiff: University of Wales Press, 2007), pp. 3–32 (11); cf. J. Gwynfor Jones, 'Henry Rowland, Bishop of Bangor', *JHSCW*, 26 (1979), 34–53.

8   See Peter Lake, *Moderate Puritans in the Elizabethan Church* (Cambridge: Cambridge University Press, 1982).

9   'A breviat ... against the clergie of the Diocese of Bangor ... Julie 1623', *Archaelogia Cambrensis*, 3rd series, 36 (1863), 283–5.

10   Dent, *Protestant Reformers in Elizabethan Oxford*, p. 239.

11   Patrick Collinson, *The Elizabethan Puritan Movement*, 2nd edn (Oxford: Clarendon Press, 1990), p. 125.

12   Collinson, *The Elizabethan Puritan Movement*, pp. 126–7.

13   See H. C. Porter, *Reformation and Reaction in Tudor Cambridge*, 2nd edn (Hemden: Archon Books, 1972), pp. 215–30.

14   Porter, *Reformation and Reaction in Tudor Cambridge*, p. 216; cf. Leif Dixon, *Practical Predestinarians in England, 1590–1640* (Aldershot: Ashgate, 2014), pp. 123–73.

15   H[enry] H[olland] (ed.), *The Works of the Reverend and Faithfull Servant of Jesus Christ Mr Richard Greenham*, 2nd edn (London: Cuthbert Burbie, 1605); cf. Kenneth L. Parker and Eric J. Carlson, *'Practical Divinity': the Works and Life of Richard Greenham* (Aldershot: Ashgate, 1998); for Henry Holland (1555/6–1603), see *ODNB*.

16   Glanmor Williams, *Wales and the Reformation* (Cardiff: University of Wales Press, 1997), p. 301.

17   For Middleton (d.1593), see *ODNB*.

18   Williams, *Wales and the Reformation*, p. 285.

19   See Introduction and Glanmor Williams, 'Bishop Richard Davies (?1501–81)', in *idem, Welsh Reformation Essays* (Cardiff: University of Wales Press, 1967), pp. 155–90.

20   Williams, *Wales and the Reformation*, p. 285.

21   See W. B. Patterson, 'William Perkins as apologist for the Church of England', *JEH*, 57 (2006), 252–69; *idem, William Perkins and the Making of a Protestant England* (Oxford: Oxford University Press, 2014), pp. 40–63.

22   See Diarmaid MacCulloch, *The Later Reformation in England, 1547–1603*, 2nd edn (London: Palgrave, 2001), pp. 38–51.

23   Peter Lake, 'Calvinism in the Church of England, 1570–1635', *Past and Present*, 114 (1987), 32–76; republished in Margo Todd (ed.), *Reformation to Revolution: Politics and Religion in Early Modern England* (London: Routledge, 1995), pp. 179–207.

24   Philip Benedict, *Christ's Churches Purely Reformed: A Social History of Calvinism* (New Haven: Yale University Press, 2002), p. 319.

25   Patterson, *William Perkins and the Making of a Protestant England*, pp. 90–113; Dixon, *Practical Predestinarians in England, 1590–1640*, pp. 61–122.

26   Richard A. Muller, *Christ and the Decree: Christology and Predestination in Reformed Theology from Calvin to Perkins*, 2nd edn (Grand Rapids: Baker, 2008), p. 6.

27   Alec Ryrie, *Being Protestant in Reformation Britain* (Oxford: Oxford University Press, 2013), p. 37.

28 See Ian Breward, *The Work of William Perkins* (Abingdon: Sutton Courtney Press, 1970), pp. 353–85, 169–257.

29 Robert Holland, 'Ymddiddan Tudur a Gronw', in Thomas Jones (ed.), *Rhyddiaith Gymraeg: Yr Ail Gyfrol, Detholiad o Lawysgrifau a Llyfrau Printiedig 1547–1618* (Caerdydd: Gwasg Prifysgol Cymru, 1956), pp. 161–73 (166); page numbers which follow are in the text. For an assessment of the pamphlet's content, see D. S. T. Clark and Prys Morgan, 'Religion and magic in Elizabethan Wales', *JEH*, 27 (1976), 31–46.

30 NLW Cwrt-mawr MS 114B; it was republished by Stephen Hughes in *Cannwyll y Cymry sef, gwaith Mr. Rees Prichard, gynt ficcer Llanddyfri* (London: Thomas Dawkes, 1681), pp. 457–68, under the title 'Dau Gymro yn Taring, yn Bell o'u Gwlad' ('Two Welshmen discoursing, far from their country').

31 Robert Holland, *Basilikon Doron by King James I: Fragment of a Welsh Translation by Robert Holland* (1604), ed. J. Ballinger (Cardiff: University of Wales Press, 1931), Introduction; for the context see Peter Roberts, 'Tudor Wales, national identity and the British inheritance', in *idem* and Brendan Bradshaw, *British Consciousness and Identity: The Making of Britain, 1533–1707* (Cambridge: Cambridge University Press, 1998), pp. 8–42.

32 J. Gwynfor Jones, 'Robert Holland a *Basilikon Doron* y Brenin Iago', in J. E. Caerwyn Williams (ed.), *Ysgrifau Beirniadol*, 22 (Dinbych: Gwasg Gee, 1997), pp. 161–88 (181); cf. Adrian Morgan, 'Llenor anghofiedig: Trem ar fywyd a gwaith Robert Holland', *Llên Cymru*, 31 (2008), 139–64.

33 Thomas Salisbury, Introduction to *Psalmae y Brenhinol Brophwyd Dafydd* (1603), in Hughes (ed.), *Rhagymadroddion 1547–1659*, pp. 108–10 (109).

34 Williams, *Wales and the Reformation*, pp. 395–6.

35 See Patrick Collinson, 'The Jacobean Religious Settlement: The Hampton Court Conference', in H. Tomlinson (ed.), *Before the English Civil War: Essays on Stuart Politics and Government* (London: Macmillan, 1983), pp. 27–51.

36 For Laud's reign at St David's, see Charles Carlton, *Archbishop William Laud* (London: Routledge, 1987), pp. 29–34; for the significance of Laud's anti-Puritan stance, see Nicholas Tyacke, *Anti-Calvinists: The Rise of English Arminianism c. 1590–1640* (Oxford: Clarendon Press, 1990), *passim*.

37 All references are taken from *Sail Crefydd Gristnogawl*, Evan Roberts's re-issue published in 1642; Merfyn Morgan (ed.), *Gweithiau Oliver Thomas ac Evan Roberts, Dau Biwritan Cynnar* (Caerdydd: Gwasg Prifysgol Cymru, 1981), pp. 227–86; page numbers in the text refer first to the pagination of *Sail Crefydd Gristnogawl* and secondly as they appear in Morgan's edition.

38 For the original text of *The Foundation of Christian Religion* see Breward, *The Work of William Perkins*, pp. 137–67.

39 See above, p. 15.

40 W. P. Griffith, *Learning, Law and Religion: Higher Education and Welsh Society, c.1540–1640* (Cardiff: University of Wales Press, 1996), pp. 42, 204–6 and *passim*.

41   Glanmor Williams, 'Bishop William Morgan and the first Welsh Bible', in *idem, The Welsh and their Religion: Historical Essays* (Cardiff: University of Wales Press, 1991), pp. 173–229 (195).

42   Diarmaid MacCulloch, *Thomas Cranmer: A Life* (New Haven: Yale University Press, 1996), p. 373.

43   Benedict, *Christ's Churches Purely Reformed*, pp. 230–54.

44   The authoritative study is J. Gwynfor Jones, *Crefydd, Cenedlgarwch a'r Wladwriaeth: John Penry a Phiwritaniaeth Gynnar* (Caerdydd: Gwasg Prifysgol Cymru, 2014).

45   Williams, 'Bishop Richard Davies (?1501–81)', pp. 159–63.

46   Gareth Lloyd Jones, *The Discovery of Hebrew in Tudor England: A Third Language* (Manchester: Manchester University Press, 1983), pp. 97–8.

47   Gruffydd Aled Williams, *Ymryson Edmwnd Prys a Wiliam Cynwal* (Caerdydd: Gwasg Prifysgol Cymru, 1986), pp. xcvi–xcvii.

48   A. O. Evans, 'Edmund Prys: Archdeacon of Merioneth, Priest, Preacher, Poet', *THSC* (1922–3), 112–68; Gruffydd Aled Williams, 'Edmwnd Prys (1543/4–1623): Dyneiddiwr Protestannaidd', *JMHRS*, 8 (1977–80), 349–68.

49   Glanmor Williams, 'William Morgan's Bible and the Cambridge connection', *WHR*, 14 (1989), 363–79 (372).

50   Nia M. W. Powell, 'Dr William Morgan and his parishioners at Llanrhaeadr ym Mochnant', *TCHS*, 49 (1988), 87–108.

51   William Morgan, '*Y Beibl Cyssegr-lan* (1588): cyflwyniad i'r Frenhines Elisabeth I', in Ceri Davies (ed. and trans.), *Rhagymadroddion a Chyflwyniadau Lladin, 1551–1632* (Caerdydd: Gwasg Prifysgol Cymru, 1980), pp. 64–70 (65).

52   Morgan, '*Y Beibl Cyssegr-lan* (1588): cyflwyniad i'r Frenhines Elisabeth I', pp. 67, 70.

53   John Penry, *The Notebook of John Penry*, ed. Albert Peel (London: Royal Historical Society, 1944), p. 64.

54   Peter White, *Predestinarianism, Policy and Polemic: Conflict and Consensus in the English Church from the Reformation to the Civil War* (Cambridge: Cambridge University Press, 1992), pp. 101–9.

55   J. Gwynfor Jones, 'John Penry: government, order and the "perishing souls" of Wales', *THSC* (1993), 47–81; *idem, Crefydd, Cenedlgarwch a'r Wladwriaeth: John Penry a Phiwritaniaeth Gynnar*, pp. 155–91.

56   MacCulloch, *The Later Reformation in England, 1547–1603*, p. 81.

57   Morgan, '*Y Beibl Cyssegr-lan* (1588): cyflwyniad i'r Frenhines Elisabeth I', pp. 66–7.

58   Williams, 'Bishop William Morgan and the first Welsh Bible', p. 193.

59   This is described vividly in Glanmor Williams, 'The ecclesiastical history of Glamorgan, 1572–1642', in *idem* (ed.), *Glamorgan County History, Vol. IV, Early Modern Glamorgan* (Cardiff: University of Wales Press, 1974), pp. 203–56.

60   Glanmor Williams, *Recovery, Reorientation and Reformation: Wales, 1415–1642* (Oxford: Clarendon Press, 1987), pp. 3–55, 165–278.

61 For a comparative study of the Reformation among the different nations of Britain, see W. Ian P. Hazlett, *The Reformation in Britain and Ireland: An Introduction* (London: T & T Clark, 2003).

62 Williams, *Wales and the Reformation*, pp. 248–79.

63 For Godwin (1562–1633), bishop of Llandaff between 1601 and 1617, see Williams, 'The ecclesiastical history of Glamorgan, 1572–1642', p. 240, and *ODNB.*

64 D. Myrddin Lloyd (ed.), 'Y Clasuron Cymraeg' , *Erthyglau Emrys ap Iwan*, vol. 2, pp. 32–6; cf. Glanmor Williams, 'Edward James a Llyfr yr Homilïau', in *idem, Grym Tafodau Tân: Ysgrifau Hanesyddol ar Grefydd a Diwylliant* (Llandysul: Gwasg Gomer, 1984), pp. 180–98.

65 *Pregethau a osodwyd allan trwy awdurdod i'w darllein ymhob Eglwys blwyf a phob capel er adailadaeth i'r bobl annyscedig. Gwedi eu troi i'r iaith Gymeraeg drwy waith Edward Iames* (Llundain: Robert Barker, 1606), p. 24; page numbers which follow are in the text.

66 For the prevalence of Roman Catholicism within the diocese, see Williams, 'The ecclesiastical history of Glamorgan, 1572–1642', pp. 232–9, 249–52 and Madeleine Gray, 'Religion and Belief, 1530–1660', in Madeleine Gray and Prys Morgan (eds), *The Gwent County History, Vol. 3, The Making of Monmouthshire, 1536–1780* (Cardiff: University of Wales Press, 2009), pp. 62–76.

67 'Our bishops ... are the very ground-work of this, our miserable confusion' (p. 61), 'I trust in the Lord Jesus to see his church flourish in Wales when the memory of our lord-bishops are buried in hell whence they came' (p. 65), *An Exhortation unto the Governors and people of Her Majesty's Country of Wales* (1588), in John Penry, *John Penry: Three Treatises Concerning Wales*, ed. and intro. David Williams (Cardiff: University of Wales Press, 1960), pp. 47–98; the rhetoric is even stronger in his *Supplication unto the High Court of Parliament* (1588), in *John Penry: Three Treatises Concerning Wales*, pp. 99–168.

68 See Patrick Collinson, 'England and International Calvinism, 1558–1640', in Menna Prestwich (ed.), *International Calvinism, 1541–1715* (Oxford: Clarendon Press, 1985), pp. 197–224 (213–16 esp.).

69 *Pregethau a osodwyd allan*, Introduction, Sig. A2v.

70 See 'Bishop Francis Godwin's Injunction for Llandaff diocese, 1603', in Kenneth Fincham (ed.), *Visitation Articles and Injunctions of the Early Stuart Church* (Woodbridge: Boydel and Brewer, 1994), pp. 1–3; cf. R. Geraint Gruffydd, 'Bishop Francis Godwin's injunctions for the diocese of Llandaff, 1603', *JHSCW*, 4 (1954), 14–22.

71 See above, p. 21.

72 Williams, *Recovery, Reorientation and Reformation: Wales, 1415–1642*, pp. 471–4.

73 Kenneth Fincham and Peter Lake, 'The ecclesiastical policy of King James I', *JBS*, 24 (1985), 169–207; Kenneth Fincham, 'Introduction', in *idem* (ed.), *The Early Stuart Church, 1603–42* (Macmillan: Basingstoke, 1993), pp. 1–22.

74 See Charles Butterworth, *The English Primers: Their Publication and Connection with the English Bible and Reformation* (New York: Octagon Books, 1971); Ian M. Green, *Print and Protestantism in Early Modern England* (Oxford: Oxford University Press, 2000), pp. 244–6.

75 R. Geraint Gruffydd, 'Catechism y Deon Nowell yn Gymraeg', *JWBS*, 7 (1950–3), 114–15, 203–7.

76 Dent, *Protestant Reformers in Elizabethan Oxford*, pp. 87–93; for Nowell (c.1507–1602), see *ODNB*.

77 Morgan, '*Y Beibl Cyssegr-lan* (1588): cyflwyniad i'r Frenhines Elisabeth I', p. 70.

78 For the introduction to the compendium, see David Powel, '*Britannicae Historiae ... et Itinerarium Cambriae*', in Davies (ed. and trans.), *Rhagymadroddion a Chyflwyniadau Lladin, 1551–1632*, pp. 48–63.

79 Among Gabriel Powel's works were *The Resolved Christian* (1600) which had gone into its seventh edition by 1617, *De Adiaphora* (1607) and the virulently anti-Catholic *Disputationem ... de Antichristi et eius ecclesia* (1607); see *ODNB*.

80 Kenneth Fincham, *Prelate as Pastor: the Episcopate of James I* (Oxford: Clarendon Press, 1990), p. 272; for Vaughan (1550–1607), previously bishop of Bangor and friend and contemporary of William Morgan, see *ODNB*.

81 J. Ballinger (ed.), *Llyfer Plygain* (1612) (Caerdydd: Gwasg Prifysgol Cymru, 1931), p. 52; page numbers which follow are in the text.

82 Williams, *Recovery, Reorientation and Reformation: Wales, 1415–1642*, pp. 406–9.

83 Williams, 'Religion and Welsh literature in the age of the Reformation', in *The Welsh and their Religion: Historical Essays*, pp. 138–72 (166–9 esp.).

84 *The Aequity of an Humble Supplication ... unto Her Majesty and this High Court of Parliament in the behalf of the Country of Wales* (1587), in David Williams (ed. and intro.), *John Penry: Three Treatises Concerning Wales*, pp. 1–45 (32).

85 Williams, *Wales and the Reformation*, pp. 72–156.

86 Patrick Collinson, *The Religion of Protestants: The Church in English Society, 1559–1625* (Oxford: Clarendon Press, 1982), pp. 92–140.

87 Williams, 'The early Stuart church', pp. 11–16.

88 Fincham, *Prelate as Pastor: the Episcopate of James I*, pp. 65–6.

89 Tyacke, *Anti-Calvinists*, pp. 87–105.

90 Benedict, *Christ's Churches Purely Reformed*, pp. 310–11.

91 Williams, 'The ecclesiastical history of Glamorgan, 1572–1642', p. 239; for the impact of Field and Laud on their diocese, see J. Morgan-Guy, 'The Diocese of St David's in the Reformation Era II: from Reaction to Restoration, 1553–1660', in William Gibson and J. Morgan-Guy (eds), *Religion and Society in the Diocese of St David's, 1485–2011* (Aldershot: Ashgate, 2015), pp. 37–62.

92 Kenneth Fincham and Peter Lake, 'The ecclesiastical policies of King James I and Charles I', in Fincham (ed.), *The Early Stuart Church, 1603–42*, pp. 23–49 (31).

93 G. Dyfnallt Owen, *Wales in the Reign of James I* (London: The Boydell Press, 1988), p. 94.

94 Fincham and Lake, 'The ecclesiastical policies of King James I and Charles I', pp. 25–6.

95 Enid P. Roberts, 'Gabriel Goodman and his native homeland', *THSC* (1989), 77–104.

96 Eryn M. White, *The Welsh Bible* (Stroud: Tempus, 2007), p. 40.

97 See J. Gwynfor Jones, 'Yr Esgob Richard Parry (1560–1623)', in *idem, Crefydd a Chymdeithas: Astudiaethau ar Hanes y Ffydd Brotestannaidd yng Nghymru,* c.*1559–1750* (Caerdydd: Gwasg Prifysgol Cymru, 2007), pp. 188–208 and *idem* in *ODNB.*

98 Richard Parry, '*Y Bibl Cyssegr-Lan,* Cyflwyniad i'r Drindod Sanctaidd, ac i'r Brenin Iago I', Davies (ed. and trans.), *Rhagymadroddion a Chyflwyniadau Lladin, 1551–1632,* pp. 101–4 (101–2).

99 Parry, '*Y Bibl Cyssegr-Lan,* Cyflwyniad i'r Drindod Sanctaidd, ac i'r Brenin Iago I', p. 102.

100 Parry, '*Y Bibl Cyssegr-Lan,* Cyflwyniad i'r Drindod Sanctaidd, ac i'r Brenin Iago I', p. 103.

101 Ceri Davies, 'John Davies and Renaissance humanism', in *idem* (ed.), *Dr John Davies of Mallwyd: Welsh Renaissance Scholar* (Cardiff: University of Wales Press, 2004), pp. 1–16 (2); for his life see Rhiannon Francis Roberts, 'Dr John Davies of Mallwyd: a biographical survey', in Davies (ed.), *Dr John Davies of Mallwyd,* pp. 17–59, and *ODNB.*

102 Davies, 'John Davies and Renaissance humanism', p. 6.

103 Quoted by Gwilym H. Jones, 'John Davies and Welsh translations of the Bible and Book of Common Prayer', in Davies (ed.), *Dr John Davies of Mallwyd: Welsh Renaissance Scholar,* pp. 208–25 (213).

104 Isaac Thomas, *Y Testament Newydd Cymraeg, 1551–1620* (Caerdydd: Gwasg Prifysgol Cymru, 1976), pp. 368–428; *idem, Yr Hen Destament Cymraeg* (Aberystwyth: Llyfrgell Genedlaethol Cymru, 1988), pp. 255–98.

105 Jones, 'John Davies and Welsh translations of the Bible', pp. 224, 225.

106 White, *The Welsh Bible,* p. 41.

107 White, *The Welsh Bible,* p. 42.

108 See above, pp. 26–7.

109 The introduction to Gruffydd Aled Williams's *Ymryson Edmwnd Prys a Wiliam Cynwal,* pp. xvii–cxcv, is the indispensable guide to his life and work.

110 Morgan, '*Y Beibl Cyssegr-lan* (1588): cyflwyniad i'r Frenhines Elisabeth I', p. 70.

111 John Davies, '*Antiquae Linguae Britannicae ... Rudimenta* (1621): Llythyr Annerch at Edmwnd Prys', Davies (ed. and trans.), *Rhagymadroddion a Chyflwyniadau Lladin, 1551–1632,* pp. 105–23 (105).

112 W. Ll. Davies, 'Welsh metrical versions of the Psalms', *JWBS,* 2 (1916–23), 276–301; Gruffydd Aled Williams, 'Mydryddu'r Salmau yn Gymraeg', *Llên Cymru,* 16 (1989), 114–32.

113 Williams, 'Edmwnd Prys (1543/4–1623): Dyneiddiwr Protestannaidd', 361.

114 Williams, 'Religion and Welsh literature in the age of the Reformation', pp. 164–5.

115 Williams, 'Edmwnd Prys (1543/4–1623): Dyneiddiwr Protestannaidd', 363.

116 See Tyacke, *Anti-Calvinists, passim.*

117 Dewey A. Wallace, *Puritans and Predestination: Grace in English Protestant Theology, 1525–1695* (Chapel Hill: University of Carolina Press, 1982), pp. 79–110.

118 Diarmaid MacCulloch, *Reformation: Europe's House Divided, 1490–1700* (London: Allen Lane, 2003), p. 516.

119 MacCulloch, *Reformation*, pp. 485–96; for the Welsh response to this crisis, see Lloyd Bowen, *The Politics of the Principality: Wales, c.1603–42* (Cardiff: University of Wales Press, 2007), pp. 85–92.

120 Williams, *Recovery, Reorientation and Reformation: Wales, 1415–1642,* pp. 478–9.

121 'A breviat ... against the clergie of the Diocese of Bangor ... Julie 1623', 283–5.

122 Quoted in J. Gwynfor Jones, 'Wales and Hamburg: the problems of a younger son', in R. R. Davies and Geraint H. Jenkins (eds), *From Medieval to Modern Wales: Historical Essays in Honour of K. O. Morgan and Ralph A. Griffiths* (Cardiff: University of Wales Press, 2004), pp. 104–22 (113–14).

123 Milbourne (*c.*1550–1624), Field (1574–1636), Murray (d.1645), Hanmer (1575–1629) and Owen (1580–1651) are noted in *ODNB*; Owen would side with the Arminian party during the 1630s.

124 Fincham, *Prelate as Pastor: the Episcopate of James I*, p. 32.

125 A. H. Dodd, 'Bishop Lewes [*sic*] Bayly, c.1575–1631', *TCHS*, 28 (1967), 13–36.

126 For the operation of 'synods' in the Jacobean Church, see Collinson, *The Religion of Protestants: The Church in English Society, 1559–1625*, pp. 122–7.

127 Quoted in E. A. B. Barnard, 'Lewis Bayly, bishop of Bangor (d.1631) and Thomas Bayly (d.1657) his son', *THSC* (1928–9), 99–132 (122).

128 See J. Gwynfor Jones, '*The Practice of Piety*: Campwaith Lewis Bayly, esgob Bangor', in *idem, Crefydd a Chymdeithas: Astudiaethau ar Hanes y Ffydd Brotestannaidd yng Nghymru, c.1559–1750*, pp. 235–61.

129 William Evans, *An Outline of the History of Welsh Theology* (London: James Nisbet, 1900), p. 16.

130 Benedict, *Christ's Churches Purely Reformed: A Social History of Calvinism*, pp. 319–20; cf. Green, *Print and Protestantism in Early Modern England*, pp. 348–51.

131 Ryrie, *Being Protestant in Reformation Britain*, pp. 22, 283.

132 Lewis Bayly, *Yr Ymarfer o Dduwioldeb* (1630), ed. John Ballinger (Caerdydd: Gwasg Prifysgol Cymru, 1930), p. 4; page numbers which follow are in the text.

133 R. T. Kendall, *Calvin and English Calvinism to 1649* (Oxford: Oxford University Press, 1979), pp. 78–80; MacCulloch, *The Later Reformation in England, 1547–1603*, pp. 72–8.

134 Robert Llwyd, *Llwybr hyffordd yn cyfarwyddo yr anghyfarwydd i'r nefoedd ... o waith Arthur Dent* (Llundain: Nicholas Okes, 1630), Sig. A6v; the foreword

(Sig.A3v–A6v) is reproduced in Hughes (ed.), *Rhagymadroddion 1547–1659*, pp. 126–31; page numbers which follow are in the text.

135 For Dent (d.1603), see *ODNB*; his volume provides the basis for Christopher Haigh's study of popular religion, *The Plain Man's Paths to Heaven: Kinds of Christianity in Post-Reformation England, 1570–1640* (Oxford: Oxford University Press, 2007).

136 See A. H. Dodd, 'Mr Myddleton, the merchant of Tower St', in S. T. Bindoff, J. Hurstfield and C. H. Williams (eds), *Elizabethan Government and Society: Essays Presented to Sir John Neale* (London: The Athlone Press, 1961), pp. 249–81; both Myddleton and Heylyn are listed in *ODNB*.

137 *Y Bibl Cyssegr-Lan, sef yr Hen Destament a'r Newydd*, Hughes (ed.), *Rhagymadroddion 1547–1659*, pp. 122–5 (123).

138 Rice Rees (ed.), *Y Seren Foreu, neu Ganwyll y Cymry, sef gwaith prydyddol y Parch. Rhys Prichard MA, gynt ficer Llanymddyfri* (Llanymddyfri: W. Rees, 1841), p. 16, stanzas 63 and 64.

139 Rice Rees (ed.), *Y Seren Foreu, neu Ganwyll y Cymry*, p. lxxv, stanza 2.

140 For the complexities concerning the canon of Prichard's verse, see Eiluned Rees, 'A bibliographical note on the early editions of *Canwyll y Cymry*', *JWBS*, 10 (1966–71), 36–41; the best recent scholarly edition of Prichard's verse is Nesta Lloyd (ed.), *Cerddi'r Ficer* (Abertawe: Cyhoeddiadau Barddas, 1994), though it only contains a small selection of the whole.

141 Although the term 'Anglican' is anachronistic, it is used here to describe Prayer Book Christianity which conformed to the ceremonies and norms of the Established Church; see Judith Malby, 'Suffering and Surviving: the Civil Wars, the Commonwealth and the formation of "Anglicanism", 1642–60', in C. Durston and J. Maltby, *Religion in Revolutionary England* (Manchester: Manchester University Press, 2006), pp. 158–80.

142 Nesta Lloyd, '*Yr Ymarfer o Dduwioldeb* a rhai o gerddi Rhys Prichard', *Y Traethodydd*, 150 (1995), 94–106.

143 Quoted in R. Brinley Jones, *'A Lanterne to their Feete': Remembering Rhys Prichard (1579–1644), Vicar of Llandovery* (Porthyrhyd: The Drover's Press, 1994), p. 22.

144 See John Spurr, *English Puritanism, 1603–89* (London: Palgrave, 1998), pp. 79–85.

145 Morgan (ed. and intro.), *Gweithiau Oliver Thomas ac Evan Roberts*, pp. xxiv–v.

146 Polly Ho, *English Presbyterianism, 1590–1640* (Stanford, CA: University of Stanford Press, 2011), pp. 129–30, 132.

147 Morgan (ed. and intro.), *Gweithiau Oliver Thomas ac Evan Roberts*, pp. xvi, xix.

148 All references are taken from *Car-wr y Cymru* (1631), in Morgan (ed. and intro.), *Gweithiau Oliver Thomas ac Evan Roberts*, pp. 21–153; page numbers in the text refer first to the pagination of the *Car-wr* and secondly as they appear in Morgan's edition.

149 Rice Rees (ed.), *Y Seren Foreu, neu Ganwyll y Cymry*, p. 498, stanza 15.

150 Ryrie, *Being Protestant in Reformation Britain*, p. 104.

151 See above, pp. 40–1.

152 See Davies (ed.), *Dr John Davies of Mallwyd: Welsh Renaissance Scholar, passim.*

153 I. D. [John Davies], *Llyfr y Resolution ... wedi ei gyfiethu i Gymraeg* (Llundain: John Beale, 1632); for an assessment of its literary merit, see R. Geraint Gruffydd, '*Llyfr y Resolution* and other pastoral literature', in Davies (ed.), *Dr John Davies of Mallwyd: Welsh Renaissance Scholar*, pp. 226–37.

154 See Brad S. Gregory, '"The True and Zealous Seruice of God": Robert Parsons, Edmund Bunny and *The First Booke of the Christian Exercise*', *JEH*, 45 (1994), 238–68.

155 Richard Baxter, *The Autobiography of Richard Baxter* (1696), ed. N. H. Keeble (London: Dent, 1974), p. 7.

156 Wallace, *Puritans and Predestination*, pp. 84–90; Tyacke, *Anti-Calvinism*, pp. 125–30, 155–7.

157 Tyacke, *Anti-Calvinism*, p. 246.

158 See Horton Davies, *Worship and Theology in England, Vol. 1: From Cranmer to Baxter and Fox, 1534–1690* (Grand Rapids: Eerdmans, 1996), pp. 92–111; for the contrasting spir40ualties of 'holiness' and 'godliness', see Collinson, *The Religion of Protestants: The Church in English Society, 1559–1625*, pp. 108–10.

159 Roberts, 'Dr John Davies of Mallwyd: a biographical survey', p. 53.

160 For Roberts (1585–1665) and Owen (?1585–1645), see *ODNB*; for Mainwaring (1590–1653), see Edward Yardley, *Menevia Sacra*, ed. Francis Green (London: Cambrian Archaeological Assoc., 1927), pp. 109–12.

161 Philip Jenkins, '"The Sufferings of the Clergy": the Church in Glamorgan during the Interregnum', *JWEH*, 3 (1986), 1–17; 4 (1987), 9–41; 5 (1988), 73–80.

162 Philip Jenkins, 'Welsh Anglicans and the Interregnum', *JHSCW*, 32 (1990), 51–9.

163 Lambeth MS 943, f.255; quoted in Thomas Shankland, 'Anghydffurfwyr ac Ymneilltuwyr cyntaf Cymru', *Y Cofiadur*, 1 (1923), 33–44 (36).

164 NLW MS 128C, f.76, cited in Geraint H. Jenkins, *Protestant Dissenters in Wales, 1639–89* (Cardiff: University of Wales Press, 1992), p. 73.

165 Edward Terrill, *The Records of a Church of Christ meeting in Broadmead, Bristol, 1640–88*, ed. W. Haycroft (London: J. Heaton, 1865), p. 6.

166 Anon., *The Life and Death of Henry Jessey* (London, 1671), pp. 9–10, quoted in R. Geraint Gruffydd, '*In that Gentile Country': The Beginnings of Puritan Nonconformity in Wales* (Bridgend: Evangelical Library of Wales, 1976), pp. 14–15.

167 Francis J. Bremer, *The Puritan Experiment: New England Society from Bradford to Edwards*, 2nd edn (Hanover, NH: University Press of New England, 1995), pp. 105–13.

168 Bremer, *The Puritan Experiment*, pp. 135–7; cf. Perry Miller, *Orthodoxy in Massachusetts, 1630–50*, 2nd edn (Boston, MA: Beacon Press, 1959), pp. 148–211.

169 Jenkins, *Protestant Dissenters in Wales, 1639–89*, p. 13.

170 William Erbury, *Apocrypha* (London: n.p., 1653), p. 8; also in John I. Morgans, *The Honest Heretique: the Life and Work of William Erbury (1604–54)* (Tal-y-bont: Y Lolfa, 2012), p. 143.

[171] For Love, see Don Kistler, *A Spectacle unto God: the Life and Death of Christopher Love (1618–51)* (Morgan, PA: Soli Deo Gloria, 1994) and *ODNB*.

[172] *The Humble Petition of Mr Erbury and the whole Principality of Wales* in Morgans, *The Honest Heretique: the Life and Work of William Erbury*, pp. 55–6.

[173] They would all play key roles in the Puritan regime of the Interregnum, see Thomas Richards, *A History of the Puritan Movement in Wales, 1639 to 1653* (London: National Eisteddfod Association, 1920), *passim.*

[174] See Lloyd Bowen, 'Wales and religious reform in the Long Parliament, 1640–2', *THSC*, N.S. 12 (2005), 36–59; *idem, The Politics of the Principality*, pp. 235–61.

[175] *Petition from many in the Principality of Wales*, in Morgans, *The Honest Heretique: the Life and Work of William Erbury*, pp. 56–9.

[176] See above, p. 61.

[177] See above, pp. 48–9.

[178] Edmund Jones, *A Sermon ...occasioned by the Death of Mr. Evan Williams ...to which is added some Account of his Life* (London: n.p., 1750), p. 86.

[179] Keeble (ed.), *The Autobiography of Richard Baxter*, p. 15.

[180] Geoffrey F. Nuttall, *The Welsh Saints, 1640–60* (Cardiff: University of Wales Press, 1957), p. 6; cf. J. T. Cliffe, *The Puritan Gentry: the Great Puritan Families of Early Stuart England* (London: Routledge and Kegan Paul, 1984), pp. 185–9.

[181] Cited in Jacqueline Eales, *Puritans and Roundheads: the Harleys of Bramton Bryan and the Outbreak of the English Civil War* (Cambridge: Cambridge University Press, 1990), p. 68.

[182] Eales, *Puritans*, p. 67.

[183] Lambeth MS 943, f.256; in Shankland, 'Anghydffurfwyr ac Ymneilltuwyr cyntaf Cymru', 36

[184] Shankland, 'Anghydffurfwyr ac Ymneilltuwyr cyntaf Cymru', 36–7.

[185] See Morgan (ed. and intro.), *Gweithiau Oliver Thomas ac Evan Roberts*, pp. xxvii–xxxii.

[186] Shankland, 'Anghydffurfwyr ac Ymneilltuwyr cyntaf Cymru', 37.

[187] For Matthews, see E. Stanley John, 'Bywyd, gwaith a chyfnod dau Biwritan Cymreig, Marmaduke Matthews a Richard Blinman' (unpublished PhD thesis, University of Wales, Bangor, 1987), and *ODNB*.

[188] Shankland, 'Anghydffurfwyr ac Ymneilltuwyr cyntaf Cymru', 38.

[189] For the Scottish debacle, see Benedict, *Christ's Churches Purely Reformed: A Social History of Calvinism*, pp. 392–5.

[190] Keeble (ed.), *The Autobiography of Richard Baxter*, p. 22.

[191] Quoted in Tyacke, *Anti-Calvinism*, p. 240.

[192] See John Morrill, 'The religious context of the English Civil War', in *idem, The Nature of the English Revolution* (London: Longmans, 1993), pp. 45–68.

[193] Tyacke, *Anti-Calvinism*, p. 243.

[194] Carlton, *Archbishop William Laud*, p. 194.

195 John Walker, *An Account of the Numbers and Sufferings of the Clergy in the late Times of the Grand Rebellion* (1714) (Oxford: John Henry and James Parker, 1862), p. 47.

196 Kenneth Fincham and Nicholas Tyacke, *Altars Restored: The Changing Face of English Religious Worship, 1547–c.1700* (Oxford: Oxford University Press, 2007), p. 259.

197 Rice Rees (ed.), *Y Seren Foreu, neu Ganwyll y Cymry*, p. lv.

198 Yardley, *Menevia Sacra*, p. 111.

199 Williams, 'Religion and Welsh literature in the age of the Reformation', p. 160.

200 Morgans, *The Honest Heretique: the Life and Work of William Erbury*, p. 47.

201 References are taken from *Sail Crefydd Ghristinogol* in Morgan (ed.), *Gweithiau Oliver Thomas ac Evan Roberts*, pp. 157–208; page numbers refer first to the pagination of the original text and secondly as they appear in Morgan's edition.

202 William Erbury, *The Great Mystery of Godliness* (London: Robert Milbourne, 1639), p. 10; also in Morgans, *The Honest Heretique: the Life and Work of William Erbury*, pp. 46–51; page numbers refer first to the pagination of the original text and secondly as they appear in Morgans's selection.

203 Morgans, *The Honest Heretique: the Life and Work of William Erbury*, p. 48.

204 Cf. Bowen, *The Politics of the Principality*, pp. 235–78 with the earlier studies by A. H. Dodd, 'Wales and the parliaments of Charles I', *THSC* (1945), 16–49; (1946–7), 57–96; *idem*, 'The pattern of politics in Stuart Wales', *THSC* (1948–9), 8–91.

205 See Philip Jenkins, 'The Anglican Church and the Unity of Britain: the Welsh Experience, 1560–1714', in Steven G. Ellis and Sarah Barber (eds), *Conquest and Union: Fashioning a British State, 1485–1725* (London: Longman, 1995), pp. 115–39.

206 Quoted in Judith Maltby, *Prayer Book and People in Elizabethan and Early Stuart England* (Cambridge: Cambridge University Press, 1998), p. 114; for the text, see Judith Maltby, 'Petitions for episcopacy and the Book of Common Prayer on the eve of the Civil War, 1641–2', in Stephen Taylor (ed.), *From Cranmer to Davidson: A Miscellany* (Woodbridge: The Boydell Press, 1999), pp. 103–68 (138–40).

2

1642–1660

The Theology of the Radical Puritans, 1642–60

Walter Cradock and the theology of free grace

The first of the seventeenth-century radical Welsh Puritans for whom we have a modestly substantial body of published works is Walter Cradock (*c.*1606–59).[1] Having succeeded William Wroth as minister of the gathered church at Llanfaches, Monmouthshire, early in 1641, by the June of that year Cradock had appealed to parliament to send godly, orthodox and effective preachers to evangelize in south Wales. Due to the success of Puritan witness in the area and the ease of passage between the Caldicot hundred and the city of Bristol, a mere few miles over the water, the links between Bristol Puritans and the Llanfaches community were strong. The outbreak of the civil war found the Llanfaches people in an invidious position. A despised minority in an overwhelmingly royalist Wales, Cradock, along with the bulk of his congregation, found it expedient to move to Bristol where they were given succour by the Congregationalists of the Broadmead Church. Worshipping together, with Cradock administering the sacraments among them, they persevered until the parliamentary garrison yielded to the king in July 1643.[2] Rather than returning to Wales, the fellowship relocated to London where they worshipped at Allhallows the Great, a staunchly Puritan congregation in Thames Street in the city, Cradock having been appointed parish lecturer. There he would remain until October 1646 when, along with Richard Symonds and Henry Walter, fellow Monmouthshire-born Puritans, he was financed by parliament to itinerate in south Wales.[3] The next five years would see him dividing his time between Wales and the capital, while he would take an increasingly significant role in the campaign to evangelize his native land.

Between 1646 and 1651 Cradock published six volumes of sermons, the first, *The Saints' Fullness of Joy*, being a single sermon preached in St Margaret's Church, Westminster, on 21 July 1646 at the request of the House of Commons and which celebrated the surrender of Oxford by the king. Despite its public context, its emphasis was on the need for personal religion and its central doctrine was that of union with Christ: 'Fullness of joy is the fruit of our union with Jesus Christ ... without union with Christ men are hypocrites ... Wherever there is righteousness and peace in the heart, there joy in Jesus Christ follows' (pp. 17–18; p. 393).[4] Cradock's reputation as a winsome preacher had already been forged, and his characteristic emphases of the pitfalls of legalism, the sheer graciousness of the gospel and the spiritual nature of church fellowship which eschewed as far as possible external forms and ordinances, are all evident in this work:

> Therefore, when I have communion with a saint, I must not look so much whether he be of such an opinion, or whether he has taken the covenant, or has been baptized once or twice or ten times ... but see if he has fellowship with the Father and with Jesus Christ. (p. 28; p. 402)

Early in the sermon he records his debt to William Wroth and refers to the intimate way that his predecessor at Llanfaches had dealt with parishioners: 'He that would convert sinners or edify saints ought to study souls as well as books' (p. 11; p. 391). Whereas in the rest of the treatise the objective truths of the faith are nowhere downplayed, for Cradock the essence of true religion is the soul's experiential appropriation of salvation: 'I would not have you to think that the union between Christ and the saints is nothing put a pure empty notion' (p. 22; p. 399).

In London the Welsh had traditionally been derided for their poverty, clannishness and rusticity, a custom that was magnified among many parliamentarians following Wales's near wholesale support for the king from the beginning of the civil war.[5] Consequently, Cradock's heartfelt plea for parliament to support the spiritual needs of his native land was even more pointed:

> And what if you should spend one single thought upon poor, contemptible Wales? It is little indeed, and little respected, yet time was the enemy

made no small use and advantage of it, how inconsiderable so ever we deem it. Oh, let not poor Wales continue sighing, famishing, morning and bleeding while you have your days of feasting, rejoicing, thanksgiving and praising God. Yet praised be our God! Some few there are among us ... who are ready and willing to spend and be spent for ... the good of their country. Oh, that you allow them some small competency of maintenance ... (p. 34; p. 406)

It was this eloquent petition which helped expedite the campaign that would lead in 1650 to the passing of the Act for the Better Propagation of the Gospel in Wales.[6]

Cradock's characteristic appeal to Christian freedom on the basis of the gracious nature of the gospel was equally apparent in his next two publications, *Glad Tidings from Heaven*, a sermon on the Great Commission in Mark 16:15, and a series on I Cor. 10:23 entitled *Gospel Liberty*, both of which appeared in 1648. His acute and incessant fear of legalism reflects his response to the tendency within Puritanism towards either despair or censoriousness. Those whose consciences had been awakened through the preaching of the gospel were in danger of being over-scrupulous in nurturing their own piety or else of judging harshly others whose religious experience did not wholly replicate their own. In order to counter both tendencies, Cradock made a sharp distinction between justification, which was dependant absolutely on the objective sacrifice of Christ, and sanctification through which the justified sinner would strive to live the moral life. To emphasize this, he drew an equally sharp contrast between the Old Testament, which he saw as being based mostly on law, and the New:[7]

Before our Lord went to heaven there was some gospel but there was much law ... In the New Testament ... we read that there was perfect gospel, or only good news and glad tidings, for the bad news was now all gone. (pp. 6, 3; pp. 356, 354)[8]

The besetting sin of legalism was to nurture what he called 'an Old Testament Spirit' which 'makes laws and ties and bonds and knots and knacks and many ridiculous things to tie and bind themselves where Christ Jesus in the New Testament has not bound them' (p. 44; p. 265).[9] Although ostensibly obedient to scripture, legalism was in fact its antithesis: 'Remember, the greatest misery to an honest heart ... is this, a misdrawing of rules out of the Word of God' (*Gospel Liberty*, p. 58; p. 274). Christ, for his part, made people free, and the New Testament spirit was one of boldness, confidence and joyfulness before its Lord.

In turning to preaching, since the time of William Perkins at least, Puritan practice had been to expound the law in order to convict hearers of their sin. This, however, was a practice of which Cradock did not approve. It was, he claimed, the gospel and not the law that awakened people's conscience and drew them to Christ:

> In the gospel poor sinners come to learn what a damnable wretched condition they are in. Whereas men without it think they are well, they do nobody hurt, they give to the poor … and the like, and yet they are going the broad way to destruction. Now we see not only by scripture but by experience, the gospel tells them that they are dead in sin, that they are children of wrath, that they are under the curse of God, going the broad way to hell. (*Glad Tidings*, p. 11; p. 359)

Of itself, the preaching of the law could so easily lead to works righteousness: 'There are so many conditions, a man must be broken and humbled and damned almost and go to the gates of hell before he can come to Christ' (*Gospel Liberty*, p. 27; p. 254). The preacher's task however was to invite everyone, awakened or not, to come to Christ: 'We are not sent to get galley slaves to the oars, or a bear to the stake, but he sends us to woo you as spouses, to marry you to Christ' (p. 28; p. 255). Grace was more effective than the law in drawing people to the Saviour, and infinitely more attractive:

> This … jumbling old and new together … routs and confounds a poor soul, as to preach terror and damnation to a sinner as a sinner. Though we may be called ministers of the gospel, yet this is a part of the ministry of the law, for the law brings curses for a sinner, and blessings for him that does well; now when we, as a sinner, damn him and curse him, we harden him and make him run further from God than before. (*Glad Tidings*, p. 52; p. 382)

Although Cradock insists on the importance of the law to which the believer, having been justified, must adhere, it is the gospel alone that leads to salvation: 'It is true that the law is necessary … but God intends not in the New Testament that it should be mixed and mingled with the gospel' (p. 52; p. 382). The preacher's task was to preach the good news of salvation and not the bad news of the law. He was charged to be a New Testament minister of grace, not an Old Testament prophet of doom:

> [It is] that Old Testament principle that is the root of all our mischief ... Whereby you will go and make laws in external things and under the gospel, where Christ has not made them, and in the meanwhile neglect or destroy love and peace and edification.(*Gospel Liberty*, p. 162; p. 341)

The wider context of these two publications was the tension between Presbyterians and Independents which had dogged the success of parliament's religious mission to the realm following the outlawing of the Book of Common Prayer in January 1644 and the eventual abolition of episcopacy in October 1646.[10] At the bidding of parliament, the Assembly of Divines had been in session since July 1643.[11] The Westminster Assembly, as it came to be known, was overwhelmingly Presbyterian in composition and sought to promote the Christianization of the realm through a learned ministry within a parish-based, non-Episcopal though still hierarchical national establishment. The Congregationalists[12] both within the assembly and without, held that godly renewal could only succeed through creating gathered congregations of so-called 'visible saints'.[13] Although Cradock held to the concept of a state-supported religious establishment, he was instinctively dubious of hierarchical religion and in matters of ecclesiastical government was incontrovertibly Congregational. Whereas he sought to minimize the difference between the two schemes: 'Presbytery and Independency are not two religions but one religion to a godly, honest heart: it is only a little ruffling of the fringe' (*Gospel Liberty*, p. 135; p. 324), nevertheless all his sympathies were with what he calls 'the Independents'.

It was this antipathy towards religious formalism which he feared that Presbyterianism no less than Episcopacy would nurture, that controlled his attitude towards both the sacraments and a learned, ordained ministry. For Cradock, the sacraments were of secondary importance for true Christian faith: 'How moderately and sparingly and covertly the Lord mentions ordinances' (*Gospel Liberty*, p. 47; p. 267). It was not only Laudians who had been obsessed with the right administration of baptism and the Lord's Supper, but there were too many godly people who were overzealous about the ordinances at the expense of the weightier matters of tolerance and love. The disciples, he states,

[m]ight ask a hundred questions, shall we do it in a river, or in a brook?, to young or to old?, in winter or in summer? Who shall do it?, and what shall his calling be?, and many such questions. But Christ lays down the sum of the doctrine and the end of it: 'In the name of the Father, and of the Son, and of the Holy Ghost', and there is no more of it. (p. 16; pp. 246–7)

The same was true of the Lord's Supper:

He has bound us that we should break bread and drink wine, that may represent the thing, but he has not bound us to bread so properly called, or to wine so properly called, for there are some countries that they have neither bread nor wine but only roots that they call bread, and they have water for their drink. (p. 24; p. 252)

It was among the Congregationalists, and latterly the Baptists, that the conviction had spread that spiritual competency rather than conventional learning was the one thing essential for the gospel ministry. One of the great criticisms levelled at the radical Welsh Puritans was their immoderate zeal to uproot the parish-based ministry and replace it with an itinerant system of unlettered preachers.[14] Although patently Cradock was learned, being able to point frequently to the meaning of the Greek text and refer in *The Saints' Fullness of Joy* to Oxford as 'that university that I had formerly known' (p. 30),[15] he had no truck with the idea that only university-trained clergy were fit to preach:

Let us not be so curious and scrupulous as to hinder people that have no degrees in the university, or, it may be, have not the knowledge of tongues … let us not pick quarrels with them to stop their mouths and so to hinder the preaching of the gospel … It is strange you should have pulpits ring with calling them tub-preachers, tinkers and cobblers. We should think better of them. Why? They are filled with good news, and they go and tell it to others. (*Glad Tidings*, p. 49; p. 380)

The vivid description in *Glad Tidings* for which Cradock is best known:

I have observed and seen in the mountains of Wales the most glorious work that I ever saw in Britain, unless it were in London; the gospel has run over the mountains between Brecknockshire and Monmouthshire, as the fire in the thatch is as much an apologia for an unlettered, lay ministry as a depiction of the success of the gospel in his native land:

> They have no ministers, but some of the wisest say there are about eight hundred godly people, and they go from one another … And shall we rail at them, and say they are tub-preachers, and they were never at the university? Let us fall down and honour God. (p. 50; pp. 380–1)

Perhaps the most jarring difference between the radical Puritans' interpretation of biblical faith and the consensus which had developed among Reformed Welsh churchmen since the time of Bishop William Morgan and Archdeacon Edmund Prys had to do with the validity of forms and liturgy, especially the Book of Common Prayer. As for the doctrines of election, the concept of God's sovereignty in salvation, the need for effective gospel preaching and the necessity for personal conversion, there was little material difference between the likes of Rhys Prichard, the vicar of Llandovery, and those of Walter Cradock and his colleagues. But as for the virtues or otherwise of the Episcopal system and the spiritual qualities of Cranmer's Prayer Book, there would be no meeting of minds. For all Cradock's ostensible moderation, he had nothing but abhorrence for the legacy of the old Established Church. Whereas John Davies of Mallwyd had counted it part of his pastoral duty to provide a serviceable Welsh translation of the Prayer Book, for Cradock the very concept of liturgical prayer was anathema:

> [As] for prayer, when it may be the poor minister's soul was full of groans and sighs, and he would have rejoiced to have poured out his soul to the Lord, he was tied to an old service book, and must read that till he grieved the Spirit of God, and dried up his own spirit as a chip, that he could not pray as he would.[16]

There was no recognition that the minister's role was *not* to groan and sigh in personal prayer but to represent through well-selected words and phrases the needs and petitions of his flock before God, or that 'an old service book' could be a more effective way for the Holy Spirit to support and animate the faithful than the momentary effusions of an undisciplined piousness.

Neither was Cradock's view a protest against Laudian formalism as such. Anything which reflected the establishment tradition or liturgical worship was ruled wholly out of court:

> So they made the Thirty Nine Articles and decrees and canons, to etch
> out the New Testament, and the minister must say this with a loud voice
> and that with a low voice and now he must sit and now he must stand
> and he must read one lesson here and one lesson there, and here he
> must read the first and then the second service ... What an abominable
> thing it is to tie the sons of God that are not babes under tutors with
> paltry things when the Spirit of God in the least saint is better able to
> determine than all the bishops. (*Gospel Liberty*, p. 49; p. 268)

Equally disconcerting was his opposition to the more conservative elements among the Presbyterians. Having followed closely the deliberations
of the Assembly of Divines, he could nowhere believe that its vision of
a reformed, hierarchical non-Episcopal church would be effective. Even
worse, if many of their leaders were purportedly godly, there were too
many in the Presbyterian party who were 'wolves in sheep's clothing',
who merely replicated the evils of the former regime:

> Usually they are prelatical men, such as were surrogates to the bish-
> ops before, double-beneficed men, rich parsons, prebends and canons;
> these men, that know not the power of godliness, whose hearts were at
> Oxford ... these are none that talk so much of Presbytery as they ...
> they study to devour the people of God: beware of them! (p. 131; p. 321)

The received view of Walter Cradock's proverbial moderation, geniality
and tenderness,[17] though not necessarily incorrect, should be qualified
in the light of this harsh and incessant anti-formalist polemic.

Cradock's final three works, a series of sermons on Rom. 8:4 entitled
Mount Zion (1649), *Divine Drops Distilled* (1650), which was an assortment of short expositions on a range of biblical texts from both Old
Testament and New, and *Gospel Holiness* (1641), sermons based on Isaiah's
vision of God in Isa. 6, although published during the early years of
the Commonwealth and when the Act for the Better Propagation of the
Gospel was further radicalizing the religious situation in Wales, reflect
mostly his characteristic convictions concerning the Spirit and the law.
The motif that runs through *Mount Zion* is that of justification by faith
alone and righteousness on the basis of the unique sacrifice of Christ:

> There is but one way, that is Jesus Christ, there is a perfect righteousness
> in him, he has fulfilled the law; get into him and be one with him, and

then we shall be able to say perfectly with Paul, 'that the righteousness
of the law might be fulfilled perfectly in us that believe'. (p. 12; p. 12)[18]

The problem with so many of Cradock's faithful hearers is that they
believed that they had somehow to complement the finished righteousness
of Christ with something of their own: 'For this is the misery, the general
misery of most Christians, that they mislay their justification: they lay it
partly upon faith and partly upon their sanctification and their holiness'
(p. 18; p. 15). The fact is that salvation was wholly dependent upon Christ
and not upon themselves or any quality of piety that they had attained:

> The law as it is, is a contract, a bond, a bargain; as it is a covenant of
> works between God and us, it is perfectly fulfilled by Christ and we are
> dead to it, we are freed from it or delivered from it. (p. 17; p. 15)

Consequently, salvation is not a synergy or a partnership. Quietness of
conscience or peace of mind could only be attained by his hearers seizing
this reality and making it their own:

> I am a just man only by the righteousness that is in Christ, that the law
> is perfectly fulfilled for me by Jesus Christ and not partly by him and
> partly by me, but only and perfectly by him. (p. 18; p. 15)
> ... My justification is built upon the death of Christ and his resur-
> rection: he has fulfilled the law and he has paid the debt and he is out of
> prison and the Father is satisfied: here is my justification and believing
> this I am happy ... Now the Lord has put it out of our hands. (p. 29; p. 21)

This was the self-same doctrine as had been taught by Welsh theologians since the days of Bishop Richard Davies: it had been enshrined in
Maurice Kyffin's 1595 version of Jewel's *Apologia Ecclesiae Anglicanae*;
it was basic to Robert Holland's translations of William Perkins early
in the century; it was luminously clear in Edward James's rendition of
Cranmer's Book of Homilies in 1606; it provided the basis for the diocesan policy of William Morgan, Lewis Bayly and their fellow Reformed
bishops; it is a staple in the metrical poetry of Archdeacon Edmund
Prys and the popular verse of Rhys Prichard; it was the centre-point
of the parochial teaching of conformists like Robert Llwyd and John
Davies and the preaching and publications of moderate nonconformists like Oliver Thomas. What appeared new in Cradock was the verve,

effectiveness and uncompromising vitality with which these convictions were applied to the lives of ordinary people through the act of preaching. Among the radical Welsh Puritans, Cradock was the preacher *par excellence*. A quarter century after his death he was described, by an admirer, of having 'a wonderful faculty of coming down and bringing with him the things of God to the meanest of his auditors'.[19] During the early years of the Evangelical Revival, a further three-quarter century ahead, popular preachers and their converts in north Wales would be known as 'Cradockites' (*Cradociaid*).[20] The rhythms of speech, studied repetitions and rhetorical skill of Cradock are all illustrated in these sermons, though his 'unusually limpid and thoughtful prose is scarcely likely to have been delivered on the stump' as it appears in the books: 'The assumption must be that Cradock fashioned his sermon notes into prose marked by an immediacy that makes for lively copy in print.'[21]

The danger of Cradock's passionate emphasis on justification by faith alone was antinomianism, the idea that somehow the law no longer had a hold on the believing Christian; indeed conservative Presbyterians like Thomas 'Gangraena' Edwards and mainstream Puritans such as Richard Baxter accused him of this very thing.[22] Cradock, however, was as insistent on the need for good works, what he called 'gospel holiness', as he was on the necessity of being justified by faith: 'We must get good works [but] after' (p. 31; p. 22), he asserted. Although justification must be accompanied by, though never confused with, sanctification, namely the individual's progressive growth in holiness, Cradock would never allow this to eclipse the truth that the Christian life was one of the humble receipt of costly forgiveness and the simple acceptance of grace. Neither was it a matter of speculation or undue curiosity as to the workings of the soul:

> I do not approve of those that do endeavour to show you too particularly and exactly how the Spirit of God works in the soul, as many men have done, but they have lost much time and have puzzled the souls of poor people.

Such conjecture 'has brought forth a deal of curiosity and needless distinctions, troubling the people of God' (p. 129; p. 121). It was enough to affirm the reality of God's calling and the individual's believing response. The fact of divine election, though rarely dwelt upon, is presupposed throughout his work: 'It is not the will of God that we should conceive that Jesus Christ did equally die for all men, and redeem all men' (p. 76; p. 93), he claimed. But this, in truth, was not our affair. The listener's response was only to act humbly in faith and be confident that he or she would be welcomed by Christ: 'As Christ Jesus has purchased salvation for the soul, so he has purchased faith for us to lay hold upon that salvation' (p. 76; p. 93). Although both faith and salvation were wholly of God, this in no way debars individuals from responding actively to the divine invitation. The gospel was no conundrum, in fact it was radiantly clear. This theme forms a refrain in *Divine Drops Distilled*: 'The gospel is a far more simple and plain thing than most people conceive it to be … The gospel is a plain, simple thing' (p. 225; p. 527).[23] Whereas false teachers would feign complicate the Christian message through metaphysical speculation, the New Testament itself was abundantly clear:

> I see the apostles preached Christ, they tell a story of a man being born
> of the Virgin Mary, apprehended by the Jews, and he was a public person,
> and bore the sins of his people, and he was put to death, and rose again
> for our justification. (p. 224; p. 527)

All we are expected to do is to respond to the gospel call in humble obedience. It was hardly surprising that 'the simplest people most commonly understand the gospel best' (p. 225; p. 528). In *Gospel Holiness*, his final work, he recalls a sight that took him back to the rolling hills of Gwent:

> I have seen poor women in the mountains of Wales (and I have often
> thought of it), they have been so poor that when they have come to the
> house to beg a little whey or buttermilk, they have been feign to beg the
> loan of a pot or a dish to put it in. So we, when we come to beg mercy
> of God, we must desire the Lord, when we have done our best, to give
> us eyes to see it, and a heart to lay it up, and a hand to receive it … We
> cannot carry one grain of grace home, unless God gives us spiritual
> buckets … Says the humble soul, Lord, I have none, thou must both give
> the water, and lend the bucket to carry it home. (p. 165; pp. 214–15)[24]

In February 1650 Cradock was the first name listed among the itinerants whose task, under the Propagation Act, was to spread the gospel message throughout Wales. Although the sermons quoted above had been delivered initially in Allhallows Church in London, they provide an insight into the nature of his specific theology of grace, a theology that would resound from pulpits in south-east Wales, his specific sphere of service, during the following years. When the Act was discontinued in 1653, he was appointed minister at Usk, a few miles from his Llangwm home. He remained influential in parliamentary circles, preaching to the Nominated Assembly in August 1653, being appointed to the government's commission on the readmission of the Jews in 1655, and presenting to Cromwell on behalf of the Welsh parliamentary loyalists *A Humble Representation and Address* (1656), pledging support for the Protector's religious policies. Along with his colleagues Vavasor Powell and Morgan Llwyd, he is said to have 'provided the leadership for a revival of Christianity at once free, expectant and spiritual'.[25] He died on 24 December 1659 and was buried beneath the chancel of St Jerome's Church, Llangwm-Uchaf, the parish where he was born.[26]

Vavasor Powell, Calvinism and chiliasm

Like Llwyd, one of Cradock's foremost converts was Vavasor Powell (1617–70), the so-called 'metropolitan of the itinerants', whose premier contribution to the Puritan movement was as an evangelist, activist and firebrand rather than as a theologian as such.[27] Born at Cnwc-las (Knucklas) in the parish of Heyope, Radnorshire, to a middling family of well-connected freeholders, he was educated at Christ's College, Brecon – Anthony Wood's reference to his having matriculated at Jesus College, Oxford, cannot be substantiated – and became a schoolmaster at Clun, Shropshire, as well as acting as an un-ordained assistant to his uncle, Erasmus Powell, the parish's rector. His conversion, instigated by contact with godly parishioners at Clun, his reading of Richard Sibbes's devotional handbook *The Bruised Reed* and especially by the preaching of 'a very famous godly preacher',[28] almost certainly Cradock who was active on the Radnorshire-Shropshire border at the time, was complete by 1639–40 by which time he had already begun preaching. It is obvious that by now vigorous lay religion or what the Puritans would refer to as 'godliness' was advancing in the border areas of south-east Wales as well as in the principal towns of Swansea, Carmarthen, Haverfordwest and Wrexham in the north, and Powell's strenuous evangelistic labours contributed to its expansion. According to his biographer, he

> did bestir himself exceedingly in preaching the gospel, labouring therein
> more abundantly then any we have known giving himself wholly to

the work both in public and private … Many by his preaching were turned to the Lord, so that Radnorshire that before was a dark country, came to have much light and in a short space many eminent professors begotten in it.[29]

Just as Cradock had found himself in Bristol after August 1642 following the outset of the civil war, Powell's zealous preaching had inflamed the royalist authorities in his own county making it expedient for him to leave for the much more parliamentary-friendly city of London. The next two years spent in the capital would seal his success as an effective preacher, especially in the parish church of St Anne and St Agnes, Aldersgate, and at Crooked Lane in the city. While there he witnessed the abandonment of the Book of Common Prayer, the dismantling of many of the structures of the Church of England, including deans and chapters leading, by 1646, to the abolition of episcopacy. Although he followed the activities of the Westminster Assembly avidly, he became increasingly disenchanted by its hierarchical bent, its favouring of a rigidly Presbyterian polity and its emphasis on a learned ministry rather than providing for the sort of rousing evangelistic preaching that would awaken men's souls. Early in 1646 parliament appointed him incumbent of the parish church in Dartford, Kent, where he immediately set about gathering a covenanted congregation of 'visible saints'. In the ecclesiastical vacuum left by the eradication of episcopacy, the only church structure that Vavasor Powell would contemplate was that of a stark and unalloyed congregationalism:

> The particular visible churches under the gospel did not consist of whole nations, countries or cities; nor of the generality and multitudes of either, but of such companies (many or few in them) that did receive and profess the doctrine of the gospel, were converted and called to be saints, separated from the world, both its sins and services; and united and given up to the Lord, and to one another, to live according to the will of God in all things.[30]

What brought him back to Wales was an invitation 'by the Church of Radnorshire' in June 1646 to act as their pastor.[31] It was served by Richard Price and John Williams, commissioners attached to parliament's Committee for Plundered Ministers and engaged in appointing Puritan clergy to replace those who had been found either morally inept or politically unacceptable to the new regime. In order to accept this invitation, Powell needed approval from the Westminster Assembly of Divines, and though he cavilled at the idea of Presbyterian ordination, nevertheless he was approved. The certificate, issued on 11 September 1646 was signed by such Presbyterian luminaries as Stephen Marshall and Christopher Love as well as the Congregationalists Joseph Caryl, Philip Nye and Jeremiah Burroughs. It confirmed that he was 'a man of a religious and blameless conversation and of able gifts for the work of the ministry', who had already been called 'to exercise his gifts in his own country of Wales ... also having the language thereof'.[32] Apart from some well-attested forays into London later in the decade and during the mid-1650s, thereafter Powell's ministry would be fulfilled primarily in Wales.

Vavasor Powell's overt political commitment and radical activism took him to the centre of the religious maelstrom of the Interregnum. Taking a respite from his parish responsibilities, he had already served with the parliamentary army against the royalist garrisons in Pembrokeshire and Oxford, and in 1648 was wounded while taking part in the siege of Beaumaris on Anglesey. By then he was highly regarded by the Cromwellian authorities, and between 1650 and 1653 took a leading if decidedly contentious part in implementing the Act for the Better Propagation of the Gospel in Wales.[33] As well as contributing to the evangelization of the populace, his published sermons *God the Father Glorified and the Work of Man's Redemption* (1650) and *Christ Exalted above all Creatures by his Father* (1651), the first preached in London before the mayor and city aldermen in December 1649 and the second before parliament in February 1650, urge the establishment of a godly Commonwealth thus paving the way for the millennial reign of Christ. With the politicization of the army following the conclusion of the First Civil War in 1646 and the fevered atmosphere which culminated in the execution of the king in January 1649, Powell's apocalypticism had become even more pronounced. The comment made by Alexander Griffith, the ejected rector of Glasebury, Breconshire, and Powell's most vitriolic critic, reflects the content of much of Powell's preaching at the time:

> Now his chief work is to preach and advance Christ's personal reign
> here on earth, being the ancient error and foppery of the chiliasts and
> millenaries, hissed and exploded out of the church of Christ in the very
> infancy thereof.[34]

Imbued with Fifth Monarchist views, he interpreted the regicide as part of the divine strategy to hasten the Second Coming, while the Republic, instituted officially on 19 May 1649, would herald the Lord's return. Just as parliamentary moderates shuddered at the execution of the monarch, they realized that any hope of recreating the Established Church along Presbyterian lines was now wholly forlorn. If the Westminster Assembly's liturgical goal of producing a Directory of Worship and its doctrinal aim of producing its celebrated Longer and Shorter Catechisms and Confession of Faith would be fulfilled,[35] its ecclesiastical ambition of establishing a nationwide network of congregational assemblies, classical presbyteries and provincial synods led by an alliance of ministers and lay elders had already dissolved.[36] In fact political power was ebbing away even from parliament to the direction of the army for whom independency in church matters had become a settled conviction. Powell was elated. The ideals for which he had striven so zealously since 1642 seemed to be coming to fruition.

Powell's chiliastic radicalism went hand in hand with a fairly conventional doctrinal Calvinism. His dispute with John Goodwin, incumbent of St Stephen's Colman Street in the City of London, on 31 December 1649, found him defending the concept of particular redemption against his opponent's conviction that Christ had died for all. 'We differ concerning election, redemption, man's will', he claimed, 'and ... falling away from grace'.[37] Goodwin was one of the most remarkable Puritan ministers of his generation.[38] A graduate of Queens' College Cambridge, he had been instituted to the bustling parish of St Stephen's in 1633 following an eight-year preparatory ministry in East Anglia. A moderate Calvinist at first, he became increasingly dissatisfied with what he now regarded as the inconsistencies of Reformed doctrine. Dispensing with the concept of Christ imputing a so-called 'alien' righteousness to the believer, he had come to interpret justification by faith as consisting solely of the forgiveness of sins. He felt that the traditional formulation had led too easily to antinomianism, that a merely forensic imputation of Christ's sinlessness was not conducive to a striving after holiness on the believer's part. On the political front, he had become the most virulent opponent of King Charles among the London clergy and virtually the only one to venture into print to justify his execution. His ecclesiasticism had become equally uncompromising. Formerly a moderate Congregationalist, by the mid-1640s he had gained notoriety as the scourge of the Presbyterians and an advocate of what was, in terms of the day, radical toleration. The function of government, he claimed, was not to privilege any one sect but to safeguard the conscientious freedom of all (albeit orthodox) Christians.

Goodwin's restless mind was at the same time taking him away from the Calvinistic consensus shared by Presbyterians and Congregationalists alike. His magnum opus entitled *Redemption Redeemed*, 'the longest and most substantial defence of Arminianism yet published in the English language' would appear in 1651, though it had become apparent since 1648 that he had broken with the moderate Calvinists' claim that pre-destination was compatible with divine justice, human agency and the universal nature of God's love.[39] If God's love was universal, he now contended, Christ's atonement could not be particular or restricted to the elect. Similarly, if man was called to respond freely to the gospel, the divine decree was relative, not absolute. In other words, grace was not, in fact, irresistible but dependent upon human cooperation. Such a doctrine had heretofore characterized the Laudian prelates and formalist High Churchmen who had been so unceremoniously stripped of their power by the present regime. To have Arminianism now appearing among the Puritans themselves was disconcerting to say the least. Although Powell retained his respect for Goodwin's integrity and erudition, he well realized what was at stake. The crux of the discussion was that, for Goodwin, God's elective will embraced all of Adam's posterity and that the Johannine contention that God so loved the world should be taken literally, whereas for Powell, 'the world' implied those who had been chosen by God and called out *from* the world: 'Jesus Christ did not die alike for every man … he did not die to redeem every man from the guilt of his sin, and from the curse of the law'.[40] The dispute was fragmented and inconclusive but it demonstrated Powell's grasp of the Calvinistic faith, and his zeal to defend it in the public arena. It also constituted 'a major episode in the history of London's Puritanism, one that revealed the crumbling of the Calvinist consensus among the godly'.[41]

In his volume *Christ and Moses' Excellency* (1650), Powell elaborated on a theme that had been developed within Reformed theology on the continent since the time of Heinrich Bullinger, Zwingli's successor at Zürich, at least, and had become a mainstay of English Puritan thought, namely covenant theology or federalism.[42] For Powell, who styles himself 'preacher of the gospel in Wales', there were two basic scriptural covenants, the gospel covenant or covenant of grace, and the legal covenant or covenant of works.[43] He is at pains to point out that the covenant of works was not that made with Adam before the Fall, but the covenant given to Moses and encapsulated in the Ten Commandments. Adam was not issued with a covenant but with a simple command: 'Do this and live'. There was no promise involved for even Adam was saved not on the basis of his own obedience but through the goodness of God's sheer grace. Thus after Adam *had* sinned, the covenant, which had already been agreed between God the Father and Christ the Son, was revealed and activated in order to ensure humankind's salvation:

> God foreseeing that man would sin … he prepared this sovereign salve … to be presently applied, and clapped to this wounded dying man, as the brazen serpent was prepared and set up before hand for them that afterwards be stung. (pp. 8–9)

Although the beneficiaries of the covenant would be humankind, or those among humankind who had been elected to life, the covenant itself was between the Father and the Son: 'It was a voluntary, well-pleasing and mutual act and agreement, between the Father and his Son Jesus Christ, such as a man makes with his own mind, concerning his own children' (p. 10). God the Father promised to endow the Son with all that was needed for human redemption, and to elect him to be head of those who had also been foreordained to obtain adoption, salvation and eternal glory. Striking the characteristic Calvinistic note, 'God's first and main end in all his actions', stated Powell, 'is his own glory, and next making out his goodness unto his creatures' (p. 12). Election itself was absolute and not dependent on God having foreknown individuals' faith, and although this was a harsh truth, given the prevalence of human sinfulness, it was unavoidable. Election, however, was not, in fact, the cause of human redemption:

> Election and reprobation are not in any sense the causes of salvation and damnation, but Christ is the proper and meritorious cause of salvation, and sin the proper and meritorious cause of damnation. Election and reprobation, they are but precedent and pre-current acts or decrees; … the causes of salvation and damnation, they come in between the decrees and the execution thereof. (pp. 15–16)

For all his discussion of election, sinfulness and damnation, Powell is keen to concentrate on the Person and Work of Christ. After discussing man's original freedom and the nature of Adam's disobedience, God, as Father, Son and Spirit, had, he claimed, made a gracious covenant with his people, while Christ

> did legally interpose and put himself between God and man, to mediate and intercede for them, and so voluntarily became obedient to the Father's will, and by undergoing, bearing and suffering the wrath and curse due to men for their sins, he took away their sins, reconciled them to God, redeemed them from the law, and delivered them from the wrath to come. (p. 25)

Following an extended exposition of the different biblical covenants with Adam, Noah, Abraham, Moses and finally with Christ, Powell explains why an atonement was necessary at all: 'Though God the Father was inclinable and propense to be at peace with and be reconcilable unto men, yet his justice put a bar to his mercy till it had a promise of satisfaction from Christ, yea till it was satisfied by him' (p. 46). He also emphasizes once more its free and gratuitous nature. Good works, moral duties and conditions are implied, but are in no way meritorious:

> The covenant of grace doth not require duties upon pain and penalty of damnation, but to express our love to Christ ... Though the covenant of grace doth require duties and performances, yet it doth not exact upon men, but where there is a sincere aim and a true desire in any, it is accepted, though they come very short in performance. (p. 99)

As Powell had claimed in his dispute with John Goodwin, the New Testament references to 'all' did not necessarily imply a concept of general redemption. Like all proponents of particular redemption, he had to exegete numerous passages which emphasize the all-embracing range of the divine humility. After having done so, he remained insistent that 'Christ redeemed the world of mankind, satisfied God's justice, obtained a way of salvation for every man, but never intended that the outward act should put every man in possession of pardon or state of justification or salvation' (p. 129).

Christ and Moses' Excellency consisted of three parts: a general assessment of the covenant and its nature, a practical explanation of the right use of the law in the Christian's life, and a history of the promises attached to the two covenants. It shows little conceptual originality and, unlike Goodwin's *Redemption Redeemed*, it quotes no patristic, Reformed or contemporary authorities. It does, however, reflect faithfully the theological consensus that had developed among the English Puritans for a half-century or so and was now being popularized in south-central Wales. Although closely reasoned, it is not devoid of occasional doxological flourishes in which Powell's compelling pulpit rhetoric can be heard:

> The whole way and path of salvation is paved with the grace of God the Father and the grace of Jesus Christ; the grace of love, the grace of good will, the grace of mercy, and the grace of Christ, his merits and obedience. So that from everlasting to everlasting, from the first minute of time ... to the last moment of eternity there was nothing, and there will be nothing but grace in men's salvation; their predestination and election, their calling and vocation, their redemption and justification, their adoption and sanctification, their confirmation and consolation, their preservation and supportation, their perseverance and glorification, flows all from free grace ... Nothing moved God to will men's salvation but his good pleasure; nothing persuaded God to send his Son Jesus Christ to work men's redemption but his mere and dear love. Observe, here is nothing of self-will, nothing of self-righteousness, nothing of self-power, neither foreseen faith nor foreseen works, no qualifications nor conditions, no preparations nor performances, no duties nor deserts of men, having so much as a voice, the least hand or place, in their salvation. The first and the last stone, yea all the materials in this glorious building of men's salvation, is hewn out of the quarry of God's unspeakable grace. (pp. 154–5)

Although '[i]t would be inappropriate to treat Powell as though he were a first rate theologian',[44] he was nevertheless an able exponent of the federal doctrines and it was through him that the covenant motif, which would subsequently become so dominant, was first introduced to the theological discourse in Wales.

Morgan Llwyd, mysticism and millennialism

The doctrinal contribution of the third principal representative of radical Puritanism in Wales, Morgan Llwyd (1619–59), coincided with the end of the Commonwealth and the beginning of the Protectorate. A markedly different thinker than either Cradock or Powell, he conjoined apocalyptic millennialism with Behemian mysticism to introduce a novel spiritual note into the development of the Christian mind in Wales. What is more, he did this in a startlingly new genre of Welsh prose which constitutes 'a fountain-head of the modern language at its purest'.[45]

Born at Maentwrog in Merionethshire, the parish where Edmund Prys, author of the metrical psalms had been so assiduous in establishing Reformed Prayer Book Protestantism a generation earlier,[46] Llwyd was the scion of a gentry family steeped in the ancient bardic tradition. A near relation (possibly his grandfather), Huw Llwyd (d.1630), had served as a professional soldier in France and the Low Countries during the reign of James I before returning to the family seat at Cynfal where he conjoined the tradition of poetic prowess with the responsibilities of a country squire. Little is known of Morgan's early years though it seems that he was sent to the Wrexham Grammar School and it was there, in 1634–5, during Walter Cradock's curacy in the parish, that he came under Puritan influence. A wonderfully evocative Welsh-language auto-biographical poem *Hanes Rhyw Gymro* ('A Welshman's Story'), penned in 1650, recalls the major stages of his life thus far: 'In Denbighshire I was converted', he says.[47] The bond between the teenage convert and his new mentor became very close, as he followed Cradock to Llanfair Waterdine where he found sanctuary in the service of Sir Robert Harley – 'In Herefordshire I served'[48] – and thereafter he spent time at Llanfaches, as a member of William Wroth's gathered congregation which Cradock would soon serve as sole minister. It was there that he married Ann, the sister-in-law of Edward Herbert of Magor who would become one of Oliver Cromwell's most steadfast Welsh supporters and the county's MP in the second Protectorate parliament of 1656.

With the outset of the First Civil War, Ann was sent to Cynfal to be cared for by his mother, while Morgan, now aged twenty-three, accompanied Cradock and the Llanfaches congregation to Bristol. The 'Welshman's Story' lists his wanderings for the next five years. Just as Huw Llwyd had served loyally with the king's forces a generation and more earlier, now Morgan committed himself equally whole-heartedly to the parliamentary cause, either as a chaplain or even as a fighting man. Glamorgan, Gloucestershire, Somerset, Hampshire, London and Kent are all mentioned as spheres of his activity, while he landed with the seaborne force in Pembrokeshire early in 1644 to support Major-General Rowland Laugharne's imposition of parliamentary control over west Wales. Later in the year he was in Portsmouth, among the 'Welsh ministers' mentioned in the Commons Journal who had been

requested to provide a preaching ministry for the forces of Sir Thomas
Myddleton who had been tasked with curtailing royalist jurisdiction in
the region of Oswestry and Montgomeryshire. The reference to 'Tref
Baldwyn' (Montgomery) in the poem indicates that he was present when
Myddleton overwhelmed the king's garrison in the town in September.
The year 1645 saw him in Bath, Chichester, Leicester, Winchester,
Guildford and Derby, while Thomas 'Gangraena' Edwards records that
in June 1646, near Oxford, one 'Floyd, newly came to be a preacher to
the troop of Major Huntingdon', spoke out in favour of 'laymen, tinkers,
weavers and cobblers' being allowed to hold forth, that 'learning was not
any means or help to understand the meaning of the scriptures', and 'that
any chamber, barn or stable' was as holy as any church building and a fit
place for the worship of God.[49] This echoed Walter Cradock's sentiments
perfectly, and shows the extent that Llwyd had rejected the conformist
consensus that had been championed by Welsh Reformed Protestants of
earlier years. That his radicalism was of the extreme kind is underlined
by the fact that, during his stay in Oxford, he had torn up a copy of the
Book of Common Prayer and burnt it publicly.[50]

An autobiographical passage in his *Llyfr y Tri Aderyn* ('The Book
of Three Birds') states that even orthodox and biblical worship, if not
accompanied by inward conviction, could become an active hindrance
to true faith:

> Previously, I heard sermons but I had never listened; I said prayers but I
> had never prayed; I sang psalms but my heart had been dumb; I took the
> sacrament but I discerned not the Lord's body; I said many things though
> never in truth or from my heart, until the rose blossomed within.[51]

In another of his 1653 tracts, *Gwaedd Ynghymru* ('A Cry in Wales'), he
goes even farther: 'If you feel you cannot pray, try even to groan before
God, but disregard your prayer book which is nothing but barenness.'[52]
Like many who react forcefully against a conventional religious upbringing, Llwyd could see no virtue at all in the Prayer Book Protestantism
that had been so carefully inculcated by Edmund Prys and others. All
his prose works convey a radical newness and a vision for the future;
even the recent past is consigned to oblivion: 'As for the Prayer Book, it
is hardly worth mentioning. It is high time to bury it, so that it infects
no one else. Behold, all things are become new.'[53] For a young man so
steeped in tradition, his violent break with his inheritance had become

absolute. The longbow, prized by Huw Llwyd as a trophy in the family home at Cynfal, symbolized all that Morgan had come to despise. In a series of strict metre couplets, all the more potent for being written in the medieval verse form, he states that the 'brown bow', although appearing sturdy, was so fragile as to splinter in his hands: '*Caniadau nhadau cyn hyn / Oedd moli'r bwa melyn*' ('The songs of my forefathers / Was to praise the brown bow').[54] Despite its fine appearance, it was now obsolete and rotten. In an accompanying free verse poem he made the same refrain:

> *Fe wasnatha'r grefydd honno*
> *Pan oedd dynion heb oleuo*
> *Ond mae'r plant yn awr yn gryfach*
> *Neu mae'r grefydd gynt yn grinach.*[55]

('That religion served its purpose before men had become enlightened / But their children are now much stronger, while the old religion is much more brittle.')

By 1647 Llwyd had returned to Wales to minister to the separatist congregation that had been gathered outside the established parish church in Wrexham. This would remain the field of his labours for the remainder of his life:

> In Wrexham Christ a vineyard had
> A vineyard of red wine,
> With truth they have been oft made glad
> The sun on them did shine.[56]

Apart from his work as an Approver under the Act for the Better Propagation of the Gospel, he would play little part thereafter in public affairs, and unlike Cradock and Powell he would remain far from the centres of power. Yet he had no qualms about supporting the more overt radicals in parliament or justifying the execution of the king. In an essay of 1649 he wrote:

> Was not the late king delinquent in chief? And was not death the condigne [*sic*] punishment? Either the parliament or he deserved to die the death who caused three hundred thousand poor souls in three kingdoms to be woefully destroyed. The guilt and fault must need be somewhere and either or both are guilty of very high treason.[57]

He expressed the same sentiment in what would become a very familiar verse:

> The law was ever above kings
> And Christ above the law,
> Unhappy Charles provoked the Lamb
> To dust he must withdraw.[58]

As well as being a means of evangelizing the people, for Llwyd and Powell (but not for Cradock) the Act for the Better Propagation of the Gospel in Wales, in operation for three years from 20 March 1650 onwards,[59] was part of the millenarian strategy to hasten the Second Coming of Christ. Whereas it was true that 'millenarianism was not a creed preached simply by cranks and imbeciles'[60] – though undoubtedly there were some among their ranks – Llwyd and Powell interpreted Colonel Thomas Pride's purge of an over-cautious and still too conservative parliament in December 1648, the subsequent government of the people by the 'Rump' or what was left of the Long Parliament, the execution of Charles I a month later and the abolition of the Upper House in March 1649, as paving the way for the coming of the Lord. Disenchanted by the inertia even of the Rump, the Welsh millennialists were heartened when Cromwell forcibly dissolved the Commons in April 1653 only weeks after the Act had run its course, and were positively ecstatic at the establishment of the Nominated Assembly or 'Barebone's Parliament' made up of 140 members chosen by the Council of Officers on the basis of recommendations made by the gathered or Independent churches. Five of the six Welsh representatives to the assembly were Fifth Monarchists as was Major-General Thomas Harrison, the first signatory to the Propagation Act and commander-in-chief of the parliamentary army in Wales. Believing, on the basis of the prophecies of Daniel and Revelation, that Rome, the last of the four great empires of Babylon, Persia and Greece, was about to fall, Christ himself would inaugurate a fifth monarchy in which peace and righteousness would dwell. All of Llwyd's earlier work is suffused with this burning revolutionary hope: 'Our Lord is coming once again, as all the scriptures say / Even so Lord Jesus quickly come and make no long delay.'[61] The only question was when? 'Fifty goes big, or fifty six, or sixty five some say, / But within man's age, hope to see all old things flung away.'[62] What was incontrovertible was that before 1660 the millennial kingdom would have arrived: *'Cyn mil a chwe chant a chwe deg / Mae blwyddyn deg yn dyfod'*[63] ('Before 1660 / A fair year will have dawned').

This, as we know, was not to be. Such was the radicalism of some within the Nominated Assembly that even Cromwell became alarmed. Moves such as the proposed abolition of the Court of Chancery and the elimination of tithes caused friction between extremists and moderates, and in the event little was achieved. Within five months of its formation, many of the assembly's own members had become exasperated by the outlandish conduct of their more militant colleagues and had petitioned Cromwell for its dissolution. On 15 December the Instrument of Government had been adopted and a day later Oliver was appointed Lord Protector. Thereafter the Commonwealth became the Protectorate. In fact moderation had triumphed over zealotry, and a semblance of responsible government had been restored. If Powell was incandescent at what he considered Cromwell's treachery, as his petition *A Word for God ... against Wickedness in High Places* (1654) makes plain, Llwyd's disappointment was more muted. His prose had already evidenced an intense inwardness that was not evident in the preaching of either Cradock or Powell, and subsequently became even more pronounced: 'When his hopes of political achievement are lost, he loses his balance and, to some extent, his way.'[64] Yet his great works of 1653, in which millenarianism and mysticism are combined, comprise the most remarkable contribution, however deviant or irregular, that had yet been made to the sum of Protestant theology in Wales.

Morgan Llwyd's two evangelistic treatises *Llythyr ir Cymru Cariadus* ('A Letter to the Beloved Welsh People') and *Gwaedd Ynghymru yn Wyneb pob Cydwybod* ('A Cry in Wales in the Face of every Conscience') and his creative volume in the form of a conversation between the Eagle, the Dove and the Raven, namely *Llyfr y Tri Aderyn* ('The Book of Three Birds'), were penned in the latter half of 1653.[65] They constitute a unified body of work which expresses a unique doctrinal scheme. The underlying theme is that of the immanence of God and the need to experience salvation by journeying within: 'Seek God within your heart, for no-one will ever see him is they do not see him within themselves'.[66] Llwyd was too soundly rooted in Puritan orthodoxy to neglect the trinitarian objectivity of God or to reject the historical reality of the gospel, but the emphasis throughout is on the God who reveals himself in the depths of the human heart and at the root of the individual's experience:

Within the life of nature you will find your spirit walking and running among the angels. Beyond that though still within is the blessed and infinite Trinity, the Father, the Word, the Spirit (or the will, the delight, and the power, all three though they are one) and the human mind can penetrate no farther. (*Llythyr*, p. 119)

The human condition, marred by sin, cannot plumb to these depths unaided. Sinfulness is a fact which needs to be overcome. Llwyd describes the fallen state of his fellow Welshmen more in terms of missing out on God's good intentions than of having rebelled grievously against him, nevertheless it remains a stark reality which renders them incapable of enjoying fellowship with him. The aim of his prose is to direct his readers and listeners – the treatise should be read aloud, he says, in order to be effective; like traditional Welsh poetry its appeal is to the ear – to the oblique reality of the inexpressible God. Men and women cannot be driven to him but allured by the One who reveals himself within: 'You know not yourself (poor man), nor the One who has made you, nor the One who has been sent to make you anew' (*Llythyr*, p. 117). (Llwyd employs the singular which is still used in modern Welsh whereas the 'thee' form in English has become obsolete). Though existing as the transcendent Lord, the all-encompassing God is continually near at hand: 'He is always close to you and keeps you forever in his sight, he hears you, he tastes you, he smells you and feels you everywhere and at all times' (*Llythyr*, p. 118).

This God, as has been stated, is inexpressible. Llwyd was uniquely sensible to the fact. Even the most exquisite prose can only suggest his reality and allude to his attributes. Llwyd's use of striking rhythmic patterns of short, image-laden, vivid clauses and sometimes simple, sometimes elaborate sentences, one tumbling after the other, is designed merely to *point* to the God who is always ready to reveal himself to the diligent seeker. Despite the author's genius as a wordsmith, the Word is beyond the words and can only be hinted at. This is exemplified in a paragraph which, in well over a score of short phrases, balances the human predicament with the divine condescension:

Eternity is long; sin is bitter; the law is as dung; the curse is cruel; ... the mind is dark; the heart is deceitful; the will is stubborn; the conscience is cunning, though blessed is he who denies himself and strives for fellowship with the Father and the Son ...

> ... God is love; Christ is gentle; his Spirit is sweet; ... his word is
> truth; his ways are perfect; his counsel is sincere; his day is long; his sight
> is keen; his arm is powerful and paradise is his bosom. (*Llythyr*, p. 120)

'[Llwyd's] interest is not in logical precision', as R. Tudur Jones stated,
'nor in academic accuracy, nor yet in intellectual comprehension of God
and his love, but in leading men into that confrontation with God who
will transform their existence'.[67] Although this God is within, creature
and Creator are not confused (though see below) nor does the Deity
forfeit his personhood. Despite the mystical tenor of the *Llythyr*, the
eschatological note is still sounded:

> The righteous who believe will *see* the coming of Jesus the King in
> his transcendent beauty, the idols will fall before him, and the present
> kingdoms will yield to the fifth monarchy ... as the holy scriptures claim
> abundantly ... This is at hand, yea at the very door, and within our own
> times it shall be witnessed. (*Llythyr*, p. 121)

Yet it is the Christ within who will be revealed to all flesh at his Second
Coming, and it is the immanent God whose transcendent glory will be
disclosed.

If the *Llythyr* is an evangelistic tract, *Gwaedd Ynghymru* is an
extended treatise on the nature of the conscience. The concept of immanence is emphasized throughout:

> The life of the soul is not in pen and ink or in words and opinions but
> in *the spirit of the living God* (which is the root of man and the strength
> of the light within) which also cries aloud from the depths of the mind.
> (*Gwaedd*, p. 127)

It was the Welsh people's plight to have been consigned to ignorance and
darkness, no less under the recent dispensation of nominal Protestantism
than under the papalism of old: 'Making do with a service book ... and
laid waste by dumb priests and bloated preachers of which there was
not one man of God among four hundred' (*Gwaedd*, p. 129). The fault of
these preachers, and the reason behind Llwyd's bitter denunciation, was
that they had failed lamentably to awaken their hearers' conscience and
thus deprive them of the blessing of salvation. The aim of the treatise,
like the mission of the Act for the Better Propagation of the Gospel,

was to do that very thing. Yet the preaching of the Word would only be effective if coordinated with the response of the voice within. Llwyd is adamant that, despite the blemish of sin and if not hopelessly seared, the human conscience is ever willing and able to respond to the divine call. Nowhere in the *Llythyr*, the *Gwaedd* or *Llyfr y Tri Aderyn* is there a trace of the Calvinistic conviction concerning election, predestination, limited atonement or the bondage of the will.[68] Rather, each listener is free to respond to the inner voice which corresponds to the call of God himself. And just as the emphasis is on the individual's ability to respond, there is an equivalence between that which is to come and that which has occurred within. The Apocalypse, although remaining an awesome event at the end of history, has already occurred in each human heart: 'A sort of day of judgement already exists in man himself, though the end of all things has yet to come' (*Gwaedd*, p. 131). The existential crisis that impinges itself on all people is between the flesh, namely all things human which militate against God, and the Spirit which gently and perpetually assists the conscience in responding to the divine love: 'No-one has ever been lost, except those who have closed their ears to the voice within' (*Gwaedd*, p. 141).

Just as the concepts of election and predestination are absent in these works, the idea of justification is mostly subsumed in the idea of union with Christ and the doctrine of sanctification through the Spirit. Formally Christ exists as the divine saviour whose sacrifice satisfied the divine righteousness and through whose blood redemption was accomplished, but the essence of Christian faith is mystical union with God through the Spirit. Not only does God exist as the divine fellowship of Father, Son and Holy Spirit, but that fellowship is shared with those who are engrafted into Christ himself: '*Immanuel … God with us* in the flesh of *the Saviour*, and in us as well' (*Gwaedd*, p. 139). In orthodox terms, Llwyd is sailing very close to the wind: the danger is that the distinction between the human and the divine is blurred. Yet it is the immanent Christ who must be born within in order for the sinful self to be displaced and for the divine presence to flourish:

> Do not think of God through your own thoughts, as the power of Christ's cross must put your own thoughts to death in order for the mind of Christ to be born within you. Instead of *your old self*, you will be granted *a new self* which is Christ himself within your fleshly heart. (*Gwaedd*, p. 143)

For Llwyd, the three necessary elements of the gospel consisted of the factual death of the historical Christ whose atoning sacrifice paid the price of the believer's redemption; 'but this is not enough if the next does not follow, namely that Christ lives within us and rules us and through us as light, comfort and strength in the bosom of our heart' (p. 143), while even this is not, of itself sufficient, as 'the root of the matter is the union between *the Father and the soul in the Spirit of his Son and in the inexpressible love,* in fact the same union as exists between God and his only Son' (p. 143). Whereas Walter Cradock had been insistent that even a modicum of faith was more than enough for the salvation of the soul, by stipulating that the essence of the gospel was in a mystical scheme which melded together justification, sanctification and union with Christ, Llwyd was in grave danger of compromising the finished work of the cross and undercutting the gratuitous nature of the good news. The simple belief that Christ had died for our sins was, he stated, 'fleshly faith'; 'the sum of the eternal gospel', on the other hand, and 'its very wellspring is *the Father within you, as your life is hidden in God himself with Christ*' (*Gwaedd*, p. 144). 'Of all the radical Puritans', according to Geoffrey F. Nuttall, 'the writer who is most consciously and consistently mystical in his language is Morgan Llwyd'.[69] For all his superb abilities, he does not wholly avoid the pitfalls of mysticism as well as conveying its purported strengths.

Llyfr y Tri Aderyn is Llwyd's longest and most ambitious work and, in literary terms, his masterpiece. Inspired by the German mystic Jakob Böhme's *Mysterium Magnum*, a commentary on the Book of Genesis, it is nevertheless a volume of striking originality and great imagination. Fashioned as an exercise in typology replete with Noah's flood, the ark and the Lord's judgement and redemption, it is both a commentary on the politico-religious crisis of the day and a work of edification and spiritual instruction: 'The pillars of the world are shaking, and fire and storm rage everywhere round about' (p. 21).[70] The three figures of the Eagle, the Dove and the Raven represent secular authority as embodied in the Cromwellian state, spiritual enlightenment as witnessed by the mission of the Independent churches, and the oppressive forces of reaction, now happily dispatched, which had been the prelatical or Established Church. The book comprises of two parts: a prolonged debate between the three protagonists which touches on the momentous events of the hour including the expected return of Christ, and a more intimate and pastorally orientated conversion in which the Dove ministers to the Eagle. Once more God is revealed as the immanent reality at the ground of each person's existence whose trinitarian personhood is ever ready to make himself known to the diligent seeker. 'How', asks the Eagle, 'is a man's mind to find rest?' 'By retreating into the inner chamber', replies the Dove, 'and that chamber is God himself within' (p. 75). Llwyd's characteristic emphasis on the perpetual nearness of the all-encompassing God, linked with the objective, visible coming again of Christ in glory, are evident once more, as is his blending of a realized eschatology with a futurist apocalyptic. On the one hand, 'From the beginning of the world to the flood there were 1656 years, wherefore I advise you (O Eagle) to be vigilant, for the time is near!' (p. 40), yet: 'Paradise is never far from you and is present wherever God's love is revealed ... while hell, and fire, and wailing, and darkness prevail in the hearts of many even as they walk upon the earth' (p. 55). Paradise is not merely an internalized state, it is also (in the guise of God's kingdom) an objective reality that is about to be inaugurated.

Despite Llwyd's emphasis on the universal benevolence of God – 'He died for all people, and all have benefit from him at all times' (p. 58) – and his conviction concerning a general rather than a particular atonement – 'There is in his heart nothing but goodwill towards all men, and a desire that no-one should be lost' (p. 84) – costly regeneration was a *sine qua non* of the spiritual life; mere morality or a superficial religiosity was insufficient: 'However pure on the outside, you must undergo transformation within, or you will be burned in all your plumage and gentility and sense of your own worth' (p. 56). Regeneration is nothing less than transference from flesh to spirit, darkness to light, bondage to freedom, the realm of demons to the company of angels and to the very presence of the divine. The strength of his rhetoric, 'in which metaphor follows metaphor in profusion',[71] along with his characteristic themes, is exemplified in the following:

> DOVE: But if a man will deny himself and follow the Lamb, the new birth, and endure to the end, and be saved, let him not extinguish the light which is in his conscience, but blow it till it shine, and let him follow the light of God, and the morning star within, and the sun will rise brightly upon him.
> EAGLE: What is that morning star?
> DOVE: The certainty of knowledge, the pledge of the Spirit, the sure eye of faith, the earnest of perfection, Jehovah's seal, and the witness of the

Three-in-One, the anchor of the soul, and all that happens when a man
in the light knows the love of God towards him, in him, and through
him, in might and in a wondrous peace. (p. 64)

The Raven, for one, found this concept alarming, not so much theologically for the doctrine of union with Christ was both orthodox and
biblical, but because of the impertinence with which the sectarians
claimed to be acquainted with the deep things of God: 'They say with
confidence that the Trinity dwells within them, making his abode among
all men' (p. 29). The Dove's response, however, was unequivocal:

> This is indeed a truth most profound. It is a tightly bound knot, a door
> which has been locked and bolted from the ages. It is, nevertheless, true.
> One scripture states that the Father dwells in us (Eph. 4:6), and another
> that the Son does the same (II Cor. 13:5), and a third, that the Holy Spirit
> finds a home in every pure, enlightened, humble, heavenly heart. And all
> the scriptures together show (and I will be bold enough to assert) that
> the Trinity is within in us, making us eternal. (p. 29)

What orthodox Puritans, to say nothing of Reformed churchmen
whether (formerly) conformist or otherwise, would have found wanting
here was a counterbalancing emphasis on the objectivity of the Trinity
and its transcendent existence beyond the experience of the believer or
a feel for the concept of the imputed or 'alien' righteousness of Christ.
The idea of the believer being *made* eternal by the indwelling Trinity is
peculiar. As the work progresses, it is clear that immanence has displaced
transcendence as the controlling theme, while faith in the God beyond
is subsumed by a mystical union with the God within.

The two movements which most closely cohere with Llwyd's progressing worldview are Behemenism, or the thought of Jakob Böhme,
and Quakerism. After 1644 many of the German mystic's works began
to be published in English, and immediately found a wide readership.
Böhme's Platonism is apparent even in Llwyd's earlier works:

> O Eagle, understand that every spirit is a substance and the visible world
> is only a shadow of the invisible world which irradiates this world; and
> the body is but a shadow, and the overlay of the spirit and the scabbard
> encasing the everlasting soul. But the Trinity remains within as the ore
> is in the ground, or a man is in his house, or a child is in the womb, or

the fire is in the furnace or the sea is in the spring, or the soul is in the
eye, so remains the Trinity within the godly. (*Llyfr y Tri Aderyn*, p. 30)

It was only after the expulsion of the Nominated Assembly, however,
and Llwyd's increasing disillusionment with the coming millennial
reign of Christ, that the German's influence becomes even more pronounced. Two of Böhme's tracts were translated by Llwyd into Welsh,
Yr Ymroddiad ('The Devotion') in 1654 and *Y Dyscybl a'i Athraw* ('The
Disciple and his Teacher') in 1655, though neither was published until
1657. By then he was in correspondence with the decidedly un-mystical
Richard Baxter, discussing the virtues of the German's books. The vicar
of Kidderminster was unimpressed. Like Sir Henry Vane, both 'purposely
and wilfully hide their minds, delivering most things in allegories ...
avoiding plain and purposeful terms', he stated: 'I have no need of riddles
to hinder my discerning'.[72] His advice to the Welshman was 'studiously
[to] avoid allegories, metaphors and uncouth phrases except where
necessity compelleth you to use them'.[73] The move towards an ever more
inward spirituality was patent in all of Llwyd's later works, *Lazarus
and his Sisters, discoursing of Paradise* (1655) and its accompanying tract
*Where is Christ?, An Honest discourse between Three Neighbours touching on
the Present Government* (1655) and his final Welsh work, *Gair o'r Gair,
neu Sôn am Sŵn* (1656) ('A Word from the Word, or an Expression from
Commotion'). In *Lazarus and his Sisters* he states: 'He is waiting and
watching to fill us with the light of life ... but for the present, silence
is better than words', while in *Where is Christ?* all religious truths have
been internalized radically:[74]

> Now the poor soul in these difficult days doth ask, what shall I do to
> have Christ, and be saved by him? First, fasten this in thy inmost mind;
> Christ to me and I to him ... then look for Christ next where he is to
> be found forever, and that is within thy heart ... and if thou thus look
> upon him, thou shalt be melted daily into his eternal love, and so become
> one with him.[75]

Christ's physical Second Advent has been transmuted into a spiritual
communion with the Christ within and paradise transposed to the eternal realm. Although *An Honest Discourse* is ostensibly a discussion of the
politics of the Protectorate, it is in fact a chastened activist's reflections
of the futility of all human schemes: 'If thou wouldst wait patiently, thou

should see, forty years in thy wilderness is but as a minute with him, with whom there is no time. Therefore learn from all this to tend thy own soul';[76] 'I well understand that there can be no calm peace in this stormy world';[77] 'God is not in the earthquake, fire or whirlwind, nor in wars, bloodshed and carnal animosities, but in the still, small, private voice';[78] 'Look in upon eternity in your own chamber, that ye may come to the ground of all things, and of yourselves.'[79] In *Sôn am Sŵn*, Llwyd reasserts the fact of God within, while all objective realities have been spiritualized:

> If you descend into yourself to the root of your own selfhood, and for-get the ruminations of your own mind and the words of men, you will discover what the gospel is ... Neither the Christ beyond nor the Christ within is the Saviour, but both together.[80]

It is here that Llwyd most approximates the teachings of the Quakers: 'It is a blasphemy against God to think that the book in your pocket, or under your arm, is God's Word, through which he created the whole world and can create a new a world within you';[81] 'Instead of any voice without, let us follow and obey the Voice and the Light which is within';[82] 'The Scriptures are the leaves of the tree of life which will heal the nations ... [but] seek assiduously the Bible that is within you.'[83] Llwyd had been in touch with George Fox as early as 1652 and had sent his emissary, John ap John, to Swarthmoor, Lancashire, in order to find out more about the Friends' teachings. Although he would never formally espouse their creed, there is no doubt that he was strongly attracted to it. Neither was it a coincidence that it was from among his own followers (and those of Vavasor Powell) that Quakerism first gained a foothold in Wales.[84] In fact John ap John (*c.*1625–97) became 'the apostle of Welsh Quakerism'.[85] Llwyd's associates found this at best unnerv-ing and at worst intolerable. John Myles, leader of the Welsh Baptists, vilified Quakers as a pestilence describing them as 'the infection of the times',[86] while Vavasor Powell feared for his friend's orthodoxy if not for his salvation:

> It will be [no] small joy to me and other saints to hear that beloved M[organ] Ll[wyd] does [not] degenerate so much in his doctrine as to hold many of the old Arminian and popish principles as free-will, perfec-tion etc., or the Socinian doctrine as to enervate the power of Christ's death and intercession.[87]

By the late 1650s Morgan Llwyd had drifted far from the mainstream of Puritan faith.

Unorthodox or not, Llwyd, who died aged thirty-nine in 1659, would retain his place in the pantheon of Welsh evangelical dissent. The classic works of 1653 were reissued regularly throughout the eighteenth and nineteenth centuries and became a mainstay of the literary revival of the twentieth.[88] When Richard Baxter in his *Catholick Communion Defended* (1684) reproached Cradock, Powell, Llwyd and Erbury for their doctrinal vagaries, he drew the sharp rebuke of an un-named defender. Although *A Winding-sheet for Mr Baxter's Dead* was published more than a decade after the last of them had passed on, their contribution was still revered. Llwyd was said to have been 'the deepest and truest Welshman, and the most absolute British orator, perhaps that ever was', whose charity, holiness and humility were in no way diminished by his 'spiritualizing of all things, and … his very impartial and unprejudiced search after truth'.[89] A century and a quarter later, Robert Jones of Rhos-lan, the Calvinistic Methodist historian, recorded north Wales's continuing debt to Llwyd for having taken vital Christianity, under the auspices of the Act for the Better Preaching of the Gospel, to that dark corner of the land. Jones, however, could make little of Llwyd's millennialism, and interpreted the chiliastic passages in his works as prophesying the dawn of the Evangelical Revival of the 1730s: 'He was a man of strong parts, renowned for his piety, profound in his insights, though there was much that was mysterious in his manner of speech, while his letters and books are sometimes hard to comprehend.'[90] For all that, he was a veritable champion of the faith who represented all that was heroic in the Welsh Protestant past. Given Llwyd's blatant deviation from the Reformed norms that had been established by Prayer Book Protestants since the reign of Edward VI and the Calvinistic consensus that would persist into the period of the Older Dissent, this was a curious opinion indeed. Yet it remained an inviolable element in the emerging identity of Nonconformist Wales.

John Myles and the Baptists

That the earliest Welsh Baptists should be included among the radical Puritans is patent from the comments of John Tombes, formerly preacher at the Temple Church but latterly champion of believer's baptism, who had been invited to Abergavenny in September 1653 to assist his co-religionists in defending their convictions. Preaching from the pulpit of St Mary's church, he claimed

that infant baptism was a nullity, a mockery; no baptism but by dipping
or plunging as lawful; all that would be saved must be re-baptized, or
baptized after profession; that there was no such thing as infant baptism
in the primitive times, but that it came in with other corruptions upon
unsound grounds.[91]

The spiritual revivalism that had been spreading through the border
areas of south-east Wales since the early 1640s created a receptivity to
novel opinions of which the Baptist faith was one. The first recorded successful Baptist missioner had been Hugh Evans, a native of Radnorshire,
who had left home to become an apprentice clothier in Worcester.
During the civil war he had moved to Coventry where he had been won
to the General or Armininan Baptist cause. Thereafter,

being zealous in the gospel, and his love much kindled towards God and
man, and hearing that his native country was destitute of that means of
salvation (that is to say) the preaching of the Word and the ministration
of the ordinance of Jesus Christ

he persuaded Jeremiah Ives, minister at the Old Jewry Church in
London, to accompany him, and they 'came to *Wales*, and performed the
work which they were sent to do'.[92] This was in 1646 and soon a Baptist
congregation was gathered from Radnorshire's Llanllŷr, Llanddewi
Ystradenni, Cefn-llys and Nantmel parishes though its doctrines
were Arminian not Calvinistic, holding to general redemption or that
Christ had died not for the elect alone but for the whole of humankind.
Communion was 'closed' or restricted to those who had been baptized on
a confession of faith.[93] It was with the advent of the Particular Baptists,
however, and their mission of 1649–52, that the Baptist faith made its
most marked impact on the religious life of south Wales.

The leader of this movement was John Myles (1621–83), a native
of Newton Clifford on the northern edge of the Archenfield district of
Herefordshire. Geographically in England, Archenfield – the ancient
kingdom of Erging – was culturally Welsh, though nothing is known of
Myles's specific family or linguistic background. After having matriculated from Brasenose College, Oxford, in 1636 when he was fifteen,
he disappears from view only to re-emerge in the summer of 1649 at
Ilston, Glamorgan, having been commissioned by the London Calvinistic
Baptists to evangelize in south Wales. Why he selected Ilston as a base

is impossible to tell, were it not that the home of Thomas Proud, his colleague in the mission, was in nearby Llanddewi, and that Puritan influence on the Gower was already fairly widespread. Nevertheless by the end of the year a particular Baptist church embodying the theological and ecclesiological precepts of the 1644 *Confession of Faith* had been established in that place. 'Thus', recounted the church book,

> it pleased the Lord to choose this dark corner to place his name here, and to honour us, undeserving creatures, with the happiness of being the first in all these parts among whom was practised the glorious ordinance of baptism, and to gather here the first church of baptized believers.[94]

The achievements of Myles's subsequent career, as an Approver of the Act for the Better Propagation and Preaching of the Gospel in Wales; his staunch support after 1653 in the face of severe radical and Fifth Monarchy dissension for Oliver Cromwell's protectorate, the anti-Quaker polemic of his *Antidote against the Infection of the Times* (1656), his appointment by the state to a Puritan lectureship at Llanelli, Carmarthenshire, and, a year later in 1657, to the incumbency of the Ilston parish church, would prove less enduring than his work in establishing the modern Baptist movement among the Welsh people. He stood, in fact, 'like a Colossus above all other Welsh Baptists in the period ... In many ways the history of early Welsh Baptists is the history of John Miles.'[95]

In theological terms, Myles's abiding contribution was in the realm of ecclesiology and in cementing Calvinism as the doctrinal norm among the Welsh Baptists.[96] Soon after establishing, by October 1649, his first congregation at Ilston, a second fellowship was planted, in January 1650, at Hay-on-Wye, Breconshire (causing dismay by drawing members from Vavasor Powell's Congregational church which was already flourishing in the locality), and a third followed within a few months at Llanharan on the northern edge of Vale of Glamorgan, being 'a golden candlestick set up in those dark parts'.[97] A general meeting for the three churches was called for November 1650 which would form the blueprint for the so-called 'association principle' or inter-congregational structure, which would typify Baptist witness both in Wales and England for the next three centuries.[98] Although the seat of authority would remain in the local gathered community, the association was structured to guard against isolationism and to perpetuate group solidarity among the churches. A fourth fellowship, at Carmarthen, west Wales, was founded in January 1651 and a fifth, in Abergavenny, Monmouthshire, in August 1652. Membership in these five congregations was around 250, each church replete with its pastor, ruling and teaching elders, deacons and 'widows' or female members with specific pastoral responsibilities. In the light of this vision, a theologically valid Christian fellowship was only possible where believers, having been baptized through immersion, covenanted together to form a community of faith. Church order was as essential a part of Christian discipleship as was conversion and individual faith. According to the general meeting convened at Llantrisant, Glamorgan, in August 1654:

> Our Lord Jesus Christ, who is the head of the church, after he had by himself purged our sins, ascended on high, gave gifts to his church, that each joint in the body might have its particular gift, and that thereby unity, peace and order be preserved for the good of the whole.[99]

Whereas the leadership of pastors and elders was important, the aim of ministry was mutual edification and the enrichment of spiritual fellowship among the body as a whole. This tight and carefully overseen network ensured a Baptist presence between west Carmarthenshire and Monmouthshire in the east which would be sturdy enough to endure the hardships that would follow the Restoration.

It was Myles's tract *An Antidote against the Infection of the Times* that laid out the basis for the movement's Calvinism. His assessment of the human condition is bleak. The starting point for the application of the gospel is to admit to the desperate malady of sinfulness through the imputation of Adam's transgression: 'Your present state is most wretched and miserable.'[100] Humankind's corruption is total and all individual acts are tainted due to each person's radical antipathy to God. Yet in order to deal with this situation, God in his mercy has sent forth a deliverer. Jesus Christ was made fit to be that deliverer through his sinless obedience, his sacrificial death and his glorious resurrection. Myles's emphasis on the doctrine of the ascension is noteworthy:

> For though satisfaction was made to divine justice by the death of Christ, and justification is obtained by his resurrection, yet glorification is only had from Christ's ascension into heaven ... for as he died once for all, so must he ever live and act for us, else we are most miserable. (p. 7)

It is through the ascension that the resurrected Christ's authority both over creation and within the church are facilitated, while the present dispensation is one of hope and expectancy. Although he had no sympathy with Vavasor Powell's chiliasm, the Second Coming was nevertheless a vouchsafed certainty though there should be no speculation as to when it would occur. Salvation was by faith alone: 'What then can be more plain than that we are justified by Christ alone without any relation to any works done by ourselves' (p. 11). Christ has fulfilled his saving mission by existing as the God-man through whom individuals are bidden to partake of the redemption: 'It is by an effectual calling alone you may come to enjoy true light and salvation' (p. 13).

The immediate threat to which the *Antidote* was a response was the growing influence of Quakerism in south Wales during the latter part of the decade.[101] That is why Myles places such a heavy stress on the absolute authority of God's Word in scripture:

> All and every of which considerations may ... work in you a reverential esteem of the sacred scriptures as that which is wholly and certainly given by the inspiration of God, and so dissuade you from being carried away by the delusions of these sad times to slight or undervalue but rather with fear and trembling to embrace them as those that are able to make you wise unto salvation. (p. 14)

It was on the basis of Holy Scripture that the godly could be made wise unto salvation, and it is the New Testament that provided them with a blueprint for the regulation of their church life. This included provision for the ministry of the gospel:

> We exhort you, in the fear of the Lord, to look upon the ministers of the gospel as God's ambassadors, to whom he hath committed the ministry of reconciliation, to woo and betroth souls to Christ ... We beseech you to observe that as long as there is a soul to be called or perfected, there must be gospel ministers. (p. 15)

Myles had a high doctrine of ministry in which those who were called to preach did so in obedience to the apostolic commission. The glory of the recent Act for the Better Propagation of the Gospel had been to release ministerial gifts for the good of the people:

> Have we not seen with our eyes in many places of this land, where
> Satan's seat hath been for many ages together, that since the enjoyment
> of our precious liberty to hold forth the Word of God to poor straying
> souls, many thousands are come to the profession of the gospel, and par-
> ticularly the poor country wherein we live may for ever bless the Lord
> and remember with thankfulness all such as were instruments for their
> souls' good in procuring that much envied and too short lived Act for the
> Propagation of the Gospel in Wales ... so in a few years such a change is
> wrought even in the darkest places, that it is wonderful to behold. (p. 16)

But again, although evangelization began with the conversion of individual souls, it was only complete when those who had been convicted
were baptized and organized themselves into full church communion:
'Baptism of believers in water [is] ordained by Christ, practised by him
as our pattern, and administered according to the said commission ...
and pattern by the primitive disciples on all believers' (pp. 22–3). The
ministry was ordained by divine commission while 'the election of ministers by the people and their ordination by elders is clear in scripture'
(p. 23). Consequently Baptist polity was congregational though isolationism was eschewed through the inter-congregational links of the
general meeting or association.

Between the Radnorshire General Baptists, Myles's Particular
Baptists and what may have been an even earlier gathering of baptized
believers located in the Olchon Valley in Herefordshire,[102] there was little wonder that John Tombes and other Baptist apologists were given a
hearing in south-east and south-central Wales during the 1650s. When
Vavasor Powell underwent believer's baptism in 1655, it was obvious
that the nature of the baptismal rite if not sacramental theology as such
had become a matter of consideration among the godly.[103] Unlike Hugh
Evans's followers and those in the Myles orbit, Powell did not believe
baptism, whether paedo-baptism or believer's baptism, to be essential
to church order. 'Outward baptism, or water-baptism', he claimed, 'is a
solemn significant dipping into, or washing with water the body in the
name of the Father, the Son, and the Holy Ghost', signifying the death,
burial and resurrection of Christ, the justification of the believer, his or
her regeneration, and the bestowal of the gifts of the Holy Spirit.

> Though baptism be not absolutely necessary to salvation, yet being com-
> manded by Christ, it is the duty of all professing and visible believers ...

to be baptized once, and that upon the first believing and conversion, and before they enter into a particular visible church, or partake of the Lord's Supper. Yet it is not baptism, but an interest in Christ, that gives any a right to either … But in this of baptism, as in many other cases, difference in persuasion and practise may well consist with brotherly love and Christian communion.[104]

In other words, although obedience to the rite was expected, it was not essential for salvation or for the right ordering of the church: 'Neither is it the proper work of baptism to confer or work grace, but to seal, confirm and increase it, much less are all those that are baptized true believers and saved'.[105] By the 1650s the divergent ecclesiologies of the Baptist movement were contributing to the rich mix of radical theology in Wales.

William Erbury

By far the most eccentric of the Welsh Puritans and 'the *enfant terrible* of the Welsh saints' was William Erbury.[106] Having resigned his Cardiff living in 1638, within two years he had drawn together a gathered church in the town and been appointed its pastor.[107] The hardship that had taken Walter Cradock and the Llanfaches congregation to Bristol at the outbreak of the civil war took Erbury to London, and between 1643 and 1649 he served as a chaplain to the parliamentary forces. It was during these years that he became thoroughly and irrevocably radicalized. Formerly a Congregationalist, he now came to reject the concept of visible church order totally while the Calvinism of his *Great Mystery of Godliness* (1639) was transmuted into the wholly unconventional idea of Christ's emerging incarnation in the very body of the saints.

'Gangraena' Edwards had related how, as early as 1645, 'one Mr Erbury that lived in Wales' had become notorious in London, the Isle of Ely, Bury St Edmunds and other parts where 'he declared himself for general redemption, that no man was punished for Adam's sin, that Christ died for all [and] that the guilt of Adam's sin should be imposed on no man'.[108] A year later such was the commotion in Oxford where Erbury was now based, that a delegation of Presbyterian divines led by Francis Cheynell, later president of St John's College and Lady Margaret Professor in divinity, was sent to restore order. The Welshman had been vigorously fomenting radical ideas among soldiers, townspeople and students, and in a series of meetings culminating in a public disputation at St Mary's, the university church, in January 1647, 'Mr Erbury['s] ... divers blasphemous errors' were officially reprimanded.[109] By now he had relinquished his status as a minister, whether Episcopal or Congregational, and described himself as a seeker.[110] He rejected the whole concept of an organized, visible church as organization demanded discipline which in turn implied compulsion, whereas God's Spirit allowed each of the saints freedom to follow their conscience in full. The essence of true faith was to affirm the reality of Christ within: 'The mystery of Christ in us ... in opposition to those huge tomes and mighty volumes of fathers, councils and commentators, treatises etc. which have been all the days of Antichrist.'[111] None of the established formulations of doctrine could do justice to the fact of the inner Christ, and it is hardly surprising that Cheynell, using the traditional categories, labelled him as Arian, Socinian and anti-Trinitarian. For Erbury the Westminster Catechism and Confession were as erroneous as any of the classic symbols of the faith:

> [t]he knowledge and worship of Christ was taught by men's traditions, forms framed by old creeds and councils, new catechisms and confessions of churches as if the scriptures and Spirit were not sufficient to teach men all the knowledge of God and Christ clear enough.[112]

It was this Spirit, witnessed to in Scripture, which would lead the saints to ever new truths: 'The mystery of God shall be more gloriously revealed in the last times, after Antichrist's destruction and deliverance of the saints from the apostasy, then ever it was by the apostles themselves at first.'[113] The apostolic age marked merely the beginning of the Christian era. Now the saints were about to witness an even more glorious revelation in which Christ would make himself known in the very body of his people: 'Christ was in the flesh of his saints ... formed in them, brought forth in them, living in them and suffering in their flesh.'[114] 'If I know anything', he continued,

> First, that the Son and the saints make one perfect man, and that the fullness of the Godhead dwells in both, in the same measure, though not in manifestation. Secondly, that the fullness of the Godhead shall be manifested in the flesh of the saints, as in the flesh of the Son. These two things, which others see as heresy and blasphemy, seems to me as truths, both in scriptures, and by that Spirit which speaks in me.[115]

Although Cheynell had no authority to prevent him from perpetrating his ideas, following the Presbyterian divines' report to parliament, the Welshman was commanded by his army superiors to leave Oxford to serve with Colonel John Lambert in his campaign in the north of England and was afterwards posted as chaplain to General Thomas Fairfax's regiment of horse.[116]

By now Erbury was becoming ever more impulsive in his views. According to his next published tract, *The Lord of Hosts, or God guarding the Camp of the Saints* (1648), the so-called 'age of apostasy' was now being brought to a close through the progressive overthrow of oppressive structures in both church and state, while the saints, empowered by the Spirit, were in the process of manifesting God's kingdom to the world: 'What is the house of God, but God dwelling in the flesh of the saints … the fullness of the Godhead dwelling in them bodily, or the Godhead embodied in their flesh.'[117] God's mission in the saints was to bring all things, spiritual and temporal, under his rule so that salvation would be experienced by all: 'The saints shall no more act for themselves but for the world also, and see how liberty may be settled on the whole earth, and foundations of justice, of righteousness and peace may be established in the nations.'[118] The Second Coming would not be a matter of the heavenly Jesus returning to earth 'as Christians carnally conceive Christ to come in the clouds', but would consist of the Christ within making himself fully known through the medium of his people thus confounding the kingdoms, states and parliaments which had too long governed by the sword and invariably oppressed the poor and the weak.[119] It was now apparent that Erbury had been drawn to a social message approximating that of the Levellers, and his contribution to the Army Council's Whitehall Debates of January 1649 (which coincided with the trial and execution of the king) was to plead for full religious toleration for all.[120] Although far from Wales, and possibly unbeknown to his fellow Welsh radicals, Erbury had diverged dramatically from the views that he had held as the Puritan minister of St Mary's Church in Cardiff a decade earlier.

Had his colleagues realized the full extent of his deviation from any semblance of Christian orthodoxy, it is very difficult to imagine his appointment in 1650 as an itinerant preacher in south Wales under the Act for the Better Preaching of the Gospel. The Act, passed on 22 February of that year, stipulated that until March 1653, a commission of seventy-one members, led by Major-General Thomas Harrison, the millenarian commander of the army in Wales, would oversee a plan for the evangelization of the whole nation. The Act's forty-three south Wales commissioners and twenty-eight in the north were chosen from among the gentry and higher yeoman class who had proven their allegiance to the parliamentary cause during the civil war, along with a handful of English-born military officers who had served under Harrison. The commission was charged with a much more radical purge of unacceptable clergy than had occurred previously. Between 1650 and 1653, 298 clergymen were deprived of their livings for a range of misdemeanours, both moral and political. 'Delinquency' and 'malignancy' signified a refusal to conform to parliament's stipulations concerning use of the Prayer Book, while the epithet 'scandalous' referred as often to a stubborn attachment to older religious usages including episcopacy as it did to moral shortcomings such as drunkenness and fornication: 'Five or more commissioners were empowered to receive charges against clergymen wanting in piety, education, or acceptable political views, and it was possible for the accused to be condemned on the evidence of two credible witnesses.'[121] The wives and children of ejected clergy were to receive a fifth of the revenue of the parishes that they had formerly served. In all it was a draconian measure, and for all its worthy aims of encouraging spiritual renewal by removing corrupt and ineffectual clergy, it became all too easy for inoffensive men to be discharged and despoiled through rumour, malice or local jealousy.

Of more strategic importance than removing unworthy ministers was providing an effective evangelistic and pastoral force in their place. Along with the seventy-one commissioners were twenty-five 'Approvers' charged with recruiting and selecting 'godly and painful men, of able gifts and knowledge for the work of the ministry, and of approved conversation for piety' in order to preach the gospel. Among the Approvers were the radicals Cradock, Powell, Llwyd, Myles, Henry Walter, Richard Symonds, Ambrose Mostyn and Jenkin Jones along with moderates like Jenkin Lloyd, Oliver Thomas and Dr John Ellis, in other words most of the Welsh Puritan elite. Due to the scarcity of acceptable and theologically educated Welsh-speaking preachers, recruitment was slow. Some men of distinction were employed: Charles Edwards, formerly of both All Souls and Jesus College Oxford, and author of *Y Ffydd Ddi-ffuant* ('The Unfeigned Faith) (1667) who would serve in Denbighshire; the Balliol graduate Richard Jones, translator of Baxter's *Call to the Converted* (*Galwad i'r Annychweledig*, 1659) who itinerated in the same area; and

Jonathan Roberts, fellow of Jesus College, whose sphere of service was the Vale of Clwyd. For every one theologically trained preacher were the many 'tub-preachers, tinkers and cobblers', prized by such radicals as Cradock, Llwyd and Symonds but despised by the upholders of the old dispensation and even, now, by some moderate Puritans who saw them as incompetent interlopers with scant respect for either true piety or decorum. Due to lack of numbers, it was much more expedient for the commissioners to send out itinerant preachers than settled ministers, the result being that parish churches were closed often for months on end while congregations made do with occasional visits from roving evangelists. For all that, the Act was cherished by many as an effective means of evangelizing the multitude, and initially William Erbury was zealous for its success.

It was not long, however, before Erbury's conscience began to chafe at receiving a state salary drawn from the tithe. Like all the itinerants under the Act, he had been in receipt of a government stipend of £100 per annum but in a letter to the approver Henry Walter entitled *The Grand Oppressor, or, the Terror of Tithes* (1652) he relates how he had been convicted of the measure's unrighteousness:

> Upon this, God began ... to roar in my spirit, and I to hear nothing within me but the cry of the oppressed, 'twas far (me-thought) from my temper to tread on a worm, or to oppress the poorest creature in the world ... Then the oppression of tithes came to my ears, and the cry of the oppressed filled my heart, telling me that I and my children fed on their flesh, that we drunk their blood and lived softly on their hard labour and sweat.[122]

From then on the three absorbing themes in his preaching would be social justice; the apostasy of the religious establishment including the leading Welsh Puritans, Cradock, Powell and Henry Walter; and the coming victory of the immanent Christ through the Holy Spirit in the flesh of the saints. By the summer of 1652 he was domiciled in Cardiff though still feverishly active as a freelance, unpaid preacher and tract-writer, and ever ready to cross metaphorical swords with his state-employed opponents. In the discourse entitled *A Scourge for the Assyrian* which followed *The Grand Oppressor* he reasserts his doctrinal convictions and took his complaints against the religious *status quo* farther while he has become contemptuous of the so-called successes of the

Propagation Act. Now he sees nothing but declension since the days of Llanfaches a decade-and-a-half earlier:

> That which you hear of so many called in Wales is not so true as the report; it is but to church that multitudes run ... but ... they are still as earthy as ever they were, as ignorant, carnal and covetous ... That light and love which was formerly in Wales in good Mr Wroth's days is dead with him.[123]

The welter of tracts that followed: *The Bishop of London, The Welsh Curate*, the *Apocrypha* and *The General Epistle to the Hebrews*, appearing in quick succession also in 1652,[124] rehearse his now familiar themes though his support for the weak and humble is more pointedly extended to the plight of his home nation: 'Wales is a poor, oppressed people, and despised also'.[125] The only one of his erstwhile colleagues to escape censure is Morgan Llwyd:

> Behold, O English, Scottish and Irish churches, ye shall shortly see what gallant spirits and noble hearts we have in Wales, a man going into the eternal Spirit, not in words and tongue but in deed and truth, as you shall shortly read in a teacher of North Wales.[126]

Llwyd had written to Erbury in June 1652, and it is obvious that the Wrexham pastor was in considerable sympathy with the older man's views: 'I do both long and profess to become a little child again, willing to learn my ABC anew, if my once dear schoolmaster Erbury can teach it me.'[127] Erbury's reference was to Llwyd's forthcoming publications which, as we have seen, emphasized the interiority of God and a mystical appropriation of the Christian salvation.

Much more typical, however, was the radical's opposition to what he believed was the carnality of much popular Puritanism whether in the matter of ordinances, doctrine or church government. His clash with David Davies, an associate of John Myles, a government-approved preacher under the Propagation Act and pastor of the Baptist church at Llanharan, was pointed. They disputed twice, at Bridgend, Glamorgan, and thereafter at Llantrisant, in mid-1652 amid much tumult: 'No sooner [had I] finished my discourse', he recalled, 'but the gentleman starts up again and begins to contradict and withstand my words the second time, to the trouble and tumult of the company.' Erbury's retort was:

'Mr Davies, you will be shortly in the fire ... and so I departed to peace.'[128]
A similar altercation occurred in Cowbridge, on this occasion with the
Congregational minister Henry Nichols. Both Erbury and his interloc-
utor published rejoinders, though Nichols's is the most interesting.[129]
Erbury, he claimed, was 'once an old English professed saint, though now
a professed opposer of all the saints, both Welsh and English'.[130] Plainly
aggrieved at what he saw as his opponent's apostasy, he complains that
he now rejected the testimony of all the godly whether Presbyterian,
Independent or Baptists, 'which did not little please the many Royalists ...
present'.[131] Though he prided himself on being a Welshman, he had to
resort to English as 'he cannot deliver himself in the Welsh tongue'.[132]
Yet despite everything, Nichols had to admit that there were many among
the godly who were indebted to Erbury's earlier ministry:

> I will not derogate so much from Master Erbury's worth and merit as to
> conclude him sterile and barren of testimony in this way, while he used
> the ordinances of the gospel, prayer, preaching etc. While he did follow
> Christ in his own way fully, the Lord did witness with his ministry ...
> There are not a few godly people that yet bless the Lord for him, who
> made him instrumental to deliver them from the power of darkness and
> so translate them into the kingdom of his dear Son.[133]

This dispute marked an end of Erbury's contribution to the history of
religion in Wales. By November 1652 he was back in London, and the
next fifteen months, until his death, aged fifty, in April 1654, a frenzy of
pamphlets would stake out his increasingly wayward and fanciful opinions.[134] Given his extreme views, it is not surprising, perhaps, that his
wife Mary became a leading Welsh Quaker, while his daughter Dorcas
accompanied James Naylor on his notorious re-enactment of Christ's
arrival at Jerusalem in 1656 for which he was indicted for blasphemy and
incarcerated for two years.[135] Yet for all that, those who knew Erbury
best were loath to criticize him too stringently. Twenty years later, the
anonymous author of *A Winding-sheet for Mr. Baxter's Dead* wrote:

> Mr Erbury then, before he was taken ill of his whimsies, was a good
> scholar, of smart parts, very serious and successful in his preaching,
> and very grave and religious in his life and practice ... A very judicious
> person, of a considerable figure, no way infected with his distemper,
> told me [that] Mr Erbury's disease lay in his head, not in his heart.[136]

Nevertheless, his legacy was on the whole dire. It also underscored the weaknesses of the radical Puritans generally. By diverging from the norms of the Welsh Reformed churchmen and by dismantling so brutally the older ecclesiastical structures, they contributed to the mayhem and anarchy which characterized the religious situation during the Interregnum. Despite being far from the main channels of activity, Wales partook fully of 'the religious bedlam [that] prevailed' at the time, and shared in the 'religious chaos' that blighted the life of the realm.[137] Even Presbyterians like John Lewis of Glasgrug, commissioner for the Propagation Act and formerly Wales's premier apologist for parliament, rued the disorder that had followed 'our late purgation of the temple', or the ejection of the conformist parish ministers from their parishes.[138] By 1656, ten years after issuing his *The Parliament Explained to Wales*, he complained that whatever good had issued from the removal of incompetent or unworthy clergy, the attitudes implicit in the words and deeds of the Puritan radicals had caused untold mischief: 'So much trouble and loss of charity I conceive is a remedy worse than the disease' (p. 5). The occasional preaching of unlettered itinerants whose grasp of the scriptures was often minimal and knowledge of theology and Christian history was deficient to say the least, had become an affront to the faith itself. Antinomianism, chiliasm, mysticism and Anabaptism had so often displaced Christian orthodoxy, while worship itself had become a matter of personal whim rather than an informed response to God's claim on the whole of life:

> People now generally mutter ... that when they customarily assemble, they come ... to serve and worship God and not merely to hear and be instructed. Now as for some thousands that are said to be converted amongst us by late preaching (my charity bids me hope, really to Christ, and praise be to God for it) yet others ... complain, that far many more thousands, for want of preaching or any other public duties of religion, and the distance and scarcity of ministers (at least such as they will attend to) are ready to make defection, and fall away to popery if not utter profanity and neglect and contempt of all religion. (pp. 4–5)

By downplaying the role of the sacraments the itinerants had overstated the significance of preaching, and even the liturgical use of the Lord's Prayer was despised as being formalistic and papistical. Those who yearned for the old ways were traduced as formalists and antichristian;

church buildings, now regarded as superstitious, had been allowed to
fall into disrepair while ancient and venerable traditions everywhere
had gone by the board:

> I humbly conceive that it would not do amiss to correspond and comply
> with the people in some of their more tolerable modes and customs ...
> and not too rigidly inveigh against them. As their aptness to observe
> some of the ancient festivals, as the nativity and resurrection of our
> Saviour and the like, referring to the great actions of our redemption, all
> the Christian churches of the world (laying aside Rome) as the Eastern
> and the Reformed churches hath ever anciently, and doth observe them,
> and the charity and hospitality of such times doth much balance the
> abuse and corruptions imputed to them; and with us in Wales the people
> generally from an ancient use much spend the time in pious hymns
> and songs, celebrating the birth and actions of Christ, which at least
> keeps them in some awe and reverence of God, and their anniversary
> course no doubt makes some more impression upon them, than not at
> all. (pp. 12–13)

It was these very customs that had been so summarily rejected by the
itinerants, while a notion had arisen which demanded that godliness and
true piety should reject tradition outright. Lewis, as a Presbyterian, had
scant sympathy with the gathered concept of the church but pleaded
instead for a comprehensive Christian establishment in which all the
baptized were placed under effective ecclesiastical discipline. It was only
thus that a national profession of faith could be achieved. The aim of
the Propagation Act, in his view, had been to ensure the spread of vital
Christianity in Wales, whereas the work of the Triers (the London-based
Committee for the Approbation of Public Preachers) from 1653 onwards
had been to provide a viable alternative to the superseded Episcopal system by appointing suitable clergy to vacant livings. What had occurred,
alas, was that too few settled clergy had been instituted while sectarianism had grown rife: 'There are those that simply imagine (like the
Donatists of old) that think none belong to God, or are to be saved, but
such of their own judgement and opinion' (p. 39). Even the word 'saints'
had become tainted:

> For my part, I heartily wish all would labour to become such in holi-
> ness and innocency of life, and to abandon all other unhappy names of

schisms and division amongst us, and once again meet in the old honest
name Christian. (p. 14)

In his correspondence with Richard Baxter, Lewis bewailed the situation
that had developed by the mid-1650s: 'Now every ignorant pretender
to preaching will strive to have the chair and will censure fathers and
all others as below themselves.'[139] He contended that 'the cause of such
extravagancies in religion in this age [are] our condemning, out of passion and prejudice, the light and traditions of the universal church, as
superstitious, popish and antichristian'.[140] This had not been the original
vision of parliament at all. Whatever good emerged from the labours of
the radicals – indeed it was they who laid the foundations of nineteenth-
century Nonconformist Wales – their immediate effect was calamitous.
Doctrinally the legacy of the radical Puritans was, at best, mixed.

The New England contribution to Welsh Puritanism: Marmaduke Matthews and Thomas Shepard's *Cywir Ddychwelwr* (1657)

It has been claimed that 'seventeenth-century Welsh Puritanism, like
nineteenth-century Welsh radicalism, cannot be fully understood apart
from the two-way transatlantic traffic in men and ideas in which both
were so deeply involved'.[141] In comparison with England, very few Welsh
people were enticed over to the New World, either to the Jamestown
colony and the Carolinas after 1607 or to separatist and Puritan New
England in the wake of the emigration of the Pilgrim Fathers in 1620.[142]
There is no doubt, however, that the project to create a community
in which the ideal of a reformed church, free from Episcopal control in
which godly discipline could be applied, exerted its appeal among
Puritans in Wales. If Marmaduke Matthews, vicar of Pen-maen in the
diocese of St David's, had left under the Laudian regime and had become
minister at Yarmouth Massachusetts in 1638, only to return as incumbent of St John's in Swansea during the Interregnum in 1652, [143] a
translation of one of the most characteristic examples of New England
Calvinism, Thomas Shepard's *The Sincere Convert* (1641), would have a
significant impact on the spread of Reformed piety in Wales during the
coming generations.

Thomas Shepard (1605–49), graduate of Emmanuel College
Cambridge, and Puritan lecturer at Earl's Colne, Essex, had been

deprived of his post by William Laud, by then bishop of London, in 1630, and following a peripatetic ministry in Yorkshire and Northumberland, had set sail for New England in 1635. As minister at Newton (soon to be called Cambridge) Massachusetts, the site of Harvard College, he would be involved in the Antinomian Controversy of 1636–8, and become one of the prime architects of New England Congregationalism.[144] *The Sincere Convert*, 'destined to become one of the most frequently reprinted of all New England sermons', set forth a morphology of conversion which provided a pattern for the spiritual experience of innumerable believers for generations to come.[145] Like many Puritans, Shepard's own conversion had been protracted and painful. Already under religious impression when he had gone up to university aged fifteen, during his first two years he became more absorbed in his studies than in his spiritual state, in fact, 'I did not regard the Lord at all unless it were at some fits.'[146] He was drawn back to a more heartfelt experience of God, mostly through the preaching of 'old Doctor Chadderton' [*sic*] – Laurence Chaderton, since 1584 master of Emmanuel – but backslid one again, '[falling] from God to loose company, to lust and pride and gaming and bowling and drinking' (p. 21), only to be restored by contemplating the divine wrath and the torments of hell. Yet even this failed to keep him in check and he returned to his worldly ways. The preaching of John Preston, Chaderton's successor, in college chapel brought Shepard to conviction once more – 'I thought he was the most searching preacher in the world' (p. 23) – but although thereafter he did his utmost to live a life of obedience, repentance and sanctity, he could find no inner relief:

> The terrors of the Lord began to break in like floods of fire into my soul. For three quarters of a year this temptation did last, and I had some strong temptations to run my head against walls and brain and kill myself. (p. 25)

Believing himself to be hopelessly damned, he was in deep despair. He did, nonetheless, persevere under Preston's ministry, and although he was told that Christ had died for his sins and that he needed to embrace him in faith, 'but yet I had no assurance that Christ was mine' (p. 27). The slow realization that Christ, though sinless, had kept the law in order that the unrighteous, who could not keep the law, could be allowed to share his righteousness, led to the breakthrough: 'I saw the Lord gave

me a heart to receive Christ, with a naked hand even a naked Christ, and
so he gave me peace' (p. 28).

There is little doubt that Shepard's tortuous experience conditioned
both how he would read scripture and analyse the motions of the soul.
Moreover this pattern would soon become pervasive throughout Puritan
New England. Shepard's concept of 'preparing' the soul for grace became
regulative within the colony: '"Preparation" meant driving the soul to
contrition and humiliation, and most of the New Englanders agreed that
it was necessary.'[147] For the minister of Newton, the efficacy of the law
would become pivotal in order for true conversion to occur. 'Within the
complex structures of Shepard's thought', the three main stages leading to
conversion were 'conviction of sin', 'compunction of sin' and 'humiliation':

> In conviction the law jolts a man into an awareness of his sins, although
> his heart may remain unaffected with 'true remorsefulness'; for a man
> may have 'sight of sin' without any 'sorrow' and 'sense' of it. In com-
> punction the 'affections and will' are aroused in such a way that the
> heart is made to 'stir toward Christ' and does not 'remain hard'. These
> stages then bring on humiliation, in which the sinner is cut off from all
> self-confidence.[148]

Only then will he truly be able to come to Christ. The *ordo salutis*, or
order of salvation, had long been decided upon among Puritans in
England, but with Shepard and his colleagues its preparatory stages
became codified to a much higher degree.[149] Following conviction and
humiliation there would come vocation, namely God's effectual call
through which the decree of election would take effect. Then there
would be saving faith in which the prepared soul would respond actively,
through its own volition, to the divine call. This, in turn, would lead to
justification in which God would impute the merits of Christ, acquitting
the sinner and accepting them as righteous. Next would come ingrafting
or union with Christ whereby the newly justified believer would partake
of the divine benefits, leading to adoption when the gift of the Holy
Spirit would be granted. This in turn led to sanctification or the creation
of a holy disposition through which the believer would grow in grace
in order for the divine image gradually to be restored, leading finally to
glorification beyond death when the ultimate blessings of heaven would
be bestowed. It is important to emphasize that the whole scheme was
pointedly Calvinistic. Although the individual was called to apply to him

or herself the benefits of salvation through attendance at the means of grace, often painful introspection and the positive act of faith, the whole process occurred in response to God's gracious elective will. None of this was meritorious in any way: 'The doctrine of preparation referred to divine activity, not to human effort.'[150] Soon this scheme in its detail would find its way to Wales.

In his preface to his version of Shepard's *Sincere Convert*, the translator, who only identifies himself as 'R. E.', shared his rationale for embarking on the task. Like the original author, he was keenly aware of the pitfalls of hypocrisy and the dangers of insincere repentance and laboured to instruct his compatriots in the truths contained 'in this excellent book'. Its doctrine, he claimed, was 'in such full accord with the Word of God and consistency of the faith that no man who truly fears God can say anything against it or oppose it any way'.[151] Its six chapters elucidate first the reality of God and his attributes; secondly that humankind, though made in the divine image, has fallen away from God; thirdly that man's state is grievous and deserving of the divine wrath and judgement; fourthly that redemption is through Christ alone; fifthly that those who will be saved are few; and finally that the cause of man's eternal ruin is himself and himself alone. God is in no way responsible or blameworthy for man's ultimate plight. Much of the book's content was routine though the author was constantly aware of the need to warn his readers of false confidence or, among the more ostentatiously religious, open hypocrisy:

> If a little religion will serve to afford credit to men, they will indeed be very religious. They will commend good men, good sermons and good books in a fulsome, zealous way. But by so doing they are only covering themselves with such fig leaves of common honesty in order to hide their nakedness. They bait their courses over with honesty as they only fish for their own credit ... Let either a minister or a faithful friend search, prove, reveal, accuse or condemn these men as rotten, though gilded, posts or unsound, hollow-hearted wretches, they will swell like toads and hiss like snakes and bark like dogs at those that had censured them being now robbed of their god, namely their good name and reputation, as their gain is now gone. (pp. 47–8)

It was in the fifth and sixth chapters, however, 'Those that are saved are few, and are saved with much difficulty', and '[t]hat the grand cause of man's final ruin, or why so many are damned and so few saved by Christ, is from themselves', that Shepard's proverbial zeal to prepare his listeners' souls for contrition and humiliation comes especially to the fore. His prose is unyielding and his repetitions are unrelenting while it is his refusal to countenance the slightest excuse among those that would justify themselves that gives the treatise its edge:

> It is a very difficult thing to be saved ... It is not wishing and desiring to be saved that will bring a man to heaven; the entrance to hell is paved with good intentions. It is not shedding a tear at a sermon, or blubbering now and again in a corner and saying your prayers again and again and crying for mercy for your sins that will get you saved. It is not 'Lord have mercy upon us' that will do you good. It is not coming constantly to church. All these are easy matters. But it is a tough work, an extremely hard matter, to be saved. (p. 199)

The truly saved soul must first go through the gate of humility, faith, repentance and the active opposition of Satan and his demons before arriving at true redemption and even then it must be aware of the dangers of self-delusion. The comforts of the gospel are in short supply in this work, and its abrupt conclusion only intensifies its dour effect. Justification is by faith alone and the dangers of a sham faith are only all too real:

> This faith is a precious faith (II Peter 1:2). Precious things cost much and we set high store on them. If you have true faith it will have cost you many a prayer, many a sob and many a bitter tear. If you ask most men how they came by their faith they will tell you, 'very easily'. When a lion sleeps a man may lay down beside it and sleep equally soundly himself, but when he awakes woe betide that man! When God is patient and silent, you may delude yourself by thinking that you really do trust in him. But woe betide you when God appears in his wrath as one day he surely will. For by virtue of this false faith, sinners take God for a dishcloth who only wipes their surface clean. This is the only use they have for such a superficial faith. They sin indeed and trust in God for mercy but in truth remain in their sins. God will revenge such contempt with blood and fire and plague. (p. 367)

The remorseless quality of Shepard's tract and R.E.'s translation and its constant warnings about the dangers of cheap grace are unbalanced and harsh, yet its effectiveness as a means of awakening the conscience cannot be doubted. It featured often in the work of Stephen Hughes during the Restoration, it would be reissued in the early eighteenth century and became one of the means, in 1737, which brought the Methodist Howell Harris into the Calvinistic fold.[152] Its weakness, pastorally, was that it had virtually nothing to say about the divine tenderness or to assure the spiritually sensitive that God was gracious and sympathetic and not only a God of wrath. Not even Vavasor Powell (and certainly not Walter Cradock whose antinomianism was in direct response to the ostensibly legalistic approach implied in the concept of preparationism) was so unrelenting on the theme of the divine retribution as R.E. It was through this volume that the more bracing features of New England Puritanism were drawn into the religious experience of the Welsh.

In the narrow interconnected world of Massachusetts Puritanism, it is virtually inconceivable that Thomas Shepard and Marmaduke Matthews did not know one another. They were almost the same age, had graduated within a year of one another, the one from Emmanuel, Cambridge, and the other from All Souls in Oxford, had both fallen foul of Laud's strictures and had emigrated to the New World, the Englishman in 1635 and the Welshman some eighteen months later. Whereas Shepard's base was in Newtown (Cambridge), Matthews ministered first at Maldon, then at Yarmouth and briefly at Hull, Massachusetts, all within easy reach of Boston. He was in the vicinity during the Antinomian Controversy and, like Shepard, had become a convinced Congregationalist.[153] After some seventeen years 'whilst I yet lived in the midst of wild men and wild beasts among the Lord's exiles in America', he had been prevailed to return 'to the land of my birth' by Colonel Philip Jones, the Commonwealth's foremost leader in south Wales and a fellow native of Llangyfelach near Swansea.[154] Since then he had been assiduous in his labours as Puritan incumbent at St John's parish in the town, though the contrast between the two spheres was stark:

> My eyes did gladly see several of those naked natives fervently praying to God, and feelingly preaching of Christ on a solemn day of humiliation … So likewise my ears did grievously hear, since my arrival to these shores, that promiscuous companies of misbelieving Britons, like a company of rotten sheep … do kick up their heads not only against Christ's church but against Christ himself. (Sig. A3r)

The theology of *The Messiah Magnified* was characteristic of much mainstream Puritanism though Matthews's ecclesiology, as displayed in a second work, *The Rending Church Member*, shows him to be on the radical wing of the movement. The doctrine of election is presupposed, though the call to repent was universal: 'God hath bound himself in the covenant of grace as in a bond, for to bestow upon as many sinners as can find in their hearts to receive both his Christ to be their Jesus and his Jesus to be his Christ' (p. 4). Like the preparationists, he held to the fact that the process of conversion would not be easy:

> Oh what a pleasantly pitiful sight it would be to see their tears to trickle, their lips to quiver, their hue to change, their joints to quake and their flesh to tremble, and above all ... to observe their weeping for their piercing of Christ, their waiting on the preaching of Christ, their questioning about Christ, their enquiring after Christ and their coming seasonably and seriously unto Christ, if possible they may be cured by Christ. (pp. 8–9)

Unlike Shepard, however, he is keen to apply the balm of the gospel to afflicted souls sooner rather than later: 'Christ Jesus, our chief kinsman, God-man blessed forever ... heals a guilty sinner of the guilt of his sin ... by the purchase of such a pardon as is signified with his own hand and sealed with his own blood' (p. 21). Although no one will come to God unless they have been called, nevertheless the elect will come readily, their captive wills having been made free by sovereign grace:

> Every one of Christ's waiting patients is a very willing person, because he is made willing to subject his own will, which is crooked and corrupt, to the immaculate will of his Creator, by ... forsaking his heart of stone, and receiving a heart of flesh, of him that works both to will and to do, out of his own good pleasure. (p. 30)

If sinners remain sinful by participating, through their own volition, in Adam's sin; by the imputation of Adam's sin and by the infusion of that sin, 'in which sense, who I was in my mother's womb, I was made a sinner who did conceive me in sin' (p. 36), they are made righteous 'by virtue of God's sacred institution, or spiritual marriage bonds, which renders the contracted convert perfectly beautiful and comely' (p. 41). Along with this comes imputation, 'that all the former faults and offences of Christ's rescued sheep are fully forgiven and forgotten' (p. 41), and infusion:

> because Christ Jesus, by the application of his holy scriptures outwardly, and his Holy Spirit inwardly, doth so crucify the body of sin, and create such a bent and a bias in the bottom of the heart of the believing hearer ... that it plainly appears that he is an upright person. (pp. 42–3)

Much more than in *Y Cywir Ddychwelwr*, Matthews emphasizes the kindness of God and the tenderness of the gospel:

> Oh that they knew that Christ Jesus, the forlorn sinner's friendly kinsman, is so kind and so full of compassion to all crying supplicants, so that he would soon make them see how he is marvellously willing to remove those blood-shedding loads from their living backs, which consist of their wickedness against God and God's wrath against them. (p. 39)

When Matthews left Wales in 1636 or 1637, Congregationalism existed at best in an embryonic form.[155] It was in New England, far beyond the reach of the ecclesiastical authorities, that the opportunity arose in which the ideal of the church as a covenanted community, maintaining godly discipline and electing its own leaders, could be put into practice.[156] Whereas the pioneers of the Congregational Way envisaged the ideal church to be a covenanted community admitting its own members with no recourse to a bishop or a presbytery, by the time of Matthews's arrival in the colony, the necessity for experiential evidence of conversion had been added to the above:

> While the voluminous separatist and anti-separatist writings make it clear that new members had to offer a profession, subscribe to the covenant, and demonstrate good behaviour, there is no mention in the period before the founding of Massachusetts, of any inquiry into the candidate's religious experiences ... [T]he new demand for signs of grace gave the New England churches a different character from the old separatist churches ... It is certain that the new system was fully established in Massachusetts by 1640.[157]

In other words, the pattern of spiritual experience that had been formalized in Thomas Shepard's *Sincere Convert* was now incorporated into an ecclesiology which would become highly significant not only in New England but in the subsequent development of religion in Wales.

It is apparent from Matthews's tract *The Rending Church Member* (1659) that however compelling the ideal of the church as a gathered community of saints: 'Can any have an approved interest in Christ's name or nature, that care not (by converting and confirming grace) to be knit to Christ himself and his Congregational church in a conjugal covenant?',[158] the reality of human imperfection could undermine even the most faultless model. 'Every one of the gospel privileges and gracious ordinances of Congregational churches', he stated, 'do produce diverse uncomfortable and unchristian contentions among inconsiderate and ill-catechized professors of godliness' (Sig. A1v). A Congregational church had first been established in Swansea by Ambrose Mostyn (1610–?63), former Puritan incumbent of Pennard, on the Gower peninsula, sometime after 1646,[159] and following his appointment as an evangelist in north Wales under the Propagation Act, it is likely that Matthews took over as its leader. By 1658, when the essay was penned, dissention had seriously weakened the fellowship and the pastor had no doubt where the fault lay:

> [T]he very first rise and reason of those ... divisions that threaten church desolation is without dispute the raw and unripe entrance ... into church estate, before they have been ashamed of, sorrowful for, and separated from, their personal and parental abominations: *Ye have brought into my sanctuary strangers uncircumcised in heart, and uncircumcised in flesh, to pollute my house.* (Sig. A1v)

The prevailing faults of these errant, if nominally converted, members was their absence from regular worship services including the Lord's Supper, their neglect in presenting their children for baptism and their disregard for a regularly constituted and scriptural ministry. The witness of such belied the reality of their profession. Whereas 'all persons that would esteem members of any reformed church are to be orderly saints' (p. 5), those saints were charged with reflecting the Christian virtues in their witness to the world and in their mutual obligations within their congregation. In this instance, that seemed not to be the case: 'The charity of some old and sundry young professors ... is so little that it is scarce visible to ordinary eyes, and that Christianity itself is less legible in their lives who walk so quite contrary to Christ's church ways' (p. 14).

Church membership entailed a sacred bond which was being repudiated openly: 'Are they in a capacity to conform to these commands who do not close with, and conjoin in, the church covenant? You know that they are far from being church-edifiers who are church-defamers, much more church-despisers' (p. 21). Not only did they absent themselves from regular worship, by so doing they debarred themselves from the benefits of the Lord's Supper:

> Can such persons be deemed fit guests, at such church-feasts, which have not admittance and abode in church-fellowship? And how can they eat often at the Lord's Table who do not eat once in a year, or in their lifetime? (p. 24)
>
> … Would you … have Christ to give you a full and free forgiveness of all your former sins, while you sinfully and willfully withhold or withdraw your personal presence from the Lord's soul-feasting Supper? Can ye possibly receive Christ's sealed pardon and withal keep your selves out of the reach of Christ's sealing appointments? Can you procure under his hand a non-obstante, or toleration for your absence from his house and non-appearance at his door posts? (pp. 29–30)

Yet it was the neglect of the sacrament of baptism that most incurred Matthews's disapproval. The baptismal doctrine presupposed in the text accorded with that of New England and English Puritanism generally.[160] The ordinance was administered by ministers only in the context of the regular Sunday worship of the community. The child would have been brought to the service by its parents and following exhortation, the minister would pour water on its head and announce that it had been baptized in the name of the Father, the Son and the Holy Spirit. Although all Puritan pastors eschewed an overtly sacramentarian theory of mediation of grace, nevertheless baptism was a seal of the infant's confirmation into the covenant community. Administration of the rite 'is that which goads and spurs faithful parents to offer their infants to fellowship with the church, in the first seal of the covenant of grace which doth seal their grafting into Christ' (p. 21). In other words, the covenant came first and membership into it thereafter. Like other Puritan ministers, Matthews reverted to Old Testament typology, in this case that of circumcision, to provide a rationale for the sacrament. Congregational polity was deeply communitarian, with solidarity within families and between generations implicit in both the rite and its concomitant theology: 'Note that children of eight days old are here called disciples of Christ, and 'tis granted by all that disciples of Christ may be baptized' (p. 22). Matthews had no compunction about referring to both active and passive faith:

> Are not the infants of believers to be accounted believing infants, seeing he stiles them so, who spake as never man spake? Is there not a passive as well as an active faith? Is not the first before the second, in all Christ's flock, yea in young infants as well as in old folks? Hath he not told and taught you, that 'tis by such a faith as is in believers infants (which is a passive faith) that the Kingdom of God is received? (p. 23)

The Spirit of Christ was, in fact, active within the covenanted community as it came together as God's people:

> Is it not as true that the least child of the covenant of grace is to be acknowledged a Christian, and a gracious child, although not for, or from any act or exercise of grace of Christianity, yet for and from the root and ground thereof, which is the gracious spirit of Christ? (p. 23)

Although this would create tensions in the New England churches when, a generation later, the discrepancy between the baptismal rite and the requirement for an adult conversion experience as a prerequisite for church membership (leading to the so-called 'half-way covenant') would become glaring,[161] the Swansea pastor was insistent that baptism and covenant solidarity was the route to church membership. In fact it was this that made parents' deliberate and persistent absence from the church fellowship so heinous an offence:

> Who can affirm that those infants do relate to Christ's elect flock, whose father have relinquished Christ's fold and do love to live out of it? Shall not the sins of such parents be visited upon their children, when his sanctifying Spirit that is in his covenant servants, shall rest in their seed, and seeds seed, from generation to generation? (pp. 37–8)

At bottom this transgression arose from a revolt against the concept of an ordained, scripturally mandated doctrine of ministry. It seems that the Swansea Congregationalists had been infected by a spirit of gross individualism or unbridled spiritualism:

Is it probable that their souls shall be preserved from going astray after Satan, who unthankfully refusing to attend on the teaching of public teachers, do reject God's ordinary means of preservation? Are they not to this day running on in apostasy, who are not related to any pastors? …
Or is it any wonder that they dare so wretchedly to wrest the sacred scriptures and to wallow in open sins, who will have no church officers to watch over their souls? (p. 38)

In the absence of an essay explicitly delineating his tradition's church polity,[162] Matthews's pastoral tract provides an invaluable insight into the theory and practice of the earliest Welsh Congregationalism.

As for the man himself, unlike his sons both of whom became 'sober conformists',[163] Matthews refused to be subject to the stipulations of the 1662 Act of Uniformity and remained in Swansea where 'he afterwards preached, by the connivance of the magistrates, in a little chapel at the end of the town'.[164] Calamy's account affords a vivid insight into his witness and personality that deserves to be quoted *in extensio*:

He was a very pious and zealous man, who went about to instruct people from house to house. All his discourse … was about spiritual things. He made no visits but such as were religious and ministerial, and received none but in a religious manner. When any came to visit him, after common salutations, he would soon enter some discourse about their souls, and when anything was brought for them to drink, it was his custom to take the glass into his hand, give solemn thanks to God for it, and drink to his friend telling him that he was heartily welcome. He would often go out on market days to the country people and speak to them about spiritual matters, some of whom received him with respect and others with contempt and scorn … He had no estate but subsisted by the piety of his children … and by the kindness of relations and friends which made him sometimes pleasantly say, he was comfortably maintained by the children of God, his own children and the children of this world. His way of preaching and catechizing had some particularities which became him, and were advantageous to many. He lived to a good age and continued useful to the last. He died about 1683.[165]

It was through his work and that, in translation, of Thomas Shepard, that New England Puritanism made its mark in Wales.

Orthodox and Prayer Book divinity during the Interregnum, 1649–60

The emerging consensus as delineated in Chapter One consisted in upholding Reformed doctrine according to the Prayer Book formularies with an accompanying commitment to Episcopal government and parish-based discipline. Effective preaching and the need to inculcate vital godliness among the flocks remained the aim of the most conscientious clergy, and whatever qualms they may have had with the Laudian bishops, there was no question of their rejecting the authority of either Church or Crown. For these men, the civil war came as a terrible shock. Rhys Prichard, the Puritanically minded vicar of Llandovery, not only sided with the king but contributed generously to the royal cause.[166] His death in 1644 saved him from falling foul of parliament's prohibitions against the former regime. There were other sound and pious clergy who felt they had no choice but to remain faithful to the old dispensation. William Nicholson, the theologically Reformed vicar of Llandeilo Fawr, declined an appointment to the Westminster Assembly of Divines on the basis of his conscientious commitment to Episcopacy and his loyalty to the king. James Ussher, archbishop of Armagh and primate of all Ireland whose impeccably orthodox Calvinism was conjoined with massive patristic learning, spent part of the First Civil War at St Donat's Castle, Glamorgan, being shielded by the Stradling family, while Jeremy Taylor, the deposed chaplain to King Charles, penned his famous *Rule and Exercises of Holy Living* (1650) and *Rule and Exercises of Holy Dying* (1651) during his sojourn at Golden Grove, Carmarthenshire, where he had been given shelter by Richard Vaughan, the second earl of Carbery.

Of the scores of Welsh clergy ejected from their parishes between 1644 and 1653 for 'malignancy', 'scandal', 'not reading the [Westminster] Directory', 'using the Prayer Book' and the like, there were not a few devout and holy men whose conscience did not allow them to support the present system.[167] Also, the fact that the commissioners of the Propagation Act found as many as 127 of the long-established ministers in south Wales and scores in north Wales including the bulk of the clergy in Denbighshire, Flintshire and Merioneth as being acceptable, listing them as 'clerk and preaching minister', 'an approved preacher', 'a good preaching minister', 'a good divine and constant preacher' and the like, showed that diligent and effective parish ministers had not become wholly extinct during the Interregnum.[168] The fact that the majority of these men conformed at the Restoration and reverted to Prayer Book worship cannot be taken as proof of bad faith. To posit a stark divide between a formalist, Arminian establishment and a doctrinally pure and religiously unblemished Puritan dissent does not square with the facts. As we have seen, virtually all of the radical Puritans diverged, sometimes grievously, from biblical orthodoxy, while much of the non-Puritan theology published in Wales during the Interregnum was in continuity with the older norms. Reformed doctrine and the call for repentance, the need for true piety and the religion of the heart remained a mainstay of Welsh theology during these years.

John Edwards (c.1606–58) was among the three score clergy to be ejected from their Monmouthshire livings by the commissioners of the Propagation Act in 1650. A native of Caldicot, he had graduated from Jesus College, Oxford, and since 1631 had served as rector of Llanmartin, Wilcreek, Tredynog and Magor, all in his home county. The reason for his dismissal is not recorded, but in his 1651 translation of Edward Fisher's *Marrow of Modern Divinity*, he laments not only his lack of finesse in written Welsh but the misery of his present situation. Having been born on the shores of the River Severn where English was rapidly replacing the native tongue, both piety and patriotism had prompted him to issue the present work. Though, to his immense distress, his lips had been sealed preventing him from fulfilling his pulpit ministry, nevertheless he felt the need to share the gospel among his countrymen through the present work. He says nothing of the current upheaval, but the introduction to his work has long been noted as a vivid description of attitudes to the Welsh language in the border areas during the mid-seventeenth century.[169] Presented to the local gentry families including the Morgans of Tredegar Park, the Kemeyses of Cefnmabli and the Williamses of Llangybi, he appealed for their support not only in the cause of godly reformation but of cultural regeneration as well:

> Of all the countries in the world, as far as I know, there is not a single nation as negligent of its language as that of the Welshman, despite the fact this his tongue deserves as much respect on account of its antiquity and richness as any other.[170]

For Edwards, writing under the pen-name of 'Siôn Tre-rhedyn', Christian obedience and national renewal went hand in hand, while 'no-one can deny that, next to the Word of God, sound literature is the most effective way to teach the people their responsibility towards God and their fellow man' (Sig. A2v). The *Marrow of Modern Divinity*, first published in 1645, was a pastorally orientated study on the pitfalls of legalism on the one hand and antinomianism on the other. Its author, Edward Fisher, was a London layman associated at different times both with Independent and Presbyterian congregations.[171] It was written in dialogue form between four characters: Nomista, the legalist, for whom salvation was dependent on good works or fulfilling the obligations of the law; Antinomista, whose overemphasis on divine grace undercut all obligations for moral or evangelical obedience; Neophytus, a young man eager for instruction; and the gospel minister Evangelista, who represented the correct balance of truth. Despite Edwards's grammatical blemishes, mostly his faulty use of mutations, it translates well into the Welsh milieu and provides a lively insight into the doctrinal tensions of the time.

In the opening section Evangelista expounds the difference between the rule of works, the rule of faith and the rule of Christ, the function of the law in the Christian dispensation and to what extent should the Decalogue remain authoritative in the life of the believer. This took him to the Book of Genesis, to Adam in the Garden of Eden and to Abraham who was justified by faith in God's gracious promises, to Moses and the covenant in the Book of Exodus, and to the luxurious use of typology throughout the Old Testament, its sacrificial motifs all referring to Christ's atoning death in the New. Even in the Old Testament, the Decalogue was never a means of salvation, rather a way of life for those who had been redeemed by the mercy and favour of God. Thereafter it was meant to 'introduce a new and better covenant, to lead men by the hand to Christ, to unmask sin, to awaken the conscience and to convict them of their own inability thus forcing them out of themselves and to Christ' (p. 58). Christ, who fulfilled the law and had repaid the debt that had been forfeited by Adam, had also imputed his righteousness to those who believed in him thus absolving them from their guilt and making them children of God. Nominista affirmed this as did Antinomista, but both fell short of a full understanding of the way in which the law functioned in the Christian life. In Nominista's case, the notional affirmation of Christ's sacrificial death together with the living of a moral, upright and religious life was rooted in his own volition rather than being based on the free grace of the cross. For all his piety and humility, he was, in fact, depending on himself for salvation and not on the Lord. Antinominista, for his part, though he revelled in the gospel and rejoiced in a full, final and objective salvation, lived a life which hardly reflected the Christian virtues: 'I have heard that your behaviour does not accord with the gospel of Christ' (p. 131). If one was in danger of self-justification, the other was guilty of hypocrisy and presumption:

> It is apparent that you, my dear Antinominista, transgress to the left, as you have not lived your life according to the rule of God's law, while it is obvious (in my view) that you, my good neighbour Nominista, have transgressed to the right, justifying yourself through trusting in your obedience to the law. (p. 135)

Although both repent of their errors in the end, it is the young man Neophytus who affords the preacher the opportunity to teach his listeners (and the author to enlighten his readers) about the true gospel way. Inevitably, given the significance of the concept of election in the religious discourse of the day, Neophytus's anxiety as to whether he was among the elect was bound to arise. His teacher is insistent that the whole tenor of the gospel was all-embracing and that Christ bids everyone to come unto him: 'Never say perhaps I am not among the elect therefore I cannot believe in Christ, but say rather that I do believe in Christ therefore am certain to have been chosen' (p. 147). Both election and reprobation were among God's secret counsels into which it was not fitting for people to pry. The gospel, on the other hand, was an open truth while Christ called upon all to come to him. Each individual's obligation was to make their salvation certain: 'The righteousness of Christ Jesus is given to all who believe; I believe, therefore his righteous belongs to me' (p. 148). Having rehearsed again the difference between Adam and Christ, the old dispensation and the new, justification by works and justification by faith and the true nature of the Decalogue in the context of the Christian faith, Evangelista summarizes the balance of scripture:

> But these laws agree in this, and they both declare 'Do this', but this is the difference. One says, 'Do this and you will live', and the other says, 'If you are alive, you will do this'. The one says, 'Do this and you will receive life', while the other says, 'Now that you have life, you will do this' ... Now that you, my neighbour Neophytus, are in Christ, make sure to receive the Ten Commandments as though from God's own hand but in Christ and not merely from the hands of Moses. Take them from Christ's hands and keep them as Christ's own laws. (pp. 186–7)

The absence of any polemical or controversial references to church government, the Prayer Book or the sacraments in Edwards's translation and its wholesale affirmation of mainstream Reformed divinity would place it ordinarily in the moderate Puritan camp. Yet for some reason Edwards, like Robert Llwyd, the godly but conformist vicar of Wrexham who, decades earlier, had been so assiduous in the provision of sound biblical literature in Welsh,[172] found himself at odds with the parliamentary regime and banished from his living. In the case of Thomas Powell, however, who was ejected from his incumbency at Cantref, Breconshire, even before the advent of the Propagation Act, we have the first Welsh-language expression of what would come to be denominated specifically as 'Anglican' theology.[173] Powell (1608–60), educated at Jesus College, Oxford, rector of his home parish of Cantref since 1635 and intimate of the poet Henry Vaughan, 'the Silurist', is reported in John Walker's *Sufferings of the Clergy* as 'a learned and orthodox man of a godly life and conversation, a constant preacher in Welsh and English'.[174] Walker's notorious bias notwithstanding, this is almost certainly a correct description of Powell's character. His *Cerbyd Jechydwriaeth* ('The Chariot of Salvation') (1657) is a commentary of the Apostle's Creed, the Ten Commandments, the Lord's Prayer, the two sacraments of baptism and the Lord's Supper replete with catechetical instruction and set prayers. As with Richard Hooker's *Laws of Ecclesiastical Polity*, the first five books of which had been in circulation since 1593, Powell's doctrine remained generally reformed: the absolute supremacy of scripture, a rejection of popery, the disavowal of a doctrine of merit and an acceptance of the concept of justification by faith alone, but in matters of ceremonial and forms including the Prayer Book, the validity of Episcopal government and a deep respect for venerable tradition, he follows what would become typical of the Anglican way.

After complaining of having been 'forbidden from preaching the gospel among you', he had set about preparing the present work in order 'to instruct some and to confirm others in the true way and the sound faith'.[175] He begins by outlining the trinitarian structure of the Apostle's Creed, by describing the church catholic as a fellowship of those called effectively by God, sanctified by his Spirit, set apart for eternal glory and bound together in a common faith. If the Nicene and Athanasian Creeds were expanded versions of the Apostle's Creed, the *Gloria Patri* was a distillation of the creed's essence. The Decalogue, though fulfilled in

Christ 'who freed us from the curse of the law when, having been made a curse in our place, he suffered an execrable death on the cross for our sins' (p. 7), remains in force as the standard of Christian conduct. The Lord's Prayer remains the pattern and standard for all true piety as it was given by Christ himself at the request of, and for the instruction of, his disciples. Although no prayer is effective apart from sincere and experiential faith, as part of the liturgy of the faithful it is designed to be used constantly. There is nothing intrinsically wrong with set or repetitive prayers including the Lord's Prayer, as long as they are offered thoughtfully and sincerely. In fact it was so often effusive and unrestrained supplications, lacking discipline or preparation, that were unsatisfactory:

> To read or recite prayers made by others can be as beneficial and accept-
> able as those we have compiled ourselves. Indeed we should often use
> the same prayers (as did our Saviour himself), as long as grace and need
> impels us. God does not delight in variation of utterance or constant
> newly-coined supplications. (p. 31)

The two dominical sacraments had been instituted by Christ and were effective for showing forth, in the face of human weakness, the reality of the spiritual life both in believers' entry into the Christian community and their retention therein. Not being operative of themselves, they were only beneficial through personal faith: 'The two essential notes through which the true Church is discerned are the sacraments and the right ministration of the Word of God; wherever these two are present and correctly administered, there exists the true Church of Christ' (p. 34). Both baptism and the Lord's Supper were essential ordinances, having been instituted by the Saviour himself, baptism being for the believers and their children while the Supper – referred to as the Lord's Supper and never as the Eucharist – was not only a reminder of Christ's sacrificial death but a partaking, in repentance, faith and the Holy Spirit, of its fruits. The biblical and evangelical nature of both these sacraments are everywhere to the fore, though Powell is insistent that only duly ordained ministers are allowed to celebrate:

> Q: Who are the lawful administrators of these sacraments?
> A: Only those who have been legitimately called to the Church's min-
> istry. It is they who are the keepers of the seals, any they alone have

been entrusted to convey and impart [the sacraments] to those who are
appropriate, and to none else. (p. 36)

Although forgiveness was freely available to all, solely on the basis of
true repentance and faith in Christ's full and perfect atonement on the
cross, Christ, however, 'has given the authority to his Church to declare
and pronounce that pardon (in his name) on whatever occasion is fitting
and legitimate' (p. 5).

The only reference, apart from the Epistle Dedicatory, to the crisis
of the times was in Powell's final prayer: 'A prayer composed on entry
to a ruined church where no sermon has been heard nor service held for
many a year' (pp. 37–9). Echoing his friend Henry Vaughan's 'Prayer in
time of Persecution and Heresy' in his bleak and poignant prose work
Mount of Olives (1652),[176] the ejected rector of Cantref entreats God:

> Be merciful to thy oppressed Church and divided Kingdom; look towards
> thy ministers who have been banished to the farthest recesses and secret
> places, and to their congregations who are wandering, like sheep without
> a shepherd, journeying here and there seeking God's Word, which is
> nowhere to be found. (pp. 38–9)

Three years earlier, Powell, along with two colleagues, had appealed
to Jenkin Jones, the radical Puritan Approver for Breconshire, to be
reinstated to their parochial charges:

> May [we] at last have the door of utterance opened, and be permitted to
> preach the gospel freely among those that do much want it and do ear-
> nestly call for it, as the parched earth after the dew and rain of heaven.[177]

Jones, keenly aware of their antipathy to the current regime, refused
the request. Consequently Powell spent his closing years awaiting the
advent of happier times. His reinstatement to his charge, along with an
appointment to a canonry at St David's Cathedral, occurred with the
Restoration, though he died on 31 December 1660, aged fifty-two, before
being able fully to resume his ministry.

The year of Cromwell's death and his son Richard's brief succession
to the position of Lord Protector – 1658 – saw a spate of works by a
single author, Rowland Vaughan, all of which propounded the emerging Anglican consensus: the supreme value of Prayer Book worship,

the significance of historical continuity within an episcopally governed church and the need to reinstate the traditional Christian festivals. Vaughan has been mentioned previously as the translator of Lewis Bayly's *Practice of Piety* under the title of *Yr Ymarfer o Dduwioldeb*, a second edition being issued in 1656.[178] The son of a distinguished north Wales family, 'the Cavalier poet of Caer-gai' (his Merionethshire estate) served as high sheriff in 1642–3 and was sufficiently zealous in the king's cause to have his home razed to the ground by parliamentary soldiers in 1645 and to be imprisoned, in Chester, for a short time some years later. Already renowned for his bardic prowess, five substantial prose translations emerged more or less simultaneously in 1658:

- *Yr Arfer o Weddi yr Arglwydd*, his rendition of *The Use of the Lord's Prayer, maintained against the Objections of the Innovators of these Times* (1646) by the minister of London's French Reformed Church, Jean d'Espagne;
- *Pregeth yn erbyn Schism*, a translation of the Oxford clergyman Jasper Mayne's *Sermon against Schism, or, the Separation of these Times* (1652). While the original had been aimed at the radical Anabaptist and Fifth Monarchy man John Pendarves, Vaughan's translation was in response to Vavasor Powell's recent altercation with George Griffith, rector of Llanymynech, Montgomeryshire, who would soon become bishop of St Asaph;[179]
- *Euchologia: neu, yr Athrawiaeth i arferol weddïo … o'r Llyfr Gweddi Gyffredin*, being his version of John Prideaux, bishop of Worcester's notes addressed to his daughters on the use of the Book of Common Prayer (1655);
- *Prifannau Sanctaidd neu Lawlyfr o Weddïau*, namely *The Holy Feasts and Fasts of the Church of England, with Mediations and Sacred Prayers* (1657) by William Brough, the Laudian dean of Gloucester, and the same author's
- *Preservative against the Plague of Schism* (1652) which Vaughan entitled *Ymddiffyniad rhag Pla o Schism*.

Along with these, he also issued during the same year two works by James Ussher, archbishop of Armagh: *Prifannau Crefydd Gristnogawl* (*The Principles of Christian Religion*, 1645) and *Y Llywbreiddiad-fodd byrr o Gristnogawl Grefydd* (*A Brief Method of the Body of Christian Religion*, 1647). In all it was a quite remarkable body of work by a layman who

professed no technical expertise in theology, residing far from the centres of learning in the fastness of rural north Wales.[180]

By now there was a yearning for peace and stability. Philip Henry
of Wrothenbury, Flintshire, who had been ordained by the Shropshire
Classis in September 1657 according to the most exacting standards of
archetypal Presbyterianism,[181] observed that by the following year 'there
was generally throughout the nation, a great change in the temper of
God's people, and a mighty tendency towards peace and unity, as if they
were by consent weary of their long clashings'. He hoped that the time
was at hand when 'Judah should no longer vex Ephraim, nor Ephraim
envy Judah, neither should they learn war any more'.[182] In truth, not
only the royalists' but even the moderate Puritans' zeal for the current
regime had mostly dissipated. It had become a settled opinion among
all but the most unwavering radicals that the parliament's religiously
motivated exertions in Wales had been at best only partially effective:
'Who cannot look with grief and sorrow at the parties and sects and
schisms and heresies that Satan has allowed to flourish, to silence sound
doctrine and its professors, and to elevate the prophets of Baal in their
place', wrote Rowland Vaughan.[183]

> When the schismatics, the spiritualists, the Quakers, the Anabaptists,
> Independents and Presbyterians sowed their tares maintaining inso-
> lently that it was the choicest wheat, and by force of arms deprived the
> Church of its ministers, I had no option but to take my sickle to cut
> away the brambles and thorns which were in danger of choking the
> sweet vines.[184]

While it was only to be expected that the cavalier Vaughan would
sound a sour note, it was echoed in different degrees even by moderate Episcopalians and others who had remained for the most part loyal
to the present government. 'For the itinerants are so few, so ignorant
and so mean', complained William Nicholson, former vicar of Llandeilo,
'that … it is as it was in the days of Eli, so now for their sakes the
sacrifice of the Lord is abhorred and the people are scattered upon
the mountains without a shepherd'.[185] Quoting the third-century
Hippolitus of Rome, he continued: 'In the last times of Anti-Christ, the
houses [of God] shall be like a cottage, the precious body of Christ and
his blood shall not be extant, the liturgy shall be extinguished [and]
the singing of psalms shall cease.'[186] For the critics of the regime what

was especially galling was that the tithe was still collected punctiliously though parishes were only fitfully served or not all: 'All sorts of people, who are sadly aggrieved to pay their tithes more strictly than ever they did, and yet have neither preaching, praying, christening, decent burials or other spiritual rites or comforts administered to them.'[187]

Whereas the formalist Alexander Griffith's pique was exacerbated by his hatred for Vavasor Powell, the chief embodiment of the Propagation Act among the people, there is ample evidence to corroborate that much of what he claimed was true: 'A man on a Lord's day may ride twenty miles through a county and not see a church door open, supplied with a constant, able, godly minister.'[188] By 1658 Jenkin Lloyd who had been instituted to the rectory of Llandysul, Cardiganshire, by the Westminster Assembly, who had functioned as an approver under the Propagation Act and later represented his county in parliament, pined for concord and harmony. Though impeccably Reformed with a marked penchant for the doctrines of election and perseverance, his exposition of Christ's seven last words from the cross included the following sentiments:

> We all believe in thee (O God) and in the same Christ, and are all bap-
> tized into him, and look to be saved by his sufferings. We agree in that
> one and only foundation; we all embrace the two Testaments, and as I
> hope, the three Creeds and many other very material points; why should
> we vary about the superstructures and circumstantials of religion? We
> believe thy mercy to be of that extent, that whosoever shall call upon thy
> name shall be saved; why should we then be so uncharitable as to exclude
> so many millions of weak but true believers … for no other reason but
> because they are not of our judgements in all things?[189]

If a decade or so earlier the more committed reformers had sup-
ported the suppression of forms, the festivals of the church year and the Prayer Book due to their having been tainted with superstition, prelacy and Laudian oppression,[190] by now the Presbyterians conceded the need to restore a biblically informed liturgy, set prayers and even, if need be (for some at least), moderate Episcopal oversight. The royalist Vaughan knew he had the sympathy of Dr John Ellis, the Puritan rector of Dolgellau, revered by John Lewis of Glasgrug as 'one of the ablest divines I know in Wales'.[191] A native of Merionethshire, DD of both universities (and of St Andrews) and formerly a fellow of Jesus College, Oxford, he had been instituted by the Westminster Assembly

to the living of Dolgellau in 1646, had served as an Approver under the Propagation Act and after 1653 functioned as the Triers' principal Welsh intermediary. Appalled that a 'gathered church' had established itself within Ellis's parish, Vaughan dedicated his translation of Jean d'Espagne's *The Use of the Lord's Prayer* to the rector.[192] For his part Ellis had become thoroughly disenchanted with the regime. 'I am persuaded that this and the rude contempts and irreverencies ... [in] divine worship', he wrote to Richard Baxter in February 1660, 'hath not been the least cause (among other great sins) of the Lord's so signal displeasure against those in late power among us, and the sudden and strange blasting of them and their greatness to the astonishment of the whole world'.[193] By then Richard Cromwell had resigned as Lord Protector, the Long Parliament had been reconvened and General Monck had opened the way for Charles II to be reinstated as king. Unsurprisingly, both Ellis and Jenkin Lloyd conformed to the Restoration settlement, the former sealing his new commitment with the publication in 1660 of his Latin exposition of the 39 Articles, *Defensio Fidei seu responsio succincta ad argumenta, quibus impugnari solet Confessio Anglicana.*[194]

It could be argued that the moderate Puritans' acquiescence in the post-1660 ecclesiastical regime was a return to the tradition established in 1594 with Maurice Kyffin's translation of Bishop Jewel's *Apologia Ecclesiae Anglicana*, perpetuated during the Jacobite decades with Robert Holland's editions of William Perkins's handbooks on experiential piety, John Davies of Mallwyd's biblical labours and Edmund Prys's metrical psalms, and solidified during the reign of Charles I through the didactic and pastoral endeavours of such conformist though quasi-Puritan clergy as Robert Llwyd and Rhys Prichard. The confluence of catechetical teaching, awakening preaching, Reformed doctrine and practical godliness combined with a deference to the formularies laid down by such Elizabethan reformers as bishops Richard Davies and William Morgan, had now been restored. Since 1640 Wales had, as it were, turned full circle.

There were, however, differences. The conscientious, spiritually awakened clergy had always been a minority and the parliamentary authorities had, in fact, done the Christian cause a favour by ejecting idle, feckless and morally reprehensible ministers even though too many exemplary Episcopalians suffered along with them. Rowland Watkyns, a fellow ejectee and neighbour of Thomas Powell of Cantref who shared his, and Henry Vaughan's, sacramental High Church piety, feared that many clergy of the worst type would return to their livings at the Restoration:

> Drones, knaves and fools, for Church-preferment look,
> Those fish, and catch it with a silver hook;
> Such workmen in Christ's vineyard will, I fear,
> More shame the work than help good labourers there.[195]

There would still be ample justification for sincerely pious folk to complain about a corrupt establishment and to call on tender consciences in the mixed multitudes within parish assemblies to 'come out from among them'.[196]

Of greater historical significance was the fact that voluntary religion and the ideal of a more charismatic, spontaneous, less hierarchical and tradition-bound concept of church fellowship had captivated the imagination and commitment of too many of the Welsh people for it to be easily uprooted. For all the radicals' zealotry and immoderation, ordinary people had been given a taste of spiritual freedom and they would not go back to the old ways. Walter Cradock, Vavasor Powell, Morgan Llwyd, John Myles, Jenkin Jones, Ambrose Mostyn, Richard Symonds and a host of others had proven themselves (despite everything) to be highly effective evangelists and powerful missionary organizers. 'Hath any generation since the apostles days', asked Powell, 'had such powerful preachers, and [such] plenty of preaching as this generation?'[197] Even such a paragon of moderation as Philip Henry concurred that, despite the 'great disorders' in civil matters during the previous decades,

> in the matters of God's worship, things went *well*. There was freedom, and reformation, and a face of godliness was upon the nation … Ordinances were administered in power and purity, and though there was much amiss, yet religion … did prevail. This … we know very well, let men say what they will of those times.[198]

In fact there would remain hundreds of converts in conventicles and cottage meetings, mostly in the larger coastal towns and the border counties, who would remain faithful to the vision of a new kind of religion that had captivated them in the two momentous decades previously. 'In short', to quote one modern authority, 'Dissent was here to stay'.[199]

Notes

1   Whereas Goronwy Wyn Owen places Cradock on 'the moderate wing of
    the Welsh Puritan movement of the 1650s', *Cewri'r Cyfamod: Y Piwritaniaid
    Cymreig, 1630–60* (Bangor: Canolfan Uwchefrydiau Crefydd, 2008), p. 103,
    Geoffrey F. Nuttall much more realistically describes him as being 'fairly
    far to the left wing of the radical party in Puritanism', *The Holy Spirit in
    Puritan Faith and Experience*, 2nd edn (Chicago: University of Chicago Press,
    1992), p. 36.
2   Edward Terrill, *The Records of a Church of Christ Meeting in Broadmead,
    Bristol, 1640–88*, ed. W. Haycroft (London: J. Heaton, 1865), p. 25.
3   *House of Commons Journal* (London: HMSO, 1802), vol. 4, p. 242; Thomas
    Richards, *A History of the Puritan Movement in Wales, 1639 to 1653* (London:
    National Eisteddfod Association, 1920), pp. 60–1.
4   Walter Cradock, *The saints fulnesse of joy* (London: Mathew Simmons, 1646),
    re-titled 'A Thanksgiving Sermon Preached before the Parliament', in *idem,
    The Works of the Late Revd Walter Cradock*, ed. Thomas Charles and Peter
    Oliver (Chester: W. C. Jones, 1800), pp. 384–406; page numbers in the text
    refer first to the original and secondly as they appear in *Works.*
5   See Lloyd Bowen, 'Representations of Wales and the Welsh during the Civil
    Wars and Interregnum', *Historical Research*, 77 (2004), 358–64; *idem, The
    Politics of the Principality: Wales, c.1603–42* (Cardiff: University of Wales
    Press, 2007), pp. 242–3.
6   Stephen K. Roberts, 'Propagating the Gospel in Wales: the making of the
    1650 act', *THSC*, N.S. 10 (2004), 57–75.
7   See Noel Gibbard, *Walter Cradock: 'A New Testament Saint'* (Bridgend:
    Evangelical Library of Wales, 1977), *passim.*
8   Walter Cradock, *Glad Tydings, from Heaven to the worst of sinners* (London:
    Mathew Simmonds, 1648); re-titled 'Good News', in *idem, Works*, pp. 353–84;
    page numbers in the text refer first to the original and secondly as they
    appear in *Works.*
9   Walter Cradock, *Gospel-libertie* (London: Mathew Simmonds, 1648);
    re-titled 'Gospel Liberty Explained', in *idem, Works*, pp. 238–352; page
    numbers in the text refer first to the original and secondly as they appear
    in *Works.*
10 Michael R. Watts, *The Dissenters: from the Reformation to the French Revolution*
    (Oxford: Clarendon Press, 1978), pp. 94–116.
11 Robert S. Paul, *The Assembly of the Lord: Politics and Religion in the Westminster
    Assembly* (Edinburgh: T & T Clark, 1985), *passim.*
12 Although the terms Independency and Congregationalism are often regarded
    as being identical, the present chapter will refer to 'Independents' as those
    who, as well as holding to a congregational church polity, pleaded for tolera-
    tion of religious opinion. This was never the view of the Congregationalists
    per se; see Francis J. Bremer, *Congregational Communion: Clerical Friendship in
    the Anglo-American Puritan Community, 1610–92* (Boston, MA: Northeastern
    University Press, 1994), pp. 139–43.

13 Geoffrey F. Nuttall, *Visible Saints: the Congregational Way, 1640–60* (Oxford: Blackwell, 1957), *passim*; Bremer, *Congregational Communion*, pp. 174–200.

14 Geraint H. Jenkins, *The Foundations of Modern Wales, 1642–1780* (Oxford: Clarendon Press, 1987), pp. 57–9; *idem, Protestant Dissenters in Wales, 1639–89* (Cardiff: University of Wales Press, 1992), p. 15.

15 This section does not appear in the version reproduced in Cradock, *Works*.

16 *Glad Tidings*, p. 29; this passage is omitted from the nineteenth-century *Works* edited by Thomas Charles and Peter Oliver, both of whom, though Methodists, were ordained clergymen in the Established Church: 'For as the Lord has abundantly owned the labours of many in past ages and in the present day, whose judgement favoured a moderate episcopacy, on this account it is not inserted', p. 368.

17 E.g. Geoffrey F. Nuttall, *The Welsh Saints, 1640–60* (Cardiff: University of Wales Press, 1957), pp. 18–36; *idem*, 'Walter Cradock (1606?–1659): the man and his message', in *The Puritan Spirit* (London: Epworth Press, 1967), pp. 118–29; Gibbard, *Walter Cradock: 'A New Testament Saint'*.

18 Walter Cradock, *Mount Zion, or the privilege and practice of the saints* (London: Mathew Simmonds, 1649); re-titled 'Mount Sion', in *idem, Works*, pp. 9–128; page numbers in the text refer first to the original and secondly as they appear in *Works*.

19 Anon., *A Winding-sheet for Mr. Baxter's dead or [tho]se whom he hath kill'd and slain in his Catholick [co]mmunion, sweetly embalmed, and decently buried again: being an apology for several ministers, viz. [Mr. E]rbury, Mr. Cradock, Mr. Vavasor Powel, & Mr. Morgan [Ll]oyd, misrepresented by Mr. Baxter to the world* (London: E. Reyner, 1685), p. 9.

20 Thomas Rees, *History of Protestant Nonconformity in Wales* (London: John Snow, 1861), p. 53.

21 Stephen K. Roberts, 'The sermon in early modern Wales: context and content', in P. McCulloch, H. Adlington and E. Rhatigan (eds), *The Oxford Handbook of the Early Modern Sermon* (Oxford: Oxford University Press, 2011), pp. 303–25 (315).

22 Thomas Edwards, *Gangraena: or a Catalogue and Discovery of many Errours, Heresies [and] Blasphemies* Part III (London: Ralph Smith, 1646), p. 163; Richard Baxter, *Catholick Communion Defended* (London: Thomas Parkhurst, 1684), p. 28; see Nuttall, *The Welsh Saints, 1640–60*, pp. 10, 20.

23 Walter Cradock, *Divine Drops Distilled* (London: Raphael Harford, 1650); re-titled 'Exposition and Observations on various texts of Scripture', *idem, Works*, pp. 405–531; page numbers in the text refer first to the original and secondly as they appear in *Works*.

24 Walter Cradock, *Gospel-holinessse, or, the saving sight of God* (London: Mathew Simmonds, 1651); re-titled 'A Saving Sight of God', in *idem, Works*, pp. 129–287; page numbers in the text refer first to the original and secondly as they appear in *Works*.

25 Nuttall, *The Welsh Saints, 1640–60*, p. 22.

26 As well as Nuttall's volume, for his biography, see Stephen K. Roberts in *ODNB*.

27 Alexander Griffith, *Strena Vavasoriensis, a New Year's Gift for the Welsh Itinerants, or a Hue and Cry after Mr Vavasor Powell, Metropolitan of the Itinerants* (London: n.p., 1654), frontispiece.

28 Autobiography in Edward Bagshaw, *The Life and Death of Mr Vavasor Powell, that faithful minister and confessor of Jesus Christ* (London: n.p., 1671), p. 4.

29 Bagshaw, *The Life and Death of Mr Vavasor Powell*, p. 107.

30 'Confession of Faith', in Bagshaw, *The Life and Death of Mr Vavasor Powell*, pp. 37–8.

31 Edward Allen et al., *Vavasoris Examen et Purgamen or, Mr Vavasor Powell's Impartial Trial* (London: Thomas Brewster and Livewell Chapman, 1654), p. 12.

32 Cited in Bagshaw, *The Life and Death of Mr Vavasor Powell*, p. 16.

33 Jenkins, *The Foundations of Modern Wales, 1642–1780*, pp. 42–83; idem, *Protestant Dissenters in Wales, 1639–89*, pp. 17–28.

34 Griffith, *Strena Vavasoriensis*, p. 5.

35 Robert Letham, *The Westminster Assembly: Reading its Theology in Historical Context* (Phillipsburg, NJ: P & R Publishing, 2009), *passim*.

36 C. G. Bolam et al., *The English Presbyterians: From Elizabethan Puritanism to Modern Unitarianism* (London: George Allen and Unwin, 1967), p. 43.

37 John Weekes (ed.), *Truth's Conflict with Error, or Universal Redemption Controverted* (London: Robert Austin, 1650), p. 6.

38 See John Coffey, *John Goodwin and the Puritan Revolution: Religion and Intellectual Change in Seventeenth Century England* (Woodbridge: The Boydell Press, 2006).

39 Coffey, *John Goodwin and the Puritan Revolution*, p. 214.

40 Weekes (ed.), *Truth's Conflict with Error*, p. 6.

41 Coffey, *John Goodwin and the Puritan Revolution*, p. 205.

42 See D. A. Weir, *The Origins of Federal Theology in Sixteenth Century Reformed Thought* (Oxford: Oxford University Press, 1990).

43 Vavasor Powell, *Christ and Moses' Excellency, or Sion and Sinai's Glory* (London: Hannah Allen, 1650), frontispiece; page numbers which follow are in the text.

44 R. Tudur Jones, *Vavasor Powell* (Abertawe: Gwasg John Penry, 1971), p. 89.

45 Nuttall, *The Holy Spirit in Puritan Faith and Experience*, p. 148.

46 See Chapter One, p. 42.

47 Morgan Llwyd, *Gweithiau Morgan Llwyd o Wynedd*, ed. Thomas E. Ellis, vol. 1 (Bangor: Jarvis and Foster, 1899), pp. 57–60 (57).

48 The link between Cradock, Powell and Llwyd and the Harleys of Brampton Bryan is discussed in detail by Nuttall, *The Welsh Saints, 1640–60*, pp. 1–17.

49 Quoted in Introduction, Morgan Llwyd, *Gweithiau Morgan Llwyd o Wynedd*, ed. J. H. Davies, vol. 2 (Bangor: Jarvis and Foster, 1908), pp. ixx–lxxx (xxix).

50 Cited by Gwyn Thomas, 'Dau Lwyd o Gynfal', in J. E. Caerwyn Williams, *Ysgrifau Beirniadol*, 5 (Dinbych: Gwasg Gee, 1970), pp. 71–98 (85).

51 Morgan Llwyd, *Llyfr y Tri Aderyn* (1653), ed. M. Wynn Thomas (Caerdydd: Gwasg Prifysgol Cymru, 1988), p. 102.

52 *Gwaedd Ynghymru yn Wyneb Pob Cydwybod*, in Llwyd, *Gweithiau Morgan Llwyd o Wynedd*, vol. 1, pp. 127–50 (146).

53 *Gwaedd Ynghymru yn Wyneb Pob Cydwybod*, p. 97.

54 'Y Bwa Melyn', in Llwyd, *Gweithiau Morgan Llwyd o Wynedd*, vol. 1, p. 38.

55 'Y Bwa Melyn', p. 40.

56 'A Song of my Beloved', in Llwyd, *Gweithiau Morgan Llwyd o Wynedd*, vol. 1, p. 88.

57 'A Justification of the Army and Parliament', in J. Graham Jones and Goronwy Wyn Owen (eds), *Gweithiau Morgan Llwyd o Wynedd*, vol. 3 (Caerdydd: Gwasg Prifysgol Cymru, 1993), pp. 38–44 (41).

58 'Charles, the Last King of Britain', in Llwyd, *Gweithiau Morgan Llwyd o Wynedd*, vol. 1, p. 55.

59 For the text see Richards, *A History of the Puritan Movement in Wales, 1639–53*, pp. 81–90.

60 Jenkins, *The Foundations of Modern Wales, 1642–1780*, p. 88.

61 'Our Lord is coming', in Llwyd, *Gweithiau Morgan Llwyd o Wynedd*, vol. 1, p. 9.

62 '1648', in Llwyd, *Gweithiau Morgan Llwyd o Wynedd*, p. 22.

63 '1648', p. 87.

64 Nuttall, *The Welsh Saints, 1640–60*, p. 53.

65 Although the *Gwaedd* was not published until 1655, the literary critic Saunders Lewis argued convincingly that all three were composed between May and October 1653 and constitute a single body of work: Saunders Lewis, 'Morgan Llwyd: trefn ar ei lyfrau', in *idem*, *Meistri'r Canrifoedd: Ysgrifau ar Hanes Llenyddiaeth Gymraeg*, ed. R. Geraint Gruffydd (Caerdydd: Gwasg Prifysgol Cymru, 1973), pp. 153–60; cf. M. Wynn Thomas, *Morgan Llwyd*, Writers of Wales (Cardiff: University of Wales Press, 1984), p. 18.

66 *Llythyr ir Cymru Cariadus* and *Gwaedd Ynghymru yn Wyneb Pob Cydwybod* are reproduced in Llwyd, *Gweithiau Morgan Llwyd o Wynedd*, vol. 1, pp. 115–23 and pp. 127–50 (122); page references will be made in the text.

67 R. Tudur Jones, 'The Healing Herb and the Rose of Love: the piety of two Welsh Puritans', in R. Buick Knox (ed.), *Reformation Conformity and Dissent; Essays in Honour of Geoffrey F. Nuttall* (London: Epworth Press, 1978), pp. 154–9 (169).

68 Despite their erudition, the attempts of R. M. Jones and Goronwy Wyn Owen to analyse Llwyd according to Calvinistic categories are ultimately unconvincing: Jones, 'Morgan Llwyd: y cyfrinydd ysgrythurol', in *idem*, *Cyfriniaeth Gymraeg* (Caerdydd: Gwasg Prifysgol Cymru, 1994), pp. 39–77; Owen, *Morgan Llwyd* (Caernarfon: Gwasg Pantycelyn, 1992) and *Rhwng Calfin a Böhme: Golwg ar Syniadaeth Morgan Llwyd* (Caerdydd: Gwasg Prifysgol Cymru, 2001).

69 Nuttall, *The Holy Spirit in Puritan Faith and Experience*, p. 148.

70   All quotations are from M. Wynn Thomas's 1988 edition; page references are made in the text.

71   Nuttall, *The Holy Spirit in Puritan Faith and Experience*, p. 148.

72   Richard Baxter to Morgan Llwyd, 10 June 1656, in Llwyd, *Gweithiau Morgan Llwyd o Wynedd*, vol. 3, pp. 98–100 (99).

73   Baxter to Llwyd, 10 June 1656, p. 100.

74   *Lazarus and his Sisters, discoursing of Paradise*, in Llwyd, *Gweithiau Morgan Llwyd o Wynedd*, vol. 1, pp. 271–93 (293).

75   *Where is Christ?* (1655), in Llwyd, *Gweithiau Morgan Llwyd o Wynedd*, vol. 1, pp. 297–309 (307).

76   *An Honest Discourse between Three Neighbours, touching the Present Government*, in Llwyd, *Gweithiau Morgan Llwyd o Wynedd*, vol. 2, pp. 211–40 (232).

77   *An Honest Discourse between Three Neighbours, touching the Present Government*, p. 235.

78   *An Honest Discourse between Three Neighbours, touching the Present Government*, p. 236.

79   *An Honest Discourse between Three Neighbours, touching the Present Government*, p. 239.

80   *Gair o'r Gair, neu Sôn am Sŵn*, in Llwyd, *Gweithiau Morgan Llwyd o Wynedd*, vol. 2, pp. 133–205 (147, 165).

81   *Gair o'r Gair, neu Sôn am Sŵn*, p. 173.

82   *Gair o'r Gair, neu Sôn am Sŵn*, p. 175.

83   *Gair o'r Gair, neu Sôn am Sŵn*, p. 177.

84   See Nuttall, *The Holy Spirit in Puritan Faith and Experience*, pp. 151–4.

85   See W. G. Norris and Norman Penney (eds), *John ap John and Early Records of Friends in Wales* (London: Friends Historical Society, 1907).

86   [John Myles], *An Antidote against the Infection of the Times, or a faithful Watchword from Mount Sion to prevent the ruine of souls* (London: T. Brewster, 1656); a facsimile version, edited by Thomas Shankland, was published by the Welsh Baptist Historical Society in 1904.

87   Powell to Llwyd, 22 April 1657, in Llwyd, *Gweithiau Morgan Llwyd o Wynedd*, vol. 3, pp. 146–7 (146).

88   M. Wynn Thomas, 'Morgan Llwyd and the Foundations of the Nonconformist Nation', in Stewart Mottram and Sarah Prescott (eds), *Writing Wales, From the Renaissance to Romanticism* (Surrey: Ashgate, 2012), pp. 111–30.

89   Anon., *A Winding-sheet for Mr. Baxter's dead*, pp. 11, 12.

90   Robert Jones, *Drych yr Amseroedd* (1820), ed. Glyn M. Ashton (Caerdydd: Gwasg Prifysgol Cymru, 1958), p. 8.

91   John Tombes, *A Publick Dispute betwixt John Tombes BD, John Cragge MA and Henry Vaughan MA touching Infant-Baptism* (London: H. Twyford, 1654), epistle dedicatory.

92   John Price, *The Sun out-shining the Moon... In answer to a lying scandalous paper published by John Moone, entitled The True Light* (London: John Price, 1658), pp. 9–10.

93 Joshua Thomas, *Hanes y Bedyddwyr Ymhlith y Cymry* (Caerfyrddin: John Ross, 1778), pp. 108–9; T. M. Bassett, *The Welsh Baptists* (Swansea: Ilston Press, 1977), pp. 14–15.

94 B. G. Owens (ed.), *The Ilston Book: earliest register of Welsh Baptists* (Aberystwyth: National Library of Wales, 1996), p. 31; for the 1644 Confession, Myles's contribution to the London Baptists' missionary endeavours and his place within contemporary Baptist life generally, see B. R. White, 'The doctrine of the church in the Particular Baptist Confession of 1644', *JTS*, N.S. 19 (1968), 570–90; *idem*, 'John Miles and the structures of the Calvinistic Baptist mission to south Wales, 1649–60', in Mansel John (ed.), *Welsh Baptist Studies* (Cardiff: South Wales Baptist College, 1976), pp. 35–76.

95 Jenkins, *Protestant Dissenters in Wales, 1639–89*, p. 30; despite the general tendency to use the form Miles, the style which the subject used invariably was Myles.

96 D. Densil Morgan, 'John Myles (1621–83) and the future of Ilston's past', in *idem, Wales and the Word: Historical Perspectives on Welsh Identity and Religion* (Cardiff: University of Wales Press, 2008), pp. 5–16; Ian Birch, *To Follow the Lambe Wheresoever he Goeth: the Ecclesial Polity of the English Calvinistic Baptists, 1640–60* (Eugene, OR: Pickwick Publications, 2017), pp. 28–30.

97 Owens (ed.), *The Ilston Book*, p. 40.

98 B. R. White (ed.), *Association Records of the Particular Baptists of England, Wales and Ireland to 1660: Part 1, South Wales and the Midlands* (London: Baptist Historical Society, 1971), pp. 1–17.

99 White (ed.), *Association Records of the Particular Baptists of England, Wales and Ireland to 1660*, p. 10.

100 Myles, *An Antidote against the Infection of the Times*, p. 1; hereafter page references will be made in the text.

101 Nuttall, *The Welsh Saints, 1640–60*, pp. 55–73; Jenkins, *Protestant Dissenters in Wales, 1639–89*, pp. 33–8.

102 Thomas, *Hanes y Bedyddwyr Ymhlith y Cymry*, pp. 66–86.

103 Tudur Jones, *Vavasor Powell*, p. 138.

104 'Confession of Faith', pp. 36–7.

105 'Confession of Faith', p. 37.

106 Jenkins, *The Foundations of Modern Wales, 1642–1780*, p. 66.

107 See Chapter One, p. 64.

108 Edwards, *Gangraena*, Part I, Division 2, p. 24.

109 Francis Cheynell, *An account given to the Parliament by the ministers sent by them to Oxford … [concerning] divers of Mr. Erbury's dangerous errours* (London: Samuel Gellibrand, 1647), p. 51.

110 See Brian Ll. James, 'The evolution of a radical: the life and career of William Erbury (1604–59)', *JWEH*, 3 (1986), 31–48.

111 [William Erbury], *Nor Truth nor Errour, nor Day nor Night … being the relation of a Public Discourse in Mary's Church at Oxford, between Mt Cheynell and Mr Erbury* (London: n.p., 1647), p. 7.

[112] [Erbury], *Nor Truth nor Errour, nor Day nor Night*, p. 6.

[113] [Erbury], *Nor Truth nor Errour, nor Day nor Night*, p. 7.

[114] [Erbury], *Nor Truth nor Errour, nor Day nor Night*, p. 4.

[115] [Erbury], *Nor Truth nor Errour, nor Day nor Night*, p. 8.

[116] John I. Morgans, *The Honest Heretique: the Life and Work of William Erbury (1604–54)* (Tal-y-bont: Y Lolfa, 2012), p. 79.

[117] William Erbury, *The Lord of Hosts, or God guarding the Camp of the Saints* (London: Giles Calvert, 1648), p. 19.

[118] Erbury, *The Lord of Hosts*, p. 32.

[119] Erbury, *The Lord of Hosts*, p. 40.

[120] For Erbury's contribution to the Whitehall Debates, see Morgans, *The Honest Heretique: the Life and Work of William Erbury*, pp. 93–7.

[121] Jenkins, *The Foundations of Modern Wales, 1642–1780*, p. 50.

[122] William Erbury, *The Grand Oppressor, or, the Terror of Tithes* (London: Giles Calvert, 1652), p. 50.

[123] William Erbury, *A Scourge for the Assyrian* (London: Giles Calvert, 1652), p. 91.

[124] For a précis, see Morgans, *The Honest Heretique: the Life and Work of William Erbury*, pp. 127–45.

[125] William Erbury, *Apocrypha* (London: n.p., 1652), p. 9.

[126] Erbury, *Apocrypha*, p. 10; for Llwyd's indebtedness to Erbury, see M. Wynn Thomas, *Morgan Llwyd: ei Gyfeillion a'i Gyfnod* (Caerdydd: Gwasg Prifysgol Cymru, 1992), pp. 103–19.

[127] Llwyd, *Gweithiau Morgan Llwyd o Wynedd*, vol. 2, p. 257.

[128] William Erbury, *A Call to the Churches, or a Packet of Letters to the pastors of Wales … with a postscript of a Welsh dispute* (1653), quoted from *The Testimony of William Erbery, left upon record for the saints of succeeding ages* (London: n.p., 1658), p. 221; the nature of this dispute is analysed in B. R. White, 'William Erbury and the Baptists', *BQ*, 23 (1969), 114–25.

[129] William Erbury, *A Dispute at Cowbridge, with Mr Henry Nichols, Pastor of an Independent Church* (London: n.p., 1653).

[130] Henry Nichols, *The Shield Single against the Sword Doubled* (London: H. Cripps and L. Lloyd, 1653), p. 5.

[131] Nichols, *The Shield Single against the Sword Doubled*, p. 8.

[132] Nichols, *The Shield Single against the Sword Doubled*, p. 10.

[133] Nichols, *The Shield Single against the Sword Doubled*, p. 32.

[134] They are analysed in full in Morgans, *The Honest Heretique: the Life and Work of William Erbury*, pp. 188–336.

[135] Christine Trevett, 'William Erbury and his daughter Dorcas: Dissenter and Resurrected Radical', *JWRH*, 4 (1996), 23–50.

[136] Anon., *A Winding-sheet for Mr. Baxter's dead*, p. 3.

[137] D. G. Hart, *Calvinism: A History* (New Haven: Yale University Press, 2013), p. 88.

[138] John Lewis, *Some Seasonable and Modest Thoughts, in order to the Furtherance and Promoting the Affairs of Religion and the Gospel, especially in Wales* (London:

N. Ekins, 1656), p. 29; page references will be made in the text; for Lewis (d.1672), see *ODNB* and *DWB.*

139 Cited in Geoffrey F. Nuttall, 'The correspondence of John Lewis Glasgrug with Richard Baxter and with Dr John Ellis, Dolgellau', *JMHRS*, 2 (1954), 120–34 (125).

140 Nuttall, 'The correspondence of John Lewis Glasgrug with Richard Baxter and with Dr John Ellis, Dolgellau', 120.

141 A. H. Dodd, 'New England influences in early Welsh Puritanism', *BBCS*, 16 (1954), 30–7 (30).

142 See A. H. Dodd, *The Character of Early Welsh Emigration to the United States* (Cardiff: University of Wales Press, 1956).

143 See Chapter One, p. 62.

144 Michael McGiffert (ed.), *God's Plot: Puritan Spirituality in Thomas Shepard's Cambridge* (Amherst: University of Massachusetts Press, 1994); for Shepard see *ODNB.*

145 Harry S. Stout, *The New England Soul: Preaching and Religious Culture in Colonial New England*, 2nd edn (New York: Oxford University Press, 2012), p. 42; for the text see J. A. Albro (ed.), *The Works of Thomas Shepard*, vol. 1 (Boston, MA: Doctrinal Tract and Book Society, 1853), pp. 9–114.

146 Nehemiah Adams (ed.), *The Autobiography of Thomas Shepard* (Boston, MA: Pierce and Parker, 1832), p. 20; hereafter page numbers are in the text.

147 E. Brooks Holifield, *Theology in America: Christian Thought from the Age of the Puritans to the Civil War* (New Haven: Yale University Press, 2003), p. 43.

148 Norman Pettit, *The Heart Prepared: Grace and Conversion in Puritan Spiritual Life*, 2nd edn (Middletown, CT: Wesleyan University Press, 1989), p. 108.

149 See W. K. B. Stoever, *'A Fair and Easie Way to Heaven': Covenant Theology and Antinomianism in Early Massachusetts* (Middletown, CT: Wesleyan University Press, 1978), *passim.*

150 Holifield, *Theology in America*, p. 44.

151 Thomas Shepard, *Y Cywir Ddychwelwr, yn datguddio y nifer bychan o'r rhai gwir gredadwy ... o gyfieithiad R. E.* (London: Thomas Brewster), Sig. A2r; hereafter page numbers are in the text.

152 David Ceri Jones, 'Calvinistic Methodism and the Reformed tradition in eighteenth century Wales', in Tadhg Ó hAnnracháin and Robert Armstrong (eds), *Christianities in the Early Modern Celtic World* (Basingstoke: Palgrave Macmillan, 2014), pp. 164–78 (169).

153 For Matthews's career, see E. Stanley John, 'Marmaduke Matthews a Richard Blinman: eu teuluoedd a'u cyfraniad', *Y Cofiadur*, 60 (1996), 3–25; the Antinomian Controversy is treated in Pettit, *The Heart Prepared*, pp. 125–57 and Stoever, *'A Fair and Easie Way to Heaven'*, pp. 21–34; for the genesis of Congregationalism see Perry Miller, *The New England Mind: the Seventeenth Century*, 2nd edn (Cambridge, MA: The Belknap Press, 1962), pp. 432–62 and Bremer, *Congregational Communion*, pp. 104–22.

154 Marmaduke Matthews, *The Messiah Magnified by the mouths of babes in America* (London: Simon Miller, 1659), Sig. A2r; hereafter page numbers are in the text.

155 Nuttall, *Visible Saints: The Congregational Way, 1640–60*, pp. 11–17.

156 Edmund S. Morgan, *Visible Saints: The History of a Puritan Idea* (Ithaca, NY: Cornell University Press, 1965), pp. 64–112.

157 Morgan, *Visible Saints: The History of a Puritan Idea*, pp. 73, 93.

158 Marmaduke Matthews, *The Rending Church Member, regularly called back to Christ and to his Church* (London: Simon Millar, 1659), p. 36; hereafter page numbers are in the text.

159 R. Tudur Jones, *Congregationalism in Wales*, ed. Robert Pope (Cardiff: University of Wales Press, 2004), p. 36.

160 See E. Brooks Holifield, *The Covenant Sealed: the Development of Puritan Sacramental Theology in Old and New England, 1570–1720* (New Haven: Yale University Press, 1974), pp. 145–59.

161 Morgan, *Visible Saints: The History of a Puritan Idea*, pp. 113–38; Holifield, *The Covenant Sealed*, pp. 169–96.

162 There seem to be no extant copies of a third publication by Matthews, namely his *New Congregational Church* (1659).

163 Mordecai (1635?–1702) became rector of Reynoldston on the Gower Peninsula and Manasses (1640–81) was appointed vicar of Swansea, see John, 'Marmaduke Matthews a Richard Blinman: eu teuluoedd a'u cyfraniad', 5–11.

164 Samuel Palmer, *The Nonconformist's Memorial ... originally written by the Reverend and Learned Edmund Calamy DD*, vol. 2 (London: W. Harris, 1715), p. 627.

165 Palmer, *The Nonconformist's Memorial*, pp. 627–8.

166 Rice Rees (ed.), *Y Seren Foreu, neu Ganwyll y Cymry, sef gwaith prydyddol y Parch. Rhys Prichard MA, gynt ficer Llanymddyfri* (Llanymddyfri: W. Rees, 1841), p. 314.

167 Richards, *A History of the Puritan Movement in Wales, 1639–53*, pp. 52–3, 115–33.

168 Richards, *A History of the Puritan Movement in Wales, 1639–53*, pp. 143–4.

169 W. J. Gruffydd, *Llenyddiaeth Cymru: Rhyddiaith o 1540 hyd 1660* (Wrecsam: Hughes a'i Fab, 1926), pp. 128–31; Henry Lewis (ed.), *Hen Gyflwyniadau* (Caerdydd: Gwasg Prifysgol Cymru, 1948), pp. 25–8; John Gwynfor Jones, 'Language, Literature and Education', in Madeleine Gray and Prys Morgan (eds), *The Gwent County History, Vol. 3, The Making of Monmouthshire, 1536–1780* (Cardiff: University of Wales Press, 2009), pp. 285–311 (294–5).

170 [John Edwards], 'Siôn Tre-rhedyn', *Madruddyn y Difinyddiaeth Diweddaraf* (Llundain: William Ballard, 1651), Epistle dedicatory; page numbers will be made in the text.

171 William Van Doodewaard, '"To walk according to the gospel": the origin and history of *The Marrow of Modern Divinity*', *PRJ*, 2 (2009), 96–114.

172 See Chapter One, pp. 48–9.

173 Cf. Judith Maltby, 'Suffering and Surviving: the Civil Wars, the Commonwealth and the formation of "Anglicanism", 1642–60', in C. Durston and J. Maltby, *Religion in Revolutionary England* (Manchester: Manchester University Press, 2006), pp. 158–80.

174 John Walker, *An Attempt towards recovering an Account of the Numbers and Sufferings of the Clergy*, Part 1 (London: J. Nicholson, R. Knaplock, R. Wilkin, 1714), p. 163; Powell is listed in *DWB*.

175 Thomas Powell, *Cerbyd Jechydwriaeth, neu Prif Byngciau Grefydd Gristnogawl wedi eu egluro a'u gosod allan* (London: Philip Chetwind, 1657), Sig. v2; page references will be made in the text.

176 Henry Vaughan, *The Mount of Olives, or Solitary Devotions* (London: William Leake, 1652), in *Henry Vaughan: Poetry and Selected Prose*, ed. L. C. Martin (Oxford: Oxford University Press, 1963), p. 131.

177 A[lexander] G[riffith], *A True and perfect relation ... concerning the Petition of the Six Counties of South Wales ... for a supply of Godly Ministers* (London: Mathew Ekins, 1654), p. 50.

178 Chapter One, p. 46.

179 For an earlier clash between Griffith and Powell, see Tudur Jones, *Vavasor Powell*, pp. 55–7.

180 For his work, see Gwyn Thomas, 'Rowland Vaughan', in Geraint Bowen, *Y Traddodiad Rhyddiaith* (Llandysul: Gwasg Gomer, 1970), pp. 231–46 and *ODNB*.

181 Described in detail in *Diaries and Letters of Philip Henry MA, of Broad Oak, Flintshire*, ed. Matthew Henry Lee (London: Kegan Paul and Trench, 1882), pp. 34–7; Thomas Richards, *Religious Developments in Wales, 1654–62* (London: National Eisteddfod Association, 1923), pp. 166–7; for Henry (1631–96) see *ODNB*.

182 Mathew Henry, *The Life of the Rev. Philip Henry* (1698), ed. J. B. Williams (Edinburgh: Banner of Truth, 1974), p. 60.

183 Rowland Vaughan, Intro. to William Brough, *Prifannau Sanctaidd neu Lawlyfr o Weddïau*, trans. Rowland Vaughan (London: Philip Chetwind, 1658), Sig. 2v.

184 Rowland Vaughan, Intro. to James Ussher, *Prifannau Crefydd Gristnogawl*, trans. Rowland Vaughan (London: Philip Chetwind, 1658), Sig. 4r.

185 William Nicholson, *A Plain but Full Exposition of the Catechism of the Church of England* (London: Nathaniel Webb and William Grantham, 1655), Sig. A1r, 'to all his loving parishioners of Llandilo-Vawr'; Bryan D. Spinks categorizes Nicholson's doctrinal views as being 'Patristic Reformed', *Sacraments, Ceremonies and the Stuart Divines: Sacramental Theology and Liturgy in England 1603–62* (Aldershot: Ashgate, 2002), pp. 139–41.

186 Nicholson, *A Plain but Full Exposition of the Catechism of the Church of England*.

187 [Alexander Griffith], *Mercurius Cambro-Britannicus, or News from Wales touching the ... propagation of the gospel in those parts* (London: n.p., 1652), p. 8; cf. *Gemitus Ecclesiae Cambro-Britannicae, or, the candle-sticks removed, by the ejectment of the ministers of Wales* (London: n.p., 1654).

188 Griffith, *A True and perfect relation ... concerning the Petition of the Six Counties of South Wales*, pp. 20–1.

189 Jenkin Lloyd, *Christ's Valedictions, or Sacred Observations on the Last Words of our Saviour from the Cross* (London: D.M., 1658), pp. 35–6.

190 See John Lewis, *Contemplations upon These Times, or the Parliament Explained to Wales* (London: Nathaniel Webb and Thomas Grantham, 1646), pp. 22–7.

191 Cited in Nuttall, 'The correspondence of John Lewis Glasgrug with Richard Baxter and with Dr John Ellis, Dolgellau', 127.

192 Rowland Vaughan, *Yr Arfer o Weddi yr Arglwydd* (London: Philip Chetwind, 1658).

193 Cited in Nuttall, 'The correspondence of John Lewis Glasgrug with Richard Baxter and with Dr John Ellis, Dolgellau', 133.

194 An English translation, *A defence of the Thirty nine articles of the Church of England written in Latin by J. Ellis ... now done into English* (London: n.p., 1700) was issued later.

195 Rowland Watkyns, 'The Priesthood', *Flamma Sine Fumo* (1662), ed. Paul C. Davies (Cardiff: University of Wales Press, 1968), p. 91.

196 Cf. Nuttall, *Visible Saints: The Congregational Way, 1640–60*, pp. 43–69.

197 Vavasor Powell, *A Word in Season* (p. 9) in *The Bird in the Cage Chirping* (London: L. C., 1661).

198 Williams (ed.), *The Life of the Rev. Philip Henry*, p. 97.

199 Jenkins, *The Foundations of Modern Wales, 1642–1780*, p. 194.

3

1660–1689

The theology of post-Restoration Anglicanism in Wales

The northern dioceses: Bangor and St Asaph

In his handbook on Christian discipleship, *Trefn Ymarweddiad Gwir Gristion, neu lwybr hyffordd i'r Cymro i rodio arno beunydd gyda'i Dduw* (1662) ('The Right Conduct of a True Christian, or the path guiding the Welshman's daily walk with his God'), Edward Wynn, rector of the Anglesey parishes of Llangeinwen and Llangaffo, confirmed his unfeigned loyalty to the Restoration settlement. Among the admonitions he issued his parishioners was that they should ask daily God's blessing not only on the elect but on 'Charles, our gracious king and sovereign, Queen Catherine, Queen Mary, Prince James and all the royal progeny, all of the lords of council and all of the officers of the king'.[1] The discipline which he evoked was bracing: a daily regime of self-examination, prayer and severe moral endeavour through which the individual, the family and the parish congregation should strive after Christ's imputed righteousness and live a life which honoured God. Human sinfulness was a radical perversion of the soul: 'Our condition is wretched and miserable for of ourselves we can do nought but offend Thee and displease Thee' (p. 12). All were, in fact, the children of Adam, afflicted and forlorn, ravaged by wholesale depravity and standing ominously under the divine wrath: 'All our strength has been dissipated, our understanding has been darkened, our conscience has been seared and our will is hostile to Thee … Our whole behaviour is blameworthy before God and man' (p. 13). Men and women's only hope was to throw themselves on God's mercy in Christ who had taken upon himself their sins, and through sincere faith and costly repentance experience forgiveness, redemption and the regeneration of the soul. Salvation was through faith alone on the basis of Christ's unique sacrifice, vouchsafed by his resurrection from the dead:

> Make us hear the joyful cry of thy salvation at all times, and may the fruits of thy grace be revealed to us. Grant us faith in thy promises, peace of conscience, joy in the Holy Spirit, zeal for good works and a sure indication of our eternal delight. (p. 14)

Wynn (1618–69), a graduate of Jesus College, Cambridge who in 1662 supplicated for his university's DD degree, had been curate to the biblical and renaissance scholar Dr John Davies at Mallwyd and, after 1644, had married his mentor's widow.[2] Despite expulsion for a temporary and unspecified lapse in 1650, he had been confirmed to the living of Llanymawddwy, Merionethshire, by the Committee for the Propagation of the Gospel in Wales, before transferring to his Anglesey living in 1658. He personified the Reformed consensus of the Welsh church prior to the Interregnum, whose commitment to Episcopal government and Prayer Book discipline matched though never overshadowed their Calvinistic orthodoxy and evangelical zeal. Like so many others, he conformed to Richard Baxter's description of 'the old common moderate sort' of Episcopalian, who were

> in doctrine Calvinists and took episcopacy to be necessary *ad bene esse ministerii et ecclesiae*, but not *ad esse*; and took all those of the Reformed that had not bishops for true churches and ministers, wanting only that which they thought would make them more complete.[3]

In theological terms, he was a conformist, moderate Puritan, keen above all to train up his people in practical godliness.

If the doctrinal underpinning of Edward Wynn's parochial practice was Reformed, the admonition to his flock included the devotional and liturgical use of the Apostles' Creed, the Litany replete with audible responses, as well as the *Te Deum*. A strict Sabbatarian, he urged his parishioners to fashion their lives on the Decalogue and, when called by their minister (*gweinidog*, not 'priest'), to prepare assiduously for partaking of the sacrament by fasting, almsgiving, the devotional reading of Matthew 26, Luke 22 and I Cor. 11, and solemn prayer. Only those who had sincerely repented of their sins and whose 'nakedness had been covered by the wedding garment and clothed with the righteousness of the Lord Jesus' (p. 100) were fit to approach his table. If the Supper was designed to confirm the saints in the Christian way, assuring them of their incorporation, through faith, into Christ's body, baptism was the sacrament of initiation, signifying 'death to sin and a new birth to righteousness, as, although we are born in sin and are the children of wrath, through baptism we are made the children of grace' (p. 126). Although he uses realistic language and concrete terms, Wynn is careful not to imply the concept of *ex opere operato*. Regeneration, though implied in the sacrament, only occurs through faith which required a considered, responsible affirmation on the part of those who in infancy had been baptized. Cranmer's sacramental realism is toned down somewhat in this exposition, but it is clear that the rector of Llangeinwen and Llangaffo strove to be faithful to the teaching of the Book of Common Prayer.

Yet for Edward Wynn the principal function of the minister was to preach the gospel. Faith came through hearing, and hearing came through the exposition of God's Word. Again and again he implores his parishioners to pray for God's blessing on their pastor's pulpit labours and that the Lord would send more labourers to gather the harvest. He also provided his flock with an appropriate prayer:

> O Merciful Father, who saw fit through the foolishness of preaching to save those who believe, may it please Thee through the power of thy Holy Spirit and the preaching of thy holy Word, to create in my heart a true and living faith, and establish me in it, through which I can take possession of Christ Jesus' merits for my justification and eternal salvation. (p. 84)

This is as good an example of the perpetuation of so-called 'Anti-Arminianism' or traditional Reformed churchmanship, within the post-Restoration Anglican Church as one could hope to find.[*] Wynn was elected member of convocation in 1661–2, canon of St Asaph in 1663 and thereafter canon chancellor of Bangor Cathedral. He died, aged fifty-one, in 1669. However pervasive the influence of a renewed Laudian-type prelacy would become in the four Welsh dioceses following the Restoration, the significance of Wynn's brand of piety should not be discounted. It would help ensure the remarkable success of the SPCK in affording godly literature during the following decades, and provide the impetus, during the next century, for the educational and evangelistic labours of Griffith Jones, Llanddowror. Not all Anglican theology in Wales – in fact remarkably little of it – would be dry, formalist and Arminian.

There is little doubt, however, that the policy re-introduced by Wynn's diocesan William Roberts, the only pre-Interregnum bishop to be restored to his diocese, was in the High Church tradition. A nephew of Gabriel Goodman, former dean of Westminster, and protégé of the late William Laud, he had been instituted to his bishopric as early as 1637 and following his expulsion in 1640 had spent the Commonwealth years quietly at his Denbighshire estate.[5] His re-establishment in 1660 led to the refurbishment of the neglected cathedral and the reinstatement of its services along sacramentalist lines; he left money in his will for the installation of an organ. His successor, Robert Price, was only in post for a few months before passing away in 1666. He was followed by Robert Morgan, a Cambridge-educated native of Montgomeryshire and former chaplain to William Roberts who, despite his pronounced royalist sympathies, had retained the Anglesey living of Llanddyfnan during the Commonwealth. Elected to the prebend of Penmynydd in the cathedral chapter at the Restoration while holding the archdeaconry of Merioneth *in commendam*, he combined his predecessor's High Church discipline with a conviction that experiential piety should not be merely a Puritan prerogative. A conscientious preacher whose unembellished, scripturally based sermons 'called for a keener awareness of the state of the soul and the overwhelming necessity of regeneration', he contributed to the post-Restoration accord which strove for spiritual renewal in the parishes along with liturgical worship according to the Book of Common Prayer.[6] This conviction was not shared by the formalist and virulently anti-Dissenting Humphrey Lloyd, dean of St Asaph, who was elected Morgan's successor in 1674, though it found an energetic supporter in Humphrey Humphreys, Morgan's son-in-law who would serve from 1680 as Bangor Cathedral's dean. A native of Penrhyndeudraeth and former fellow of Jesus College, Oxford, Humphreys would become by far the most impressive cleric in the diocese. Ordained in Bangor Cathedral by Bishop Morgan in 1670, he displayed administrative ability, scholarly acumen, spiritual insight and rare pastoral sensitivity. His election as Lloyd's successor in 1689 was greeted with much satisfaction: 'Humphreys … claimed to know every parish and clergyman in Bangor when he was promoted from dean to bishop'.[7] Unlike his predecessor, he would prove unstinting in his support for the SPCK and did more than anyone to enhance the reputation of the Established Church in the diocese and beyond.

The High Church, sacramentalist emphasis favoured during the episcopate of Humphrey Lloyd is reflected in works published by two north Wales clergymen in the early 1680s, namely *Unum Necessarium: Ymarferol Athrawiaeth Gweddi* (1680) ('The One thing Necessary: A Practical Doctrine of Prayer') by John Thomas, rector of Penegoes near Machynlleth, and *Egwyddor i rai Ieuaingc i'w cymhwyso i dderbyn y Cymmun Sanctaidd yn fuddiol* (1682) by Edward Lloyd, the aged incumbent of Llangower in the neighbouring diocese of St Asaph who, despite the upheaval of the Commonwealth, had served his flock on the shores of Bala Lake since as far back as 1639. (His son, William Lloyd, would become in turn bishop of Llandaff, Peterborough and Norwich; see below.) This was a translation of *A Book for Beginners, or a help to young communicants* (1680) by Simon Patrick, the dean of Peterborough and later bishop of Ely. The accent in both these volumes is not so much on the necessity to respond to the preached Word but on holy living and obedience, especially to established order, made manifest primarily through prayer and the frequent partaking of the Lord's Supper. Free will and the universal extent of Christ's sacrifice are taken for granted, and the doctrine of election does not feature at all. With the tumult of the civil wars having receded, by now the canon to judge all things spiritual was scripture, apostolic tradition and the dispassionate application of detached reason. Episcopal grace is highly valued: 'Through the laying on of the bishop's hands', claimed Lloyd, 'more divine grace is dispensed establishing and strengthening your Christian endeavour, so that you will belong to God for ever more.'[8] The piety elucidated in these works presupposes a synergy between human effort and divine grace and the aim is moral progression and gradual spiritual growth: 'As I have already committed myself to keeping my promises, I can happily and faithfully obey the divine will in all things, and through the help of thy Holy Spirit I can grow daily until I reach thy eternal kingdom.'[9] Whereas Lloyd's treatise is measured and serene, Thomas frequently supplements his often valuable comments on the discipline of prayer – 'What is prayer? In short, prayer is the regular and earnest lifting up of the heart to God the Father who is always ready and able to hear and to answer'[10] – with barbed references to Romanists and Dissenters:

> The papists in their darkened superstition, in an unknown tongue, mumble scores of Ave Marias and Pater Nosters. It is said that Macarius prayed fifty times a day, one Paulus made three hundred supplications in a single morning and Sisinus prayed constantly doing nothing else for three whole years. (p. 7)

The benchmark of true spirituality was the Prayer Book which contains 'our own Church's exceedingly excellent prayers, which are like crutches for a lame man and a life jacket allowing he who cannot swim to reach the shore' (Sig. A3v). As for the Dissenters, it was they, 'loathsome hypocrites', who during the late troubles became drunk on the blood of a justly instituted king 'who is now blessed, a saint and glorious martyr in heaven' (p. 34). For all its righteous anger, there is nothing in Thomas's work that compares with the lyrical vignette, reminiscent of the famous introduction to Erasmus's Greek New Testament of 1519, in which the aged rector of Llangower visualizes the reciting of psalms among the faithful:

> There is nothing more satisfying than to hear the labourer sing them when following the plough, the sailor on the deck of his ship, the boatman as he rows, the weaver as he weaves, the gentlewoman as she spins, the miner spade in hand, the children at play, in fact all who have taken them as with their mothers' milk and have learned since childhood to recite the sweet music of these holy songs.[11]

It was in the two northern dioceses of Bangor and St Asaph – the disastrous interlude under Bishop Glemham, 1667–70, notwithstanding (see below) – that the institutional renewal of the Church proved most effective. Each of the Bangor diocesans, as we have seen, was not only scholarly, diligent and accomplished, but they were Welsh-speaking natives of the region and, in Humphrey's case particularly, deeply rooted in its cultural mores. Likewise, the new bishop of St Asaph, George Griffith, was a native of Anglesey whose education at Westminster School and Christ Church, Oxford (where he was awarded the DD in 1634), had done nothing to lessen his commitment to the Church in his native land. Described as being a 'Low-Churchman', his doctrinal views had been well attested in his dispute with the radical Puritan Vavasor Powell at Welshpool in July 1652.[12] The point of contention between them had not been the nature of the gospel, on which they agreed, but whether congregationalism or the parish system best reflected God's will for the governance of his church and whether the church should be composed of committed believers or 'saints' or whether it was a wider gathering of all those who had been baptized. Appointed archdeacon of St Asaph in 1632 and rector of Llanymynech in the same diocese, he retained his living during the Interregnum though his diocesan post had been terminated with the abolition of episcopacy in 1646. During the dispute Griffith described himself as 'an Episcopal Presbyterian',[13] holding to Archbishop Ussher's concept of a non-prelatical episcopacy in which the bishop shared authority with his fellow clergy.[14] Although his detractors accused him of refusing to abandon the surplice, of still using the cross in baptism, of referring to churches as consecrated buildings and administering the sacrament to immoral parishioners (all of which illustrated that, at a parish level with the incumbent still *in situ*, the church in the Diocese of St Asaph had functioned more or less as usual during the Interregnum), he regarded himself as being a regularly ordained minister of a reformed and biblically sound church.[15] For Griffith, a congregational polity would be inherently schismatic; its establishment would unchurch those who had been baptized and confirmed on the basis of a credible confession of faith: 'The scripture speaketh of two sorts of saints, some of special calling and election of grace, others by general vocation to, and profession of the name of Christ.'[16] In the judgement of charity, all who had made such a profession were to be treated as true believers. Liturgical prayer (which was anathema to Powell) not only preserved order and decency in worship but had been sanctioned by Christ himself in Luke 11. When challenged to explain how the image of Christ was wrought on the soul, he answered 'instantly without prompting, "Inwardly by the Spirit, outwardly by the Word"'.[17] This could hardly be faulted even by his most zealous opponents. Doctrinally, therefore, he held to a middle-of-the-road Reformed Protestantism, and this would be the tenor of his diocesan policy following his nomination to the see in October 1660 and his installation a month later.[18]

Gweddi'r Arglwydd wedi ei hegluro ('The Lord's Prayer explained') (1685), a series of twenty-two short sermons expounding the Lord's Prayer issued posthumously in George Griffith's name by William Foulkes, rector of Llanfyllin, encapsulates the tone of the bishop's pastoral teaching and conveys the nature of doctrinal instruction within the diocese at its best between the Restoration and the accession of William and Mary in 1689. 'The soul of prayer is faith,' he claimed, 'but its articulation is its body.'[19] Formalism must be avoided and no prayer is valid if it does not issue from the work of the Spirit within, yet this does not invalidate the use of forms; in fact such forms are essential for true prayer to be profitable. Recollecting, possibly, the abrasive altercation with Vavasor Powell and his supporters years earlier, he emphasized the need for deference in matters of the spirit:

> This caused the Church from the outset, following the example of her Lord, to teach the people set forms, while general councils ordained that no prayers should be used apart from those hallowed by steadfast use and authorized by the Church herself. (p. 15)

God's fatherhood, his sanctity, his glory and transcendence are strongly emphasized, while the individual petitions offered the opportunity to teach his hearers about the divine attributes and the different names of God contained in scripture. As with the work of Edward Wynn in the neighbouring diocese of Bangor, Griffith entreats them to pray for renewal among the faithful:

> To the extent that God works these things within us and we learn that through the preaching of his Word and the ministry of his Church, we implore that he would bless our parishes by providing us with teachers of righteousness, proven by God and blameless before men, rightly dividing the word of truth. (p. 42)

By praying for the coming of the kingdom, namely the kingdom of his grace, his power and his glory, God's purposes will be fulfilled partially in the course of human history but ultimately beyond it. The souls of the righteous, their sins having been forgiven and perfected through divine grace, would be blessed though still awaiting the resurrection when the whole of creation would be renewed: 'God's kingdom then will have arrived when he will rule over all and in all, there will no longer be disobedience or rebellion or any tendency to evil or aversion to God' (p. 48); Satan himself will have been dethroned and the consummation of all things would have occurred. The only condition was that his hearers would come to Christ:

> No-one can come to him in their own strength, but having been regenerated by his Spirit, taught by his Word, nourished by his sacraments

and truly repentant, they will be led to the kingdom of his grace and thus enjoy the promised blessings of his everlasting kingdom. (p. 51)

For God's will to be done on earth as it was in heaven, the faithful were charged with striving to be obedient to his commandments knowing full well that Christ alone had fulfilled them in total. At this juncture Griffiths could not resist displaying his erudition. Quoting Cyprian and other patristic authorities, he expatiated on the difference between God's secret will and his revealed will and the meaning of the phrases *De hâc voluntate nec opus est petere, nec rectè aut piè quicquam est petere* and the like, before returning to simple Welsh in order to urge his listeners to fulfil their duty:

> Even though no one but Christ himself could accomplish the law in full and do God's will perfectly, yet every true Christian has it in his heart, like David, to follow God's commandments to the end ... Thereby the spirit of grace (which according to the promise has been poured out in greater abundance under the gospel) will comfort them and help them, and by so doing God, through the merits of Christ (who fulfilled the law for us and in our place), will make up for that which we cannot do. (p. 67)

Although sacramental teaching is not prominent in Griffith's exposition, the petition concerning 'our daily bread' prompted him to offer instruction on the Lord's Supper. Here he is nearer to Cranmer's doctrine (and Calvin's) than to Zwingli, and in treating the sacrament of baptism, unlike Edward Wynn, he does not balk at the idea of baptismal regeneration or, in this context, of the real presence. Just as God provides earthly bread for his creatures, he has appointed spiritual bread for those who have been born anew.

> After vivifying them through baptism, he gave them food for their sustenance, namely the Lord's Supper, to feed their souls in the sure hope of eternal life. For it has been promised that whoever partakes of this sacrament according to Christ's mandate, that he will feed them through the virtue of his crucified body and his shed blood ... For this purpose Christ himself is active in the sacrament of the communion of the Lord's body and blood. And this communion cannot be of absent things but of present things; there could be no Lord's Supper were the Lord's body and blood not present. (pp. 102–3)

Christ's spiritual presence is to be found in the bread, though he offers no metaphysical explanation after the fact. Echoing I Cor. 12:27, he is insistent that the believer can only feed on Christ through faith: '[He] is present to feed us in the sacrament through a spiritual union between the worthy partaker and Christ, and a sacramental union between the body and blood of Christ and the external elements of the sacrament' (p. 103). Whereas the doctrine is catholic, he eschews totally the Roman concept of *ex opere operato*. For Griffith, the classic Protestant teaching of the *Ecclesia Anglicana* since the days of Thomas Cranmer and the 39 Articles included a high doctrine of both the sacrament and the Word. Although it had been reported to William Sancroft, Archbishop of Canterbury, in June 1678, that the clergy of the St Asaph diocese were mostly 'illiterate and contemptible',[20] there were others among them, not least William Foulkes (who also served as a canon in the cathedral as well as rector of Llanfyllin),[21] who strove earnestly to make his late diocesan's teaching a reality in the parishes. It was instruction such as this that typified the ministry of the more conscientious clergy of the day.

George Griffith was followed in the see in 1667 by Henry Glemham, formerly dean of Bristol, who had been traduced by Samuel Pepys as being 'a drunken swearing rascal and a scandal to the Church'.[22] His preferment had been due to the influence at court of his niece Barbara Villiers, countess of Castlemain and mistress of Charles II. It was with a sense of relief that he, in turn, was replaced in 1670 by Isaac Barrow, a pronounced Laudian in churchmanship and formerly bishop of Sodor and Man. Despite being an active reformer, repairing the fabric of the cathedral and the bishop's residence in St Asaph and attempting to find fresh sources of income in order to improve the impoverished nature of the diocese, his ignorance of Welsh and generally alien disposition militated against his effectiveness in the post.[23] Nevertheless one highly significant work of theology which appeared from a diocesan author during this period, in 1672, was a superior translation of the High Church Richard Allestree's immensely popular devotional handbook *The Whole Duty of Man* (1657) by John Langford, the rector of Efnechtyd in Denbighshire. Intended to show 'the very meanest reader' how 'to behave himself so in this world that he may be forever happy in the next',[24] its prescription of morality, duty and effort is balanced by an emphasis on divine grace fed by regular Prayer Book worship and the sacrament which was becoming characteristic of emerging 'Anglican' piety: '*The Whole Duty* epitomized the commonsensical, non-controversial, brand of theology on offer in the Restoration Church of England'.[25] Its seventeen chapters on duties to God, to oneself and to one's neighbour were divided in a way which allowed the book to be read through three times each year, while it also contained many pithy, succinct and biblically informed prayers. Of all devotional manuals issued during the later Stuart era, *Holl Ddledswydd Dyn* was the most generally acceptable. Promoted vigorously by the SPCK and appreciated by churchman and Dissenter alike, it was republished frequently and remained popular well into the eighteenth century.[26] Although patently 'Anglican', it was in no way formalist or over-sacramental, while its orthodox, biblical tone presupposed shared truths such as repentance, justification by faith and the need to appropriate personally the fruits of Christ's atoning sacrifice.

> Although the whole of humankind through the sin of Adam is under the judgement of eternal damnation, yet God saw fit to take pity on our wretchedness, and sent forth his Son to make a new covenant with us who had broken the original covenant … By taking our sins upon himself, not Adam's alone but the sins of all humankind, we are called to repent and obey his commandments, so that we too shall be forgiven and delivered from eternal damnation and hell … and by benefiting from his sacrifice, all our sins will be pardoned no matter how extensive and frequent they have been.[27]

Along with William Foulkes, John Langford and their like, another St Asaph cleric whose pastoral zeal could not be faulted was David Maurice (1626–1702), vicar of Abergele and Betws-yn-Rhos and some-time rector of Llanarmon-yn-Iâl and Llanasa. The son of a former dean of St Asaph, he graduated from Jesus College, became chaplain at New College and proceeded to the Oxford DD, thereafter he won respect for his support for the disadvantaged within his parishes and for bringing education to the needy. His sermon *A Bruised Reed*, Mat. 12:20, delivered at St Asaph Cathedral in 1688 (a Welsh version would be published in 1700), showed pastoral sensitivity of a high degree. Keen to assure his parishioners that even the weakest faith, if sincerely held, was enough to secure salvation, he emphasized the tenderness of Christ and the gracious nature of the gospel. A sense of assurance did not necessarily accompany what was, in fact, a real dependence on Christ for the forgiveness of sins:

> [Many] think they have no faith because they want the *assurance of*
> *faith* ... which is not of the essence of faith but a consequent of it, and
> a reflex act of the soul upon itself attained by a long continued course
> of holy and close walking with God which few believers have. But faith
> is a recumbent act of the soul upon Christ, and is usually expressed by
> the instance of one, that, having suffered shipwreck, cast himself upon a
> floating plank of the ship, and there sticks in a trembling, doubtful hope
> of coming ashore.[28]

Like Edward Wynn at Bangor, the tenor of this very engaging treatise is Reformed. Maurice holds to the fact that grace, though often
imperceptible, is nonetheless irresistible and that the saints, despite
their weaknesses, will be preserved to the end. The sacraments are not
mentioned though the preaching of the Word is deemed essential for
securing salvation. Although Maurice was held in esteem by the High
Church William Lloyd, Barrow's successor as diocesan, his name being
forwarded to Archbishop Sancroft as Lloyd's possible successor,[29] he
had also preached the funeral sermon for William Jones, the Dissenting
minister of Denbigh.[30] He and Jones had married two sisters. Despite
Maurice remaining a conscientious conformist, the two men shared doctrinal as well as familial bonds.

Another exceedingly profitable work though more in the vein of
The Whole Duty of Man was *Y Rhybuddiwr Christnogawl* (1689), a fine
translation made by the drover poet Edward Morris, Perthi-llwydion,
Denbighshire, of John Rawlet's *Christian Monitor* (1686).[31] Rawlet, a
Church of England clergyman who, although being a staunch conformist, remained a protégé of the nonconforming Richard Baxter,[32] had
risen from unpropitious beginnings and retained a clear sympathy for
the dispossessed. His handbook on Christian sanctification was brief,
clear and winsomely written and aimed at baptized if nominal members
of the Established Church: 'In sum, a good Christian is he who believes
resolutely in the Creed, and is careful to keep the commandments.'[33] It
calls its readers (or listeners: he expects its contents to be shared by
its owners with the illiterate) to improve on their baptismal vows
by living blameless lives based upon the gospel to which they had access
by faithful attendance at their parish church. The gospel message of
redemption, 'that our heavenly Father has taken pity upon us and sent
his Son from his bosom to be our saviour and redeemer, to rescue us
from our sins and so deliver us from ruin' (p. 10), was the only basis on

which the individual could live a life of virtue and usefulness to himself, his family and his neighbour:

> Let us not believe that Christ has died for our sins in order to make us free to live in them. No indeed; He has come to redeem us *from* our sins, not that we should remain *in* them ... Christ accounts no-one as his friends but those that keep his commandments and to those alone does he grant forgiveness and salvation. (p. 12)

The author urges the didactic use of the Prayer Book liturgy and its rhythm of prayer, praise, sacrament and Word. By attending faithfully the means of grace, worshippers would be in a position to exercise the obedience of faith which alone leads to salvation: 'It is through faith that we are granted forgiveness, through faith that we attain salvation, and true faith issues forth in obedience and makes us true and dutiful disciples of Jesus Christ' (p. 30). Although the human situation is dire, God's tender goodness both in the gospel and through the ministry of the Holy Spirit is such that he draws people to himself readily granting grace to repent and believe. Rawlet's concern for the poor shines through from every page, and it was probably this that attracted Morris, a layman and cultured artisan, to undertake the translation: 'Remember that Christ died for the poor as well as for the rich, and those who are bereft of an earthly inheritance will inherit the kingdom of heaven if they are rich in faith and love towards God' (p. 29). Those who had few of life's advantages were reticent to come to the Lord's Table:

> Do not say that you cannot come to communion for want of fine clothes, but come in the wedding garment that the gospel provides, namely a humble, contrite and grateful heart; as such you will be made welcome at the Lord's Table. (pp. 46–7)

For both author and translator, this volume was part of the campaign to spread gospel knowledge among the populace which had become such a central concern of earnest Christians during the late Stuart era:

> For those who desire further instruction, next to Holy Scripture I suggest that pious, useful book *The Whole Duty of Man*. This is my firm desire, that every poor family in the realm would be provided with a copy

along with a Bible and Book of Common Prayer which can be purchased very cheaply. (p. 61)

The Welsh translation had been sponsored by Margaret Vaughan of Llwydiarth, the matriarch of one of the key landed families of north Wales,[34] and it is striking that the author urges the gentry to do their utmost to support the poor by distributing edifying and evangelistic literature among them (pp. 62–3). This call would soon be heeded by such influential laymen as Sir John Philipps and John Vaughan of Derllys, Carmarthenshire, the principal Welsh supporters of the SPCK, thus instigating the subsequent phase of religious development among the people of Wales. As for Morris's volume, it would become nearly as popular as *Holl Ddledswydd Dyn* being reissued in 1699, 1706, 1789 and 1805.[35]

Whereas the translations of John Langford and Edward Morris were exercises in pastoral divinity, an original work by another St Asaph cleric, Rondl Davies, vicar of Meifod, was pointedly polemic. Davies (d.1691) had been instituted to his Montgomeryshire living by the Triers in 1647 and was affirmed there under the new regime by Bishop George Griffith in August 1661.[36] His earnest treatise *Profiad yr Ysbrydion, neu Ddatcuddiad Gau Athrawon, a rhybudd i'w gochelyd* ('Trying the Spirits, or an Exposure of False Prophets, and a warning to beware of them') (1675) is an apologia for the integrity of the Established Church in the face of Dissenting, notably Quaker, intransigence. Despite the hardships of the Clarendon Code, Quakerism remained in a fairly flourishing state in mid Wales at least until the crippling exodus to Pennsylvania after 1681, and was especially active in the parishes around Davies's home.[37] Indeed his daughter, Prudence, had even joined the local meeting and would later marry one of its members, a lowly blacksmith by trade. Although personal considerations undoubtedly coloured his attitude – 'Righteousness demands that those who are inferior remain subject to those above them', he asserted indignantly; 'Were this not the case anarchy would prevail'[38] – none the less there were serious doctrinal issues at stake as well. For the vicar of Meifod, the religious norm for all loyal subjects was that enshrined in the 39 Articles and the Book of Common Prayer which was being assailed by Papists on the one side and Dissenters on the other. Roman Catholics, he claimed, held to works righteousness and an inherent faith in the infallible authority of the pope. 'Holy Scripture', however, 'shows clearly that we are justified not by our own righteousness but by the righteousness of Christ which is imputed to us' (pp. 12–13). Transubstantiation is patently unbiblical; in the Lord's Supper we are bidden to partake of Christ spiritually, not corporeally: 'In the sacrament the outward signs, namely the bread and the wine, refer to the reality to which they signify, the body and blood of Christ of which we must partake worthily' (p. 28). All this is contained in the Book of Common Prayer which, faithfully reflecting the biblical Word, is our only trustworthy guide to salvation.

As for the sectaries, Davies was as apprehensive of the social levelling implicit in their witness as he was of their doctrinal stance. The calamity of the civil war was that it had challenged the bulwark of divinely instituted authority. The king was the Lord's anointed and to have risen up against him had been treason against God. Yet his main complaint against even moderate Dissent – the Quakers and the Anabaptists were clearly beyond the pale – was that they were in schism against what was a sound, scriptural and godly church. 'The means of grace and hence salvation', he averred, '(thanks be to God), are available in every parish church in Wales' (p. 116). Each possesses the liturgy, the creed, the Ten Commandments, the Psalms, stipulated readings from the Old Testament and the New, the two sacraments ordained by Christ himself, the homilies as well as conscientious preaching by duly instituted ministers which, were it heeded and acted upon in repentance and faith, would lead unquestionably to salvation: 'This accords with Christ's gospel, being "the power of God to salvation for all who believe" Rom. 1:15' (p. 116). How, therefore, could anyone judging fairly contemplate forsaking the established church of the realm? 'Such was the view of that learned man [John] Calvin who asserted that were the Word and sacrament to be found within a parish gathering, then undoubtedly the true church would be present' (p. 116). Consequently Dissenters were guilty of schism, an unlawful separation from the true church of God. With a battery of patristic references, mostly from Cyprian, the third-century bishop of Carthage, and Augustine's treatises against the Donatists, Davies claimed emphatically that the Established Church was the true church of the realm. As it possessed the pure Word of God and the faithful administration of baptism and the Lord's Supper, 'there is no doubt that she is a true Church of Christ wherein salvation is to be found' (p. 129).

Prayer Book worship as postulated by Davies along with the continued reception afforded to Langford's translation of *The Whole Duty of Man* and Edward Morris's version of *The Christian's Monitor* coincided with the marked improvement in diocesan life signalled by the institution in 1681 of William Lloyd, previously canon of Salisbury, prebendary of St Paul's and an energetic vicar of St Martins-in-the-Fields, Westminster. Although he had been born in Berkshire, his father's family was from Anglesey and Lloyd retained strong links with the Bangor diocese where he had held *commendam* livings, including the deanery of the cathedral, a decade earlier. A graduate and former fellow of Jesus College, Oxford, he well realized both the spiritual and cultural needs of his new diocese. By now the staunchly High Church (though resolutely anti-Catholic) nature of the diocese had been confirmed, and the new bishop, a vociferous anti-papal polemicist, was content to uphold it. (He had been ordained both priest and deacon clandestinely at Oxford at the height of the Commonwealth, consequently his High Churchmanship was beyond reproach.[39]) He immediately instigated sweeping reforms. He met with his clergy in synod in June 1681, consulting them about what 'things are amiss in the church and how every fault might be mended, and what is well may be improved'. Rural deans were appointed and incumbents were charged with compiling a *notitia*, listing conditions within their parishes, the numbers of households, the ages of those under sixteen, the level of Christian instruction that they had attained and whether they had been confirmed, the number of marriages performed during the previous year, who was under excommunication and the amount of money that had been spent on charities and pious causes, along with 'all those things which you think fit to impart for my information, or wherein you desire my advice'.[40] It was something of a novelty to have a bishop who not only took communion with his clergy but who dined with them as well. Although bracing, the new regime was very effective. In a second synod in 1683 among the topics discussed was 'the more decent and orderly administration of the holy offices'. In marked contrast to his two predecessors, Lloyd took seriously his responsibility to use Welsh, the only language that most of his flock could understand. He soon became sufficiently proficient 'to read it, to administer the sacraments, to confirm them and to officiate publicly among them in their own tongue, which was a means not only to render him more serviceable but of mightily endearing him to his people'.[41] A complex and contradictory figure, his surprisingly approachable attitude to the leading Dissenters within the diocese, including the Quakers, will be discussed below.

The diocesan renewal which occurred under William Lloyd inspired William Foulkes not only to issue the sermons of George Griffith, as we have seen, but to translate for the benefit of his fellow clergy and their parishioners a remarkable catechism which had recently been published by Thomas Ken, the bishop of Bath and Wells. In 1685 the ascetic and spiritually minded Ken who, along with Lloyd was one of the seven bishops to be imprisoned and later acquitted for their opposition to James II's second Declaration of Indulgence (1688),[42] published his *Practice of Divine Love*, a devotional exposition of the Church Catechism, along with a handbook entitled *The Church Catechism, with directions for prayer*, in which he encouraged his people to devise their own prayers using phrases culled from the Book of Common Prayer and other approved liturgies, and showed them how it could be done. Whereas the catechism itself follows the pattern of virtually all catechisms of the period, including an exposition of the Creed, the Decalogue, the Lord's Prayer and the sacraments,[43] the *Practice of Divine Love* manifested an intense sense of Christocentric devotion which was practically baroque in style: 'No other contemporary catechism has such a "devotion of rapture" which recalls the medieval "Bone Jesu" tradition, but is an authentically seventeenth-century devotion, Puritan as well as Caroline.'[44] Foulkes's fervent translation, *Esboniad ar Gatechism yr Eglwys neu Ymarfer o Gariad Dwyfol*, which included the *Directions for Prayer* (*Cyfarwyddiadau i Weddi*), appeared in 1688. Under the article 'crucified, dead and buried' in the Creed, he implores:

> O Thou merciful wonder, God incarnate on the cross, by what names shall I adore thee, all are too short, too meagre to express thee, love alone, there is nought but love that will reach thee, thou art love, O Jesus, thou art all love, O most tender, most sweet, most pure, dearest love, soften, sweeten, refine, love me into all love like thee!
>
> By the love of thy cross, O Jesus, I live, in it alone will I glory, that above all else will I study, that before all things will I value; by the love of thy cross I will take up my cross daily and follow thee; I will persecute, torment and crucify my sinful affections and lusts, which persecuted, tormented and crucified thee; and if thy love calls me to it, I will suffer on the cross for thee, as thou hast done for me.[45]

In the main, in devotional matters and aids for practical religion, the clergy and parishes of the two northern dioceses of the Established Church were well served during these decades. Alas (with one shining exception which will be treated below) the situation was not nearly so propitious in the south.

The southern dioceses: St David's and Llandaff

The largest of the Welsh sees and one of the most extensive within the province of Canterbury was St David's, covering the counties of Carmarthenshire, Cardiganshire and Pembrokeshire as well as much of Brecon and Radnorshire towards the English border. It was proverbially poor and its last pre-Restoration bishop, Roger Mainwaring, had died in 1653. In the meantime 'the Church of England in the diocese, as elsewhere, did not disappear as go underground'.[46] Although as many as 127 of its clergy had been dispossessed during the Commonwealth regime,[47] there is little evidence of clandestine ordinations or even of much overt use of the superseded Book of Common Prayer, but the fact that parochial and diocesan structures were re-established so swiftly in 1660 shows that the older tradition must have remained robust. The man chosen to lead the diocese at the Restoration was the sixty-eight year old William Lucy, a native of Hampshire and former rector of Highclare in that county, who, while at Cambridge in 1620 had provoked notoriety by vociferously opposing the Church of England's Reformed consensus.[48] An anti-Calvinist animus and absolutist concept of Episcopal authority had characterized his career ever after and were displayed to much effect in his *Treatise on the Nature of a Minister* (1670), written in 1650 but published two decades later in response to the New England Congregationalist Thomas Hooker's *Survey of the Summe of Church Discipline* (1648). Although assiduous in his labours in his new sphere and generous in paying for repairs to the collegiate chapel in Brecon, the bishop's houses at Brecon and Abergwili as well as the cathedral itself, his seventeen-year reign at St David's ensured that he became best known for nepotism, a cantankerous nature, the Anglicization of the see and zeal for implementing the most repressive aspects of the Clarendon Code.

Lucy's nepotism became blatant through his appointment soon after his consecration of his son Spencer as prebendary, cathedral treasurer and rector of Pen-y-bryn, Cardiganshire, two other sons, George and Robert, as joint-registrars of the diocese, and a fourth son, Richard, as cathedral chancellor.[49] His belligerent temperament came to the fore in his clash with William Nicholson, former vicar of Llandeilo, who had been appointed bishop of Gloucester while at the same time holding the archdeaconry of Brecon, and thereafter in a further protracted altercation with Thomas Aubrey, his diocesan chancellor.[50] As archdeacon, Nicholson believed that he had the right to hold regular visitations and collect the relevant dues which he proceeded to do, first at Michaelmas

1663 and again in the autumn of 1664. To this Lucy objected bitterly and complained to Gilbert Sheldon, Archbishop of Canterbury. The bishops of London and St Asaph were called in to arbitrate and adjudicated in his favour by which time his reputation for obduracy had been well established. It was further entrenched through his feud with Thomas Aubrey, whose brother, Sir John Aubrey of Llantrithyd, Glamorgan, was one of the Archbishop of Canterbury's intimates: 'Gilbert Sheldon ... and Sir John Aubrey [had] contracted a great friendship at Oxford in their youth, which continued to their deaths'.[51] Aubrey had been appointed to his post by Roger Mainwaring, Lucy's predecessor, in 1641 and was keen to return to his post when the Commonwealth regime was terminated. The bishop, however, was insistent in establishing his own protégé, John Cruso, rector of Great Yarmouth, in the position. Aubrey took the matter first to the king, then to the Court of Arches, later to the Archbishop of Canterbury (who quite despaired of the problem) and finally to the Barons of the Exchequer, with Lucy insisting throughout that all previous arrangements had been abrogated and that appointment to the position was in his gift and his alone. The case remained unsettled even at Aubrey's death in 1673 which allowed Cruso to take up the post which he would hold until his demise in 1681.

The placing of non-Welshmen in key positions within the diocese was characteristic of Lucy's policy – Timothy Halton of Bristol followed Nicholson as archdeacon of Brecon and Henry Falconbridge became diocesan chancellor in 1681 – all of which served to estrange the post-Restoration establishment from the people. There is little wonder that a later commentator claimed that Lucy's 'lack of wisdom and quick temper did no little damage to the Church at a critical point in its history'.[52] Like Humphrey Lloyd in St Asaph, Lucy was uncompromising in his response to Dissent. He showed no sympathy with those who could not, for conscience's sake, accept the Restoration settlement, and was ruthless in implementing the stipulations of the Clarendon Code which enforced religious uniformity according to the norms of a prelatical, hierarchical and inflexible state church.[53] Not that that deterred Dissenters from fulfilling what they saw as their calling. Lucy was regularly exasperated at their impertinence. 'Preach these fellows do everywhere', he exclaimed in his correspondence with Gilbert Sheldon in February 1672.[54] He spent the last five years of his life virtually housebound and died, aged eighty-five, in 1677, and was buried at the collegiate church at Brecon.

Apart from the denominationally unspecific works produced by Stephen Hughes of Meidrim which will be treated in the following section, and aside from one work of Church of England apologetic, no explicitly Anglican theology emerged from the southern dioceses between the 1660s and the 1680s. What did occur, however, was a change in the leadership of the diocese which opened the way for a surprising rapprochement between churchman and Dissent which was expressed in the literature that was published after 1670.[55] Lucy's successor was William Thomas (1613–89), who, although born in Bristol, had deep family roots in the borough of Carmarthen where his grandfather had served as alderman, mayor, recorder and MP. Following elementary education in the town where he was taught by Morgan Owen, latterly the Laudian bishop of Llandaff, he proceeded to Jesus College, Oxford, where he was instituted into the High Church, anti-Puritan tradition which by the 1630s had come to characterize the institution's churchmanship. Although ordained at Oxford, he was presented with the livings of Pen-y-bryn, Laugharne and Llansadyrnin in the diocese of St David's, and fell foul of the authorities during the Commonwealth by refusing to abstain from using the Book of Common Prayer.[56] He was nevertheless allowed to retain his clerical status within the diocese as he preached an assize sermon at Carmarthen in 1657 which was subsequently published.[57] In 1660 he was swiftly restored to his former livings – he had held Laugharne even under the Puritan dispensation – and in August of that year he was appointed precentor of St David's Cathedral by which time, as a former fellow of Jesus, he had been awarded the Oxford DD. For most of Lucy's ascendancy, however, he had served as dean of Worcester to which he had been presented in 1665, and it was not until January 1678, following his predecessor's death, that he returned as bishop of his home diocese. The conciliatory nature of his attitude to Dissent became obvious in his unexpectedly cordial relations with the Congregationalist Stephen Hughes (of which more will be said below), though he retained both his High Church theology and an unwavering commitment to the doctrinal norms of the post-Restoration establishment.

The one example of specifically Anglican apologetic to emerge from south Wales during these decades came from Thomas's pen, namely his *Apology for the Church of England in Separation from it* (1679), which had been composed two decades earlier, 'rather huddled … in the eclipse of the Church of England, in a time of discomposure'.[58] Unlike some examples of the genre, the *Apology* was measured, fair-minded and charitable. 'My duty', he claimed, had been 'to assist the cause, the honour of my mother, the Church of England, especially in the distress, the umbrage of her persecution', but to do so in a restrained and temperate way:[59]

> I have in this Apology entirely avoided not only virulency of passion, but also acrimony of style, recollecting the grave, candid animadversion of Mr Hooker. There will come a time when three words uttered with charity and meekness will receive a more blessed reward than three thousand volumes written with disdainful sharpness of wit. (Sig. A4r)

Written as a series of answers to the questions of an unnamed Dissenting minister, Thomas rehearses what he deems to be the truth and virtue of the Established Church, and responds to the interlocutions of his correspondent. By setting out his criteria, namely the Word of God as interpreted by the universal tradition of Christendom, 'it is the golden rule of Vincentius Lyrinensis, that which is asserted in all Christian churches in all ages is truly catholic and venerable' (p. 19), he hopes to achieve clarity and a measure of agreement. The dialogue does not commend episcopacy or any specific form of church government; it does not discuss ordination or the nature of the sacraments and says nothing about liturgy or the value of the Book of Common Prayer. It centres, rather, on the legitimacy (or otherwise) of a parochially based national church and the justification (or not) of forsaking it in order to establish voluntary congregations of gathered 'saints'. Like all apologists for the Church of England, the bishop held to its catholic wholeness, its apostolic quality and its antiquity. Whereas Romanists assailed it on the one side and 'our Reformed brethren' on the other, 'I affirm the national Church of England to be constituted according to the Word of God and the primitive institution' (p. 31). Although he accepted that it was less than perfect and would not excuse the faults and corruptions of its individual members, it still commanded his allegiance: 'Having owned and reverenced the Church of England as a chaste matron, as a venerable mother in her lustre, I shall not desert nor brand her as an impure harlot in her eclipse' (p. 32). If these words reflected the situation as it had existed during the Interregnum, his present position agreed with his former views:

> As for the doctrine and discipline of the Church of England, which
> upon mature examination my conscience hath constantly dictated
> to me to be the best constituted reformed church in the world, most
> untainted, unbiased for principles of piety and loyalty (the pillars of
> church and state) of exactest correspondence with Christ's signal pre-
> cept. (Sig. A10v)

The treatise is, on the whole, repetitive and somewhat one-sided.
We hear Thomas's responses but not the Dissenting minister's counter-
arguments. Much is taken up with a fairly exhaustive exposition of
biblical texts, with one side stressing the need for doctrinal purity and
upright morality and the other arguing that the Church of England
was doctrinally pure while scripture never countenanced the concept of
separation. Like Israel in the Old Testament, the followers of Jesus in
the gospels and the early Christian community as delineated in the Book
of Acts, the Epistles and the Book of Revelation, the church has always
been a mixed multitude containing both true and false professors, while
schism had always been considered injurious and unjustified. There was
a deep continuity between the New Testament and the expanding church
communities of Asia and Europe during the early Christian centuries.
The parochial system was itself a venerable institution tracing its beginnings to the third century, while the conversion of Constantine ensured
that church and empire would thereafter cohere. The ancient British
Church was born of this inheritance, while the Reformation under
Henry VIII to Queen Elizabeth had purged it of such medieval aberrations as papal supremacy, pardons, merits, images and pilgrimages. The
Bible had been made available in the vernacular while 'the people were
instructed, weaned, not constrained, not scared out of their superstition' (p. 49). In what had become a characteristically Anglican appeal
to historical continuity, Thomas commends his church as reflecting the
way in which God had bestowed his blessings upon the realm while to
secede from this body would be perilous in the extreme: 'Beware lest
yourself be embarked in a floating vessel, while the Church of England
is fixed on a rock' (p. 77).

> Visible profaneness being recorded in every visible church, specified
> in scripture without the effect, or attempt at severing, disjointing in
> celebrating God's ordinances, renders your separation as inexcusable
> as it is unwarrantable. (p. 78)

For Thomas, one of the principal weaknesses of separatists was their judgementalism:

> You deny most of our parochial churches to be in the state of salvation. They stand or fall to their own master. Yourself must appear before the same dreadful tribunal. *Judge nothing before the time, until the Lord come, who will bring to light the hidden things of darkness.* I pray suspend your judgement till the Day of Judgement. Then the sheep shall be sorted, severed from the goats. Till then touching the damnation of others it becomes you to be a sceptic rather than a critic. (pp. 57–8)

As long as the Word was preached and the sacraments were administered according to the scriptural pattern, the Church, he claimed, preserved its validity. He quotes the views of William Perkins and Arthur Hildersham, the non-separating Puritans of an earlier era, in order to back his claim: 'Mr Perkins concludeth that no man can separate from the Church of England with a good conscience, since it teacheth, obeyeth and believeth the doctrine of the prophets and apostles' (p. 82). What made a church pure was not a putative moral excellence on the part of its members but simple faith in the Word of God and obedience to his commandments: 'That those assemblies that enjoy the Word and doctrine of salvation, though they have many corruptions remaining in them, are to be acknowledged as true churches of God, and such as none of the faithful may make separation from' (p. 88).

Thomas's opponent, nevertheless, remained adamant that parish gatherings fell well short of the biblical ideal. 'A church', the Dissenter claimed, 'that generally consists of ignorant, profane and scandalous persons, and scoffers therein, is a degenerate church, and not safely to be communicated with' (p. 162). In his view, 'such are generally the people of the parishes of England and Wales, as sad experience testifieth' (p. 162). Thomas, however, rejected this decisively: 'You aggrieve it as a solecism in religion that a company of ignorant drunkards, swearers, Sabbath breakers are saints. Is this your best character to decipher a parochial ecclesiastical assembly?' (p. 139). His opponent's view, he claimed, was subjective, jaundiced and cynical. It was not for him to cast aspersions on others. When the Word was preached and the sacraments honoured, God would indeed bring forth fruit: 'Though the outward fruit be blasted to your eye, yet there may be secret buds and blossoms discernible to God and acceptable in Christ not withstanding those apparent witherings' (p. 166). That was not to say that often the pastoral situation within the parishes was acceptable or that discipline should not be applied, but at bottom the Church itself was sound: 'I appeal to Calvin's judgement. We do not less esteem it a church for this defect; we persist in its communion. We aver it not lawful for men to segregate, to separate themselves from it' (pp. 157–8). What should be aimed at was discipline, not separation. Affirming the reformed character of the national church and its affinity with continental Protestantism he averred: 'With unity and humility of spirit we may uprightly renounce the errors and vices of any members of the Church, but not renounce the Church itself for the errors and vices of any of its members' (pp. 168–9). If the Established Church was too often guilty of immorality, the besetting sin of the Dissenters, he suggested, was censoriousness and pride: 'I wish from my soul your separation were as guiltless for spiritual trespasses as our parishes are guilty of carnal' (p. 177). It would be better for them both not to be overly critical of the other: 'I pray God of all hands pierce us with a deep mournful apprehension of our own personal offences, that our parochial assemblies may be more sober and devout, and that your separate churches may be more humble and charitable' (p. 177). What is remarkable about this treatise is that an avowed High Churchman, steeped in the Laudian tradition and wholly committed to the Restoration compact, shows such moderation and an appreciation of a viewpoint to which he was so conscientiously opposed. Thomas's predecessor William Lucy and his colleague and contemporary Humphrey Lloyd, bishop of Bangor, would have bristled at his sentiments. Rather than traducing his opponent however, he affirms their shared Christian faith:

> Lastly, I shall assure you of a reciprocal love. Our affections may be linked, though our opinions are not. And though we are not both members of a separated church on earth, yet I hope, by the sacred merits of our blessed Redeemer, we shall be both in the same congregated church in heaven: where in a full quire of angels, all notes shall be tuned to an exact harmony, no jar of faction, no descant of division, but entire unisons, where our anathemas shall be exchanged to anthems, our censures to alleluia. (pp. 228–9)

In a truculent and contentious age, rarely did Christian charity sound a more engaging note than this.

It was a great blow to Welsh Christianity when, in August 1683, William Thomas was translated to the see of Worcester. While there he gained a reputation for generosity towards the poor who were fed daily at his door and twice weekly in the city's gaol. Still staunch in his loyalty to the Established Church, he engaged the respect of the redoubtable Richard Baxter, as venerable a nonconformist as Thomas was a conformist. He died, aged sixty-six, in 1689. His replacement at St David's was the Englishman Lawrence Womack, archdeacon of Suffolk, who remained for a mere three years, 1683–6, while his successor, John Lloyd, principal of Jesus College, Oxford, died before taking office to be replaced by the notorious Thomas Watson, a Yorkshireman, who would be suspended from office in 1694, deprived of his see five years later and died in excommunication, if 'very rich', in 1717.[60] Had it not been for the witness of William Thomas and, as we shall see, the cross-party exertions of Stephen Hughes, Thomas Gouge and the Welsh Trust, the lower clergy and laity of the most extensive of the Welsh dioceses would have had precious little in the way of support in order to ensure the 'promotion of piety' within their parishes during these years.

The one remaining Welsh see was that of Llandaff. Its first Restoration bishop was Hugh Lloyd, a Cardiganshire man who, despite being a fellow of Jesus College in the 1620s and taking the Oxford DD in 1638, seems to have had an undistinguished career as a Glamorgan rector as well as holding sinecure livings in north Wales. Imprisoned for a time following his support for the king at the Battle of St Fagan's in 1648, his appointment to the see was due to his connections with a powerful network of Glamorgan gentry who had shown tenacious loyalty to the crown during the civil war.[61] Elected bishop in October 1660 when he was also restored as non-resident archdeacon of St David's to which he had been appointed in 1644, at seventy-one he was probably too old to have made much of an impact on the see, though his previous 'innocuousness' and 'obscurity' suggests that he would have been an indifferent diocesan even had he been a younger man.[62] He was though, in the view of Francis Davies, a nephew of his successor, 'a very pious, learned, charitable and primitive good man', and was seventy-eight when he died.[63]

Like Lloyd his successor, also called Francis Davies, had been a fellow of Jesus College and a Glamorgan clergyman who, as rector of Llantrithyd, seat of Sir John Aubrey and intimate of Gilbert Sheldon,

Archbishop of Canterbury, had been at the very centre of the covert Anglican network which would prove so powerful in south Wales at the Restoration. Having been deprived of his livings during the Commonwealth, he divided his time between London and his native Glamorgan where he supported himself as a schoolmaster, and in 1660 was appointed archdeacon of Llandaff, the most powerful clerical position within the diocese. He succeeded to the bishopric in 1667 being consecrated on 24 August. Zealous in enforcing discipline among his clergy, he devoted himself mainly to restoring the fabric of the previously dilapidated cathedral and refurbishing the bishop's residence at Mathern, Monmouthshire. He died, aged seventy, in 1675, and was buried at the cathedral.[64] He was succeeded, in turn, by William Lloyd (not to be confused with William Lloyd, bishop of St Asaph 1680–92), a native of Llangower, Merionethshire, whose father, Edward Lloyd, would translate Simon Patrick's devotional manual, *A Book for Beginners, or a help to young communicants* in 1682.[65] Already a preacher at Gray's Inn and prebendary of St Paul's Cathedral, he spent a brief four years at Llandaff before transferring to the see of Peterborough in 1679 and then to Norwich in 1685. His reputation was primarily secured as one of the Non-Juring bishops who refused to accept the legitimacy of William III and his wife Mary as joint-monarchs in 1688 choosing rather to remain loyal to the Stuart dynasty.[66] Despite his proficiency in the Welsh language and his upbringing in rural Merionethshire, his contribution to the sum of religion and theology in Wales was minimal. He would be the last native Welsh bishop of Llandaff until Richard Lewis in 1883 and the last fluently Welsh-speaking head of the diocese until the enthronement of Joshua Prichard Hughes in 1905.

The final name to be mentioned is William Beaw (1615–1705), a Berkshire man, whose colourful life as a cavalryman during the civil wars, the banished Charles II's emissary to the Danish court and mercenary service in the pay of the Russian czar, hardly fitted him for the uneventful life of a bishop in Wales.[67] Ordained in 1660 to a New College living in Addlerbury, Oxfordshire, he was elected to his 'little bishopric' in June 1679 as a belated reward for his services to the king. Shocked at the poverty of his see and knowing virtually nothing about his new sphere of responsibility, he spent the next two decades ruing his bad fortune, canvassing for preferment, ideally to Hereford or Litchfield but even *in extremis* to St Asaph were he had fought during the civil war, and spending more and more time at Addlebury which he had been allowed to keep *in commendam* along with the parish of Bedwas in Monmouthshire and St Andrews, Glamorgan, in order to supplement his income. Aged sixty-five when he was installed, twenty years later he lamented that he had 'sat stooping and bowing almost the space of the life of a man'.[68] He died in February 1705 at the advanced age of ninety, having 'like other senile prelates put out to grass in Wales, simply lapsed into inactivity'.[69]

If the two north Wales dioceses witnessed something akin to a modest renewal in church life following the Restoration, the evidence from south Wales is less sanguine. The fact that the structures of the pre-Commonwealth Established Church were so quickly restored shows that, despite all hardships, it was far from having been destroyed, while the relief felt by most of the populace with the return of the king was widespread and palpable. Whereas it may well be that many incumbents laboured assiduously among their flocks preaching conscientiously, catechizing the young and administering pastoral care to all, numerous parishes were pitifully poor and it was a constant struggle to ensure that they received a living wage.[70] During his brief tenure at St David's, Lawrence Womack was shocked at the temerity of over-advantaged non-residents who placed 'illiterate curates for scandalous stipends' in their livings while keeping their hands firmly on more lucrative parishes elsewhere.[71] He was shaken by the poverty that some of his clergy had to endure, while in Llandaff at the end of the century, Thomas Price, rector of Merthyr Tydfil, bewailed the fact that '[m]any poor clergymen are not able to purchase more than bare food and raiment for their families'.[72] One of the two foci of renewal, Thomas Gouge's Welsh Trust, was only partially Anglican – Thomas Gouge was a London Presbyterian and anyway 'Bishop Lucy was unenthusiastic about Gouge's Welsh Trust'[73] – while the successes of the other, the SPCK, did not begin to register in the southern dioceses until early in the eighteenth century. There were no south Wales equivalents in either language to the devotional literature that had emanated from the north between 1660 and 1688. It was left to the Congregationalist Stephen Hughes to champion the cause of inter-denominational literature in post-Restoration Wales. Paradoxically it was through the labours of Stephen Hughes and his fellow Dissenter Charles Edwards that the theology of Rhys Prichard, John Jewel, Lewis Bayly, James Ussher, John Davies of Mallwyd and other orthodox Church of England men would circulate in south Wales and beyond in the decades following 1662.

Theology and post-Restoration Dissent

The critique of Prayer Book worship

Of the leading radical Welsh Puritans, Vavasor Powell alone ventured into print following the momentous changes of 1660. His reputation as a firebrand ensured that he would be a marked man under the new regime, and whereas the bulk of the moderate Puritans welcomed the return of the exiled king, by April 1660, the month before Charles II landed at Dover, Powell had already been incarcerated at Shrewsbury.[74] Following General Monck's reconvening of the Long Parliament in February twelve years after it had been expelled by Pride's Purge in 1648, the Solemn League and Covenant had been reinstated, plans for a Presbyterian national church had been revived and all former oaths of loyalty to the Commonwealth had been abrogated.[75] The dominance, however, of Episcopalians in the next elected parliament which met for the first time on 25 April, scuttled the idea of a future established church governed by the Westminster Confession and run on Presbyterian lines. On 1 May this parliament (or 'convention', as it had not been called by the king) voted to reinstate the House of Lords and invite King Charles to return to his realm. By then even the 'conditional royalists', the Presbyterians (in the main) who had envisaged an enhanced role for parliament along with the king, in the new dispensation, began to worry about the possibility of an oppressive re-established prelacy and a return to pre-1640 norms. The Declaration of Breda, however, also published in May, in which the king had promised a 'free and general pardon' for most of those who had taken up arms against the monarchy during the civil wars and assured 'liberty to tender consciences' in matters of religion, restored Presbyterian confidence. By now their ideal was for 'comprehension' or the creation of a broad-based national church with pastoral or non-territorial bishops who would govern in tandem with their presbyters as had been envisaged by Archbishop Ussher a decade-and-a-half previously. The most that the 'gathered churches', the Congregationalists, Baptists and Quakers, could hope for was 'toleration' or 'indulgence', namely to be allowed to exist side-by-side with the new establishment. By the summer the London Presbyterians were calling for a reduced episcopacy on Ussher's model, revision of the Book of Common Prayer and that ceremonial such as clerical dress and kneeling at communion should not be imposed by law but left to the individual conscience. At the same time royalist views were hardening, and it was becoming increasingly apparent that there would be no leeway on the matter of diocesan episcopacy or anything less than wholesale uniformity in matters of worship. The vacant sees were already being filled and whatever was being deliberated in the metropolis, in Wales the reversion to the *status quo ante* was well under way: 'Without waiting for the outcome of the discussions in London, the sounds and sights of the national church abolished in 1645 were gradually returning through the summer and autumn of 1660.'[76]

While this was occurring, having been released from Shrewsbury gaol on 25 June, Powell had redoubled his preaching efforts in mid Wales and was rapidly accused of fomenting 'sedition, rebellion and treason'.[77] He was rearrested in late July, not least because of his putative links with the republican General John Lambert's rebellion of three months earlier, and this time was imprisoned at Welshpool. Apart from a short period in early 1661, he would remain under lock and key for the next seven years, being incarcerated at Shrewsbury, the Fleet in London and at Southsea Castle in Hampshire. It was during this period that Powell issued his next two works, the vigorous tract *Common Prayer-Book No Divine Service* in 1660 and an apologia for his contribution to the Cromwellian evangelistic project evocatively entitled *The Bird in the Cage Chirping* in 1661.

Typical of all the radical Puritans, Powell would have no truck at all with written liturgies generally or with the Book of Common Prayer in particular.[78] For him prayer was spiritual whereas written liturgies were inherently carnal:

> How inconsistent with the day and light of the gospel is this service, God having sent his Word more fully and plainly to direct his ministers and people, and given his Spirit in a more abundant measure to … enable them to call upon him.

Indeed, 'How little good (if any at all) hath been done by the long use of the Service Book, though men have prayed long by it.'[79] As well as enunciating explicitly theological reasons for his critique, namely that the Holy Spirit, alone and unmediated, enabled the believing soul to communicate with God, he also cited the lessons of history: 'Whether some now may not intend by the re-establishing of this book to oppose and pull down that excellent and gracious spirit of prayer and preaching which God hath poured out upon his ministers', the fact was that formal liturgies has always been 'a snare and net against all preachers and people that out of conscience cannot conform thereto' (p. 3). In truth 'this book hath been so much idolized by the generality of men' that there had been no alternative but to banish it (p. 3). Turning to scripture, he declared that imposed and formalistic prayer was idolatrous and as such prohibited under the Second Commandment while in the New Testament it came under the rubric of the vain repetition which was censured in Matt. 17 and Mark 7. Scripture itself provided sufficient example as to how the sincere believer should pray to God in the Spirit, while duly ordained ministers, if anointed by the Lord, should possess the requisite gifts to be able to lead their congregations in prayer. It was only carnal ministers, bereft of a true calling, who could not offer extempore prayer: 'Such are like Jeroboam's simpletons, the blemished priests under the law and the dumb dogs which the prophet reproves' (p. 7). As for the faithful, they needed to be edified which could only be done according to the precepts of Holy Scripture itself: 'How can they tie up themselves strictly to those forms, without limiting, stinting, and quenching the Spirit?' (p. 9) For Powell there was no doubt that 'stinted liturgies or Common-Prayer Books are the ordinances, traditions, and rudiments of men' (p. 9).

Along with the unspiritual nature of liturgical prayer, to have mixed multitudes of the godly and ungodly indiscriminately worshipping together in parish gatherings nurtured hypocrisy. The imposition of such practices was deeply scandalous and not a matter of *adiaphora* or 'things indifferent':

> Either such liturgies or Common Prayers are indifferent or not indifferent; if indifferent, then they are not to be imposed upon Christians, but they are to be left to their liberty (as Christians were left by the Apostles) but if it is not indifferent, then unless a prescript can be shewed from God (it being in his service) it is no less than will-worship, forbidden, Col. 2.23. (p. 10)

As for the claim that the Lord's Prayer, taught by Christ himself, was formal if not formalistic and in essence liturgical, he rejects the premise entirely: 'The Lord's Prayer (so called) though it be not denied but that it may be used by any godly men (though not in the way it is by most, at the end of their own) yet it will be hard to prove it to be a form' (p. 11). Its context was the Sermon on the Mount and as such was never meant to be turned into a stilted, unbending matter of form, while the different, indeed conflicting versions in Matt. 6 and Luke 11 showed that it was not intended for repetitive liturgical use. In fact there was no evidence of it ever having been used in the regular worship of the New Testament church. Likewise, in responding to the claim that a written prayer, like the use of crutches, could be helpful to weak believers, he rejected this contention as well: 'It is rather a hindrance than help for people would, if it were not for such forms, seek the Spirit of God, which would be given to help them' (p. 14). Only graceless people needed such fleshly supports; those who had been granted saving grace needed no crutches: 'Lame persons when they are cured, hang up their crutches on the Cross and leave them behind them to shew they are cured' (p. 15). For Vavasor, the chief evil of all liturgies (especially the Book of Common Prayer) was that they served to convince people that by repeating a form of words, however thoughtlessly, they were in a right relation with God: 'It hath tended to harden many Papists in their false religion … and ignorant scandalous people among ourselves [into] thinking that they are true Christians by conforming thereto' (p. 16). The Commonwealth regime had been wholly correct in banning the Prayer Book's use, and what was appropriate during the Interregnum was equally appropriate now.

As well as making these general points, Powell displayed a working knowledge of Cranmer's Prayer Book by making a discriminating critique of its contents. He condemned the use of the term Sunday 'and other days of the week by the names of the Saxon idols' (p. 18) preferring the scriptural term, 'the Lord's day' and the like; he challenged the validity of dedicating festivals to the saints and the archangels; he abhorred the use of the title 'priest' for the minister; he disapproved of the fact that the *Te Deum* and the *Benedictus* retained their Latin names rather than being translated into the vernacular while their repeated use in worship partook of the vain repetition to which he already referred. He condemned the

> many tautologies therein, the words, 'Good Lord deliver us' used eight times and the words, 'We beseech thee to hear us good Lord' used one and twenty times; and using the Lord's Prayer five times or more in one morning service. This is vain repetition, forbidden in Matt. 6.6. (p. 19)

The Creed, though ostensibly orthodox, included some references such as Christ having descended to hell, which were theologically dubious.

Even worse was the profligate use of the litany, responsive readings, and the collects: 'This chopping and miming of prayer between the priest and the people in many places which are more like charmers than Christian prayers' (p. 20). In all it was more akin to a mockery than the offering of true devotion. In matters of both ceremonial and doctrine, the Prayer Book was clearly in error. The New Testament said nothing about the function of godparents in baptism, the use of the ring in marriage or stipulate whether people should stand, sit or kneel in worship. The practice of kneeling to receive Holy Communion implied an idolatrous devotion to the consecrated elements which was clearly papistical in essence as was use of the sign of the cross in baptism. The declaration that each baptized infant was regenerate manifested the unscriptural (and Romanist) concept of *ex opere operato*: 'What clearer proof can be desired to prove that the sacrament doth confer grace than this?' (p. 27). Equally scandalous was the implication that at their burial all parishioners, whether godly or not, could count on being numbered among the faithful: 'To say of every one buried, "This our dear brother here departed", they have a large faith that can believe that all they bury are such' (p. 30). In all, the Book of Common Prayer was an aberration which had no place in the worship of the truly biblical church.

He concluded his treatise with an extensive list of 'Arguments to prove that lord bishops or diocesan bishops ... are contrary to the Word of God and ... consequently unlawful' (p. 31). It took little aptitude to compare the simple and comparatively unstructured ministerial system of the New Testament, even as seen in the Pastoral Epistles, with the hierarchical organization of the Church of England which Powell had known in the past and was being reconstituted in the present. He shows no sympathy for the concept of historical development and makes little attempt to engage with the extensive scholarly literature, patristic, medieval or modern, with which other Puritan leaders such as John Owen and Richard Baxter fashioned their ecclesiological views. For Vavasor all that was needed was in the Bible, and the New Testament was unequivocal on the matter: 'It will evidently appear that the lordly diocesan bishops and their power are unwarrantable and unscriptural if we compare them with the bishops mentioned in scripture' (p. 39). The root of all past and present evils were with the papacy, while the Established Church, though claiming to be biblical, had never genuinely reformed itself according to the Word of God:

> Scripture finds lord bishop neither in name nor power nor in that rank
> and order they place themselves ... though you thus reckon: first the
> pope; secondly the cardinal; thirdly the archbishop; fourthly the dioc-
> esan bishop; there you find them in their proper place but not in the
> scripture. (p. 37)

His final appeal, as could be expected, was for his opponents to bring
their ecclesiology to the bar of the Word of God and (surprisingly,
given his unadorned Biblicism) to the historical example of the primitive church:

> They that read the history of the church (written by Eusebius, Sympson
> etc.) will easily discern the differences between the bishops of the three
> first centuries, and our diocesan bishops. The controversy is not about
> the name ... but about the power of bishops ... If the Word of God be a
> perfect rule (as it is) what need we go any further? Bring your episcopal
> metal to this touchstone, and if it will hold here we will honour it with
> its grey hairs and receive and reverence it as the right heir. If not, we
> must say with Gerhard, 'Antiquity without truth is but a cypher'. (p. 44)

Vavasor's apologia for the parliament-sponsored campaign connected
with the Act for the Better Propagation of the Gospel in Wales between
1650 and 1653 namely his *Bird in a Cage Chirping* had been concluded
during his imprisonment in the Fleet in the spring of 1661. For nearly a
decade he had been accused of appropriating for his own use funds that
had been raised through the tithe even though, following the expulsion
of the clergy, so many of the parish churches had been virtually aban-
doned. The general criticism had been that talk of evangelizing Wales
had been a shallow pretence for personal self-seeking by a clique of military adventurers. The Puritans had been corrupt hypocrites, flourishing
while real pastors were reduced to penury; 'Puritanism', it was said, 'was
a manifestation not of zeal but of greed, tyranny, sedition and impiety'.[80]
In fact 'Wales had been the scene of some of the most blatant examples
of persecution and corruption on the part of the Puritan regime', a view
that Powell now felt compelled to challenge.[81] As well as being a defence
of the part that he had played in the implementation of the Act, the *Bird
in the Cage* was aimed at emboldening his followers during the persecution that he felt was about to descend upon them. Although it was not
yet clear what form the Established Church would take, the very fact that

he had been arrested while the authorities had scattered his mid Wales followers abroad augured badly for the future. Whether Episcopalian or Presbyterian, any national church which compelled people to join was bound to be oppressive. It would be the saints' privilege to bear all opposition with fortitude and good cheer while persecution would in fact purify the cause of its weaknesses:

> But my faithful fellow-travellers, let us not be troubled that the wind now blows in our faces ... A day of close discovery and through trial is come, or coming upon us, and the leaves of profession are like to hide hypocrisy no longer.[82]

Along with a pointed criticism of Quakerism, the doctrinal content of Vavasor's narrative occurs near the beginning. The Quakers, whose presence in mid Wales had already become considerable, were a threat due to their rejection of all objective criteria by which to adjudge the knowledge of God. The radical subjectivity of 'the inner light' abrogated the need for the Bible, the sacraments and in the end the objective, historical work of Christ on the cross. 'The Quakers', he claimed, 'generally deny the scripture to be the Word of God ... [b]ut beloved you are better taught, and I hope will still retain your love of, diligence and delight in, and zeal for this word of God' (p. 5). The difference between the Friends' 'inner light' and the Calvinistic orthodoxy which he had long espoused was total, and in a long passage he describes the content of his own creed and that which had become the basis for his teaching in mid Wales and farther afield:

> Be steadfast in those truths which you have been taught ... concerning God and his attributes, Christ and his offices, the Holy Spirit and its manifestations, the decrees of God before time, the two covenants (viz. the law and the gospel), the wretched state of all men by nature and out of Christ; the freeness of God's grace in opposition to man's free will; the doctrine of justification by the imputed righteousness of Christ, apprehended and received by faith; sanctification (distinct from justification) wrought by the Spirit in us; perseverance, assurance and growth in grace by virtue of our union with Christ, and his spiritual indwelling and operating in us; living Godlily, righteously and soberly in this present world; denying ourselves, following Christ, shunning sin, resisting Satan, separating from the world in matters of God's

worship; not meddling with nor mingling the traditions of men with
God's truths ... (pp. 6–7)

For Powell doctrine and church fellowship went hand in hand, and it was
incumbent upon the true believer to separate from both the world and a
worldly church in order to offer pure worship, to enjoy true fellowship
and to preserve a vital witness to the gospel:

> joining yourselves to, and continuing in the fellowship of saints and
> using carefully and conscientiously all the ordinances of Christ as
> preaching, hearing, and expounding scriptures; keeping up public, fam-
> ily, and private prayers; prophesying and singing of psalms, hymns and
> spiritual songs in the churches; repetition of sermons, observing the
> Sabbath, baptism and the Supper of the Lord and upon occasion, days
> of solemn fasting, or rejoicing ... according to the blessed commands
> of Jesus Christ. (p. 7)

Despite everything that had happened since Cromwell's appointment as Lord Protector which had thwarted Fifth Monarchist hopes
for the immanent return of Christ, Powell remained unwavering in his
millennialist faith:

> Withal expecting the destruction of Antichrist, the restauration of the
> Jews, the coming kingdom and reign of Christ and still remembering
> your latter end, the immortality of your precious souls, believing the
> resurrection of the body, the judging of all and the salvation of the
> righteous. (p. 7)

He still held tenaciously to the millennial hope: 'I am persuaded of and
expect [the Fifth Monarchy] will be, and, as many ancient and modern
learned men have unanswerably proved, will begin before Christ the
monarch will himself appear' (p. 36). In all, and aside from the chiliastic
speculation, it was a clear précis of Powell's militant Calvinism and
would provide the doctrinal basis for much Welsh Dissent during the
testing times that were about to descend.

The impact of the Act of Uniformity, 1662
The unsurreptitious return to ecclesiastical normality which occurred
during the summer and autumn of 1660 masked a hardening of attitudes

towards those who still yearned for a broad-based and accommodating religious compact. The process of reclaiming livings that had been appropriated by Commonwealth incumbents had begun as early as April, but with the passing of the Act for Confirming and Restoring Ministers in September there was nothing to prevent a wholesale restoral of the situation that had prevailed in 1642. By then there was an 'unmistakable oscillation of feeling in favour of the old order'.[83] The laws under which Vavasor Powell and other radicals had been apprehended such as the Act of Uniformity and the Conventicles Act were not newly minted but had been passed as far back as the Elizabethan era. It were as though the Commonwealth and the Interregnum had never existed. Where possible, Wales's few conscientious Presbyterian incumbents bided their time, awaiting the result of discussions in the capital between their leaders and representatives of the restored Episcopalian hierarchy, but when on 28 November the reconvened parliament rejected the Declaration of Breda, namely Charles's plan to conciliate with a wider range of religious opinions, the ideal of a comprehensive national church seemed even more forlorn. The abortive uprising of January 1661 when the Fifth Monarchist John Venner broke into St Paul's Cathedral proclaiming Christ alone as king further convinced the authorities of the pernicious nature of all nonconforming religion, while the enthronement of Charles II with full Episcopal pomp on 23 April set the seal on the unity between an emboldened prelatical church and the state. A vivid snapshot of the way in which even moderate Puritans viewed the situation is seen in the letter of Samuel Jones, Presbyterian minister of Llangynwyd, Glamorgan, to Richard Baxter six days after the coronation:

> This only I shall say, that from those sad instances that occur in the most reformed parts and cities of the nation, you may take aim what to conclude of those rude and darker corners where generally the very form of godliness is as much hated as the power of it is little understood. We bless the Lord and pray him to bless his majesty for that liberty we have hitherto enjoyed in the free exercise of our ministry. A blessed respite his majesty's declaration afforded us though against the heart of those among whom we live. Oh how many a mouth hath it kept open, powerfully and indeed (as it were) valedictorally to preach the blessed gospel to the consciences of a poor mad, wild, dead people … And though the ark of the church should be tossed from one extreme to the other, yet

when God himself is both mast, stern and anchor to it, it shall at length
be tossed upon Ararat.[84]

The next round of elections on 8 May established the so-called
'Cavalier Parliament' in which Presbyterian presence was minimal. It
promptly declared void the Solemn League and Covenant (Charles I's
late agreement with the Scots to introduce a Presbyterian church-
establishment throughout the realm), commanding its statutes to be
burned by the common hangman, stipulated that all MPs should take
the sacrament according to the Book of Common Prayer and that the
bishops were to be restored to their former places in the House of Lords.
There was to be no conciliation with any religious conviction apart from
an undiluted hierarchical prelacy. The attempted *modus vivendi* between
the bishops led by Gilbert Sheldon of London, later Archbishop of
Canterbury, and the Presbyterians led by Edmund Calamy and Richard
Baxter[85] at the Savoy Conference between April and July 1661 led to
deadlock. Whereas the Presbyterians demanded a substantial revision
to the Book of Common Prayer and rejected the concept of Episcopal
re-ordination which would have nullified their former ministry, the
bishops remained insistent that the church should worship uniformly
according to the rubrics of the Prayer Book under the jurisdiction of a
diocesan hierarchy.[86]

On 19 May 1662 when the Act for the Uniformity received the royal
assent, the worst fears of the moderates came to pass. Not only was the
unrevised Book of Common Prayer set out as the sole basis for worship,
it now contained liturgical celebrations for the anniversary of the death
of Charles I 'the blessed martyr' (30 January) and the birth and restoration of Charles II (29 May). Sole blame for the 'great mischiefs ... of
the late unhappy troubles' was laid at the feet of those who had refused
to worship according to the postulated liturgy, whereas 'nothing con-
duceth more to the settling to the peace of this nation ... than a universal
agreement to the public worship of Almighty God'. For the authors of
the Act, there could be no social and political harmony without strict
religious uniformity. Public worship was required by all, and if it did not
accord to the most detailed conditions of the Book of Common Prayer,
it was deemed illegal. What was more, every clergyman in the realm
was required 'openly and publicly ... to declare his unfeigned assent and
consent to the use of all things' prescribed therein, while the only form
of ordination to be countenanced was through the laying on of hands by

a bishop. Since the Elizabethan era only a general assent to the Prayer Book had been required of the clergy, but now things had changed fundamentally: '[T]he Act broke decisively with England's history since the Reformation by recognizing the validity only of episcopal orders.'[87] Those clergy who would not fulfil these obligations before 24 August 1662, the feast of St Bartholomew, were to be deprived of their livings.

Whatever was true for the rest of the kingdom, in Wales 'The Great Ejectment' of 1662 was merely the culmination of a process which had begun two years earlier. As Presbyterianism had never embedded itself among the Welsh, most of those who found themselves outside the limits of the Act belonged rather to the 'gathered churches' of Congregationalists, Baptists and Quakers. Few of those inducted to livings after 1653, when the Propagation Act had come to an end, had been ordained by a bishop, a handful had been ordained by a Presbyterian classis and only a minority had received the imprimatur of the Westminster Assembly of Divines. The gathered congregations of Baptists, Independents or unaffiliated believers had been drawn together through the exertions of peripatetic evangelists or the organizational skills of the likes of Vavasor Powell, John Myles or Jenkin Jones. According to Powell's estimate in 1661:

> [I]n the beginning of the wars there was but one or two gathered congregations in all Wales, and in some counties scarce one that made profession; yet it hath pleased the Lord so to bless the weak means there that there were lately (and hope are still) above twenty gathered churches, in some two, in some three, some four or five hundred members with their officers, differing little in opinion and faith and walking in love and the fear of the Lord.[88]

Over two decades earlier the first congregation had gathered at William Wroth's Llanfaches. Thereafter groups of saints formed themselves into church order in Walter Cradock's Monmouthshire, in William Erbury's Cardiff; various groups of Baptists, some closed communion, others open communion, some Calvinist and others Arminian, had come together in Breconshire; Myles's followers were to be found not only there but in Carmarthenshire, Glamorgan and in the western part of Monmouthshire; Powell's followers were to be found in mid Wales, including Radnorshire, parts of Cardiganshire and Montgomeryshire, while in north Wales Morgan Llwyd's gathered church at Wrexham

had been established early in the 1650s. It may be there were others as
well, especially in the thriving towns, mostly on the southern coast or
near the English border, where the Puritan message had found a modest
response. None of these groups had taken the form of a reformed parish,
and those episcopally ordained Puritans who had fought shy instinctively of disorder and disruptiveness had already conformed, hoping to
fulfil their ministry within the structures of the Established Church.
It was only the small knot of convinced Presbyterians, Philip Henry
in Flintshire,[89] John Jones in Llanarmon, Denbighshire, Samuel Jones in
Llangynwyd and the like, who held out until 'Black Bartholomew', hoping against hope for the establishment of a broad-based national church
in which they could conscientiously serve. Alas, it was not to be.

During the next decade the laws passed under the direction of the
Lord Chancellor, Edward Hyde, the first earl of Clarendon, impacted
harshly on the Dissenting ministers and those laypeople who refused
to withdraw from the gathered churches. The Corporation Act of 1661
had already required all municipal officials to take communion according
to the Book of Common Prayer, thus excluding nonconformists from
holding public office. The 1664 Conventicle Act, revised in 1670, forbade
more than five people outside the same family from joining together
for religious purposes thus making non-Anglican congregational worship illegal, while the Five Mile Act of 1665 prevented Commonwealth
ministers from living within five miles of the churches in which they
had previously served. The Quaker Act of 1662 had already targeted
the most recalcitrant group of Welsh Dissenters, those in fellowship
with the Society of Friends, while along with Baptists and
Congregationalists the code also penalized those who remained loyal
to 'the Old Faith', the Catholicism of the Church of Rome.[90] In all some
130 former Commonwealth incumbents were relieved of their livings
between 1660 and 1662,[91] a number of whom emerged as leaders in the
network of clandestine congregations which perpetuated the Dissenting
message in post-Restoration Wales.[92] Tracing the bounds of that network is not an easy task. The very nature of preserving a witness in
a time of persecution made congregations wary of advertising their
existence. Nevertheless the list of conventicles returned by the bishops of St Asaph and Llandaff to Lambeth Palace in preparation for the
renewal of the Act in 1670 (those from Bangor and St David's have not
survived); the licences for Dissenting places of worship issued under the
Indulgence of 1672; Henry Maurice's catalogue of Welsh congregations

appended to Bristol's Broadmead Church Records in 1675, along with traditions preserved by Edmund Calamy in his account of the ejected ministers of 1702, by Joshua Thomas in his *Hanes y Bedyddwyr ymhlith y Cymry* ('A History of the Baptists among the Welsh') (1778) and the evidence of various early church books, afford a glimpse of the strength and extent of Welsh Dissent during this period.

North Wales

Apart from the border town of Wrexham, the Puritan cause had achieved little success in north Wales. Consequently, within the diocese of Bangor, there seems to have been no Dissenting witness at all in Anglesey after 1662 and only a single church in Caernarfonshire, a Congregational gathering at Llanarmon and Llangybi along with a meeting place in the Caernarfon home of Ellis Rowland, ejected vicar of Clynnog Fawr, and another at Llangïan on the Llŷn Peninsula registered under the 1672 Indulgence.[93] This was despite the fact that the parliamentary cause had attracted significant support from some of the county's substantial landed families during the Interregnum. In neighbouring Merionethshire, scattered believers formerly linked with Wrexham were not constituted into church order until the early 1670s when Hugh Owen of Bronclydwr near Harlech, graduate of Jesus College, Oxford, and heir of a local gentry family, became its pastor and leader of the county's Congregationalists.[94] Only five places were registered as places of worship in 1672, including Cynfal, the childhood home of Morgan Llwyd.[95]

In the diocese of St Asaph, Llwyd's Wrexham church was now led by John Evans, a former member of Balliol College Oxford who, although having been clandestinely ordained by Roger Mainwaring, the Laudian bishop of St David's, had long turned radical and in 1670 would marry Vavasor Powell's widow. 'A person of great sobriety and godliness'[96] in the view of his admirers, for the bishop of St Asaph he ruled over 'schismatics many'.[97] The only other Dissenting gathering in the county was in Denbigh and the Vale of Clwyd, initially pastored by William Jones, a former approver under the Propagation Act, who was obliged to leave the town in 1665 under the requisites of the Five Mile Act. His later contribution to the 'promotion of piety' would be through his Welsh translations of the works of Thomas Gouge (see below). Ten licences were issued in the county under the 1672 Indulgence, including the home of Jonathan Roberts, former Commonwealth incumbent at Llanfair Dyffryn Clwyd.[98]

Although Henry Maurice stated that in neighbouring Flintshire '[t]here has been no professing people in all these late times', it would be remiss not to list the contribution of Philip Henry, the remarkable non-separating Presbyterian of Wrothenbury and Broad Oak in the parish of Bangor Is-coed.[99] Having been called before the Flintshire assizes as early as September 1660 for refusing to read the Book of Common Prayer, he had been obliged to vacate his living a year later and thereafter found himself unable to yield to the requirements of the Act of Uniformity. He could neither conscientiously submit to Episcopal re-ordination nor could he affirm unreservedly the content of the Prayer Book. A regular attender at public worship in his parish church after 1662 (though he refused to take communion which would have entailed him having to kneel), on Sundays he would nevertheless preach at home to his family and a few invited hearers though seeking never to contravene the demands of the Conventicle Act. Despite initial reluctance, he had his home at Broad Oak licenced as a Presbyterian meeting place under the Indulgence of 1672: 'By both temperament and conviction Henry was intensely law-abiding ... Separatism he abhorred, he could never become the pastor of a congregation gathered independently and outside the Church of England.'[100] 'I do not conform to the liturgy ... as a minister to read it, that I may bear my testimony against prelacy', he claimed. 'I do conform to the liturgy as a private person to hear it in public assembly that I bear my testimony against Independency.'[101] It was a highly principled stance which exasperated conformists, to whom he showed unfailing deference, as much as it did his fellow nonconformists. Although he respected those of the Congregational way, he could never join them for, he claimed, 'they unchurch the nation ... they pluck up the hedge of parish order [and] they ... allow persons to preach who are un-ordained'.[102] Emboldened after 1675, he preached in the licenced conventicles and administered the Lord's Supper to gatherings of believers, though he still longed for a broad-based, inclusive national church and would never be wholly at ease outside it.[103]

The one remaining Welsh county within the diocese was Montgomeryshire.[104] In 1669 the bishop had listed eight conventicles within its bounds, two of which were Quaker.[105] The teacher in the Llanfyllin conventicle, which consisted of both open communion Baptists and Congregationalists, was Vavasor Powell who was to pass away, aged only fifty-three, during that year. Only five licences were issued in 1672, and three years later Henry Maurice bewailed the low state of Powell's geographically extensive cause: 'Upon [Powell's] great trials and troubles it was much scattered and made desolate', yet by then Henry Williams (of Ysgafell), one of the itinerant's lieutenants, had been chosen successor.[106] Such, therefore, was the extent of north Wales Dissent in the two decades following the Restoration.

It had been in north Wales during the same period that the Established Church had best risen to the challenge of institutional renewal and pastoral care, and with the advent of William Lloyd as St Asaph's bishop in 1681 the pace of reform quickened. One of his first undertakings was to enter into dialogue with Dissenters, the Montgomeryshire Quakers, the Flintshire Presbyterians and the Wrexham Independents, with a mind to drawing them back into the Established Church. 'Persecution was very sharp and severe in several places about this time', recalled the Quaker leader Richard Davies, 'but this new bishop thought to take a more mild way to work by summoning all sorts of Dissenters to discourse with him'.[107] After two decades of oppression by the authorities, this was an unexpected turn. The first conference, at Llanfyllin, Montgomeryshire, on 22–3 September, was with the Quakers who were represented by Charles and Thomas Lloyd of the celebrated Dolobran family.[108] The discussion, which was held at the town hall in the presence of a large and enthusiastic crowd, ranged widely but came to centre on the validity of the sacraments, baptism in particular which, being an external ordinance, was for the Friends unnecessary for salvation. The bishop was aided by Humphrey Humphreys, dean of Bangor, and the lay historian Henry Dodwell both of whom were 'very learned men'.[109] As the two parties reasoned from contrary premises there is little wonder that no agreement was reached, but Lloyd was impressed by the quality of his opponents' testimony: 'He said that he expected not to find so much civility from the Quakers; he highly commended Thomas Lloyd and our Friends came off with them very well.'[110] A later meeting with Davies served to deepen the prelate's respect, indeed affection, for that stalwart, although there would never be a rapprochement between Bishop Lloyd and the most recalcitrant of the Dissenting sects within the see.

If the Quakers were the most radical of the Dissenters, the Presbyterians were the most law-abiding and conservative. The conference with their representatives occurred at Oswestry a week later. The bishop's party once more included the learned dean of Bangor and Henry Dodwell whose erudition on this occasion was matched by that of their opponents, Philip Henry, Jonathan Roberts and James Owen. Henry's education had taken him from Westminster School to Christ Church, Oxford, where he had been taught by both the High Church Episcopalian Henry Hammond and the scholarly Puritan John Owen before proceeding to the rigours of Presbyterian ordination by the Shropshire Classis in July 1657.[111] Roberts, 'a plain man of great integrity and a very good scholar', had been a sizar at Clare College, Cambridge, before transferring to Oxford where he had graduated and been appointed fellow of Jesus College in 1648.[112] There is no record of where or how he was ordained, but he had served as an itinerant under the Propagation Act and was later presented to the living of Llanfair Dyffryn Clwyd. Like Henry he had been summoned before the Great Session for refusing to lead worship according to the Book of Common Prayer, in his case in September 1661, but unlike his colleague he was incarcerated briefly in Denbigh gaol. In 1672 his home at Llanfair was licenced as a meeting place under the Indulgence.[113]

The youngest of the three, James Owen, was a twenty-seven-year-old Carmarthenshire man whose spiritual formation had occurred under the pressures of the post-Restoration regime. One of the first to be grounded in the Classics, theology and modern languages at Samuel Jones's academy at Brynllywarch, Glamorgan, he had been trained for ministry under the Congregationalists Stephen Hughes in south Wales and Hugh Owen in the north, where he had been charged with the pastoral care of the saints gathered in the Pwllheli area of Caernarfonshire. Since 1676 he had been based in Oswestry, assisting with the oversight of those who had been gathered under the ministry of Rowland Nevett, though he had preaching responsibilities in the Vale of Clwyd as well. Despite his youthfulness, he had gleaned exceedingly wide experience of Welsh Dissent in both south and north Wales. The exigencies of persecution had blurred the distinction between Congregationalist and Presbyterian though Owen assured Bishop Lloyd that his ordination, which occurred in October 1677, had been according to Presbyterian rites: 'I was ordained by presbyters whose ordination I took upon as valid.'[114] Following the Glorious Revolution Owen would combine his Oswestry ministry with the teaching of students, and his academy, like that of Samuel Jones, became revered for its scholarly excellence.[115] Latterly a member of the Cheshire Classis, he would become a towering figure in the Presbyterianism of Lancashire and the Welsh borders, with works such as *A Plea for Scripture Ordination* (1694), *Moderation a*

Virtue (1703) as well as publications in Welsh, cementing his reputation as one of the principal proponents of late seventeenth- and early eighteenth-century Presbyterianism.[116]

The essence of the debate, held on 27 September 1681 and run on typically scholastic lines with theses and syllogisms, had to do with the nature and authority of ordination and what the New Testament taught concerning episcopacy: 'I do desire ... that you would give some satisfactory account of your title to the ministry which you exercise, and also of your reason for your separation from the Church of England', stated Bishop Lloyd, and asked 'by what right is it that you take upon you the ministry?'[117] Much of the discussion had to do with the exposition of biblical texts: Acts 20, I Timothy 3, II Cor. 13, and whether Paul envisaged ordination as an apostolic rite vested in his own hands as the *episcopos* or whether this function was shared with other presbyters. 'The grand question proposed and discussed', according to James Owen's biographer, 'was whether ordination by such diocesans as have uninterrupted succession of canonical ordination down from the Apostles, be so necessary that churches and ministry are null without it?'[118] The tenor of the discussion was balanced, reasoned and of a high intellectual standard. Each side could quote to purpose, comparing apposite texts in Greek as well as in English, even touching on the dating of the Epistle to the Ephesians in relation to the Thessalonian correspondence.[119] Biblical exegesis on both sides was supported by a wide knowledge of patristic sources. As expected, neither side could concur with the other, though the debate did result (for the time being) in a degree of mutual forbearance. Charles Owen (James's brother and biographer) described Lloyd as an 'excellent and learned prelate, being a declared enemy to persecution' who 'studied to reduce the Dissenters in his diocese by mild and Christian methods', while Lloyd, writing to Henry a week later, appreciated his moderation and irenic spirit: 'He said he did not look upon me as σχισματικός [a schismatic] but only as παρασυνάγωγος [a separatist], and if I were in his diocese he did not question but he should find out some way to make me useful'.[120]

For all his ostensible fairmindedness, Lloyd was not nearly as sympathetic to the Wrexham Congregationalists. Although he persevered through the summer of 1682 in attempting to persuade all of these groups to conform, John Evans, the Wrexham pastor, was impervious to both his allure and his blandishments. 'I am very much troubled for the poor souls at Wrexham', Lloyd informed Archbishop Sancroft in

November 1682: 'They were horribly poisoned by one Vavasor Powell in the late wretched times.'[121] Evans had married Powell's widow, and the bishop's frustration with them both could barely be concealed. He had no compunction about using the Conventicle Act against them, and were it not for the ineffectiveness of the local magistrates they would be already under lock and key. A month later he repeated his complaints against 'that impudent conventicle in Wrexham', but soon the situation would deteriorate.[122] The Rye House Plot of spring 1683 in which a group of former republicans and aggrieved noblemen conspired to topple the king, caused outrage not least among the bishops, while 'Anglican paranoia in the provinces grew to new heights'.[123] Those in high office turned obsessively suspicious of Dissent, no one more than the bishop of St Asaph who vilified (in his correspondence with Sancroft at least) those whom he had previously courted. '[James] Owen, the Oswestry preacher' was the target of special opprobrium, while 'every Protestant Dissenter, as those bloody wretches are pleased to call themselves' were seen to be party to the conspiracy: 'For 'tis visible that all this while we have been treating with these sectaries, it has been God's wonderful providence that when they mustered in their conventicles they had not come out to cut our throats.'[124] According to his biographer, '[t]hese were the letters of a very frightened man'.[125] Although he would show a renewed consideration especially for Philip Henry and the Quaker Richard Davies during the coming years, any hope for reconciliation had been squandered.[126] Whereas for Anglicans William Lloyd would be revered as 'one of the most learned, laborious and successful bishops that ever occupied the see of St Asaph',[127] his 'proud spirit, violent temper and enormous egotism'[128] would blight his memory in Dissenting historiography for generations to come.[129]

South Wales

In the county of Brecon, which had seen considerable Puritan activity during the Commonwealth,[130] five licences were issued in 1672, one at the Llanafan-fawr home of Thomas Evans, ejected minister of Maesmynys, two for the town of Talgarth and two others.[131] Although Henry Maurice (whose knowledge of the area's Dissent was extensive) notes that there was only one gathered church in the county, namely that of Llanigon 'consisting mostly of Independents in judgement and partly of Baptists their communion being founded upon union unto Christ as far as may be, according to the rule of gospel love',[132] other fellowships established decades before still exerted their presence.[133] The church to which Maurice alludes (and of which he was the pastor) was that which had been gathered by the ubiquitous Vavasor Powell, but there was also the Arminian Baptist congregation located on the border with Radnorshire at Cwm, Llanddewi Ystradenni, and led by Henry Gregory;[134] the closed communion Calvinistic Baptist cause at Olchon and Llanigon which had been planted by John Myles;[135] along with the open communion Calvinistic Baptist fellowship which met at the home of Thomas Evans at Pentre near Llanafan-fawr.[136] The amorphous nature of these churches, house meetings and congregations, which often spilled over county boundaries, reflected the fractured nature of Dissenting witness at the time. As Eryn White has stated: 'It was a situation that made it difficult for either a Presbyterian or an Independent [or Baptist] organisation to develop properly ... as each church was in reality a loose federation of different congregations.'[137] These Breconshire congregations had a presence in neighbouring Radnorshire, Montgomeryshire and Herefordshire, while the same pattern was replicated in the other southern counties.[138] Rather than being 'local churches', some of these were somewhat unwieldy county or cross-county gatherings.

Still within the diocese of St David's, Henry Maurice noted the existence of several informal gatherings of the godly in Cardiganshire but only one regularly established church, 'that which meets at Llan[badarn Fawr] being the first original gathered church in this county, of the judgement commonly called Independent but very moderate'.[139] This was in the north of the county but he neglects to mention the apparently flourishing fellowship centred on Cilgwyn in the Aeron Valley to the south with branches at Llanarth, Lampeter, Betws Bledrws, Llanbadarn Odwyn and Abermeurig, the existence of which during the 1650s and later is testified to in the church book.[140] Five of the nine licences granted for Cardiganshire in 1672 were for preaching houses in this area.[141] The key person in neighbouring Carmarthenshire is Stephen Hughes in whose name two licences were issued in 1672, one as teacher of the conventicle meeting at Llansteffan and another for the gathering at Pencader.[142] Maurice describes him as 'pastor of the original church that was in this county, and are properly Independent in their judgement not much differing from Presbyterianism'.[143] The Mynydd Bach (Capel Isaac) church book records that the church there was first gathered during the 1650s, listing fifteen members along with its pastor, Stephen Hughes,[144] while Maurice also lists the portion of the Llanigon (Breconshire) church which met near Llandovery who 'intended to make choice of Mr Rees Prytherch, a worthy, well qualified person, for their pastor'.[145] The cross-county nature of these geographically expansive churches is well illustrated in the fact that Maurice mentions under Carmarthenshire a branch of John Myles's Ilston church, namely Llangennech near the Glamorgan border, and a branch of the recently established Baptist church whose centre was at Rhydwilym in Pembrokeshire.[146]

That a Baptist church, closed communion and Calvinist in creed, could be established in Pembrokeshire in 1668 illustrates both the zealous nature of post-Restoration Dissent and the ineffectual way in which legal restrictions were being implemented: 'Persistent, proactive persecution of religious Dissenters of whatever shade of opinion had ... hardly been a characteristic of the country's civil authorities at any time.'[147] William Jones, the Commonwealth incumbent ejected from the living of Cilmaenllwyd in 1660, had been won over to the Baptist cause by Jenkin Jones when (it is said) they shared a cell during that year in Carmarthen goal.[148] After having been baptized by immersion, he began doing likewise, on the Pembrokeshire-Carmarthen border, in August 1667. Within a year thirty members had been gathered into fellowship and by 1689 there were 113 from as many as thirty-eight parishes in Pembrokeshire, Cardiganshire and Carmarthenshire.[149] According to Thomas Richards: 'The new Ilston was greater than the old. His [William Jones] work was sincere, substantial and abiding; all Baptists between Carmarthen and the Teifi may be reckoned in direct, though distant, succession, his disciples.'[150] The county's Congregationalists were the disciples of Peregrine Phillips, a local man educated at Jesus College, Oxford, who had been active in radical Puritan circles during the civil wars. Although inducted to various livings under the Commonwealth, he pastored a gathered congregation at Llangwm as well as acting as parish minister there, only relinquishing his incumbency in August 1662 on refusal to conform.[151] He remained pastor of the gathered congregation throughout the 1660s though Maurice recorded that 'it has been much shattered of late years between the troubles of the times and the Quakers'.[152] According to Edmund Calamy:

> He was a gracious and laborious servant of Jesus Christ and was useful in his whole neighbourhood. He took no small pleasure in reconciling differences. He continued in service to the very last, preaching twice the very Lord's day before his death, September 17, 1691, aged sixty-eight.[153]

Only three licences had been issued for the county in 1672.[154]

The counties of Glamorgan and Monmouth were divided between the two dioceses of St David's and Llandaff though county and diocesan boundaries did not coincide. Glamorgan saw the highest number of ejections between 1660 and 1662, twenty-three ministers and clergymen from a total of 130 throughout Wales, six of whom subsequently conformed.[155] In his replies to Archbishop Sheldon in 1669, Francis Davies, bishop of Llandaff, lists eight illegal conventicles in the part of the county over which he had jurisdiction, three of which were Quaker and the others containing an assortment of Congregationalists and Baptists. The largest, with over 300 members (if his informants could be believed), was in Merthyr Tydfil, 'a mixed rabble', led by 'Henry William Thomas who knows only the Welsh tongue and hath been during the late Rebellion a captain against the king'.[156] Curiously there is no mention of Dissenting presence in Cardiff, William Erbury's former sphere of labour (though there were two Quaker conventicles in the neighbouring parishes of Llandaff and Canton) and, as it lay within the diocese of St David, the town of Swansea, an important Puritan centre during the Commonwealth and Protectorate, was not mentioned. Given the strength of Puritan activity during the Interregnum it was hardly surprising that as many as twenty-six licences were issued throughout the county in 1672, four of which were for meeting places in Swansea.[157] Three years later Henry Maurice mentioned 'the church that meets at Swansea, gathered at first by Mr Ambrose Mostyn; they are all Independents in judgement for aught I know, Mr [Daniel] Higgs being their pastor'.[158] Stephen Hughes, Daniel Higgs and Marmaduke Matthews, the New England Congregationalist who had returned to his native Swansea in 1654 before being ejected from the parish church of St Mary's in 1662,[159] had each been licenced to hold worship at their homes under the Indulgence. Although it contained Congregationalists as well as Baptists, the Baglan congregation which was listed both by Bishop Davies and Maurice[160] had emerged from the Ilston church and was led by Lewis Thomas who had succeeded as pastor after John Myles had left for Massachusetts in 1663.[161] Thomas had also been licenced to preach in Swansea under the Indulgence. Both Henry Maurice and Bishop Davies also noted the presence at Llangynwyd of a Presbyterian congregation led by the learned Samuel Jones, 'a godly, well-qualified, moderate person',[162] who would represent in south Wales the judicious doctrinal orthodoxy which was being championed in north Wales by Philip Henry and James Owen.[163]

Which only left Monmouthshire. Bishop Davies's report to Archbishop Sheldon in 1669 listed twenty illegal conventicles between Caldicot and Shirenewton in the east of the county, Bedwas, Mynydd Islwyn and Bedwellty to the north and Abergavenny, Gofilon and Llanwenarth to the west, all of which included Baptists, Congregationalists and Quakers of whom 'many ... were in actual arms in the late Rebellion or bred up under such'.[164] The twenty-four licences issued in 1672 reflects the spread of Dissenting presence in the county (apart from the Quakers who resolutely refused to avail themselves of the Indulgence), [165] while in 1675 Henry Maurice referred to the evolution that had occurred in William Wroth's original church at Llanfaches, one branch at Llangwm and Llantrisant having become Baptist and the other, although still Congregational, worshipping now at Magor 'in the moors, towards [the] Severn Sea'.[166] He also mentioned the Congregationalists of Mynydd Islwyn, Newport and Blaenau Gwent and the Baptists of Llanwenarth who shared fellowship with their co-religionists over the border in Olchon, Herefordshire, and at Llanigon in Breconshire, illustrating once more the sprawling, unwieldy shape of many Dissenting churches during these decades.

If this was the geographical pattern of Welsh Dissent by the mid-1670s, it remains difficult to judge how many of the Welsh people regarded themselves as committed Dissenting worshippers. Although scholars have shed serious doubt on the dependability of some of its Welsh evidence,[167] by far the best source to ascertain the movement's numerical strength is the census made by Henry Compton, bishop of London, in 1676 in order to gauge the purported threat, both Catholic and Dissenting, to the hegemony of the Established Church. The census showed that in the Bangor diocese there were 247 Dissenters, in St Asaph 463, in St David's 2,401 and in Llandaff 905. Fifty-two Dissenters were adjudged to be living in the Welsh-speaking border parishes of the diocese of Hereford.[168] Consequently in a total Welsh population of some 371,000, there were 1,085 adherents to the 'Old Faith' of the Catholic Church, 4,240 Protestant Dissenters and as many as 153,000 who conformed to the Established Church.[169] In other words, Welsh Protestant Dissenters 'were in a tiny minority' while the vast bulk of the population remained loyal to the reconstituted Church of England.[170] It is important to bear this in mind when analysing the spread of religious knowledge and theological understanding during the post-Restoration years.

Dissent and 'the Promotion of Piety' c.1670–89

With the disappearance of Jenkin Jones from the historical record after 1661, the death of Ambrose Mostyn in 1663 and John Myles's emigration to the American colonies in the same year followed by Vavasor Powell's demise in 1670, the generation of Puritan leaders who had been most active during the Interregnum had come to an end. The following generation was less radical though no less energetic while the problems they faced were more immediate and pressing. Those who held out for Presbyterian values have already been mentioned: Philip Henry, Samuel Jones and James Owen; the mantle of Congregationalist leadership fell on Stephen Hughes and Henry Maurice, while the most prominent Baptists were now William Jones and Lewis Thomas.

It has been claimed that 'Samuel Jones was, in many respects, the most eminent of all the Welsh Nonconformist ministers of the seventeenth century'.[171] His correspondence with Richard Baxter has already been referred to.[172] A native of Denbighshire, he had been educated at All Souls, Merton and Jesus College where he was elected fellow in 1652. Already acquainted with Philip Henry, an Oxford contemporary though at Christ Church, he took Presbyterian orders under the auspices of the Fourth Somerset Classis at Taunton in 1657 (probably through the influence of Joseph Alleine of Lincoln College and Corpus Christi who had left Oxford in 1655 to become assistant to George Newton, vicar of St Mary Magdalene church in the town). Later that year he was instituted to the incumbency of Llangynwyd, Glamorgan. Having married into the family of Rice Powell of Goetre-hen in 1660, one of the many Glamorgan gentry families which had taken a Puritan stand during the Commonwealth, he and Mary, his wife, took up residence at Brynllywarch within the parish which would remain the family home for the rest of his life.

Family connections afforded him both the financial stability and the practical support to withstand the worst of the post-Restoration opposition. He remained staunch if courteous in his refusal to bow to the entreaties of Hugh Lloyd, the High Church bishop of Llandaff and Francis Davies, his archdeacon (and successor), to conform and accept a living in their gift. His character as 'a Christian of the primitive stamp, always meek and humble, loving and peaceable' was evident in 1665 in the measured tone of his response to their offer.[173] He listed his reservations under four heads: first, that to accept that 'any book whatsoever (referring to the Book of Common Prayer) ... can justly lay claim to an unfeigned assent of the understanding and consent of the will to all and everything contained in it' was patently unreasonable, especially as the liturgy, by including the *filioque* clause in the Athanasian Creed, unchurched Greek Christendom and denied its adherents salvation, while it claimed conversely that all who were buried according to its own conventions were imbued with 'the sure and certain hope of salvation'.[174] Secondly, that in the matter of ceremonies, the Established Church had no right to impose rites that had no basis in scripture, or if regarded as *adiaphora* or matters indifferent neither ecclesiastical nor secular law should bind the conscience of worshippers and ministers. Thirdly, that to force ministers who had undertaken the solemn vows of ordination, albeit by presbytery, to be re-ordained by the hands of a prelatical episcopacy, was not only to nullify the validity of their previous ministry but to act in opposition to all of the best Protestant churches of Europe as well as the Church of England herself since the days of Archbishops Cranmer and Bancroft. Fourthly, that to constrain the consciences of fellow Christians in matters appertaining to worship and salvation when scripture allowed freedom, was inherently scandalous:

> Seeing the least evil of sin is not knowingly to be done to avoid the greatest evil of suffering, or to compass the greatest good thereby; whether a minister forcing himself against his light in all or any of these or the like particulars, God may not justly ... follow him with terrors of conscience to his grave? As by obvious instances within late experience, it is almost demonstrably apparent.[175]

As well as undertaking a preaching ministry – under the Indulgence as many as five licences were taken out in his name, at Cowbridge, Margam, Goetre-hen and Llangynwyd along with his Brynllywarch home[176] – Jones's main reputation was as principal of the academy that he had established at Brynllywarch by 1672.[177] According to Calamy: 'He was a great philosopher, a considerable master of the Greek and Latin tongues and a pretty good orientalist, an excellent casuist, well read in the modern controversies and a very useful preacher.'[178] He retained cordial relations with successive bishops of Llandaff as well as with the conformist clergy, including 'my loving neighbour' John Hutton, a Jesus College contemporary and his successor as vicar of Llangynwyd, to whom he bequeathed his copy of *The History of the Council of Trent* 'as a token of deserved respect for his friendship and neighbourhood for many years'.[179] Despite remaining a convinced non-conformist, he related in 1696: 'I confess I had then, and I have still, a very honourable respect for the able and the conscientious ministers of the Church of England, and do profess an agreement with all that are sound in their faith and holy in their life and conversation.'[180] This would remain a characteristic of the leaders of Welsh Dissent, including the Congregationalist Stephen Hughes, throughout these decades. It was a world away from the intemperate radicalism of William Erbury, Morgan Llwyd and Vavasor Powell and would accord with the sober Reformed churchmanship that had typified the best of Welsh theology between 1588 and 1642. Surprisingly, given both his erudition and his zeal, Samuel Jones published nothing. It was left to his colleagues, Stephen Hughes and Charles Edwards especially, to supply the reading public with devotional literature during these decades. This they did with assiduousness and remarkable success.

Stephen Hughes (1622–88) had been born in Carmarthen, the largest town in south Wales, into a fairly prosperous merchant family long imbued with Puritan convictions.[181] After his education at the local grammar school though not, it seems, at university, in 1650, under the provision of the Act for the Propagation of the Gospel, he was presented with the living of Merthyr four miles to the west of his home town, taking the place of its former incumbent who had been ejected for 'drunkenness and malgnancy'.[182] In August 1654, following the termination of the Act, he was transferred by the Triers to the living of Meidrim, a few miles away, which became the base for a wide itinerant ministry throughout the county.[183] Like Walter Cradock, but unlike Vavasor Powell and Morgan Llwyd, he was wholly supportive of the Protectorate and had an aversion to the radicalism of the millenarians and the Quakers. With the Restoration he was obliged to quit his living, and as a conscientious Congregationalist there was no question of his either seeking Episcopal ordination or of adhering to the stipulations of the Act of Uniformity. After leaving Meidrim in the spring of 1661, he returned to Carmarthen, and in 1665, aged forty-three, he married Catherine Bowen, the daughter of a substantial Puritan family, and moved to her Swansea home. Despite the stipulations of the Five Mile Act which prevented Dissenting preachers from living within five miles of any corporate town or parliamentary borough, Swansea had, in fact, become 'a city of refuge' for the ejected clergy, and among its 292 Dissenters (far more than in any other Welsh town and more than in the whole diocese of Bangor) were such prominent leaders as Marmaduke Matthews, Daniel Higgs and now Hughes himself.[184] Like others among his Dissenting colleagues, he benefitted from the half-hearted application of the penal laws and the sympathy shown by many in authority to those whom they regarded as upright and principled citizens whatever differences they had with the present regime. His appearances before the archdeacon's court in December 1667 for holding an illegal conventicle at Llansteffan and in June 1670 for keeping school without an Episcopal licence led to fines, but otherwise were fairly inconsequential. They did nothing to impede either his itinerant preaching or his pastoral work building up congregations at Llansteffan, Tre-lech, Pencader, Capel Isaac, Pentre-tŷ-gwyn and Llanedi.[185]

Hughes's first venture into evangelism through print occurred in 1657 with his publication of a selection of Rhys Prichard's popular verse. Prichard, the vicar of Llandovery, had died at the outset of the civil war, but his reputation for godliness and vital religion was still fresh decades later. It was a sign of the Congregationalist's moderation and expansiveness that he had no qualms about publishing the works of an avowed royalist and churchman whose Reformed piety, nevertheless, had been admired by all:

> Take no umbrage at certain terms which are used in this book, such as calling a congregation a church, a minister a priest, morning-prayer matins and the like. This was wholly acceptable during the author's day, and even now it should cause little offence. Certainly none of us should expend any zeal in tussling over matters like these but should contend, rather, for the faith once given to the saints, namely the doctrines necessary for salvation.[186]

Hughes's own theology was a very earnest form of evangelical Calvinism with the call to costly repentance well to the fore. He felt an affinity with Prichard who, despite being a resolute conformist, held the same doctrinal truths while pressing on his parishioners the need for true conversion and a vital personal faith. In all of his prefaces to the vicar's works – 1659, 1670, 1672 and 1681 – he provided a precis of the books' contents and urged his readers to repent of their sins and turn to Christ. Prichard's verses elaborate on the sinfulness of the people, the dire state of those who persist in sin, the multifarious ways in which people deceive themselves that they are in a right relationship with God despite being unconverted, that salvation is in Christ alone, and that faith is only validated by issuing forth in sanctification, good works and the keeping of God's commandments. 'Take heed to what is written here concerning true faith', concluded Hughes,

> as there are many who think they have faith merely by believing that there is a God, that Christ is his Son and that He has died for their sins, though they have never repented of their sins or changed their ways or lived consciously to please God. They should beware lest they deceive themselves.[187]

True faith was through costly repentance and a lively appropriation of Christ by means of an experienced faith. The gospel, however, was readily available for those who would turn and live.

Hughes's emphasis during the 1660s was on preaching and pastoral work, and it was then that his reputation was consolidated as a winsome if uncompromising evangelist. According to Calamy:

> He was a plain, methodical and affectionate preacher, and instilled much upon the great and substantial things of religion. He seldom preached without melting into tears, which often drew tears from his auditors. He affected to preach in the darkest corners, and in places where the people had ignorant readers that could not preach. His moderation and lively preaching recommended him to the esteem of the sober part of the gentry, by whose connivance he often preached in public [= parish] churches, which were much thronged with hearers from the neighbouring parishes … He had very great seals to his ministry, in the numbers that were reclaimed from their sinful ways, and became serious Christians.[188]

Even then he sensed the evangelistic importance of the written word, and urged his readers to acquaint themselves with the body of theological and didactic literature that had been made available in Welsh during the previous generation:

God placed it upon the hearts of some to translate into Welsh such English books as the *Pathway to Heaven*, the *Practice of Piety*, *Mr Perkins' Catechism* etc., and on the hearts of others to compose, in our language, small books of their own such as *Carwr y Cymry* ["The Welshman's Kinsman"], *Drych i Dri Math o Bobl* ["A Mirror for Three Types of People"], *Cydgordiad y Scrythyrau* ["A Scriptural Concordance"] and *Cannwyll y Crist* ["Christ's Candle"], the reading of which has brought no small benefit to many. That benefit is also to be had by perusing *Y Cywir Ddychwelwr* ["The True Convert"] and Bishop Ussher's Catechism which have recently been translated into Welsh.[189]

Whereas Prichard had used verse as an evangelistic tool, Hughes was insistent that potential converts should learn to read in order to access the scriptures and devotional manuals for themselves. In order to create a literate people he stressed the need for education which brought him, by the early 1670s, into contact with Thomas Gouge's 'Welsh Trust'.

The absence of educational provision following the collapse of the system set up initially under the Act for the Propagation of the Gospel and continued under the Protectorate created a vacuum only partially filled by the establishment of schools, both with and without Episcopal permission, after the Restoration. Glamorgan, reported Bishop Hugh Lloyd after receiving his first Articles of Enquiries for his diocese in 1662, 'was utterly destitute of schools', while the move to provide education came not primarily from the bishops but from the labours of individuals, many of whom were Dissenters.[190] In his report to Lambeth Palace in February 1672, Bishop Lucy of St David's complained to Archbishop Sheldon that '[d]espite law and coercion', the Dissenters within his diocese were unrelenting in establishing elementary schools.[191] (For the 308 parishes in the diocese, there were a mere ten officially licenced parish-based schools, while in Bangor under the unflinchingly anti-Dissenting Humphrey Lloyd, there was a paltry five.) This was the situation into which Thomas Gouge (1605–81) came.[192] The philanthropic Gouge, a non-doctrinaire Presbyterian and 'one of the most moderate nonconformists',[193] having reluctantly quit his living of St Sepulchure's, Southwark, in 1662, had been won to the cause of evangelism in Wales through the influence of Joseph Alleine of Taunton, the friend of Samuel Jones and author of the widely read *Alarm to the Unconverted* (1672). Although an Englishman, Alleine 'had an eye for the poor Welsh', though due to his poor health, he was prevented from going among them.

The reading of this [however] did so inflame the zeal of ... Mr Thomas
Gouge (as he himself told me) that he was restless in his spirit, till (having settled his affairs about London) he had liberty and opportunity to
persecute this design. Since which time he has made many journeys both
into South and North Wales where he hath done much good.[194]

Whereas some of the Welsh bishops were at best indifferent to providing means for the people to learn to read and at worst – due to their
antipathy to Dissent – actively opposed, there were other individuals
who looked beyond sterile divisions in order to encourage the spread of
Christian orthodoxy of an all-embracing kind. Among Gouge's associates in the capital were such key establishment figures as John Tillotson,
dean and later Archbishop of Canterbury, Edward Stillingfleet, canon
of St Paul's, and Simon Patrick, at the time prebendary of Westminster
and later bishop of Ely. He was equally friendly with such broadminded
and influential Dissenters as Richard Baxter, the biblical commentator
Matthew Poole and the theologically Arian businessman and philanthropist Thomas Firmin. With their backing, along with that of the
Lord Mayor of London and the court of aldermen, he secured sufficient
funds to establish a trust, the mission of which was to establish schools in
Wales and disseminate Welsh Bibles along with evangelistic literature. He
was equally successful in attracting the support of key Welsh politicians
like Sir Edward Harley, MP for Radnor, Sir Edward Mansell, Sir John
Trevor, Sir Trevor Williams, MP for Monmouth, and Pembrokeshire's
Sir Erasmus Philipps. Although this grated on the bishops: Lloyd of
Bangor described Gouge as an 'itinerant emissary of the leading sectaries' whose only aim was to draw 'the credulous common people into a
disaffection to the government and liturgy of the Church',[195] by 1675
over eighty schools had been founded in twelve of the thirteen Welsh
counties with well over 2,000 boys and girls being taught to read and
write (albeit in English rather than the vernacular). What is more, thirty-
two Welsh Bibles, 479 copies of the New Testament and 500 copies of
Holl Ddyledswydd Dyn, John Langford's translation of Richard Allestree's
The Whole Duty of Man, had been distributed.[196] If bishops Lucy and
Humphrey Lloyd reviled him, many of the parish clergy were happy to
support his venture, while John Tillotson was unstinting in his praise;

That he might manage the distribution of this great charity with his own
hands, and see the good effect of it with his own eyes, he always once,

but usually twice a year, at his own charge travelled over a great part of
Wales, none of the best countries to travel in. But for the love of God and
men he endured all that, together with the extremity of heat and cold …
not only with patience but with pleasure … Wales may as worthily boast
of this truly apostolical man as of their famous St David.[197]

In order to expedite his vision, Gouge needed the help of
Welsh-speaking colleagues, and these he found principally in Stephen
Hughes and Charles Edwards.[198] The preface to Hughes's 1672 edition
of Rhys Prichard's works shows how his and Gouge's views cohered.
Dedicated to William Thomas, dean of Worcester (and later bishop
of St David's), Hugh Edwards, vicar of Llangadog, Carmarthenshire,
and William Lloyd, rector of St Petrox, Pembrokeshire, along with the
Dissenters David Thomas of Margam and Samuel Jones, he emphasizes
the wide common ground between orthodox and godly conformists and
their nonconformist brethren. He praises Thomas especially for his practical support in bringing out a recent vernacular edition of the New
Testament, the Psalms and the Welsh translation of Perkins's *Catechism*.
His future aim was to publish the whole Welsh Bible, which had become
scarce, at an affordable price for the benefit of all. One of the founding principles of the Reformation had been that God's Word should be
made known in the language of people. The preface is, in fact, a warm
panegyric in praise of the Bible and an impassioned appeal to the Welsh
bishops to facilitate the publication and dissemination of Scriptures
among the common people. He charges them to do this

> [f]or the glory of God, for the sake of Jesus Christ who yearns for the
> salvation of sinners, for the precious souls of the people who, in many
> parts of Wales, dwell in darkness and in the shadow of death, for the
> honour of the Christian faith … and for the joy of all who fear God
> within this kingdom.[199]

Hughes's characteristic tolerance was expressed in the conclusion
to his composite volume *Cyfarwydd-deb i'r Anghyfarwydd* (1677) ('An
Instruction for the Uninformed'):

> We have good reason to believe that there are among us many minis-
> ters, both conformists and nonconformists, who are as learned, as able,
> as godly, as vigilant of the lambs of Christ which have been committed

to their care as anywhere else in Christendom. And God forbid that I breathe a single word against their holy calling, or their persons, or even suggest any criticism which would provoke people to blame such reverend servants who are faithful to God according to their knowledge, their calling and their situation, whatever their opinion in inconsequential matters that may be in dispute among us.[200]

By then his campaign to evangelize through literature, funded by the Welsh Trust, had expanded substantially. A reprint of Robert Holland's version of Perkins's *Catechism* had appeared in 1672 along with two translations by Richard Jones (1603–73), the Denbigh schoolmaster, namely Henry Oasland's *Christian Daily Walk* (1660) entitled *Rhodfa Cristion*, and *Amdo i Babyddiaeth*, Baxter's anti-papal tract, *A Winding-Sheet for Popery* (1567).[201] Hughes's compendium, *Tryssor i'r Cymry* (1677) ('A Treasure for the Welsh') contained a new edition of Robert Llwyd's 1629 translation of Arthur Dent's *Sermon on Repentance* (*Pregeth ynghylch Edifeirwch*), a second edition of Oliver Thomas's *Drych i Dri Math o Bobl* ('A Mirror for Three Types of People') which had first appeared in 1648, along with Richard Jones's translation of Baxter's *Now or Never* (1662) entitled *Bellach neu Byth*, a treatise on the believer's need to be justified by faith in Christ. His *Cyfarwydd-deb i'r Anghyfarwydd* of the same year contained a new version of Robert Holland's early (1599) translation of William Perkins's tract on the Lord's Prayer, *Agoriad Byrr ar Weddi'r Arglwydd* ('A Short Exposition of the Lord's Prayer'), a new version of Oliver Thomas's 1631 *Car-wr y Cymry* ('The Welshman's Kinsman') and a Welsh translation of Vavasor Powell's *Saving Faith set forth in Three Dialogues* (1651), namely *Ymddidanion rhwng Crist a'r Publican, rhwng Crist a'r Pharisaed, a rhwng Crist a'r Credadyn ammheus*. A year earlier Richard Jones had issued a translation of Gouge's *Christian Directions* (1672) entitled *Hyfforddiadau Christianogol*, while William Jones (d.1679) – not the Baptist – another Denbigh Puritan who forfeited his living at the Restoration, translated the same author's *A Word to Sinners and a Word to Saints* (1668) as *Gair i Bechaduriaid a Gair i Sainct*, along with his *Principles of Christian Religion* (1645) which he released as *Principlau neu Bennau y Grefydd Ghristianogol*.[202] All these were didactic works expounding the same doctrinal convictions shared by orthodox Protestants of all stripes (apart from formalists and rank Arminians). 'Early modern Protestantism was a *broad-based* religious culture', according to Alec Ryrie. 'The division between puritan and conformist Protestants, which has been so important in English historiography, almost fades from view when examined through the lens of devotion and lived experience.'[203] This is also true of the evidence from Wales. What Hughes had achieved in this short burst of frenetic activity was to re-establish continuity with the theological tradition which had been developed steadfastly among Welsh Protestants from 1588 onwards, and had been disrupted, in part, by the upheavals of the civil wars and Interregnum and later imperilled by intransigent forces after 1662. In short, the hard-won legacy of the first four decades of the century was being restored.

The final figure to be noted among those who strove to 'promote piety' through the written word during these years is the exquisite littérateur Charles Edwards (c.1628–after 1691). A native of Llansilin, on the Denbighshire-Shropshire border, he was educated at All Souls and Jesus College, Oxford, and in 1650 was appointed itinerant in north-east Wales under the Propagation Act. Thereafter he proceeded to the living of Llanrhaeadr-ym-Mochnant (celebrated as the place where William Morgan had translated the 1588 Welsh Bible) where he married (probably) the daughter of his predecessor, the Presbyterian Oliver Thomas, author of *Car-wr y Cymry*. Deprived of the living in 1660, two years before the implementation of the Act of Uniformity, he submitted to the Oath of Allegiance and afterwards lived 'as privately and inoffensively as I could'. According to his short – and melancholy – autobiography: 'I often went to hear the conformists in public, and seldom joined in private worship with any greater number than the law allows of, and never meddled with any designs to disturb the government.'[204] In other words, like Philip Henry and other moderate nonconformists, he refused to contravene the laws laid down under the Clarendon Code though he never submitted to Episcopal ordination, while in 1672 he was licenced under the Indulgence (temporarily it seems) 'to be a general Pr[esbyterian] teach[er] at Oswestry in Salop'.[205] Everything about him underlines the fact that, in ecclesiastical matters, he was nonaggressive and restrained, supporting parochial worship under the current regime:

My disposition was moderate … towards the established ecclesiastical government, acknowledging its usefulness in exhibiting the Scriptures and prayers to these nations in their vulgar tongues, upholding learning, and a deal of smooth and grave praying and preaching and melodious singing which I hope by some are devoutly improved.[206]

His career as an author began in 1667 with the publication of his slim volume describing the history of Protestant Christianity entitled *Y Ffydd Ddi-ffuant* ('The Unfeigned Faith'). A larger version was issued in 1671 but it was the third edition, *Y Ffydd Ddi-ffuant, sef hanes y Ffydd Gristianogol a'i Rhinwedd* ('The Unfeigned Faith, being a history of the Christian Faith and its Virtue'), which became a classic. The ninety-page abridgment of Foxe's *Acts and Monuments* of 1667 was transformed into a 400-page treatise containing a history of Christianity from the early years, a narrative assessing the development of the faith in Wales, and a presentation of the essence of Reformed piety set forth in a magnificent prose style.[207] Part One begins with a description of the ancient world and the way in which the divine decree was manifested in the history of Israel and the coming of Christ (chapters 1 to 3). The apostolic age was one of patent spiritual success: 'As through the preaching of the apostles in a short time each kingdom was filled with Christians, as so many barns are filled with grain during the few short weeks of harvest.'[208] There was a deep continuity between the old dispensation and the new, though now the fulfilment had occurred: 'The New Testament remained veiled within the Old, but now the Old has been revealed in the New, and, like the sun over Africa, gives forth light without a shadow' (p. 28). Success brought the inevitable reaction, though through the martyrdom of Ignatius of Antioch, Polycarp and others and the works of Justin Martyr (including the *Dialogue with Trypho the Jew*) and his colleagues, Christian witness was sustained and its intellectual as well as moral integrity was undergirded (chapters 4 to 6). Edwards had not only learned from the Apostolic Fathers and Apologists, but was keen to convey the substance of their writings to his readers. The same was true of the work of other patristic authors, Cyprian, Tertullian and Origen especially. The following chapters (7 to 9) are replete with extended quotations from the pre-Nicene Fathers including Tertullian's aphorisms:

> If the Tiber overflows its banks, if the Nile does not rise in order to irrigate the fields, if the earth quakes and famine and pestilence follow, soon they're all screaming: 'Throw the Christians to the lions!' (p. 62)
>
> As often as you mow us down the more numerous we become; the blood of the Christians is seed (p. 65)

and punctuated with Edwards's own striking metaphors:

> After this the church experienced a time of peace which in turn gener-
> ated pride and discord among the Christians just as a shaft between two
> clouds lights up the weeds amidst the corn (p. 70)
>
> ... As the summer draws the flies, so dissension and jealousy grow
> from indolence. (pp. 71–2)

Up till then the church had been a despised if potent minority, but
with the conversion of Constantine, 'that godly emperor' (p. 75), on
having seen the sign *In hoc vince*, 'In this conquer', 'the Christian faith
expanded like the wheat at the beginning of summer when the cold of
winter has passed' (p. 74). This took Edwards to the Arian controversy,
the Council of Nicaea in 325 and the contribution of such giants as
Ambrose, Augustine and Chrysostom (chapter 10). He also includes a
remarkable chapter (11) expounding the religion of Islam and the life
of the Prophet Mohammed replete with a synopsis, the first ever in
Welsh, of the Koran. (It had first been translated into English in 1649
by Alexander Ross, chaplain to Charles I.) The following four chapters
(12 to 15) took him into the Middle Ages, with an emphasis on renewal
movements such as the Albigenses, the Waldensians and the Lollards
and on proto-reformers such as Wycliffe and Huss, and then to Erasmus
and the dawn of the Reformation and the 'witnessing' – *pro-testare* – at
the Diet of Spyer in 1529, 'and for that they were called Protestants'
(p. 115). As for Luther, who died in 1546, nearly thirty years after having nailed his ninety-five theses to the door of the Wittenberg church:

> Although he had suffered much, Luther died with his head on his pillow,
> in tranquillity, after twenty nine years having preached profitably, hav-
> ing prayed effectively, having written with genius, having been delivered
> from many trials and having lived a holy life. (p. 116)

Calvin, he claimed, 'was one of the purest preachers and the most replete
of grace and learning since the time of the apostles' (p. 118), but the
Genevan reformer had not stood alone: among his contemporaries were
Beza, Knox, Bilney and others. The Reformation had been championed in
England first under Henry VIII and Edward VI, and despite the setback
under Mary Tudor, was to thrive during the reign of Queen Elizabeth.
In treating his own century, Edwards is reticent about the civil war,
claiming that its wounds were still fresh (p. 148), but he was insistent
that presently the state of Christianity was buoyant:

We can say confidently that knowledge of the gospel has never been clearer, the scriptures and good books have never been more readily and cheaply available, preachers, even since the time of the prophets and apostles, have never been more able than they are now throughout the kingdoms of the west, indeed wherever there has been renewal and religious freedom. (p. 148)

Part of the originality of Part One was that it introduced readers to the names and writings of the Early Church Fathers – Edwards would later publish a compendium of excerpts from the patristic writers in English entitled *Fatherly Instructions, being Select Pieces of the Writings of the Primitive Christian Teachers* (1686) – which broke with the stark Biblicism of the earlier Welsh Puritans and placed current Protestant faith within an historical continuum that was far more extensive than usual. In chapters 16 to 20 he advanced a theory of Welsh nationhood which was at once providential and patriotic. Having drunk deeply from David Powel's *Historie of Cambria* (1584) and Percy Enderbie's *Cambria Triumphans, or Brittain in its Perfect Lustre* (1661), he fashioned his own analysis of the history of the faith in Wales, taking his cue from Bishop Richard Davies's celebrated 1567 '*Epistol … at y Cembru*' ('Epistle to the Welsh'), which had been so persuasive in convincing Welsh Christians during the preceding century that the Reformation had been the natural successor of the early Celtic Church whereas medieval Rome had, in fact, been an interloper.[209] Edwards had re-issued Davies's tract along with a new edition of Maurice Kyffin's 1595 translation of Bishop Jewel's *Apologia Ecclesiae Anglicanae*, namely *Deffynniad Ffydd Eglwys Loegr* under the exhilarating title *Dadseiniad Meibion y Daran* ('An Echo of the Sons of Thunder') in 1671. Even more potent had been his discovery of the sixth-century monk Gildas, whose *De Excidio Britanniae* ('On the Fall of Britain') had been published by Polydore Vergil in 1525. Following his monastic exemplar, Edwards held that when Wales or 'Britain', like Israel of old, had been obedient to its Lord its people had been blessed, but when they had hardened their hearts against him, judgement had followed. Such was the power of Gildas on his imagination that he fashioned his historical narrative in the light of the monk's prophetic motif. Indeed, he called the concluding part of *Fatherly Instructions*, in which he applied the sixth-century jeremiad to the contemporary situation, 'Gildas Minimus'.[210] Chapter 17 of *Y Ffydd Ddi-ffuant* consisted of a summary of Gildas's volume while the surrounding chapters elucidated Edwards's providential interpretation of the history of the Welsh nation.[211] Although his countrymen should always beware that they would be judged for their sins, nevertheless a merciful God had blessed them profusely:

> Since the Scriptures came among us in Welsh, our nation has prospered more than ever before. God has granted us peace. This present generation knows nothing of the woeful misfortunes that were inflicted on our forefathers. The English, who were formerly like ravenous wolves, have become tender shepherds and nearly as kind to us as we are to one another. (pp. 209–10)

For Charles Edwards, like all of his compatriots since the Tudor era, the incorporation of Wales into the English state had brought untold benefits.

Following two chapters of rational apologetic extolling 'The sure truth of the Christian faith' (20 to 21), Edwards begins Part Two, 'The Virtue of the Faith', which constitutes the most compelling assessment of the human predicament under sin and the remedial work of Christ and the gospel as had yet appeared in vernacular prose. These chapters (22 to 29) 'include some of the most brilliant prose ever composed in Welsh ... This is writing that takes one's breath away, work which is sweepingly, consummately splendid':[212]

> As our first parents (who were once wholesome) became tainted by the sinful pestilence when they stood in the breath of the infernal Serpent, the foul disease poisoned their seed ever after, while the corrupted sap from the trunk of the tree (namely Adam) soured all the branches (to wit, his descendants) bringing forth rotten fruit, that is lives hostile to the will of God. (p. 260)

Thereafter, in an escalating proliferation of imagery, Edwards pictures the consequences of the Fall: all have been effected, the nations of Christendom and beyond; all ages, whether young or old; all categories of people, irrespective of social status, while humankind's very equilibrium had been wholly overthrown: 'In his fall man's head has plunged downwards while his belly has gone atop (such a pitiful posture!); his lust now is stronger than his reason' (p. 265). Having influenced mind and will, body and soul, sin engenders its own condemnation: 'The defilement of sin is snakelike, having a sting in its tail. In the wake of its merriment comes savagery, choleric bitterness is mixed with the dregs of the wine; such is the truth experienced by each conscience and soul' (p. 277). Unremitting gloom is hardly conducive to creating great literature nor to effective evangelism, yet the expansive comparisons, extended similes and imaginative pliability that are such a characteristic of Edwards's work turns his diagnosis of the blighted condition of the human soul into prose of the most arresting kind. Neither does he stay too long with the sombre reality of sinfulness.

The concluding chapters move inexorably from the strain involved in drawing individuals away from the lure of their lusts and relish of their trespasses to the ultimately irresistible work of grace which guarantees the victory of Christ and the gospel. God is gracious despite humankind's rebellion, and Christ has come among them, and through the sacrifice of the cross has fulfilled the demands of righteousness and achieved salvation for the elect: 'Thus he purifies his people not only of the guilt which had weighed down their conscience, but of the pollution which had defiled their hearts and their lives' (pp. 295–6). Through the gift of the Holy Spirit, the preaching of the Word and the ministry of Christ's faithful servants, salvation had been made freely available to all who would avail themselves of it. (In the mystery of election it was only some, however, who would do so). For those who were to come broken-spirited, 'pleading to God to be cleansed from all sin through the blood of Christ', forgiveness, comfort and release was assured unreservedly (p. 316). Despite Edwards's melancholic cast of mind, these superbly accomplished chapters are suffused with a quiet confidence in the divine benevolence which makes the book's tenor ultimately affirming and positive. The author's training in classical rhetoric is obvious throughout – he provided his readers with instructions, in an appendix, as how to recognize the different figures of speech – yet his aim was not to produce timeless literature but simply to save souls: 'Clearly designed to penetrate the mind and lodge in the memory, these ... [passages] remind us that the main concern of Edwards was to create an affective rhetoric powerful enough to effect a profound transformation in people's lives.'[213] The final chapters (26 to 29) constitute a call to scriptural holiness, an appeal to all who have experienced justifying grace to live their lives in grateful response to Christ, their Lord, knowing that despite their manifest imperfections that the saints will persevere to the end:

Lastly my dear Wales, consider, yes consider eternally that God deserves
your willing obedience; it is He who has created you, redeemed you and
sustains you. He has been a benevolent Father to us all, so it is fitting
that we give to him our utmost as his tender children … He is our king
of exceptional majesty and deserves our respect. And to him be glory
forever. Amen. (p. 383)

Along with Anglicans of the 'holy living' school, it was through the
workmanlike prose of Stephen Hughes, Richard Jones and William Jones
and the literary brilliance of Charles Edwards, underwritten by Thomas
Gouge's Welsh Trust and the patronage of sympathetic clerics and
laymen, that orthodox doctrine and biblical piety were disseminated
among the Welsh during the latter period of the Stuart era. Moreover,
'[f]rom the standpoint of the history of ideas, these books exer-
cised a great influence … since they provided the foundation for a
Welsh-language Protestant theological culture'.[214]

The post-Restoration consensus

In terms of both piety and doctrine, there was a vast amount of common
ground between Anglican and Dissenter in post-Restoration Wales. The
extreme partisan enmity posited by current political controversy and
later denominational historiography for the most part did not exist. It is
true that the most fanatical High Church zealots would always despise
Dissenters while those on the Powellite wing of radical Dissent would
have no truck with churchmen of any stripe, yet the bulk of the faithful
(whether they attended the parish church or a conventicle) yearned for
concord and accommodation. Recent scholarship in the area of English
church history has made clear 'that the Anglican piety of the Restoration
was far from tepid',[215] while the evidence shows that among ordinary
Christians in late seventeenth-century Wales, vital godliness was far
from lacking.[216] The conciliatory spirit that characterized Stephen
Hughes's leadership among the Congregationalists and the constructive eirenicism of such senior churchmen as St David's William Thomas
and Humphrey Humphreys in Bangor was exhibited in their mutual
desire to bring their compatriots to a saving faith in Christ. 'The Church
is under a strange judgement being so barren when her breasts are so
full', wrote Charles Edwards in 1677. 'Ephraim's fate was that her womb
aborted and her breasts were so parched. But today Zion, though fertile,

cannot bear children for her heavenly spouse. Though the milk of the Word is plentiful, there is but little sign of increase among us.'[217] All zealous evangelists were dismayed that the common faith of Protestant Christendom was less effective than they strove for it to be.

Not only was there substantial communality across ecclesiastical boundaries, but there was considerable continuity with the doctrinal norms of the pre-civil war church. For all but the most radical Protestants, mostly Quakers, Baptists and extreme Independents, there was unanimity in the need to maintain political stability and strengthen social bonds. Indeed, '[t]he moral message of the Restoration church was essentially what it had been in the 1650s, a message of personal piety and political quiescence'.[218] The morally bracing High Church sacramentalism of Welsh Anglican theology during the 1670s and 1680s was not wholly dissimilar to the Reformed faith as exemplified by those like Bishop Lewis Bayly, Robert Llwyd of Chirk, Dr John Davies of Mallwyd and Rhys Prichard, vicar of Llandovery, a half-century earlier. Although liturgical and Episcopalian, it was Word-centred, incontrovertibly Protestant and pointedly conversionist. Formalist it was not:

> This union with Christ through faith was the crux of seventeenth-century religion. It provided the theological and emotional assurance of the Christian's salvation as a sinner; it united theology and piety by connecting a logical account with a religious experience.[219]

This remained the essence of Welsh theology, whether Anglican or Dissenting, during these years:

> The bulk of the literature of inward experience published [in Wales] in this period was outstanding in its emphasis on the 'psychological vivisection' of the soul, on the subjective awareness of sin, on the Christocentric nature of faith, and on the practical fruits of the growth of grace in the regenerated soul.[220]

The idea that somehow post-Restoration piety was formalistic, notional or barrenly moralistic is patently wrong. Moralism, in the context of Reformation theology, is an unwarranted trust in good works or actions performed by the natural powers of individuals without the grace of the gospel. The Protestant Reformation was a wholesale rejection of such a view. All the preaching, teaching, catechizing and literature produced by Welsh theologians since the days of William Salesbury and Bishop Richard Davies centred on the absolute truth of the sinner's justification by faith alone on the basis of the atoning sacrifice of Christ. This was the article upon which the church would stand or fall. The same convictions animated the labours of virtually all the authors and evangelists whose work has been assessed above.

What differed was the context. Following the execution of Charles I and the Interregnum there was a feeling abroad that the very pillars of church and state were being shaken and that morality itself was under threat. The social radicalism of William Erbury, the lurid millennialism of Morgan Llwyd and Vavasor Powell and the uninhibited antinomianism of Walter Cradock did little to allay people's fears. There was no wonder that the anti-Quaker diatribes of such Restoration Anglicans as Rondl Davies, the vicar of Meifod,[221] were so impetuous, while the prominence given by the moderate Dissenters Stephen Hughes and Charles Edwards to the doctrine of sanctification and the need for moral rectitude was as pronounced as their belief in the necessity of justification by faith alone. The stern ascetical teaching of post-1662 Anglicanism was, for its part, an inevitable response to the excesses of the Great Rebellion while its religious seriousness paralleled Puritanism at its most severe: 'Anglican piety was a regime of introspective, almost morbid self-examination, penitence and thanksgiving, of private and household devotion, and it was the necessary foundation of "holy living".'[222] For Richard Allestree and his Welsh disciples, the translators of *The Whole Duty of Man* and other works of the 'holy living' school, stark asceticism fed by strict Prayer Book worship and sacramental piety could only function on the basis of a sure faith in the divine mercy: 'Far from demoting religion to the mere pursuit of virtue, the theology of "holy living" demanded a rigorous pursuit of Christian perfection while constantly reiterating the impossibility of overcoming sin.'[223] As John Walsh so perceptively pointed out, a half-century later it would become one of the taproots of the Evangelical Revival.[224] Redemption through the blood of Christ was at its very heart. If it seemed sometimes to blur the distinction between justification and sanctification, to downplay the doctrine of election in favour of the obedience of the human will and to accentuate discipline, worship and right conduct, it did so in the knowledge that God remained sovereign in the process of salvation and that the integrity of the Christian life should be maintained. For Welsh

Anglicans and Dissenters alike, the yoke of Christ was not something to be taken on lightly.

Notes

1   Edward Wynn, *Trefn Ymarweddiad Gwir Gristion, neu lwybr hyffordd i'r Cymro i rodio arno beunydd gyda'i Dduw* (Llundain: n.p., 1662), p. 11; hereafter page numbers in the text.

2   For Wynn, see *DWB*.

3   Matthew Sylvester (ed.), *Reliquae Baxterianae* (London: Thomas Parkhurst, 1696), I, ii 29; quoted in Ann Whiteman, 'The Restoration of the Church of England', in Geoffrey F. Nuttall and Owen Chadwick (eds), *From Uniformity to Unity, 1662–1962* (London: SPCK, 1962), pp. 19–68 (43).

4   Stephen Hampton, *Anti-Arminians: The Anglican Reformed Tradition from Charles II to George I* (Oxford: Oxford University Press, 2008), *passim*.

5   For William Roberts (1585–1665) see *DWB* and *ODNB*.

6   Geraint H. Jenkins, *Literature, Religion and Society in Wales, 1660–1730* (Cardiff: University of Wales Press, 1978), p. 22; for Morgan (1608–73), see *DWB* and *ODNB*.

7   William Jacob, 'Part Two: 1660–1780', in Glanmor Williams, William Jacob, Nigel Yates and Frances Knight, *The Welsh Church from Reformation to Disestablishment, 1603–1920* (Cardiff: University of Wales Press, 2007), pp. 65–208 (89); cf. *DWB*, *ODNB* and E. G. Wright, 'Humphrey Humphreys (1648–1712), Bishop of Bangor and Hereford', *JHSCW*, 2 (1950), 72–86.

8   [Simon Patrick], *Egwyddor i rai Ieuaingc i'w cymhwyso i dderbyn y Cymmun Sanctaidd yn fuddiol*, trans. Edward Llwyd (Rhydychen: n.p., 1682), p. 15.

9   [Patrick], *Egwyddor i rai Ieuaingc*, p. 29.

10   John Thomas, *Unum Necessarium: Ymarferol Athrawiaeth Gweddi* (Llundain: n.p., 1680), p. 4; hereafter page numbers in the text.

11   [Patrick], *Egwyddor i rai Ieuaingc*, p. 121.

12   Ian M. Green, *The Re-establishment of the Church of England, 1660–63* (Oxford: Oxford University Press, 1975), p. 90; for Griffith (1601–67), see *DWB*, *ODNB*.

13   Anon., *A Welsh Narrative … containing a Narration of the Disputation between Dr Griffith and Mr Vavasor Powell, near New-Chappel in Montgomeryshire, July 23, 1652* (London: John Brown, 1653), p. 4.

14   James Ussher, *The Reduction of Episcopacie unto the form of Synodical Government* (London: Nicholas Bernard, 1656); see Alan Ford, *James Ussher, Theology, History and Politics in early-modern Ireland and England* (Oxford: Oxford University Press, 2007), pp. 223–56.

15   Anon., *A Relation of a Disputation between Dr Griffith and Mr Vavasor Powell* (London: Livewell Chapman, 1653), p. 2.

16   Anon., *A Welsh Narrative*, p. 17.

17   Anon., *A Welsh Narrative*, p. 18.

18 See G. Milwyn Griffiths, 'The Restoration in St Asaph: the Episcopate of Bishop George Griffith, 1660–66', *JHSCW*, 12 (1962), 9–27; 13 (1963), 27–40.

19 [William Foulkes], *Gweddi'r Arglwydd wedi ei hegluro, mewn amryw ymadroddion neu Bregethau Byrion, o waith y Gwir Barchedig Dad George Griffith DD, Diweddar Esgob Llanelwy* (Rhydychen: Y Theatr, 1685), p. 9; hereafter page numbers in the text.

20 Bodleian Library Tanner MS 146, f. 39; Thomas Richards, *Wales under the Penal Code, 1662–87* (London: National Eisteddfod Association, 1925), p. 142.

21 For Foulkes (d.1691), see *DWB*.

22 Quoted in Richards, *Wales under the Penal Code*, p. 135.

23 For Barrow (1613–80) see *ODNB*; such was the sense of embarrassment that Glemham's episcopate only gleans a desultory five lines in D. R. Thomas, *A History of the Diocese of St Asaph*, vol. 1 (London: James Parker, 1874), p. 111, and is not even mentioned in the shorter version, *idem, Diocesan Histories: St Asaph* (London: SPCK, 1888).

24 [Richard Allestree], *Holl Ddledswydd Dyn ... Ynghyd a Defosiynau Neillduol ar amryw Achosion*, trans. John Langford (Llundain: R. Royston, 1672), Sig. A3r; for Langford (1650?–1716?), see *DWB*.

25 John Spurr, *The Restoration Church of England, 1646–89* (New Haven: Yale University Press, 1991), pp. 283–4; cf. Horton Davies, *Worship and Theology in England, Vol. 1: From Cranmer to Baxter and Fox, 1534–1690* (Grand Rapids: Eerdmans, 1996), pp. 112–13; Ian M. Green, *Print and Protestantism in Early Modern England* (Oxford: Clarendon Press, 2000), pp. 353–5.

26 Jenkins, *Literature, Religion and Society in Wales, 1660–1730*, pp. 243, 257, 258, 274, 278.

27 [Allestree], *Holl Ddledswydd Dyn*, pp. 17–20.

28 David Maurice, *The Bruised Reed, or a sermon preached at the Cathedral Church of St Asaph, for the support of weak Christians* (Oxford: The Theatre, 1700), p. 27; the occasion of its being delivered, in 1688, is explained in the 'Letter to my Parishioners', which introduces the Welsh version, *idem, Cynffwrdd i'r Gwan Gristion, neu'r Gorsen Ysig, mewn pregeth* (Rhydychen: Y Theatr, 1700), pp. 3–8; for Maurice see *DWB*.

29 Bodleian Library Tanner MS 31, f. 294; 32, f. 69; Jenkins, *Literature, Religion and Society in Wales, 1660–1730*, p. 215.

30 Samuel Palmer, *The Nonconformist's Memorial ... originally written by the Reverend and Learned Edmund Calamy DD*, vol. 2 (London: W. Harris, 1715), p. 601.

31 For Morris (1607–89), see *DWB*.

32 For Rawlet (1642–86) and his links with Baxter, see *ODNB*; the significance of the original version of the *Monitor* is noted by Green, *Print and Protestantism in Early Modern England*, pp. 358–9.

33 [John Rawlet], *Y Rhybuddiwr Christnogawl, yn cynnwys Annogaeth Ddifrifol i Fuchedd Sanctaidd*, trans. Edward Morris (Rhydychen: John Hall, 1689), p. 36; hereafter page numbers in the text.

34 See *DWB s.n.* Vaughan family of Llwydiarth, Montgomeryshire.

35 Eiluned Rees, *Libri Walliae: a Catalogue of Welsh Books and Books Printed in Wales, 1546–1820,* vol. II (Aberystwyth: National Library of Wales, 1987), p. 519.

36 See *DWB*.

37 J. Gwynn Williams, 'The Quakers of Merioneth during the seventeenth century', *JMHRS,* 8 (1978–9), 122–56, 312–39; Geraint H. Jenkins, 'The Friends of Montgomeryshire in the Heroic Age', *Montgomeryshire Collections,* 76 (1988), 17–30.

38 Rondl Davies, *Profiad yr Ysbrydion, neu Ddatcuddiad Gau Athrawon, a rhybudd i'w gochelyd* (Rhydychen: H. Hall, 1675), p. 75; hereafter page numbers included in the text.

39 A. Tindal Hart, *William Lloyd, 1627–1717: Bishop, Politician, Author and Prophet* (London: SPCK, 1952), pp. 14–15; for a more recent assessment of Lloyd's contribution, see *ODNB.*

40 Thomas, *Diocesan Histories: St Asaph,* p. 89.

41 Erasmus Saunders, *A View of the State of Religion in the Diocese of St David's* (1721) (Cardiff: University of Wales Press, 1949), p. 40.

42 William Gibson, *James II and the Trial of the Seven Bishops* (London: Palgrave Macmillan, 2009).

43 Ian M. Green, *The Christian's ABC: Catechisms and Catechizing in England, 1530–1740* (Oxford: Clarendon Press, 1996); Ken's *Directions for Prayer* is noted on p. 483.

44 E. Gordon Rupp, *Religion in England, 1688–1791* (Oxford: Clarendon Press, 1986), pp. 13–14.

45 [Thomas Ken], *Esboniad ar Gatechism yr Eglwys neu Ymarfer o Gariad Dwyfol, a gymmonwyd er lleshad Esgobaeth Baddon,* trans. William Foulkes (Rhydychen: n.p., 1688), p. 39.

46 John Morgan-Guy, 'The Diocese of St David's in the Reformation era II: from Reaction to Restoration, 1553–1660', in William Gibson and John Morgan-Guy (eds), *Religion and Society in the Diocese of St David's 1485–2011* (Aldershot: Ashgate, 2015), pp. 37–62 (61).

47 Thomas Richards, *A History of the Puritan Movement in Wales, 1639 to 1653* (London: National Eisteddfod Association, 1920), pp. 115–25.

48 Nicholas Tyacke, *Anti-Calvinists: The Rise of English Arminianism c. 1590–1640* (Oxford: Clarendon Press, 1990), p. 46; for Lucy's (1594–1677) career, see *ODNB.*

49 William Gibson, '"The most glorious enterprises have been achiev'd": the Restoration Diocese of St David's 1660–1730', in Gibson and Morgan-Guy (eds), *Religion and Society in the Diocese of St David's,* pp. 92–128 (94).

50 The most detailed assessment remains Thomas Richards, 'The troubles of Dr William Lucy', *Y Cymmrodor,* 38 (1927), 142–83.

51 Philip Jenkins, 'Welsh Anglicans and the Interregnum', *JHSCW,* 32 (1990), 51–9 (51).

52 R. Tudur Jones, 'Religion in Post-Restoration Brecknockshire, 1660–88', *Brycheiniog,* 8 (1962), 11–66 (29).

53 The Code incorporated the following: the Corporation Act (1661), the Act of Uniformity (1662), the Quaker Act (1662), the Conventicle Act (1664) and the Five-Mile Act (1665).

54 Bodleian Library Tanner MS 146, f. 113; quoted in W. T. Morgan, 'The Prosecution of Nonconformists in the Consistory Courts of St David's', *JHSCW*, 12 (1962), 28–54 (44).

55 See R. Tudur Jones, 'Relations between Anglicans and Dissenters: the Promotion of Piety, 1670–1730', in David Walker (ed.), *A History of the Church in Wales* (Penarth: Church in Wales Publications, 1976), pp. 79–102.

56 See *ODNB s.n.* William Thomas (1613–89).

57 William Thomas, *The Regulating of Law Suits, Evidences and Pleadings: an Assize Sermon preached at Carmarthen, 16 March 1656* (London: Gabriel Bedell and Thomas Collins, 1657).

58 Bodleian Library Tanner MS 146, f. 121, letter to Archbishop Sancroft.

59 William Thomas, *An Apology for the Church of England, in point of Separation from it, by the Reverend Father in God, William, Lord Bishop of St David's* (London: William Leach, 1679), Sig. A3v; page numbers which follow are in the text.

60 For Watson (1637–1717), see *ODNB*; for his tenure at St David's, and that of Womack, see Gibson, '"The most glorious enterprises have been achiev'd": the Restoration Diocese of St David's 1660–1730', pp. 96–101.

61 See Jenkins, 'Welsh Anglicans and the Interregnum'; *idem, The Making of a Ruling Class: the Glamorgan Gentry, 1640–1790* (Cambridge: Cambridge University Press, 1983), pp. 101–33.

62 Green, *The Re-establishment of the Church of England, 1660–63*, p. 95; for Lloyd (1589–1667), see *DWB* and *ODNB*.

63 Philip Jenkins, '"The sufferings of the clergy": the Church in Glamorgan during the Interregnum, Part Two, the Account of Francis Davies', *JWEH*, 4 (1987), 9–41 (31).

64 For Davies (1605–75), see *DWB, ODNB* and E. T. Davies, 'The Church of England and Schools, 1662–1774', in Glanmor Williams (ed.), *Glamorgan County History, Vol. IV, Early Modern Glamorgan* (Cardiff: University of Wales Press, 1974), pp. 432–68.

65 See above p. 171.

66 For the context, see Rupp, *Religion in England, 1688–1791*, pp. 5–28; Lloyd is noted on p. 11; for Lloyd (1637–1710), see *ODNB*.

67 See Bickham Sweet-Escott, 'William Beaw: a Cavalier Bishop', *WHR*, 1 (1963), 397–411; he is not listed in *ODNB*.

68 Bodleian Library, Rawlinson Letters, MS 94, f. 29.

69 Jenkins, *Literature, Religion and Society in Wales, 1660–1780*, p. 3.

70 Philip Jenkins, 'Church, nation, language: the Welsh Church, 1660–1800', in Jeremy Gregory and John Chamberlain (eds), *The National Church in Local Perspective: The Church of England and the Regions, 1660–1800* (Woodbridge: Boydell and Brewer, 2002), pp. 265–84.

71 Bodleian Library Tanner MS 32, f. 119; quoted in Jenkins, *Literature, Religion and Society in Wales, 1660–1780*, p. 7.

72 Quoted in Davies, 'The Church of England and Schools, 1662–1774', p. 438.

73 Gibson, '"The most glorious enterprises have been achiev'd": the Restoration Diocese of St David's 1660–1730', p. 117.

74 For his career during these years, see R. Tudur Jones, *Vavasor Powell* (Abertawe: Gwasg John Penry, 1971), pp. 166–79; *idem*, 'The sufferings of Vavasor', in Mansel John (ed.), *Welsh Baptist Studies* (Cardiff: South Wales Baptist College, 1976), pp. 76–91.

75 For the political and constitutional developments, see N. H. Keeble (ed.), *'Settling the Peace of the Church', 1662 Revised* (Oxford: Oxford University Press, 2014), pp. 1–29.

76 Keeble (ed.), *'Settling the Peace of the Church', 1662 Revised*, p. 12.

77 Edward Bagshaw, *The Life and Death of Mr Vavasor Powell, that faithful minister and confessor of Jesus Christ* (London: n.p., 1671), p. 129.

78 For the differences between radical and moderate Puritans on this question, see Geoffrey F. Nuttall, *The Holy Spirit in Puritan Faith and Experience*, 2nd edn (Chicago: University of Chicago Press, 1992), pp. 66–74 and Horton Davies, *The Worship of the English Puritans*, new edn (Morgan, PA: Soli Deo Gloria, 1997), pp. 98–114.

79 Vavasor Powell, *Common Prayer-Book No Divine Service, or XXVIII reasons against ... Imposing any Human Liturgies*, 3rd edn (London: Livewell Chapman, 1661), p. 2; hereafter page numbers in the text.

80 Philip Jenkins, '"The sufferings of the clergy": the Church in Glamorgan during the Interregnum, Part One, Introduction', *JWEH*, 3 (1986), 1–17 (13–14).

81 Jenkins, '"The sufferings of the clergy": the Church in Glamorgan during the Interregnum, Part One, Introduction', 7.

82 Vavasor Powell, *The Bird in the Cage Chirping ... and a brief narrative of the former Propagation and late Restriction of the Gospel ... in Wales* (London: L.C., 1661), p. 3; hereafter page numbers will be placed in the text.

83 Thomas Richards, *Religious Developments in Wales, 1654–62* (London: National Eisteddfod Association, 1923), p. 327.

84 Samuel Jones to Richard Baxter, 29 April 1661: N. H. Keeble and Geoffrey F. Nuttall (eds), *Calendar of the Correspondence of Richard Baxter*, vol. 2 (Oxford: Clarendon Press, 1991), p. 13.

85 Although he had been episcopally ordained, Baxter was the most vocal of those who argued for a comprehensive national church; Geoffrey F. Nuttall, *Richard Baxter* (London: Thomas Nelson, 1965), pp. 64–113.

86 See E. C. Ratcliff, 'The Savoy Conference and the revision of the Book of Common Prayer', in Nuttall and Chadwick (eds), *From Uniformity to Unity, 1662–1962*, pp. 89–148.

87 Keeble (ed.), *'Settling the Peace of the Church', 1662 Revised*, p. 17.

88 Powell, *The Bird in the Cage Chirping*, pp. 11–12.

89 Although forced to vacate his living in September 1661 through the Act for Confirming and Restoring Ministers, Henry always regarded himself as belonging to those who had been ejected on Bartholomew's Day.

90 For the extent of Welsh Catholicism, see Geraint H. Jenkins, *The Foundations of Modern Wales, 1642–1780* (Oxford: Clarendon Press, 1987), pp. 141–8.

91 R. Tudur Jones and B. G. Owens, 'Anghydffurfwyr Cymru, 1660–62', *Y Cofiadur*, 31 (1962), *passim*.

92 The best recent assessments of the fortunes of Welsh Dissent between 1660 and 1689 are Geraint H. Jenkins, *Protestant Dissenters in Wales, 1639–89* (Cardiff: University of Wales Press, 1992), pp. 39–71 and Eryn M. White, 'From Ejectment to Toleration in Wales, 1662–89', in Alan P. F. Sell (ed.), *The Great Ejectment of 1662: Its Antecedents, Aftermath and Ecumenical Significance* (Eugene, OR: Pickwick Publications, 2014), pp. 125–82.

93 Thomas Richards, *Wales Under the Indulgence, 1672–75* (London: National Eisteddfod Association, 1928), p. 144; for Rowland (1621–91), see *DWB*.

94 For Owen (1640–1700), see R. T. Jenkins, *Hanes Cynulleidfa Hen Gapel Llanuwchllyn* (Y Bala: Robert Evans, 1937), pp. 33–42, *DWB*, *ODNB*.

95 Richards, *Wales Under the Indulgence, 1672–75*, pp. 149–51.

96 Henry Maurice's account in E. B. Underhill (ed.), *Records of a Church of Christ meeting in Broadmead, Bristol, 1640–87* (London: Hanserd Knollys Society, 1867), pp. 511–18 (513).

97 Lambeth MS 639; cited in G. Lyon Turner (ed.), *Original Records of Early Nonconformity under Persecution and Indulgence*, vol. 1 (London: Fisher Unwin, 1911), p. 4; for Evans (1628–1706), see *DWB*.

98 Richards, *Wales Under the Indulgence, 1672–75*, pp. 146–9.

99 Underhill (ed.), *Records of a Church of Christ meeting in Broadmead*, p. 514.

100 Geoffrey F. Nuttall, 'The Nurture of Nonconformity: Philip Henry's Diaries', *THSC*, N.S. 4 (1998), 5–27 (11).

101 Matthew Henry Lee (ed.), *Diaries and Letters of Philip Henry MA, of Broad Oak, Flintshire* (London: Kegan Paul, 1882), p. 277.

102 Lee (ed.), *Diaries and Letters of Philip Henry MA, of Broad Oak, Flintshire*.

103 For Henry (1631–96), see Mathew Henry, *The Life of the Rev. Philip Henry* (1698), ed. J. B. Williams (Edinburgh: Banner of Truth, 1974), and *ODNB*.

104 The town of Oswestry, though in England (Shropshire), was also in the see of St Asaph; in 1672 a licence was issued to Rowland Nevett, its Commonwealth vicar who two decades earlier had assisted Walter Cradock as an Approver under the Propagation Act; Richards, *Wales Under the Indulgence, 1672–75*, p. 99; *idem, A History of the Puritan Movement in Wales, 1639–53*, pp. 99–100.

105 Lambeth MS 639; in Lyon Turner (ed.), *Original Records of Early Nonconformity under Persecution*, vol. 1, pp. 3–4.

106 Underhill (ed.), *Records of a Church of Christ meeting in Broadmead*, p. 517; for Williams (1624–84), see *DWB*.

107 Richard Davies, *An Account of the Convincement, Exercises, Services and Travels of that Ancient Servant of the Lord, Richard Davies*, 3rd edn (Philadelphia: Joseph Cruickshank, 1770), p. 204.

108 For Charles (1638–98) and Thomas (1640–94), see *DWB s.n.* Lloyd (Family) Dolobran.

109 Davies, *An Account*, p. 207.

[110] Davies, *An Account*, p. 207; Thomas Lloyd would later become the chief executive of the new Quaker colony of Pennsylvania.

[111] Lee (ed.), *Diaries and Letters of Philip Henry*, pp. 34–8.

[112] Henry, *The Life of the Rev. Philip Henry*, p. 153; for Roberts (*c.*1630–84), see Thomas Rees, *History of Protestant Nonconformity in Wales* (London: John Snow, 1861), pp. 150–1.

[113] See above, p. 197.

[114] Henry, *The Life of the Rev. Philip Henry*, p. 381.

[115] G. Dyfnallt Owen, 'James Owen a'i Academi', *Y Cofiadur*, 22 (1952), 3–36; 'James Owen's Academy, Oswestry and Shrewsbury (1690–1706)', Dr Williams Library, Dissenting Academies Database online.

[116] For Owen (1654–1706), see *DWB*, *ODNB*.

[117] Henry, *The Life of the Rev. Philip Henry*, p. 380.

[118] Charles Owen, *Some Account of the Life … of the Rev. James Owen* (London: John Lawrence, 1709), p. 31.

[119] A transcript was published in Henry, *The Life of the Rev. Philip Henry*, Appendix 17, pp. 380–93.

[120] Owen, *Some Account of the Life … of the Rev. James Owen*, p. 29; Lee (ed.), *Diaries and Letters of Philip Henry*, p. 309; at the time Henry's residence was in the diocese of Chester.

[121] Bodleian Library Tanner MS 146, f. 33; quoted in Hart, *William Lloyd*, pp. 49–50.

[122] Bodleian Library Tanner MS 25, f. 151; Hart, *William Lloyd*, p. 50.

[123] David Appleby, 'From Ejectment to Toleration in England, 1662–89', in Sell (ed.), *The Great Ejectment of 1662*, pp. 67–124 (113).

[124] Lloyd-Baker MSS, Hardwick Court, Gloucester, Lloyd to Sancroft, 17 July 1683; quoted in Hart, *William Lloyd*, p. 48.

[125] Hart, *William Lloyd*, p. 47.

[126] See Hart, *William Lloyd*, pp. 46, 52, 186–7.

[127] Thomas, *A History of the Diocese of St Asaph*, vol. 1, p. 125.

[128] Hart, *William Lloyd*, p. 249.

[129] E.g. R. Tudur Jones, *Congregationalism in Wales*, ed. Robert Pope (Cardiff: University of Wales Press, 2004), pp. 65–6.

[130] Pennar Davies, 'Episodes in the History of Brecknockshire Dissent', *Brycheiniog*, 3 (1957), 11–65.

[131] Richards, *Wales Under the Indulgence, 1672–75*, pp. 154–5.

[132] Underhill (ed.), *Records of a Church of Christ meeting in Broadmead*, p. 512.

[133] See Tudur Jones, 'Religion in Post-Restoration Brecknockshire, 1660–88', 40–65.

[134] Joshua Thomas, *Hanes y Bedyddwyr ymhlith y Cymry* (Caerfyrddin: John Ross, 1778), pp. 112–17; for Gregory (?1637–?1700), see *DWB*.

[135] Thomas, *Hanes y Bedyddwyr ymhlith y Cymry*, pp. 66–76.

[136] Thomas, *Hanes y Bedyddwyr ymhlith y Cymry*, pp. 122–4; cf. Owain Jones, 'The Anabaptists of Llanafan-fawr and Llysdinam', *Brycheiniog*, 18 (1978–9), 71–7; for Thomas Evans (1625–68), see *DWB*.

137 White, 'From Ejectment to Toleration in Wales, 1662–89', p. 158.
138 For licences issued in those counties, see Richards, *Wales Under the Indulgence, 1672–75*, pp. 151–2, 162–5.
139 Underhill (ed.), *Records of a Church of Christ meeting in Broadmead*, p. 512.
140 J. Morgan Jones (ed.), 'Llyfr Eglwys y Cilgwyn', *Y Cofiadur*, 1 (1923), 22–31.
141 Richards, *Wales Under the Indulgence, 1672–75*, pp. 155–6.
142 Richards, *Wales Under the Indulgence, 1672–75*, pp. 156–7.
143 Underhill (ed.), *Records of a Church of Christ meeting in Broadmead*, p. 512.
144 E. D. Jones (ed.), 'Llyfr Eglwys Mynydd Bach', *Y Cofiadur*, 17 (1947), 3–50.
145 Underhill (ed.), *Records of a Church of Christ meeting in Broadmead*, p. 513; for Prytherch (?1620–99), see *DNB s.n.* Prydderch, Rhys.
146 Underhill (ed.), *Records of a Church of Christ meeting in Broadmead*, pp. 512–13.
147 White, 'From Ejectment to Toleration in Wales, 1662–89', p. 150.
148 This, at least, is the tradition, see Rees, *History of Protestant Nonconformity in Wales*, pp. 256–9.
149 Rhydwilym Church Book, NLW Deposit MS 127A; Richards, *Wales Under the Penal Code*, pp. 106–14: B. G. Owens, 'Rhydwilym Church 1668–89: a Study in West Wales Baptists', in John (ed.), *Welsh Baptist Studies*, pp. 92–107; for William Jones (d.1690) and Jenkin Jones (1623–?), see *DWB*.
150 Thomas Richards, 'Nonconformity from 1620 to 1715', in J. E. Lloyd (ed.), *A History of Carmarthenshire*, vol. 2 (Cardiff: The London Carmarthenshire Society, 1939), pp. 133–84 (151).
151 Richards, *Religious Developments in Wales, 1654–62*, p. 488.
152 Underhill (ed.), *Records of a Church of Christ meeting in Broadmead*, p. 517.
153 Palmer, *The Nonconformist's Memorial ... originally written by the Reverend and Learned Edmund Calamy DD*, vol. 2, pp. 631–2; Phillips (1623–91) is noted in *DWB* and *ODNB*.
154 Richards, *Wales Under the Indulgence, 1672–75*, pp. 161–2.
155 Glanmor Williams, 'The Dissenters in Glamorgan, 1660–c.1730', in *idem* (ed.), *Glamorgan County History, Vol. IV, Early Modern Glamorgan*, pp. 468–533 (497–8 esp.).
156 Lambeth MS 639; in Lyon Turner (ed.), *Original Records of Early Nonconformity under Persecution*, vol. 1, p. 45.
157 Richards, *Wales Under the Indulgence, 1672–75*, pp. 158–9; Williams, 'The Dissenters in Glamorgan, 1660–c.1730', pp. 498–9.
158 Underhill (ed.), *Records of a Church of Christ meeting in Broadmead*, p. 514; for Ambrose Mostyn (1610–63), see *DWB*, *ODNB*, and for Daniel Higgs (d.1691) see *DWB*.
159 See above, Chapter Two, p. 143.
160 Lyon Turner (ed.), *Original Records of Early Nonconformity under Persecution*, vol. 1, p. 47; Underhill (ed.), *Records of a Church of Christ meeting in Broadmead*, p. 514.
161 Thomas Richards, 'Bedyddwyr Cymru yng nghyfnod Lewis Thomas', *TCHB* (1916–19), 3–46; Thomas (d.1704) has an entry in *DWB*.

[162] Underhill (ed.), *Records of a Church of Christ meeting in Broadmead*, p. 515; Lyon Turner (ed.), *Original Records of Early Nonconformity under Persecution*, vol. 1, p. 47.

[163] For Samuel Jones (1628–97), see D. R. L. Jones, 'Fame and obscurity: Samuel Jones of Brynllywarch', *JWRH*, 1 (1993), 41–65; *DNB, ODNB*.

[164] Lyon Turner (ed.), *Original Records of Early Nonconformity under Persecution*, vol. 1, pp. 44–9 (45).

[165] Richards, *Wales Under the Indulgence, 1672–75*, pp. 159–61.

[166] Underhill (ed.), *Records of a Church of Christ meeting in Broadmead*, p. 516.

[167] E.g. Elizabeth Parkinson, 'Interpreting the Compton Census returns of 1676 for the Diocese of Llandaff', *Local Population Studies*, 60 (1998), 44–57.

[168] Anne Whiteman (ed.), *The Compton Census of 1676: A Critical Edition* (Oxford: Oxford University Press, 1986), pp. 243–61, 457–523; cf. Thomas Richards, 'The Religious Census of 1676', *THSC* (1927), 1–110.

[169] For the lacunae and aberrations in the returns, see Jenkins, *Protestant Dissenters in Wales, 1639–89*, pp. 57–8 and White, 'From Ejectment to Toleration in Wales, 1662–89', pp. 140–1.

[170] Jenkins, *Protestant Dissenters in Wales, 1639–89*, p. 58.

[171] Rees, *History of Protestant Nonconformity in Wales*, p. 259.

[172] See above, pp. 202–3.

[173] Palmer, *The Nonconformist's Memorial... originally written by ... Edmund Calamy DD*, vol. 2, p. 624.

[174] Cited in Rees, *History of Protestant Nonconformity in Wales*, p. 261.

[175] Rees, *History of Protestant Nonconformity in Wales*, p. 263.

[176] Richards, *Wales Under the Indulgence, 1672–75*, p. 158.

[177] 'Samuel Jones' Academy, Brynllywarch (c.1672–97)', Dr Williams Library, Dissenting Academies Database online.

[178] Palmer, *The Nonconformist's Memorial... originally written by ... Edmund Calamy DD*, vol. 2, p. 624.

[179] The will is transcribed in Jones and Owens, 'Anghydffurfwyr Cymru, 1660–62', p. 46.

[180] Rees, *History of Protestant Nonconformity in Wales*, p. 266.

[181] Geraint H. Jenkins, 'Apostol Sir Gaerfyrddin: Stephen Hughes, c. 1622–88', *Y Cofiadur*, 54 (1989), 3–23; Glanmor Williams, 'Stephen Hughes (1622–88), "The Apostle of Carmarthenshire"', *CA*, 37 (2001), 21–30; also *DWB* and *ODNB*.

[182] Richards, *A History of the Puritan Movement in Wales, 1639–53*, p. 124.

[183] Richards, *Religious Developments in Wales, 1654–62*, pp. 17, 21.

[184] Richards, *Wales under the Penal Code, 1662–87*, pp. 37–8.

[185] J. Dyfnallt Owen, 'Camre cyntaf Anghydffurfiaeth ac Annibyniaeth yn Sir Gaerfyrddin, 1660–1710', *Y Cofiadur*, 13 (1936), 3–56.

[186] *Rhan o waith Mr Rees Prichard, gynt ficer Llanddyfri yn Sir Gaerfyrddin, a osodwyd allan er daioni'r Cymry* (Llundain: Thomas Brewster, 1659), Sig. A4r; the Preface is dated March 1657.

187 *Y drydedd rhan o waith Mr Rees Prichard, gynt ficer Llanddyfri* (Llundain: Thomas Dawks, 1670), Sig. A7r.

188 Palmer, *The Nonconformist's Memorial ... originally written by ... Edmund Calamy DD*, vol. 2, pp. 621–2.

189 *Rhan o waith Mr Rees Prichard*, Sig. A3v; the detail of Hughes's literary contribution is assessed in G. J. Williams, 'Stephen Hughes a'i gyfnod', *Y Cofiadur*, 4 (1926), 5–44.

190 Quoted in Davies, 'The Church of England and Schools, 1662–1774', p. 449.

191 Bodleian Library Tanner MS 146, f. 138; Lucy to Archbishop Sheldon, 20 February 1672; quoted in M. G. Jones, *The Charity School Movement: A Study in Eighteenth Century Puritanism in Action* (Cambridge: Cambridge University Press, 1938), p. 286.

192 R. Buick Knox, 'The Bible in Wales: The Life and Labours of Thomas Gouge', *CH*, 2 (1978), 38–43.

193 Richard L. Greaves, art. in *ODNB*.

194 Samuel Clark, *The Lives of Sundry Persons in this later Age ...* (London: Thomas Summers, 1683), pp. 141–2; for Alleine (*c.*1624–68), see *ODNB*.

195 Bodleian Library Tanner MS 40, f. 18; Lloyd to Archbishop Sheldon, 10 August 1676; quoted in Jones, *The Charity School Movement*, p. 286.

196 See p. 222 above; M. G. Jones, 'Two accounts of the Welsh Trust, 1675 and 1678', *BBCS*, 9 (1939), 71–80.

197 John Tillotson, *A Sermon Preached at the Funeral of the Reverend Mr Thomas Gouge, 4 November 1681* (London: Brabazon Aylmer, 1682), pp. 92–3.

198 For Edwards's contribution to the work of the Welsh Trust, see G. J. Williams's Introduction to *Y Ffydd Ddi-ffuant, sef hanes y Ffydd Gristianogol a'i Rhinwedd* (1677) (Caerdydd: Gwasg Prifysgol Cymru, 1936), pp. xxxvi–xlix.

199 *Gwaith Mr Rees Prichard, gynt Ficer Llanddyfri ... ynghyd a Phedwaredd Ran* (London: J. Darby, 1672), Sig. A16v.

200 *Cyfarwydd-deb i'r Anghyfarwydd* (Llundain: Thomas Dawks, 1677), p. 152.

201 For Jones, Balliol graduate and schoolmaster in Denbigh under the Propagation Act, see *DNB* and Cynthia S. Davies, 'Richard Jones: Crefftwr o Gymro', in J. Gwynfor Jones (ed.), *Agweddau ar Dwf Piwritaniaeth yng Nghymru yn yr Ail Ganrif ar Bymtheg* (Lampeter: Edwin Mellen Press, 1992), pp. 167–202.

202 For Jones, see *DWB*; his funeral sermon was preached by David Maurice, vicar of Abergele, see p. 178 above.

203 Alec Ryrie, *Being Protestant in Reformation Britain* (Oxford: Oxford University Press, 2014), p. 6.

204 Charles Edwards, *An Afflicted Man's Testimony Concerning his Troubles* (London: n.p., 1691), p. 8.

205 Lyon Turner (ed.), *Original Records of Early Nonconformity under Persecution*, vol. 1, p. 550.

206 Edwards, *An Afflicted Man's Testimony*, p. 18.

207 The authoritative analysis is by Derec Llwyd Morgan, 'A critical study of the works of Charles Edwards, 1628–?1691' (unpublished DPhil dissertation,

Oxford University, 1967), *idem*, *Charles Edwards* (Caernarfon: Gwasg Pantycelyn, 1994) and *ODNB*.

208 Edwards, *Y Ffydd Ddi-ffuant, sef hanes y Ffydd Gristianogol a'i Rhinwedd*, p. 23; page numbers which follow are in the text.

209 See Introduction, pp. 3–4.

210 Charles Edwards, *Fatherly Instructions, being Select Pieces of the Writings of the Primitive Christian Teachers, translated into English, with an appendix entitled 'Gildas Minimus'* (London: n.p., 1686).

211 See Derec Llwyd Morgan, 'Dau Amddiffynnydd i'r Ffydd', in J. E. Caerwyn Williams (ed.), *Ysgrifau Beirniadol*, 5 (Dinbych: Gwasg Gee, 1970), pp. 99–111.

212 Morgan, *Charles Edwards*, pp. 40, 42; cf. M. Wynn Thomas, 'Seventeenth-century Puritan writers: Morgan Llwyd and Charles Edwards', in R. Geraint Gruffydd (ed.), *A Guide to Welsh Literature, c.1530–1700* (Cardiff: University of Wales Press, 1997), pp. 190–209.

213 Thomas, 'Seventeenth-century Puritan writers', p. 203.

214 Tudur Jones, *Congregationalism in Wales*, p. 76.

215 John Spurr, 'The Church, the societies and the moral revolution of 1688', in John Walsh, Colin Haydon and Stephen Taylor (eds), *The Church of England c.1689–c.1833* (Cambridge: Cambridge University Press, 1993), pp. 127–43 (143).

216 The revisionist, indeed iconoclastic thesis of Geraint H. Jenkins, echoing partially Mary Clement's earlier researches on the history of the SPCK, shows that spiritual vitality pre-dated the Methodist revival by many decades; Jenkins, *Literature, Religion and Society in Wales, 1660–1780, passim; idem, The Foundations of Modern Wales, 1642–1780*, pp. 173–212; cf. Mary Clement, *The SPCK and Wales, 1699–1740* (London: SPCK, 1954), especially Chapter Two, 'The renewal of religious life', pp. 48–73.

217 Edwards, *Y Ffydd Ddi-ffuant*, p. 361.

218 Spurr, *The Restoration Church of England, 1646–89*, p. 264.

219 Spurr, *The Restoration Church of England, 1646–89*, p. 280.

220 Jenkins, *Literature, Religion and Society in Wales, 1660–1780*, pp. 133–4.

221 See above, pp. 180–1.

222 Spurr, 'The Church, the societies and the moral revolution of 1688', p. 138.

223 Spurr, 'The Church, the societies and the moral revolution of 1688', p. 140.

224 John Walsh, 'Origins of the Evangelical Revival', in G. V. Bennett and J. Walsh (eds), *Essays in Modern English Church History* (London: Adam and Charles Black, 1966), pp. 132–62; *idem*, '"Methodism" and the Origins of English-Speaking Evangelicalism', in Mark A. Noll, David W. Bebbington and George A. Rawlyk (eds), *Evangelicalism: Comparative Studies of Popular Protestantism in North America, the British Isles and Beyond* (Oxford: Oxford University Press, 1994), pp. 19–37.

4

1689–1760 (i)

Anglican piety during the reign of William and Mary

The piety that fed the devotion of the bulk of the faithful during the reign of William and Mary (1689–1702) was rooted in the sacramental doctrines of the High Church divines.[1] The Catholic James II who had become sovereign at the death of his brother, Charles II, in 1685, had so incensed the realm by his intrigues that key figures in church and state had invited his daughter, Mary, princess of Orange and her Dutch husband, William, to take possession of the throne in order to secure the Protestant succession. The prince and his army landed at Torbay, Devon in November 1688 and a month later James, having realized the hopelessness of his situation, vacated the throne and fled to France. Following the Convocation Parliament of January 1689 and the passing of the Bill of Rights which safeguarded parliamentary privilege and forbade any potentially arbitrary rule by successive sovereigns, the couple were installed as joint-monarchs, and on 11 April were crowned in Westminster Abbey by Henry Compton, bishop of London. Of enormous significance for the subsequent history of religion in the realm was the passing of the Toleration Act in May, much to the chagrin of virtually all of the Anglican hierarchy and its clerics, exempting Protestant Dissenters from the penalties of those statutes which had been aimed at suppressing their existence since 1662.[2] The statutes themselves, however, remained in force.

Although there was some Tory coolness towards the new joint-rulers, mostly among a section of the Pembrokeshire gentry and the circle around Sir Watkin Williams Wynn, baron Wynnstay, in north-east Wales,[3] for the most part the Welsh welcomed the new regime.[4] If there was one Welsh churchman, William Lloyd (1627–1717), bishop of

St Asaph, who was among the 'seven bishops' who had refused to sanction James's Declaration of Indulgence, granting freedom of worship to Catholics (and Protestant Dissenters) in May 1688 and was consequently arrested for sedition, tried and acquitted,[5] his namesake William Lloyd (1637–1710), bishop of Norwich – a native of Merionethshire who had, a decade-and-a-half earlier, served briefly as Llandaff's diocesan[6] – had shown *his* loyalty to the concept of hereditary monarchy by refusing to pledge allegiance to William and Mary. Like William Sancroft, Archbishop of Canterbury, being bound by his previous vow to be faithful to James as the realm's divinely appointed king, he could not conscientiously swear obedience to the new monarchs. As with the other Non-Jurors, he believed that by reneging on their previous vows, the clergy, indeed the Church of England as a body, was guilty of the grave sin of schism.[7] As a result, he along with Sancroft, seven other bishops and some 400 clergy were deprived of their sees and livings and deposed. Although only a handful of the Welsh clergy followed their lead – four in St Asaph, four in Llandaff, a half-dozen in St David's and one in Bangor[8] – it was a sign of the turbulence of the times. In the main, however, the Welsh Church accepted the new dispensation and persevered with its ministrations to the people.[9]

The brand of edifying literature which appeared during the last decade of the seventeenth century and the years beyond demonstrated how the piety of the 'holy living' school had now become the norm. Along with a second edition (1699) of Edward Morris's *Rhybuddiwr Christnogawl* ('The Christian Counsellor'),[10] among the books published were translations of works by William Sherlock, William Howell, William Beveridge, John Williams, bishop of Chichester, William Assheton and Theophilus Dorrington. Sherlock, master of the Temple and a leading London clergyman (he would later become dean of St Paul's) had penned his *Practical Discourse Concerning Death* (1689) during the succession controversy as he agonized, like the bishop of Norwich, whether to forgo his previous allegiance in order to swear the oath of obedience to the new king and queen.[11] The treatise itself had nothing to do with the constitution but was wholly concerned with personal religion. It was this that drew Thomas Williams (1658–1726), vicar of Llanrwst in the diocese of St Asaph and later rector of Denbigh, in 1691 to issue a Welsh version for the sake of his compatriots. The 'holy living' motif was patent throughout: 'What value is teaching or admonition if we do not follow a holy life?', he asked. 'It is essential that

we live lives of virtue and true piety.'[12] Liturgy as such did not feature
plainly in this exposition, though baptism as the pledge of the believer's
obedience to Christ and the Lord's Supper as a means of grace were
emphasized as being essential in order to live the consecrated life. The
stress though was on true repentance, sincere faith and the taking up
of one's cross in discipleship:

> This is our comfort, that Christ did for us what we could not do for our-
> selves, that purchasing immortality for us all through his wounds on the
> cross, his agony and his blood, thereafter quickened us and lifted us up
> to new life through his gracious Spirit. But as we first must die before
> we can enter into immortality, it is as clear as the sun that we are to
> live our lives in this world as a preparation for entering into the next.[13]

The same theme was underlined in *Y Llyfr Gweddi Gyffredin, y
Cydymmaith Goreu* (1693), a translation by Evan Evans, another St Asaph
clergyman, of the Oxford cleric William Howell's *The Common Prayer
Book, the best Companion in the House as in the Closet as well as in the Temple*
(1692). As well as being 'a pillar of the kingdom', Sir John Wynn of
Watstay (later re-named Wynnstay), one of the chief landowners of
north Wales to whom the book was dedicated, was described by the
translator as 'a faithful son of our Mother, the Church of England'.[14]
However important the public worship of God, the life of faith could only
be maintained fully by family prayer and private devotion. As a leader
in his community, Sir John was charged with supporting the clergy in
their duty of 'engendering the devotions of the common people and the
ignorant among our countrymen'.[15] The Prayer Book was prized not
only as a source of the liturgy but its prayers were deemed authoritative
'as they are the words of that church which is the most glorious and
perfect among all the Protestant churches'.[16] The same conviction was
central to the next published work, *Pregeth ynghylch Godidawgrwydd a
Defnyddiaeth Llyfr y Gweddiau Cyffredin* (1693), a translation of William
Beveridge's enormously popular *Sermon Concerning the Excellency and
Usefulness of the Common Prayer*, though in this public liturgy would
take centre stage.

Beveridge (1637–1708), vicar of St Peter Cornhill in the City of
London, who would later become a leading advocate of the SPCK and
between 1704 and his death earn the respect of Welsh churchmen
through his exertions as bishop of St Asaph, represented the consensus

view of Restoration Anglicanism. He was orthodox in faith, Protestant in conviction, holding to the Prayer Book liturgy, Episcopalian though more in a pragmatic than an ideological sense, but staunch in the belief that the post-1662 Church was a *national* church, representing the people as a whole. His was a 'true "Anglicanism", rooted in ecclesiology and theology, with a compelling vision of personal and communal piety, and widely disseminated among the [people].'[17] This vision was elucidated most clearly in the *Excellency and Usefulness of the Common Prayer* which had been preached at the consecration of the newly rebuilt Wren church of St Peter Cornhill in 1681. The sermon not only established his reputation as a champion of the Restoration consensus but would serve as a benchmark for the emerging 'Anglicanism' ever after.[18] The text was I Cor. 14:26, St Paul's admonition to the Corinthian church that 'all things should be done for edification'. The theme was the nature of public worship and it would have been clear to all of his hearers that the foremost element in the Christian's deportment was a lively and considered participation in the liturgy of the Book of Common Prayer.

For Beveridge, the concept of set prayer was patently biblical. The temple worship of the Old Testament and the psalms, the synagogue devotion as portrayed in the New Testament gospels and especially the example of Jesus himself in the Lord's Prayer were precedent enough. But there were pragmatic considerations as well, that the rhythm of the spiritual life rooted as it was in the reality of human weakness presupposed the need for set forms, aids and encouragements. These had all been provided for by the Fathers and Reformers and enshrined in the Prayer Book: 'My task is to prove that the divine service contained in the *Book of Common Prayer*', he stated, 'and now used by the Church of England is effective for the edification of all who use it and conforms to the rule set down by the Apostle in our text.'[19] The four points that illustrated the Book's virtues were its language, its content, its structure and its ordering. As a Protestant text it was written not in Latin but in the tongue of the people, which in this case (in the unidentified translator's words) was Welsh:

> You will know that the whole service is set forth in Welsh, the language which is used mostly among the common people in this Principality and that which virtually everyone understands and can thus be edified by its means. (p. 26)

The Welsh used was not a patois or mere dialect but pure Welsh, understood by all, 'thus the weakest man in the congregation who but understands his mother-tongue can be edified just as much as the finest scholar' (p. 28). As for the Book's content, it was simple, straightforward, unadorned and clear. Its teaching was biblically informed and doctrinally sound, while the recitation of the Apostles' Creed, the Nicene Creed and the Athanasian Creed ensured that worshippers would be grounded in the true, catholic and apostolic faith. By the constant and thoughtful repetition of the Ten Commandments the moral lives of believers would be reinforced while their devotion would be nourished by the recurrent use of the Lord's Prayer. The collects, the litany, the *Gloria* and other prayers provided diversity and variation, while all the supplications were made either in the name of Christ or of the Holy Trinity. Structurally the Prayer Book delivered a balance between confession, thanksgiving, supplication and praise while the absolution following the General Confession assured true penitents that their sins had been forgiven:

> Now, looking upon ourselves as those who have been redeemed from our trespasses through our repentance and our faith in Christ, and consequently having been reconciled with God, we are bold enough to address him as our Father, humbly calling upon him in the words that He himself has given us. (p. 51)

Although sacramental, the theology of the sermon is not sacerdotal. The minister who absolves the penitents is there to assure them of the gospel promises, that Christ, through his passion and sacrifice, offers salvation to all who had turned from their sins and put their trust wholly and unreservedly in him. The Lord's Supper was the pledge of this truth and the ordering of the service led to this as its climax:

> The highest mystery of our religion is the sacrament of the Lord's Supper as it sets out for us the death of God's Son, and for this reason the place where the sacrament is administered is, and always has been, the prime place within the church. (p. 61)

For Beveridge the parish church was itself a consecrated building and the most sacred place therein was the chancel where the Lord's Table (the word 'altar' is not used) was situated: 'The chancel in our Christian churches corresponds to the holy of holies in the temple' (p. 63).

Partaking of the sacrament in that place contributes to the believer's edification. Posture is also important: standing for the recitation of the Creed and the gospels and kneeling for prayer. Although this is all set forth in the form of an exposition of a text, Beveridge has virtually nothing to say about the place of the sermon in the context of worship. The preaching of the Word of God is presupposed rather than commended and explained. For him and those who shared the Restoration consensus, holy living was mostly a matter of obedience, personal piety and prayer: '[T]he primary purpose of private devotion ... was to prepare the individual for the public worship of the Church and above all for the Lord's Supper.'[20] The Welsh version has no reference at all to the identity of the (undoubtedly clerical) translator or to the circumstances of its translation, but it refutes, whether intentionally or not, virtually every paragraph in Vavasor Powell's fiery *Common Prayer-Book No Divine Service* of a generation before.[21] Memories of the civil war plainly rankled still:

> All that I will say is that the spirit which provoked people to refute the Common Prayers provoked them to rise up against the king, to take away the possessions and the lives of others contravening both justice and the law, and in the end to murder one of the most pious kings that ever lived. (pp. 80–1)

Despite the doctrinal affinities between Anglican and Dissenter in post-Restoration Wales, by the 1690s the divide between the two traditions was widening markedly.

The abundant devotional literature of post-Restoration Welsh Anglicanism was not only in accord with the liturgical uses of the Book of Common Prayer but was preoccupied with the motifs of repentance and self-examination which figured so largely in the 'holy living' ideal. As this centred on the sacrament of the Lord's Supper, it is not surprising that the question of 'worthy receiving' would loom large. Although the theologians of the Church steered clear of any theoretic explanation of the mode of Christ's presence in the Eucharist – though they rejected totally the Romanist doctrine of transubstantiation – the bishops and clergy were insistent that only 'worthy believers' would receive spiritual benefit from partaking in the consecrated bread and wine. Unlike Dissenters who administered the sacrament only to those who could testify to the experience of conversion, Restoration Anglicans urged those who strove towards godliness to partake of the sacrament in order to *be* converted. Like New England Puritans, they too had a concept of 'preparationism', but for them it was impossible to discern how sincere spiritual striving cohered with divine election or when, in fact, it occurred. Like the sermon, the liturgy and the set prayers, the sacrament was a means of grace and although it could not, of itself, engender conversion, it could be taken up into the process of conversion and lead the faithful to eternal life.

Yet before experiencing the consolations of faith, all prospective converts with even a modicum of spiritual sensitivity were challenged by St Paul's warning in I Cor. 11:29: 'But let a man examine himself ... for he that eats and drinks unworthily, eats and drinks damnation to himself, not discerning the Lord's body.' The dilemma of the 'holy living' school was that its stout concentration on sinners' unworthiness was in danger of preventing them from accessing the very thing that would lead to true holiness, namely faith in Christ's atoning sacrifice on their behalf. It was for this reason that in 1698 Michael Jones, curate of the Flintshire parish of Hope, issued his translation of the Irish clergyman Edward Synge's *An Answer to all the Excuses and Pretences which men ordinarily make for not coming to the Holy Communion* (1697). Taking as his text Luke 14:15–24, Jesus's parable of the great banquet, he outlined both the plausible reasons and the unacceptable excuses that people used for not partaking of the Lord's Supper. There were four of them. First, that some deemed themselves too sinful to come to the holy table; secondly, that others lacked time and opportunity to prepare themselves for worthy partaking; thirdly, that still more felt that however meticulous, their preparation would be insufficient to do justice to what was expected of the true penitent; and fourthly, that having partaken in the past, they felt no discernible improvement in their lives and it would be impertinent to come to the table again. Jones made short shrift of the second excuse, but the others were more weighty. Holy living, he claimed, never implied nor required absolute moral perfection. What it did require was the active obedience and humility which affirmed Christ's costly obedience to which the sacrament witnessed:

> If it is in any man's ability (at least any man who has not through a long course of wickedness so displeased God that he has withdrawn his grace) through the grace and strength that God offers him constantly in order to repent of his sins and improve his life, he should so strive and not regard this as a hindrance between him and the sacrament.[22]

For the bruised conscience, however, this was cold comfort. The awakened sinner's dilemma was that he could never be sufficiently sure that his striving and improvement were enough, and that despite all he would be eating and drinking damnation to himself. The curate from Hope, however, was insistent that Christ had died for sinners and that all they needed to do was to grasp the divine forgiveness for themselves. There was a difference between sin and scrupulosity, and 'unworthiness' could become a false scruple when it prevented the humble sinner from affirming Christ's death for his (or her) salvation:

> In conclusion I have only one thing to say, namely that even though it is a great sin to partake of the Holy Communion unworthily, that is, without true repentance, it is no less a sin to despise and scorn the ordinance that Christ himself has appointed and commanded to keep in remembrance of his death and sufferings which were borne for us.[23]

The Welsh clergy were charged with maintaining a difficult balance between welcoming to the table parishioners who desired to live an amended life and reprimanding others who were openly and insistently profane. None, however, was of the opinion that 'holy living' of itself was sufficient for salvation: 'Our Lord Jesus Christ has died for our sins and through his merits and his suffering alone can we expect of God forgiveness of sins and eternal life.'[24] Salvation came through the merits of Christ or not at all.

The same theme was apparent in John Morgan, the vicar of Aberconwy's 1699 translation of *A Brief Exposition of the Church Catechism* by John Williams, bishop of Chichester.[25] Its five sections on the baptismal vow, the Creed, the Decalogue, the Lord's Prayer and the two sacraments was typical of the Anglican catechisms of the period and reinforced the doctrinal consensus which had already established itself among Welsh churchmen. Although patently orthodox and scriptural, with an obvious animus towards Roman Catholicism, faith and obedience were well to the fore. The doctrine of justification is not treated separately, while the catechumens were taught that by grace alone they were progressively enabled to respond to the divine offer of salvation through the sacrifice of Christ and live the Christian life. Although the Holy Spirit was given 'to sanctify me and all of God's elect people', the older Reformed emphases of foreordination and the divine decree are muted, and the idea that grace is irresistible is not countenanced.[26]

Whereas baptism signified regeneration, without true repentance the rite itself is void. It may be that baptism makes us 'children of grace', but it is not automatically effective:

> Q: Is baptism itself sufficient for salvation?
> A: No, without the regeneration which it signifies, it is empty.[27]

Salvation was by faith and faith presupposed strenuous repentance leading to conversion. The sacrament of the Lord's Supper signified a vital union with Christ in his sacrifice designated as his body and blood, though this too demands a real turning away from sin: 'It is only a living faith in God's mercy through Jesus Christ that we can receive forgiveness of our trespasses.'[28]

Before assessing the most accomplished contribution to the 'holy living' tradition yet issued in Welsh, there are three other texts which deserve mention. *Duwiolder ar Ddydd yr Arglwydd* (1700) ('Piety on the Lord's Day') was a short composite volume taken from portions of works by William Assheton, vicar of Beckenham in Kent. Its translator, an un-named 'Priest of the Church of England', took it upon himself to issue the work as 'A short counsel to urge you to partake more regularly of the sacrament of the Lord's Supper, the mysterious banquet of the soul'.[29] The sacramental, churchly tone of the treatise is pronounced, while the preaching of the Word is construed very much as a liturgical event:

> Were heeding the Word of God only a matter of listening to the sermon, where would that leave the psalms, the hymns, the lessons, the epistle and the gospel? The sermon is but the making known of the Word of God along with counsels and admonitions based upon it.[30]

The climax of worship, however, is the Lord's Supper: 'Therefore prepare yourselves, and come forth to the Lord's Table and the eternal Father will say, "Rejoice; your sins are forgiven".'[31] David Maurice's rendition of Theophilus Dorrington's *Familiar Guide to the right and profitable receiving of the Lord's Supper* (1695) and George Lewis's translation of John Tillotson's tract, *A Persuasive to frequent communion in the Holy Sacrament of the Lord's Supper* (1685), both reinforced the High Church emphasis on the key importance of holy communion as a means of grace as well as underlining the need for worthy partaking on the one hand and warning against an overscrupulous conscience of the other. 'Our duty', wrote Maurice, the scholarly vicar of Abergele,

> is to receive these elements which as God's sure pledge of his blessings [of forgiveness of sins, sanctification and the hope of glory] according to his conditions, being an outward expression on our part that we have agreed to do what is asked of us, and if there is no inner obedience along with the external profession, it is no less than rank hypocrisy rendering us guilty of the body and blood of Christ.[32]

Tillotson's fear, as expressed by George Lewis (*c.*1640–*c.*1709), vicar of Abergwili in the diocese of St David's, was more that good people would neglect the sacrament than bad people would partake of it unworthily. Due to imprudent zeal in the past, a feeling had arisen that it was only those of a very high level of sanctity who were fit to come to the table: 'Thus the neglect of this sacrament among Christians has grown so general that a great many people, through superstitious reverence and awe, have allowed it to fall into shameful neglect.'[33] For the archbishop there was something absurd about the contention of so many 'timorous Christians' that 'the danger of unworthy receiving was so great that the safest thing is not to receive it at all'.[34] Even a superficial perusal of St Paul's first letter to the Corinthians should convince the faithful that, despite the moral laxity of that church, its members were nowhere told to refrain from partaking of the sacrament. They were urged, rather, to examine themselves and strive for improvement:

> If this be a good reason to abstain from the sacrament, for fear of performing so sacred an action in an undue manner, it were best for a bad man to lay aside all religion and to give over the exercise of all the duties of piety, of prayer and of reading and hearing the Word of God, because there is an equal danger in the unworthy and unprofitable use of any of these ordinances.[35]

Like baptism, the sacrament of the Lord's Supper had been ordained by God for the church's benefit, and it was incumbent upon all to partake in obedience and in humble faith:

> The neglect of the sacrament is not the way to prevent these sins but, on the contrary, the constant receiving of it with the best preparation we

can is one of the most effectual means to prevent sin for the future, and to obtain the assistance of God's grace to that end. And if we fall into sin afterwards, we may be renewed by repentance *for we have an advocate with the Father Jesus Christ the righteous, who is the propitiation for our sins* … If we prepare ourselves as well as we can, this is all God expects.[36]

The masterpiece of the 'holy living' literature, however, was *Rheol Buchedd Sanctaidd* (1701), Ellis Wynne's magnificent translation of Jeremy Taylor's classic *The Rule and Exercises of Holy Living*. Taylor (1613–67), protégé of William Laud, chaplain in ordinary to Charles I and among the foremost of the Caroline divines, had spent much of the Interregnum in Wales where he had been taken prisoner by parliamentary forces following the siege of Cardigan Castle in 1645. Following his release he had remained in south-west Wales, first as a schoolmaster at Newton Hall near Llandeilo and then as chaplain to Richard Vaughan, second earl of Carbery, at his seat at Golden Grove in the same vicinity. It was there that he produced his life of Christ, *The Great Exemplar* (1649) and his exquisite devotional works *The Rule and Exercises of Holy Living* (1650) and *The Rule and Exercises of Holy Dying* (1651). Both became bestsellers and were soon issued as a single work which reached its ninetieth edition in 1695. At the Restoration he was appointed bishop of Down and Connor and had died, aged fifty-four, in 1667.[37] Ellis Wynne (1671–1734), a Merionethshire gentleman and graduate of Jesus College, Oxford, who would take deacon's orders in 1704 and a year later become rector of parishes near his Harlech home, dedicated his translation to Humphrey Humphreys, bishop of Bangor. The preface mentioned the importance of religious literature in the vernacular, the Welsh versions of *The Whole Duty of Man* and *The Book of Resolution* and now the present volume, all of which gave instructions as how to reach the realm of glory:

> In order to do so, your Creator has sent his Son to redeem you through his precious blood, his Spirit to sanctify you through the secret ministrations of his Word and sacraments, along with the spiritual books that he has provided for your country.[38]

The volume's four sections, a chapter-length introduction leading to a chapter on Christian charity, a third chapter on Christian righteousness and a final chapter on what Taylor calls 'Christian religion' translated by Wynne as *duwioldeb*, 'piety' or 'godliness', are subdivided into manageable portions interspersed with written prayers. Centring on the cultivation of personal sanctity, the text steers away from controversial points of divinity (until the final section) while the author's rejection of the imputation of Adam's sin to his posterity which, he believed, relieved individuals from taking responsibility for their own souls, and his antipathy towards Calvinism generally, are not wholly apparent. The serenity of the prose belies the turbulence in which it was written, when the king had been beheaded, the Prayer Book had been outlawed, episcopacy had been banned and much of the structure of the national church had been abolished. 'When his servants are persecuted', he claimed, evoking memories of clandestine Anglican worship during the 1640s, 'God would bless their exertions even if they meet in dens in the earth or in caves, though his usual way is to be present with them in consecrated buildings appointed for the purpose' (p. 25). For those who would live the life of piety, baptismal regeneration is presupposed, while the chapters on charity and righteousness are replete with counsels as to how, through moral exertion, the reader should attain holiness of life: 'When God gives his Spirit to those who are baptized and truly confirmed to be in communion with him, our bodies become temples in which the Holy Spirit dwells' (p. 71). The ethical standard demanded of the worshipper was high and there is little wonder that John Wesley, on reading *Holy Living* in Oxford in the 1730s, doubted whether he was converted at all.[39] The drumbeat rhythm that reverberates throughout this sonorous prose is the believer's duty to God: 'It is infallibly certain that there is heaven for all of the godly, and for me among them, if I do my duty' (p. 176).

Although the bulk of the book has to do with the privileges and profit of personal devotion, it moves by the final section to the obligation of public, communal worship. The circumstances in which it was written precluded any blatant reference to the Book of Common Prayer, nevertheless the author emphasizes the significance of the liturgy:

> Do not fail to be present at the public hours and places of prayer, arriving at church early and with good cheer, in reverence and gladness, waiting patiently and listening attentively to the sermon. In no way should you neglect taking communion whenever it is offered as this is the great solemnity of thanksgiving and the proper climax of each Sunday. (pp. 201–2)

The Christian calendar should provide the context for public worship with the feasts and fasts of the church year, saints' days and the points listed in the Creed: the nativity celebrating Christ's birth, the passion, the resurrection at Easter, the ascension to God's right hand, the descent of the Spirit at Pentecost being high points in the worshipper's life: 'The memories of the saints are precious to God and so they should be for us … Holy days are to be kept in order to give thanks for the lives of the saints, the apostles and the martyrs' (p. 203). The Arminian theology which undergirds the writing becomes more explicit by the closing chapter. Election, though a scriptural truth, is conditional. Grace can be forfeited. Perseverance is not granted automatically, it must be worked at strenuously. Regeneration does not necessarily guarantee eternal life. Although regeneration occurs only once, through the rite of baptism, it must be improved upon or its benefits will be lost: 'We repent, or rise from death but once, but from sickness many times, and by the grace of God we may be pardoned if we do so repent' (p. 237). For Taylor salvation was a synergy, a matter of cooperation between human effort aided by grace, and by God himself:

> We are but once to change our whole state of life … from that of sin and death, from the body of corruption, to the life of grace, to the possession of Jesus, to the kingdom of the gospel, and this occurs in the baptism of water, or in the baptism of Spirit when the right is verified by God's grace coming upon us, and by our obedience to the heavenly calling when we work together with God …
>
> … A hearty endeavour and an effective general change will secure a pardon; the unavoidable infirmities, the past evils, the present imperfections and short interruptions against which we watch and pray and strive being accounted to the cross and paid by the holy Jesus. (pp. 237–8)

However essential private devotion is to the life of holiness, the true climax of all worship is the partaking of the Lord's Supper, for

> the sacrifice of the cross which Christ offered for all the sins and all the needs of the world is represented to God by the minister in the sacrament, and offered up in prayer and sacramental memory, after the manner that Christ himself intercedes for us in heaven … [while] the benefits of that sacrifice are conveyed to all who communicate worthily. (p. 256)

Never before had such a high concept of Eucharistic grace been exhibited in Welsh theology,[40] and in the context of the eighteenth century it remained exceptional. On the basis of his other works (including the classic *Gweledigaethau'r Bardd Cwsg*, 'Visions of the Sleeping Bard' (1703)), Ellis Wynne held to a much more conventional position, High Church and sacramental certainly, but more in keeping with the Protestant churchmanship of centrist Anglicanism.[41] Yet there is no doubt that his superb rendering of Taylor's work contributed substantially to the richness of religious discourse in Welsh at the dawn of the eighteenth century.

Whereas the analysis above has depended on published works,[42] there is no doubt that ordinary parish clergy, where possible, were in substantial accord with the theology that those works propounded. The besetting weakness of the clergy was (on the whole) not their lack of piety but their poverty. In his correspondence with John Chamberlayne, secretary to the newly established Society for the Propagation of Christian Knowledge (the SPCK) in October 1700, Robert Wynne, vicar of the north Wales parish of Llanddeiniolen, 'complains of the poverty of the clergy in those parts'.[43] This fact was reiterated by Arthur Bedford, rector of Bristol's Temple Church, the following January who noted that 'the great ignorance and atheism' which was still all too prevalent in south Wales was due to 'the contempt of the clergy occasioned by the small provision for them'.[44] 'The account you give ... is very melancholy', Chamberlayne replied, 'nor do we hope to have it mend[ed] till a better provision be made for the clergy there whose learning will be proportionable to their means of attaining it'.[45] Although they faced enormous hardships, and despite there being more than a few rogues and reprobates among them,[46] it was for the most part the clergy who engendered the 'genuine and deep renewal of devotion' which characterized these years.[47] On the basis of his extensive research into the MS sermons of Welsh Anglicans of the period, Geraint H. Jenkins has described the tenor of their teaching: 'The awfulness of sin, the vanity of earthly joys, the brevity of human existence, and the paramount need for repentance were the themes which stocked most clerical repertories. The greatest stress of all, however, was laid on the terms of salvation.'[48] The introspective, penitential, morally disciplined character of Restoration religion and more especially its uncompromising call for the appropriation of the benefits of Christ's passion through personal faith, remained the *sine qua non* of parochial preaching well into the eighteenth century.

What is more, the 'puritan ethos' which 'manifested itself as a deep religious mood or an intense emotional tone' that had characterized the post-Restoration consensus shared by churchman and Dissenter alike would soon to be energized by the influence of continental Pietism and the exertions of the SPCK.[49] During the reign of Queen Anne (1702–14) and beyond, the modest 'renewal of religious life' already underway would be maintained.[50]

Pietism, the SPCK and Anglican pastoral theology, 1702–c.1714

The 'moral revolution' which emerged from within this ethos of religious seriousness following the political changes of 1689 was a reaction against the dissolute and worldly spirit in the metropolis and in the court especially which had itself been a reaction against what had been perceived as Puritan repression during the Commonwealth regime.[51] One of its most zealous proponents was Sir John Philipps (c.1666–1737), fourth baronet of Picton Castle, Pembrokeshire, whose father Sir Erasmus Philipps (d.1697) had expressed his Puritan convictions through his work as a commissioner for the Act for the Better Propagation of the Gospel in 1650–3.[52] Now articulated in the guise of post-Restoration Anglicanism, Sir John's deep piety led him, as MP for the Pembroke Boroughs, to introduce several measures for moral improvement through parliament, including the Blasphemy Act of 1698 making it an offence to deny publicly the doctrine of the Trinity and the 'Bill for the More Effective Suppressing of Vice and Immorality', the so-called (and ill-fated) 'Immorality Bill' of 1699 aimed at curbing prostitution. That his moral stance was fuelled by an experiential spiritual commitment is clear from his affirmation of the labours of the continental Pietists, August Hermann Franke (1663–1727) especially, and his support for evangelism, both at home and abroad, through the SPCK.

'Pietism', it has been said, 'was an answer to the problems of religious establishments in the doldrums'.[53] Just as there was a widespread frustration that the Church of England as a national church was failing to turn its baptized members into committed Christian disciples, Franke and his mentor, Philipp Jakob Spener (1635–1705) had striven to renew a state Lutheranism in the German regions that had become morally flabby and spiritually effete. Their emphasis on the need for individual conversion ('the New Birth') rather than a notional dependence on the doctrine of justification by faith, formally declared, the gathering together of earnest Christians for mutual edification and an optimistic missional orientation towards the future, inspired many not only in continental Europe but beyond.[54] Among Franke's projects was a mission to Tranquebar in India for which the Llanddowror clergyman Griffith Jones would volunteer. When news that a catechism in Portuguese, the first work to be printed in Tranquebar, arrived, Philipps informed his wife that it 'had filled us with surprise and holy joy'.[55] It was Philipps, his colleague John Vaughan of Derllys, senior clerics like John Jones,[56] dean of Bangor and John Evans,[57] Jones's diocesan, along with influential parish clergy such as Thomas Thomas,[58] rector of Merthyr near Carmarthen, James Harris,[59] vicar of Llantrisant in the diocese of Llandaff, as well as Philipps's brother-in-law, Griffith Jones, Llanddowror, who, by ensuring the success of the SPCK, would spread religious literacy and schooling for the poor during the coming decades.

One of the most significant results of the Toleration Act of 1689 was that it changed the Church of England from being 'the *national* church' to what has been described as 'merely the *established* church' of the land.[60] By legalizing Protestant Dissent even though it remained a tolerated rather than a fully accepted entity, the Anglican Church had lost its post-1662 *raison d'être* as the sole legitimate church within England and Wales: 'During the 1690s, the clergy of the Church of England became divided along political, ideological and ecclesiological lines that would have been scarcely conceivable to their predecessors in the Restoration church.'[61] The clergy's dilemma was either to accept the fact that the state, not the church, had become the primary agent of moral and spiritual unity leaving the church, although established, as a more or less voluntary body with a pastoral role providing the people with salvation. Either this or to return to the *status quo ante* when the absolute unity between the church and the state was still intact. The Whigs chose the first course and the Tories the second. Notwithstanding the discreet cooperation between some key Welsh Anglicans and moderate Dissenters during the 1670s and 1680s, Restoration churchmen had been, for the most part, very wary of voluntary religion. On the other hand, an element of voluntaryism had been part of the genius of the Reformation from the beginning. Conventicles, lay associations and voluntary groups had always characterized Protestant witness, indeed for the Pietist leaders Spener and Franke, groups of renewed individuals, *collegiae pietatis*, were essential for the rebirth of the state church. In

fact in London 'religious societies' of pious laymen under clerical control and inspired by Anthony Horneck, preacher at the Savoy Chapel,
had contributed to the deepening of devotion during the 1670s.[62] It
was in this spirit that the SPCK had been established by Thomas Bray
(1658–1730), rector of Sheldon near Birmingham, in March 1699, with
the twofold aim of founding charity schools 'for teaching poor children
to read and write and to repeat and understand the Church Catechism'
and to distribute affordable and easily understood literature 'in order to
diminish the gross ignorance of the principles of the Christian religion'.[63]
Four of its five founder members had links with Wales: Bray himself
was of Welsh descent whose early education had been at the Oswestry
Grammar School;[64] Sir Humphrey Mackworth, lawyer, industrialist
and later MP for Cardiganshire, lived at Neath; the jurist John Hook,
serjeant-at-law, had been chief justice of Caernarfonshire; while Colonel
Maynard Colchester, though resident in Gloucestershire, had sponsored
schools in Brecknock and Radnorshire. Within two years the society
had ninety subscribing members based in London, and an increasing
host of corresponding (i.e. non London-based) members, consisting of
clergy and godly laymen throughout the country, eager to expedite
its programme and values.[65] As one of its earliest members, both as a
subscriber and a correspondent, Sir John Philipps would remain the
society's driving force in Wales until his death in 1737.

Since the expiry of the system established by the Welsh Trust following the demise of its instigator, Thomas Gouge, in 1681,[66] there had
been little provision for popular elementary education in Wales. The
range of schools which did exist was partial, sectional and catered for
very few: parochially based private schools, grammar schools in the
market towns, elementary schools run by Dissenting ministers, along
with academies providing an intellectually bracing curriculum for young
men, mostly prospective ministers in the Dissenting churches who had
been debarred from the two English universities.[67] There was very little
for the children of the poor. For religion to be vitally effective, it was
realized that an efficient system of elementary education was essential.
In Wales, the SPCK's call for the establishment of charity schools met
with an immediate and widespread response. Between 1699 and 1727,
ninety-six schools would be set up: forty-three during the first decade,
forty-four between 1711 and 1720, and nine thereafter, most of which
were in Pembrokeshire, Carmarthenshire and Glamorgan.[68] The curriculum in these schools was the Bible, the Catechism and, for senior

pupils, that staple of Restoration Anglicanism *The Whole Duty of Man*.
There would be four classes in the larger schools, the first offering basic
instruction in spelling and reading; the second teaching the Book of
Psalms and the New Testament; the third covering the rest of the Bible
along with writing; and in the fourth boys would be taught arithmetic
and girls taught needlework, knitting, weaving and spinning. Practical
subjects such as husbandry and, in the coastal areas, seamanship, were
also included though an intimate knowledge of the Catechism was inculcated throughout. On completing the programme and where possible,
care would be taken to provide pupils with apprenticeships. Meals would
be supplied as well as clothes for the poorer children. Teaching would be
gratis. When not undertaken by the clergy (often in order to augment
their meagre stipends), authorized teachers would be appointed. Every
teacher was required to be

> a member of the Church of England, of a sober life and conversation, not
> under the age of twenty-five, one that frequents the Holy Communion,
> hath a good government of himself and his passions, of a meek temper
> and humble behaviour, of a good genius for teaching, who understands
> well the ... principles of the Christian religion, ... who can write a good
> hand and who understands the grounds of arithmetic.[69]

Each school, which was to be self-funded, would be maintained by the
munificence of the gentry and other wealthy patrons, by senior clergy
and by voluntary subscriptions within the parishes. The society would
ensure that each school was provided with books and other teaching aids
and would be inspected regularly. The most shining example of support
came from John Philipps who not only established twenty-two of the
thirty-one schools in Pembrokeshire and a handful in Carmarthenshire,
but paid the teachers' salaries, clothed the pupils and arranged for them
to be fed: 'The importance of Sir John Philipps' contribution cannot be
too greatly emphasised.'[70] John Vaughan and Sir Humphrey Mackworth
also contributed generously, as did the dean of Bangor and such philanthropic gentlewomen as Lady Dorothy Jeffreys in north-east Wales
and Mrs Edward Vaughan in Montgomeryshire. The system worked
exceptionally well during the first two decades of the century though
thereafter, due to the society's disinclination to become involved in the
deepening split between High Church Tories and low church Whigs,
its effectiveness declined. Nevertheless while it lasted, it perpetuated

'a programme of evangelical philanthropy which would reassert the spiritual and political primacy of the Church of England in the nation'.[71]

Yet it was through the society's support for literature that the profile of orthodox theology in Wales would be most marked. For its supporters the link between personal and public morality, referred to often as 'the reformation of manners', and the inculcation of sound doctrine was unassailable. In 1700 William Young, a lay correspondent from Wrexham, suggested to secretary Chamberlayne how the 'corruptions of the age' could be remedied: 'Discipline must be restored, catechising seriously applied to, and the magistrate be vigorous and resolved in punishing vice.'[72] For catechesis to be effective, catechisms and other improving literature would need to be distributed, and in February 1701 John Evans, bishop of Bangor, was requested to provide a list of the Welsh books already available as a basis for deciding what the next step in publishing should be. The list was remarkably free from doctrinal bias, its thirty-seven titles representing works from Puritan, Reformed and 'holy living' schools.[73] The society soon responded to the perceived need and by November 1704 it had urged a re-issue of Beveridge's sermon on the usefulness of Common Prayer and sponsored George Lewis's translation of Tillotson's *Persuasive to Frequent Communion*.[74] By July 1705 Thomas Williams, rector of Denbigh, informed the society that he had begun translating Beveridge's *Exposition of the Church Catechism*, published a year earlier for use by the clergy of St Asaph, though the Welsh version would not be available till 1708, the year the bishop died.[75] It would be followed two years later by his rendition of the High Church divine William Assheton's *A Brief Exhortation to the Holy Communion*[76] while the society then sponsored the republication of three texts which had long proved their worth: a fourth printing of Rowland Vaughan's translation of Lewis Bayly's classic *The Practice of Piety*;[77] a second edition of John Langford's version of *The Whole Duty of Man*[78] and a new rendering of John Davies of Mallwyd's *Llyfr y Resolusion*.[79] Such was their popularity that a fifth printing of both *The Practice of Piety* and John Davies's volume were issued in 1713 with a new imprint of Assheton's *Exhortation* appearing in 1715.

The remarkable effectiveness in distributing this literature was achieved through the increasing network of corresponding members of the SPCK and their adjuncts, making it plain that there was abroad a thirst for improving works of practical divinity. If Sir John Philipps had been the key figure ensuring the success of the society's educational exertions, '[t]he chief patron of Welsh books throughout South Wales, and indeed throughout the country as a whole, was John Vaughan of Derllys'.[80] Vaughan (1663–1722), Justice of the Peace and one-time mayor of Carmarthen, was related to John Philipps by marriage and shared his vibrant Pietistic faith and deep reformist convictions.[81] His constant refrain in the correspondence was that appropriate literature should be made available, that he would sponsor its translation and distribution, and that libraries should be established in strategic centres where clergy and the public would be allowed to borrow from the ever expanding range of titles that were appearing. By 1714 each of the four Welsh dioceses had its own lending library: Carmarthen for St David's, Cowbridge for Llandaff and the cities of Bangor and St Asaph for the two north Wales sees. The ideal was for the more easily consumed litera-ture to be distributed gratis while bulkier, more expensive items should be available for loan. Along with the titles mentioned above, among the most popular shorter works sponsored by the society (especially in south Wales) during these years was Moses Williams, later vicar of Defynnog's translation of Robert Nelson's *An Exercise … explaining the nature of Confirmation*[82] – this was underwritten by Edmund Tenison, archdeacon of Carmarthen – and in north Wales Ellis Wynne's version of the Kentish clergyman John Lewis's celebrated *The Church Catechism Explain'd.*[83]

The most ambitious undertaking was the rector of Denbigh's trans-lation of the Non-Juror Robert Nelson's exhaustive *Companion for the Festivals and Feasts of the Church of England.*[84] The tone of the teach-ing remained in the High Church, 'holy living', mode, though it never degenerated into mere moralism. Self-examination, costly repentance, partaking of the Lord's Supper as the principal means of grace were there to engender conversion and strengthen personal faith. 'Strive to make your salvation certain', urged Samuel Williams, vicar of Llandyfrïog in the diocese of St David:

> Now is the proper time, while the day of grace remains, while Christ still waits at the door, open to him and do everything he requires of you so that you will be forgiven your sins, justified by his righteousness and thereafter live a holy life.[85]

Despite the still incessant mention of poverty in the SPCK correspond-ence and the realization that many challenges remained, nevertheless these efforts at spreading scriptural knowledge and inculcating true piety were paying dividends. Indeed, Edward Samuel (1674–1748), rector of Betws Gwerfyl Goch in the St Asaph diocese, was virtually rapturous in his assessment of the country's spiritual state:

> May God be blessed that the light of the gospel is shining as brightly in Wales as anywhere, that ever more godly, useful, printed books are available, and that we now have better preachers among us than at any time for a thousand years.[86]

Yet even he realized that much more work needed to done: 'We also see that irreligion, contention and loveless-ness, heresy, immorality and corruption are all too common in this vicinity and farther afield.'[87] In fact the ground was being prepared thoroughly for an even more widespread reformation and what would become a uniquely intense spiritual revival. In the meantime, however, both external pressures and internal difficulties served to slow down the progress of renewal.

Orthodoxy and piety during the early Hanoverian period, c.1714–40

After 1714 the renewal of piety fuelled by the zeal of key individuals both clerical and lay, the exertions of the SPCK and manifested in the increasing availability of sound literature began to wane. The structural weaknesses that had blighted the Welsh Church since the Reformation were compounded by the political changes of the Hanoverian reign. The translation of John Evans, bishop of Bangor, to the Irish see of Meath in 1716 and the transfer of John Wynne, bishop of St Asaph, to Bath and Wells in 1727, marked the end of the practice of having Welsh (and Welsh-speaking) bishops governing Welsh dioceses.[88] From now on the trend would be to appoint careerist, Whig-supporting bishops, many of whose hearts, and futures remained in England.

The turnover of Hanoverian bishops was high with some being in post for unseemly short spans of time. In 1723 Richard Reynolds, chaplain to George I, retained the Bangor see for a matter of months before proceeding to Lincoln; Elias Sydall, a zealous supporter of the Whig regime, was both appointed to and left St David's (for Gloucester) in 1731, while Mathias Mawson's tenure at Llandaff lasted a winter, 1739–40, before his departure for Salisbury in the following spring.

In 1742 Edward Willes stayed at St David's for less than a year before leaving for Bath and Wells, and in 1743 the latitudinarian John Thomas persevered a matter of months at St Asaph before his translation to Lincoln. Even for those who waited longer, their eyes were almost invariably on more prestigious and lucrative destinations elsewhere. On his appointment to Bangor in 1728, Thomas Sherlock's retort, "tis pity this b[isho]prick should be only a bridge to a better', typified the view of many of his brethren.[89] Though a High Church Tory and pastorally conscientious bishop, by 1734 he was happily ensconced in Salisbury. Between 1724 and 1729, while serving as Llandaff's diocesan, Robert Clavering, formerly Regius Professor of Hebrew at Oxford, retained his canon's stall at Christ Church along with the *commendam* deanery of Hereford. However pressing his calls in Wales, he continued to reside 'in luxury and ease in Christ Church with his young wife, where he eats, drinks and [be]gets children'.[90] Almost inevitably, by 1729 he had progressed to Peterborough. Philip Bisse remained in post (at St David's) for three years before departing for Hereford in 1713, while William Baker (Bangor 1723–7; thereafter to Norwich), Francis Hare (St Asaph 1727–31; then to Chichester) and Samuel Lisle (St Asaph 1744–8; then to Norwich) maintained their Welsh sees each for four years only.

When the House of Lords was not in session, all bishops were expected to be in their dioceses in order to hold confirmations, to conduct visitations and to ordain new clergy. Some diocesan heads were more conscientious in this than others. The latitudinarian Benjamin Hoadly, although admittedly disabled, managed to visit Bangor only once during his occupancy of the see between 1715 and 1721 – he proceeded to Hereford in 1721 and to Salisbury two years later – while the corpulent bibliophile and scholar Thomas Tenison was too ill to fulfil his duties at St Asaph following his appointment in 1732. He remained in Oxford throughout, retaining his canonry at Christ Church until his death in 1735.[91]

There were others, however, who fulfilled their obligations scrupulously and brought credit to their calling. Despite failing to restore the cathedral's fabric and delegating many responsibilities to a skilled team of rural deans, John Tyler's oversight at Llandaff between 1706 and 1724 was on the whole commendable.[92] Before his departure for Ely in 1714, William Fleetwood had been an exemplary bishop of St Asaph where he had succeeded William Beveridge in 1708. His *Charge to the Clergy of St Asaph* (1710) underlined the high standards he required of his clerics.

They were expected to catechize the young diligently, to preach gospel truth plainly, to promote piety and eradicate vice. They were not to pander to the powerful within their parishes by preaching in English rather than Welsh. Not surprisingly perhaps, he engendered more respect than affection among his clergy, yet his effectiveness as a diocesan could not be gainsaid.[93] The same standards were perpetuated between 1714 and 1727 during the presidency of John Wynne, his successor. Adam Ottley was sixty-eight years old when he arrived at St David's in 1713 having served for decades as archdeacon of Shropshire. He set about with determination revitalizing the see, restoring the previously uninhabitable Episcopal palace at Abergwili, setting high standards in his visitation charges of 1714, 1717 and 1723, and appointing worthy local-bred prelates to key posts within the diocese. A staunch supporter of the SPCK, along with John Vaughan of Derllys he facilitated the distribution of improving literature within the parishes and patronized Theophilus Evans's translations of works by the High Church authors William Ward and Thomas Bisse. Dying in October 1723, he had chosen to be buried not in Shropshire, from where he hailed, but at Abergwili, thus cementing the link with the diocese that he had led with such distinction for ten years.[94] Before his translation to Coventry and Litchfield in 1731, Richard Smalbroke, a Warwickshire man, maintained the norms instituted at St David's by Ottley, his predecessor, replicated his zeal and mastered the vernacular sufficiently well to be able to lead confirmation services in Welsh.[95] In the main each of these prelates served the Established Church in their adopted land competently and well.

The main drawback faced by the Welsh Church both before and after the accession of George I in 1714 was its endemic administrative weakness, the debilitating poverty of its four dioceses and often ineffective, indeed sometimes negligent, Episcopal oversight. However strenuous the labours of its lay reformers and more conscientious clerics, efficient Christian witness and pastoral care were hampered by these factors.[96] The unwieldy structures had hardly changed since medieval times, while profits from the dissolution of the monasteries had not gone towards administrative reform but into the pockets of lay impropriators, mostly already wealthy landowners, who inherited with the monastic properties the right to appoint clergy to serve the benefices for which they were now responsible. Most of the impropriators were more interested in amassing gain for themselves than in paying the clergy a living wage. Tithe money from many benefices had also been transferred to cathedral chapters, not only in Wales (some went to the English dioceses of Gloucester, Chester, Coventry and Litchfield) and to Oxford and Cambridge colleges. As most of the monastic lands had been in south Wales, impropriation affected the sees of St David's and Llandaff the worst. In north Wales the post-Reformation bishops had preserved the right to appoint to benefices which meant that clerical poverty would not be as pressing a problem as it became in the south. By the eighteenth century and despite the Queen Anne's Bounty, which was meant to augment the salaries of clergy in benefices that yielded less than £50 per annum, clerical stipends in Welsh parishes remained scandalously low, a situation that led to the prevalence of pluralism, or holding more than one living at the same time, and its attendant scourge, non-residency.

There remain two remarkable assessments of the faults and failings of the Church, in the southern dioceses at least, issued at the time, the first being Griffith Jones's scorching apologia for his extra-parochial evangelism addressed to Bishop Ottley in July 1715, and the second was Erasmus Saunders's more measured but no less poignant *View of the State of Religion in the Diocese of St David* of 1721.

Griffith Jones (1684–1761), rector of Llandeilo Abercywyn, Carmarthenshire, latterly of Llanddowror, had been brought before the diocesan authorities for preaching in other men's parishes without their consent. In an extraordinarily virile and eloquent defence of his actions, the thirty-two year old clergyman portrayed the spiritual needs of the diocese in the starkest terms. To the accusation that

> I have transgressed the limits prescribed by your lordship and that repeated accounts have been received of my persisting in the same irregular way of preaching and attended with crowds of people, directly contrary to the canons and of ill-consequence to the peace of the church[97]

he claimed that he had never ventured abroad without first being invited by the incumbent, and had always done so in order to support and not undermine the regularly instituted parochial ministry. Whatever zeal he had expended had been strictly according to his ordination vows and for the good of the people's souls:

> My solemn vows and promises at the time of my ordination; the love of God; the requests of the clergy, and the deplorable necessity of perishing

multitudes move me with compassion and constrain me sometimes to preach abroad where desired, in order to endeavour the rescuing of some souls as firebrands out of the fire (p. 83)

... Nor am I aware how it can be of ill consequence to the peace of the church, whereas I directly aim at its peace and tranquillity, and have nothing more in view than the chiefest peace of all, i.e. a reconciliation of men to God in order to obtain the peace which passeth all understanding. (p. 84)

Whatever the qualms and 'implicit suggestions of my hyper-canonical neighbours' (p. 84), there were needs within the diocese which were not being met. In an impassioned appeal to the bishop he claimed that 'there are not a few to be met within every corner ... that are utter strangers to Christ and his gospel, knowing not the Ten Commandments nor the Lord's Prayer' (p. 85). Whereas there was no doubt that some of the clergy were fulfilling a faithful ministry, that was not, by a long chalk, true of them all:

It is far from me to revile any of them or to deny that there are several painful divines (thanks to God for them!) that endeavour sincerely to discharge their duty, but several more there are that, I am afraid, do not. (p. 85)

The reasons for their failure were varied, but pluralism and non-residency were plainly a bane. There were good men who were being overworked and grievously underpaid, generally due to the stinginess of impropriators. Being 'pinched with poverty and forced to officiate in three or four parishes', they 'cannot pretend to do well in either, and thus are the children left uncatechised and the people in some places for months, yea for near twelve months, without a sermon' (p. 85). There were others, alas, who were not nearly so deserving of sympathy: those 'that do not understand our language and consequently no better than barbarians and no more edifying nor less odd than Welsh in England or Latin in France'; those who were partial to 'empty speculations, high and lofty or quaint phrases, scholastical or controversial divinity above the reach of ordinary capacity'; there were High Churchmen 'pleading with warmth for our Holy Mother whilst our duty to the Heavenly Father is but coldly or hardly mentioned'; and worse still, those who preached 'a little sober morality (which a pagan philosopher would have preached much better), without any intimation of repentance, regeneration' and the like (p. 85).

However much clerical poverty subverted spiritual effectiveness, what was most pernicious was a carnal or unconverted ministry: 'It is … much better to have the plague in the parish as the countenance of a profane profligate or a sensual epicure of a minister' (p. 84), he said. 'Can he be heartily desirous of converting others who is unconverted himself?' (p. 86), he asked. 'Is he likely to fight against Satan with all his might that is a servant of Satan himself? Or is he likely to do any great harm to Satan's kingdom whilst he is a member of it?' (p. 86). Such a scathing indictment was not likely to make Jones popular among his less committed colleagues, but he was now so emboldened that nothing would hold him back:

> And yet many, even too, too many, are thus profaners in your lordship's diocese (to the great detriment and scandal of religion) need none other witness to prove it to those that know them than their adultery, drunkenness, the neglect of domestic worship and their common swearing in conversation. (p. 86)
>
> … I crave your lordship's favourable interpretation of this freedom I take. I have no pleasure to inveigh against any of my brethren … and it is not without some pains that I overcome flesh and blood to be thus sincerely plain … [but] it is the mere necessity of souls and my desire of their salvation, the prosperity of the church and the flourishing of piety in this diocese which forced me to this unmodesty, if some such hard name must be given it. (p. 87)

There is no record of Bishop Ottley's direct response to this mighty epistle, but the insightful nature of Griffith Jones's critique and his searing sincerity did him no lasting harm. He was not without powerful support, not least from John Dalton, squire of Clog-y-frân, Llanddowror, John Vaughan of Derllys and later his daughter, Madam Bridget Bevan, and especially Sir John Philipps.[98] As for Jones himself he feared no man: 'None can cultivate a wilderness without sometimes being scratched by the thorns and briars' (p. 88). As will be shown below, he would become a key figure in the spiritual development of the Welsh Church during the succeeding decades.

A gentler but no less heartfelt appraisal was issued in 1721 by Erasmus Saunders (1670–1724), vicar of Blockley, Gloucestershire, prebendary of Brecon in the St David's diocese and a native of Pembrokeshire. In his appeal to George, prince of Wales, and through him to parliament, he made a sobering assessment of the state of religion in his home diocese, listed its needs and suggested how they should be met. 'We, the poor people of this obscure part of the Church and nation', he wrote, were in dire need of aid, and although spiritual renewal could only ultimately come from above, it was incumbent upon the governors of the Established Church, 'that Church which is the glory of the Reformation', not to depend on voluntary giving through charities such as the SPCK, but to play their part in ensuring its financial viability and institutional flourishing.[99]

Among the most obviously pressing needs was to provide a living wage for the clergy, especially incumbents of the more impoverished livings and the curates, and to ensure the upkeep of church buildings: 'So great are the desolations of religion in this country; so many of our churches are in actual ruins' (p. 4). Many buildings were in such a dilapidated state as to 'only serve for the solitary habitations of owls and jackdaws' (pp. 23–4). As for the payment of the clergy, the practical challenges of serving multiple parishes compounded their problems: 'Stipends … are so small that a poor curate must sometimes submit to serve three or four churches for ten or twelve pounds a year, and that perhaps when they are almost as many miles distant from one another' (p. 24). In order to provide services in these distant parishes on a Sunday, they would be 'forced to a kind of perpetual motion, and like hasty itinerants to hurry about from place to place'. This indeed was 'the hard case of our poor unhappy curacy-pluralists' (p. 25). Yet the wonder was that the clergy still achieved so much in the face of such hardships and humiliations, that young men were still offering themselves for ordination and that the people were being served:

> [N]otwithstanding these discouragements, there are, God be thanked, several clergymen among us, that by their virtue and steady application, surmount the difficulties they meet with, find means to be well accomplished, and to adorn their station for the sake of welldoing, and to be no less eminent for their pastoral care and diligence, than others are for their neglect and scandal. (p. 27)

Saunders, a keen advocate of the SPCK and fervent in his practical support of its labours, partook earnestly of that renewal of devotion which had characterized Welsh religion a generation earlier. Yet he was painfully aware of its limitations and that despite everything, reformed piety had yet to win over the bulk of the people. The Bible had been available in the vernacular since 1588, the Prayer Book liturgy had become familiar to worshippers while the conventions of the Established Church had become an accepted part of everyday life. In fact, '[b]y the eighteenth century the Anglican Church had become widely accepted in Wales and seems to have been held in some affection'.[100] But this was not enough. The ordinary people were open to truth. Indeed, they were genuine in their commitment to religion as they knew it, and had a sincere and worthy sympathy for the ministrations of the establishment:

> There is, I believe, no part of the nation more inclined to be religious and to be delighted with it than the poor inhabitants of these mountains. They don't think it too much when neither ways nor weather are inviting, over cold and bleak hills, to travel three or four miles or more on foot to attend the public prayers and sometimes as many more to hear a sermon, and they seldom grudge many times for several hours together in their damp and cold churches to wait the coming of their minister who, by occasional duties in his other curacies, or by other accidents may be obliged to disappoint them, and to be often variable in his hours of prayer. (p. 32)

As well as attending services, in the absence of the clergy the people would read to one another from religious texts and instruct one another accordingly: '[I]t is not uncommon to see servants and shepherds, as they have an opportunity, strive to do these good offices to one another' (p. 32.). Along with this they would sing simple, home-spun verses, usually in harmony and with responses,

> which they call *haslingod*, or *carolion*, which generally consist either of the doctrinal or historical parts of scripture, or of the lives and worthy acts of some eminent saints, whose extraordinary piety and virtue they thereby endeavour to illustrate and recommend to themselves and others. (p. 33)

These devotional practices, and others such as crossing themselves and praying at the graves of their forefathers, though reminiscent of the customs of the primitive Christians, were, nonetheless, mingled with the remains of popery such as praying to the saints and the Holy Virgin, peregrinations to holy wells, and prayers for the departed. In fact true religion was mixed with superstition and conventionality. However sincere the devotions of the faithful, they were yet lacking in the purity of true biblical faith:

> And thus it is that the Christian religion labours to keep ground here, superstition and religion, truth and error are so very oddly mixed that it should be in charity concluded to be rather the misfortune than the fault of many that they are mixed. For the generality are, I am afraid, more obliged … to their religious observances of these ancient customs, or to the instructions they derive from their *haslingod*, or the Vicar of Llanymddyfri's poems … than any benefit received by the catechising and preaching of a regular ministry. (pp. 36–7)

The basic problem was that, despite having the Bible, the Book of Common Prayer and a plethora of sound literature, and notwithstanding the labours of generations of fine teachers, preachers, clergy and bishops, the Protestant Reformation had not yet wholly taken root in the life of the nation:

> If we have not yet quite unlearned the errors of our popish ancestors, it is because the doctrines of the Reformation begun about two hundred years ago in England have not yet effectively reached us, nor is it indeed likely that they ever should without a fit and learned clergy. (p. 37)

By allowing pluralism, non-residency and the wholly inappropriate appointment of non-Welsh speakers to the more lucrative livings and key diocesan posts, the Church had done itself a grave disservice. Equally serious was the general devaluing of a well-endowed, parochial ministry, 'for as religion can't subsist without a clergy, neither can a clergy without a maintenance, and that proportioned not only to bare necessity but with some regard to the dignity of the function' (p. 92). Even now the clergy, despite its blemishes, were doing the best they could. Indeed in many cases their exertions were heroic: 'That there have been, that there are still even in this obscure corner, many honest and good men who labour under these difficulties, is too well known a truth to be denied' (p. 72). Yet they clearly required support while the Church itself stood in need of comprehensive renewal.

The literature which continued to be published and distributed for the benefit of Welsh readers remained for the most part in the 'holy living' vein, much of it still much concerned with sacramental religion and worthy partaking of the Lord's Supper,[101] though by the 1720s there occurred a marked hardening in its High Church character. In 1719 Griffith Jones, vicar of Bodfari and thereafter of Denbigh (and not to be confused with his namesake at Llanddowror), issued the first of three tracts emphasizing the catholic nature of the Church of England, the apostolic succession of its ministry and the perils of schism. God had ordained a single church to be the ark of his salvation, represented in the sovereign's realm by the establishment. Moreover, under the divine dispensation, it was governed not by presbyters, as the Dissenters would have it, but by bishops: 'It appears from scripture that our saviour committed the government of the church to his apostles, and that they delegated that ordinary part of their authority to particular persons who were since distinguished by the name of bishops.'[102] This was not a matter of expediency but of deep theological import: 'Bishops were anciently called apostles, the apostles' successors, the offspring of the apostolical seed', this being in direct contradistinction to 'your doctrine of parity'.[103] An expanded Welsh version of the tract which appeared in 1722 was even more pugnacious, adding a rationale for Anglican use of such extra-biblical practices as the sign of the cross in baptism, kneeling to take communion, confirmation and the use of godparents, keeping lent and celebrating saints' days as well as the celebrant's wearing of the surplice. For the vicar of Bodfari, all were justifiable according to venerable tradition, their significance being ceremonial rather than doctrinal. The call, however, was for Dissenters to return to the bosom of the Mother Church: 'Your obligation is to return to the communion of the established Church of England.'[104] A third essay of 1728 repeated the substance of the previous two, laying out clearly the logic of the High Church position:

> That we may be saved according the rule of God's revealed will, we must be members of Christ's church; that we are members of Christ's church we must be partakers of the sacraments, which be instituted to initiate and confirm us therein, by making them the ordinary and stated means of conveying to us his divine grace; that we may partake of the sacraments, they must be administered by persons duly commissioned; lastly, that these persons may be duly commissioned, they must be ordained by

those who derive this authority in a continued and uninterrupted succession from the apostles, as they did theirs from our Saviour.[105]

Although Dissenters claimed to have the sacraments, their effectiveness was at best dubious due to the invalid nature of their institution. There were, in fact,

> just grounds to question whether baptism of the Lord's Supper as administered by them be really sacraments or no; nay, a strong presumption that they are not. In regard in all probability, they have no power in dispensing them for want of a due and valid commission.[106]

Although he virtually unchurched non-episcopalian communions, on the basis of the reality of God's non-covenanted grace he stopped short of denying the validity of Dissenters' salvation. There was no doubt, however, that all non-Anglicans remained in grave peril: 'You cannot join with a separating congregation without sinning against God for thereby to incur the guilt of a causeless separation which is the sin of schism.'[107] The Dissenters needed to repent and return to the one true church. This note of stridency, increasingly common during the 1720s and 1730s, quashed any attempt to find common ground between churchmen and Dissenters. However, this was not the only theology that appeared at the time.

William Beveridge, former bishop of St Asaph, had been quite singular among late seventeenth-century High Church divines in holding together a high doctrine of the church and sacraments with a staunchly Reformed doctrine of redemption. For him there could be no blunting of the distinction between justification and sanctification; salvation was not a matter of cooperating with prevenient grace but of being grasped miraculously by the mystery of election, albeit an election manifest openly in the Person and Work of Christ. This was clear in James Davies's (Iaco ab Dewi) 1717 translation of *Private Thoughts upon Religion, Digested into Twelve Articles, with Practical Resolutions form'd thereon* (1709), a compendium of the bishop's theology published shortly after his death. The first seven articles covered the doctrine of God as Trinity, humankind's fall in Adam, Christ's perfect obedience to the divine law in order to secure human redemption, his atoning sacrifice and resurrection, leading to Article Eight: 'I believe that I am justified only by the merits of Christ imputed to me, and that my nature is sanctified by the Spirit of Christ implanted in me.'[108] Whereas most High Church divines shied away from the concept of imputation, preferring the idea that justification was subsumed into the process of sanctification, that sin had only weakened rather than incapacitated the will and that faith itself was a human work,[109] Beveridge was insistent that salvation was the result of sovereign grace alone: 'How is it possible for me to be justified by good works, when I can do no good works, until I have first been justified myself?' (p. 72). Far from being a human work, faith was a gift; only by affirming the gift could I profit from salvation. My own righteousness was as filthy rags. It was only through the righteousness of Christ imputed to my soul, could I access the benefits of salvation: 'No; I believe no-one can deserve a thing from God, only he who can do more than is asked of him, and that is beyond the means of any creature' (p. 73). The wonder of the gospel was that God himself, in the Person of his Son, had taken it upon himself not only to live a perfect life in full obedience to the claims of the divine law, but to face the divine wrath, namely God's righteous anger in response to sin, and through his sacrifice offer an atonement to the Father. It was this righteousness, completely underserved and achieved apart from us, which is imputed (not imparted) to us, and upon which alone we can rely:

> Whose righteousness? Our own righteousness? No! God's righteousness, originally his, but through imputation made ours. And this is the *only* way that we can be said to share God's righteousness, namely through that of Christ's (p. 79)

For Beveridge it was on the basis of this that 'holy living' could be achieved. Sanctification followed justification but remained separate from it. It was only thereafter that the life of obedience, with God the Holy Spirit operating within the believer, that he or she could strive to live a life of holiness, being refashioned slowly to the image of Christ. Although the bishop aligned himself with the High Church divines, espousing a high doctrine of sacramental grace in both baptism and the Lord's Supper (Article Nine), while the section entitled 'Practical Resolutions' – more than half the book – emphasized the importance of living a holy life, this shows that Reformed theology had not been wholly eclipsed among Welsh Anglicans during the early eighteenth century.

Unlike the *Private Thoughts* (which was issued in a second Welsh-language edition in 1726), the 1723 translation of Beveridge's

The Great Necessity of Public Prayer and Frequent Communion (1708) emphasized the importance of public worship and of regular and sincere partaking of the Lord's Supper, thus replicating the teaching that had appeared in 1693 in the Welsh version of his *Sermon Concerning the Excellency and Usefulness of the Common Prayer.*[110] Here it was the High Church divine rather than the Reformed theologian that was on display. The essay on public prayer described the place that public worship had in the life of the early church, invariably described by High Churchmen as 'Primitive Christianity', and however important personal religion and private devotion were for individuals, they should be balanced by the corporate, liturgical and churchly aspects of faith. The essay on frequent communion repeated the usual pastoral advice concerning unworthy partaking of the sacrament. Whereas the Prayer Book stipulated that all baptized church members should come to the table at least three times a year, including Easter, the primitive practice had been to partake daily when possible, and certainly each Sunday and on holy days as well. For the bishop this should be the parochial ideal, while no one should neglect what was the principal means of grace: 'Whenever we are invited to this spiritual wedding we must come, sure to be dressed in our wedding garment, with such a temper and disposition of mind as becomes the place, the company and the feast itself.'[111]

The impression gained by reading the literature of the later 1720s and 1730s was that the zeal which had been notable a generation earlier was dissipating. Improving works, again in the High Church tradition, were still being published,[112] and the SPCK was still doing its best to distribute them to the needy, but there was little sign of widespread religious renewal. Many of the more ardent supporters of reform were passing on: John Vaughan of Derllys died in 1722; Erasmus Saunders passed away in 1724; John Jones, dean of Bangor, in 1727; James Harris, the SPCK's most dedicated agent in Glamorgan, died in 1728 followed by Sir John Philipps in 1737. For Griffith Jones of Llanddowror, this was a huge blow.[113] He had lamented four years earlier in February 1733, 'how numerous and shameless, … how common and impudent the despisers and oppressors of serious piety are in our days', bewailing 'the tide of iniquity which now flows so fast upon us', but the loss of the most pious leader in the public life of south Wales was grievous indeed.[114] The spiritual situation was only set to get worse. 'That ancient thing called religion', he informed Madam Bridget Bevan in June 1737, had now been 'almost exploded out of conversation, except for the purpose of ridicule'.[115] Doctrinally the Achilles heel of the 'holy living' school (to which the rector of Llanddowror did not adhere) was its aversion to the concept of justification by faith alone. The result was that the heavy emphasis on human cooperation with divine grace in the matter of salvation could all too often degenerate into works righteousness or mere moralism. Even partaking of the sacrament could become an empty rite. During the 1690s and 1700s this had never been the case. The correct balance between costly obedience, a subjective striving for repentance and an objective salvation wrought by God on the basis of the sacrifice of Christ had been preserved. By 1730 or so, though there was still a formal adherence to atonement doctrine and the necessity of divine grace, moralism and conditionality had tended to emerge. The words of the evangelical parson Thomas Jones of Southwark: 'We have preached morality so long that we have hardly any morality left, and this moral preaching has made our people so very immoral that there are no lengths of wickedness which they are not afraid of running into', could equally well be applied to Wales.[116] Although the bulk of the clergy remained orthodox – there is no evidence of latitudinarianism or liberal theology gaining ground in the parishes – the incipient threat was formalism. This was not all the story: vital piety would still exist, the Evangelical Revival did not emerge in a vacuum and there would remain much continuity between 1689 and the 1750s, but by the 1730s there does seem to have occurred a waning of spirituality. Nevertheless a vision for renewal remained: the one person who was most responsible for turning it into a reality was the Llanddowror clergyman, Griffith Jones.

Practical godliness and theology: Griffith Jones, *c.*1712–61

Not for nothing have historians referred to 'this starchy, introspective Anglican clergyman', 'an austere, peevish and humourless man', as 'the greatest Welshman of the eighteenth century and one of the chief benefactors of the Welsh nation'.[117] A figure of unique inventiveness, prodigious energy, granite-like spirituality and dogged resolve, he – and not the bishops or anyone else within an ecclesiastical establishment to which he cleaved with such unswerving loyalty – succeeded in transforming a poor, marginal and only partially lettered nation into 'one of the most literate countries in the modern world'.[118] The instigator of 'the most striking experiment in mass religious education undertaken anywhere in Great Britain or its colonial possessions in the eighteenth century', he was also a preacher, pastor and evangelist for whom sound doctrine, anointed by the Holy Spirit, was the means of renewing the church and saving the people.[119] Already revered as an orator as early as the 1710s, by the middle decades of the eighteenth century he would come into his own.

The youngest son of a moderately prosperous if obscure farmer, John ap Griffith and Elinor, his wife, of Pant-yr-efel, Pen-boyr, Carmarthenshire, Jones was born in 1684[120] and baptized soon after at Cilrhedyn Church in neighbouring Pembrokeshire. Educated at Carmarthen Grammar School, he had already been converted – an event referred to scathingly if accurately by John Evans, rector of Eglwys Gymun, the man who would become his most malicious critic – and called 'to be a chosen vessel … [and] a peculiar instrument for rescuing many souls that were now far gone on their way to that place of torment'.[121] Rather than progressing to university, he was ordained deacon by George Bull, bishop of St David's, in September 1708 and held successively the curacies of Pen-y-bryn, Pen-rhydd and Laugharne (where he was also employed as teacher in the local SPCK school) before being appointed rector of Llandeilo Abercywyn, Carmarthenshire, in 1711. Five years later, in July 1716, Llanddowror was added to his charge, a living in the gift of his principal benefactor, Sir John Philipps. All these places were within a small compass in the south-western portion of the county where he would remain until his death, aged seventy-seven, in April 1761.

He first appears on the public record in the files of the SPCK for 24 October 1712 in relation to the mission at Tranquebar:

> That there's a very worthy clergyman in Carmarthensh[ire] whose name is Jones that has lately discovered an inclination to go to Tranquebar and for that end is desirous to acquaint himself with the Portuguese language and would gladly receive a Portuguese grammar if it can be procured.[122]

The Tranquebar mission on the Malabar coast near Madras had been established in 1706 by King Frederick IV of Denmark, a man imbued deeply with Pietist principles. It was to be the first organized Protestant mission in India and, heavily dependent on Halle-trained evangelists, it bore all the hallmarks of the Pietist faith. As the movement's leader August Hermann Franke had already forged strong links with the SPCK having been elected a corresponding member as early as 1700, it was natural that Sir John Philipps would seek support for the mission among those whom he knew. This was especially true since the Danish venture had virtually merged with the Anglican mission attached to the East India Company at nearby Fort St George.[123] Although excited by the prospect of evangelizing overseas – a very novel concept among British Protestants at the time – and despite having begun to teach himself Portuguese, further reflection made him believe that he should redouble his efforts at home. According to the society's record: '[T]hough he labours under many inconveniences and among others, that the little flock committed to his charge would be deprived of the ministry of God's Word during his absence.'[124] In fact, he seems to have had second thoughts: ''tis not the belief of his unmeetness and insufficiency only which hinders him from resolving upon the mission to Malebar, but likewise the extremely miserable blindness of his own country'.[125] After months of indecision, including visiting London to meet with the mission's officers where he was offered the post, and conferring regularly with Sir John Philipps, in November 1713 he finally declined 'upon the prospect he had of doing more service in his native country than he can propose to do abroad'.[126] Thereafter his unquenchable zeal was poured into evangelizing his needy compatriots in south-west Wales.

The fact that Griffith Jones's effectiveness as a preacher had registered by that time is confirmed by a letter to the SPCK written by John Dalton, squire of Clog-y-frân, Llanddowror, on 25 February 1713. Not only was he having an impact on his own parishioners but on congregations everywhere in the vicinity.

> The worthy and reverend Griffith Jones still goes on with an indefatigable industry and earnestness to press Christian knowledge and practice upon the hearts and lives not only of the people under his charge [but] his auditors everywhere when he is invited to preach God's Word.[127]

What was most striking to Dalton was not the jealousy that his ministry was inflaming in 'the generality of negligent and ignorant clergy and gentry of which sort this country does most lamentably abound', but his popularity among the ordinary people: 'His endeavours and excellent advice are most approved among the generality of the vulgar sort of people, who mostly appear to have a hungering and thirsting after the sincere milk of the Word' (p. 274). At last it seemed that Reformation truth was beginning to reach the lives of the populace at a deep spiritual level. He would soon be summoned before the bishop for the irregularity of preaching beyond his home parish, but his insistence of having done so only when invited is clear from Dalton's account:

> When Mr Jones is invited to preach anywhere, and also when he preaches in his own church, in which there does not belong as parishioners save ten or twelve small families, it is to be admired what a numerous congregation he has to minister to ... Having generally above five or six hundred auditors, nay sometimes a thousand, a number not to be met with in Wales beside on the like occasion. It mostly consists of such who seem very desirous of being instructed in the plain and familiar dialect of their native tongue. (p. 274)

Dalton had never seen the like, and part of the evangelist's appeal was his mastery of the vernacular: 'It is certain that Mr Jones is one of the greatest masters of the Welsh tongue that ever Wales was blessed with, both in respect of fluency of speech and eminency in scriptural and Christian knowledge' (p. 274). It seems that as no time before, certainly not since the Puritan period, had such a powerful and effective evangelist been raised in the Welsh Church. Dalton's aim was to have the SPCK use its influence to procure a bishop's licence, or even permission by the Archbishop of Canterbury, for the rector of Llandeilo Abercywyn to preach abroad without restraint: 'It is a great pity that all the doors of his neighbouring churches are not open to so good a man, especially upon holidays on which there is no service read but in very few churches, and hardly ever a sermon' (p. 274). Such a practice, he claimed, 'might be a means of awakening not only the drowsy clergy, but their people also out of that dead sleep they now seem to be in' (p. 275).

Such being the nature of religious establishments everywhere, it was unlikely that this wish would ever be granted. In May 1713 Bishop Ottley mentioned to his diocesan registrar, his nephew also named Adam Ottley, 'a great disorder of late' concerning 'Mr Jones of Llandeilo Abercywyn's going about preaching on weekdays, sometimes in churches and sometimes in churchyards and sometimes on the mountains to several hundreds of auditors'.[128] The upshot of the affair, as related by Sir John Philipps ('I see it is high time to repair to my diocese' Ottley had retorted, writing from London) was 'a sort of trial before the bishop of St David's at Carmarthen where several of the clergy appeared against

[Mr Jones of Laugharne], whose principal accusation was his neglecting his own cure and intruding himself into the churches of other ministers without their leave'.[129] Despite the tumult, deplored by Edward Jones, the diocese's chancellor, as the work 'of this busy enthusiast' encroaching 'on other men's cures', the accused seems to have been more or less exonerated.[130] The popularity and effectiveness of his ministry was once again underlined. 'That he had preached twice or thrice without the walls of the church' was admitted, 'the reason of which was because the church was not large enough to contain the hearers, which sometimes amounted to three or four thousand people'.[131] Indeed Ottley had been informed that on the first Thursday in April 1714, such was the throng at Llanwenog, Cardiganshire, that the doors of the parish church had had to be 'broken open',[132] while years later John Evans, Eglwys Gymyn, recalled that as a lad he had been unable to gain entrance to the church at Laugharne where he went to hear Griffith Jones, as the crowd had been too dense.[133] In all it was obvious that Griffith Jones's ministry, even before being instituted to the parish of Llanddowror, was quite extraordinarily powerful.

Griffith Jones's apologia addressed to Bishop Ottley was dated 11 July 1715,[134] and for the next decade-and-a-half he appears in the minutes of the SPCK (of which he became a corresponding member in 1716) chiefly as being in receipt of Welsh Bibles for distribution among his parishioners.[135] In 1718 he took a three-week journey in the company of Sir John Philipps throughout Wales, north-east England, the Scottish borders and back through the Midlands, in order to meet with many of the SPCK's members, and by so doing not only confirmed his stature within the society but also cemented his already strong relationship with his mentor.[136] Two years later, on 11 February 1720, he married Sir John's sister, Margaret. Apart from the evidence of a few MS sermons,[137] we know little of the detail of his ministry during the 1720s, but his name re-appears in the minutes of the SPCK on 22 September 1731 requiring financial help for the establishment of 'a Welsh school' at Llanddowror in order to teach the contents of the Welsh Bible gratis. Thereafter his name is mentioned repeatedly in connection with the schools, so much so that on 26 January 1737, it was recorded, 'that the Welsh schools … increase beyond their ability to manage'.[138] Before accounting for the development of the circulating schools and their significance in inculcating biblical doctrine among the populace, it is important to describe the theological underpinning of Jones's ministry and how, by the middle of the eighteenth century, it would contribute to a renewal of the Puritan and Reformed faith within mainstream Welsh Anglicanism.

According to his earliest biographer, Henry Phillips of Tre-lech, Carmarthenshire, who, following his conversion in 1737 (under the exhortation of Howell Harris) became a regular worshipper at Llanddowror's parish church, Griffith Jones 'preached up faith and repentance judiciously and was a strenuous asserter of the absolute necessity of the new birth and gospel holiness both in heart and life'.[139] Moreover

> [h]e steadily relied for final acceptance ... on a better righteousness than his own, even the glorious and transcendently rich perfect right-eousness of Jesus Christ, imputed unto him for his justification. This was the rock of his hope and crown of his rejoicing.[140]

That this was an accurate assessment of his theological position is pat-ent from his voluminous correspondence with Madam Bridget Bevan throughout the 1730s. The Pietist spirituality shared by Sir John Philipps and John Vaughan of Derllys was inherited by Bridget, Vaughan's youngest daughter, who in 1721 (a year before her father died) married the barrister Arthur Bevan of Laugharne, recorder of the Carmarthen Boroughs and its MP. Already members of the landed elite, the couple moved in fashionable circles in London and Bath, where she was eager to use her connections to further the religious, educational and philanthropic concerns which had been so close to her father's heart. In fact, according to Glanmor Williams, this 'lady of rank and sub-stance', became something of 'a poor man's Countess of Huntingdon'.[141] Be that as it may, she certainly took over responsibility for the oversight of the SPCK's schools in Carmarthenshire, and came increasingly to value and rely on Griffith Jones's spiritual counsel. In effect the rector of Llanddowror became her de facto confessor while she undoubtedly became his soul-friend. Once he went so far as to state that '[i]t may be of great benefit for very dear and intimate Christian friends, in a private, prudent and humble manner, to unbosom their souls and make known to each other such particular sins and temptations as haunt them, and therefore to pray with and for one another', though the tone of their correspondence was unfailingly decorous, chaste and unrelentingly doctrinal.[142]

Whereas the 'holy living' school tended to fuse justification with sanctification and blur the distinction between Christ's imputed righteousness and human, if faith-induced, obedience, Griffith Jones was adamant that sinners were saved by grace alone. In other words a radical concept of sin demanded an absolute doctrine of redemption. For him sin was not a superficial blemish on the surface of life but a profound perversion of the soul. 'Nothing is plainer from the whole current of the Holy Scriptures', he claimed, 'that all men are dead in trespasses and sins, spiritually dead through the mortal wound of sin and the sentence of death which the divine law has passed upon it'.[143] All of humankind is implicated in the fall of Adam and as such every aspect of life has been effected: 'Human nature being corrupted by the apostasy of our first natural parents, what better inclinations can we by nature derive from them but such are fleshly, corrupt and sensual.'[144] Men and women are not just flawed and damaged but in utter enmity with God, the knowledge of which can be devastating: 'Nothing can affect the soul of man so grievously as the heavy pressure of sin and its guilt and break to pieces the sturdiest heart.'[145] The malaise of sin incurs spiritual death. Sin cannot be assuaged, it can only be forgiven, while the only answer to death is rebirth and resurrection: 'No death is so frightful as to be dead to the things of God, nor is there anything but the enjoyment [of that] above equal to a life of faith in communion with him.'[146] All of which depended on the finished work of Christ. It is Christ who, by living a sinless life in full obedience to the divine law, offered himself up as an atonement to the Father, and following his death, resurrection and ascension to glory, now gives himself to believers as their saviour and friend:

> When the guilt and greatness of our offences affright us from God, when we are full of doubt and fear that the righteous and holy God will not accept such great offenders as we are, then must faith apply to Christ as our alone and sufficient remedy, who hath washed away our guilt, paid our debt, bore our punishment and by his own death purchased our pardon. He is a surety and saviour to the humble penitent sinner. He hath taken from him the terrible curse and condemnation of sin, and justifies the sinner by his own righteousness wherewith he clothes the soul as with a glorious robe, that his vileness may not appear.[147]

Such a salvation could never be wrought by the individual through his or her own striving or morality, it could only be accepted freely as a gift from God. Human righteousness or formal religion meant nothing in the presence of grace:

> As we are all conceived and born in sin, those seeds of rebellion or rebellious principles which we brought in our nature into this world, however covered or refined and polished they may be with moral qualities or other acquirements, yet still continue irreconcilable to the pure and holy precepts of Jesus Christ, till renewing grace is admitted to have its perfect work in the soul.[148]

For Jones, the choice between death and life was stark, and where the gospel was concerned, there could be no dissembling:

> There are but two states that men can possibly be in, one saving and the other damning, a state of sin and a state of grace, and all men are included in one or the other. Most men live in a state of wrath and enmity, having their inclinations contrary and averse to God and to ways of holiness, living in obedience to their own corruptions, walking after the flesh … wallowing in sin … minding nothing but to make provision for the flesh to fulfil the lusts thereof. Some few others are in a state of favour and friendship with God, who walk not after the flesh but the spirit, and mind the things of the spirit, who place their desire and delight upon higher and better things, that is, upon things that concern the spiritual life, who endeavour to walk with God in humble obedience to his holy will unto all well pleasing, and would not willingly have so much as an inward motion swerving from God.[149]

The aim of his labours was that the parishioners of Llandeilo Abercywyn and Llanddowror, the many who made their way from afar to listen to him, enthralled by such a lively and uncompromising exposition of gospel truth, would forsake their sinful ways and embrace the good news.

The character of Griffith Jones's piety was not speculative or theoretic but wholly practical, emphasizing conversion, regeneration, union with Christ and holiness of life: 'No abiding comfort can be found', he would insist, 'but by pursuing true godliness as it is in Jesus'.[150] It was essential for all individuals to be born anew. 'Happiness cannot be conveyed to us in any other way', he claimed, 'than by planting in us a like disposition and nature with God, which in scripture is called the new man, new heart, new spirit, new creature, new birth and the divine nature'.[151] This was not our work but the work of the Holy Spirit, active within: 'The Spirit is the author of the new birth, and it is by him that the work of regeneration must be carried on to perfection.'[152] If Christ's righteousness needs to be imputed to us, the Holy Spirit, or Christ within, needs to be imparted to each believing soul: 'It is by means of a spiritual regeneration from the second Adam, our Lord Jesus Christ, and from a spiritual ingrafture by faith in him, that we can produce fruit that is acceptable to him.'[153] This conversion 'is a renewing or remodelling of our inward frame and disposition, changing the bent of our souls from carnal and perishing to spiritual and eternal joys';[154] similarly it is 'the powerful workmanship of the Holy Spirit whereby the soul is deeply impressed with God's image, and the whole man brought to a complete conformity to his holy will'.[155] Such a change would lead to 'a willing, solemn, full and unreserved dedication of ourselves to Jesus Christ and to God through him, with a firm trust for every necessary grace and mercy, and with a resolved adherence to him whatever it may cost'.[156] Being at enmity with the flesh, the process would inevitably be painful though ultimately joyful and comforting:

> His Spirit is at work within them, working in them softness of heart, a mournful sense of their hardness, a spiritual thirst and striving after holiness in heart and in life, enabling them to labour hard to forsake every sin, to obtain and exercise every grace, to practice and perform every duty, to use all means and to delight much in those that affect the spirits and bring them nearest to God, and to bear most willingly every burden of suffering from love and faithfulness to him.[157]

Such were the blessings of spiritual union with Christ in the soul:

> Our union with Christ, from which fountain of all comforts flow our covenant relation to God, forgiveness of sin, justification, everlasting peace, adoption, access before the throne of prayer, and eternal life and everything that pertains to it.[158]

Again and again, Griffith Jones pressed upon his hearers the need for a living faith. Mere morality or formal religiosity were not sufficient:

> The faith which gives us a happy interest in Christ and everything that is his, is not what some through stupid ignorance may imagine it

to be, namely a blind confidence and ungrounded hope of mercy, or a vain trust that all will be well, though they are dead or slothful in their duties and strangers to the power of godliness, and continue to live in conforming to this world and under the power of their own vanity and corruption.[159]

For such a serious-minded cleric, conventional religion was a curse and hypocrisy was all too easy even for many who were assiduous in attending public worship: 'The most regular conversation, the most commendable actions and the best morality, even at its most eminent height of excellency, if they be not produced by this divine bent in the soul, are all vile hypocrisy and false disguise.'[160] 'How few there be', he cried,

> that know what it is to be Christians indeed, which, I am sure, is noth-ing less than to live a life of faith to God and so, upon good grounds, to make, by the grace of faith, a comfortable application of the Son of God to themselves on all occasions.[161]

Nevertheless, despite the challenges of the Christian life, there were those who had applied themselves and experienced the miracle of regen-eration: 'They who embark on a religious course of life, and set out in a channel where tide and contrary winds and force of the stream are all against them, so that they cannot get an inch on without labouring at the oars.'[162] Yet by persevering the blessing had been granted, faith had been kindled in their hearts, and they had experienced the reality of Christ within: 'These breathings of the inward man', he claimed, 'are the soul and life of religion, without which outward religious duties are but vain oblations'.[163] Such exertion is surely worthwhile:

> Is not religion the design and end of our being and the chief intention of all God's mercies to us? Is it not of the greatest importance and necessity and of the greatest weight and consequence? Have we not a God to please, a soul to save, an account to make, a heaven to seek and a hell to flee from?[164]

Far from being an imposition it was privilege and joy. 'It is God and his Christ with the Holy Spirit that is our all in this, the everlasting and ever flowing fountain of bliss', he told Madam Bevan. 'It is from this fund of all-sufficiency that we must be supplied with all we want, all graces and mercy, all peace and pardon, all help and wisdom, all our righteousness, sanctification and redemption.'[165]

The 'holy living' school had no monopoly on strict morality or the call to pursue a bracing ethical code but Reformed theologians also emphasized the need for self-denial and the mortification of the flesh. For them, however, this followed on after justification by faith alone and as a function of the doctrine of sanctification. 'Self-denial and mortification', wrote Jones, 'is nought else but to deny and kill vice and all inclinations that favour or minister strength to our lusts which keep back our love from God.'[166] Obedience remained essential in order to live a life of holiness and faith: 'It is not talking, desiring, praying, repenting nor believing but obeying that God requires.'[167] Although salvation was by grace alone, nevertheless in the gospel scheme, obedience was vital still: 'Our obedience to the law of God is made the *gospel condition* of our interests in the merits of Christ.'[168] As for religious feelings, they were no substitute for an obedient faith: 'A steady bent of our hearts and lives heavenwards is a surer ground of comfort than a rapturous fit of sensible joy.'[169] Yet obedience always led the believer back to the source of all true blessing, namely the Person and Work of Christ:

> It is faith, and faith only, that points out to the sinner a way of escape from his dismal and distracting prospect of eternal wrath and punishment ... It is the infinite mercy of God in the merits of Christ, firmly believed and applied by faith, that is the only remedy which can give light and comfortable hope to the despairing soul.[170]

Only then could religious feelings be relished, 'that inward sense of divine love that we have at times felt in our souls',[171] and the knowledge of the gospel 'digest[ed] upon our minds till we feel its influence inflaming our affections and kindling a burning love in our hearts'.[172]

It is very obvious that Griffith Jones was a Reformed or Puritan theologian and in no way a High Church divine. Nowhere in his correspondence with Madam Bevan does he mention the ceremonial aspect of religion, the importance of liturgy, the feasts of the church year, episcopacy or the function of consecrated buildings. He alludes to baptism only in the context of mortification, 'the baptismal vow of renouncing the flesh and the world as well as the devil',[173] and never equates it with regeneration, while his Eucharistic doctrine is decidedly memorialist or 'low', verging on the Zwinglian (though he does, in fact, mention Christ's active presence in the rite):

> The Lord's Supper was ordained to be a solemn commemoration of our Lord's death and passion, and to keep up a lively and affectionate remembrance of it in our minds until his coming again. It was also to be a solemn renewing of the holy covenant in which Christ, on his part, makes a solemn delivery of himself to us, and with himself peace, pardon, adoption, his spirit of grace and eternal life to every worthy receiver.[174]

In the correspondence as in his ministerial practice, his emphasis is almost exclusively on the preaching of the Word and the discipline of prayer. Neither does he ever mention his sources. According to Henry Phillips, 'Mr Jones made the study of divinity the main point of his pursuit and ... by a close and diligent application became well versed in the writings of the most eminent divines, whether at home or abroad.'[175] That he had mastered the body of Puritan theology there can be no doubt, while his subsequent published expositions of the Prayer Book and Church Catechism are determinedly Reformed in character. It was the remarkable success of the circulating schools, and the insatiable need to provide easily understood reading matter for their pupils, that ensured that the doctrinal predilections of a single Carmarthenshire clergyman would challenge the hegemony of the 'holy living' school and, by the 1750s, renew an older Calvinistic consensus within the Established Church in Wales.

The circulating schools and the theology of *The Welch Piety*

By 1731, when Griffith Jones established his first charity school in Llanddowror, the SPCK's educational policy in Wales had withered almost to nothing.[176] Whereas the society had been willing enough to sponsor religious literature in Welsh, it had perpetuated the Welsh Trust's practice, common in the 1680s, of educating through the medium of English. While that had been acceptable initially, in the market towns at least, it had become clear by the 1720s that this was of only limited use. Welsh was still the only language understood by the bulk of the people while the most pressing need was among the poor. The society had done sterling service since 1714, primarily through the scholarly and practical exertions of Moses Williams, later vicar of Defynnog, in providing thousands of copies of new editions of the Welsh Bible, proving how keen ordinary people were to possess copies of the scriptures in their own tongue.[177] Yet despite owning copies of the Bible and even with regular preaching, the more conscientious among the clergy realized that vital piety had yet to reach the hearts and minds of the majority.

In his initial letter to Sir John Thorold of Lincolnshire, who would become one of the principal benefactors of the circulating school movement, in March 1738, Griffith Jones related how the first school had been established. Realizing the need to inculcate religious knowledge among his people beyond the regular gospel ministry, he had gathered together both the youth and willing adults in the parish on the Saturday before the monthly communion in order to examine them in the catechism 'but also in a system of divinity'.[178] This was done simply and sensitively, especially as there were those who were embarrassed to show their ignorance in the company of their neighbours. Those who did attend were 'discoursed with in an easy, familiar and very serious way about every answer they made, explaining it clearly to their understanding, and strongly applying to their conscience' (p. 1). Soon others, especially the poor, came for instruction, 'and at length would not be content without it' (p. 1). By providing bread bought with money from the Sunday collection, these classes became even more popular, especially among the very needy: 'Being come together, and placed orderly in a row to receive the bread, a few plain and easy questions were asked them, with great tenderness and caution not to puzzle them or give them blush' (p. 2). Many of the attendees learned their catechism rapidly, began memorizing scripture for themselves and were soon advanced 'in all knowledge needful to salvation' (p. 2). Attendance at Sunday services, including the Lord's Supper, rose, but more importantly the level of understanding and spiritual discernment increased as well. Yet it soon dawned on Jones that in order for the catechism to be understood, it was essential that the poor were taught to read: 'In this way … it came to be discovered here how deplorably ignorant the poor people are who cannot read even when constant preaching is not wanting, where catechising is omitted' (p. 2). Consequently catechizing came to be accompanied by a drive towards literacy, and the more the catechumens learned to read, the more effective the evangelistic work became.[179]

Following this initial success at Llanddowror, he expanded the experiment to include neighbouring parishes, 'and divine providence was not wanting to bring in benefactions to support them' (p. 3). News of the achievement spread quickly, indeed

> it pleased God to increase their success and number all along … in so much that this last winter and the present spring the number of these schools has amounted to seven and thirty, and some three masters, who are obliged to keep a methodical list of the names, place of abode, ages, quality, and condition in the world … of all the men, women and children taught in them. (p. 3)

Having now become impossible for Jones to do the teaching himself, he began employing instructors, all on a shoe-string budget, selecting, vetting and training them and sending them to needy parishes to set up school, all the while making sure that he had attained the incumbents' permission. Each school would be held in each place for some eight to ten weeks, between September and May, the least busy time in the agricultural year, and for those who could not attend during the day there would be classes during the evenings. Of the 2,400 pupils that had been taught by 1738 throughout the south Wales counties of Carmarthen, Cardigan, Pembroke and Brecknockshire,

> very few … could say so much as the Lord's Prayer when they first came to school, and many of them could, in six or eight weeks' time, not only read tolerably but repeat by heart all the Church Catechism in their native Welsh language and make pretty good answers to plain and familiar questions concerning all the necessary points of faith and practice in a system of divinity, which the masters are to instruct them in for some hours every day, about the time of morning and evening prayer. (pp. 3–4)

The venture was run strictly on Church of England lines while the SPCK had provided, readily and generously, hundreds of copies of the Bible, the Psalter and the Church Catechism: 'It is visible that a great reformation from immoral heathenism and rude conversation is wrought in them' (p. 4), he claimed, and appreciation by the better part of the clergy had been universal.

His second letter to Thorold, dated 16 August 1739, repeated many of the same sentiments: 'Serious men in the ministry have experiences and complained much of it, that without catechising (which is not very practicable when the people cannot read), preaching is in a manner lost

and thrown away upon them' (p. 16), and once more described the plight
of the people:

> How void of that necessary Christian knowledge the generality of the
> people are in this country … In many parts here … few can say the
> Creed and the Lord's Prayer, and others say them so corruptly as scarce
> to be understood. (pp. 14–15)

Yet the schools were going from strength to strength, extending their
remit beyond south-west Wales to Radnorshire and Montgomeryshire
in mid Wales, Glamorgan and Monmouthshire in the east and even to
Merionethshire in north Wales. What was more, 'these schools never
intrude or force themselves, but are given where desired, and therefore
are generally very welcome and kindly received everywhere' (p. 21). As
well as ensuring that they were provided with an abundance of Bibles
and catechisms, Jones had also begun writing his own textbooks, one
being on the theology and practice of prayer, the other being a simple
primer in doctrine, 'a *Scripture Body of Divinity* in a catechetical method'
(p. 22), which would be published before long. As it would transpire, his
Galwad at Orseddfaingc y Gras ('A Call to the Throne of Grace') (1738) and
Hyfforddwr at Orseddfaingc y Gras ('An Instructor to the Throne of Grace')
(1740) would go into multiple printings to become the most widely used
aids to prayer ever, while his five-volume *Hyfforddiad i Wybodaeth Iachusol*
('An Instruction in Sound Knowledge') (1741–6), being an exposition,
replete with copious scriptural references, of the Creed, the Decalogue,
the Lord's Prayer and the two sacraments as found in the Catechism
in the Book of Common Prayer, would become the most extensively read
Welsh doctrinal compendium to appear thus far.

Jones's concluding letter to Thorold, dated 11 October 1739, includes
his celebrated apologia for teaching the Welsh people 'who neither
are, nor (humanly speaking) can be qualified … to receive necessary
instructions to secure their eternal salvation in any other language than
their own British tongue' (p. 32). As well as emphasizing the practicali-
ties of the situation, 'We cannot help thinking that English sermons to
Welsh congregations are neither less absurd nor more edifying than
Welsh preaching would be in the centre of England or Latin services in
the Church of Rome' (p. 41), he makes an impassioned rationale for the
integrity of Welsh nationhood as part of the biblical economy and divine
plan. Whereas there were those who expected Wales, as a conquered

nation, to be absorbed inexorably into the English state and its language to wither away, that, for Jones, was not going to happen. Like its sister Hebrew, Welsh was part of the divine dispensation: 'She has not lost her charms nor chasteness, remains unalterably the same she was four thousand years ago, still retains the beauties of her youth, grown old in years but not decayed' (p. 51). Moreover, Jones's wholly counter-cultural exegesis of the Tower of Babel story in Genesis 11, where the confusion of tongues is not seen as a judgement but as part of the divine condescension in order to create humility among the nations, would become part of the theological basis for modern Welsh nationalism.[180] Yet for all his warm, and often blunt, patriotism: 'I was born a Welshman, and have not unlearned the simple honesty and unpoliteness of my mother tongue, nor acquired the oiliness of the English language', Jones's overriding concern was for the salvation of his people and their reconciliation with God through Christ.[181] This aim which would only be achieved by the spreading abroad of biblical knowledge:

> It is the Word of truth, contained in the sacred volume, that is the great and appointed instrument to raise the dead in sin unto a life of righteousness, and whereby we come to be born of God, and begot or born again unto a lively hope, and to an inheritance that fadeth not away. (p. 6)

Sir John Thorold (d.1748), the eighth baron of Cranwell, Lincolnshire, was but one of the landed and professional class that Griffith Jones looked to for support. 'For years', wrote Eryn White, 'he wheedled, cajoled and pleaded with the Welsh gentry for money to fund his venture'.[182] In fact, due to the poverty of Wales to say nothing of the apathy of so many in the Welsh landed class, he was forced to go farther abroad and seek backing, via the SPCK network, in England. The aim of his annual report, *The Welch Piety*,[183] a clear echo of *Pietas Hallensis*, August Franke's account of the charity schools established at Halle a generation earlier, was not only to chart the development of the movement but to beg for adequate financial support. For the poor teaching would be gratis, but tutors needed to be employed, salaries (even as modest as £3–£4 per annum) needed to be paid, schoolrooms needed to be rented and books, though heavily subsidized by the SPCK, needed to be purchased. Money was, on the whole, forthcoming, from generous English philanthropists as well as from Sir John Philipps and, following his death, Madam Bevan, but the one category conspicuously absent from the list of supporters were the senior Welsh clergy: 'During his career he saw nine bishops come and go in St David's, not one of whom saw fit to acknowledge, let alone support or praise, his enterprise.'[184] There is, however, ample evidence of ordinary parish clergy, despite their small stipends, contributing according to their means, while collections were often made in the parishes in order to finance the work.

Between 1738 and his death in 1761, nine volumes of the *Welch Piety* were issued biennially, each listing how the schools had fared during the previous two years, and after 1751–2 detailed testimonials from appreciative clergy were included as well. These were invariably fulsome, while the one sour note, namely John Evans's bilious *Some Account of the Welsh Charity-Schools, and the Rise and Progress of Methodism in Wales* (1752), 'a nasty vicious piece of propaganda, a character assassination of Griffith Jones and an attempt to bring the episcopate against the movement', was more than offset by the unvarnished praise of appreciative laymen and grateful parish priests.[185] 'Who is this man Evans, author of this pamphlet?' asked an astounded William Morris to his brother Richard, the London-based Anglesey litterateur: 'His invective is bitter enough; courtesy would be more fitting. There's no doubt that old Griffith Jones, Llanddowror, is doing a huge amount of good and deserves respect and sympathy from all men, however fallible he may be.'[186] By then the schools were becoming as numerous in north Wales, especially in Caernarfonshire and Anglesey, as they were in the south. 'By degrees', recalled the Methodist historian Robert Jones, Rhos-lan, in 1820, 'the charity schools spread to most parts of Wales, and great were the blessings that ensued'.[187] Of the 650 or so clergy in the four Welsh dioceses between 1740 and 1760, it has been estimated that nearly 300 showed their active support for his venture.[188] It was these men, along with the schoolmasters who did so much to ground pupils in the content of Jones's catechetical handbooks, who spearheaded a Reformed renewal in the Welsh Church: 'The Welsh clergy who supported these schools did so with a full understanding of their evangelical nature, and had every wish to further that quiet but authentic revival of spiritual life that was taking place through these schools in their parishes.'[189] By 1761, in all some 3,395 schools had been set up in just under 1,600 different places, having taught 158,237 scholars. This total did not include occasional attenders. 'The most critical of recent estimates', according to Glanmor Williams, 'places the numbers taught to read within twenty-five years at 200,000, at a time when the population of Wales numbered probably between 400,000 and 500,000. This is, by any standards, an immense achievement. Given the difficulties confronting Griffith Jones, it is even more astounding.'[190] 'The business of the Welsh schools', Jones had claimed,

> [is] to teach the serious and sober knowledge of the articles and duties of religion as they are stated in our Bibles, Creeds and Catechisms, urging the necessity of conversion from sin unto God in Jesus Christ, with holiness of heart and life, and practical godliness as the necessary fruit of saving faith.[191]

It seemed as though in Wales, the Reformation ideal of a nation renewed according to the norms of *sola fides*, *sola gratia* and *sola scriptura* was at last being fulfilled.

The 'scripture body of divinity' which was used in the circulating schools was Jones's *Hyfforddiad i Wybodaeth Iachusol* ('An Instruction in Sound Knowledge'), which came out in five parts between 1740 and 1746. Written by 'a Minister of the Church of England', it began by staking out the needs of the day: 'Such is the pity that so many souls are dying, and going under the eternal pains of the second death for want of being instructed.'[192] By explaining the Church catechism this could be prevented. He aimed to help clergy, schoolmasters and heads of households in their task so that 'the power of religion and the spirit of godliness are renewed once more' (p. vii). He challenges both open immorality and a dead or notional faith: 'How, indeed, can your repentance and your faith and your love be true and sincere if bereft of the right fruit and actions and work which are implied in them?' (p. ix). As the opening section of the catechism concerned baptism, its initial questions mentioning the role of godparents standing surety for the child, 'thus I was made in my baptism a member of Christ, a child of God and an inheritor of the kingdom of heaven' (p. 4), that is where Jones begins. Ostensibly, for a Reformed theologian, this wording posed problems. Although he could affirm the role of godparents on the basis of evidence from the early church, he had no truck with the Catholic concept of baptismal regeneration or the idea that grace was operative automatically, *ex opera operato*, which, on the face of it, the catechism implied. He is insistent that the rite itself is empty if, when the candidate came of age, they did not make its reality their own, an act that would be confirmed by the laying on of the bishop's hands. Jones interprets baptism as a covenant rite bound up with the sin of Adam and redemption in Christ:

> After our first parents broke the covenant of works, God revealed to them the covenant of grace, to save man from his sin and wretchedness through Jesus Christ, who was shown to them after their fall by saying that the seed of the woman, namely Christ, would smite the head of the serpent who deceived them, being the devil. (p. 14)
>
>   … The first Adam is our covenant head in the covenant of works in which all his natural offspring went under the judgement of death. But Christ, the second Adam, is our covenant head in the covenant of grace in whom his spiritual children are granted freedom and life. (p. 16)

What baptism does is to promise all who had undergone the rite that through the covenant of grace they, too, would be engrafted into Christ, made children of God and heirs to the kingdom of heaven. But how could an external rite be made a means of accessing spiritual blessings? Because God had ordained its effectiveness through the Holy Spirit:

> The catechism does not teach that baptism itself made me a member of Christ, a child of God and an heir of the kingdom of heaven, but that I was accepted in a visible means to the rights of these privileges, being brought under the oversight of the covenant of grace when I was baptized, through which the children of the covenant were sealed. (p. 20)

'Baptism, like circumcision of old', he claimed, 'is the sign and seal of the covenant which includes justification by faith' (p. 20). There is no concept of *ex opera operato* at work. The 'ordinance' (Jones's word) needs to be used correctly and according to God's will as pointing forward to the reality of personal faith: 'Many seeds lay hidden in the earth for many years before germinating; so too are many of God's promises in his Word before they are fulfilled.' (p. 20)

The church, however, is a mixed multitude of those who are real saints and others whose profession is merely nominal. This is inevitable, and indeed shown clearly in scripture. There is no scriptural warrant for forsaking the visible church though salvation was reserved for those who improved on their baptism and made faith a living reality of their own. This leads to union with Christ which is the basis of all other blessings. Baptism, he claimed, was the sign of spiritual union 'in which our souls are joined with Christ through his Spirit and we partake of the gifts that Christ purchased, just as the members are one with the body' (p. 21). Thereafter the *Instruction* details those blessings and explains their meaning: forgiveness of sins, justification, adoption, receipt of the Spirit, the gift of prayer, protection of the heavenly angels, strength in the face of suffering, fortitude in death and the promise of resurrection. The key to all these is a vital faith: 'Saving faith is the gift of God's grace in the heart through the ministry of the Word which allows us to accept Christ as he gives himself to us' (p. 60). Such faith sanctifies the heart, enlightens the mind, captures the will and renews the affections. What was true of Philipp Spener's *ordo salutis* ('order of salvation') among the continental Pietists was paralleled in Wales by the teaching of the circulating schools: 'Here was the framework of an elaborate theological sequence, and still more, a dynamic view of the Christian life against which it would be the business of the class leaders everywhere to assist the faithful to test their progress.'[193] Such was the system popularized in the schools and affirmed by their teachers and many of the clergy, with baptism as the outward sign of Christian initiation:

> I believe that the oversight of the ordinances of the covenant and the ministry of the gospel in the visible church into which I am accepted in baptism, is what is meant by a state of salvation, through which salvation is to be had in everything to which the faith appertains, though many reject it and are lost. (p. 86)

The emphasis throughout the treatise, however, is not on eternal damnation but on the positive blessings of true faith.

The topic covered in Part Two is the Creed, 'I believe in God the Father Almighty', and like all orthodox theologians, Jones sets out to explain God's trinitarian reality and its significance. He begins by listing the divine attributes and God's work as Creator, not only of the world but of the angels and of humankind. Having been created by God Adam fell, which allows the author scope to explore once again the covenantal link between Adam, his descendants and the promise of Christ. In the context of the second article, 'and in Jesus Christ, his only Son, our Lord', he treats the offices of Christ as prophet, priest and king, the nature of faith, the substantive relation between the Father and the Son, his conception through the Holy Spirit, and his lordship. This, in turn, leads to Christ's humanity and passion: 'As Christ suffered to the utter-most, the powers of darkness were allowed to assail him to the fullest degree and God himself hid his face, leaving him devoid of all comfort, when our punishment was laid upon him.'[194] The atoning sacrifice is sufficient for all, though there is no mention, either here or anywhere else in Jones's corpus of work, of specific election. Predestination is presupposed rather than explained and never becomes a matter for speculation. 'As Christ's suffering was a sufficient propitiation for all, do all people, through Christ, share in God's mercy and salvation?' (p. 68), he asks. The answer is 'No'. Faith must be applied and the general gospel call must be heeded. This vocation precedes regeneration, forgiveness of sins, justification, the gift of faith, sanctification and adoption. Then comes the article on the resurrection, ascension and heavenly session: 'His sitting at the right hand of the Father, signifies his ascension, clothed in our humanity, to the highest place of honour' (p. 88), which in turn advances to the judgement of all mankind in righteousness and the doctrine of the Second Coming. In the concluding articles on the Holy Spirit and the Holy Catholic Church, Jones finds himself defending the Anglican position against the sects:

> Q: Are all who are within the church holy people?
> A: No they are not; there are many sinful and hypocritical people as well as saints in the visible church in this world, who will go to destruction in the Last Day. (p. 126)

The church's holiness is rooted in the preaching of the Word rather than the personal holiness of its individual members, the Holy Spirit through the Word pledging Christ's presence among his people despite unbelief and sin, while its catholic nature guarantees that there is a place within its fellowship for all. The 'notes' of the church are its ministry, understood not in prelatical terms but as the ministry of the Word; its ordinances including preaching, the sacraments and prayer; sound doctrine; and evangelical discipline. Despite the inevitable presence of nominal professors within such a mixed community, 'everyone who wishes to be a real member should strive to be truly converted' (p. 137). The 'communion of saints' mentioned next points to one of Griffith Jones's most treasured doctrines, union with Christ: 'The saints' union with Christ is the most essential subject for the true Christian's comfort and salvation, as our eternal life depends upon it' (p. 144), which leads

finally to the Creed's statement on 'the forgiveness of sins, the resurrection of the body and the life everlasting'.

The next section of the Catechism included the Ten Commandments
which Jones proceeded to expound in Part Three. As justification was by
faith alone, the Decalogue functioned as a means whereby sinners were
convicted of their sins, led to Christ being the only one who had ever
lived his life in full obedience to its stipulations, and as a rule of obedience
for those who had come to believe: 'I should consider that it is through
faith and not the works of the law through which I am justified before
God, and that it is impossible for my obedience to be perfect or sinless in
this present world.'[195] Whereas the ceremonial law of the Old Testament
had been abrogated, the moral law remained in force. The first table of
the law, or the first to the fourth commandments, taught our responsibilities to God, and the second table, commandments five to ten, conveyed
our responsibility to our neighbours. The fifth commandment, 'honour
thy father and mother', is applied not only to our natural parents, but to
all in authority: 'We should honour all according to their calling, especially those who are placed above us who are accounted in the scriptures
as our parents' (p. 66). Although as an Anglican clergyman the rector of
Llanddowror was establishment-minded, he always had an acute sense
of social justice and a sincere sympathy for the poor and oppressed.[196]
Those in authority were charged with governing fairly and justly and
with protecting the poor and dispossessed, and if servants were to obey
their masters, rulers were answerable to God for those in their employ.

Jones is most vigorous, however, on the role of the ministry:

> The work and the calling of ministers is the most onerous work in the
> world as it is given to them to serve between God and men in the matter
> of their salvation, and as such the scriptures express our duties towards
> them very clearly and weightily. (p. 73)

Just as the minister was commanded to live a blameless life and be an
example to the flock, those under his care were to respect him and
obey his precepts. Sensitive to the challenge of the Dissenting sects, he
exhorts the faithful not to forsake 'the godly ministers' of the Established
Church, 'and so sadden and dishearten them by gadding after other
teachers which is a sure sign of a fickle, unstable spirit' (p. 86). Not all
ministers, alas, were godly. Jones had an exalted ideal of the ordained
ministry and dreaded the idea of anyone entering it unworthily:

> Every minister is decreed with not rushing forth into the service of
> God's church until he has first made sure that he is a true Christian. Just
> as no-one could become a priest under the law if he were not a member
> of the tribe of Levi, no-one should become a minister of the gospel if he
> is not yet of the family of faith. (p. 73)

The rest of the exposition is taken up with the commandments concerning murder; adultery, in which he expatiates, though not in a prurient
fashion, on the evils of prostitution, incest, bigamy, homosexual acts,
rape and bestiality, and emphasizes the mutual obligations between
husbands and wives; theft; bearing false witness and coveting others'
property.

Part Four, published concurrently with the above, expounded the
next section in the catechism, namely the Lord's Prayer.[197] This allowed
Jones to present a precis of the teaching contained in his immensely
popular treatises *Galwad at Orseddfaingc y Gras* ('A Call to the Throne
of Grace') and *Hyfforddwr at Orseddfaingc y Gras* ('An Instructor to the
Throne of Grace') published a few years earlier, both of which were
practical introductions to personal, family and public prayer. The treatise begins with instructions as to how to pray, it notes the difficulties
encountered in prayer, it lists scriptural examples of prayers of praise,
confession and supplication, and shows the ways in which God responds
to them all. Beginning with the first petition he explicates the doctrine
of God's fatherhood, leading to the petitions concerning the divine name;
the coming kingdom; the doing of God's will on earth as in heaven; the
benefits of providence in the gift of daily bread; the forgiveness of trespasses; temptation and the forsaking of evil leading to the doxology. In
all this is a more succinct discourse than its predecessors which presents
a clear, practical, no-nonsense and useful teaching on the discipline of
prayer.

Part Five, the final instalment of Jones's *Instruction* which also
appeared in 1746, deals with the conclusion of the catechism's teaching,
namely the sacraments of baptism (which Jones deals with once more)
and the Lord's Supper. As in Part One, he contextualizes the sacraments
by placing them firmly within the covenant of grace and the first twenty
pages are taken up with a detailed elaboration of covenantal or the so-
called 'federal' theology.[198] As for the question, 'Who, in truth, is within
the covenant of grace?', the answer is: 'We have not been given to know
who they are by name, those names being written in the Book of Life;

such mysteries belong to God alone.'[199] Grace presupposes election and the sovereign will of God. The gospel call, however, is restricted to no one. All of those within the visible and professing church are called to believe. By embracing Christ in faith, a new law is implanted in their hearts and they are born again. The two sacraments of baptism and the Lord's Supper testify to this faith: 'Through the sacraments appointed by Christ, the covenant is sealed' (p. 23). To the extent that grace is essential for salvation, the seals of grace, namely the sacraments, are essential as well: 'They are essential in a general, not an indispensable way', he says. 'The penitent thief on the cross went to paradise without partaking of the sacraments as it was not feasible for him to do so. It is through neglect of the sacraments, not deprivation, that we will be damned' (p. 24).

According to the classic definition, the sacraments are 'outward and visible signs of an inward and spiritual grace, ordained by Christ himself, pledging that we shall receive that grace' (p. 25). He is careful not to lock grace within a physical rite as God alone is sovereign and grace is a spiritual, not a material reality. Baptism is linked in scripture with regeneration, but can never be manipulated by the human will. Sacramental grace is never independent of the gift of faith. Like circumcision in the Old Testament, baptism is a covenantal rite for those within the church and their children, administered by immersion but more often the sprinkling of water. Although infants cannot yet exercise faith, they are baptized within the church community as a pledge and promise of their exercising saving faith on coming of age. As for the role of godparents, the use of ceremony and the like, these are the *adiaphora* or non-essentials of faith and should never cause undue contention among Christians: 'Many minor circumstances in the ordinances of religion have not been laid down with certainty in scripture, but it has been left to the wisdom of the churches to arrange as is constructive and suitable' (p. 40). What is not in contention is that only ministers, set aside for the purpose, are allowed to serve at either the table or the font: 'No-one is to administer the sacraments ordained by God within his church but those who have been called validly and legitimately to the ministerial office' (p. 2).

Turning to the Lord's Supper, Jones emphasizes once more that a physical rite, though ordained by Christ and connected firmly with the reception of the Holy Spirit, cannot be effective of itself without the active faith of the recipient: 'It is not because they possess a natural virtue that they do us good, but through the blessing of Christ alone the sacraments become profitable' (p. 58). Scripture, however, along with the Book of Common Prayer and the Church catechism, uses concrete and realistic language to describe the sacraments, and that language has meaning:

> The faithful receive the body and blood of Christ truly and surely, though in a sacramental way, that is that they receive the visible signs for the correct and effective use, and they do this truly and surely, signifying and sealing for them invisible blessings. These signs signify nothing nor do the seals seal anything for those who have no faith. (p. 62)

Along with the doctrinal teaching, Jones is keen to emphasize the need for the faithful to partake of the sacrament regularly, humbly and, following due preparation, confidently as well. As with the adherents of the 'holy living' school, he treats the problem of worthy reception.

> Q: After you have considered these things and examined yourself, can you be confident that you are fit to come to the Lord's Supper?
> A: If by examining myself I find that the beginnings of these graces within, even if they are as yet feeble, frail and weak, I am allowed to hope sincerely that I am not wholly unfitted to approach the Lord's Table. (p. 86)

Even the weakest faith, if directed to its true object, namely Christ dying for one's sins, is sufficient to save a penitent's soul.

> The sum of the worthiness and merit that the gospel asks in those who come to the Lord's Supper is that they approach this ordinance mindfully, respectfully and with true humility through faith in Christ. (p. 86)
> … It is those who are rash and presumptuous that are unfit for the Lord's Supper, but the weak and fearful Christian who still has an anguished journey ahead, is most fitted to be strengthened and comforted by the spiritual meal that has been prepared for him. (p. 87)

Following the publication of the final part of the *Instruction*, in 1748 a composite volume entitled *Drych Difinyddiaeth, neu Hyfforddiad i Wybodaeth Iachusol* ('A Mirror of Divinity, or an Instruction in Sound Knowledge') was issued comprising the five parts of the *Instruction* within a single set of covers which would become the staple text for use in the circulating schools for the next two decades.[200] Along with these, a shorter version, *Esboniad Byr ar Gatechism yr Eglwys* ('A Short Exposition of the Church Catechism') was issued in 1752 and again in 1762, 1767 and 1778, with a bilingual catechism entitled *Instructions for the Young Christian, or Addysg i'r Cristion Ieuaingc*, aimed at those schools in the anglicized or border districts, having appeared in 1750. No other single Welsh author had ever produced such a quantity of published work which, due to the rapidly expanding popularity of the circulating schools and, since 1735, the progress of the Evangelical Revival, ensured that Jones's interpretation of Church doctrine was gaining a hearing throughout the land.

Although it was incontrovertibly Anglican and true to the 39 Articles and the Book of Common Prayer, nevertheless Jones's interpretation was selective at best. As has been noted, he had virtually nothing to say on such matters as episcopacy, church government, consecrated buildings, ceremony, vestments or the feasts and festivals of the church year. He barely mentions the rite of confirmation and nowhere does he explain its significance. Although his handbooks on prayer contain detailed instruction on how to pray replete with innumerable scriptural references, he never expounds such aspects of Cranmer's Prayer Book as the litany, the *Gloria*, the *Te Deum*, the collects, the General Confession or the General Thanksgiving. High Church theology was not expunged due to Griffith Jones's exertions, nor did the 'holy living' school cease to exist. Howell Harris and his fellow parishioners in Talgarth had been steeped in High Church teaching, this being the accepted emphasis among many pious and conscientious clergy including Pryce Davies, his vicar. It is no coincidence that the revivalist's conviction and conversion between Easter Sunday and Whitsun 1735 revolved around the whole reality of worthy reception of the Lord's Supper, while his first attempts at exhorting sprung from his reading, in the presence of eager listeners, of that 'holy living' classic *The Whole Duty of Man*.[201] Some 'holy living' literature continued to appear, though by the 1740s the former flood had been reduced to a trickle,[202] while the triple phenomena of the Revival, the rise of Methodism and the circulating schools, would cause High Church theology to be eclipsed by evangelical Calvinism of a vibrant kind.

The last twenty years of Griffith Jones's life coincided with the first phase of the Evangelical Revival in Wales. Although its leaders revered the older man, a strained and fractious relationship would prevail between them which will be assessed in the final chapter. As for Jones, despite the jealousy of John Evans and the lamentable aloofness of the bishops, he had consolidated his reputation as a venerated Christian leader. If formerly the object of disdain: 'I have lived long enough', he had written in 1736, 'to know that in almost all, if not every congregation, I have more judges and censors than honest hearers', two decades later his contribution had come to be lauded virtually by all.[203] Indeed, '[n]o churchman in eighteenth century Wales was as highly regarded, even loved, as Griffith Jones'.[204] Following his wife's death in 1755, he was taken in by Madam Bevan, and notwithstanding the mounting peevishness of old age – even as a younger man 'he could be opinionated, self-willed, domineering and filled with his own importance'[205] – he spent his declining years at her Laugharne home and under her care.

Those who had come under his direct influence idolized him still. Henry Phillips would never forget the 'unassuming solemnity and seriousness in his face ... the fire and zeal, chastened with modesty kindled in his eyes', that he had witnessed in the pulpit at Llanddowror in the late 1730s, when 'his hearers could feel their blood thrill within them'.[206] In a report published in the *Glasgow Weekly History* describing the religious situation in Wales in 1742, the Dissenting minister Edmund Jones, Pontypool, had written: 'Among the clergy is the famous Griffith Jones, one of the most excellent preachers in Great Britain for piety, good sense, diligence, moderation, zeal, a mighty utterance, the like whereof I never heard.'[207] Three years later as a lad of fifteen, John Thomas, who would later become a Congregational minister in Radnorshire, walked the thirty-five miles from his home in order to meet his hero and hear him preach: 'His manner of speech and his appearance won my heart as though I had seen an angel of God.'[208] Peter Williams, a contemporary of Howell Harris and Daniel Rowland and a fellow leader among the Welsh Methodists, had been taken to Llanddowror as a child where his pious mother had wanted him to hear the famous rector preach.[209] Mary Francis, wife of the hymnist William Williams Pantycelyn had been converted under Jones's ministry and had left home to live in Llanddowror in order to benefit from his ministry. According to the recollection of Thomas Charles, he 'remained her prime counsellor in all things relating to salvation'.[210] Charles himself, the second generation Methodist father 'of Bala', a native of Llanfihangel Abercywyn, the parish adjoining Jones's Llandeilo Abercywyn, had received his first spiritual impressions during the 1770s under the tutelage of a local layman Rhys Hugh who had been converted under Griffith Jones's ministry a generation earlier.[211] In all the influence of Griffith Jones would persist.

His principal legacy, however, was among those tens of thousands of ordinary people many of whom may have never heard of him at all. It has been said that '[f]or the first time in the history of Wales, large numbers of farmers, craftsmen, and labourers, together with their sons and daughters, were given the opportunity to learn to read'. In fact Griffith Jones's scheme, for which he expended enormous sacrifice, energy and ingenuity for some thirty years, 'helped to create a literate peasantry'.[212] It was this literate peasantry, animated by the spirit of revival, which would transform the history of the nation and contribute to the paradox noted by W. R. Ward: 'A sustained campaign to assimilate Wales to the English language, culture and religious establishment generated by way of reaction a religious revival which ended by being Welsh, evangelical and dissenting.'[213] It is to Dissent and the Evangelical Revival that we finally turn.

Notes

[1]   Philip Jenkins, 'The Anglican Church and the Unity of Britain: the Welsh Experience, 1560–1714', in Steven G. Ellis and Sarah Barber (eds), *Conquest and Union: Fashioning a British State, 1485–1725* (London: Longman, 1995), pp. 115–38; Jenkins refers to 'the High Church triumph, 1690–1714', pp. 136–7.

[2]   See Roger Thomas, 'Comprehension and Indulgence', in Geoffrey F. Nuttall and Owen Chadwick (eds), *From Uniformity to Unity, 1662–1962* (London: SPCK, 1962), pp. 189–254; John Spurr, *The Restoration Church of England, 1646–89* (New Haven: Yale University Press, 1991), pp. 376–9.

[3]   Peter D. G. Thomas, 'Jacobitism in Wales', *WHR*, 1 (1960), 279–300.

[4]   Craig D. Wood, 'The Welsh response to the Glorious Revolution', *JWRH*, 1 (1989), 21–39.

[5]   See Chapter Three, pp. 209–11.

[6]   See Chapter Three, p. 192; he would later become bishop of Lichfield and Coventry and then bishop of Worcester.

[7]   E. Gordon Rupp, *Religion in England, 1688–1791* (Oxford: Clarendon Press, 1986), pp. 5–28.

[8]   Their names are listed by Thomas Richards, *Piwritaniaeth a Pholitics, 1689–1719* (Wrecsam: Hughes a'i Fab, 1927), pp. 17–22.

[9]   This was true of the Church of England as a whole; the reasons are delineated in William Gibson, *The Church of England, 1688–1832: Unity and Accord* (London: Routledge, 2001), pp. 28–69.

10 This was Morris's translation of John Rawlet's *Christian Monitor*, see Chapter Three, pp. 178–80.

11 For Sherlock (1639–1707), see *ODNB*.

12 *Ymadroddion Bucheddol ynghylch Marwolaeth, o Waith Dr Sherlock a gyfieithiwyd yn Gymraeg gan Thomas Williams MA* (Rhydychen: Thomas Jones, 1691), Sig. A1v; for Williams, see *DWB*.

13 *Ymadroddion Bucheddol ynghylch Marwolaeth*, p. 36.

14 [William Howell], *Y Llyfr Gweddi Gyffredin, y Cydymmaith Goreu yn y Tŷ a'r Stafell*, trans. by 'E.E.' (Rhydychen: L. Litchfield, 1693), Sig. A1v; for Howell (1656–1714), see *ODNB*.

15 [Howell], *Y Llyfr Gweddi Gyffredin*.

16 [Howell], *Y Llyfr Gweddi Gyffredin*, Sig. A6v.

17 Spurr, *The Restoration Church of England, 1646–89*, pp. 112–13.

18 Paul Avis, *Anglicanism and the Christian Church* (Edinburgh: T & T Clark, 1989), pp. 171–2.

19 William Beverids [*sic*], *Pregeth ynghylch Godidawgrwydd a Defnyddiaeth Llyfr y Gweddïau Cyffredin* (Llundain: J.R., 1693), p. 26; hereafter page numbers are in the text.

20 John Spurr, 'The Church, the societies and the moral revolution of 1688', in John Walsh, Colin Haydon and Stephen Taylor (eds), *The Church of England c.1689–c.1833* (Cambridge: Cambridge University Press, 1993), pp. 127–43 (138).

21 Chapter Three, pp. 195–9.

22 [Edward Synge], *Attebion i'r Holl Wag Escusion a wnae llawer o bobl yn erbyn dyfod i dderbyn y Cymmun Bendigedig … a gyfieithiwyd i'r Gymraeg gan Michael Jones* (n.p.: Thomas Jones, 1698), pp. 8–9; for Synge (1659–1741), see *ODNB*.

23 [Synge], *Attebion i'r Holl Wag Escusion a wnae llawer o bobl yn erbyn dyfod i dderbyn y Cymmun Bendigedig*, p. 29.

24 [Synge], *Attebion i'r Holl Wag Escusion a wnae llawer o bobl yn erbyn dyfod i dderbyn y Cymmun Bendigedig*, p. 5.

25 For John Morgan (1662–1701), see *DWB* and J. T. Jones, 'John Morgan, Ficer Aberconwy', *Y Llenor*, 17 (1938), 16–30; for John Williams (1633–1709), see *ODNB*.

26 *Eglurhad Byrr ar Gatechism yr Eglwys … o waith y Gwir barchedig Dad yn Nuw, John Williams, Escob Caer-gai, wedi ei gyfiethio gan John Morgan, ficer Aberconwy* (Llundain: Matthew Wooton, 1699), p. 11.

27 *Eglurhad Byrr ar Gatechism yr Eglwys*, p. 68.

28 *Eglurhad Byrr ar Gatechism yr Eglwys*, p. 72.

29 [William Assheton], *Duwiolder ar Ddydd yr Arglwydd, wedi ei gyfieithu er mwyn Cymru gan Offeiriad o Eglwys Loegr* (Amwythig: Thomas Jones, 1700), p. 2; for Assheton (1642–1711), see *ODNB*.

30 [Assheton], *Duwiolder ar Ddydd yr Arglwydd, wedi ei gyfieithu er mwyn Cymru gan Offeiriad o Eglwys Loegr*, p. 14.

31 [Assheton], *Duwiolder ar Ddydd yr Arglwydd, wedi ei gyfieithu er mwyn Cymru gan Offeiriad o Eglwys Loegr*, pp. 27–8.

32 Theophilus Dorrington, *Arweiniwr Cartrefol i'r Iawn a'r Buddiol Dderbyniad o Swpper yr Arglwydd ... a gyfieithiwyd i'r Gymraeg gan Ddafydd Maurice DD* (Llundain: B. Aylmer, 1700), p. 23; for Dorrington (1654–1715), rector of Wittersham in Kent, see *ODNB*; Maurice's *Cynffwrdd i'r Gwan Gristion, neu'r Gorsen Ysig, mewn pregeth* (Rhydychen: Y Theatr, 1700), was treated in Chapter Three, pp. 177–8.

33 [John Tillotson], *Annogaeth i gymmuno yn fynych yn y Sacrament Sanctaidd o Swpper yr Arglwydd ... a gyfieithiwyd i'r Gymraeg gan G[eorge] L[ewis]* (Llundain: n.p., 1704), p. 8; for Lewis, see *DWB*.

34 [Tillotson], *Annogaeth i gymmuno yn fynych yn y Sacrament Sanctaidd o Swpper yr Arglwydd*, p. 12.

35 [Tillotson], *Annogaeth i gymmuno yn fynych yn y Sacrament Sanctaidd o Swpper yr Arglwydd*, p. 16.

36 [Tillotson], *Annogaeth i gymmuno yn fynych yn y Sacrament Sanctaidd o Swpper yr Arglwydd*, pp. 19–20.

37 See H. Trevor Hughes, *The Piety of Jeremy Taylor* (London: Macmillan, 1960); H. B. Porter, *Jeremy Taylor Liturgist* (London: SPCK, 1979); Henry R. McAdoo, *Jeremy Taylor, Anglican Theologian* (Armagh: Historical Society of the Church in Ireland, 1997).

38 Ellis Wynne, *Rheol Buchedd Sanctaidd, yn dangos y Moddion a'r Arfeu i ynnill pob Gras ... ynghyd â Gweddïau, gan Jeremy Taylor DD* (1701) (Caerdydd: Gwasg Prifysgol Cymru, 1928), Sig. A4v; hereafter page numbers are in the text.

39 Nehemiah Curnock (ed.), *The Journal of John Wesley*, vol. 1 (New York: Eaton and Mains, 1909), p. 42, quoted in Horton Davies, *Worship and Theology in England, Vol. 1: From Cranmer to Baxter and Fox, 1534–1690* (Grand Rapids: Eerdmans, 1996), pp. 110.

40 For the detail of Taylor's doctrinal scheme, see Henry R. McAdoo, *The Eucharistic Theology of Jeremy Taylor Today* (Norwich: Canterbury Press, 1988).

41 For Wynne's literary contribution, see Gwyn Thomas, *Y Bardd Cwsg a'i Gefndir* (Caerdydd: Gwasg Prifysgol Cymru, 1972); idem, *Ellis Wynne*, Writers of Wales (Cardiff: University of Wales Press, 1984) and *ODNB*.

42 Among other publications in this vein were *Blaenor i Ghristion* (Llundain: Matthew Wooton, 1701), John Williams, curate of Llanfrothen's translation of Thomas Tenison's *A Christian Guide*, a succinct commentary on the Apostle's Creed along with prayers for private devotion; for Tenison (1636–1715), see *ODNB*; *Cymorth i'r Cristion a Chyfarwyddid i'r Gŵr Ieuangc* (Mwythyg: Thomas Jones, 1704), an anonymous translation of William Burkitt's *A Poor Man's Help and Young Man's Guide*; for Burkitt (1650–1703), vicar of Dedham, Essex, see *ODNB*; and *Hynodeb Eglwysydd Cywir* (Llundain: J. Dowling, 1712), William Rowlands's translation of the anonymous *The Character of a True Churchman*.

43 Mary Clement (ed.), *Correspondence and Minutes of the SPCK relating to Wales, 1699–1740* (Cardiff: University of Wales Press, 1952), p. 9.

44   Clement (ed.), *Correspondence and Minutes of the SPCK relating to Wales*, p. 10.

45   Mary Clement, *The SPCK and Wales, 1699–1740* (London: SPCK, 1954), pp. xv–xvi.

46   See Walter T. Morgan, 'Yr Eglwys Sefydledig yng Nghymru, 1700–35', in Gomer M. Roberts (ed.), *Hanes Methodistiaeth Galfinaidd Cymru*, vol. 1, *Y Deffroad Mawr* (Caernarfon: Llyfrfa'r Methodistiaid Calfinaidd, 1973), pp. 43–80 (68–72 esp.); Geraint H. Jenkins, *Literature, Religion and Society in Wales, 1660–1730* (Cardiff: University of Wales Press, 1978), pp. 5–6.

47   Rupp, *Religion in England, 1688–1791*, p. 289.

48   Jenkins, *Literature, Religion and Society*, p. 22; see also his wider assessment of the 'Preaching of the Word' among Welsh Anglicans, pp. 1–24.

49   Jenkins, *Literature, Religion and Society*, p. 43.

50   Clement, *The SPCK and Wales, 1699–1740*, pp. 48–73.

51   D. W. R. Balman, *The Moral Revolution of 1688* (New Haven: Yale University Press, 1957), *passim*; Spurr, 'The Church, the societies and the moral revolution of 1688', pp. 127–8.

52   Thomas Richards, *A History of the Puritan Movement in Wales, 1639–53* (London: National Eisteddfod Association, 1920), p. 93.

53   W. R. Ward, 'Evangelical awakenings in the North American world', in S. J. Brown and T. Ticketts (eds), *The Cambridge History of Christianity: Enlightenment, Reawakening and Revolution, 1660–1815* (Cambridge: Cambridge University Press, 2006), pp. 329–47 (329).

54   See Carter Lindberg (ed.), *The Pietist Theologians: An Introduction to Theology in the Seventeenth and Eighteenth Centuries* (Oxford: Blackwell, 2005), pp. 1–20.

55   Clement (ed.), *Correspondence and Minutes of the SPCK relating to Wales*, p. 205.

56   For Jones (1650–1727), see *DWB*.

57   Evans (?1651–1724), bishop of Bangor and thereafter of Meath in Ireland, is listed in *ODNB* and *DWB*; also E. D. Evans, 'John Evans, bishop of Bangor, 1702–16', *THSC*, N.S. 7 (2000), 44–65.

58   For Thomas (c.1660–1722), see Clement (ed.), *Correspondence and Minutes of the SPCK relating to Wales*, p. 8, n. 33.

59   Mary Clement, 'Pennod newydd o hanes Eglwys Loegr ym Morgannwg gyda chyfeiriad neilltuol at James Harris, Llantrisant (1663–1728)', *Seren Gomer*, N.S. 37 (1945), 35–8, 65–8, 77–85.

60   Spurr, *The Restoration Church of England, 1646–89*, p. 78.

61   Spurr, *The Restoration Church of England, 1646–89*, p. 78.

62   Rupp, *Religion in England, 1688–1791*, pp. 290–5.

63   'A General Plan of the Constitution of a Protestant Congregation or Society for Propagation of Christian Knowledge', quoted in Clement, *The SPCK and Wales, 1699–1740*, p. xii.

64   H. P. Thompson, *Thomas Bray* (London: SPCK, 1954), pp. 1–2, also *ODNB*.

65   Craig Rose, 'The origins and ideals of the SPCK, 1699–1716', in Walsh, Haydon and Taylor (eds), *The Church of England c.1689–c.1833*, pp. 172–90.

66   Chapter Three, pp. 221–2.

67 See Gareth Elwyn Jones and Gordon W. Roderick, *A History of Education in Wales* (Cardiff: University of Wales Press, 2003), pp. 25–37.

68 All statistics have been gleaned from the appendices to Clement, *The SPCK and Wales, 1699–1740*.

69 'Account of the Charity Schools' (1704) from NLW Boderwyd MS 15, quoted in Clement, pp. 8–9.

70 Clement, *The SPCK and Wales, 1699–1740*, p. 13.

71 Rose, 'The origins and ideals of the SPCK, 1699–1716', pp. 179–80.

72 Clement (ed.), *Correspondence and Minutes of the SPCK relating to Wales*, p. 9.

73 Listed in Clement, *The SPCK and Wales, 1699–1740*, pp. 162–4.

74 Clement (ed.), *Correspondence and Minutes of the SPCK relating to Wales*, p. 232.

75 William Beveridge, *Eglurhaad [sic] o Gatecism yr Eglwys ... wedi ei gyfieithu* [gan Thomas Williams] (Llundain: Edmund Powell, 1708).

76 William Assheton, *Annogaeth ferr i'r Cymmun Sanctaidd*, trans. Thomas Williams (Llundain: Edmund Powell, 1710).

77 Lewis Bayly, *Yr Ymarfer o Dduwioldeb ... a gyfieithiwyd yn Gymraeg o waith Row[land] Vaughan* (Mwythig: Thomas Jones, 1709).

78 *Holl Dd[y]ledswydd Dyn ...a gyfieithiwyd yn Gymraeg gan Jo. Langford ... yr ail argraffiad* (Llundain: Edmund Powell, 1711); a new translation by Edward Samuel would be issued in 1718.

79 *Llyfr y Resolusion ... Cyfieithiwyd o'r Saesneg i'r Gymraeg gan Dr John Davies o Fallwyd* (Mwythig: Thomas Jones, 1711).

80 Clement, *The SPCK and Wales, 1699–1740*, p. 36.

81 See Mary Clement, 'John Vaughan (1663–1722), Cwrt Derllys, a'i waith', *THSC* (1942), 73–107 and *DWB*.

82 [Robert Nelson], *Ymarferol-waith yn egluro natur Conffirmasiwn ... a gyfieithiwyd i'r Gymraeg gan Foses Williams* (Llundain: n.p., 1711); at the time Williams (1685–1742: see *DWB, ODNB*) was curate in Chiddingstone in Kent.

83 [Ellis Wynne], *Catechism yr Eglwys, wedi ei egluro ... a gasglwyd gan John Lewis .... O'r pummed argraphiad* (Mwythig: John Rogers, 1713); for Lewis (1675–1747), see *ODNB*.

84 [Robert Nelson], *Cydymaith i Ddyddiau Gwyliau ac Ymprydiau Eglwys Loegr ... a gyfieithiwyd yn Gymraeg gan Thomas Williams* (Llundain: W. Bowyer, 1712); Nelson (1656–1715), philanthropist, lay-theologian and biographer of George Bull, bishop of St David's, is listed in *ODNB*.

85 [Samuel Williams], *Amser a Diwedd Amser, yn Ddau Draethawd* (Llundain: Ebenezer Tracey, 1707), p. 211; for Williams (*c.*1660–*c.*1722), see *DWB*.

86 Hugo Grotius, *Gwirionedd y Grefydd Gristnogol ... a Gyfieithiwyd gan Edward Samuel* (Mwythig: John Rhydderch, 1716), Sig. A3; Samuel is listed in both *DWB* and *ODNB*.

87 Grotius, *Gwirionedd y Grefydd Gristnogol*.

88 For Wynne (1665–1743), a native of Flintshire, former Regius Professor of divinity at Oxford and principal of Jesus College, see *ODNB* and William Gibson, '"A Welsh Bishop for a Welsh See": John Wynne of St Asaph, 1714–27', *JWEH*, 1 (1984), 28–43.

89 Quoted in Edward Carpenter, *Thomas Sherlock 1678–1761: Bishop of Bangor, Salisbury and London* (London: SPCK, 1936), p. 128.

90 C. E. Doble (ed.), *Remarks and Collections of Thomas Hearne*, vol. 9 (Oxford: Clarendon Press, 1909), pp. 283–4.

91 The careers of most of the above are listed in *ODNB*.

92 See B. M. Lodwick, '"Poor Llandaff" during the episcopate of John Tyler, 1706–24', *Morgannwg*, 49 (2005), 34–61; Tyler's dates were ?1640–1724.

93 D. R. Thomas, *A History of the Diocese of St Asaph*, 2 vols (London: James Parker, 1874), pp. 132–3; for Fleetwood (1656–1723), see *ODNB*.

94 For Ottley (1655–1723), see *ODNB* and William Gibson, '"The most glorious enterprises have been acheiv'd": the Restoration Diocese of St David's', in William Gibson and John Morgan-Guy (eds), *Religion and Society in the Diocese of St David's, 1485–2011* (Aldershot: Ashgate, 2015), pp. 92–128.

95 Smalbroke (1672–1749) is listed in *ODNB*; cf. Gibson, '"The most glorious enterprises have been acheiv'd": the Restoration Diocese of St David's', pp. 106–9.

96 For an excellent assessment, see Eryn M. White, '"A Poor, Benighted Church"? Church and Society in mid-eighteenth century Wales', in R. R. Davies and Geraint H. Jenkins (eds), *From Medieval to Modern Wales: Historical Essays in Honour of K. O. Morgan and R. A. Griffiths* (Cardiff: University of Wales Press, 2004), pp. 123–41; for a more indulgent view, see William Jacob, 'Episcopal administration', 'The Welsh clergy', 'The state of the parishes', in Glanmor Williams, William Jacob, Nigel Yates and Frances Knight, *The Welsh Church from Reformation to Disestablishment, 1603–1920* (Cardiff: University of Wales Press, 2007), pp. 82–164.

97 NLW Ottley Papers 100; transcribed in *TCAS*, 24 (1933), 82–9; hereafter page numbers are in the text.

98 For Dalton (1677–1724), see Mary Clement, 'Teulu'r Daltoniaid, Pembre, Sir Gaerfyrddin', *CCH*, 29 (1944), 1–12.

99 Erasmus Saunders, *A View of the State of Religion in the Diocese of St David's* (1721) (Cardiff: University of Wales Press, 1949), pp. 3, 11; hereafter page numbers are in the text. For Saunders, see *ODNB*, *DWB*.

100 White, '"A Poor, Benighted Church"? Church and Society in mid-eighteenth century Wales', p. 123.

101 William Vickers, *Cymdymmaith i'r Allor, yn dangos anian ac angenrheidrwydd ymbaratoad sagrafennaidd, modd y derbyniom y Cymmun Bendigaid, a gyfieithiwyd gan Foses Williams* (Llundain: Joseph Downing, 1715); another version appeared in 1721 translated by John Jones, curate of Llansanffraid; also William Fleetwood, *Y Cymmunwr Ystyriol, neu eglurhad athrawiaeth sacrament Swpper yr Arglwydd*, trans. Michael Jones (Llundain: John Downing, 1716).

102 Griffith Jones, *A Short View about the Controversy about Episcopacy* (Chester: W. Cooke, 1719), p. 9.

103 Jones, *A Short View about the Controversy about Episcopacy*, pp. 9, 12.

104 Griffith Jones, *Golwg Byrr o'r Ddadl ynghylch Llywodraeth yr Esgobion* (Mwythig: John Rhydderch, 1722), p. 12.

105 Griffith Jones, *Short and Plain Considerations to Convince Men of the Danger of Separating from the Communion of their Parish Churches* (London: n.p., 1728), pp. 1–2.

106 Jones, *Short and Plain Considerations to Convince Men of the Danger of Separating from the Communion of their Parish Churches*, p. 4.

107 Jones, *Short and Plain Considerations to Convince Men of the Danger of Separating from the Communion of their Parish Churches*, p. 4.

108 *Meddylieu Neillduol ar Grefydd, Dosbarthedig mwyn [sic] Deuddeg Pwngc, a Bwriadeu Gweithadwy Seiliedig arnynt, gan Gwilym Beveridge DD, o gyfieithiad Iaco ab Dewi* (Llundain: William Mears, 1717), p. 71, hereafter page numbers are in the text; for James Davies, 'Iaco ab Dewi', see Garfield H. Hughes, *Iaco ab Dewi (1648–1722)* (Caerdydd: Gwasg Prifysgol Cymru, 1952), *DWB*, *ODNB*.

109 See Alister E. McGrath, 'The Emergence of the Anglican Tradition on Justification', *Churchman*, 98 (1984), 28–43; *idem, Iustitia Dei: A History of the Christian Doctrine of Justification: from 1500 to the present day* (Cambridge: Cambridge University Press, 1986), pp. 105–11.

110 See above, pp. 247–50.

111 William Beveridge DD, *Prif Ddledswyddau Christion, sef Angenrhaid a Mawrlles Gweddi Cyffredin a Mynych Gymmuno, o gyfieithiad Edward Samuel* (Mwythig: John Rhydderch, 1722), p. 85.

112 E.g. *Prydferthwch sancteiddrwydd yn y Weddi Gyffredin ... o waith Thomas Bisse DD, o gyfieithiad Theophilus Evans* (Mwythig: John Rhydderch, 1722); anon., *Llythyr oddiwrth Weinidog at ei Blwyfolion* (Llundain: Joseph Downing, 1727); Peter Nourse, *Athrawiaeth yr Eglwys, yn cynnwys XII o dractiau bucheddol, o gyfieithiad E[dward] S[amuel]* (Caerlleon: Roger Adams, 1731); Offspring Blackall, *Pwyll y Pader, neu Eglurhad ar Weddi'r Arglwydd*, trans. Theophilus Evans (Mwythig: Thomas Durston, 1733).

113 Edward Morgan (ed.), *Letters of the Revd Griffith Jones to Mrs Bevan, late of Laugharne, near Carmarthen* (London: Whittaker and Co, 1832), pp. 198–201, letter to Madam Bevan, 11 January 1737.

114 Morgan (ed.), *Letters of the Revd Griffith Jones to Mrs Bevan*, p. 21, letter to Madam Bevan, 15 February 1733.

115 Morgan (ed.), *Letters of the Revd Griffith Jones to Mrs Bevan*, p. 242, letter to Madam Bevan, 26 June 1737.

116 Quoted by John Walsh, 'Origins of the Evangelical Revival', in G. V. Bennett and J. D. Walsh (eds), *Essays in Modern English Church History* (London: Adam and Charles Black, 1966), pp. 132–62 (140–1).

117 Geraint H. Jenkins, '"An old and much honoured soldier": Griffith Jones, Llanddowror', *WHR*, 11 (1983), 449–68; cf. Glanmor Williams, 'Religion, Language and the Circulating Schools of Griffith Jones, Llanddowror (1683–1761)', in *idem, Religion, Language and Nationality in Wales: Historical Essays* (Cardiff: University of Wales Press, 1979), pp. 200–16.

118 E. Wyn James, 'Griffith Jones (1684–1761) of Llanddowror and his "Striking Experiment in Mass Religious Education" in Wales in the Eighteenth

Century', in Reinhart Siegert (ed.), *Educating the People through Reading Material in the Eighteenth and Nineteenth Centuries* (Bremen: Edition Lumière, 2012), pp. 275–92 (283).

119   Glanmor Williams, 'Language, Literature and Nationality in Wales', in *Religion, Language and Nationality in Wales*, pp. 127–47 (136).

120   Not, apparently, in 1683 as most earlier historians had claimed, see Emlyn Dole, 'Trichanmlwyddiant geni Griffith Jones', *Y Traethodydd*, 139 (1984), 196–9.

121   John Evans, *Some Account of the Welsh Charity-Schools, and the Rise and Progress of Methodism in Wales* (London: n.p., 1752), p. 14.

122   Clement (ed.), *Correspondence and Minutes of the SPCK relating to Wales*, p. 52.

123   For the background, see E. D. Evans, 'A Providential Rescue? Griffith Jones and the Malabar Mission', *JWRH*, 8 (2000), 35–42.

124   Clement (ed.), *Correspondence and Minutes of the SPCK relating to Wales*, p. 57.

125   Clement (ed.), *Correspondence and Minutes of the SPCK relating to Wales*, p. 57.

126   Clement (ed.), *Correspondence and Minutes of the SPCK relating to Wales*, p. 62.

127   Bodleian Library Rawlinson MS 743; transcribed as 'A Letter Concerning Griffith Jones', in *BBCS*, 10 (1939–41), 273–5 (274). Hereafter page numbers are placed in the text.

128   NLW Ottley Papers 1627, quoted in E. D. Jones, 'The Ottley Papers', *NLWJ*, 4 (1945), 61–74 (66).

129   Clement (ed.), *Correspondence and Minutes of the SPCK relating to Wales*, p. 72.

130   NLW Ottley Papers 139, cited in *TCAS*, 24 (1933), 81.

131   Clement (ed.), *Correspondence and Minutes of the SPCK relating to Wales*, p. 72.

132   NLW Ottley Papers 1627, quoted in Jones, 'The Ottley Papers', 66.

133   Evans, *Some Account of the Welsh Charity-Schools*, p. 19.

134   See above, pp. 247–50.

135   Clement (ed.), *Correspondence and Minutes of the SPCK relating to Wales*, pp. 82, 99, 105, 108, 125.

136   J. H. Davies, 'A diary of a journey … by Revd Griffith Jones', *CCH*, 7 (1922), 10–14.

137   NLW Add MS 24B, sermon on Eph. 1:18, preached at Llandeilo Abercywyn 14 October 1722; sermon on Romans 2:28–9, 'The circumcision of the heart', preached at Cynwyl, 1 January 1724.

138   Clement (ed.), *Correspondence and Minutes of the SPCK relating to Wales*, p. 176.

139   [Henry Phillips], *A Sketch of the Life and Character of the Reverend and Pious Mr Griffith Jones of Llanddowror* (London: W. Oliver, 1762), p. 9; for Phillips (1719–89), a teacher in the charity schools who later became a Baptist minister in Salisbury, see *DWB*.

140   [Phillips], *A Sketch of the Life and Character of the Reverend and Pious Mr Griffith Jones of Llanddowror*, p. 20.

141   Williams, 'Religion, Language and the Circulating Schools of Griffith Jones', p. 203; for Bridget Bevan (1698–1779), see *DWB*, *ODNB*.

142   Morgan (ed.), *Letters of the Revd Griffith Jones to Mrs Bevan*, p. 122; 16 February 1736.

143 Morgan (ed.), *Letters of the Revd Griffith Jones to Mrs Bevan*, p. 32; 30 March 1733.

144 Morgan (ed.), *Letters of the Revd Griffith Jones to Mrs Bevan*, p. 139; 29 May 1736.

145 Morgan (ed.), *Letters of the Revd Griffith Jones to Mrs Bevan*, p. 235; 25 May 1737.

146 Morgan (ed.), *Letters of the Revd Griffith Jones to Mrs Bevan*, p. 274; 6 January 1738.

147 Morgan (ed.), *Letters of the Revd Griffith Jones to Mrs Bevan*, p. 51; 12 May 1733.

148 Morgan (ed.), *Letters of the Revd Griffith Jones to Mrs Bevan*, pp. 242–3; 26 June 1737.

149 Morgan (ed.), *Letters of the Revd Griffith Jones to Mrs Bevan*, pp. 107–8; 2 January 1736.

150 Morgan (ed.), *Letters of the Revd Griffith Jones to Mrs Bevan*, p. 268: 3 January 1738.

151 Morgan (ed.), *Letters of the Revd Griffith Jones to Mrs Bevan*, p. 41; 22 April 1733.

152 Morgan (ed.), *Letters of the Revd Griffith Jones to Mrs Bevan*, p. 282; 14 February 1738.

153 Morgan (ed.), *Letters of the Revd Griffith Jones to Mrs Bevan*, p. 109; 2 January 1736.

154 Morgan (ed.), *Letters of the Revd Griffith Jones to Mrs Bevan*, p. 17; 30 January 1733.

155 Morgan (ed.), *Letters of the Revd Griffith Jones to Mrs Bevan*, p. 127; 17 April 1736.

156 Morgan (ed.), *Letters of the Revd Griffith Jones to Mrs Bevan*, p. 15; 6 January 1733.

157 Morgan (ed.), *Letters of the Revd Griffith Jones to Mrs Bevan*, p. 118; 6 February 1736.

158 Morgan (ed.), *Letters of the Revd Griffith Jones to Mrs Bevan*, p. 216; 2 April 1737.

159 Morgan (ed.), *Letters of the Revd Griffith Jones to Mrs Bevan*, pp. 239–40; 25 May 1737.

160 Morgan (ed.), *Letters of the Revd Griffith Jones to Mrs Bevan*, p. 18; 30 January 1733.

161 Morgan (ed.), *Letters of the Revd Griffith Jones to Mrs Bevan*, p. 49; 12 May 1733.

162 Morgan (ed.), *Letters of the Revd Griffith Jones to Mrs Bevan*, p. 230; 25 May 1737.

163 Morgan (ed.), *Letters of the Revd Griffith Jones to Mrs Bevan*, p. 138; 29 May 1736.

164 Morgan (ed.), *Letters of the Revd Griffith Jones to Mrs Bevan*, p. 55; 20 May 1733.

165 Morgan (ed.), *Letters of the Revd Griffith Jones to Mrs Bevan*, p. 56; 20 May 1733.

166 Morgan (ed.), *Letters of the Revd Griffith Jones to Mrs Bevan*, p. 61; 30 March 1734.

167 Morgan (ed.), *Letters of the Revd Griffith Jones to Mrs Bevan*, p. 71; 16 July 1734.

168 Morgan (ed.), *Letters of the Revd Griffith Jones to Mrs Bevan*, p. 72; 16 July 1734.

169 Morgan (ed.), *Letters of the Revd Griffith Jones to Mrs Bevan*, p. 263; 3 January 1738.

170 Morgan (ed.), *Letters of the Revd Griffith Jones to Mrs Bevan*, p. 235; 25 May 1737.

171 Morgan (ed.), *Letters of the Revd Griffith Jones to Mrs Bevan*, p. 86; 10 August 1735

172 Morgan (ed.), *Letters of the Revd Griffith Jones to Mrs Bevan*, p. 46; 27 April 1733.

173 Morgan (ed.), *Letters of the Revd Griffith Jones to Mrs Bevan*, pp. 112–13; 9 January 1736.

174 Morgan (ed.), *Letters of the Revd Griffith Jones to Mrs Bevan*, p. 58; 26 March 1734; cf. p. 31; 30 March 1733; for Zwingli's doctrine of the Lord's Supper, see W. P. Stephens, 'The theology of Zwingli', in D. V. N. Bagchi and D. Steinmetz (eds), *The Cambridge Companion to Reformation Theology* (Cambridge: Cambridge University Press, 2004), pp. 80–99.

175 Phillips, *A Sketch of the Life and Character of the Reverend Mr Griffith Jones*, p. 5.

176 For the context, see Eryn M. White, 'Popular schooling and the Welsh language, 1650–1800', in Geraint H. Jenkins (ed.), *The Welsh Language before the Industrial Revolution* (Cardiff: University of Wales Press, 1997), pp. 318–41.

177 Jenkins, *Literature, Religion and Society in Wales, 1660–1730*, pp. 60–6; John Davies, *Bywyd a Gwaith Moses Williams 1685–1742* (Caerdydd: Gwasg Prifysgol Cymru, 1937), pp. 50–75.

178 [Griffith Jones], *Welsh Piety: or the needful Charity of Promoting the salvation of the Poor, being an account of the Rise, Method and Progress of the Circulating Welsh Charity Schools ... in Three Letters to a Friend* (London: J. Hutton, 1740), p. 1; hereafter page numbers are in the text.

179 Jones's textbook for teaching literacy to the poor, *Cyngor Rhad yr Anllythrennog*, was published in 1737.

180 R. Tudur Jones, *The Desire of Nations* (Llandybïe: Christopher Davies, 1974), pp. 131–33; cf. E. Wyn James, '"The New Birth of a New People": Welsh Language and Identity and the Welsh Methodists, *c.*1740–1820', in Robert Pope (ed.), *Religion and National Identity: Wales and Scotland, c.1700–2000* (Cardiff: University of Wales Press, 2001), pp. 14–42.

181 Griffith Jones, *Letter to a Clergyman* (London: John Oliver, 1745), p. 50.

182 Eryn M. White, *The Welsh Bible* (Stroud: Tempus, 2007), p. 63; for Thorold, see W. Moses Williams, *The Friends of Griffith Jones* (London: Hon. Soc. of Cymmrodorion, 1939), pp. 29–36 and *ODNB s.n.* Thorold Family.

183 Following the first edition of 1739, the spelling used was 'Welch' rather than 'Welsh'.

184 Jenkins, 'An old and much honoured soldier', 461; Robert Williams, treasurer of Bangor Cathedral and Andrew Edwards, its chancellor, were the most senior Welsh clerics to be listed among the schools' benefactors; W. Moses Williams, *Selections from the Welch Piety* (Cardiff: University of Wales Press, 1938), p. 126.

185 Roger L. Brown, '"Spiritual Nurseries": Griffith Jones and the Circulating Schools', *NLWJ*, 30 (1997), 27–49 (34).

186 J. H. Davies (ed.), *The Letters of Lewis, Richard, William and John Morris, 1728–65*, vol. 1 (Aberystwyth: J. H. Davies, 1908), p. 171; this is my translation from the Welsh.

187 Robert Jones Rhos-lan, *Drych yr Amseroedd* (1820), ed. G. M. Ashton (Caerdydd: Gwasg Prifysgol Cymru, 1958), p. 104.

188 Brown, 'Spiritual Nurseries', 29–31.

189 Brown, 'Spiritual Nurseries', 42.

190 Williams, 'Religion, Language and the Circulating Schools of Griffith Jones', pp. 207–8; for the detailed statistical and geographical evidence, see W. T. R. Pryce, 'The Diffusion of the "Welch" Circulating Schools in Eighteenth-Century Wales', *WHR*, 25 (2011), 486–519.

191 Griffith Jones, *A Further Account of the Welsh Charity Schools* (London: J. Hutton, 1740), p. 23.

192 [Griffith Jones], *Hyfforddiad i Wybodaeth Iachusol o Egwyddorion a Dyledswyddau Crefydd ... yng Nghatecism yr Eglwys ... y Rhan Gyntaf ... gan Weinidog o Eglwys Loegr* (Llundain: n.p., 1740), p. vi; page numbers which follow are in the text.

193 W. R. Ward, *Christianity under the Ancien Régime, 1648–1789* (Cambridge: Cambridge University Press, 1999), p. 79.

194 [Griffith Jones], *Hyfforddiad i Wybodaeth Iachusol o Egwyddorion a Dyledswyddau Crefydd ... yng Nghatecism yr Eglwys ... yr Ail Ran ... gan Weinidog o Eglwys Loegr* (Llundain: n.p., 1743), p. 55; page numbers which follow are in the text.

195 [Griffith Jones], *Hyfforddiad i Wybodaeth Iachusol o Egwyddorion a Dyledswyddau Crefydd ... yng Nghatecism yr Eglwys ... y Drydedd Ran ... gan Weinidog o Eglwys Loegr* (Llundain: n.p., 1746), p. 55; page numbers which follow are in the text.

196 This is emphasized in Jenkins, 'An old and much honoured soldier', 459–61.

197 [Griffith Jones], *Hyfforddiad i Wybodaeth Iachusol o Egwyddorion a Dyledswyddau Crefydd ... yng Nghatecism yr Eglwys ... y Bedwaredd Ran ... gan Weinidog o Eglwys Loegr* (Llundain: n.p., 1746).

198 For federal theology, see R. Tudur Jones, 'Athrawiaeth y Cyfamodau', in D. Densil Morgan (ed.), *Grym y Gair a Fflam y Ffydd: Ysgrifau ar Hanes Crefydd yng Nghymru* (Bangor: Canolfan Uwchefrydiau Crefydd yng Nghymru, 1998), pp. 9–16.

199 [Griffith Jones], *Hyfforddiad i Wybodaeth Iachusol o Egwyddorion a Dyledswyddau Crefydd ... yng Nghatecism yr Eglwys ... y Bummed Ran ... gan Weinidog o Eglwys Loegr* (Llundain: n.p., 1746), p. 20.

200 It would be reissued in 1749, 1763, 1792 and into the nineteenth century, see Eiluned Rees, *Libri Walliae: A Catalogue of Welsh Books, 1546–1820*, vol. 1 (Aberystwyth: National Library of Wales, 1987), p. 359.

201 Geraint Tudur, *Howell Harris: from Conversion to Separation, 1735–50* (Cardiff: University of Wales Press, 2000), pp. 13–22.

202 Jeremy Taylor, *Ystyriaethau o gyflwr dyn, yn y byd hwn ac yn y byd sydd i ddyfod*, trans. G. Wynne (Caer: Roger Adams, 1731); a second edition of John Jones's version of William Vickers, *Cymdymmaith i'r Allor, yn dangos anian ac angen-rheidrwydd ymbaratoad sagrafennaidd, modd y derbyniom y Cymmun Bendigaid* (Mwythig: John Rhydderch, 1738) with a third printing in 1753; William Assheton, *Trefn am Dduwiolder am Ddydd yr Arglwydd*, trans. R. Lloyd (Mwythig: Stafford Prys, 1747), which was a much attenuated version of a work that had first been issued in 1700, see p. 253.

203 Morgan (ed.), *Letters of the Revd Griffith Jones to Mrs Bevan*, p. 183; 1 November 1736.

204 Jenkins, 'An old and much honoured soldier', 466.

205 Williams, 'Religion, Language and the Circulating Schools of Griffith Jones', p. 215.

206 Phillips, *A Sketch of the Life and Character of the Reverend Mr Griffith Jones*, pp. 6, 7.

207 Quoted in D. Ambrose Jones, *Griffith Jones Llanddowror* (Wrecsam: Hughes a'i Fab, 1923), p. 118.

208 Ioan Thomas, *Rhad Ras* (1810), ed. J. Dyfnallt Owen (Caerdydd: Gwasg Prifysgol Cymru, 1949), p. 46.

209 Gomer M. Roberts, *Bywyd a Gwaith Peter Williams* (Caerdydd: Gwasg Prifysgol Cymru, 1943), p. 13.

210 Gomer M. Roberts, *Y Pêr Ganiedydd (Pantycelyn), Cyfrol 1, Trem ar ei Fywyd* (Aberystwyth: Gwasg Aberystwyth, 1949), p. 96.

211 D. E. Jenkins, *Life of the Rev. Thomas Charles BA of Bala*, vol. 1 (Denbigh: Ll. Jenkins, 1908), pp. 29–30.

212 Geraint H. Jenkins in *ODNB, s.n.* 'Griffith Jones'.

213 W. R. Ward, *The Protestant Evangelical Awakening* (Cambridge: Cambridge University Press, 1992), p. 316; cf. *idem, Christianity under the Ancien Régime, 1648–1789*, pp. 136–9.

5

1689–1760 (ii)

The faith of the Older Dissent

Congregationalists and Presbyterians

On 24 May 1689 when the Toleration Act received its royal assent, Wales's Protestant Dissenters breathed a collective sigh of relief. 'Liberty of conscience', recorded the church book of the Independent congregation at the Cilgwyn, Cardiganshire, 'was made legal in the year 1689 by the Toleration Act'.[1] Its stipulations did not cover non-Trinitarians to say nothing of the monarchs' Roman Catholic subjects, nor did it clarify the position of Dissenting schools and academies. Dissenters were denied entrance to public office while prospective students who could not conform to the rubrics of the Church of England were still barred from the English (though not the Scottish) universities. However, 'for the most part Dissenters were now able to go about their daily business without fear of the informer, the constable or the magistrate'.[2] As long as its meeting houses were registered and its ministers assented to the doctrinal clauses of the 39 Articles, orthodox Dissent was free to worship in peace and function unmolested under the protection of the law. It would become, in effect, an alternative if lower-status establishment.[3] Although harassment at a local level did not always cease, especially during the reign of Queen Anne, while in 1714 'the wild and bigoted rabble' of pro-Stuart rioters destroyed Wrexham's Presbyterian New Meeting, damaged the town's Congregational chapel and smashed the Congregational meeting house at Llanfyllin, Montgomeryshire, on the whole Welsh Dissenters were allowed to cultivate their congregational life as they pleased.[4] Following the oppression of the post-Restoration decades it was a welcome respite indeed.

The sprawling, multi-branched and often cross-county nature of Dissenting witness which had developed after the Restoration was perpetuated into the new era. It would not be until 1718 when the survey collated by Dr John Evans, minister of London's Hand Alley Presbyterian Church and secretary of the Committee of the Three Denominations, would reveal the extent of that witness throughout the kingdom,[5] but there was likely to have been little fluctuation in size or spread of Welsh Dissent between 1689 and approximately 1715. According to R. Tudur Jones's computations, Congregationalists (who were virtually indistinguishable from the Presbyterians as listed by John Evans) had some sixty churches which were manifested as eighty or more congregations, branch-congregations and house meetings; the Baptists' dozen churches were comprised of twenty-one congregations and branches; with the Quakers, who were now seriously depleted in numbers, assembling at some twenty-six venues, mostly in mid Wales, though their established meetings were considerably less than this. Baptist strength was in north Pembrokeshire and on the Carmarthen-Cardiganshire border, mid-Glamorgan, west Monmouthshire as well as parts of Radnorshire, while the Independents were also strongest in west Wales, namely in Pembrokeshire, Carmarthen and Cardiganshire; in Breconshire in mid Wales; Glamorgan and Monmouthshire in the south, as well as having a limited presence in such north Wales towns as Pwllheli, Ruthin, Denbigh and Wrexham. By 1715 the Dissenting denominations had an estimated membership of some 17,700 which, although a still small proportion as a whole, had expanded from the 1 per cent recorded in 1676 to nearly 4 per cent of the population.[6] In fact, these figures 'reveal that Welsh Dissent was a small but influential minority'.[7]

The post-Restoration doctrinal consensus forged by Stephen Hughes and others which had characterized Anglicans and Dissenters during the 1680s continued up to and beyond the turn of the century. The new crop of Congregational ministers who took charge of the churches at the time – David Penry at Tirdwncyn, Swansea; Rhys Prydderch who took over from Henry Maurice at the Breconshire church; William Evans (latterly head of the academy at Carmarthen) at Pencader; David Edwards at Abermeurig, Cae'ronnen and Cellan in mid Cardiganshire and Daniel Phillips at Pwllheli, all of whom were ordained in 1688[8] – had received their ministerial formation during the 1670s and 1680s and shared the values and social standing of their mentors. They were 'sober, knowledgeable and well-to-do men', steeped in the Puritan ethos of Stephen Hughes and James Owen, whose piety was more solid than exuberant and who prized restraint and a catholic spirit very highly.[9] For them 'moderation' was truly 'a virtue'.[10] The literature which they issued underscored both the morality that had characterized the consensus and its theology. Two translations of short works by Thomas Gouge, both of which appeared in 1693, emphasized the need for true faith to issue forth in charity and good works,[11] and that church members should be diligent in providing financial support for their ministers,[12] while another translation, this time of the Taunton Presbyterian Joseph Alleine's *Sure Guide to Heaven*, pressed the need for all men and women to be truly converted. The evangelical Calvinism which had fired the peripatetic ministry of the movement's preachers during the 1670s and 1680s was applied with equal fervency to the upcoming generation. Its basis was God's gracious election of sinners to righteousness:

> It is only the elect who will be born again. Only those who have been called will come to Christ, and only those sheep given to him by the Father will respond to his call. That which corresponds to eternal election is the effective call.[13]

This, however, should never be made an excuse for doubting whether one was among the elect. The sinner should not begin with the doctrine of election but with the gospel message which was open to all:

> If you are sure of your call, you will never doubt your election ... God's sovereign design may be mysterious but his promises are clear... Do not be perturbed by wondering whether you are elect or not but strive instead to repent and to believe.[14]

It was preachers such as these, 'men of real piety, good learning and zealously active to save immortal souls', who preserved the link between post-Restoration Dissent and the ebullience which would come to characterize the Evangelical Revival in decades to come.[15]

The sacramental piety that had been shared by High Churchmen and Calvinist alike was displayed most forcefully in the works of Thomas Baddy. A native of Wrexham, he had been grounded in Reformed divinity at Richard Franklin's academy at Rathwell, Yorkshire, before returning in 1693 to pastor the Congregational cause in the town of Denbigh. As well as being a pioneer in Welsh-language Dissenting hymnology in whose compositions the sacramental note was well to the fore,[16] he maintained the Eucharistic doctrine of Reformed Christendom through his translations of the work of Thomas Doolittle. A Presbyterian minister and eager disciple of Richard Baxter, Doolittle had first published his popular *Treatise Concerning the Lord's Supper* in 1667 which Baddy re-titled *Pasc y Christion* ('The Christian's Passover'). Its sixteen chapters and three concluding dialogues formed an extended commentary on the words of the institution to the Lord's Supper in I Cor. 11:23–5. Whereas much of the treatise offered pastoral advice to weak and needy believers, it also explained the meaning of the rite. The Lord's Supper in the Dissenting tradition was not a converting ordinance, rather it was for those who had already repented of their sins and come to Christ: 'Conversion must precede the partaking of this holy ordinance which has been given by God not to effect grace but to strengthen it.'[17] Although the words of institution did in fact speak of commemoration: 'Do this in remembrance of me', this was no mere memorialism but a function of the believer's union with Christ: 'This is not a bare historical remembrance on the surface of the mind, as even the demons remember Christ's passion in such a way' (p. 22). Rather, it is the means by which the benefits of the gospel are sealed in the Christian's heart: 'Is this ordinance not God's own great seal which confirms to your soul the immense and eternal blessings of the covenant of grace?' (p. 28). If the believer is called to remember, God the Holy Spirit is himself active in the very action of partaking of the sacrament: 'Is it not here that God pours himself out into the hearts of his people?' (p. 42). For Baddy, the sacrament was

> a sure conveyance of all the blessings of the gospel and the gifts purchased through the death of Christ along with God's great seal which assures your soul that it will receive the benefits of the covenant of Christ ... (p. 28)
>
> This sacrament is a commemoration of the passion of our Lord where he himself witnesses your conscience how he has died for your sins; it is an elucidation of his love where he assures you of how much he loves you; it is a foretaste of the heavenly blessings of which you too will undoubtedly partake. (p. 29)

Far from being an *aide memoire* or merely exhibiting externally the truths of the gospel, the rite signified 'my union with Christ and enjoyment of him, my feeding on Christ through faith whereby the grace of

God's Spirit enlivens my soul' (pp. 168–9). Thus the full teaching of Calvin's *Institiutio* was shared among the Congregational faithful, and others, during the early decades of the eighteenth century.[18]

As well as expounding Calvinist sacramentalism, Baddy's publications encouraged the self-analysis which had become *de rigueur* among both Puritans and High Churchmen of the 'holy living' school. A year after *Pasc y Christion*, he issued his version of William Dyer's *A Cabinet of Jewels* (1663), a series of sermons on the titles of Christ from the Old Testament prophecy, 'Unto us a child is born', Isa 9:6–7, along with an assortment of other essays; this he called *Cyfoeth i'r Cymry* ('A Bounty for the Welsh'), while in 1713 he published *Dwys-ddifrifol Gynghor i Hunanymholiad*, his translation of Thomas Wadsworth's *Serious Exhortation unto Self-Examination* (1687), an unremitting call to holiness based on the apostle Paul's plea in II Cor. 13:5, 'Examine yourselves as to whether you are in the faith'. Like his sacramental essay, both became very popular, *Cyfoeth i'r Cymry* being re-issued in 1714, 1731 and 1740, and *Dwys-ddifrifol Gynghor* also in 1740. Along with Thomas Doolittle, both Dyer and Wadsworth had been Presbyterian clergy, ejected from their parishes following the Act of Uniformity, who had spent the post-Restoration years ministering as best they could in the city of London and its environs.[19] Their works, in the guise of Baddy's prose, were 'marked by a mood of uneasy restlessness, with the reader granted not a moment's peace'.[20] Such readers were 'urged to probe inwardly, burrow down into every nook and cranny of the soul to uncover [their] sins and look for signs of grace'.[21] The peril of this teaching was that it could stoke an overscrupulous conscience, spiritual morbidity and an all-too-minute psychological introspection in which the gospel note was eclipsed and assurance of the divine forgiveness was forgotten. For the most part, however, by reminding his readers of the objective work of Christ and the doctrine of justification by faith alone, Baddy preserved the balance between the divine initiative and the believer's striving for holiness which characterized Dissenting spirituality in the years leading to the Evangelical Revival.

High and moderate Calvinism

The evangelical Calvinism which provided the doctrinal underpinning for late seventeenth- and early eighteenth-century Welsh Dissent was moderate and centrist. A Welsh version of Richard Baxter's posthumous *Grand Question Resolved and Instructions for a Holy Life* (1692) appeared in 1693,[22] while Baxter's ameliorating version of strict Puritanism had resonated widely,[23] especially among those ministers who retained a feel for Presbyterian values despite holding to the common polity of Welsh Congregationalism. James Owen, who represented this view most palpably, had issued his translation of the Westminster Shorter Catechism in 1691 which was reprinted in 1701 and 1705,[24] while William Evans, an occasional conformist, head of the Carmarthen Academy and one for whom Archdeacon Tension had high hopes of drawing into the Established Church,[25] published his own commentary on the same catechism in 1707.[26] Another version, identical apart from matters appertaining to baptism, was published by Abel Morgan, minister at Blaenau Gwent, for the use of the Baptist churches soon after.[27] Another book in the same vein, a translation of Thomas Vincent's *Explicatory Catechism* (1673) also based on the same work, appeared in 1719.[28] The Shorter Catechism, which was circumspect in its dealing with the doctrine of election, eschewed any mention of double predestination and centred mostly on expounding the meaning of the covenant of grace, remained a mainstay of the movement's teaching during this period. Inevitably perhaps, a reaction occurred, first in Wrexham and then at Henllan Amgoed on the Carmarthenshire-Pembrokeshire border.

The year 1690 had seen the republishing of the works of Tobias Crisp, the early seventeenth-century London clergyman whose emphasis on salvation by grace without recourse to works of the law was seen to promote antinomianism, to engender spiritual self-deception and undercut morality. Among the English Puritans, the one who had set his face most firmly against antinomianism had been Richard Baxter as evidenced by his *Aphorisms of Justification* (1649),[29] his earliest published work, while his final volume, *The Scripture Gospel Defended …* *against the Libertines* (1690), issued a year before his death, was in response to the rekindling of what he believed to be Crisp's errors. By then his staunchest ally and the one upon whom his mantle would fall was Daniel Williams (*c.*1643–1716), a native of Wrexham and Dr John Evans's predecessor as minister of Hand's Alley Presbyterian church in Bishopsgate. Williams continued Baxter's crusade by publishing in 1692 his *Gospel-Truth Stated and Vindicated*, insisting that even though salvation was by grace alone, the very nature of grace inculcated holiness, obedience and indeed good works in its recipients, while true faith necessarily implied compliance with the gospel's law. Not surprisingly, and like Baxter before him, he was accused of works-righteousness and

Arminianism and a pamphlet war, 'the Crispian Controversy', ensued.[30] Among its consequences was that the Wrexham church, founded during the Commonwealth as a gathered congregation under Morgan Llwyd and led during the post-Restoration oppression by John Evans,[31] would split into two, the Baxterian-Williams section forming a Presbyterian church ('the New Meeting'), the remainder, which already comprised of both Independents and Baptists, becoming a specifically Congregational gathering ('the Old Meeting').[32] The reactionary tone of those who opposed the consensual and moderate Calvinism championed by Williams was seen in *Baxterianism Barefac'd* (1699), an inflammatory work by Thomas Edwards of Rhual and member of the Old Meeting. Whereas that book, like those of the supporters of Crisp, magnified election and sovereign free grace, it did little to convince opponents that this new strain of High Calvinism could prevent antinomianism, eternal justification and other such erroneous views. According to Joshua Thomas, the Baptist historian, Edwards was a man of 'learning, talent, understanding and piety',[33] and after his death in 1700 a measure of doctrinal tranquillity was restored to the town's Dissenting community with both churches, although still worshipping apart, drawing together where possible on the basis of those convictions which they held in common.

The Crispian Controversy had been one element in a complex of issues which put paid to the so-called 'Happy Union', the short-lived attempt between 1690 and 1695 to create a united Dissenting front in England and Wales.[34] Thereafter the Presbyterians and Congregationalists, especially in London though less so in the provinces, tended to diverge. The one came to emphasize even more than previously church government by elders and synods; the need for a trained and learned ministry; preparation for church membership in terms of moral integrity and a grounding in sound, biblical doctrine; and moderate Calvinism as its theological norm. The other revelled in the 'gathered church' inheritance or the sovereign right of each individual fellowship to govern itself without recourse to rule by a synod of elders; spiritual gifts rather than formal learning as a prerequisite for the preaching of the Word; an experience of conversion rather than doctrinal orthodoxy and a bare confession of faith in order to partake of the Lord's Supper; and High Calvinism as its yardstick for truth. As classic Presbyterianism had never really taken root, the situation in Wales during the post-Restoration decades had always been very open, with elements of both traditions existing in harmony and side by side.

Henry Maurice's refrain in his report on the state of Welsh Dissent in 1672, that many fellowships were 'of the judgement called Independent *but very moderate*' (Llanbadarn, Cardiganshire), or 'Independent in their judgement *not much differing from Presbyterianism*' (the Carmarthenshire Church), typified the situation in the country at large.[35] The same would be true by the turn of the century and beyond, while after 1700 even in Wrexham, between the Old Meeting and the New Meeting, concord would prevail. Alas, this tranquillity would be disturbed, in south-west Wales at least, by 'the Henllan secessions' of 1707 to 1709.

It is on the basis of two key publications which appeared nearly twenty and twenty-five years after the events described that we know the detail of what occurred at Henllan during the first decade of the century. In 1727 Matthias Maurice, Congregational minister at Rothwell, Northamptonshire, a zealous evangelist and unabashed High Calvinist, published his *Byr a chywir hanes Eglwys Rhydyceished yn eu nheilltuad o Henllan, trwy y blynyddoedd 1707, 1708, 1709* ('A short and correct history of the church at Rhyd-y-ceisiaid in its withdrawal from Henllan through the years 1707, 1708, 1709'), which was challenged five years later by an even more vigorous essay, *Golwg ar y Beiau* ('A View of the Faults') by another expatriate Welsh pastor, Jeremy Owen (*fl.* 1704–44), Presbyterian minister at Barnet, Hertfordshire.[36] Maurice (1684–1738), a tailor from Llanddewi Efelffre, Pembrokeshire, began preaching at the Congregational church at Henllan, Carmarthenshire, around 1706 and trained for ministry at the Carmarthen Academy under William Evans. He would subsequently become minister at Olney, Buckinghamshire, and in 1714 succeed his compatriot, the High Calvinist Richard Davis at Rothwell where he would remain for the rest of his life.[37] In his work he narrates how, on the death of Henllan's minister, 'God's dear servant Mr Dafydd Lewis of Cynwil' (p. 41), Lewis Thomas, a teaching elder in the congregation, began preaching in a way that shed new light on the doctrines of the faith and gained a following among a portion of the members of which Maurice was one. Others, however, questioned this new emphasis and began challenging its supporters, and before long 'the great truths of eternal election, particular redemption, the effective work of the Spirit in converting those who were elect and redeemed, and their perseverance in a state of grace to the end, were cast aside' (p. 42). Soon two factions had formed, one of which coalesced around Lewis Thomas for whom the High Calvinist truths had become highly precious, but were deemed by the others as being plainly heretical:

When we said that God in his eternal counsel preordained everything
in the world that came to pass, they said that we made God the author
of sin ... When we said that faith and repentance were not terms or
conditions of the covenant of grace to be performed in order to earn
God's favour and eternal life, they said that we advocated dispensing
with both faith and repentance. (p. 44)

The debate was fuelled by literature, 'erroneous books which turned
the gospel into a new law and as such a covenant of works under the
guise of the covenant of grace' (p. 44), a clear reference to the works
of Baxter and Daniel Williams, which led Maurice's opponents 'to take
every opportunity to speak out against us, that we were abolishing
the law and were therefore antinomians' (p. 44). This in turn inspired
them to master the literature that the Crisp controversy had evoked:
Edward Fisher's *Marrow of Modern Divinity*, Elisha Coles's *Practical
Discourse on God's Sovereignty*, Isaac Chauncy's *Doctrine which accords to
Godliness* and his *Neonomianism Unmask'd*, 'a learned and godly riposte
to Daniel Williams' despicable book' (p. 45), while 'several godly men
in England, having heard the cry of our persecution, gave us every
encouragement to go forward in the name of the Lord' (p. 45). In order
to decide on the matter, the case was taken to a series of synods of neighbouring Congregational churches, the first at Pencader and the next at
Tre-lech, and the High Calvinist section found, much to their chagrin,
that the judgement of their peers went against them. Recollecting the
crisis decades later, this represented (for Maurice) the victory of quasi-
Presbyterian oppression over the Independent ideal of sovereignty of
the local fellowship, and as such was anathema:

For if Christ's church is true, it is there [= in the local church gather-
ing] that the seat of judgement has been set up, according to Christ's
order and God's wisdom, and not in any so-called synod of man's design.
(p. 46)

By now, 'amidst the clamour of terms, conditions, synodical authority,
heresies, schisms ... separations and the like' (p. 47), peaceful co-existence
had become impossible, until the words of Jeremiah – 'Repay them,
O Lord, according to the works of their hands!' (Lamentations 3:64)
– in a final thunderous rebuke from the Henllan pulpit, made secession inevitable. The upshot was the founding at Rhyd-y-ceisiaid, in the

neighbouring parish of Llangynin, sometime in 1709, of an unambigu-
ously Independent church of High Calvinist conviction in which Lewis
Thomas was ordained minister.

The response, when it came, was devastating. Jeremy Owen in his
treatise supplied detail that Maurice had failed to declare. First, that
following Dafydd Lewis's death in 1705, the church had in fact chosen
and ordained his successor who was none other than Owen's father,
D. J. Owen (1651–1710) who, like Lewis Thomas, had already served the
congregation for years as a teaching elder. What Jeremy did not mention but was known by all, was that D. J. Owen was the elder brother of
the most revered and intellectually distinguished minister of his generation, namely James Owen of Oswestry. In other words, the Henllan
church had affirmed the centrist Calvinism and moderate churchmanship
that had become a norm among the Welsh Congregationalists since
the Restoration. Secondly, and supporting his contention with a welter
of historical examples, that the so-called synods that Maurice had traduced were in no way over-authoritarian or coercive but true to the New
Testament and primitive Christian practice of tendering advice to fellow
churches when it had been sought. And thirdly, that Maurice himself
had been a considerable object of censure throughout the period of tension. Despite everything, Maurice had not joined the new fellowship
at Rhyd-y-ceisiaid, either when the initial secession occurred or when
others had left at the ordination of Jeremy Owen as Henllan's minister in
1711 following his father's death, but he was still exercising his freedom
as a preacher within his home church and propounding what were, for
the moderate Calvinists, patently erroneous views. Such was the strain
that guidance from neighbouring churches had been sought once more.
Two more synods were convened, one again at Tre-lech and the other
at Henllan itself, which declared 'that Mr Maurice should be silenced *pro
tempere* until his head is cooler and his heart is improved'.[38]

Advice had also been requested from within the wider Dissenting
network. The first letter, quoted by Owen *in extensio*, was from fellow
Congregationalists in Bristol urging Maurice 'to uphold truth and God's
peace by behaviour which was more circumspect, sober and wise' (p. 59),
followed by similar missives from Barnstable and Bideford. These letters were dated July and August, while in September Maurice's case was
discussed by Somerset Congregationalists meeting in Shepton Mallet,
and then in Exeter. According to the records of the United Brethren
(Congregationalists and Presbyterians) of Devon and Cornwall: 'An

account of some proceedings in Wales against Mr Matthias Maurice for harsh expressions, viz. of our being justified from eternity, of God's willing sin, and his ill conduct in thrusting himself into Mr Jeremy Owen's pulpit.'[39] This was not done in a corner but showed that Welsh Dissent saw itself very much part of a wider, more expansive community of faith, while the Crispian theology was now being deemed a declension from the moderate Calvinism which Congregationalists had estimated as orthodoxy since the time of Stephen Hughes.

That which made Owen, Williams and Baxter such implacable opponents of High Calvinism was, at root, its deterministic view of the doctrine of election and its subjectivist understanding of faith, that faith was not an act of the will but a mere affirmation that Christ had already achieved all that was needed for salvation. There was no truth in the accusation that the Henllan church had cast aside 'the great truths of eternal election, particular redemption, the effective work of the Spirit in converting those who were elect and redeemed, and their perseverance in a state of grace to the end' as Maurice had claimed (p. 62). According to Jeremy Owen, that had remained the prevailing view of all orthodox Calvinists and constituted the regular teaching at the Henllan church both before and after he had been called to take his father's place. It was the secessionists, rather, who had turned their back on John Calvin and 'departed for the tents of the Crispites and the Davisites [a reference to Richard Davis, Matthias Maurice's Hyper-Calvinist predecessor at Rothwell]' (p. 62). For Owen, the idea that Adam's fall had been pre-destined (the so-called supralapsarian view) made God the author of sin which was 'a blasphemous verdict' (p. 72), while his opponents held to such an absolutist view of God's elective will as virtually to over-ride sinners' need to repent of their sins and actively to embrace Christ. Such concepts as 'eternal justification' not only cut the nerve of gospel preaching and undermined morality, but were a grotesque caricature of the true faith:

This alone is what I say: neither faith nor repentance is necessary if it is true that (according to their doctrine) they have been justified since eternity, neither can sin be accounted against them. 'Christ has done everything in our place, and there is nothing at all for us to do to be saved': these are words I heard with my own ears at Henllan ... [If this is true] they are hardly likely to heed the warning to flee from the wrath to come when they have been told that they are no longer under

that wrath and have never so been since eternity! Is *this* the treasured
doctrine of the gospel? (pp. 77–8)

For Jeremy Owen at least, it was this that was behind the Henllan secessions: 'When they could no longer have their sweet doctrine pure and
unadulterated, then they withdrew' (p. 78).[40]

Although they would spend their careers far beyond the borders
of Wales, both Maurice and Owen would continue to contribute to
Dissenting life in the country of their birth. Maurice, as has been noted,
was inducted to the Independent charge at Olney, Buckinghamshire, in
1713 before being ordained a year later as Congregational minister at
Rothwell in neighbouring Northamptonshire. He would remain there for
the rest of his life. Along with *Monuments of Mercy* (1729), his history of
the Congregational cause at Rothwell, and his *Modern Question Modestly
Answer'd* (1738), his most celebrated work would be *Social Religion
Exemplify'd* (1737), a handbook which fused a spirit of devotion with a
description of Independent church order and would prove immensely
popular among English (and Welsh) Congregationalists well into the
nineteenth century.[41] His nemesis, Jeremy Owen, had been trained for
ministry under James Owen at Oswestry, and would thereafter share
his uncle's scholarly bent as well as his moderate doctrinal stance.[42]
Having resigned from the Henllan pastorate following an unspecified
moral lapse (for which he had been disciplined and was restored), he
took a teaching position in London around 1715, and pastored churches
at Petworth in Sussex (1721–6), Barnet near London (1726–32) and
Princes Risborough, Buckinghamshire (1733–44). His *Traethawd i brofi
ac i gymell ar yr holl Eglwysi y Ddyledswydd Fawr Efangylaidd o Weddïo dros
Weinidogion* (1733) ('An Essay to prove and to urge upon the Churches
the Great Evangelical Responsibility of Praying for their Ministers')
was not only a solemn appeal to support the gospel ministry among
the Congregationalists in his native land, but an impeccable example of
the purest Welsh prose.[43] His emigration to America in 1744, where he
died at an unknown date and location, proved a loss to the Dissenting
cause in both England and in Wales.[44]

The fact that High Calvinism in doctrine along with uncompromising Independency became one strand in Welsh Congregational life after
1710 is evidenced by two volumes which emerged from the Crispian
Controversy. They were Howel Powel's translation of Elisha Coles's
Practical Discourse of God's Sovereignty (1673) and Matthias Maurice's

version of Isaac Chauncey's *The Doctrine which is according to Godliness* (1694).[45] Maurice we have met. Powel (*c.*1678–1716) had trained at William Payne's Independent academy at Saffron Walden, Essex, and was ordained at Beili-halog, Breconshire, in 1700. According to one source: 'He was a learned and cultured man with a gift for expounding the gospel to country audiences.'[46] He left Wales to settle at Cohensey, New Jersey, in 1712 and died there four years later. Both works appeared in 1711 and show that a fairly rigid doctrinal scheme which foregrounded election and an absolute concept of the divine sovereignty was by then gaining ground.

'The doctrine of election', claimed Powel, 'contains the sum and substance of the gospel'.[47] Through it God, in his sovereign freedom, has chosen from among the bulk of humankind, all of whom, through their rebellion in Adam, had fallen into sin, some to be redeemed in Christ for the sake of his own glory. It is 'the work of the Lord's eternal love, his desire to choose his own, designating them for everlasting life' (p. 49). It was a wholly unconditional act, based neither on any potential merit that the elect may have had nor on the divine pre-perception of faith or obedience on their part. It depended, rather, on God's sheer loving kindness and grace. The doctrine is, in sum, 'heaven's great charter, God's particular act of undeserved compassion towards his chosen ones, entrusted to Christ for their eternal good' (p. 49). As well as being undeserved this decree was eternal, through which the elect 'were ordained to eternal life before the world began' (p. 50). 'Election', he maintained,

> is the fundamental great law of the gospel ... It is unchangeable in itself and demands that all other laws concur with it. For its sake everything else exists, and in it God purposes the greatest glory for himself ... Were this aim to fail, the whole of creation would not be sufficient to make up the loss. (p. 62)

Powel was keen to defend God from the accusation of capriciousness or arbitrary mercy and he did so by maintaining that no one had a claim on God's love. All people were, after all, sinners, deserving nothing but the divine condemnation, and just as Christ, the second Person of the Holy Trinity, had been elected by the Father first to take flesh and then to bear the sins of the world, so God's people, 'those who were given to Christ each by their name as well as in number' (p. 68), has been chosen to receive the gift of salvation. This has nothing to do with their worthiness but with his own free and sovereign grace:

> Election is a victory which comes from neither east, west nor south but from God. As such it casts down the one and exalts the other. Thus it chooses some and rejects others. No-one can say to him 'What are you doing?' or 'Why did you punish me thus?' For just as election always signifies more than merely those who are chosen, so it holds out the full authority of he who chooses, to take whom he so wills, owing no account to any but himself. (p. 78)

In other words, God is wholly sovereign in his design. Although Powel spends many pages parrying the obvious questions: how can such a doctrine square with the universal love of God; the explicit scriptural claim that God wishes all people to come to repentance and be saved (I Tim. 2:4, II Peter 3:9); that good works are made redundant, and the like, he is adamant that the doctrine is rooted in scripture and it alone does full justice to both God's holy love and his perfect righteousness. According to the gospel plan all are bidden to come to Christ; any saving response they make is proof that they are among the chosen:

> You who have affirmed and accepted this truth, and after much soul-searching have discovered within yourselves signs that you are among his elect, you should take comfort in it. May the joy of the Lord be your strength! Eat your bread heartily and drink your wine (or your water if you so choose) with a jubilant heart in the sure knowledge that you are acceptable in God's eyes. (p. 125)

The remainder of the book expounds some of the main tenets of Reformed orthodoxy, namely particular redemption, effectual calling and the perseverance of the saints, all of which derive from elective grace. Christ, according to this scheme, has not died for all but for the elect alone: 'Their number is set and cannot be broken by adding some and subtracting others' (p. 128). Just as election is unconditional, Christ's atoning death is restricted to the chosen: 'There is none but the elect alone who are granted the saving fruits of redemption' (p. 154). Consequently the divine grace is irresistible while the saints will never fall away but will persevere to the end: 'Therefore you can be sure that you will arrive safely in the land of promise' (p. 176). All of these truths: effective calling, particular redemption and the perseverance of the saints, are the result of an un-thwarted, gratuitous love: 'As Christ gave himself a ransom for the elect, redemption is also of grace and is wholly free' (p. 176).

Maurice's volume was in two parts, Part One being in the form of a catechetical commentary on each of the main points of the Calvinistic scheme, and Part Two on the application of the divine law in the context of an Independent or Congregational church polity. Of the thirty-three chapters in Part One, the most substantial, chapter seven, was a long and intricate exposition of the divine decrees, followed, in chapter eighteen, by an extensive assessment of the covenant of grace. After first treating the doctrine of scripture, God and his attributes, and the Holy Trinity, the author launches into an extended and philosophically sophisticated account of election, predestination and the decrees. The basic truth about God is his sovereignty. Both love and righteousness are derivative of the fact. 'Predestination as such', he claims, 'is neither an act of mercy nor of justice but of sheer sovereignty'.[48] On this basis God chooses both to love his elect and to manifest his righteousness. Through this decree he elects some to salvation and others, namely the reprobate, to perdition. 'Election', he claimed, 'necessarily implies reprobation' (p. 61). The grim doctrine of double predestination had always been a point of consternation and felt by many, even within the Reformed constituency, to be more speculative than biblical. It would yet cause controversy and mark one of the divisions between High and moderate Calvinists. Maurice, however, was happy to affirm the starker view. Election to life was 'when a certain determinate number of angels ... and men ... are predestined to the praise of the glory of God's grace' (p. 63). The idea that God is responsible for sin is rejected firmly. The fact that he allows sin does not mean that he is its cause. Sin is, however, a stark reality which is dealt with through the Father's election of the Son to take human corruption upon himself on the cross. For those who had experienced the blessings of salvation, the truth of the doctrine was the cause of ceaseless praise: 'For all who are godly, the consideration of predestination and election in Christ is full of sweet, pleasant and unspeakable comfort' (p. 69).

Apart from the sections on the decree and the covenant of grace, most of the chapters are succinct, straightforward and replete with appropriate scriptural references. After treating the outworking of election in creation and providence, the volume expounds the creation of

Adam both as the first man and the covenant head of all of humankind:
'all mankind were seminally in him' (p. 108); the covenant of works; the
doctrine of the fall; the reality of sin, its propagation and consequences:
'Original sin is not a matter of merely following Adam as the Pelagians
vainly believe, but it is the corruption deep within the nature of every
man' (p. 110). Adam had been bound by the covenant of works whereas
'the covenant of grace was made with Jesus Christ as the second Adam,
and in him the elect as his seed' (p. 124). However universal the extent of
the fall, redemption in Christ does not include everyone. To the question
as to whether Christ died for all, the answer is unequivocal: 'No; none
but those who, of his sheer good pleasure, have been elected to eternal
life' (p. 124). This, in turn, leads to chapters on the nature of Christ; his
incarnation; the threefold office of prophet, priest and king; his passion
and exaltation; the application of redemption through the work of the
Holy Spirit; a rich if short exposition (in chapter twenty-eight) of
the believer's union with Christ; effective calling; justification; adoption;
sanctification and glorification. The undergirding truth is that of the
divine sovereignty and its concomitant, the absolute bondage of the human
will: 'The condition of man since the fall is not only so impotent but his
depraved nature is so obstinately contrary to God that he will not nor
cannot prepare his heart to faith and calling upon God' (p. 207). Yet the
consolation of the godly is that their very godliness is proof that election has been effective in their lives. 'They who have been elected and
accepted in the Beloved, effectually called, justified and sanctified by his
Spirit, can neither totally nor finally fall away from a state of grace but
shall certainly persevere to the end and be saved' (p. 258).

The preaching of the gospel and the application of the Word

Whether High or moderate, the unambiguous theological standpoint
of orthodox Welsh Dissenters, Baptists as well as Congregationalists,
during the first three decades of the century was Calvinism. For them
God's sovereign grace in election was the only reality powerful enough
to raise sinners from the dead. 'We see here for whom Christ suffered',
reasoned John Jenkins, Baptist minister at Rhydwilym, in 1721.

> It was for his elect, those given him by the Father in the eternal cov-
> enant. He did not suffer for all men, for He says to some, 'You are not of
> my flock, nor do you recognize my voice.' It was on behalf of the elect
> that Christ suffered, the elect alone.[49]

His colleague Enoch Francis, foremost Welsh Baptist preacher of his generation, also proclaimed the absolute sovereignty of God in salvation. 'The Lord', he maintained, 'gives grace only to those whom he wills, in the way he wills, when he wills'.[50] 'Election', he stated in a treatise of 1733, 'is that part of God's immutable, eternal and all-wise decree, that he, of his free grace and immeasurable love, fore-ordained a certain number of men through Christ to eternal salvation'.[51] Yet this did not hamper evangelism even among the High Calvinists, as the only way for hearers to know whether they were among the elect was by their being afforded the opportunity to respond to the gospel call. Preaching from the Rhydwilym pulpit in 1722, this time on the apostle Paul's exhortation to the Ephesians to rise from their slumber, John Jenkins cried:

> Have we been raised with Christ or have we not? If we have, have you heard his voice calling unto you? 'What', says someone, 'How could we hear his voice?' Did you not hear him calling unto you through his Word and Spirit: 'Yes!', says one, 'we heard him speak to some, but we know not how to reply, whether He addressed us or not'. Do you not know that Lazarus, when he heard the voice bidding him to come hither, he came forth. The Lord speaks thus to all whom He resurrects with Christ.[52]

In order to respond effectively to such a message, the gospel first of all needed to be preached. 'Among the many responsibilities that God has laid upon men through the gospel', wrote Howel Powel in an essay of 1709, 'there is none more profitable than heeding the preaching of his Word'.[53] Although he complained that there were all too many among the congregations who were not sufficiently attentive to their ministers, nevertheless faith came through hearing and salvation through the proclamation of the Word: 'The pastor's office is to preach, and what is required of the flock is that they listen.'[54] Those who did not listen could hardly blame the ministers if their refusal laid within themselves. 'When we find the preaching of the Word unprofitable', wrote Benjamin Meredith, Baptist minister at Llanwenarth, Monmouthshire, in 1721, 'we should test ourselves to discover what fault lies within us, preventing God from blessing us with his presence'.[55] The evidence, however, among Dissenters at this time, is that preaching was, on the whole, both arresting and effective. Enoch Francis, for one, was 'extremely gifted in winning hearers, being well received everywhere'.[56] In a rousing sermon on Ephesians 5:14, 'Awake, O sleeper, and arise from the dead', his stress on his listeners' inability to rise of themselves is never used as an excuse for unbelief. The fact of spiritual death is squarely faced: 'The man who is dead in his sin ... is like a corpse, he knows nothing of his state.' He must first be touched by God: 'When the Lord ... in his glorious salvation says, as he did to Lazarus, "Come forth", so he who is spiritually dead must first hear the call of Christ before he is made alive.' It was the sinner's duty to obey the call. 'Let us make sure that we are awake and not asleep', he urged.[57] Jacob Rees, Baptist minister at Pen-y-fai, Glamorgan, in a sermon on Hebrews 10:22, issued a similar appeal. 'What prevents a man from turning to God?' he asked. 'A fear of losing the respect and friendship of carnal friends when starting out on the road to religion?' This, he claimed, was a small price to pay for eternal salvation: 'Remember that the ministers of the gospel are ready to do all they can to assist you; remember that the Spirit of God is yet at work.'[58] It was the Holy Spirit, active through the preaching of the gospel, which applied the benefits of Christ's atoning sacrifice to the elect. 'Christ's death is sufficient to save all mankind', claimed Francis, 'though it is only effective for the elect; and the reason that it is only effective for them is due to the particular work of God's Spirit within'.[59] For preachers and listeners alike, God's Spirit was active in the proclamation of the Word: 'The promise of salvation is for all who believe in the Son and who walk in his ways. There is no discrimination; God's revealed will is man's only rule.'[60]

The call to conversion, whether through pulpit appeals or from the written page, continued to be made. Some preachers were stern, others were more alluring. John Jenkins warned his Rhydwilym congregation that the Day of Judgement would find out those 'hypocrites who only appear to be godly yet who remain within the church'.[61] Within a few months he was constrained to repeat his warning: 'You are not a step nearer by being baptized in water if you have not first received grace from God for your souls.'[62] 'Sin', exclaimed Abel Francis, cousin of Enoch, with admirable rhetoric on a summer's day in 1731,

> is more acrid than death because it is the sting of death. It is blacker than the devil because it was sin which turned the devil into the devil. It is hotter than hell because it is sin which heats hell's furnaces. Sin is undoubtedly worse than anything imaginable![63]

James Owen's treatise on the goodness and severity of God first issued in 1687, with its lurid and wide-ranging *exemplae* picturing the fate of those upon whom the divine displeasure had descended – atheists, apostates, persecutors, drunkards, sexual deviants and the like – retained its popularity, being re-issued in 1715, 1721 and 1745. By elucidating not only on the temporal (to say nothing of the eternal) misfortunes of the impenitent but also of the remarkable providences, the answered prayers and startling conversions granted to the faithful, his aim was to bring his readers to repentance:

> The purpose of this book is not to cause you to marvel but to engender within you a fear of God's judgements, a love for God's compassion and to urge you to persevere in the truth of the gospel in the day of your distress.[64]

Jenkin Jones, soon to become notorious for introducing Arminianism into Welsh Dissent, was nevertheless earnest in exhorting sinners to flee from the divine wrath and to embrace salvation with all their might. His vivid translations of works by Matthew Meade and Thomas Vincent, two ejected ministers whose nonconformity had cost them dearly after the Restoration, show that he was not squeamish in reminding his readers of the consequences of sin. To be formally religious, morally exemplary or even to have had the most sublime spiritual impressions was not enough. Like Agrippa in his response to Paul's pleading in Acts 28, an 'almost Christian' was sure to be damned:

> You who are professors of Christ's gospel, stand back and look on in dismay. If those who have surpassed us in all virtues have yet fallen short of heaven, where does that leave us? If those foolish virgins (in Matthew 25) have professed the gospel faithfully and fruitfully, have gone forward with their profession of faith and walked ever more worthy of it, if these are 'almost Christians', dear God!, what of ourselves?[65]

True Christianity was a matter of deep repentance, sincere faith and above all else costly obedience on the basis of Christ's atoning blood shed for all. His second work, *Dydd y Farn Fawr* ('The Great Day of Judgement'), his version of Thomas Vincent's apocalyptic treatise first published in 1667, was based on the concluding words of the New Testament: 'Surely I am coming quickly, Amen; even so, "Come quickly

Lord Jesus!'" (Revelation 22:20). The doctrine of the Second Coming not only gave hope to the redeemed but struck fear into the unrepentant. Christ would judge in righteousness, and the need was for all to forsake their sins and fall upon his mercy:

> Look for the appearance of the Lord with an *eye of hope* ... let this hope be an anchor fastened within the vail, to stay your sinking hearts in the midst of those fierce storms which so often beat upon you in the world; and look with an *eye of desire* ... long for Christ's appearance, send up your wishes often to heaven. O! when shall we see the heavens opened, and behold our Lord in his glory? When shall we hear the trumpet sound and be gathered by the angels from all the corners of the earth? When shall we put off this dust and corruption and be clothed with robes of immortality? When will the Lord Jesus come down ... and receive us to himself, that where he is there we may be also? Christ has spoken from heaven to earth, 'Surely I come quickly'. Let there be an echo back from earth to heaven: 'Amen, even so come Lord Jesus, come quickly!'[66]

Whether they were frightened into repentance through a vivid fear of the divine righteousness or drawn gently towards Christ through the appeal of grace, the aim was the same. 'Through the preaching of the Word', claimed Enoch Francis, 'the Lord works conversion; through the preaching of the Word souls are cut down from the wild branch of corrupt nature and grafted into the true vine, Jesus Christ'.[67]

By now memories of the post-Restoration oppression were fading, in some cases nearly to extinction. The leaders who came to maturity during the first two decades of the century had been formed by experiences which were significantly different from those of their immediate forebears. They were gifted, conscientious and would become widely influential in their individual spheres. They included (among the Congregationalists): James Lewis (1674–1747), ordained in 1706 at Pencader as successor to William Evans; Philip Pugh (1679–1760), whose long and distinguished ministry in the extensive mid Cardiganshire church from 1709 onwards would have such a salutary effect on Daniel Rowland, curate of Llangeitho and instigator of the Evangelical Revival in Wales; Christmas Samuel (1674–1764), ordained in 1711 to serve the church at Pant-teg, Carmarthenshire; James Davies (d.1760), ordained at Troedrhiwdalar, Breconshire, in 1712 before progressing to Cwm-y-glo, Merthyr Tydfil where he would stand out not only as an apologist for Calvinism but as a consummate evangelist. There were others as well.[68] For the Baptists Enoch Francis (1688–1740), since 1707 preacher and then minister at the Teifi-side church between Carmarthen and Cardiganshire, excelled not only as a pastor but as a missioner: 'His most precious subject', recalled Joshua Thomas, 'was peace and joy through the blood of Christ'.[69] Over in east Glamorgan, Morgan Griffiths (1679–1738), minister at the Hengoed church, was equally revered for pastoral wisdom as for evangelistic zeal: 'His sermons were usually short, ordered, intelligent and most constructive, yet always sweet and acceptable, clear and memorable',[70] while in Monmouthshire, Miles Harry (1700–76), ordained at Blaenau Gwent in 1729, would become 'the outstanding Welsh Baptist minister of his time'.[71]

Yet these men differed from their predecessors. Whereas Stephen Hughes and his pupils had tried, within the bounds of conscience, to do common cause with pious High Churchmen, currently a 'mutual excommunication between two coherent patterns of Christian faith and order' was, whether discernibly or imperceptibly, taking place.[72] During the first quarter of the eighteenth century, the brisk proclivity for preaching and evangelism within the small communities of Protestant Dissent fuelled by varying blends of Calvinist thought, and the concurrent renewal of heart religion and sacramental piety fed by the exertions of the SPCK among their much more numerous Anglican neighbours, were diverging drastically. Each would evolve, into, during and beyond the Evangelical Revival, independently of one another. Not even the modest parish-based Calvinistic renewal of the 1750s in the spirit of Griffith Jones could engender a reconciliation between them. Both would contribute richly and constructively to the development of theology and spirituality in Wales, but they would do so in parallel though very much apart from one another.

Baptismal controversies

In his history of the Baptist Association, Joshua Thomas recounts the meeting convened by the London ministers in September 1689 in order to support 'their brethren in the country who had been so long in the storms and tempests of persecution'.[73] Among the 150 who attended were six from Wales: William Jones and Griffith Howells from the Pembrokeshire church of Rhydwilym; William Pritchard and Christopher Price from Abergavenny in Monmouthshire; and Lewis

Thomas and Francis Giles from Swansea. The most significant result of this convocation was the publishing of a confession of faith, based on the Baptist Confession of 1677, which would become the normative standard of belief among the English Particular Baptists into the nineteenth century and, in some cases, well beyond.[74] Echoing both the Westminster Confession (1647) and the Congregational Declaration of Savoy (1657), though substituting the articles on infant baptism for those which reflected Baptist practice of the immersion of believers on the basis of a personal profession of faith, its teaching would encapsulate the essence of Welsh Baptist orthodoxy for generations to come.[75]

There is no doubt that even during the post-1662 repression, the one Baptist church which not only held its own but increased in strength and membership was 'the famous and excellent church of Rhydwilym',[76] established in 1668 'in the very teeth of the penal code'.[77] Constantly active even during the Restoration years, after the Toleration Act it redoubled its evangelistic efforts and soon baptisms administered by its ministers, John Jenkins, George John and Thomas David Rees, were occurring in profusion.[78] As it transpired evangelistic zeal turned into inter-Dissenting proselytization, and tensions arose as to who should be the correct subjects of baptism, whether infants or believers, and how the rite should be administered, through sprinkling or total immersion. Following much heart-searching, dispute and deliberation, a meeting was arranged at Pen-y-lan near the Frenni Fawr in Pembrokeshire sometime in 1692, and two preachers, John Thomas, Congregational minister at Llechryd and a convinced paedo-baptist,[79] and John Jenkins, the Rhydwilym pastor, were chosen to debate the matter. Thomas, somewhat to the surprise of his supporters, took as his text Mark 16:18, Christ's commission to evangelize and baptize; they thought that he would have been better served by preaching on the concept of family solidarity according to the precepts of covenant theology. He was followed the next day by Jenkins who expounded the same text. Whereas the earlier debates had been inconclusive, many were won over by Jenkins's reasoning, and were soon baptized by immersion and joined the Rhydwilym church. The principal convert was John Phillips, previously a member at Llechryd, whose home at Cil-cam in the parish of Eglwys-wen would become the meeting place of a new Baptist cause, Cilfowyr, established in 1704 with an initial membership of sixty-eight. The Congregationalists, plainly disconcerted by this move, called upon their most learned theologian, the redoubtable Samuel Jones, head of

the academy at Brynllywarch, Glamorgan, to issue an apologia for infant
baptism. Now in his mid-sixties and irenic by nature,[80] Jones excused
himself and transferred the task to perhaps his most able pupil, the by
now equally formidable James Owen, who was happy to take up the
cudgels to defend the Reformed faith against Baptist innovations: 'It is
probably fair to say that there existed in late seventeenth-century Wales
no more able an advocate nor more learned a disputant than Owen.'[81]

Bedydd Plant o'r Nefoedd, neu Draethawd am Natur a Diben Bedydd
('Infant Baptism from Heaven, or an Essay on the Nature and Purpose
of Infant Baptism') (1693), twenty-one chapters and over two hundred
pages in length, was the first ever detailed assessment of the doctrine of
baptism in Welsh. For its author, there was a deep continuity between
the two testaments, and what was true of the nation of Israel in the
Old was applied to the Christian church in the New. As Abraham,
father of the faithful, was never envisaged apart from his children,
God's call affirmed family solidarity: 'God made this covenant of grace
with Abraham and his seed, that is, with his children.'[82] What began with
Abraham, and Noah before him, was true of those who came after them:
'The Jews knew that they were the children of promise, and that promise
extended to their offspring' (p. 44). The sign of the covenant was circumcision, made on all males eight days after their birth, while the Christian
rite which paralleled this was baptism though for females as well as for
males: 'Circumcision signified rebirth, namely the circumcision of the
heart. Not that all who were circumcised would be born again, but God,
in his own time, would bless his ordinance in order to regenerate his
elect according to his promise' (pp. 50–1). Not only did baptism mark
out the children of the Christian faithful as being within the covenant,
but it was the sign which distinguished between Christians, Jews and
those who had been born into families of no faith at all:

> In the same way baptism is a sign of the differentiation between the
> church, the Jews and the unbelieving pagans ... God had formerly put
> them under the mark of his ownership. Where, therefore, are they now?
> If they are the Lord's, let him put his mark upon them still, to show that
> they have been separated from unbelievers. (pp. 58–9)

Holiness meant separation, and baptism was the external sign of the
community that had been called apart or sanctified to the Lord. Whereas
the children of the faithful were expected, in the years of discretion, to

make Christianity their own by personal repentance and an individual act of faith, they were nevertheless uniquely advantaged by being included within God's covenantal design. Christ had, after all, blessed the little children, and all believers would have to become like little children in order to enter the kingdom of God. Neither was there any reason why God could not regenerate children in their infancy. Many children of the promise could not recall a time when they did not believe in Christ: 'It is an easy thing for God to endow a child with holiness' (p. 106). The rite of infant baptism and the mystery of election were tightly entwined:

> All of the children of the faithful are within the bonds of the promise, though we know that God will bestow his grace upon the elect alone, often when they are still children. As to who will be among the elect, it is for God to decide, though it is his will that we baptize all into the promise … It is enough to know that God's promise belongs to the children of the faithful, and that they are members of his visible church through which the line of election customarily runs. (p. 112)

As well as reasoning doctrinally on the basis of covenant thought, Owen was adamant that the baptism of infants accorded with the letter of scripture. Although many New Testament converts were baptized as believers, the Book of Acts described family baptisms such as that of the Philippian gaoler, when not only the paterfamilias but his dependents were baptized as well: 'God's way from the beginning was to accept whole families into the covenant, the children being accepted along with their parents, so it was in the New Testament and so it remains' (p. 134). However, as a Presbyterian he was also very comfortable with the concept of venerable tradition not apart from but in harmony with the scriptural norm. Like his nephew Jeremy in his later altercation with Matthias Maurice, James is not averse to making a show of his erudition. Irenaeus, Tertullian, Cyprian and Calvin are all marshalled in Latin (as are the Greeks Origen, Chrysostom and Gregory Nazianzus, in Latin as well!), in order to show that the primitive and the Reformation church affirmed catholic baptism, a rite which had been richly blessed throughout the centuries: 'The Lord has blessed the baptism of infants as a means of continuing true religion and perpetuating the Christian church from the days of the apostles to our own' (p. 165). As for the mode of baptism, sprinkling or affusion must have been the scriptural way. Biblical Palestine was barren. Water was at a premium. Even the Jordan was less a river than a stream. John the Baptist would not have immersed his converts surely, while the household baptisms in the Book of Acts hardly required a large amount of water? And was not going into water over one's head in winter life-threatening and potentially a breach of the sixth commandment, 'Thou shalt not kill'?, while baptizing females naked or near-naked was incontrovertibly a breach of the seventh commandment, 'Thou shalt not commit adultery'!

Owen became most animated, however, when discussing the concept of re-baptism. Both theologically and according to church practice, baptism is inherently unrepeatable. 'Baptism', he claims, 'is God's holy ordinance which can only be administered once' (p. 176). To reject this is to rebel against the Lord: 'Those who refuse to believe in the plenitude of the covenant of grace and children's right to be sealed by that covenant, they sin against the divine promise, God's command and a myriad of scriptural examples' (p. 177). For Owen ecclesiology was no small matter. Regular church order was essential to Dissenting faith. Like all his fellow Congregationalists, James Owen was a High Churchman in the Older Dissenting mode. The sacraments, whether baptism of the Lord's Supper, were not to be downplayed, discarded or abused. True salvation and sound churchmanship went hand in hand. For a baptized person who had been brought up piously within the covenant of grace to reject his or her original baptism in order to be re-baptized was a grave sin. It denoted spiritual pride and was a blow against catholic order within the church. Re-baptism was inherently schismatic:

> By allowing yourself to be re-baptized, you cut yourself off not only from this congregation but from the catholic church in all lands and ages on the face of the earth, the church that has been purified through water and the Word, and which endures in the unity of baptismal faith. (pp. 183–4)

Such was the Oswestry scholar-minister's apologia for infant baptism.

A year later, whether in response to Owen's volume or not, the first ever Welsh-language treatise on believer's baptism appeared, namely *Bedydd gwedi i amlygu yn eglir ag yn fyddlon [sic] yn ôl Gair Duw* ('Baptism elucidated clearly and faithfully according to God's Word'), a rather poor translation of the very popular *Baptism Discovered Plainly and Faithfully according to the Word of God* (1672) by John Norcott, former minister of the Particular Baptist church at Wapping.[83] There is no detail of the translator or what occasioned its publication, though the presence of a Welsh Baptist delegation at the London conference of 1689 shows that there were links between the movement and their co-religionists in the metropolis at the time. It is a short work of fifty pages or so, explanatory rather than polemical in tone, setting out reasons for the Baptist position. Unlike Owen's work it is not weightily theological but biblical and plain. The reason why Christians should seek baptism is, quite simply, because Jesus was baptized by John in the Jordan. Those who sought John's baptism were old enough to know what they were doing, having come of their own volition, while the very fact that they were in a river suggested that they would have been immersed. Indeed the Greek word *baptizō* meant 'to be immersed', while Paul's emphasis in Romans and Colossians on being buried and resurrected with Christ shows immersion to have been essential in the New Testament rite: 'If there be not a burial under water to show Christ's burial, the meaning of the ordinance is lost.'[84] As well as patterning their lives on Christ's example, the essence of Christian baptism is to show forth unity between believers and their Lord in his death and resurrection: 'As the servant puts on his master's clothes to show that he is in his service, so in baptism we put on the raiment of the Lord; he clothes us from top to toe.'[85] This is what baptism was all about.

Marred as it was (in the Welsh version) by an atrocious prose style, the great virtue of the book was its brevity and its conceptual clarity. Rather than engaging in complex doctrinal debate, it set forth a simple, New Testament rationale for believer's baptism. Had the Welsh been better, it would probably have become an effective means of propagating the Baptist faith in late seventeenth- and eighteenth-century Wales. The magisterial response to James Owen, however, came two years later with Benjamin Keach's *Goleuni gwedi torri allan Ynghymru, gan ymlid ymmaith dywyllwch* ('Light broken forth in Wales, dispelling darkness'). If Norcott's work was succinct and peaceable, Keach's tome of 350 small-print pages was prolix and pugnacious. Infant baptism, he claimed, 'sprang from the anti-Christ's apostasy',[86] while his fellow Baptists were warned 'not to be deceived with a little filthy dross rather than the refined gold of Christ Jesus, nor allow your Lord's pure wine to be mixed with the stagnant water of a malodorous pool' (p. xxvi).[87] The gloves were off and fighting had already begun.

Benjamin Keach (1640–1704), a self-taught preacher who had been arrested and pilloried during the post-Restoration oppression

for refusing to renounce his millenarian views, had been ordained as
a General or Arminian Baptist minister in London in 1669 but soon,
under the influence of the Particular Baptist leaders William Kiffin and
Hanserd Knollys, came to espouse Calvinist views and in 1672 founded
a Particular Baptist church at Horsleydown, Southwark.[88] A prolific
author and hot controversialist who crossed swords with Quakers,
Anglicans, Presbyterians, Congregationalists and not infrequently with
his fellow Baptists as well, he was nonetheless highly esteemed within
the Calvinistic Baptist fraternity and was among the convenors of the
London convention of 1689 and signatories of its Confession of Faith. It
was through this link, possibly facilitated by Robert Morgan, one of the
joint-ministers of the Baptist church in Swansea and an acquaintance of
his, that he was prevailed upon to defend the Welsh brethren.[89] Before
this could be done Owen's volume had to be translated into English
while his reply had then to be turned back into Welsh. This, no doubt,
was why it did not appear until 1696 when it was accompanied also by
Keach's original English version.[90]

The substance of the work is in the twenty-five exhaustive chapters
which explore the rite and the theology of baptism from all conceivable angles but his response to Owen's treatise is in the twenty-five
page introduction. As a Calvinist Keach rejected neither the doctrine
of election nor the covenantal scheme, but he did reject the deductions
that the paedo-baptists had drawn from them: 'That the children of the
faithful, merely by being the children of the faithful, should be within
the covenant of grace we vehemently deny' (p. ii). God is a God of righteousness and as such chooses according to his sovereign will. There are
no special privileges accorded to the children of believers: 'Can anybody
seriously think that the promise is limited to the carnal seed of believers?' (p. ii), he asked. Due to the effect and prevalence of original sin
and the mysterious workings of the electing God, it was just as likely
that the children of believers would be among the damned as those who
had never been raised in a Christian home. If Paul is to be believed in
Ephesians 2, by nature even the children of the faithful are the children
of wrath. They could just as well be of the seed of the serpent as the
seed of the woman in Genesis 3. There is no basis to believe that election runs in line with any spurious promise made within the covenant
of grace: 'What doctrine is this? You out-do all the Arminians that I
have ever met!' (p. iv). Faith is a gift granted by the sovereign God to
the elect individual, and in order to practise faith that person needed

to repent and believe: 'A believer's faith justifies and saves only himself, not his children' (p. iv). Christians, however, should take comfort
in the doctrine of election as its stated counterpoint is the preaching
of the gospel to all. Let the gospel be preached and the children exhorted
to turn to Christ in faith: 'Our doctrine cuts off no-one, whether a
believer's child or not, who is within the covenant of salvation. If God
has elected the children of the faithful, they *will* be saved' (p. iv).[91] As for
James Owen and others who so grievously misunderstood and abused
the divine covenants, 'you strive to introduce an external, relative covenant according to the flesh' (p. v).

For Keach a true church was made up of believers alone, entry
therein being made on a credible and experiential profession of faith
sealed by the rite of total immersion in water: 'Neither believers seed
nor unbelievers seed ought to be baptized or allowed membership in the
visible church until they believe in Christ' (p. v). It is not the covenant as
such that gives a person the right to baptism but faith in Christ according to the gospel command. 'We deny', he repeated, 'that our infants are
in the covenant of particularity which God made with Abraham and his
natural seed as such' (p. vi). 'Their true inheritance is by faith, that it
might appear to be of grace and not in circumcision, nor in baptism, but
by faith alone' (p. vii). Whereas the paedo-baptists held to a virtually
uninterrupted continuity between the Old Testament and the New, true
Christianity was based on grace and not on the works righteousness of
the former dispensation. Circumcision was a human rite bound up with
all that had been superseded in the Jewish faith: 'They had the shadow,
we and the believers among our children have the substance; they had
the shell, we have the kernel' (p. vii). The grave mistake of the infant baptizers was that they built their church fellowship on an arm of flesh, the
material reality of an external rite, whereas God's church was spiritual.
Entry was not actually by baptism at all, it was by the internal conviction of faith in the heart. Adult baptism should, however, be undergone
not as being necessary to salvation but as a voluntary act of obedience
to Christ's commission in Matthew 28: 'Fleshly descent during gospel
times signifies nothing at all in the matter of gospel church membership' (p. ix), he claimed. Baptism is a voluntary rite of obedience, not an
external rite that guarantees the divine blessing:

> It would be the will and command of Christ in the New Testament that
> infants should be baptized only if they had that right. But since there is

not the least intimation given in all God's Word that it is his pleasure
they should be baptized, it must be a piece of will-worship to do it. (p. x)

In the background of this aggressive refutation of James Owen's classically Reformed rationale for infant baptism was the concurrent controversy over the works of Tobias Crisp. As a High Calvinist, Keach had no patience with the moderating doctrines of Richard Baxter and Daniel Williams, and had sensed, correctly, that Owen was one with them. What the High Calvinists feared above all else was that religious acts and activities when not directly empowered by the sovereign Spirit of God, would imperil the concept of justification by faith alone. Faith itself, if seen as a human action, was in danger of compromising the truth that salvation was wholly of God. Grace, being the work of God's sovereign will, was unconditional. The idea of a baptismal covenant 'sits only with Baxterian errors and Mr Williams' *new scheme* which renders the covenant of grace conditional according to the covenant of works' (p. xvii). The idea of covenant baptism springs directly from 'this grand Baxterian error' (p. xvii) which implied nothing less than justification by works of the law: 'Mr Baxter and Mr Williams plainly declare that the terms and conditions of the covenant of grace must be performed by such that would be justified' (p. xviii). Jewish religion was a religion of works, and it was plain that the infant baptizers were still under the law: 'Nothing can be clearer than this, that the infant's baptism covenant is of the same nature as the covenant of circumcision, namely a conditional, legal covenant: "Do this and you will live"' (p. xxi). The only baptism that the New Testament prescribed was an external ordinance, the voluntary rite of individual believers immersed of their own volition signifying personal faith and membership of the visible church: 'Christ's baptism only belongs to believers who are renewed, regenerated and have union with Christ and are in a justified state before being baptized' (p. xx). Consequently paedo-baptism was to be rejected outright: 'The nature of their perceived baptismal covenant is quite repugnant to the true baptismal covenant instituted by Christ, and is therefore pernicious' (p. xxi). As well as challenging James Owen by name, Keach called upon all Welsh Congregationalists: 'May it not be worth your most serious thoughts to consider how the doctrine of infant baptism is a direct violation of the holy precepts of our blessed Saviour' (p. xvii).

It would be six years later when James Owen responded to Keach's treatise, but his 1702 volume, *Ychwaneg o eglurhad am fedydd plant bychain*

('Some further explanation on the baptism of infants') merely traversed the same ground as before, repeated the same doctrinal convictions, warned his opponent of the baleful effects of schism and sectarianism and derided his scholarship. For all his purported erudition, the London author was, in Owen's view, little more than a charlatan and 'the light that broke forth in Wales' was in fact 'jet-black darkness'.[92] As Geraint H. Jenkins pointed out: 'There was ... a strong whiff of social snobbery involved in this literary vendetta.'[93] Socially the Welsh Baptists were less exalted than their neighbouring Congregationalists while they could never match the academic prowess or intellectual self-confidence of those ministers who had been trained in the Presbyterian academies. As for the controversy itself:

> The merits and demerits of paedo-baptism were evidently highly conten-
> tious issues, touching off the very deepest emotions. The whole issue
> could raise irrational fears and correspondingly deep passions, and it
> could force sensible, godly men to lapse from sober comment and rea-
> soned arguments to the level of personal denigration and vendetta.[94]

Yet the Baptist faith, nor the Congregational cause, did not suffer overtly from this altercation. If anything it infused energy into the opposing sides and provided a bevy of arguments, both for and against the rite and its contrasting set of theological criteria, which, in the fullness of time, provided the Welsh Dissenting communities with ample doctrinal ballast.

When the next baptismal controversy occurred, in south-east Wales more than a generation later, both the Baptist and the Congregational churches were in a fairly flourishing state. The champions on each side, Edmund Jones, at that time an un-ordained preacher at the Independent church at Pen-maen, Monmouthshire, and Miles Harry, who would be set apart to assist in the ministry among the Blaenau Gwent Baptists in 1729, could take it for granted that their numerous listeners were well versed in the main points in contention between the rival baptis-mal schemes. 'There was much zeal expended on both sides', recorded Joshua Thomas, 'especially by two young ministers, Mr Miles Harry and Mr Edmund Jones'.[95] The controversy became so heated that a truce was called, at Merthyr Tydfil in 1728, and representatives from both sides signed a document promising to ratchet down the rheto-ric, respect one another's opinions and emphasize what, as evangelical

Dissenters, they held in common: 'There were several ministers present, some concessions made, one forgave the other and agreed in future to aim at the glory of God, the honour of the gospel and the preserving of each other's reputation.'[96] The truce held until 1732 when Fowler Walker, Congregational minister at Abergavenny (and one of the signatories of the peace document) published, in both English and Welsh, his *Defence of Infant Baptism*, based the baptismal clauses of the Westminster Catechism: 'The Reverend Mr James Owen's treatise on infant baptism, in Welsh, and his answer to Mr Keach being very scarce, I was prevailed with', he claimed, somewhat disingenuously one suspects, 'to suffer this little treatise to come abroad'.[97] The volume is, in effect, a precis of Owen's earlier works replete with patristic citations in Latin, biblical terms in Greek and the occasional aspersion on the inability of Baptist apologists to understand the original tongues: 'This we often hear from those who know not the original, and therefore take it upon trust from their learned brethren, the number of which in these parts are very few.'[98] The rejoinder, the short unattributed pamphlet *Remarks on some Reproachful and Scandalous Passages, in a Pamphlet lately published on … Infant Baptism by Mr Fowler Walker* (1732), also issued in both languages,[99] came almost immediately, along with a translation of a tract by Charles Doe, *Rhessymau eglyr pa ham nad taenelliad babanod* (1732) ('Clear reasons why one should not sprinkle infants'), before David Rees, a native of Glamorgan, Baptist minister at Limehouse, London, and like James Owen educated under Samuel Jones at the academy at Brynllywarch, expended 222 pages of solid biblical, doctrinal and historical erudition in contesting Walker's strictures one by one.[100] Unlike Benjamin Keach, few could fault Rees's scholarship or his tone, while his publication brought to an end for the time being the sporadic Welsh Dissenting disputes over baptism.

The significance of these debates was to show that there was considerable liveliness, both practical and doctrinal, in the churches at the time, and that Welsh Dissent, though still very much a minority movement, was energetic, self-confident and bold in asserting its convictions in the public sphere. If it was still disdained by Anglican critics[101] and ignored even by the most pious and dedicated supporters of the SPCK, it underlines the fact that vital Christianity was an undiminished factor in early eighteenth-century Wales. If it would contribute to the vitality of the Evangelical Revival when it broke out in the mid-1730s, it would not be until the 1770s and 1780s, however, that Dissent would begin to be wholly transformed and become massively influential in the future history of Wales.[102]

The Arminian crisis

According to Thomas Rees writing in 1861, all former controversies paled into insignificance in comparison to 'the Great Arminian Controversy' which began in earnest during the late 1720s.[103] This was not because Arminianism would be necessarily inimical to evangelical religion as such, as John Wesley's movement and the 'New Connexion' of English General Baptists would later show, but because this strain of Arminianism was more rationalistic in tone and would lead inexorably to Arianism and, by the beginning of the following century, to a fully blown Unitarianism.[104] 'This unhappy agitation', wrote Rees, 'in the course of a few years, divided the Nonconformist body into two hostile, antagonistic and irreconcilable parties'.[105]

The first to come out in favour of the Arminian system was Jenkin Jones (1700?–42), a preacher at the Pantycreuddyn Independent church in Cardiganshire. He had trained at the Carmarthen Academy under James Perrot (d.1733), a close friend of Jeremy Owen, and although Perrot was never anything less than a moderate Calvinist in the Baxterian mould, during his tenure, 1719–33, the academy would become something of a breeding ground for Arminian ideas.[106] Whether he came to espouse those views during his college years, 1720–2, or after, by then Jones's unease with Calvinism had become public and he was barred from the Pantycreuddyn pulpit by his minister, James Lewis.[107] Having married well, however, he was in a position to build a meeting house, at Llwynrhydowen on his wife's land, and, having gathered a congregation there, he was ordained in 1726. Although excluded from some pulpits, he was still free to preach in sympathetic congregations, and soon Arminian tenets were being openly promoted among the Cardiganshire Independents. His pamphlet *Cyfrif Cywir o'r Pechod Gwreiddiol* (1729) ('A Correct Account of Original Sin') rejected outright the concepts of unconditional election, particular redemption and the bondage of the will, while a summary of his views, 'that to impute Adam's sin to those who could not possibly have been guilty of it' was cruel and immoral, along with the idea of God holding men and women responsible for the sin of Adam being inherently irrational, was contained, contested and discarded in its slim though ferocious rejoinder, *Cyfrif Cywiraf o'r Pechod Gwreiddiol* (1730) ('The Most Correct Account of Original Sin'), joint-written by James Lewis and Christmas Samuel of Pant-teg.[108] By then such opinions were gaining traction, and individual congregations – Llechryd, Llan-y-bri and Carmarthen; Ciliau Aeron, Cilgwyn and Cae'ronnen – were deciding against the traditional Calvinism, whether moderate or High, in favour of a much more reductionist scheme.

The corrosive effects of Arminianism were next felt in some of the branches of Philip Pugh's extensive mid Cardiganshire church. Timothy Davies, ordained as his assistant in 1737, would become much influenced by the new movement and became especially close to David Lloyd, Jenkin Jones's nephew and successor. Pugh (who refused to attend Lloyd's ordination at Llwynrhydowen in 1745) was a moderate, Presbyterian-leaning Calvinist whose disdain for Hyper-Calvinism, listed in his 'Ten Points against Antinomianism',[109] was offset by his even deeper abhorrence for the new Arminianism:

> I look upon myself as one that stands alone. Many are inclining to what they call the New Scheme, which I am assured is not the way of God. For I see the tendency of it is entirely to set up man rather than the free grace of God.[110]

Spirituality was waning even among his own people, personal religion was growing slack and worldliness was effecting the church's witness. A spirit of rationalism was abroad while the Arminian preachers, he claimed, 'are intent on destroying the faith of the gospel through their cleverly devised fables'.[111] After his death the branches at Ciliau Aeron, Cilgwyn and Cae'r onnen would become Arminian, later Arian, then Unitarian churches.[112]

Further east, after the ordination of David and John Williams to assist David Thomas in the ministry of the Cefnarthen Independent church on the border between Carmarthenshire and Breconshire in 1730, the congregation found itself being taught contradictory truths by the Williamses who were Arminians, and Thomas who held to the old ways. The tensions would become palpable. When Howell Harris, the Methodist revivalist, visited the area to preach in July 1739 he complained that the results were minimal, 'it being a congregation in a sad confusion through Arminianism being brought there'.[113] A year later the Calvinists seceded to worship at Clunpentan, and in 1749 at a newly instituted Calvinistic church at Pentre-tŷ-gwyn, among whose elders were John Williams, father of the Methodist hymn writer William Williams of Pantycelyn.[114] Cefnarthen had originally shared the pastorate with the church at Cwm-y-glo, Merthyr Tydfil. Its minister from 1730 was James Davies, previously of Troedrhiwdalar, who was joined as his assistant two years later by Richard Rees, a student at the Carmarthen Academy. Although the two men worked in harness for some years, Davies's zealous evangelical Calvinism grated with Rees's increasingly rationalistic tenets and in 1747 a section of the church seceded to form the Arminian (later Arian, then Unitarian) church at Cefncoedycymer.[115] Davies, on the other hand, became one of the means whereby Welsh Congregationalism would be increasingly revitalized by the energies of the Evangelical Revival.

It was not among the Independents alone that the reaction against Calvinism would occur. According to the association minutes at Llangloffan, Pembrokeshire, in 1729, 'Arminian doctrines now gave uneasiness to the Baptists'.[116] The meeting at the Hengoed association a year later 'was uncomfortable. There were very warm debates on general redemption and other articles connected with it.'[117] The Llanwenarth association letter of 1731 'noted … how happy the ancient Britons were till the errors of Pelagius and Arminius came in like a flood'.[118] At Blaenau Gwent in 1732, 'joy was expressed because the churches did strive together against errors, excluding those who extended redemption beyond election'.[119] The dispute was led in the south-west by Abel Francis, cousin of the Calvinist minister Enoch Francis, a person of 'restless and disputatious turn and of considerable ability', and preaching assistant in the Teifi-side church.[120] In a sermon delivered in mid-1732, he listed his recently adopted convictions concerning free will, election as a divine response to human striving, Christ's all-encompassing atonement and the possibility of falling from grace: 'One can sin the Holy Spirit away.'[121] These opinions created much consternation in the church, and led Enoch Francis (as we shall see) to set out the Welsh Baptists' mediating position on the truths of salvation. Even this, however, failed to win Abel around, and unable to sway his fellow members, 'about 1736 [he] went gradually off to those paedo-baptists, who were with him for general redemption'.[122]

These disputes failed to split any of the west Wales churches, but things did not go so smoothly in the east. The 'warm debates' recorded at the association in 1730 found a focus in the deliberations of Charles Winter (1700–73), assistant minister at the Hengoed church in

Glamorgan, variously described as 'a pious and intelligent man whose disposition was not quarrelsome', a man 'amiable and worthy ... greatly beloved by his people and much esteemed by his neighbours', and 'a good and inoffensive man'.[123] He had shown independence of mind early by choosing not to seek training at the Bristol Baptist College but under James Perrot at Carmarthen. 'Seek and you shall find, says Christ', he is reported to have said: 'Do not seek in case you find, says prejudice.'[124] His name had been connected with the move against Calvinism since 1730, at least. It was during that year's meeting of the association held at his home church that he had been challenged for holding 'that man can be saved by his own strength without God's grace'. His rejection of the accusation was total: 'I have always held that man has nothing except that given him through the grace of God.'[125] This rejoinder, however, was not sufficient to allay the fears of his fellow members, for instead of electing him pastor following the death of Morgan Griffiths in 1738, he was passed over in favour of Griffith Jones, a Calvinist from Pen-y-fai. Nevertheless, he retained his status as assistant, and for ten years, until Jones's emigration to Pennsylvania,[126] the two men worked together harmoniously. But when it became apparent in 1749 that the church was intent on passing him over a second time, his disappointment gave way to contention. According to Miles Harry he became 'more astringent in his spirit and harsher in his comments concerning those who took a differing view'.[127] 'The greatest and most common fear in the world', he asserted, 'is the fear of truth. Most men flee from it, but they do so at their peril.'[128] Winter was no longer willing to flee; the time had come to make an issue of his Arminianism. After having refused to moderate his views, he, and two dozen of his fellow members, were excommunicated. They established a General Baptist church at Craig-y-fargod, not far from Merthyr Tydfil, electing Charles Winter their pastor. This too, years later, would become Unitarian. He ministered there until his death, aged seventy-three, in April 1773.

Welsh Baptist preachers, for the most part, did not have the academy training which the Congregationalists had maintained during and beyond the Restoration. 'It is the general opinion of the Baptists in Wales', wrote Joshua Thomas, 'that grace and ministerial abilities are gifts from God, and that God, as in the days of the apostles, calls both learned and unlearned men to fulfil this office'.[129] That being the case, the unlearned did not always possess the background or doctrinal finesse to decide on the finer points of the Calvinism to which they instinctively (and confessionally) held. Following the Crisp controversy, for instance, some found it easier to embrace the more unambiguous High Calvinist scheme than to contend for the nuances of the moderate brand. In 1716 Philip John, a preaching assistant in the Rhydwilym church, contended that 'it is neither lawful nor correct for the people to pray for forgiveness of sins, but to pray to God to convince them that their sins had been forgiven since eternity',[130] a reference to the concept of eternal justification which, like antinomianism, had been one of the sticking points between High and moderate Calvinism. It was the prevalence of High Calvinism and its perceived immoderation, harshness and lack of balance which contributed to the Arminian backlash among Congregationalists and Baptists alike. 'Antinomianism has frequently been preached by the ... theologically untrained', stated Geoffrey F. Nuttall, though he made the equally irrefutable point that whereas antinomianism may be Calvinism's peril, antinomianism was *not* Calvinism.[131] The one leader who was chosen to delineate the Baptist position on these matters was Enoch Francis.

For Francis the Calvinistic convictions concerning the divine sovereignty, election and the bondage of the human will were incontrovertibly true, but the gospel system was, nevertheless, sufficiently open to allow leeway in understanding and application. His 1733 treatise *Gair yn ei Bryd, neu Ychydig o Eglurhad ar Ddirgeledigaethau ... yr Ysgrythur am Arfaeth Duw* ('A Word in Season, or Some Explanation on the Scriptural Mysteries concerning God's Decree') attempted 'in his mild and affectionate way', to balance the ideas of God's sovereignty with the call for sinners freely to repent and turn, and the concept of a limited atonement or Christ's death in place of the elect, with the seemingly obvious scriptural truth that Christ had died to save all mankind.[132] One of the implications of this was that election, while in no sense denied, was presented in a more guarded, less dogmatic, manner. Metaphysical theorizing was kept to a minimum. The discrepancy between God's general desire for repentance and the fact that many seemed to reject the gospel (a rejection which, according to the logic of Calvinism must also be rooted in God's design) was explained in terms of God's twofold will. God's revealed will was that all men should repent and be saved. That some, perhaps many, were not saved was due to God's secret design:

> Who the elect are and who the reprobate are is part of God's secret counsel and has not yet been revealed. And as his revealed will and not

his secret will has been given us a rule of life, the door of hope is still
held open for all men who, as sinners, come to Christ. (p. 31)

It was no part of the preacher's duty to anticipate God's secret will: 'It
is not for us to look towards the decree of God as a rule of life but to the
word of the gospel' (p. 37). The move, therefore, is to the all-embracing.
The promise of salvation is for all who believe in the Son and who walk
in his ways: 'There is no discrimination; God's revealed will is man's
only rule' (p. 29).

Practically, this involved a shift of emphasis from the divine mechan-
ics of election to human responsibility. Even though Christ's death was
efficient, it seemed, only in the experience of the elect, it was sufficient
to save all of humankind. Because Christ's atonement was sufficient,
because unrepentant sinners would be damned not through God's active
will but because of their own sin, because only God's revealed will was
of practical importance, Francis could say:

The man who does not believe in Christ but who rejects him, ignoring
all offers of grace and mercy to the end, there is no decree strong enough
to save him. But he who believes in Christ and who lives according to
the holy rules of the gospel remaining faithful to the end ... there is no
decree which will ever prevent him from enjoying eternal blessedness.
(p. 30)

It was not the decrees which should be of experiential importance
to Welsh Baptist preachers but their hearers' personal response. In
Francis's view, perdition should not be thought of as a positive act
of God's will. In other words, there was no 'double predestination':
'According to God's secret council some are left to choose their own
way, and God does not work as strongly in them as in others. He is
obliged to no-one' (p. 58). The obvious desire here was to scotch the
implication that God is, in any way, the author of sin. 'Neither does the
Apostle say', he continued, '"Jacob I have loved and Esau I have hated"
before they ever committed good or evil' (p. 29). Election manifested
itself not independently of individuals' actions in history but in tandem
with them. Men and women remained moral beings: they had not been
eternally conditioned to reprobation apart from their actions in history.
Were they to be damned, the fault would be their own. So Francis could
implore his Rhydwilym hearers in 1722 to secure their own salvation:

'The man who rejects Christ is the most pitiful of all men.' It was they who rejected Christ, not Christ them: 'Return to him for you have forsaken the best place of all.'[133]

Although this restrained if manifestly evangelistic Calvinism was not devoid of theological ambiguities and would retain its ability to cause offence,[134] by 1745 it had established itself as the received orthodoxy among the Welsh Baptists. Its public victory was acclaimed following the two-day conference near Llandysul Bridge in that year when five preachers were charged with expounding 'the Five Points': Timothy Thomas, Aberduar, on Original Sin; Evan Thomas, Moleston, on Unconditional Election; Morgan Harry, Blaenau Gwent, on Limited Atonement; Thomas Edwards of Llanwenarth on Effectual Calling; and David Thomas, Cilfowyr, on the Perseverance of the Saints. 'Thereafter', noted Joshua Thomas, 'controversy on these matters came to an end'.[135] The scheme provided the doctrinal motivation for vigorous gospel preaching, and especially when touched by the spirit of the Evangelical Revival, it would prove a potent means in the extension of Dissent. It paralleled the non-speculative Calvinism championed among the Congregationalists by Jeremy Owen, Philip Pugh, James Davies and Edmund Jones, and cohered with the doctrinal stance that flourished at the Bristol Baptist College from the mid-1720s on:

> From the very beginning Particular Baptists had been evangelical in their Calvinism ... At the end of the [seventeenth] century this Evangelical Calvinism still gripped the minds and hearts of many Particular Baptists ... and under the leadership of [its president] Bernard Foskett in the next century Evangelical Calvinism was vigorously continued by those who came into contact with him and the students he trained at the Bristol Academy.[136]

The Bristol College would become a magnet for young Welshmen preparing for ministry, and half of the seventy or so who trained during the course of Foskett's time as president, 1720 to 1758, would be Welsh.[137] The undisputed link between Wales, Foskett, and the Baptist Western Association to which the Bristol College belonged, would be Miles Harry.[138] He was also so enamoured with this version of Calvinism that when Alvery Jackson, the Yorkshire minister issued his treatise *The Question Answered* (1752) on the theme, he could not contain himself: 'Mr Harry was so zealous for inviting sinners to Christ, and was so interested in Mr Jackson's book ... that he undertook a long journey to meet its author.'[139] In fact, 'the evangelical understanding of Calvinism proved to be the most powerful force in the development of Miles Harry as a Baptist leader in Wales'.[140] But it was not a novelty; it was the shared inheritance of early eighteenth-century Welsh Baptists and found its most effective exponents in Enoch Francis, Morgan Griffiths as well as Harry himself. On the eve of the Revival, the bulk of Welsh Dissenting ministers shared the same open, missionary and expansive Calvinist faith.

Dissenting spirituality on the eve of the Evangelical Revival

In his lyrical description of New Testament ecclesiology in *Social Religion Exemplify'd* (1737), Matthias Maurice applied the scriptural ideal to the current life of the Independent cause:

> The churches or congregations were many, and the bishops were as many, for every particular church had its bishop or pastor. Many of them might be small, their outward appearance mean, but their real glory did lie in this, that God in Christ was their glory in the midst of them.[141]

If zeal for purity of doctrine was intended to ensure the spiritual health of church members and discipline their moral uprightness, the corporate nature of Dissent's congregational polity was designed to engender Christian fellowship. This was true for both the Congregationalists and the Baptists. The Confession of Faith of the Rhydwilym church confined membership to those 'that did receive and profess the doctrine of the gospel, were converted and called to be saints', and 'separated from the world both its sins and services to live accordingly to the will of God'.[142] After having been 'called to be saints' and having 'separated from the world', they were expected to be 'united and given up to the Lord and to one another to live according to the will of God in all things'.[143] The key difference between Baptist polity and that of the Independents was in the matter of the subject and mode of baptism, otherwise they were as one. As for the Independents: 'How beautiful the order of Congregational churches', rhapsodized Maurice.

> It answers ... the blessed rule in the written Word, it is in everything suited to promise edification, fixes a proper duty upon every member, encourages the greatest diligence and leads to the greatest humility ...

Of all the forms of church government and order pleaded for in the world, this alone is fitted to subsist and flourish under persecution. Where all other forms must dwindle and vanish … this discovers itself to be alone of divine institution.[144]

Evidence shows that baptisms, whether that of infants in the Congregational churches or of believers among the Baptists, occurred regularly, sometimes in profusion, during these years. Philip Pugh was recorded as having baptized 680 during his long ministry in the mid Cardiganshire church between 1709 and 1760, and these were not the only ones as his assistants would regularly administer the sacrament as well.[145] On reaching the years of discretion and having satisfied the churches of their spiritual competence, many of these were received into full membership. Not that this occurred automatically. Although Evan Thomas Evan had appeared before the congregation at the Mynydd Bach church in February 1745, 'we delayed to receive him', records the church book, 'until we would endeavour to catechize him better and bring him to more knowledge in the fundamentals or principles of religion'.[146] The same pattern of accepting into membership only those who were deemed competent, is to be found among the other Congregational churches at the time.[147] For those who were deemed worthy however, their reception was a solemn and memorable occasion. 'The fixed day came', recounted Matthias Maurice, 'they looked upon it as the greatest day of their lives, the day of their public espousals'.[148] Having made a public profession of faith, related the stages of their spiritual journey and affirmed the church covenant, the minister would pray over them, offer them the right hand of fellowship and receive them into membership, 'and at the conclusion they all said "Amen"'.[149] The same was true among the Baptists, though immersion preceding church membership was deemed essential. 'Christ suffered [by being buried] in the depths of the earth and the Christian in the depths of God's grace', stated John Jenkins, 'and only those who have been buried in grace are suitable to be buried in water, they alone'.[150]

Often this entry into membership occurred not only in the context of Christian nurture and the regular gospel preaching of the churches, but following local revivals. These occurred among the Baptists at Llanwenarth in 1719,[151] at Hengoed and Blaenau Gwent between 1725 and 1727,[152] and at Abertillery a year later where it had been kindled 'in that neighbourhood by means of the popular preaching of Mr Enoch

Francis and Mr Morgan Griffiths'.[153] The same pattern was visible in
west and mid Wales: at Newcastle Emlyn in 1735,[154] and at Cilfowyr,[155]
Rhydwilym[156] and Pentre,[157] all between 1740 and 1741. A similar pattern was apparent among the Congregationalists: there were revivals at
Pen-maen, Monmouthshire in 1720,[158] at Capel-Issac, Carmarthenshire,
in 1735,[159] while scores of converts were added to some of Philip Pugh's
branch churches in Cardiganshire annually between 1729 and 1734, thus
pre-dating the conversion of both Howell Harris and Daniel Rowland.[160]
Of the generation of ministers who came to the fore at the time – the
Congregationalists Edmund Jones (1702–93) who would be ordained at
Pen-maen in 1734, Lewis Rees (1710–93), later to serve at Llanbryn-mair
and Tirdwncyn following his ordination at Blaen-gwrach in 1738, and
the Baptist Timothy Thomas (1720–68) of Aberduar – Thomas Rees,
the nineteenth-century historian of Nonconformity, would claim:

> These young ministers were revivalists in the fullest sense of the term.
> A religious awakening had been actually commenced by their instrumen-
> tality as early as the year 1730, which was extending year after year, so
> that Mr Howell Harris and his coadjutors had only to blow into a flame
> the fire already kindled.[161]

The evidence, therefore, is that pre-Revival Welsh Dissent was
in good heart and in a healthy state: 'The Older Dissenting churches
were upright, compact, disciplined societies. They produced discerning,
enlightened theologians and carefully self-disciplined, deeply devotional
members.'[162] Evangelism remained a priority, the gospel was being
preached, there was a consensus (among the Calvinists at least) as to
what constituted sound doctrine, the youth was being nurtured in the
faith, gospel discipline was being applied, church membership was growing while spiritual commitment was often bolstered through localized
awakenings. Yet this may not have been the whole truth.

In recounting the state of religion in Wales before the advent of
the Evangelical Revival, the picture painted by the Methodist William
Williams, who had been brought up as a Congregationalist, was unre-
mittingly bleak: 'God had for long years become unknown throughout
the land', he claimed, 'the Spirit of the Lord had departed from whole
congregations, ministers could do nothing but preach to the stones'.[163]
Spiritual deadness, worldliness, barren controversies, self-regard and
a host of other woes had descended like locusts, destroying all before

them. Religious professors had become cynical, materialistic and self-serving: 'Animosity, malice and bigotry reigned; throughout the churches it was night, night, night! Although there were many trumpets, some of which were golden, from Holyhead to Cardiff, virtually no-one paid them heed.'[164] Whether the fruit of post-Revival hyperbole or not, something must have caused Williams's assessment to have been so severe. There were others who could hardly have been accused of anti-Dissenting exaggeration, who knew that, to a certain extent at least, things were amiss. 'There have been in the churches', lamented John Harry, Baptist pastor at Blaenau Gwent, 'and among Aaron's seed many spiritual lepers',[165] while Enoch Francis counselled his fellow ministers to 'take the utmost care to plant no-one in Christ's vineyard who has not first been implanted into Christ'.[166] Nominal commitment and spiritual hypocrisy were constant threats to the churches' health. Despite receiving scores into membership in the 1730s, Philip Pugh had bemoaned the fact that spirituality was waning, personal religion was growing slack and worldliness was affecting the church's witness. 'Among my own people', he confessed, 'how few are there that are serious Christians ... Most of them are in heart ... Arminians and formalists',[167] while Edmund Jones complained bitterly in 1741 of 'the lukewarmness and worldliness of Dissenters'.[168] It was Jeremy Owen, however, in the most literary accomplished treatise of the whole period, whose critique was the most acute. In calling for support for the Congregational ministry, he bewailed the fact that 'iniquity abounds, and that the love of many has waxed cold':

> True and sincere zeal for pure religion, and an ardent love for God's ordinances, have been wholly extinguished ... Since being allowed unbounded freedom, churches, which blossomed in the times of persecution, have declined almost to nothing. Good men, who were once faithful and useful, have been taken from us, while only some of those who have risen to take their place are possessed in any way of the same spirit or form. Few of the progeny of godly parents come up to expectation. They follow not the example that was given them, nor fulfil the prayers that were offered for their souls. Many families who were once renowned for godliness, and gloried in the Christian name, have decayed in such a parlous way. Poisonous weeds now grow where once rose the trees of righteousness. Unbelief has followed on from living faith, cold callousness after the most fervid zeal.[169]

Owen, from his home in Buckinghamshire, may have been reflecting the current malaise of English Dissent as it had been conveyed in Strickland Gough's *Enquiry into the Causes of the Decay of the Dissenting Interest* (1730) and Philip Doddridge's reply, *Free Thoughts on the Most Probable Means of Reviving the Dissenting Interest occasion'd by the Late Enquiry into ... its Decay* (1730),[170] but his heart remained with his compatriots in west Wales and his analysis of their situation may have been equally apt. Few would have believed, had they known, that when a general awakening did arrive, it would begin not in the neat chapels and orderly meeting houses of evangelical Dissent but from within the bounds of an ostensibly compromised Established Church.

The Evangelical Revival

The conversion and early doctrinal views of Howell Harris
On 30 March 1735, Howell Harris, a twenty-one year old Breconshire schoolmaster, listened to his parson exhorting his parish congregation to prepare themselves for Holy Communion the following Sunday:

> And in answering objections which people make against going to it, viz. our being not fit etc., I resolved to go to the Lord's Table the following Sunday being Easter Sunday. And by his saying, 'if you are not fit to come to the Lord's Table, you are not fit to come to church, you are not fit to live, not fit to die', I was convinced, and resolved to leave my outward vanities.[171]

Although conventionally religious and an observant member of the Church of England, Harris's main interests were worldly, though, by heeding the exhortation of Pryce Davies, the vicar of Talgarth, he 'resolved to be more serious and thoughtful' (p. 13). He began to reform his life immediately, and despite being afflicted with a deep sense of unworthiness, he partook of the sacrament, for the first time, on Easter Sunday, 6 April. The next few weeks were ones of introspection and sometimes despair. Avidly reading devotional manuals such as Richard Allestree's *The Whole Duty of Man* (1658) and Brian Duppa's *Holy Rules and Helps to Devotion* (1675), rather than being comforted he felt the divide between true holiness and his own inherent sinfulness was becoming wider day by day: 'I was convinced, that in every branch of my duty to God, to myself and my neighbours, I was guilty and had fallen short' (p. 13). His regime was now strict and unrelenting: prayer, fasting, public worship at every possible opportunity, and self-denial, but with no sense of comfort or relief. What struck him in reading Lewis Bayly's *Practice of Piety* (1611), still in use well over a century after its first publication, was 'that if we go to the sacrament, simply believing in the Lord Jesus Christ, we should receive forgiveness of all our sins' (p. 13). For Bayly, the basis of the sinner's reconciliation with God was that Christ had satisfied the divine justice through his sacrifice on the cross, and that the way to salvation was by faith, a simple trust in him:[172]

> [On] the following Whit Sunday, at the sacrament, May 25th 1735, I went thither, labouring and heavy laden under the guilt and power of my sins ... I was convinced, by the Holy Ghost, that Christ died for me, and that all my sins were laid on him; I was now acquitted at the bar of justice, and in my conscience; this evidenced itself to be true faith, by the peace, joy, watchfulness, hatred to sin, and fear of offending God, that followed it. (p. 14)

Yet even now Harris felt overcome by temptations and fears that his peace of mind would fade, that he would relapse into unbelief. The confirmation of his conversion experience occurred on 18 June in the church at Llangasty, a few miles from his home, where he was teaching school:

> I felt suddenly my heart melting within me like wax before the fire with love to God my saviour ... then was a cry in my inmost soul, which I was totally unacquainted with before, Abba Father! I could not help calling God my Father; I knew that I was his child and that He loved me and heard me. My soul being filled and satiated, crying, 'tis enough, I am satisfied. Give me strength and I will follow Thee through fire and water. (pp. 15–16)

This sealing of the Spirit or 'impartation of the spirit of adoption' freed him from all remaining doubts and emboldened him to persevere with the work on which he had already embarked, namely as an 'exhorter', or lay-evangelist, intent on sharing the gospel with others and helping save his contemporaries' souls.[173]

The youngest of three brothers, Harris was born on 23 January 1714 to Howell and Susannah Harris, at their farmstead home of Trefeca Fach, near Talgarth.[174] Unlike his elder brother Joseph who became a senior official at the Royal Mint and Thomas, the middle brother, who became a prosperous tailor and businessman in London, Howell remained at home and, following training at the grammar school at Llwyn-llwyd, not far away, he took up the work of school teaching. Although he harboured the vague ambition of becoming a clergyman, his conversion inspired him to persuade his family and friends to join him in reading extracts from the pious literature in which he was now immersed. Having read of his duty to visit the sick and infirm, he began calling on his neighbours to read to them as well, and soon invitations came to visit homes where groups of people would turn out to listen, enthralled by what this earnest young schoolmaster had to say. By autumn 1735 he had become more emboldened, and was now evangelizing openly in Talgarth and the neighbouring parishes, warning people of the consequences of sin, of their need to repent and embrace salvation: 'Now the fire of God did so burn in my soul, that I could not rest day nor night without doing something for my God and Saviour; nor could I go with satisfaction to sleep, if I had not done something for His glory that day' (p. 21). Neither was he averse to criticizing immorality and worldliness, especially among the gentry and the clergy.

Struck by his zeal, sincerity and effectiveness, more and more people were being convicted of their sins and experiencing the joy of forgiveness; attendance at public worship had increased dramatically, and the signs were that a real (if localized) spiritual awakening was underway. Whereas many were impressed by this spirit of rejuvenation, others were less sanguine. By Christmas opposition was beginning to stir. The one who voiced that opposition most pointedly was none other than Pryce Davies, Harris's own vicar. In February 1736 he wrote:

> When first I was informed that you took upon you to instruct your neighbours at Trefecca on a particular occasion – I mean, of the nature of the sacraments – and enforce their duty by reading a chapter out of that excellent book *The Whole Duty of Man*, I thought it proceeded from a pious and charitable disposition. But since you are advanced so far as to have your public lectures from house to house, and even within the limits of the Church, it is full time to let you know the sin and penalty you incur by so doing. The office you have freely undertaken belongs not to the laity any farther than privately in their own families … it is an easy matter to seduce ignorant and illiterate people, and by cunning

insinuations from house to house, induce them to embrace what tenets you please. I have yet one heavy crime to lay to your charge, which is this: that after you have expatiated ... upon *The Whole Duty of Man* to your auditors, which, in my opinion, is wrote in so plain and intelligible a manner that it is incapable of paraphrase, unless it be to obscure and confound the author's meaning, you concluded with a long extemporary prayer, with repetitions, tautologies etc. Pray consider how odiously this savours of fanaticism and hypocrisy.[175]

For his High Church vicar, Harris was contravening ecclesiastical law by preaching without having been commissioned, he was undermining the authority of the ordained ministry and by practising extemporary rather than liturgical prayer, was acting like a Dissenter. For the established clergy of the eighteenth century nothing was more odious than 'enthusiasm', while folk memories of the upheavals of the civil war and Commonwealth a century earlier remained potent even then.

Shaken by this unexpected response, he did desist for a while, especially as Davies had threatened to inform the bishop of his irregularities, 'which will prove an unmoveable obstruction to you ever getting into holy orders'.[176] Harris had gone up to Oxford in the previous November with a view to preparing for the ministry, but no sooner had he arrived that he returned home: his heart was not in it. His call, rather, was to evangelize locally and seek ordination, possibly, some time again. He had described vividly the by then powerful and aggressive nature of his ministry, in his diary a month later:

> I would raise my voice with authority, and terror and awe would be visible on the faces of all who heard. I would go to the Talgarth fairs and broach no opposition in condemning the blasphemers and vain-swearers ... A commission had been given me to cut and slash sinners in the most fearsome way ... My texts, mostly, were death and judgment, and I would say little of Christ. I was so occupied that I had no time to read apart from a page or two here and there. But when I came among the people I was given freedom to declare with great seriousness though by nature I am shallow and frivolous.[177]

There is little wonder that Pryce Davies was perturbed: this was far beyond a little private counselling. His dependence on divine provision rather than careful preparation was the mark of the enthusiast: 'No one could mistake Harris for anything else but an enthusiast', stated Geoffrey F. Nuttall, '[and] as near a specimen of pure enthusiasm as we are likely to meet'.[178] Yet it was through him that now, in Wales, the vitality of the Evangelical Revival was beginning to be felt.

Reeling from his vicar's rebuff, the young exhorter was courted by the local Dissenters, the Independents at Tredwstan and the Baptists at Trosgoed, but although he was drawn to their warm piety, he saw himself (despite everything) as a loyal son of the Anglican Church. As it happened, when it became known that he was consorting with the Dissenters, his popularity declined sharply. He still, however, felt impelled to continue his mission, and by late spring he was being invited to address cottage meetings further afield. By now he had relinquished his job as a schoolmaster. It was only then that he was told of the labours of Anglican clergy in other parts of the diocese of St David's whose ministry was more attuned to renewal and revitalization than that of his own parish priest. They were Thomas Jones (1689–1772), curate of Cwm-iou, Monmouthshire, latterly a correspondent of the English revivalist George Whitefield, and Griffith Jones.[179] In a quandary as to his next step, he wrote to Griffith Jones (whom he had never met) and in May 1736, he left for Llanddowror in order to meet the man himself. Despite not yet having reached canonical age, discussion centred on the possibility of Harris's obtaining holy orders. Realizing the younger man's religious seriousness and hearing of his evangelistic successes, Jones was probably keen to channel his energies into parish ministry. Following this initial meeting, the rector of Llanddowror promised to do what he could to help.

On returning home, Harris was pleasantly surprised to find that the attitude of Pryce Davies and other local clergymen towards him had softened. They, too, may have realized his potential value within the Church were his irregularities to be curbed and his enthusiasm disciplined. In July, with their support and that of Thomas Jones and Griffith Jones, he applied to Nicholas Claggett, bishop of St David's, for ordination but was turned down, possibly due to his youth but perhaps because of untrammelled zeal. A fortnight spent at Llanddowror in August afforded an insight into the attitude of Griffith Jones (now well into middle age) towards overzealous and injudicious evangelism. Edward Dalton, an older man than Jones even, from a distinguished Carmarthenshire family and faithful member of the Llanddowror congregation, urged Harris to nurture the spirit of moderation. Reflecting, though in a more blatant way, his rector's views, he considered revivalistic excesses as 'fanaticism, the work of the devil' and the result of spiritual pride.[180] Chastened and perplexed, he followed Jones's advice to open a school and begin teaching once more.

The most important step in his developing ministry was the establishing of fellowship meetings in order to nurture new converts in the faith. What the *collegiae pietatis* were to the Continental Pietists and the 'band meetings' and 'class meeting' would become to the followers of John Wesley, the 'society meetings' would be to the expansion and consolidation of Calvinistic Methodism in Wales.[181] Writing to Griffith Jones on 8 October, he stated: 'Private societies begin to be formed. I have not [been] six nights at home since I came down. I hope they take root.'[182] By the winter more societies had been planted. John Games, precentor of Talgarth parish church, was employed in going round the area instructing young people in the singing of psalms, and Harris decided to accompany him: 'I laid hold of this opportunity; when he had done teaching them to sing, I would give them a word of exhortation, and thereby many were brought under convictions, and many religious societies were by these means formed.'[183]

As both Games and Harris were active Anglicans, and the purpose of their going about was to improve the worship of the parish churches, this activity was readily accepted. It was through the singing classes that Harris went around Christmas to Wernos farm, between Brecon and Builth. It was there, he would claim, that the first 'permanent society' was formed. In November 1738 he wrote: 'Our country seems budding now. In our county [Breconshire] two societies; three or four in Monmouthshire, some likely to be in Glamorgan and Montgomeryshire, two or more in Carmarthenshire, one in Herefordshire; vast many in Cardiganshire.'[184] By 1740 there were as many as fifty throughout south Wales, but they all went back to Wernos, in late December 1736: it was there, he recalled, in 1745 'all this great work that has spread itself over Wales ... began, and the first society settled'.[185]

Along with the establishment of fellowship meetings, two other significant matters would occur in Harris's development during 1737–8: his espousal of Calvinism as his underlying doctrinal scheme, and a much greater level of clarity concerning his loyalty to the Established Church.

The High Church piety espoused by his vicar and affirmed by his devotional reading was in the 'holy living' tradition, emphasizing obedience as well as faith. Although tainted, the human will was free to cooperate with God's grace, while both faith and obedience were essential

in order to live the Christian life. Little prominence was given to election, predestination or the sheer gratuity of divine grace. As a layman,
untrained in theology, there had been no reason for Harris to question
this scheme: 'His idea of salvation during this early period was simple:
repentance, faith and the accomplishment of duty towards God and man.
There was little mention of the significance of Christ's death.'[186] In his
discussion with the Dissenters, however, he had been introduced to an
alternative doctrinal system. In it the will was bound, not free; sinfulness
was far more deeply entrenched in the human heart than he had realized,
while salvation was wholly of grace (*sola gratia*) on the basis of God's
eternal decree. On coming to understand it, this corresponded much
more exactly with his own spiritual experience. His perusal of the Welsh
translation of the Puritan Thomas Shepard's *Sincere Convert*, a new edition having been re-issued some years earlier, only served to confirm this
view.[187] After having been convicted of sin, he knew that even his most
vigorous moral striving brought him no closer to God. Salvation, when
it came, was wholly gratuitous, not through his own obedience but on
the basis of Christ's atoning sacrifice in which he was allowed to believe.

Already moving in this direction, during the summer of 1737 he
made the acquaintance of another revivalistically inclined clergyman,
Thomas Lewis, curate of Merthyr Cynog, Breconshire, who preached
the Calvinistic scheme. This was in keeping with the Reformed nature
of Elizabethan Anglicanism, especially eleven to fifteen in the Articles of
Religion and Archbishop Cranmer's 'Homily on Salvation'. Like Thomas
Jones of Cwm-iou, Lewis was a Calvinist, and both men were totally
loyal to the formularies of the Established Church. On theological
grounds, there was no need to question the integrity of the mother
church. Thereafter, and despite frequent doctrinal vagaries, Harris would
see himself in continuity with 'our good old orthodox Reformers and
Puritans'.[188] Although this would never impinge on his later friendship
with John and Charles Wesley who, even after their evangelical conversions always upheld the Arminianism of their High Church upbringing,
it would ensure that Welsh Methodism, like that of Whitefield and the
countess of Huntingdon, would run along Calvinistic lines.[189]

During the summer of 1737 Harris relinquished once more his job
as a settled schoolmaster and accepted Griffith Jones's offer to super-
vise the now expanding network of circulating schools in neighbouring
Radnorshire. This allowed him the freedom to itinerate (something of
which Jones did not approve), while his new doctrinal certitude allowed

him to emphasize not election as such, but the doctrine of atonement and the central importance of Christ's sacrificial death. Consequently, the Revival became even more intense: 'It was during the latter half of 1737 that his open-air ministry, and possibly the Revival itself, began in earnest.'[190] More and more societies were being established while converts were being counted not in scores but in hundreds and more, over ever expanding parts of south and mid Wales. Notwithstanding continuing difficulties, Harris was becoming more settled in his identity as a lay exhorter within the Established Church.

During this time he had been clarifying his views concerning the strengths and weaknesses of the Church. He found little wanting in its doctrinal basis, its liturgical life or (apart from the desire for more frequent celebration) its provision of the Lord's Supper. Its deficiencies, he claimed, could be made up for by delivering more intimate spiritual fellowship: 'meeting together as a society to consult about points of salvation [and] self-examination', more pointed preaching on the necessity of the new birth, more vigorous catechetical instruction ensuring that its baptized members were better instructed in the faith, and more discrimination in allowing communicants to partake of the Lord's Supper.[191] Yet all in all, the Church was sound. As well as being the church of his upbringing, it was from among its members that so many were being won to the faith; very few of the new converts showed any desire to join the Dissenters: 'I was converted myself in this ruined Church, and was fed here … [while] its principles appear to me to be sound.'[192] It was around then that he heard of the remarkable renewal which had been occurring in neighbouring Cardiganshire quite independently of his own exertions. It too was having its deepest effects among the adherents of the Established Church, its focus being the preaching of the twenty-five-year-old clergyman Daniel Rowland. Never having met, Harris heard him preach for the first time at Defynnog, Breconshire, on 13 August 1737: 'Upon hearing the sermon, and seeing the gifts given him and the amazing power and authority with which he spoke, and the effects it had upon the people … my heart burned with love to God and to him.'[193]

Daniel Rowland

Rowland, the younger son of Daniel Rowland (*c.*1659–1731) who, like his father before him, was a Cardiganshire clergyman, had been born in 1711 in the village of Nantcwnlle where his father was rector of the parish of Llangeitho. Having received his preliminary education locally, he proceeded to Hereford Grammar School and thereafter to ordination.[194] Ordained deacon on 10 March 1734, he was installed as curate at Llangeitho and Nantcwnlle, and in the same year married Elinor Davies (d.1792) of Caerllugest, near Llangeitho. Unlike Daniel, she had been brought up a Dissenter, the granddaughter of a Dissenting minister and member of the mid Cardiganshire church pastored by Philip Pugh. They would have seven children, including a son, Nathaniel, who became leader of the Welsh Methodists after his father's demise. Rowland remained in these curacies for many years, serving under his brother, John Rowland, and subsequently (and somewhat incongruously) under his own son, also called John.

Rowland was ordained priest in August 1735 by which time he had undergone a profound spiritual conversion. Unlike Harris who was a compulsive writer and kept a detailed diary throughout his life, we know little as to when or how Rowland's conversion occurred, though it was probably late in 1734 or early in 1735. Papers for the official biography, which had been commissioned by the countess of Huntingdon, were lost, while the traditions preserved by his nineteenth-century biographers conflict with one another. The name Griffith Jones occurs in more than one, and a story has it that he was convicted by hearing a sermon by the rector of Llanddowror at Llanddewi-brefi Church, some five miles from his Llangeitho home. Certainly Rowland visited Llanddowror during that winter, and there is evidence that he substituted for Jones in his pulpit at the time. After this, the whole tenor of Rowland's ministry changed. He suddenly became effective and popular, and such was the vehemence of his preaching that he became known as 'the angry cleric' (*yr offeiriad crac*):

> The excitement made on the minds of the people under his preaching from the very beginning of his conversion was most surprising. The impression on the hearts of most persons was so awful and distressing, as if they saw the end of the world drawing near, or as if they perceived hell ready to swallow them up! His fame went through all the country, and the people went from all parts to hear him. Not only were the churches filled, but also the churchyards too. It is said that people were under such deep convictions under his sermons, unable to stand, lay down on the ground ...[195]

The dramatic effect of such preaching was in accord with the new emphases of both the Great Awakening in America and the Evangelical

Revival in England. Jonathan Edwards had induced paroxysms of fear in Northampton, Massachusetts, in 1732 having preached on 'sinners in the hands of an angry God', while the most vivid impressions would soon be wrought on George Whitefield's hearers by his preaching of the divine law.[196] From the evidence of his early published sermons, Rowland seems not to have preached on hell as such though he and his colleagues did emphasize the consequences of contravening the law: 'What is common to them all [viz. Methodist conversion narratives] is often a strong sense of hell, and this seems to be induced less by hell-fire preaching than the subjects' own innate belief and conscience which appear to have required little to arouse them.'[197] This was true of the early revival in Wales. What was incontrovertible was that people in their scores were being convicted of their sins. The need was for a comparable preaching of grace and forgiveness. It was through the wise counsel of Philip Pugh that Rowland was urged to apply the gospel even as he continued to propound the law:

> Preach the gospel to the people, dear sir, and apply the balm of Gilead, the blood of Christ to their spiritual wounds, and show the necessity of faith in the crucified saviour ... If you go on preaching the law in this manner, you will kill half the people in the country, for you thunder out the curses of the law, and preach in such a terrific manner, than no-one can stand before you.[198]

By late 1735, Llangeitho had become a focus for revivalist activity in west Wales while there too fellowship or society meetings were convened. Thereafter it would become a centre for pilgrimage for Methodists throughout the land, who would journey for miles (sometimes across Cardigan Bay from north Wales) to hear him preach, to be present in his services and to receive communion from his hands. By 1736–7 Rowland was not confining himself to his curacy but was beginning to itinerate, crossing parish boundaries with the gospel message. As with Harris in neighbouring Breconshire, the results were remarkable. Though still comparatively localized and small scale, the Welsh Evangelical Revival had arrived.

Structure, organization and deepening doctrinal tensions, 1738–52
The meeting between Harris and Rowland in August 1737 would prove highly significant for the future development of the movement. Despite

their differences in ecclesiastical status, the one being a lay exhorter and the other a clergyman in full priest's orders, each affirmed the similarities between the activities which had flourished in their respective localities during the previous two years, and realized their significance. They felt a ready bond with one another and agreed that, as far as possible, they should work together to advance the spread of popular godliness and ensure that fellowship and pastoral oversight should be provided in society meetings. In fact 'the Defynnog meeting turned two embryonic religious awakenings into a more concerted movement with some semblance of centralized organization'.[199] Soon Harris was visiting Llangeitho while Rowland was emboldened to leave his parochial responsibilities in the hands of his brother John, and take the gospel to the people even if it meant intruding into other men's parishes and preaching in the open air. By early 1739, in response to an initial letter from George Whitefield, Harris reported of the progress of 'the great revival' in Cardiganshire, 'a sweet prospect' in his native Breconshire and neighbouring Monmouthshire, and many 'well-wishers to the cause of God' in Montgomeryshire and Glamorgan.[200] What had been especially significant was the warm cooperation between the revivalists and Dissenting ministers, especially in Monmouthshire and Glamorgan. Hearing of his missionary success, sympathetic Dissenters such as the Congregationalists Rees Davies of Abergavenny, Edmund Jones, and James Davies of Merthyr, and the Baptist Miles Harry, had invited Harris to their localities in order to itinerate, and throughout 1738 the impact of his evangelization had been considerable. 'The two day service with us has been attended with marvellous success', wrote David Williams, Congregational minister at Caerphilly:

> The churches and meetings are crowded, Sabbath-breaking goes down ... I cannot but forbear thinking (without any partiality) but that your coming here was from God, and that God himself, in the might and power of the Spirit, was pleased to come with you.[201]

This paralleled the sympathy that Philip Pugh had shown to Rowland in Cardiganshire, and it boded well for the promotion of the Revival as a cross-denominational phenomenon, bridging the divide between Dissent and Church. This cooperation was not, however, to last.

In December 1738, George Whitefield, fresh from his first American journey,[202] had contacted Howell Harris:

> Though I am unbeknown to you in person, yet I have long been united
> to you in spirit, and have been rejoiced to hear how the good pleasure
> of the Lord prospered in your hands. Go on, my dear brother, go on,
> be strong in the Lord and in the power of his might, and the spirit of
> Christ and of glory shall rest upon you more effectually which has, and
> still is, opening doors before you, for preaching the everlasting gospel.[203]

Just as Harris had been thrilled to hear of the progress of the gospel
under Rowland a year earlier, he was not only encouraged that another
ordained Anglican cleric had affirmed his still irregular itinerancy in
such glowing terms, but that a key leader of the Revival in England
with such strong links with the Great Awakening in America saw
fit to contact him.[204] Harris replied immediately and by March 1739
Whitefield had visited Wales twice where he met with the societies of
the south-east and took the opportunity to preach, often to very large
crowds, where he could. The Englishman's admiration for Harris – both
were twenty-five years old – was unstinting. Harris was, he claimed,

> a burning and shining light ... in those parts, a barrier against profane-
> ness and immorality and an indefatigable promoter of the true gospel
> of Jesus Christ ... he has been, I think, in seven counties, and has made
> it his business to go to wakes etc. to turn people from such lying vani-
> ties. Many alehouse people, fiddlers, harpers etc., Demetrius like, sadly
> cry out against him for spoiling their business ... But God has blessed
> him with inflexible courage ... and he still continues to go on from
> conquering to conquer ... His discourses [*sic*] generally in a field, but
> at other times from a well, a table or anything else. He has established
> nearly thirty societies in South Wales and still his sphere of action is
> enlarged daily.[205]

The blossoming friendship between the two men led to Harris being
invited to observe and partake of the Revival's work in London, and following two heady months in mid-1739, he made the acquaintance of its
leaders: the Wesley brothers, John Cennick, the Moravians Count von
Zinzendorf and James Hutton, and others. This served not only to raise
his profile within the English movement but to integrate what was hap-
pening in Wales within a movement which now stretched from Bohemia
and Saxony to New England, Georgia and the Carolinas.[206] Following
his return organizational structures were put in place, careful oversight

of the burgeoning society meetings, now placed into area divisions, was arranged, and in October 1740 a 'Society of Ministers' was convened in order to provide leadership. Indeed '[b]etween 1739 and 1741, the Welsh revival enjoyed a period of steady if unspectacular growth, closely superintended by Harris and Rowland'.[207] By now the name 'Methodist' was being used to delineate the organization,[208] and its presence had extended to south Cardiganshire and Pembrokeshire; it had raised some thirty-two exhorters who were involved in evangelism and pastoral work, while sixteen ordained ministers, both Anglican clergymen and Dissenting pastors, had consented to share in its leadership.

Religious revivalism is notorious for its fissiparousness, and by 1741, inevitably perhaps, tensions had come to the fore. In England, not least in the capital, a grievous divide had opened up between the Arminian Wesleys and the Calvinists Whitefield and Cennick on the perennially problematic subject of election and predestination, while the somewhat idiosyncratic Moravians had already broken with the rest of the move-ment in order to pursue their own vision.[209] Following the breach with the Wesleys, Whitefield cleaved even closer to his new Welsh breth-ren and was appointed moderator of the first joint association of the English and Welsh Calvinistic Methodists, at Watford, Caerphilly, in January 1743. By then the Welsh movement had undergone a crisis of its own. Harris, the only layman among the leaders, overcompensated by being overbearing and authoritarian. Although deferential to the clerical Rowland, he was often vexed by his colleague's light-hearted demean-our which he interpreted as being frivolous and unspiritual. Rowland, for his part, often found Harris arrogant and egotistical. He had little patience with what was becoming an obsession, namely that the con-verts' experience of saving faith should be accompanied by a sense of assurance. This idea was foreign to the pastoral theology of moderate Calvinism, Harris having imbibed it while in London from his contacts with the Moravians. The Dissenting ministers were also offended by his abrasive personality, while increasingly his dogmatic insistence that Methodism was essentially a renewal movement within the Established Church rather than a more broad-based evangelistic body open to all, would cause a rift. In fact, fundamental differences in ecclesiology were coming to the surface. In 1742 when Edmund Jones instituted the Defynnog society as an autonomous, self-governing Independent church, the Dissenting ministers withdrew from the movement, and thereafter Methodism and Dissent would go their separate ways.[210] Nevertheless the movement, by now highly structured and efficient, did not suffer over much. The publication of its first handbook, *Sail, Dibenion a Rheolau y Cymdeithasau ... a ddechreuasant ymgynnull yn ddiweddar yng Nghymru* (1742), ('The Foundation, Aims and Rules of the Societies .... having lately come together in Wales') laid out the character and characteristics of the organization as well as its regulations, and made it crystal clear that its members were faithful adherents of the Established Church whose only desire was to deny themselves, take up their cross and follow the Lamb.[211]

Since their first meeting in August 1737, the two principal revivalists had worked together harmoniously and effectively. The fact that their circles of activity were different, Rowland principally in Cardiganshire and west Wales and Harris in Breconshire, mid Wales and the south-east, prevented tensions from arising between two ambitious and headstrong young men. (Although we lack the abundant documentary evidence that exists for Harris, Rowland too had a reputation for wilfulness and obstinacy.) The first sign of what would become a constant trend occurred in the association meeting in March 1742 when they clashed publicly over a point of doctrine. In Harris's view the covenant of grace had been between God and his Son, whereas Rowland, reflecting the orthodox position, insisted that it had been between God and his people, namely the elect. It was the belligerent tone of the protagonists and the public nature of their disagreement, however, which caused the most consternation. In the following association Harris contended vocally that assurance was essential to saving faith – his own experience in the past had suggested that this was *not* the case – whereas Rowland was equally insistent that although assurance was preferable, personal faith was valid even without it. Again, the most worrying aspect of this debate for those present was its vehement, public nature: 'What I was afraid in him', wrote Harris, 'was his feeding hypocrites and what he feared in me was my overthrowing the little ones' (Diary, 18 March 1742).[212] Thereafter Harris became much more critical of Rowland, suspecting him of levity and lacking in the spirit of devotion, while others began rebuking Harris for his apparent failings: 'Since I left you I was grieved much concerning your conduct towards Mr Rowlands', wrote the Glamorgan exhorter Thomas Price in April 1742; 'There is another thing which appears to me as an error in you that your spirit is a little too imperious.'[213] Although harmony was restored and cooperation continued throughout 1743, by 1744 darker clouds were beginning to fill the sky.

For much of 1743 Harris had been in London, deputizing for Whitefield at the Tabernacle, headquarters of the metropolis's Calvinistic Methodists, and on his return he was much more insistent on the significance of his status as a leader within the joint movement. Indeed 'by the end of 1744 he was becoming obsessed with the idea'.[214] Along with this, he was emphasizing concepts that the Welsh Methodists found alien and disturbing. The phrases 'the blood of Christ', 'the wounds of Christ', 'the blood of the Lamb', although ostensibly biblical, were used by the Moravians (in whose company Harris had been) in an obsessive, unbalanced way, and on his return these phrases became more prevalent in his preaching. He even began talking of 'the blood of God', suggestive of the Patripassian heresy, that on the cross God the Father had suffered and not just the human nature of Christ, the divine Son. Although he protested that he was not under Moravian influence and that he remained loyal to trinitarian orthodoxy, the suspicion was that he was becoming heretical, a wariness shared by Rowland whose doctrinal perceptiveness was second to none. These fears were exacerbated by Harris's insistence that God was blessing profusely his preaching on this theme: 'I had more power than ever to show the Blood of Christ … I never had such liberty to preach Blood – Wounds – the Blood of God – Blood, Blood and Blood again' (Diary, 26 February 1745). The grotesque nature of his preaching had now come well to the fore. What is more, he now came to champion the idea that those who had not felt 'the power of the blood' were in a backslidden state and the only way for the movement to prosper was by emphasizing even more pointedly the theology of Christ's wounds. By mid-1745 he saw the evidence for declension everywhere, and felt led to 'purify' the societies by disciplining members harshly. There are repeated diary entries throughout that year and the next of his preaching in a 'cutting' way, and of his turning members out of the societies, mostly for a spirit of worldliness and lack of commitment. He hardly realized how unpopular he was becoming, especially as he was convinced that he had been led to impose heightened discipline by the direct impulse of the Holy Spirit. In effect, to oppose him was to oppose God, and all the while he was preaching on the divine blood: 'I'll go out as far as I can to declare this fountain, this blood, crying Blood, Blood, Blood, Blood', he wrote at Llandinam in 1746, 'and the Spirit came down like a mighty shower' (Diary, 15 May 1746).

Rowland, who lacked totally the quality of enthusiasm and was by far the better theologian of the two, had been surprisingly indulgent to

Harris's speculations, but at the associations in April and June 1746, he took his colleague to task openly. Moravianism had become a problem for the Welsh Methodist movement, especially in Pembrokeshire, while one of Harris's most trusted supporters, the powerful preacher James Beaumont, was advocating a mystical theology heavily influenced by Moravian ideas.[215] Rowland was unsparing in his criticism of Harris, accusing him of being tainted with Moravianism on the one hand and by Beaumont's antinomianism on the other. By now the breach was public, and thereafter, in each association meeting, criticisms would abound. The fact that Harris was even more truculent in claiming divine sanction for his opinions: 'I had this [the theology of the divine blood] from God and not from man', served to worsen the situation, as did his accusation that Rowland was overly dependent on book learning rather than the direct inspiration of the Lord. Harris's absence from Wales in London during the autumn improved the situation for a while, as it did when he deputized for Whitefield during 1747, but the underlying problems remained the same: unbalanced preaching on the divine blood, an imperious, condemnatory and harsh spirit, a conviction of his special status as a leader within the movement, and the idea that he was being directly led by God. By 1748 an even more disturbing element became apparent, namely Harris's claim to be able to discern the inward state of an individual's heart whatever the nature of his or her moral conduct. Objective criteria were now yielding to extreme subjectivism. It was then that Madam Sidney Griffith arrived on the scene.

While preaching in north Wales in October 1748, Harris first met Mrs Sidney Griffith, the wife of a Caernarfonshire squire.[216] One of the few members of the Welsh landed class to be drawn to the revival movement, she had been converted by Peter Williams, one of the newer generation of Methodist itinerants, a year earlier and was zealous in her new-found faith. February 1749 found her, along with her maid, at Llangeitho from whence she progressed, unannounced, to Trefeca and accepted the invitation to stay for two nights. Following her return home the two met again in July, this time at Pwllheli on another of Harris's preaching tours of the north. There had been nothing untoward in their relationship: he treated her as he would any other keen convert though he was flattered at having a spiritual admirer from among the gentry. Eager to attend the Llangeitho association in August, she accompanied Harris to south Wales. 'This', it has been said, 'was to be a journey that [he] would never forget'.[217] By now his relations with Rowland had soured markedly. The two men had clashed spectacularly at Carmarthen during the preceding May while the Trefeca revivalist's unpopularity even among his own converts had become acute. He had been virtually ostracized by the so-called 'clerical party' which by now included such influential individuals as Howell Davies, Peter Williams and William Williams,[218] though he retained his status within the movement due to his incessant pastoral labours, his itinerancy and the undoubted effectiveness of his evangelistic preaching. Having spent time at the Llangeitho association, Mrs Griffith joined Harris for a further journey through Carmarthenshire; in all, duly chaperoned by her maid, they spent three weeks in one another's company. Anne Harris, whom the revivalist had married in 1744, was deeply uncomfortable with her husband's behaviour though he seemed oblivious to its effect either on her or on the reputation of the Methodist movement as a whole.[219] People were being scandalized, and though his diaries suggest that their association was of a platonic nature, it was clear that he had become infatuated by his new companion: 'We had but one soul, one heart, one will, one judgment, one affection and that here I could open up my whole heart and nowhere else' (Diary, 28 July 1749). Even his most implacable opponents within the Methodist leadership never suspected the relationship of being adulterous – for those outside the movement it was a different matter entirely – yet the tensions between Anne, her husband and Sidney Griffith became intolerable. It had become obvious by early 1750 that the situation could not continue: 'By now, Harris was showing clear signs of a serious personality disorder; his megalomania, though clothed in spiritual terms ... suggested a loss of mental balance.'[220] With Madam Griffith exercising the gift of prophecy, and Harris, ever the enthusiast, heeding her every word, the whole movement was in danger of imploding: to quote Geraint Tudur again: 'While it could be said that the burden of Revival work had very nearly destroyed the man, it can also be said that the man came very near to destroying the Revival.'[221] By now the societies and the lay exhorters, even in Breconshire, were abandoning Harris in their droves. Although he tried desperately to retain power, it was in vain.

The final breach came at the Llanidloes association in May 1750. He was challenged directly by Rowland and William Williams, and thereafter leadership of the Revival in Wales passed to the former. Their complaint was never the mystical influence of Madam Griffith as such; rather that Harris had caused inordinate contention among the brethren, that he had lost his balance doctrinally, and through an overbearing harshness, had forfeited his authority over the movement at large. The doctrinal critique was made pointedly in the brief pamphlet *Ymddiddan rhwng Methodist Uniawn-gred ac un Camsyniol* (1750) ('A Discourse between an Orthodox and Erroneous Methodist') in which Rowland not only shows his grasp of patristic theology but lists the heresies of which Harris was guilty: Patripassianism or the idea that God the Father was capable of suffering; Eutychianism or the confusion of the two natures within the Person of Christ; Sabellianism, in which the three Persons of the Trinity become sub-personal modes of being; and antinomianism which downgrades the function of the law in the Christian faith: 'Please do not treat the Fathers, the authors of our Church's constitution, that excellent old theologian Athanasius, indeed the whole body of orthodox divines as though they were foolish, ignorant and obscure!'[222] To make matters worse, Harris claimed that far from being heretical, these ideas had been directly revealed to him by God. In other words, even had it not been for Madam Griffith, a division within the movement's ranks would have occurred. Beleaguered and realizing that the fate of the Methodist movement was at stake, he called his supporters together at Trefeca in June: 'All seemed to see we must separate before we can be united' (Diary, 7 June 1750). Thereafter 'Harris's people' (*Pobl Harris*), vastly outnumbered by 'Rowland's people' (*Pobl Rowland*), would divide.[223] A final blow (felt more by Harris than his supporters) was the death of Mrs Griffith, in London, in May 1752. Her mentor, then in very poor health, renounced his itinerancy and retired to Trefeca. It seemed an ignominious end to what had been a dramatic and vigorous phase in the history of the Revival in Wales.

By 1750 over 420 Calvinistic Methodist societies had been established, the great majority in the south, mid Wales and the south-west. On the basis of this, it is reckoned that the movement as a whole had a membership of 10,000 to 12,000,[224] in the context of the Welsh population at the time, a not insignificant figure. Despite everything it was still growing, and doing so in parallel with, and to an extent intertwined with, the considerable expansion of Griffith Jones's circulating schools and *their* impact on the everyday parish ministry within the Welsh Church.[225] Although *The Welch Piety* is deafeningly silent on the subject of either Methodism or the Revival, and virtually none of the clergy whose fulsome letters of support contained in each volume were known as Methodists as such, there can be little doubt that a widespread and popular spiritual renewal, fed by conversionist preaching and Calvinistic literature, was well underway. And although Dissent would not begin to be truly transformed until the 1770s and 1780s, it too was expanding during these years. In short, there can be no question that 'Protestant piety' was being 'successfully communicated … to large sections of the population of Wales, something that had evaded Welsh Protestants for well over two centuries'.[226] At long last the Reformation as a popular movement was taking root.

Religion and theology in Wales by 1760

By 1760 Welsh Dissent, though expanding steadily, maintained continuity with the movement as it had existed a half-century earlier. The Baptists' dozen churches which had been listed by Dr John Evans in 1718 had expanded to twenty,[227] while the Congregationalists' sixty churches were now nearer eighty, six of which were former Methodist societies.[228] The theology which underpinned their outreach was also in continuity with the temperate, evangelical Calvinism which pre-dated the Revival. Gospel preaching, already a mainstay of their mission, was being influenced more and more by the spirit of the awakening while the virtues of gathered church autonomy were proving attractive to some who had been touched by the Revival's flame. As early as 1736 William Herbert, Baptist minister at the church of Trosgoed had implored his neighbour Howell Harris to '[s]eparate from the profane world'. He disparaged the Established Church, to which Harris so zealously cleaved, as

> a public house which is open to all commers … Don't the Scripture tell me that the church is like a *garden enclosed*, a *spring shut up*, a *fountain sealed* … If so 'tis different from a common field where every noisesome beast may come.[229]

He urged the young reformer not to turn his clean sheep out onto the common to be contaminated, 'to a field full of scabby ones which made them rot and scabby as ever', among 'a parcel of wanton goats' under hireling clergy, but to join the Dissenters among whom he could preserve spiritual purity and doctrinal integrity: 'I think I ought not go to please men any farther than the Word of God doth allow me, or else I am not like to be as true and faithful servant of Christ as I ought be.'[230] Even though Harris, along with the bulk of the Methodist movement, had refused to be beguiled, as the years progressed it had proved difficult to prevent some ardent souls from succumbing to the Dissenting temptation. Some Methodist exhorters, chafing at the clericalism of their leaders, were ordained as Congregational ministers: Milbourne Bloom (d.1766), at Pant-teg, Carmarthenshire, in 1745; Jenkin Morgan (d.1762), at Watford, Caerphilly, in 1746; Morgan John Lewis (c.1711–71), at New Inn, Monmouthshire, in 1756; and Isaac Price (c.1735–1808) at Troedrhiwdalar, Breconshire, in 1758. Each would play an important role in expanding the Dissenting cause.[231] Evan Williams, conscious that the Dissenters among whom he had been raised had 'greatly lost the power of religion and were become lukewarm', was drawn back into the Congregationalists' service by Edmund Jones who realized his immense evangelistic gifts:

> If it be so, brother (and I did not deny that it was not) then you should not leave us in this evil state, but zealous and lively men such as you are should come among us, to stir us up and mend us.[232]

Williams's unabated evangelistic zeal took him to north Wales where he faced cruel persecution, and his untimely death, aged twenty-nine, in 1748, deprived Dissent of an extraordinary talent, yet it was through men like these that the dangers of conventionality and nominal profession were largely overcome.

By mid-century the rumbling tensions that had always characterized the situation between the Established Church and Dissent were far from abating. Both High and Reformed Churchmen registered their disapproval of those who persisted in what they believed was still a state of schism. Theophilus Evans, vicar of Llangamarch and author of the famed history of the Welsh nation, *Drych y Prif Oesoedd* ('A Mirror of the Early Ages') (1716), laid the blame for the Methodistical 'enthusiasm' which was presently blighting so much of his communion squarely at the door of the low church Puritanism which had infected the Church since Elizabethan times. The bane of the establishment had been 'popular government by lay-elders and a parity of ministers' along with 'the rigid doctrine of absolute and unconditional decrees of election and reprobation', favoured now not only by 'our present sectarists', descendants of the dreaded Oliver whom he tarred with 'a mixture of hypocrisy, cant and enthusiasm',[233] but by the odious Dissenters who, since 1662, had been beyond the ecclesiastical pale: 'Those Puritans were men of fierce and ungovernable zeal, violently attached to the rigid Geneva doctrine ... whereby man is made a mere machine, only passive and consequently unaccountable for any action, as not being a free agent.'[234]

Although the High Church Arminian doctrines of Evans were aeons away from the Reformed convictions of Griffith Jones, the rector of Llanddowror was equally critical of the pretentions of Protestant Dissent. Painting the Welsh Baptists with the Münsterite brush, he described in lurid terms how the 'new, impudent and contentious sect of Anabaptists', which had risen in Germany two centuries before, 'had announced with barefaced insolence that God had told them to destroy all the princes, governors and unawakened sinners everywhere and wash their hands in the blood of the unrighteous, so that they might become rulers over all the earth'.[235] Resenting the echo of civil war radicalism and suggestion of Baptist disloyalty to the Hanoverian state, Timothy Thomas, the Aberduar minister, accused Jones of 'trying to arouse the government against us'. Referring to the Stuart rebellion of 1745, he claimed that 'parliament and king know who their most loyal subjects are. The government knows well enough whether it was the Church of England or the Dissenters who were most loyal during the late rebellion'.[236] As in 1696 when the Baptists had called on the services of the London minister Benjamin Keach to defend them from their detractors,[237] now it was John Gill, Keach's successor at the Horsleydown Church in Southwark, who came to the defence. Although he too bristled at the retailing of 'the old stale story of the German Anabaptists and their errors, madness and distractions', maintaining that 'they were a people that scarce agreed with us in anything, neither in their civil nor their religious principles nor in baptism itself',[238] the substantial point had to do with ecclesiology and the matter of schism:

> Whereas Dissenters from the Church of England are frequently charged with schism, and their separation is represented as unreasonable, and they are accounted an obstinate and contentious people, it may be proper to give some reasons why they depart from the Established Church. (p. 3)

Listing those reasons: that it is a national establishment rather than a voluntary body; that it encompasses both the faithful and the profane; that the sound doctrine enshrined in its formularies is hardly ever proclaimed: 'Since two thousand godly and faithful ministers were turned out at once, Arminianism has generally prevailed and scarce anything else than Arminian tenets and mere morality are preached' (p. 5); that its doctrine of baptism and the Lord's Supper are erroneous; that its liturgy and ceremonial are unfaithful to the Word of God; that its officers are unscriptural: 'The scripture knows nothing of archbishops and diocesan bishops, of archdeacons and deans, of prebends, parsons, vicars and curates' (pp. 9–10); that it wants in discipline and that its Prayer Book worship is shackled to such human innovations as fasts, feasts and saints' days. In short 'the Church of England has neither the form nor matter of a true church' (pp. 11–12) and as such Protestant Dissenters are conscience bound to withdraw from its fellowship. The same point had been made succinctly by Timothy Thomas two years before: 'The Holy Spirit commands us to come out from amongst them and be separated.'[239] Griffith Jones's contention, that Dissenters were like the New Testament Diotrephes, 'who "doth not receive the brethren, and forbiddeth them that would, and casteth them out of the church" (III John 10)' made minimal impression on the Aberduar pastor.[240] 'Schism and separation from God's church is undoubtedly a serious sin', he retorted, 'but if you refer to Protestant Dissenters separating from the Church of England, I do not regard this as sin'.[241]

As well as crossing swords with Griffith Jones, Timothy Thomas was best known as one of his generation's most accomplished pastor-theologians. His two works of the late 1750s, an essay on assurance and a very able handbook on justification by faith, conveyed the doctrinal standards not only of his own denomination but of Calvinistic Dissent generally. To be assured of one's salvation was not only implicit in the gospel scheme, but was both personally beneficial and added to the confidence of the churches' mission: 'Wherefore, brethren, be diligent in making your calling and election sure, for if you do these things you will never fail' (II Peter 1:10). The doctrinal framework was, once more, federal or covenantal theology. Believers should strive to know that Christ had died for their sins, that those sins had been imputed to Christ and that, in turn, they had been reconciled to God. It is only thus that they would know that their names had been written in the Book of Life and that they were among the elect. Although believing is an act of the will, it can only be enabled by God's Spirit: 'It is our responsibility to use the means of grace, especially listening to the Word, through which God generates faith.'[242] Such is the basis of 'the assurance of our calling or our transformation from a state of nature to a state of grace'

(p. 11). This assurance elicits thankfulness and an attitude of humility, practical confidence in living the Christian life and courage in the face of adversity and death. Although it is essential to look within, 'Examine yourselves, whether you be in the faith, prove yourselves' (II Cor. 13:5), Thomas is keen to eschew extreme or morbid introspection and urges his readers to balance any untoward inwardness by looking outwards towards Jesus Christ. It is only thus that the Holy Spirit will be allowed to do his sanctifying work: 'If we experience the work of the Spirit, namely sanctification active within and we perceive that our hearts are slowly moving into accord with God's Word, we can be assured that we are among God's children' (p. 35). Like all centrist Calvinists, Thomas feared antinomianism; holiness was a requirement for the Christian life: 'Strive to be holy, yea, make sanctity your friend in all things' (p. 35). Yet he was keen to distance himself from the Anglican 'holy living' school and its propensity to collapse sanctification into justification and imperil the concept of justification by faith alone: 'I am not saying that holiness is the basis of our salvation or of the assurance of salvation; that is only granted through God's love and mercy and the merits of Jesus Christ' (p. 36). Although the aim must be to be sure of one's election and calling, Thomas showed immense pastoral sensitivity to the weak in faith and those who were just embarking on their Christian pilgrimage:

> Do not adjudge yourselves to be bereft of grace just because you have not yet achieved assurance, and do not think that you are devoid of faith if you do not yet have the fullness of faith, for not every believer knows that he is a believer even when he is in possession of true faith. (p. 46)

Assurance is only part and not the sum of the life of faith.

It was apparent by 1760 that the concerns of the Evangelical Revival, not least the appropriation of personal faith through the preaching of the gospel, were at the forefront of Dissenting discourse, and in his *Wisg Wen Ddisglair* (1759) ('The Shining White Robe'), Thomas set out the essentials of the concept of justification by faith. The 350-page octavo volume consists of a dozen chapters, four describing the state of humankind before and after the fall, two delineating the sinner's need to be justified before God, one on the Person and Work of Christ, another on the act of justification, two on when and how this occurs, another on the effects of justification and a closing chapter on the doctrine of sanctification. It is wholly in keeping with the historical verities of the Reformed faith, especially as set out in the Westminster Shorter Catechism, the Baptists' 1689 Confession of Faith and the doctrinal sections of the Church of England's Articles of Religion.[243] Justification, he claims, is the sovereign act whereby Christ, having lived his life in perfect accord with God's law, took upon himself the sins of his people. Having done this he offered himself as a sacrifice to God thereby satisfying the divine righteousness on which basis those for whom he had died were accounted righteous in God's eyes. It is a forensic or judicial act having to do with the sinner's status before God:

> After the Lord put all our sins upon Christ so that he, who knew not sin was made sin for us, he [= Christ] accounted us God's righteousness in him. And as all our sins were put upon him, he being our Surety, God saw fit to impute the righteousness that he had achieved to us. (p. 138)

Thomas is well aware of the problems involved in the doctrine: that it tends to foreground God's righteousness over his love; that it is in danger of undercutting morality by emphasizing the concept of imputation rather than inviting the sinner to contribute somehow to the process of salvation; and that it was said to engender spiritual passivity in believers. Nevertheless he is adamant that the doctrine was totally biblical, that given the reality of human sinfulness and the divine righteousness it was both logical and inevitable, while its basic presupposition was God's undeserved love towards his elect. Although the doctrine was wholly judicial, having to do with the Christian's status before God, it was complemented by a range of other doctrines including adoption, union with Christ and sanctification, through which the Holy Spirit is infused or imparted into believers' souls, enabling them to make their own contribution to the Christian life. He eschews High Calvinism by rejecting the concept of eternal justification:

> Although the sinner's justification may be said in one way to have occurred when Christ paid the ransom for them, that is when Christ died for their sins ... their specific justification occurs when they come to believe in Christ (pp. 199–200)

and by insisting that saving faith is an act of the will:

> Such faith, in its very nature, is the light, and especially the living spir-
> itual power which sees and knows Christ as one's all-sufficient Savior,
> and knowing this fleeing to him, taking hold of him and trusting him
> for justification and for life. (p. 158)

The main difference between the theology of the Welsh Methodists
and that of Protestant Dissent was one of soteriological intensity. 'The
Methodists', according to Derec Llwyd Morgan, 'in their preaching and
teaching, and in defending their beliefs, placed the greatest emphasis on
those principles which particularly and specially concerned salvation'.[244]
At first, rather than training up their own authors, they turned to those
with whom they felt affinity within the Revivalist International. The
first work to be commissioned by the association was a 1743 translation
of the Scottish evangelical Ralph Erskine's *Law-Death and Gospel Life*,
a treatise based on Gal. 2:17. [245] Here the function of the law, in typical
Lutheran fashion, was to convict its hearers of their sins: 'Through the
law comes knowledge of sin, and as I, through the law, am convinced that
I am a guilty, abject sinner, I have died to any hope of being justified by
means of the law.'[246] The only way to access salvation is not through any
moral striving of my own but by throwing myself on the divine mercy
in Christ: 'The basis of the believer's freedom from the demands of the
law as a covenant of works or condition of life is Christ's perfect obedience to the law on his behalf' (p. 23). By being made alive to God, the
believer is consequently made dead to the law in the sense of depending
upon it for salvation:

> The believer, therefore, is dead to the law in its imperative and con-
> demning guise, and has been made free in Christ. I have no fear or
> compunction in claiming that all the demands, the requirements and the
> authority of the first covenant have fallen upon Christ and that he has
> fulfilled them to the uttermost. (p. 28)

The moral implications of this spiritual transaction is that the
Christian, though free from the oppression of the law as a means of
self-justification, is now obliged to live in loving obedience to the precepts of the gospel:

> While the form of the law as a covenant of works has been so trans-
> formed, the law, now in Christ's hand, is nothing but love, wholly of

grace, and therefore compels man effectually to holiness, to live his life for God. (p. 85)

Although they are dead to the law as a means of salvation, believers are alive to Christ in whom the law has been fulfilled and as such are charged with living a life of thankfulness, obedience and moral integrity: 'In a word, if you have died to the law, you have been made alive to God ... and have been drawn sweetly to the law as a rule of conduct' (p. 109). 'Take note, there were no dead branches in Christ as the true vine. Those who believe in him are careful to bring forth good works and be obedient all his commandments' (p. 114). Again, there is nothing new in this apart from an element of clarity, immediacy and intensity. The Methodist gospellers emphasized the need to respond to the evangelical message with unsurpassed passion.

The next volume of Methodist apologetic was a composite work by the Erskine brothers, Ebenezer as well as Ralph, *Christ in the Arms of the Believer* by Ebenezer, a popular assessment of saving faith based on Luke 2:28, and a short sermon on the nature of the covenant by Ralph expounding Psalm 74:20. Much the same themes are rehearsed as before: 'There are no dead branches in Christ the true vine; those who believe in him are vigilant in good works and follow all his precepts',[247] though the experiential aspect of faith is even more prominent:

> We can praise God having *felt* the assurance of his love, his grace and his salvation ... Felt assurance is the immediate knowledge that we have come to believe in Christ, or the soul's lively reflection that it has been embraced by Christ. (p. 38)

All the Calvinistic truths are mentioned: election, the sovereignty of God and the absolute bondage of the human will, but nothing is allowed to blunt the evangelistic message or to prevent sinners from embracing Christ:

> Although we have no ability to believe, yet we must strive to believe. The way in which God's Spirit creates faith in the souls of his elect is by making them conscious of their inability so that they turn over everything to his hand. He will work *his* actions in and through *us*. (p. 59)

And finally: 'The basis of your damnation on the Day of Judgment will not be that you are not among the elect but that you have chosen not to believe' (p. 60).

The Welsh Methodists' preference for improving literature initially written by their Scottish colleagues continued with William Williams of Pantycelyn's 1759 translation of Ebenezer Erskine's treatise *The Assurance of Faith* based on Heb. 10:22. Williams had already embarked upon his career as an author by publishing his early hymn collections *Aleluia* (1744), *Hosanna i Fab Dafydd* (1751) ('Hosanna to the Son of David') and *Rhai Hymnau Newyddion* (1757) ('Some New Hymns'), along with his remarkable Christological poem celebrating creation and redemption *Golwg ar Deyrnas Crist* ('A View of Christ's Kingdom') in 1756. His most significant works, however, would appear after 1760 which is beyond the scope of the present study.[248] By then the revival was a generation old and had generated deep pastoral problems along with undoubted spiritual successes. One abiding question was: when the first flush of exuberance had abated, what was left for the converts to grasp? Erskine's six chapters treated the nature of faith, the basis of assurance and the difference between often transitory religious impressions and genuine rootedness in divine truth. It was a relief for converts to be told that doubt was part of the discipline of faith but following the subsiding of excitement and feelings, doubt should not be allowed to degenerate into despair and unbelief:

> Truly, if there were not some overall certainty in faith acting upon the unalterable covenant, in such cloud and dismal dispensations, I know not what could keep the believer from descending into utter desolation. But true faith will venture the soul's safety upon the strong plank of promise, even when conscious supports are quite dashed to pieces by the angry billows of outward and inward troubles like two seas crashing upon the believer.[249]

The fact that a second edition of this work appeared within a year shows that these were matters of import not only for Methodists but others as well, as the Dissenting Timothy Thomas's *Y Garreg Wen, neu Draethawd bychan ymherthynas i Siccrwydd* (1757) ('The White Stone, or a Short Essay pertaining to Assurance') had already shown.

Although Methodism functioned within the context of the Established Church, its relationship with the parent body was ambiguous from the start. Howell Harris and Daniel Rowland (though to a lesser degree) had no compunction about itinerating across parish boundaries, while the system of oversight that they devised was wholly independent of diocesan structures and free of parochial control. The intense fellow-ship engendered within the society meetings was meant to supplement the normal round of sacramental and Eucharistic worship within the parish churches, though it could, in practice, supersede Prayer Book worship *in toto*. Conversely, conventional parishioners could find exuberant Methodist presence in their local churches disconcerting, while clergy who were unsympathetic to evangelical truth could exacerbate latent hostilities which were waiting to erupt. Even among clergy who *were* committed to the evangelical faith, Methodist irregularities were some-times a matter of grave contention. Griffith Jones, for one, was bitingly critical of the Methodists' cavalier disregard for sobriety and general ecclesiastical norms. 'Our new itinerant preachers are exceedingly erro-neous, harsh, conceited and disorderly', he opined to Madam Bridget Bevan on 23 April 1741, 'and have, as I am informed, no appearance of that soberness and humility ... that becomes true godliness'.[250] He was critical in equal measure of Harris, Rowland and his own curate, Howell Davies, who was beginning to come to the fore as a Methodist leader in Pembrokeshire: 'So much work is cut out for me by their enthusiastical and incredible fooleries and such deplorable want of judgment.'[251] Two days later he voiced the same reproach:

> Several of our Methodists and some of their chiefs plainly discover them-selves very defective in common sense, common manners and veracity or common honesty, and indulge a very arrogant, proud, railing and slandering temper. Such has been their behaviour towards everybody who, in the gentlest manner, have talked with them about their very gross absurdities which can never pass for religion with any but the grossly ignorant.[252]

Thirty years earlier he been accused of enthusiasm and lack of ecclesi-astical decorum himself, but, along with the crabbed wisdom of middle age, he realized that, without the support of the gentry, the bulk of his fellow clergy and the people at large, his grand vision for evangelizing the nation through the circulating schools would come to naught: 'I am in no degree a favourer of their rude enthusiasm which is so void of com-mon civilities and moral conversation that none who is acquainted with the spirit of the gospel can approve of.'[253] When he heard that George Whitefield intended to visit Llanddowror in April 1743, he remained very wary indeed:

> I hope Mr W[hitefield] is not a false minister nor, so far as I know, are his doctrines false, but the absurdities [and] errors of several of his followers, and his misconduct can't be approved by judicious Christians ... I wish these people had such a modest opinion of themselves as to consider a little more about the way they observe the better sort of other persons shy of entering into their scheme.[254]

If this was the case with such an unabashed evangelical as Griffith Jones, the revivalists could expect virtually nothing from the High Church clergy. Devotional literature in the 'holy living' mode was still being produced; a new edition of William Vickers's Eucharistic primer *Cydymmaith i'r Allor* ('A Companion to the Altar') was published in 1738 with a second imprint in 1753, followed by a fresh version of William Assheton's *Duwiolder am Ddydd yr Arglwydd* ('Piety on the Lord's Day') in 1747,[255] but none of this could compete either in bulk or popularity with Griffith Jones's many catechetical handbooks and the varied Calvinistic volumes emanating from the authors of Methodism and especially Dissent. Theophilus Evans's doctrinal strictures in his splenetic *History of Modern Enthusiasm* (1752), and even more so in the expanded version of 1757, seemed by now to be very jaded indeed: 'Sudden and instantaneous calls leads men to neglect the means of salvation, gradual improvements and growing in grace', he claimed, while 'the presumptuous doctrine of the assurance of pardon ... and the certainty of salvation does naturally fill the head with spiritual pride'.[256] By now High Church theology had run to seed, degenerating into cliché and invective, while the richness and spiritual seriousness that it had lent to the religious discourse in Wales a half-century earlier had mostly dissipated:

> The gross antinomian doctrine, maintained by most of the Methodists (and by all the Moravian party) gives too much encouragement to all manner of immoralities and vice ... Their depreciating of works and teaching justification by faith alone without any regard to good works, does naturally lead people to disregard of moral duties ... to think them no part at all of the Christian religion.[257]

For the most part Evans's strictures simply did not ring true.

Another High Churchman, Thomas Ellis, fellow of Jesus College, Oxford and vicar of Holyhead, had conveyed the fears of the establishment in the face of Methodist advance in his *Gair o Gyngor … mewn perthynas i'r Schismaticiaid sy'n ymneilltuo oddi wrth Eglwys Loegr* (1747) ('A Word of Counsel … in relation to the Schismatics who are separating from the Church of England'). After describing briefly the content of the orthodox biblical faith, he claimed that everything essential for salvation was contained in the Articles and Prayer Book of the Established Church of the realm. This Church, 'the glory of Christendom, of which there is no purer in all the world', requires nothing of its members save that they believe the gospel, cleave to its formularies and live according to God's holy Word.[258] Why, therefore, should anyone adhering to the Christian faith, feel compelled to forsake its fellowship? However fervent the Methodists' contention that they were loyal to the Church of England, the very fact that they set up their own conventicles and appointed alternative leaders of their own, gave lie to their claim:

> It is inexcusable that her enemies, the schismatics (by which ever name they choose to call themselves) … see fit to traduce and disparage us throughout the land, declaring that we, within her communion, are unfit even to recite the Lord's Prayer, in fact that we are blind and lost. (p. 7)

With a welter of colourful rhetoric, Ellis accused the Methodists of a catalogue of sins: arrogance, spiritual pride, pharisaic conceit, deceiving the weak, hoodwinking the impressionable, challenging established authority and undermining apostolic order. They were guilty of 'the immense sin of barefaced schism, namely rending the unity of the body of the Church and unravelling the bond of peace and perfect love that unites the Christians of the world' (p. 8). True piety could never be equated with fanaticism and raw enthusiasm, while only hypocrites took it upon themselves to teach others when they had never been called, trained and duly instituted to the teaching office: 'Your teachers are nothing less than false prophets' (p. 12). Venerable tradition had always dictated that worship should be celebrated in consecrated buildings while established Anglicans, still haunted by the spectre of the Great Rebellion, were fearful of lay religion in un-licenced venues: 'Are there no more reputable places for Christians to congregate for religious purposes than your private houses or hedgerows or barns?' (p. 14). Who were these hot gospellers come among us for the first time as though Christian truth were totally unknown? 'Were we all in darkness before the advent of these unschooled strolling preachers?' (p. 15). With a catena of biblical quotation, Ellis strove to convince his readers that they should beware of wolves in sheep's clothing: 'Is not this new sect a confused mixture of the errors of the Quakers, the Presbyterians, the antinomians and other such schismatics of their ilk?' (p. 16). His aim, despite everything, was to draw the Methodists, whom he viewed as virtual Dissenters, back into the fellowship of the Mother Church. He did eventually accept that contemporary Anglicanism had sometimes fallen short in terms of the morality of its clergy and the commitment of its members but there was no doubt that the Church of England was basically sound: 'If you are a schismatic, return quickly to the bosom of the orthodox Church, for the love of Christ and the good of your own soul' (p. 19).

There is no evidence that either Thomas Ellis or Theophilus Evans were anything less than devoted and conscientious parish priests. Ellis was among Griffith Jones's most steadfast north Wales supporters and a careful pastor of his flock,[259] while Evans is revered not only as a popular author and historian but as a diligent and considerate churchman.[260] Yet their paranoid response to the Methodist 'threat' suggested that all was not well with the Established Church of the day. The structural and economic weaknesses enunciated in Chapter Four persisted while the turnover of political and Anglophone appointees to the four Welsh sees was unending. These were the 'Anglo-bishops' (*yr Esgyb Eingl*), berated and denounced by the snubbed and gifted cleric Evan Evans, 'Ieuan Fardd', in his (unpublished) 'Grievance of the Principality of Wales and the Church'.[261] Of the sixteen bishops who served between 1740 and 1760, three remained in post for less than a year-and-a-half (Mathias Mawson at Llandaff, 1740, before being translated to Chichester; Edward Wiles at St David's 1743–4, before proceeding to Bath and Wells, and John Thomas, appointed to St Asaph but never consecrated before transferring to Lincoln in 1744); eleven moved to other lucrative English sees (Nicholas Clagett, St David's 1732–43, to Exeter; Isaac Maddox, St Asaph 1736–43, to Worcester; Samuel Lisle, St Asaph 1744–8 to Norwich; Zachary Pierce, Bangor 1748–56, to Rochester; John Gilbert, Llandaff 1740–8 and Robert Hay Drummond, St Asaph, 1748–61, both to Salisbury; Thomas Herring, Bangor 1737–42 and Matthew Hutton, Bangor 1743–7, both to York and then to Canterbury; and Richard Trevor, St David's 1744–52 to Durham), while only two, Edward

Cressell, Llandaff 1749–55, and Anthony Ellys at St David's, 1752–61, died in office while in Wales. It goes without saying than none was Welsh-born while Hay Drummond and Trevor were conspicuous in their contempt for the Welsh language. Although these prelates visited their dioceses during the summer when the House of Lords was in recess, virtually their only direct contact with their flocks was for confirmations. Evan Evans's censure was merciless:

> What instruction can Welsh children, who do not understand English, receive from an Anglo-Welsh bishop's pompous parade of confirmation? For though a few of them who have been at school can like parrots repeat their catechism in that language, yet I am sure but a small number understand what they say, no more than they learned it in Arabic. What a solemn mockery is this, calculated to amuse the simplicity of our countrymen with outward shew and pageantry.[262]

Yet it was not the presence, or absence, of high ecclesiastical dignitaries on which the reputation and pastoral effectiveness of the Welsh church depended but on the quality of spiritual care in the parishes, and there the record was, in places, grim. The situation in England during the first decades of the Evangelical Revival can be replicated in Wales:

> The satirical writers may have caricatured, but they did not invent the less pleasant clerical types which abounded. There are too many ugly and precise examples almost accidentally portrayed in the pages of John Wesley's *Journal* for us to doubt that immoral, drunken and bigoted clergy were to be found in numbers which perhaps passed the danger level.[263]

In his 1730 visitation, the rural dean of Penllyn and Edeirnion in the diocese of St Asaph described Robert Edwards, the rector of Llandderfel, as 'a wretch and a monster', negligent, drunken, sexually immoral and an attempted murderer to boot,[264] while James Thomas, vicar of Llanfihangel Rhos-y-corn and two other parishes in the diocese of St David's, was presented to the consistory court in December 1732 for 'drunkenness and neglect of duties'. It was alleged that he often sat up the whole night drinking, and that 'Henry Thomas saw James Thomas and one Mr Evan Davies, clerk, drinking ale with John Evan in the latter's house ... Thomas vomited three times, giving great offence to

Henry Thomas who paid his reckoning and departed'. This conduct was compounded by the vicar's public declaration that 'he would not come to officiate [in Rhos-y-corn] in winter neither would he come at any other time unless he thought fit'.[265] Even the court's hearing seems to have had no effect. The churchwardens grew desperate and hired Evan Jones, a curate from Talley, who duly conducted the services and preached every Sunday. All went well until Easter Day 1733 when Thomas, who had not been near the church for several months, turned up during the service, presumably to collect his Easter Offering. Seizing the Prayer Book from the hapless curate he threw him out of the church. The next Sunday he turned up again and did the same. Evan Jones did not risk a third ejection: he stayed peacefully at home in Talley. It was only with the death of the incumbent in 1742 and the establishment of a circulating school in the parish that a semblance of decency and ministerial fidelity was restored.

Such blatant occurrences may have been the exception, but there is ample evidence for not only the exemplary ministry of many of the clergy but of the profligacy of others as well. In a detailed letter to David Lloyd, incumbent of Llandefalle, Breconshire, in June 1741, Howell Harris praised 'the laborious, experimental, pious and successful' among the neighbourhood's clergy, but he warned that 'the scandalous lives and bitter persecuting spirit of many of them should make every sober thinking person rather mourn for them than endeavour to justify them'. It was for the conscientious clergy to expose these people, surely? 'When their drunkenness, swearing, pride and malice are exposed, it is exposing the Church. God forbid that *these* should be the Church!'[266] Six months earlier, on his third visit to Bala in north Wales, Harris had been met by a mob of irate locals led by Robert Jones, vicar of Llanycil, who had set upon him viciously, pelting him with stones and thrashing him with batons, until the blood was flowing. Fortified by 'a barrel of drink' provided by Jones, they had been rallied in order 'to defend the Church'. 'On hearing the call that all that loved the Church should come to gather to defend her, many townsfolk came together and joined his army.'[267] Soon after, when on his way to Pwllheli in neighbouring Caernarfonshire, he attended worship at Llannor and heard an extraordinary sermon about himself. John Owen, vicar of the parish and chancellor of Bangor Cathedral, a man 'famous for a troublesome litigious temper and of an obscure, mean family',[268] unaware that the evangelist was in the congregation, warned his parishioners against the 'accursed heretic', 'minister of Satan', 'enemy of God and his Church and all mankind' that was about to come among them: 'He urged his listeners solemnly, for love of God, his Church and their country, to stand resolutely against this awful man who was intent on destroying not only their property but their immortal souls.'[269] When Harris made himself known after the end of the service, he was assailed by the congregation in the churchyard and was fortunate to escape unscathed.

Only a few of the clergy went to this length of violence in their opposition to the spread of Methodism, but during the 1740s persecution was an undoubted factor in the story. 'It must be admitted', wrote one Welsh Anglican historian, 'that the record is stark and clear'.[270] The stoking up of resentment against converts and their exhorters who were redoubling their efforts knowing that their cause was gaining ground took literary as well as sermonic form. William Roberts, sexton of the church at Llannor and intimate of the vicar John Owen, issued his satiric interlude or popular play *Ffrewyll y Methodistiaid* ('Scourge of the Methodists') around 1745 which lampooned the Methodists mercilessly. Among the *dramatis personae*, along with Harris and George Whitefield was Jenkin Morgan, a teacher in Griffith Jones's circulating schools who would later be ordained a Congregational minister. Not only does the play justify the abuse of the Methodists but positively revels in it.[271] Despite this (or perhaps, partly, because of it), by 1750 Methodism had begun to take root in north Wales just as it had established itself a decade earlier in many parts of the south. In June 1749 William Richard, a Cardiganshire itinerant, described the response of his preaching at Penmachno, 'a very dismal place among the rocky mountains' some twelve miles from Bala: 'I marvelled to see so many poor assembled together ... It melted my heart to see hundreds of such poor ignorant creatures in such a wild country flocking together to hear the gospel.'[272] By then active persecution had abated, and not only un-ordained itinerants but regular Methodist clergy led now by Peter Williams, ordained deacon by the bishop of St David's in 1745 who had thrown in his lot with the Methodists in 1747, were making an ever deeper impression on the counties of the north. 'Mr Peter Williams is extraordinary liked in these parts', wrote one of Howell Harris's correspondents in July 1747, 'and I hope he will come to us once a quarter. If he could be settled here for some time, the Dissenters would (I believe) decrease as fast as they have increased in this country [Anglesey] and Llŷn.'[273] It was not that conventional Anglicans were any less critical of Methodist irregularity: for many the critique made by Thomas Ellis's *Gair o Gyngor ... mewn perthynas i'r Schismaticiaid* ('A Word of Counsel ... in relation to the Schismatics) was as pertinent as ever.[274] But even they realized that conventional Anglicanism had failed, sometimes dismally, to provide its nominal members to say nothing of the poor and dispossessed who had been beyond their reach, with a satisfying spiritual commitment and a vibrant faith:

> Had the Church been capable of responding to the needs of the people, and had the clergy performed their duties more faithfully and diligently, the need for itinerant lay preachers might never have arisen. Methodism filled a felt need: a sense of spiritual vacuum. Given the fact that the Church failed to respond in a positive way, and given the determination of the Methodists to put the salvation of souls before the preservation of the external structures of the Church, the conflict was unavoidable. It is noticeable that, where the local clergy accepted the Methodist priority of salvation over structure and truth over tradition, the representatives of the two camps were able to cohabit and co-operate.[275]

This was exemplified clearly by the response of Thomas Jones, vicar of Trefriw in the Conwy Valley, to Methodist itinerants who had been proselyting in his parish early in 1749. Although he challenged their canonical authority and winced at their outlandish ways, he nevertheless accepted that they were only intent on doing good. 'I am for my part', he claimed, 'an enemy to enthusiasm, an enemy to hypocrisy and imposture, but a friend to true religion, piety and virtue and all lawful ways of promoting the same be the persons concerned in the good work of what denomination they will'.[276]

Along with the Evangelical Revival, the most significant aspect of Welsh religious life by 1760 was the spread and success of Griffith Jones's circulating schools. According to the bishop of Bangor's visitation returns of 1749, there were thirty-one schools in his diocese while the *Welch Piety* recorded that the trend would continue throughout the next decade.[277] Despite the poverty of the see, financial hardship among the clergy and other pervasive ills, the unobtrusive pastoral and theological renewal associated with Griffith Jones's venture was paying solid dividends. The question with which we shall conclude this narrative is: to what extent was that broad renewal implicit in the mission of the Established Church from the beginning? Geraint H. Jenkins's revisionist thesis, published in 1978 in his landmark *Literature, Religion and*

Society in Wales, 1660–1730 and restated with aplomb in 'The Spirit of Enthusiasm', chapter nine of his *The Foundations of Modern Wales, 1642–1780* in 1987 was that far from being a novelty commencing in 1735, materials for the so-called 'Revival' had been laid down in the extensive literary and pastoral exertions of both Anglicans and Dissenters well before, and that vital piety had been implicit in their witness all the time. Whereas this view had (and still has) much to commend it, the reaction against the older 'Methodist view of history' meant that all elements of continuity were privileged while the originality and the innovative quality of the Evangelical Revival were severely downplayed.[278] Soon afterwards Jenkins's namesake, Philip Jenkins, on the basis of his researches on the Glamorgan gentry and the High Church party during the Commonwealth, Restoration and thereafter,[279] accentuated the general spiritual ebullience among Welsh Anglicans during the seventeenth and eighteenth centuries suggesting that the tradition was constantly renewing itself throughout. 'The period between about 1680 and 1730' was, he claims, 'a golden age for the Welsh Church', while 'the best evidence for the vigour of the church was the Evangelical Revival itself'.[280] This, in turn, has provided a boon for more recent Anglican historians who have underplayed the significance of Protestant Dissent, soft-pedalled or rationalized the weaknesses of the Established Church, overlooked the Episcopal disdain under which Griffith Jones fulfilled his vision for renewal, and ignored the deep ambiguities that existed between the Revival and the Church. 'Methodism in Wales', claims William Jacob, 'was an outcome of the pastoral revival of the Established Church'.[281] This view has been taken to extreme and incredulous lengths by William Gibson (in his treatment of the diocese of St David's) who has questioned whether there ever *was* an Evangelical Revival at all.

> If there was a revival – and this is increasingly open to question – it was begun in the 1670s and provided the momentum for a later generations in the 1740s. Before John Wesley set foot in Wales in 1739 and before George Whitefield visited in the same year, before Howel Harris' conversion in 1735 and Daniel Rowland began his preaching, there was a Church in Wales which was already alive and awake.[282]

Enough, surely, has been discussed in this and previous chapters to show how much of a travesty this claim is. All too often theological vitality was manifest in the Established Church in the context of formality, indifference and sometimes open opposition while despite its flaws, Dissent was not wholly devoid of virtue and verve. The successors of those who had found themselves, for conscience's sake, outside the establishment also had a significant contribution to make.

✠

'The rise of Pietism and Evangelicalism', according to David Hempton, 'marked the beginning of the end of the confessional age of the magisterial Reformation, and may be regarded as the second stage of the history of Protestantism'.[283] It has been our concern in this study to follow the way in which, after the publication of the Welsh Bible in 1588, the bases of a vernacular Protestant culture were laid down, how the theological principles of the Reformation – *sola fides, sola gratia* and *sola scriptura* – fared through the vicissitudes of the seventeenth and early eighteenth centuries, and how by 1760 it had become a popular and influential movement. The next volume will take the narrative forward from beyond Hempton's second stage to account for Protestantism's nineteenth-century triumph and by 1900, the age of philosophical Idealism and incipient secularism, to assess the first signs of its ominous decline.

Notes

1 J. Morgan Jones (ed.), 'Llyfr Eglwys y Cilgwyn', *Y Cofiadur*, 1 (1923), 22–31 (28).

2 Michael R. Watts, *The Dissenters: from the Reformation to the French Revolution* (Oxford: Clarendon Press, 1978), p. 264.

3 A point argued forcibly and irrefutably many years ago by Bernard Lord Manning, 'Congregationalism in the Eighteenth Century', in *Essays in Orthodox Dissent* (London: Independent Press, 1939), pp. 171–95; *idem*, 'Some characteristics of the Older Dissent', *Congregational Quarterly*, 5 (1927), 286–300.

4 Diary of the Revd John Kenrick, transcribed and quoted in A. N. Palmer, *A History of the Older Nonconformity of Wrexham and its Neighbourhood* (Wrexham: Woodhall, Mincham and Thomas, 1888), pp. 63–4 (64).

5 The detail of which is analysed in Watts, *The Dissenters: from the Reformation to the French Revolution*, pp. 267–89.

6 R. Tudur Jones, 'Yr Hen Ymneilltuwyr', in Gomer M. Roberts (ed.), *Hanes Methodistiaeth Galfinaidd Cymru*, vol. 1, *Y Deffroad Mawr* (Caernarfon: Llyfrfa'r Methodistiaid, 1974), pp. 13–42 (15–16).

7 Geraint H. Jenkins, *The Foundations of Modern Wales, 1642–1780* (Oxford: Clarendon Press, 1987), p. 195.

8   The details of their ministry are listed in the respective entries in *DWB*.

9   R. Tudur Jones, *Congregationalism in Wales*, ed. Robert Pope (Cardiff: University of Wales Press, 2004), p. 80.

10   See James Owen, *Moderation a Virtue, or the Occasional Conformist Justified* (London: A. Baldwin, 1703).

11   *Traethawd ynghylch Gweithredoedd Da ac Elusenau, o waith Mr Thomas Gouge* (Llundain: Thomas Whitledge a William Everingham, 1693).

12   *Rhessymau Ysgrythurawl yn profi mai Dyledswydd pob math o Wrandawr yw cyfrannu ... tuag at Gynhaliaeth cysurus eu Gweinidogion, o waith Mr Thomas Gouge* (Llundain: Thomas Whitledge a William Everingham, 1693).

13   Joseph Alleine, *Hyfforddwr Cyfarwydd i'r Nefoedd, neu Wahoddiad Difrifol i Bechaduriaid droi at Dduw* (Llundain: Thomas Whitledge a William Everingham, 1693), p. 22.

14   Alleine, *Hyfforddwr Cyfarwydd i'r Nefoedd*; a second edition would be published in 1723; for Alleine (1634–68), see *ODNB*.

15   Owen, *Moderation a Virtue*, p. 11.

16   Garfield H. Hughes, 'Emynyddiaeth gynnar yr Ymneilltuwyr', *Llên Cymru*, 2 (1953), 135–46; Tudur Jones, *Congregationalism in Wales*, pp. 83–4; for Baddy (d.1729), see *DWB*.

17   *Pasc y Christion, neu Wledd yr Efengyl, wedi ei chyhoeddi mewn traethawd ynghylch Swpper yr Arglwydd ... gan Thomas Doolittle, wedi ei Gymreigio gan T[homas] B[addy]* (Llundain: n.p., 1703), p. 16; for Doolittle (1630–1707), see *ODNB*.

18   The work would be re-issued twice, in 1739 and 1740.

19   For Dyer (1623–96) and Wadsworth (1630–76), see *ODNB*.

20   Geraint H. Jenkins, *Literature, Religion and Society in Wales, 1660–1730* (Cardiff: University of Wales Press, 1978), p. 128.

21   Jenkins, *Literature, Religion and Society in Wales*.

22   *Dattodiad y Cwestiwn Mawr ... Athrawiaethau i Fuchedd Sanctaidd, o waith y difinydd parchedig Mr. Richard Baxter* (Llundain: Thomas Whitledge a William Everingham, 1693); no translator's name appears either on the title page or in the text.

23   See J. I. Packer, *The Redemption and Restoration of Man in the thought of Richard Baxter: a Study in Puritan Theology* (Vancouver: Regent College Publications, 2003).

24   *Egwyddorion a Sylfeini'r Grefydd Grisnogol wedi eu crynhoi allan o Catechism ... y Gymanfa o Ddifinyddion yn Westmisnter*, trans. James Owen (Llundain: Edward Brewster, 1691).

25   G. Milwyn Griffiths, 'A Visitation to the Archdeaconry of Carmarthen, 1710', *NLWJ*, 18 (1974), 287–311 (294).

26   *Egwyddorion y Grefydd Grisnogol yn Gymraeg ... megis eu gosodwyd hwynt allan mewn Catechism Byr gan y Parchedig Gymanfa o Ddifinyddion yn Westminster ... gyda rheolau byrrion*, trans. William Evans (Mwythig: John Rogers, 1707).

27   *Egwyddorion y Grefydd Gristnogol yn Gymraeg, er lleshad Ieuengctid Cymru*, trans. Abel Morgan, 2nd edn (Bristol: John Grabham, 1759); Abel Morgan

(1673–1722) left Wales to become minister of the Pennepeck Church in Pennsylvania in 1711, see *DWB*.

28 *Eglurhaad o Gatechism Byrraf y Gymanfa … o waith Thomas Vincent, a gyfieithi-wyd i'r Gymraeg gan J[ohn] P[ugh]* (Trefhedyn: Isaac Carter, 1719).

29 See Packer, *The Redemption and Restoration of Man in the thought of Richard Baxter*, Chapter 14, 'The Errors of Antinomianism', pp. 351–70.

30 See Peter Toon, *The Emergence of Hyper-Calvinism in English Nonconformity, 1689–1765*, new edn (Eugene, OR: Wipf and Stock, 2011), pp. 49–69; for Williams, see *ODNB*.

31 This was the John Evans who had married Vavasor Powell's widow who would become the father of Dr John Evans, Daniel Williams's successor as minister of the Hand's Alley Church.

32 Palmer, *A History of the Older Nonconformity of Wrexham*, pp. 53–5.

33 Joshua Thomas, *Hanes y Bedyddwyr Ymhlith y Cymry* (Caerfyrddin: John Ross, 1778), p. 152; Edwards's (1649–1700) contribution is noted in *DWB*.

34 See Roger Thomas, 'The Break-up of Dissent', in Geoffrey F. Nuttall et al., *The Beginnings of Nonconformity* (London: The Hibbert Trust, 1964), pp. 53–60; Watts, *The Dissenters: from the Reformation to the French Revolution*, pp. 289–97.

35 See above Chapter Three, p. 212; italics added.

36 *Byr a chywir hanes Eglwys Rhydyceished*, an appendix to his volume *Y Wir Eglwys yn cyrchu at y nod nefol* (n.p.: 1727), was republished in *Y Cofiadur*, 3 (1925), 41–9 while *Golwg ar y Beiau … ym mherthynas i'r rhwygiad a wnaeth-pwyd yn Eglwys Henllan* (Caerfyrddin: NT ac I. W, 1732–3) was republished, with an introduction by R. T. Jenkins, by the University of Wales Press in 1949; all page references in the text are to the republished versions.

37 For Richard Davis and Maurice's Rothwell ministry, see Geoffrey F. Nuttall, 'Northamptonshire and *The Modern Question*: a turning-point in eighteenth century Dissent', in *Studies in English Dissent* (Weston Rhyn: The Quinta Press, 2002), pp. 205–30; Maurice is listed in *DWB* while the authorita-tive study of his life and work is Wynford Thomas, 'Matthias Maurice a'i Eglwysoleg' (unpublished PhD dissertation, University of Wales Trinity Saint David, 2011).

38 Jeremy Owen, *Golwg ar y Beiau*, ed. R. T. Jenkins (Caerdydd: Gwasg Prifysgol Cymru, 1949), p. 58.

39 Minutes for 4–5 September 1711, quoted in Nuttall, 'Northamptonshire and *The Modern Question*', p. 215.

40 The stages in the dispute are explored in detail by Thomas Richards, 'The Henllan secessions', in J. E. Lloyd (ed.), *A History of Carmarthenshire*, vol. 2 (Cardiff: The London Carmarthenshire Society, 1939), pp. 165– 70.

41 See R. Tudur Jones, *Congregationalism in England, 1662–1962* (London: Independent Press, 1962), pp. 132–3.

42 See G. Dyfnallt Owen, 'James Owen a'i Academi', *Y Cofiadur*, 22 (1952), 3–36 and 'James Owen's Academy, Oswestry and Shrewsbury (1690–1706)', Dr Williams Library, Dissenting Academies Database online.

43   See Saunders Lewis, 'Jeremi Owen', in *Meistri'r Canrifoedd: Ysgrifau ar Hanes Llenyddiaeth Gymraeg*, ed. R. Geraint Gruffydd (Caerdydd: Gwasg Prifysgol Cymru, 1973), pp. 248–58; R. Tudur Jones, 'Cofio'r Gwas', in *Ffydd yn y Ffau* (Abertawe: Gwasg John Penry, 1973), pp. 26–31.

44   For Owen, see *DWB* and Marian G. Thomas, 'Astudiaeth o waith Jeremi Owen' (unpublished MA dissertation, University of Wales, Aberystwyth, 1975).

45   See *ODNB* for the doctrinal views of both Coles (1608–88) and Chauncey (1632–1712).

46   J. Dyfnallt Owen in *DWB*.

47   *Traethawd Y marferol am Gyflawn-Awdyrdod Duw ... o waith Mr Eliseus Cole ... wedi ei gyfieithu gan H[owel] Powel* (Caerludd: I'r cyfieithydd, 1711), p. 49; hereafter page numbers are in the text.

48   *Yr Atrawiaeth [sic] y sydd yn ôl Duwioldeb ... gan Isaac Chauncy ... wedi ei gyfieithu i'r Gymraeg gan Matthias Maurice* (Llundain: Edmund Powel, 1711), p. 61.

49   NLW MS 10589A, sermon on John 10:27; for Jenkins (1656–1733), see *DWB*.

50   NLW MS 10589A, sermon preached at Rhydwilym, 24 February 1724; for Francis, see *DWB*, *ODNB*.

51   Enoch Francis, *Gair yn ei Bryd, neu ychydig o eglurhad ar Ddirgeledigaethau ... yr Ysgrythur am Arfaeth Duw* (Caerfyrddin: N[icholas] T[homas], 1733), p. 5; the doctrinal stance of the Baptists is assessed in D. Densil Morgan, 'Welsh Baptist theology, c.1714–60', *JWEH*, 7 (1990), 16–25.

52   NLW MS 10589A, sermon on Eph. 5:14, Rhydwilym, April 1722.

53   Introduction to John Edwards, *Y Gwrandawr, neu Lyfr yn dangos pa gynheddfau reidiol i wrando y Gair a Bregethir ... o gyfieithiad H[owel] Powel* (Llundain: Edmund Powel, 1709), Sig. A2; John Edwards (1637–1716), was the Calvinist incumbent of Holy Trinity Church, Cambridge, see *ODNB*.

54   Edwards, *Y Gwrandawr, neu Lyfr yn dangos pa gynheddfau reidiol i wrando y Gair a Bregethir*, p. 5.

55   Benjamin Meredith, introduction to John Bunyan, *Pechadur Jerusalem yn Gadwedig* (Henffordd: William Parkes, 1721), p. vii; for Meredith (1700–49), see *DWB*.

56   Thomas, *Hanes y Bedyddwyr ymhlith y Cymry* (1778), p. 387.

57   NLW MS 10589A, sermon preached at Rhydwilym, 24 February 1723.

58   NLW Cwrt Mawr MS 68A; for Jacob Rees (d.1772), see Joshua Thomas, *Hanes y Bedyddwyr ymhlith y Cymry*, trans. Benjamin Davies, 2nd edn (Pontypridd: Benjamin Davies, 1885), pp. 458–9.

59   Francis, *Gair yn ei Bryd*, pp. 77–8.

60   Francis, *Gair yn ei Bryd*, p. 29.

61   NLW MS 10589A, sermon on Ecclesiastes 12:14, 13 January 1722.

62   NLW MS 10589A, sermon on Romans 6:4, April 1722.

63   NLW MS 9913A, sermon on Matthew 16:26, June 1731; for Abel Francis (d.c.1743), see *DWB*.

64   James Owen, *Trugaredd a Barn, neu yn agos i Drichant o Siampleu rhyfeddol o farnedigaethau Duw ar yr Annuwiol*, 2nd edn (Llundain: n.p., 1716), Sig. A4.

65   Matthew Meade, *Llun Agrippa, neu'r o fewn ychydig Gristion wedi ei ddadguddio*, trans. Jenkin Jones (Caerfyrddin: N[icholas] Thomas, 1723), p. 20; the original work was entitled *The almost Christian discover'd: or, the false professor tryed and cast* (1662); for Meade (1628–99), see *ODNB*.

66   Thomas Vincent, *Dydd y Farn Fawr, neu sain yr Udgorn Diwethaf, sef ymddangosiad dilys a disymmwth Crist i farnu'r byd ... wedi ei gyfieithu a'i gyfaddasu gan Jencin Jones* (Caerfyrddin: Nicholas Thomas, 1727), p. 356; for Vincent (1634–99), see *ODNB*.

67   Enoch Francis, *Gwaith a Gwobr ffyddlon weinidogion yr Efengyl, neu bregeth a bregethwyd mewn Cymmanfa o weinidogion ... yn Llangloffan* (Caerfyrddin: Isaac Carter, 1729), p. 16.

68   E.g. John Kenrick (1684–1745), who took Presbyterian orders in 1707 being ordained by Matthew Henry as minister of Wrexham's New Meeting, Henry Davies (1696–1766), ordained at Blaen-gwrach in 1718 and Henry Palmer (1679–1742) ordained at Henllan in 1721, all of whom are listed in *DBW*; cf. Tudur Jones, 'Yr Hen Ymneilltuwyr'; *idem, Congregationalism in Wales*, pp. 79–109; for Pugh, see also T. Eirug Davies, 'Philip Pugh a'i lafur yn y Cilgwyn', *Y Cofiadur*, 14 (1937), 16–36 and E. D. Jones, 'Philip Pugh', *Diwinyddiaeth*, 15 (1964), 62–9.

69   Thomas, *Hanes y Bedyddwyr ymhlith y Cymry*, 2nd edn (1885), p. 376.

70   Thomas, *Hanes y Bedyddwyr ymhlith y Cymry* (1778), p. 387; for Griffiths, see William Richards, *The Welsh Nonconformists' Memorial* (London: n.p., 1820), pp. 249–60.

71   Entry in *DWB*.

72   E. Gordon Rupp, *Religion in England, 1688–1791* (Oxford: Clarendon Press, 1986), p. 72.

73   Joshua Thomas, *A History of the Baptist Association in Wales* (London: n.p., 1795), p. 21.

74   Roger Hayden, 'The Particular Baptist Confession of 1689 and today', *BQ*, 32 (1988), 403–17.

75   *Cyffes Ffydd, wedi ei gosod allan gan henuriaid a brodyr amryw Gynulleidfaoedd (wedi eu bedyddio ar broffes o'u ffydd) yn Llundain a'r wlad; wedi ei gyfieithu gan R[ees] D[avid]* (Caerfyrddin: N[icholas] Thomas, 1721); see D. Densil Morgan, 'Cefndir, Cymreigiad a Chynnwys Cyffes Ffydd 1689', *TCHB* (1990), 19–34; reprinted in *Y Deugain Mlynedd Hyn: Diwinydda yng Nghymru, 1972–2015* (Bangor: Cyhoeddiadau'r Gair, 2015), pp. 18–37.

76   Thomas, *A History of the Baptist Association in Wales*, p. 41.

77   Thomas Richards, 'Nonconformity from 1620 to 1715', in Lloyd (ed.), *A History of Carmarthenshire*, vol. 2, pp. 133–84 (150); see B. G. Owens, 'Rhydwilym Church, 1668–89: a study of West Wales Baptists', in Mansel John (ed.), *Welsh Baptist Studies* (Cardiff: South Wales Baptist College, 1976), pp. 92–107.

78   Thomas, *Hanes y Bedyddwyr ymhlith y Cymry* (1778), pp. 420–1.

79 (*fl.* 1680–1712), listed in *DWB.*

80 See Chapter Three, pp. 216–18.

81 Geraint H. Jenkins, 'James Owen versus Benjamin Keach: a Controversy over Infant Baptism', *NLWJ*, 19 (1975), 57–66 (59).

82 James Owen, *Bedydd Plant o'r Nefoedd, neu Draethawd am Natur a Diben Bedydd* (Llundain: F. Collins, 1693), p. 40; hereafter page numbers are in the text.

83 For particulars of his life (d.1676) and the significance of his volume, which would be reissued many times during the next two centuries, see Geoffrey F. Nuttall, 'Another Baptist ejection (1662): the case of John Norcott', in William H. Brackney, Paul S. Fiddes and John H. Y. Briggs (eds), *Pilgrim Pathways: Essays in Baptist History in Honour of B. R. White* (Macon, GA: Mercer University Press, 1999), pp. 185–8.

84 *Bedydd gwedi i amlygu yn eglir ag yn fyddlon, yn ôl gair Duw ... gan Ioan Norcott* (Llundain: William Marshall, 1693), p. 19.

85 *Bedydd gwedi i amlygu yn eglir ag yn fyddlon, yn ôl gair Duw*, p. 19.

86 Benjamin Keach, *Goleuni gwedi torri allan Ynghymru, gan ymlid ymmaith dywyllwch: Cariad y Sais tuag at yr Hên Gymry, gan gynnwys atteb i lyfr yr hwn a elwir Bedydd plant o'r nefoedd ... gan Mr James Owen* (Llundain: William Marshall, 1696), p. xxii; hereafter page numbers are in the text.

87 Keach's standard defence of believer's baptism was entitled *Gold Refin'd, or Baptism in its Primitive Purity* (London: Nathaniel Crouch, 1689).

88 See *ODNB* and D. B. Riker, *A Catholic Reformed Theologian: Federalism and Baptism in the thought of Benjamin Keach, 1640–1704* (Carlisle: Paternoster Press, 2009).

89 Thomas, *Hanes y Bedyddwyr ymhlith y Cymry*, 2nd edn (1885), p. 112; for Morgan (1621–1710), see *DWB.*

90 Benjamin Keach, *Light broke forth in Wales expelling darkness, or the Englishman's Love to the Antient Britains, being an answer to a book entitled Children's Baptism from Heaven, published in the Welch tongue, by Mr James Owen* (London: William Marshall, 1696).

91 The covenant of salvation was that made in eternity between the Father and the Son in order to save the elect. The covenant of grace was the means whereby the elect, through the preaching of the gospel, were effectively called.

92 James Owen, *Ychwaneg o eglurhad am fedydd plant bychain* (Llundain: F. Collins, 1702), p. 16.

93 Jenkins, 'James Owen versus Benjamin Keach: a Controversy over Infant Baptism', 63.

94 Jenkins, 'James Owen versus Benjamin Keach: a Controversy over Infant Baptism', 61.

95 Thomas, *Hanes y Bedyddwyr ymhlith y Cymry* (1778), p. 239.

96 Thomas, *A History of the Baptist Association in Wales*, p. 46.

97 Fowler Walker, *A Defence of Infant Baptism wherein the arguments for it ... are briefly offered ... [and] Objections against it are answered* (London: n.p., 1732),

p. iv; the Welsh version was entitled *Bedydd Plant yn cael ei ymddiffin ... a'r Gwrthresymmau ... yn cael eu hateb* (Llundain: Richard Hett, 1732).

98 Walker, *A Defence of Infant Baptism*, p. 45.

99 *Adnodau ar rai lleoedd, cableddus a sarhaus ... ar fedydd plant gan Mr Fowler Walker* (Llundain: n.p., 1732).

100 David Rees, *Infant Baptism no Institution of Christ ... in answer to Mr Fowler Walker's ... Defence of Infant Baptism* (London: Aaron Ward, 1734); for the author, see *DWB* and Hugh Matthews, 'David Rees, Limehouse (1683–1748): an eighteenth century London Welsh preacher', *THSC* (1983), 81–96.

101 Theophilus Evans, *Cydymddiddan rhwng dau wr yn ammau ynghylch Bedydd-plant* (Llundain: Joseph Downing, 1719); Griffith Jones [of Denbigh], *Short and Plain Considerations to Convince Men of the Danger of Separating from the Communion of their Parish Churches* (London: n.p., 1728).

102 See D. Densil Morgan, '"Smoke, fire and light": Baptists and the revitalization of Welsh Dissent', *BQ*, 32 (1988), 224–32; Tudur Jones, *Congregationalism in Wales*, pp. 110–31.

103 Thomas Rees, *History of Protestant Nonconformity in Wales* (London: John Snow, 1861), p. 297.

104 Cf. Geoffrey F. Nuttall, 'The influence of Arminianism in England', in *The Puritan Spirit* (London: Epworth Press, 1967), pp. 67–80; the Welsh evidence is discussed on pp. 70–2.

105 Rees, *History of Protestant Nonconformity in Wales*, p. 297.

106 Dewi Eirug Davies, *Hoff Ddysgedig Nyth* (Abertawe: Gwasg John Penry, 1976), pp. 31–44; both Jones and Perrot are listed in *DWB*, Jones in *ODNB* as well.

107 Lewis had been ordained at Pencader in 1706 and would retain pastoral responsibility for both Pencader and Pantycreuddyn.

108 James Lewis and Christmas Samuel, *Y Cyfrif Cywiraf o'r Pechod Gwreiddiol ... [yn cynnwys] rhyw papuryn yn dwyn yr enw Cyfrif Cywir o'r Pechod Gwreiddiol* (Caerfyrddin: Isaac Carter, 1730), pp. 2, 25.

109 Eirug Davies, 'Philip Pugh a'i lafur yn y Cilgwyn', 20–2.

110 Jones, 'Philip Pugh', 65.

111 Eirug Davies, 'Philip Pugh a'i lafur yn y Cilgwyn', 23.

112 T. Oswald Williams, *Hanes Cynulleidfaoedd Undodaidd Sir Aberteifi* (Llandysul: Gwasg Gomer, n.d), pp. 5–14, 35–51.

113 Quoted in Gomer M. Roberts, *Y Pêr Ganiedydd [Pantycelyn], Cyfrol 1, Trem ar ei Fywyd* (Aberystwyth: Gwasg Aberystwyth, 1949), p. 42.

114 Tudur Jones, *Congregationalism in Wales*, p. 106.

115 For Rees (1707–49), see *DWB* and Tom Lewis, *History of the Hen Dŷ Cwrdd Cefn Coed y Cymer* (Llandysul: Gomerian Press, 1947).

116 Thomas, *A History of the Baptist Association in Wales*, p. 44.

117 Thomas, *A History of the Baptist Association in Wales*, p. 44.

118 Thomas, *A History of the Baptist Association in Wales*, p. 45.

119 Thomas, *A History of the Baptist Association in Wales*, p. 45.

120 Richards, *The Welsh Nonconformists' Memorial*, p. 271; see also *DWB*.

[121] William Herbert, *Nodiadau ar Bregeth Mr Abel Francis yng Nghwm Wysg, gerllaw Trecastell, 13 Awst 1732* (Aberhonddu: John Morgan, 1775), p. 20.

[122] Thomas, *A History of the Baptist Association in Wales*, p. 47.

[123] Thomas, *Hanes y Bedyddwyr ymhlith y Cymry* (1778), p. 212; Richards, *The Welsh Nonconformists' Memorial*, pp. 268, 277; Rees, *History of Protestant Nonconformity in Wales*, p. 299.

[124] NLW Iolo MS 13145A (Llanofer c58).

[125] Jacob Isaac, 'Charles Winter', *The Monthly Repository* (1806), 114.

[126] Thomas, *Hanes y Bedyddwyr ymhlith y Cymry* (1778), p. 210.

[127] Thomas, *Hanes y Bedyddwyr ymhlith y Cymry* (1778), p. 214.

[128] NLW Iolo MS 13145A (Llanofer c58).

[129] Thomas, *Hanes y Bedyddwyr ymhlith y Cymry* (1778), p. 64.

[130] Edward Evans, 'Yr Ymraniad yn Hengoed', *Yr Ymofynnydd* (1847), 149–53 (149).

[131] Geoffrey F. Nuttall, 'Calvinism in Free Church History', in *Studies in English Dissent*, pp. 51–64 (62, 61).

[132] Thomas, *A History of the Baptist Association in Wales*, p. 46; hereafter page numbers from *Gair yn ei Bryd* are included in the text.

[133] Sermon on John 6:68, preached at Rhydwilym 1722, *Trysorfa y Bedyddwyr* (1828), 19.

[134] See 'To the Baptized Ministers, and to all that were with them at the Consultation at Usk, about the Five Points included in Elisha Cole', Thomas Williams, *To the Society of People called Baptists* (n.p.: 1745), pp. 8–16; Morgan, 'Welsh Baptist theology, c.1714–60', 16–25.

[135] Thomas, *Hanes y Bedyddwyr ymhlith y Cymry* (1778), p. 391.

[136] Roger Hayden, *Continuity and Change: Evangelical Calvinism among ... Baptist ministers trained at Bristol Academy, 1690–1791* (Milton under Wychwood: Baptist Historical Society, 2006), pp. x, xi.

[137] Geoffrey F. Nuttall, 'Welsh students at the Bristol Baptist College, 1720–97', *THSC* (1978–9), 171–99; Hayden, *Continuity and Change: Evangelical Calvinism among ... Baptist ministers trained at Bristol Academy*, pp. 98–103.

[138] Hayden, *Continuity and Change: Evangelical Calvinism among ... Baptist ministers trained at Bristol Academy*, pp. 96–7.

[139] Thomas, *Hanes y Bedyddwyr ymhlith y Cymry*, 2nd edn (1885), p. 484; for Jackson's views, see Pater Naylor, *Calvinism, Communion and the Baptists: A Study of English Calvinistic Baptists from the late 1600s to the early 1800s* (Carlisle: Paternoster Press, 2003), pp. 177–8.

[140] Hayden, *Continuity and Change: Evangelical Calvinism among ... Baptist ministers trained at Bristol Academy*, p. 97.

[141] Matthias Maurice, *Social Religion Exaplify'd, in an Account of the first settlement of Christianity in the city of Caerludd* (London: James Buckland, 1737), p. 19.

[142] NLW Deposit MS 127A, Rhydwilym church book, p. 23.

[143] NLW Deposit MS 127A, Rhydwilym church book, p. 23.

[144] Maurice, *Social Religion Exaplify'd*, pp. 105–6.

[145] Eirug Davies, 'Philip Pugh a'i lafur yn y Cilgwyn', 17.

146 Morgan Jones (ed.), 'Llyfr Eglwys y Cilgwyn', 16.

147 Cf. E. D. Jones (ed.), 'Llyfr Eglwys Mynydd Bach', *Y Cofiadur*, 17 (1947), 3–50; E. D. Jones, 'Copi o Lyfr Pant-teg, Abergwili', *Y Cofiadur*, 23 (1953), 18–70.

148 Maurice, *Social Religion Exaplify'd*, p. 95.

149 Maurice, *Social Religion Exaplify'd*, p. 97.

150 NLW MS 10589A, sermon on Romans 6:4.

151 NLW Deposit MS 409B, Llanwenarth church book, pp. 175–6.

152 Thomas, *Hanes y Bedyddwyr ymhlith y Cymry* (1778), pp. 230, 232.

153 Edmund Jones, *A Geographical, Historical and Religious Account of the Parish of Aberystruth* (Trevecca: n.p., 1779), p. 99.

154 Thomas, *Hanes y Bedyddwyr ymhlith y Cymry*, 2nd edn (1885), p. 380.

155 NLW Deposit MS 1110B Cilfowyr church book, p. 107.

156 NLW Deposit MS 127A, Rhydwilym church book, pp. 94–7.

157 Thomas, *Hanes y Bedyddwyr ymhlith y Cymry*, 2nd edn (1885), pp. 471–5.

158 Jones, *A[n]... Account of the Parish of Aberystruth*, p. 98.

159 Rees, *History of Protestant Nonconformity in Wales*, p. 302.

160 Rees, *History of Protestant Nonconformity in Wales*, p. 302.

161 Rees, *History of Protestant Nonconformity in Wales*, p. 302, p. 303; for Edmund Jones, Lewis Rees and Timothy Thomas, see *DWB* while Jones and Thomas are also listed in *ODNB*.

162 Tudur Jones, *Congregationalism in Wales*, p. 107.

163 *Ateb Philo-Evangelius* (1762), Garfield H. Hughes (ed.), *Gweithiau William Williams Pantycelyn*, vol. 2 (Caerdydd: Gwasg Prifysgol Cymru, 1967), pp. 13–32 (15).

164 Hughes (ed.), *Gweithiau William Williams Pantycelyn*, p. 15.

165 Ioan Harri, *Rhai Datguddiadau o'r Nefoedd Newydd ar Ddaear Newydd* (Caerfyrddin: Nicholas Thomas 1725), p. 19; for John Harry (*c.*1674–1737), see Thomas, *Hanes y Bedyddwyr ymhlith y Cymry*, 2nd edn (1885), p. 412.

166 Francis, *Gwaith a Gwobr Ffyddlon Weinidogion yr Efengyl*, p. 17.

167 Jones, 'Philip Pugh', 65.

168 NLW Calvinistic Methodist Collection, letter 362, Edmund Jones to Howell Harris, 7 August 1741; Boyd S. Schlenther and Eryn M. White, *Calendar of the Trevecka Letters* (Aberystwyth: National Library of Wales, 2003), p. 57.

169 Jeremy Owen, *Traethawd i brofi ac i gymell ar yr holl Eglwysi y Ddyledswydd Fawr Efangylaidd o Weddïo dros Weinidogion* (Llundain: W. Wilcins, 1733), pp. 114–15.

170 Watts, *The Dissenters: from the Reformation to the French Revolution*, pp. 382–93; Robert Strivens, *Philip Doddridge and the Shaping of Evangelical Dissent* (Farnham: Ashgate, 2015), pp. 149–50.

171 Benjamin LaTrobe (ed.), *Brief Account of the Life of Howell Harris Esq* (Trevecka: 1791), p. 13; hereafter page numbers are in text.

172 See above, Chapter One, pp. 45–8.

173 See Eifion Evans, *Howel Harris, Evangelist* (Cardiff: University of Wales Press, 1974), *passim*.

174 The standard biography is Geraint Tudur, *Howell Harris: From Conversion to Separation, 1735–50* (Cardiff: University of Wales Press, 2000).

175 NLW Calvinistic Methodist Collection, letter 65, 27 February 1736; Roberts (ed.), *Hanes Methodistiaeth Galfinaidd Cymru*, vol. 1, *Y Deffroad Mawr*, p. 98.

176 NLW Calvinistic Methodist Collection, letter 65, 27 February 1736; Roberts (ed.), *Hanes Methodistiaeth Galfinaidd Cymru*, vol. 1, *Y Deffroad Mawr*, p. 98.

177 Quoted in Richard Bennett, *Blynyddoedd Cyntaf Methodistiaeth* (Caernarfon: Llyfrfa y Cyfundeb, 1909), p. 72.

178 Geoffrey F. Nuttall, *Howel Harris 1714–73: the Last Enthusiast* (Cardiff: University of Wales Press, 1965), p. 3.

179 Eifion Evans, 'Thomas Jones Cwm-iou (1689–1772)', *CCH*, 8 (1984), 24–30.

180 Bennett, *Blynyddoedd Cyntaf Methodistiaeth*, pp. 102–3.

181 The authoritative study is Eryn M. White, *Praidd Bach y Bugail Mawr: Seiadau Methodistaidd De-Orllewin Cymru* (Llandysul: Gwasg Gomer, 1995).

182 NLW Calvinistic Methodist Collection, letter 87 to Griffith Jones, 8 October 1736; Boyd and White, *Calendar of the Trevecka Letters*, p. 12.

183 Quoted in Evans, *Howel Harris, Evangelist*, p. 21.

184 LaTrobe (ed.), *Brief Account of the Life of Howell Harris*, p. 109.

185 Tudur, *Howell Harris: from Conversion to Separation, 1735–50*, p. 33.

186 Tudur, *Howell Harris: from Conversion to Separation, 1735–50*, p. 38.

187 Thomas Shepard, *Y Cywir Ddychwelwr, yn datguddio y nifer bychan o'r rhai gwir gredadwy [gadwedig?]*, trans. Thomas Humphrey, 2nd edn (Caerfyrddin: Nicholas Thomas, 1727); for the first edition see above, Chapter Two, pp. 135–7.

188 NLW Calvinistic Methodist Collection, letter 1295 to James Erskine, 19 February 1745; Schlenther and White, *Calendar of the Trevecka Letters*, p. 209; it is transcribed in Gomer M. Roberts (ed.), *Selected Trevecka Letters, 1742–7* (Caernarfon: Calvinistic Methodist Bookroom, 1956), pp. 163–8 (166).

189 See David Ceri Jones, Boyd S. Schlenther and Eryn M. White, *The Elect Methodists: Calvinistic Methodism in England and Wales, 1735–1811* (Cardiff: University of Wales Press, 2012), *passim*.

190 Tudur, *Howell Harris: from Conversion to Separation, 1735–50*, p. 42.

191 NLW Calvinistic Methodist Collection, Diary 23, 18 March 1737.

192 NLW Calvinistic Methodist Collection, Diary 23A, 9 April 1737.

193 NLW Trefeca MS 3186; Tudur, *Howell Harris: from Conversion to Separation, 1735–50*, p. 42.

194 For biographical details, see Eifion Evans, *Daniel Rowland and the Great Evangelical Awakening in Wales* (Edinburgh: Banner of Truth Trust, 1985) and Eryn M. White in *ODNB*.

195 Evans, *Daniel Rowland and the Great Evangelical Awakening in Wales*, p. 40.

196 For an overview of the eighteenth-century awakening in its transatlantic guise, see David Ceri Jones, *The Fire Divine: An Introduction to the Evangelical Revival* (Nottingham: IVP, 2015).

197 Henry D. Rack, *Reasonable Enthusiast: John Wesley and the Rise of Methodism* (London: Epworth Press, 1989), p. 197

198 Evans, *Daniel Rowland and the Great Evangelical Awakening in Wales*, p. 43.

199 Jones, Schlenther and White, *The Elect Methodists: Calvinistic Methodism in England and Wales, 1735–1811*, p. 13.

200 NLW Calvinistic Methodist Collection, letter 136, 8 January 1739; Schlenther and White, *Calendar of the Trevecka Letters*, p. 20.

201 NLW Calvinistic Methodist Collection, letter 112, 12 June 1738; Schlenther and White, *Calendar of the Trevecka Letters*, p. 17; for Williams (1709–84), see *DWB*.

202 For Whitefield, see Harry H. Stout, *The Divine Dramatist: George Whitfield and the Rise of Modern Evangelicalism* (Grand Rapids: Eerdmans, 1991); Frank Lambert, *Pedlar in Divinity: George Whitefield and the Trans-Atlantic Revivals, 1737–70* (Princeton, NJ: Princeton University Press, 1994) and Geordan Hammond and David Ceri Jones (eds), *George Whitefield: Life, Context and Legacy* (Oxford: Oxford University Press, 2015).

203 NLW Calvinistic Methodist Collection, letter 133, 20 December 1738; LaTrobe (ed.), *Brief Account of the Life of Howell Harris*, p. 112.

204 For this aspect, see especially David Ceri Jones, *'A Glorious Work in the World': Welsh Methodism and the International Evangelical Revival, 1735–1750* (Cardiff: University of Wales Press, 2004).

205 Whitefield's Journal; quoted in Roberts (ed.), *Hanes Methodistiaeth Galfinaidd Cymru*, vol. 1, *Y Deffroad Mawr*, pp. 110–11.

206 See especially W. R. Ward, *Early Evangelicalism: A Global Intellectual History, 1670–1789* (Cambridge: Cambridge University Press, 2006).

207 David Ceri Jones, 'A Glorious Morn? Methodism and the rise of Evangelicalism in Wales, 1735–62', in Mark Smith (ed.), *British Evangelical Identities Past and Present*, vol. 1 (Milton Keynes: Paternoster, 2008), pp. 97–113 (105).

208 See however Eryn M. White, '"The People called Methodists": Early Welsh Methodism and the Question of Identity', *JWRH*, 1 (2001), 7–20.

209 See the pertinent sections in Rack, *Reasonable Enthusiast: John Wesley and the Rise of Methodism* and Colin Podmore, *The Moravian Church in England, 1728–60* (Oxford: Oxford University Press, 1998).

210 The classic study remains R. T. Jenkins, 'Yr Annibynwyr Cymreig a Hywel Harris', in *Yng Nghysgod Trefeca: Ysgrifau ar Hanes Crefydd a Chymdeithas yng Nghymru yn y Ddeunawfed Ganrif* (Caernarfon: Llyfrfa'r Methodistiaid Calfinaidd, 1968), pp. 9–37; for the rift with the Baptists Miles Harry and William Herbert, see Tudur, *Howell Harris: from Conversion to Separation, 1735–50*, pp. 76–7, 98–100.

211 *Sail, Dibenion a Rheolau y Cymdeithasau ... a ddechreuasant ymgynnull yn ddiweddar yng Nghymru* (Bristol: Felix Farley, 1742), Sig. Av.

212 The tensions are mapped thoroughly in Tudur, *Howell Harris: from Conversion to Separation, 1735–50*, Chapter Seven, 'Controversy and Division', from which all quotations are taken.

213 NLW Calvinistic Methodist Collection, letter 544, 27 April 1742; Schlenther and White, *Calendar of the Trevecka Letters*, p. 17; transcribed in Roberts (ed.), *Selected Trevecka Letters, 1742–7*, p. 10.

214 Tudur, *Howell Harris: from Conversion to Separation, 1735–50*, p. 160.

215 Geraint Tudur, '"Like a right arm and a pillar": the story of James Beaumont', in Robert Pope (ed.), *Honouring the Past and Shaping the Future: essays in honour of Gareth Lloyd Jones* (Leominster: Gracewing, 2003), pp. 133–58.

216 For the biographical detail, see Eryn M. White's entry in *ODNB*.

217 Tudur, *Howell Harris: from Conversion to Separation, 1735–50*, p. 199.

218 Howell Davies (?1717–70), leader of the movement in Pembrokeshire, William Williams (1717–91), the hymnist, and Peter Williams (1723–96), chief clerical itinerant and Bible expositor, each have entries in both *DWB* and *ODNB*.

219 For the longsuffering Anne, see Geraint Tudur, '"The king's daughter": a reassessment of Anne Harris of Trefeca', *JWRH*, 7 (1999), 55–76.

220 Tudur, *Howell Harris: from Conversion to Separation, 1735–50*, p. 216; Chapter Eight, 'The Prophetess', presents a uniquely insightful analysis of the whole affair.

221 Tudur, *Howell Harris: from Conversion to Separation, 1735–50*, p. 223.

222 Daniel Rowland, *Ymddiddan rhwng Methodist Uniawn-gred ac un Camsyniol* (1750), reissued in Morris Davies (ed.), *Deuddeg Pregeth gan y Parchg Daniel Rowland* (Dolgellau: D. B. Jones, 1876), pp. 332–9 (338).

223 See Jones, Schlenther and White, *The Elect Methodists: Calvinistic Methodism in England and Wales, 1735–1811*, pp. 97–122; Eryn M. White, '"A Breach in God's House": The Division in Welsh Calvinistic Methodism, 1750–63', in Nigel Yates (ed.), *Bishop Burgess and his World* (Cardiff: University of Wales Press, 2007), pp. 85–102.

224 Jones, Schlenther and White, *The Elect Methodists: Calvinistic Methodism in England and Wales, 1735–1811*, p. 78.

225 See above, Chapter Four, pp. 289–303.

226 Jones, '"A Glorious Morn?" Methodism and the rise of Evangelicalism in Wales, 1735–62', p. 111.

227 Thomas, *Hanes y Bedyddwyr ymhlith y Cymry* (1778), p. 463.

228 Tudur Jones, *Congregationalism in Wales*, p. 106; they were Brychgoed (Defynnog) (1742), Groes-wen (1745), Aberthin (1749), New Inn (1751), Mynydd Islwyn (1758) and Aber (Breconshire) (1760).

229 NLW Calvinistic Methodist Collection, letter 92, 8 January 1736; Schlenther and White, *Calendar of the Trevecka Letters*, p. 13.

230 NLW Calvinistic Methodist Collection, letter 92, 8 January 1736; Schlenther and White, *Calendar of the Trevecka Letters*, p. 13; for Herbert (1697–1745), see Thomas, *Hanes y Bedyddwyr ymhlith y Cymry*, 2nd edn (1885), pp. 428–30.

231 All are listed in *DWB*.

232 Edmund Jones, *A Sermon Preached from John V: 28–9, occasioned by the Death of Mr Evan Williams, Preacher of the Gospel in Wales* (London: n.p., 1750), p. 77; Williams (1719–48) is listed in *DWB*.

233 Theophilus Evans, *The History of Modern Enthusiasm from the Reformation to the Present Times* (London: W. Owen, 1752), pp. 9, 24–5.

234 Evans, *The History of Modern Enthusiasm from the Reformation to the Present Times*, p. 11; for Evans (1693–1767), see *DWB, ODNB*.

235 Griffith Jones, *Llythyr ynghylch y Ddyledswydd o Gateceisio Plant a Phobl Anwybodus* (Llundain: n.p., 1749), p. 14; for the Münster debacle, see Diarmaid MacCulloch, *Reformation: Europe's House Divided, 1490–1700* (London: Allen Lane, 2003), pp. 204–12.

236 Letter to Griffith Jones, 30 January 1749, transcribed in *Greal y Bedyddwyr* (1830), 8.

237 See above, pp. 342–5.

238 John Gill, *Rhessymau yr Ymneillduwyr am wahanu oddiwrth Eglwys Loegr, a achlysurwyd gan Lythyr ynghylch y ddyledswydd o gateceisio plant* (Llundain: George Keith, 1751), p. 15, hereafter page numbers are in the text. The corresponding English version was entitled *The Dissenters' Reasons for Separating from the Church of England, in response to a Welch clergyman's Letter on ... Catechising Children*; for Gill (1697–1771), see *ODNB*.

239 Letter to Griffith Jones, 30 January 1749, *Greal y Bedyddwyr* (1830), 8.

240 Griffith Jones, *Bedydd yr Ail-Fedyddwyr heb sail iddo yng Ngair Duw* (Llanelli: n.p., n.d.), p. 20.

241 Letter to Griffith Jones, 30 January 1749, *Greal y Bedyddwyr* (1830), 8.

242 Timothy Thomas, *Y Garreg Wen, neu Draethawd bychan ymherthynas i Siccrwydd* (Caerfyrddin: Evan Powell, 1757), p. 9; hereafter page numbers are in the text.

243 Timothy Thomas, *Y Wisg Wen Ddisglair, Gymmwys i fyned i Lys y Brenhin Nefol* (Caerfyrddin: Evan Powell, 1759), Sig. A2; hereafter page numbers are in the text.

244 Derec Llwyd Morgan, *The Great Awakening in Wales*, trans. Dyfnallt Morgan (London: Epworth Press, 1988), p. 182.

245 Jones, *A Glorious Work in the World'*, p. 99; for Ralph Erskine (1684–1752), see *ODNB*.

246 [Ralph Erskine], *Traethawd am Farw i'r Ddeddf a Byw i Dduw* (Bristol: Felix Farley, 1743), p. 11; hereafter page numbers are in the text.

247 *Crist ym Mreichiau'r Credadyn ... gan y Parch. Ebenezer Erskine MA, a Dadl Ffydd ar Air a Chyfammod Duw ... gan y Parch. Ralph Erskine MA* (Caerfyrddin: John Ross, 1744), p. 1; hereafter page numbers are in the text; for Ebenezer Erskine (1680–1764), see *ODNB*.

248 For English assessments of this body of work, see Morgan's *The Great Awakening in Wales*, Glyn Tegai Hughes, *Williams Pantycelyn*, Writers of Wales (Cardiff: University of Wales Press, 1983) and Eifion Evans, *Bread of Heaven: the Life and Work of Williams Pantycelyn* (Bridgend: Bryntirion Press, 2010); also H. A. Hodges, *Flame in the Mountains: Williams Pantycelyn, Ann Griffiths and the Welsh Hymn*, ed. E. Wyn James (Tal-y-bont: Y Lolfa, 2017).

249   *Siccrwydd Ffydd, wedi ei agoryd a'i gymhwyso, sef sylwedd amryw bregethau ar Heb. 10:22 gan y Parch. Ebenezer Erskine MA … wedi ei gyfieithu gan William Williams, gweinidog o Eglwys Loegr* (Caerfyrddin: Evan Powell, 1759), p. 34.

250   NLW MS 6137; cited in Gomer M. Roberts, 'Griffith Jones' opinion of the Methodists', *CCH*, 35 (1950), 53–6 (54).

251   NLW MS 6137, 17 May 1741.

252   NLW MS 6137, 55, 19 May 1741.

253   NLW MS 6137, 24 May 1741.

254   NLW MS 6137, 53, 19 April 1743.

255   William Vickers, *Cydymmaith i'r Allor, yn dangos y modd y derbyniom y Cymmun Bendigedig*, trans. John Jones, 2nd edn (Mwythig: Thomas Durston, 1738), 3rd edn (1753); William Assheton, *Trefn am Dduwiolder am Ddydd yr Arglwydd*, trans. R. Lloyd (Mwythig: Thomas Durston, 1747).

256   Theophilus Evans, *History of Modern Enthusiasm, from the Reformation to the Present Times*, 2nd edn (London: W. Owen, 1757), p. 77.

257   Evans, *History of Modern Enthusiasm, from the Reformation to the Present Times*, p. 90.

258   Thomas Ellis, *Byr Grynhoad o'r grefydd Gristionogol ynghyd â gair o gyngor i'r Schismaticiaid sy'n ymneilltuo oddi wrth Eglwys Loegr* (Dulyn: n.p., 1747), p. 7; page numbers are in the text; for Ellis (1712–92), see *DWB*.

259   See *DNB* and W. Moses Williams, *The Friends of Griffith Jones* (London: Hon. Soc. of Cymmrodorion, 1939), pp. 71–5; Ellis's dates were 1712–92.

260   Geraint H. Jenkins, *Theophilus Evans (1693–1767): y dyn, ei deulu, a'i oes* (Caerfyrddin: Adran Gwasanaethau Diwylliannol Dyfed, 1993).

261   See Geraint H. Jenkins, 'Yr Eglwys "Wiwlwys Olau" a'i beirniaid', *Ceredigion*, 10 (1985), 131–46.

262   NLW MS 2009B, quoted in Gerald Morgan, 'Ieuan Fardd (1731–88): Traethawd yr Esgyb Eingl', *Ceredigion*, 11 (1990), 135–45 (142); for Evan Evans (1731–88), see *DWB* and *ODNB*.

263   E. Gordon Rupp, 'Introductory Essay', in Rupert Davies and E. Gordon Rupp (eds), *A History of the Methodist Church in Great Britain*, vol. 1 (London: Epworth Press, 1965), pp. xii–xl (xxiii).

264   G. Milwyn Griffiths (ed.), 'A Report of the Deanery of Penllyn and Edeirnion by the Revd John Wynne, 1730', *Merioneth Miscellany*, 1 (Dolgellau: Merioneth Historical and Record Society, 1955), pp. 5–29 (25).

265   Cited in Patrick Thomas, *The early history of St Michael's Church, Rhos-y-corn* (Carmarthen: published privately, 1998), p. 4.

266   NLW Calvinistic Methodist Collection, letter 343, Howell Harris to David Lloyd, 14 June 1741; Boyd and White, *Calendar of the Trevecka Letters*, p. 54.

267   John Hughes, *Methodistiaeth Cymru*, vol. 1 (Gwrecsam: Hughes, 1861), p. 99; for Harris's own account of the altercation from his diary, see Tudur, *Howell Harris: from Conversion to Separation, 1735–50*, pp. 126–7.

268   Bangor University Henllys MS 630; quoted by R. T. Jenkins in art. John Owen (1698–1755), *DWB* where he also states that 'Owen is remembered as an unremitting foe of Methodism'.

269 Robert Jones Rhos-lan, *Drych yr Amseroedd* (1820), ed. Glyn M. Ashton (Cardiff: University of Wales Press, 1958), p. 36.

270 Gwynfryn Richards, 'The Diocese of Bangor during the rise of Welsh Methodism', *NLWJ*, 21 (1979), 179–224 (181).

271 See the introduction in William Roberts, *Ffrewyll y Methodistiaid* (c.1745), ed. A. Cynfael Lake (Caerdydd: Gwasg Prifysgol Cymru, 1998), pp. ix–xxxiii.

272 NLW Calvinistic Methodist Collection, letter 1874, William Richard to Howell Harris, 20 June 1749; Boyd and White, *Calendar of the Trevecka Letters*, pp. 315–16; transcribed in Gomer M. Roberts (ed.), *Selected Trevecka Letters, 1747–97* (Caernarfon: Calvinistic Methodist Bookroom, 1962), pp. 36–8 (36).

273 NLW Calvinistic Methodist Collection, letter 1675, William Jones (Trefollwyn) to Howell Harris, 2 July 1747; Boyd and White, *Calendar of the Trevecka Letters*, p. 276; Gomer M. Roberts, *Bywyd a Gwaith Peter Williams* (Caerdydd: Gwasg Prifysgol Cymru, 1943), p. 28.

274 See above, pp. 288–9.

275 Tudur, *Howell Harris: from Conversion to Separation, 1735–50*, p. 230.

276 NLW Calvinistic Methodist Collection, letter 1848, Thomas Jones to the Methodist itinerants, 23 February 1749; Boyd and White, *Calendar of the Trevecka Letters*, p. 311; transcribed in Roberts (ed.), *Selected Trevecka Letters, 1747–97*, pp. 29–31 (30–1).

277 Richards, 'The Diocese of Bangor during the rise of Welsh Methodism', 213–18.

278 Cf. D. Densil Morgan, 'Continuity, Novelty and Evangelicalism in Wales, c. 1640–1850', in Michael A. G. Haykin and Kenneth J. Stewart (eds), *The Emergence of Evangelicalism: Exploring Historical Continuities* (Apollos: Nottingham, 2008), pp. 84–102.

279 *The Making of a Ruling Class: the Glamorgan Gentry, 1640–1790* (Cambridge: Cambridge University Press, 1983); *A History of Modern Wales, 1536–1990* (London: Longmans, 1992).

280 Philip Jenkins, 'Church, Nation and Language: the Welsh Church, 1660–1800', in Jeremy Gregory and Jeffrey S. Chamberlain (eds), *The National Church in Local Perspective: The Church of England and the Regions, 1660–1800* (Woodbridge: The Boydell Press, 2003), pp. 265–84 (266).

281 William Jacob, 'Methodism in Wales', in Glanmor Williams, William Jacob, Nigel Yates and Frances Knight, *The Welsh Church from Reformation to Disestablishment, 1603–1920* (Cardiff: University of Wales Press, 2007), pp. 165–83 (165).

282 William Gibson, '"The most glorious enterprises have been achiev'd": the Restoration Diocese of St David's 1660–1730', in William Gibson and John Morgan-Guy (eds), *Religion and Society in the Diocese of St David's, 1485–2011* (Aldershot: Ashgate, 2015), pp. 92–128 (128).

283 David Hempton, *The Church in the Long Eighteenth Century* (London: I. B. Taurus, 2011), p. 144.

Bibliography

Volumes

Avis, Paul, *Anglicanism and the Christian Church* (Edinburgh: T & T Clark, 1989).

Bagchi, D. V. N. and D. Steinmetz (eds), *The Cambridge Companion to Reformation Theology* (Cambridge: Cambridge University Press, 2004).

Ballinger, J. (ed.), *Llyfer Plygain* (1612) (Caerdydd: Gwasg Prifysgol Cymru, 1931).

Balman, D. W. R., *The Moral Revolution of 1688* (New Haven: Yale University Press, 1957).

Bassett, T. M., *The Welsh Baptists* (Swansea: Ilston Press, 1977).

Baxter, Richard, *The Autobiography of Richard Baxter* (1696), ed. N. H. Keeble (London: Dent, 1974).

Bayly, Lewis, *Yr Ymarfer o Dduwioldeb* (1630), ed. John Ballinger (Caerdydd: Gwasg Prifysgol Cymru, 1930).

Benedict, Philip, *Christ's Churches Purely Reformed: A Social History of Calvinism* (New Haven: Yale University Press, 2002).

Birch, Ian, *To Follow the Lambe Wheresoever he Goeth: the Ecclesial Polity of the English Calvinistic Baptists, 1640–60* (Eugene, OR: Pickwick Publications, 2017).

Bolam, C. G. et al., *The English Presbyterians: From Elizabethan Puritanism to Modern Unitarianism* (London: George Allen and Unwin, 1967).

Bowen, Lloyd, *The Politics of the Principality: Wales, c.1603–42* (Cardiff: University of Wales Press, 2007).

Bremer, Francis J., *The Puritan Experiment: New England Society from Bradford to Edwards*, 2nd edn (Hanover, NH: University Press of New England, 1995).

Breward, Ian, *The Work of William Perkins* (Abingdon: Sutton Courtney Press, 1970).

Carlton, Charles, *Archbishop William Laud* (London: Routledge, 1987).

Carpenter, Edward, *Thomas Sherlock 1678–1761: Bishop of Bangor, Salisbury and London* (London: SPCK, 1936).

Clement, Mary (ed.), *Correspondence and Minutes of the SPCK relating to Wales, 1699–1740* (Cardiff: University of Wales Press, 1952).

Clement, Mary, *The SPCK and Wales, 1699–1740* (London: SPCK, 1954).

Cliffe, J. T., *The Puritan Gentry: the Great Puritan Families of Early Stuart England* (London: Routledge and Kegan Paul, 1984).

Coffey, John, *John Goodwin and the Puritan Revolution: Religion and Intellectual Change in Seventeenth Century England* (Woodbridge: The Boydell Press, 2006).

Collinson, Patrick, *The Religion of Protestants: The Church in English Society, 1559–1625* (Oxford: Clarendon Press, 1982).

Collinson, Patrick, *The Elizabethan Puritan Movement*, 2nd edn (Oxford: Clarendon Press, 1990).

Cradock, Walter, *The Works of the Late Revd Walter Cradock*, ed. Thomas Charles and Peter Oliver (Chester: W. C. Jones, 1800).

Davies, Ceri (ed. and trans.), *Rhagymadroddion a Chyflwyniadau Lladin, 1551–1632* (Caerdydd: Gwasg Prifysgol Cymru, 1980).

Davies, Ceri (ed.), *Dr John Davies of Mallwyd: Welsh Renaissance Scholar* (Cardiff: University of Wales Press, 2004).

Davies, Dewi Eirug, *Hoff Ddysgedig Nyth* (Abertawe: Gwasg John Penry, 1976).

Davies, Horton, *Worship and Theology in England, Vol. 1: From Cranmer to Baxter and Fox, 1534–1690* (Grand Rapids: Eerdmans, 1996).

Davies, Horton, *The Worship of the English Puritans*, new edn (Morgan, PA: Soli Deo Gloria, 1997).

Davies, J. H. (ed.), *The Letters of Lewis, Richard, William and John Morris, 1728–65*, vol. 1 (Aberystwyth: J. H. Davies, 1908).

Davies, John, *Bywyd a Gwaith Moses Williams 1685–1742* (Caerdydd: Gwasg Prifysgol Cymru, 1937).

Davies, Rupert and E. Gordon Rupp (eds), *A History of the Methodist Church in Great Britain*, vol. 1 (London: Epworth Press, 1965).

Dent, C. M., *Protestant Reformers in Elizabethan Oxford* (Oxford: Oxford University Press, 1983).

Dixon, Leif, *Practical Predestinarians in England, 1590–1640* (Aldershot: Ashgate, 2014).

Doble, C. E. (ed.), *Remarks and Collections of Thomas Hearne*, vol. 9 (Oxford: Clarendon Press, 1909).

Durston, C. and J. Maltby (eds), *Religion in Revolutionary England* (Manchester: Manchester University Press, 2006).

Eales, Jacqueline, *Puritans and Roundheads: the Harleys of Bramton Bryan and the outbreak of the English Civil War* (Cambridge: Cambridge University Press, 1990).

Edwards, Charles, *Y Ffydd Ddi-ffuant, sef hanes y Ffydd Gristianogol a'i Rhinwedd* (1677), ed. G. J. Williams (Caerdydd: Gwasg Prifysgol Cymru, 1936).

Evans, Eifion, *Howel Harris, Evangelist* (Cardiff: University of Wales Press, 1974).

Evans, Eifion, *Daniel Rowland and the Great Evangelical Awakening in Wales* (Edinburgh: Banner of Truth Trust, 1985).

Evans, Eifion, *Bread of Heaven: the Life and Work of Williams Pantycelyn* (Bridgend: Bryntirion Press, 2010).

Fincham, Kenneth, *Prelate as Pastor: the Episcopate of James I* (Oxford: Clarendon Press, 1990).

Fincham, Kenneth (ed.), *Visitation Articles and Injunctions of the Early Stuart Church* (Woodbridge: Boydel and Brewer, 1994).

Fincham, Kenneth and Nicholas Tyacke, *Altars Restored: The Changing Face of English Religious Worship, 1547–c.1700* (Oxford: Oxford University Press, 2007).

Ford, Alan, *James Ussher, Theology, History and Politics in early-modern Ireland and England* (Oxford: Oxford University Press, 2007).

Gibbard, Noel, *Walter Cradock: 'A New Testament Saint'* (Bridgend: Evangelical Library of Wales, 1977).

Gibson, William, *The Church of England, 1688–1832: Unity and Accord* (London: Routledge, 2001).

Gibson, William, *James II and the Trial of the Seven Bishops* (London: Palgrave Macmillan, 2009).

Gibson, William and John Morgan-Guy (eds), *Religion and Society in the Diocese of St David's, 1485–2011* (Aldershot: Ashgate, 2015).

Green, Ian M., *The Re-establishment of the Church of England, 1660–63* (Oxford: Oxford University Press, 1975).

Green, Ian M., *The Christian's ABC: Catechisms and Catechizing in England, 1530–1740* (Oxford: Clarendon Press, 1996).

Green, Ian M., *Print and Protestantism in Early Modern England* (Oxford: Oxford University Press, 2000).

Griffith, W. P., *Learning, Law and Religion: Higher Education and Welsh Society, c.1540–1640* (Cardiff: University of Wales Press, 1996).

Gruffydd, R. Geraint, *'In that Gentile Country': The Beginnings of Puritan Nonconformity in Wales* (Bridgend: Evangelical Library of Wales, 1976).

Gruffydd, R. Geraint, *The Translation of the Bible into the Welsh Tongue* (London: BBC, 1988).

Haigh, Christopher, *The Plain Man's Paths to Heaven: Kinds of Christianity in Post-Reformation England, 1570–1640* (Oxford: Oxford University Press, 2007).

Hammond, Geordan and David Ceri Jones (eds), *George Whitefield: Life, Context and Legacy* (Oxford: Oxford University Press, 2015).

Hampton, Stephen, *Anti-Arminians: The Anglican Reformed Tradition from Charles II to George I* (Oxford: Oxford University Press, 2008).

Hart, A. Tindal, *William Lloyd, 1627–1717: Bishop, Politician, Author and Prophet* (London: SPCK, 1952).

Hart, D. G., *Calvinism: A History* (New Haven: Yale University Press, 2013).

Hayden, Roger, *Continuity and Change: Evangelical Calvinism among … Baptist ministers trained at Bristol Academy, 1690–1791* (Milton under Wychwood: Baptist Historical Society, 2006).

Hempton, David, *The Church in the Long Eighteenth Century* (London: I. B. Taurus, 2011).

Henry, Mathew, *The Life of the Rev. Philip Henry* (1698), ed. J. B. Williams (Edinburgh: Banner of Truth, 1974).

Henry, Philip, *Diaries and Letters of Philip Henry MA, of Broad Oak, Flintshire*, ed. Matthew Henry Lee (London: Kegan Paul and Trench, 1882).

Ho, Polly, *English Presbyterianism, 1590–1640* (Stanford, CA: University of Stanford Press, 2011).

Hodges, H. A., *Flame in the Mountains: Williams Pantycelyn, Ann Griffiths and the Welsh Hymn*, ed. E. Wyn James (Tal-y-bont: Y Lolfa, 2017).

Holifield, E. Brooks, *The Covenant Sealed: the Development of Puritan Sacramental Theology in Old and New England, 1570–1720* (New Haven: Yale University Press, 1974).

Holifield, E. Brooks, *Theology in America: Christian Thought from the Age of the Puritans to the Civil War* (New Haven: Yale University Press, 2003).

Holland, Robert, *Basilikon Doron by King James I: Fragment of a Welsh Translation by Robert Holland* (1604), ed. J. Ballinger (Cardiff: University of Wales Press, 1931).

Hughes, Garfield H., *Iaco ab Dewi (1648–1722)* (Caerdydd: Gwasg Prifysgol Cymru, 1952).

Hughes, Garfield H. (ed.), *Gweithiau William Williams Pantycelyn*, vol. 2 (Caerdydd: Gwasg Prifysgol Cymru, 1967).

Hughes, Garfield H. (ed.), *Rhagymadroddion 1547–1659* (Caerdydd: Gwasg Prifysgol Cymru, 1967).

Hughes, Glyn Tegai, *Williams Pantycelyn*, Writers of Wales (Cardiff: University of Wales Press, 1983).

Hughes, H. Trevor, *The Piety of Jeremy Taylor* (London: Macmillan, 1960).

Jenkins, Geraint H., *Literature, Religion and Society in Wales, 1660–1730* (Cardiff: University of Wales Press, 1978).

Jenkins, Geraint H., *The Foundations of Modern Wales, 1642–1780* (Oxford: Clarendon Press, 1987).

Jenkins, Geraint H., *Protestant Dissenters in Wales, 1639–89* (Cardiff: University of Wales Press, 1992).

Jenkins, Geraint H., *Theophilus Evans (1693–1767): y dyn, ei deulu, a'i oes* (Caerfyrddin: Adran Gwasanaethau Diwylliannol Dyfed, 1993).

Jenkins, Philip, *The Making of a Ruling Class: the Glamorgan Gentry, 1640–1790* (Cambridge: Cambridge University Press, 1983).

Jenkins, Philip, *A History of Modern Wales, 1536–1990* (London: Longmans, 1992).

Jenkins, R. T., *Hanes Cynulleidfa Hen Gapel Llanuwchllyn* (Y Bala: Robert Evans, 1937).

Jenkins, R. T., *Yng Nghysgod Trefeca: Ysgrifau ar Hanes Crefydd a Chymdeithas yng Nghymru yn y Ddeunawfed Ganrif* (Caernarfon: Llyfrfa'r Methodistiaid Calfinaidd, 1968).

John, Mansel (ed.), *Welsh Baptist Studies* (Cardiff: South Wales Baptist College, 1976).

Jones, D. Ambrose, *Griffith Jones Llanddowror* (Wrecsam: Hughes a'i Fab, 1923).

Jones, David Ceri, *'A Glorious Work in the World': Welsh Methodism and the International Evangelical Revival, 1735–1750* (Cardiff: University of Wales Press, 2004).

Jones, David Ceri, Boyd S. Schlenther and Eryn M. White, *The Elect Methodists: Calvinistic Methodism in England and Wales, 1735–1811* (Cardiff: University of Wales Press, 2012).

Jones, David Ceri, *The Fire Divine: An Introduction to the Evangelical Revival* (Nottingham: IVP, 2015).

Jones, Gareth Elwyn and Gordon W. Roderick, *A History of Education in Wales* (Cardiff: University of Wales Press, 2003).

Jones, Gareth Lloyd, *The Discovery of Hebrew in Tudor England: A Third Language* (Manchester: Manchester University Press, 1983).

Jones, J. Gwynfor (ed.), *Agweddau ar Dwf Piwritaniaeth yng Nghymru yn yr Ail Ganrif ar Bymtheg* (Lampeter: Edwin Mellen Press, 1992).

Jones, J. Gwynfor, *Crefydd a Chymdeithas: Astudiaethau ar Hanes y Ffydd Brotestannaidd yng Nghymru, c.1559–1750* (Caerdydd: Gwasg Prifysgol Cymru, 2007).

Jones, J. Gwynfor, *Crefydd, Cenedlgarwch a'r Wladwriaeth: John Penry a Phiwritaniaeth Gynnar* (Caerdydd: Gwasg Prifysgol Cymru, 2014).

Jones, M. G., *The Charity School Movement: A Study in Eighteenth Century Puritanism in Action* (Cambridge: Cambridge University Press, 1938).

Jones, R. Brinley, *'A Lanterne to their Feete': Remembering Rhys Prichard (1579–1644), Vicar of Llandovery* (Porthyrhyd: The Drover's Press, 1994).

Jones, R. M., *Cyfriniaeth Gymraeg* (Caerdydd: Gwasg Prifysgol Cymru, 1994).

Jones, R. Tudur, *Congregationalism in England, 1662–1962* (London: Independent Press, 1962).

Jones, R. Tudur, *Vavasor Powell* (Abertawe: Gwasg John Penry, 1971).

Jones, R. Tudur, *Ffydd yn y Ffau* (Abertawe: Gwasg John Penry, 1973).

Jones, R. Tudur, *Congregationalism in Wales*, ed. Robert Pope (Cardiff: University of Wales Press, 2004).

Jones, Robert, *Drych yr Amseroedd* (1820), ed. Glyn M. Ashton (Caerdydd: Gwasg Prifysgol Cymru, 1958).

Keeble, N. H. and Geoffrey F. Nuttall (eds), *Calendar of the Correspondence of Richard Baxter*, vol. 2 (Oxford: Clarendon Press, 1991).

Keeble, N. H. (ed.), *'Settling the Peace of the Church', 1662 Revised* (Oxford: Oxford University Press, 2014).

Kendall, R. T., *Calvin and English Calvinism to 1649* (Oxford: Oxford University Press, 1979).

Kistler, Don, *A Spectacle unto God: the Life and Death of Christopher Love (1618–51)* (Morgan, PA: Soli Deo Gloria, 1994).

Kyffin, Maurice, *Deffynniad Ffydd Eglwys Loegr* (1595), ed. W. Pritchard Jones (Bangor: Jarvis and Foster, 1908).

Lake, Peter, *Moderate Puritans in the Elizabethan Church* (Cambridge: Cambridge University Press, 1982).

Lambert, Frank, *Pedlar in Divinity: George Whitefield and the Trans-Atlantic Revivals, 1737–70* (Princeton, NJ: Princeton University Press, 1994).

Letham, Robert, *The Westminster Assembly: Reading its Theology in Historical Context* (Phillipsburg, NJ: P & R Publishing, 2009).

Lewis, Saunders, *Meistri'r Canrifoedd: Ysgrifau ar Hanes Llenyddiaeth Gymraeg*, ed. R. Geraint Gruffydd (Caerdydd: Gwasg Prifysgol Cymru, 1973).

Lewis, Tom, *History of the Hen Dŷ Cwrdd Cefn Coed y Cymer* (Llandysul: Gomerian Press, 1947).

Lewys, Huw, *Perl Mewn Adfyd* (1595), ed. W. J. Gruffydd (Caerdydd: Gwasg Prifysgol Cymru, 1929).

Lindberg, Carter (ed.), *The Pietist Theologians: An Introduction to Theology in the Seventeenth and Eighteenth Centuries* (Oxford: Blackwell, 2005).

Llwyd, Morgan, *Gweithiau Morgan Llwyd o Wynedd*, ed. Thomas E. Ellis, vol. 1 (Bangor: Jarvis and Foster, 1899).

Llwyd, Morgan, *Gweithiau Morgan Llwyd o Wynedd*, ed. J. H. Davies, vol. 2 (Bangor: Jarvis and Foster, 1908).

Llwyd, Morgan, *Gweithiau Morgan Llwyd o Wynedd*, ed. J. Graham Jones and Goronwy Wyn Owen, vol. 3 (Caerdydd: Gwasg Prifysgol Cymru, 1993).

Llwyd, Morgan, *Llyfr y Tri Aderyn* (1653), ed. M. Wynn Thomas (Caerdydd: Gwasg Prifysgol Cymru, 1988).

McAdoo, Henry R., *The Eucharistic Theology of Jeremy Taylor Today* (Norwich: Canterbury Press, 1988).

McAdoo, Henry R., *Jeremy Taylor, Anglican Theologian* (Armagh: Historical Society of the Church in Ireland, 1997).

MacCulloch, Diarmaid, *Thomas Cranmer: A Life* (New Haven: Yale University Press, 1996).

MacCulloch, Diarmaid, *Tudor Church Militant: Edward VI and the Protestant Reformation* (London: Allen Lane, 1999).

MacCulloch, Diarmaid, *The Later Reformation in England, 1547–1603*, 2nd edn (London: Palgrave, 2001).

MacCulloch, Diarmaid, *Reformation: Europe's House Divided, 1490–1700* (London: Allen Lane, 2003).

McGiffert, Michael (ed.), *God's Plot: Puritan Spirituality in Thomas Shepard's Cambridge* (Amherst: University of Massachusetts Press, 1994).

McGrath, Alister E., *Iustitia Dei: A History of the Christian Doctrine of Justification: from 1500 to the present day* (Cambridge: Cambridge University Press, 1986).

Maltby, Judith, *Prayer Book and People in Elizabethan and Early Stuart England* (Cambridge: Cambridge University Press, 1998).

Manning, Bernard Lord, *Essays in Orthodox Dissent* (London: Independent Press, 1939).

Miller, Perry, *Orthodoxy in Massachusetts, 1630–50*, 2nd edn (Boston, MA: Beacon Press, 1959).

Miller, Perry, *The New England Mind: the Seventeenth Century*, 2nd edn (Cambridge, MA: The Belknap Press, 1962).

Morgan, D. Densil, *Wales and the Word: Historical Perspectives on Welsh Identity and Religion* (Cardiff: University of Wales Press, 2008).

Morgan, D. Densil, *Y Deugain Mlynedd Hyn: Diwinydda yng Nghymru, 1972–2015* (Bangor: Cyhoeddiadau'r Gair, 2015).

Morgan, Derec Llwyd, *The Great Awakening in Wales*, trans. Dyfnallt Morgan (London: Epworth Press, 1988).

Morgan, Derec Llwyd, *Charles Edwards* (Caernarfon: Gwasg Pantycelyn, 1994).

Morgan, Edmund S., *Visible Saints: The History of a Puritan Idea* (Ithaca, NY: Cornell University Press, 1965).

Morgan, Edward (ed.), *Letters of the Revd Griffith Jones to Mrs Bevan, late of Laugharne, near Carmarthen* (London: Whittaker and Co, 1832).

Morgan, Merfyn (ed.), *Gweithiau Oliver Thomas ac Evan Roberts, Dau Biwritan Cynnar* (Caerdydd: Gwasg Prifysgol Cymru, 1981).

Morgans, John I., *The Honest Heretique: the Life and Work of William Erbury (1604–54)* (Tal-y-bont: Y Lolfa, 2012).

Morrill, John, *The Nature of the English Revolution* (London: Longmans, 1993).

Muller, Richard A., *Christ and the Decree: Christology and Predestination in Reformed Theology from Calvin to Perkins*, 2nd edn (Grand Rapids: Baker, 2008).

Naylor, Pater, *Calvinism, Communion and the Baptists: A Study of English Calvinistic Baptists from the late 1600s to the early 1800s* (Carlisle: Paternoster Press, 2003).

Noll, Mark A., David W. Bebbington and George A. Rawlyk, *Evangelicalism: Comparative Studies of Popular Protestantism in North America, the British Isles and Beyond* (Oxford: Oxford University Press, 1994).

Norris, W. G. and Norman Penney (eds), *John ap John and Early Records of Friends in Wales* (London: Friends Historical Society, 1907).

Nuttall, Geoffrey F., *Visible Saints: the Congregational Way, 1640–60* (Oxford: Blackwell, 1957).

Nuttall, Geoffrey F., *The Welsh Saints, 1640–60* (Cardiff: University of Wales Press, 1957).

Nuttall, Geoffrey F. and Owen Chadwick (eds), *From Uniformity to Unity, 1662–1962* (London: SPCK, 1962).

Nuttall, Geoffrey F. et al., *The Beginnings of Nonconformity* (London: The Hibbert Trust, 1964).

Nuttall, Geoffrey F., *Howel Harris 1714–73: the Last Enthusiast* (Cardiff: University of Wales Press, 1965).

Nuttall, Geoffrey F., *Richard Baxter* (London: Thomas Nelson, 1965).

Nuttall, Geoffrey F., *The Puritan Spirit* (London: Epworth Press, 1967).

Nuttall, Geoffrey F., *The Holy Spirit in Puritan Faith and Experience*, 2nd edn (Chicago: University of Chicago Press, 1992).

Nuttall, Geoffrey F., *Studies in English Dissent* (Weston Rhyn: The Quinta Press, 2002).

Owen, G. Dyfnallt, *Wales in the Reign of James I* (London: The Boydell Press, 1988).

Owen, Goronwy Wyn, *Morgan Llwyd* (Caernarfon: Gwasg Pantycelyn, 1992).

Owen, Goronwy Wyn, *Rhwng Calfin a Böhme: Golwg ar Syniadaeth Morgan Llwyd* (Caerdydd: Gwasg Prifysgol Cymru, 2001).

Owen, Goronwy Wyn, *Cewri'r Cyfamod: Y Piwritaniaid Cymreig, 1630–60* (Bangor: Canolfan Uwchefrydiau Crefydd, 2008).

Owen, Jeremy, *Golwg ar y Beiau*, ed. R. T. Jenkins (Caerdydd: Gwasg Prifysgol Cymru, 1949).

Owens, B. G. (ed.), *The Ilston Book: earliest register of Welsh Baptists* (Aberystwyth: National Library of Wales, 1996).

Packer, J. I., *The Redemption and Restoration of Man in the thought of Richard Baxter: a Study in Puritan Theology* (Vancouver: Regent College Publications, 2003).

Palmer, A. N., *A History of the Older Nonconformity of Wrexham and its Neighbourhood* (Wrexham: Woodhall, Mincham and Thomas, 1888).

Patterson, W. B., *William Perkins and the Making of a Protestant England* (Oxford: Oxford University Press, 2014).

Paul, Robert S., *The Assembly of the Lord: Politics and Religion in the Westminster Assembly* (Edinburgh: T & T Clark, 1985).

Penry, John, *The Notebook of John Penry*, ed. Albert Peel (London: Royal Historical Society, 1944).

Penry, John, *John Penry: Three Treatises Concerning Wales*, ed. David Williams (Cardiff: University of Wales Press, 1960).

Pettit, Norman, *The Heart Prepared: Grace and Conversion in Puritan Spiritual Life*, 2nd edn (Middletown, CT: Wesleyan University Press, 1989).

Pierce, James, *The Life and Work of William Salesbury, A Rare Scholar* (Tal-y-bont: Y Lolfa, 2016).

Podmore, Colin, *The Moravian Church in England, 1728–60* (Oxford: Oxford University Press, 1998).

Porter, H. B., *Jeremy Taylor Liturgist* (London: SPCK, 1979).

Porter, H. C., *Reformation and Reaction in Tudor Cambridge*, 2nd edn (Hemden: Archon Books, 1972).

Prichard, Rhys, *Cerddi'r Ficer*, ed. Nesta Lloyd (Abertawe: Cyhoeddiadau Barddas, 1994).

Rack, Henry D., *Reasonable Enthusiast: John Wesley and the Rise of Methodism* (London: Epworth Press, 1989).

Rees, Eiluned, *Libri Walliae: a Catalogue of Welsh Books and Books Printed in Wales, 1546–1820* (Aberystwyth: National Library of Wales, 1987).

Rees, Rice (ed.), *Y Seren Foreu, neu Ganwyll y Cymry, sef gwaith prydyddol y Parch. Rhys Prichard MA, gynt ficer Llanymddyfri* (Llanymddyfri: W. Rees, 1841).

Rees, Thomas, *History of Protestant Nonconformity in Wales* (London: John Snow, 1861).

Richards, Thomas, *A History of the Puritan Movement in Wales, 1639–53* (London: National Eisteddfod Association, 1920).

Richards, Thomas, *Religious Developments in Wales, 1654–62* (London: National Eisteddfod Association, 1923).

Richards, Thomas, *Wales under the Penal Code, 1662–87* (London: National Eisteddfod Association, 1925).

Richards, Thomas, *Piwritaniaeth a Pholitics, 1689–1719* (Wrecsam: Hughes a'i Fab, 1927).

Richards, Thomas, *Wales Under the Indulgence, 1672–75* (London: National Eisteddfod Association, 1928).

Richards, William, *The Welsh Nonconformists' Memorial* (London: n.p., 1820).

Riker, D. B., *A Catholic Reformed Theologian: Federalism and Baptism in the thought of Benjamin Keach, 1640–1704* (Carlisle: Paternoster Press, 2009).

Roberts, Gomer M., *Bywyd a Gwaith Peter Williams* (Caerdydd: Gwasg Prifysgol Cymru, 1943).

Roberts, Gomer M., *Y Pêr Ganiedydd (Pantycelyn), Cyfrol 1, Trem ar ei Fywyd* (Aberystwyth: Gwasg Aberystwyth, 1949).

Roberts, Gomer M. (ed.), *Selected Trevecka Letters, 1742–7* (Caernarfon: Calvinistic Methodist Bookroom, 1956).

Roberts, Gomer M. (ed.), *Selected Trevecka Letters, 1747–97* (Caernarfon: Calvinistic Methodist Bookroom, 1962).

Roberts, Gomer M. (ed.), *Hanes Methodistiaeth Galfinaidd Cymru*, vol. 1, *Y Deffroad Mawr* (Caernarfon: Llyfrfa'r Methodistiaid, 1974).

Roberts, William, *Ffrewyll y Methodistiaid (c.1745)*, ed. A. Cynfael Lake (Caerdydd: Gwasg Prifysgol Cymru, 1998).

Rupp, E. Gordon, *Religion in England, 1688–1791* (Oxford: Clarendon Press, 1986).

Ryrie, Alec, *Being Protestant in Reformation Britain* (Oxford: Oxford University Press, 2013).

Salesbury, William, *Oll Synnwyr pen Kembero ygyd* (1547), ed. J. Gwenogvryn Evans (Bangor: Jarvis and Foster, 1902).

Salesbury, William, *Kynniver Llith a Ban* (1551), ed. John Fisher (Cardiff: University of Wales Press, 1931).

Saunders, Erasmus, *A View of the State of Religion in the Diocese of St David's* (1721) (Cardiff: University of Wales Press, 1949).

Schlenther, Boyd S. and Eryn M. White, *Calendar of the Trevecka Letters* (Aberystwyth: National Library of Wales, 2003).

Spinks, Bryan D., *Sacraments, Ceremonies and the Stuart Divines: Sacramental Theology and Liturgy in England 1603–62* (Aldershot: Ashgate, 2002).

Spurr, John, *The Restoration Church of England, 1646–89* (New Haven: Yale University Press, 1991).

Spurr, John, *English Puritanism, 1603–89* (London: Palgrave, 1998).

Stoever, W. K. B., *'A Fair and Easie Way to Heaven': Covenant Theology and Antinomianism in Early Massachusetts* (Middletown, CT: Wesleyan University Press, 1978).

Stout, Harry S., *The Divine Dramatist: George Whitfield and the Rise of Modern Evangelicalism* (Grand Rapids: Eerdmans, 1991).

Stout, Harry S., *The New England Soul: Preaching and Religious Culture in Colonial New England*, 2nd edn (New York: Oxford University Press, 2012).

Strivens, Robert, *Philip Doddridge and the Shaping of Evangelical Dissent* (Farnham: Ashgate, 2015).

Terrill, Edward, *The Records of a Church of Christ meeting in Broadmead, Bristol, 1640–88*, ed. W. Haycroft (London: J. Heaton, 1865).

Thomas, D. R., *A History of the Diocese of St Asaph*, 2 vols (London: James Parker, 1874).

Thomas, D. R., *Diocesan Histories: St Asaph* (London: SPCK, 1888).

Thomas, Gwyn, *Y Bardd Cwsg a'i Gefndir* (Caerdydd: Gwasg Prifysgol Cymru, 1972).

Thomas, Gwyn, *Ellis Wynne*, Writers of Wales (Cardiff: University of Wales Press, 1984).

Thomas, Ioan, *Rhad Ras* (1810), ed. J. Dyfnallt Owen (Caerdydd: Gwasg Prifysgol Cymru, 1949).

Thomas, Isaac, *Y Testament Newydd Cymraeg, 1551–1620* (Caerdydd: Gwasg Prifysgol Cymru, 1976).

Thomas, Isaac, *William Morgan and his Bible* (Cardiff: University of Wales Press, 1988).

Thomas, Isaac, *Yr Hen Destament Cymraeg* (Aberystwyth: Llyfrgell Genedlaethol Cymru, 1988).

Thomas, Joshua, *Hanes y Bedyddwyr ymhlith y Cymry*, trans. Benjamin Davies, 2nd edn (Pontypridd: Benjamin Davies, 1885).

Thomas, M. Wynn, *Morgan Llwyd*, Writers of Wales (Cardiff: University of Wales Press, 1984).

Thomas, M. Wynn, *Morgan Llwyd: ei Gyfeillion a'i Gyfnod* (Caerdydd: Gwasg Prifysgol Cymru, 1992).

Thompson, H. P., *Thomas Bray* (London: SPCK, 1954).

Toon, Peter, *The Emergence of Hyper-Calvinism in English Nonconformity, 1689–1765*, new edn (Eugene, OR: Wipf and Stock, 2011).

Tudur, Geraint, *Howell Harris: from Conversion to Separation, 1735–50* (Cardiff: University of Wales Press, 2000).

Turner, G. Lyon (ed.), *Original Records of Early Nonconformity under Persecution and Indulgence*, vol. 1 (London: Fisher Unwin, 1911).

Tyacke, Nicholas, *Anti-Calvinists: The Rise of English Arminianism c. 1590–1640* (Oxford: Clarendon Press, 1990).

Vaughan, Henry, *Henry Vaughan: Poetry and Selected Prose*, ed. L. C. Martin (Oxford: Oxford University Press, 1963).

Walker, David (ed.), *A History of the Church in Wales* (Penarth: Church in Wales Publications, 1976).

Wallace, Dewey A., *Puritans and Predestination: Grace in English Protestant Theology, 1525–1695* (Chapel Hill: University of Carolina Press, 1982).

Walsh, John, Colin Haydon and Stephen Taylor (eds), *The Church of England c.1689–c.1833* (Cambridge: Cambridge University Press, 1993).

Ward, W. R., *The Protestant Evangelical Awakening* (Cambridge: Cambridge University Press, 1992).

Ward, W. R., *Christianity under the Ancien Régime, 1648–1789* (Cambridge: Cambridge University Press, 1999).

Ward, W. R., *Early Evangelicalism: A Global Intellectual History, 1670–1789* (Cambridge: Cambridge University Press, 2006).

Watkyns, Rowland, *Flamma Sine Fumo* (1662), ed. Paul C. Davies (Cardiff: University of Wales Press, 1968).

Watts, Michael R., *The Dissenters: from the Reformation to the French Revolution* (Oxford: Clarendon Press, 1978).

Weir, D. A., *The Origins of Federal Theology in Sixteenth Century Reformed Thought* (Oxford: Oxford University Press, 1990).

White, Eryn M., *Praidd Bach y Bugail Mawr: Seiadau Methodistaidd De-Orllewin Cymru* (Llandysul: Gwasg Gomer, 1995).

White, Eryn M., *The Welsh Bible* (Stroud: Tempus, 2007).

White, Peter, *Predestinarianism, Policy and Polemic: Conflict and Consensus in the English Church from the Reformation to the Civil War* (Cambridge: Cambridge University Press, 1992).

Whiteman, Anne (ed.), *The Compton Census of 1676: A Critical Edition* (Oxford: Oxford University Press, 1986).

Williams, Glanmor, *Welsh Reformation Essays* (Cardiff: University of Wales Press, 1967).

Williams, Glanmor, *Reformation Views of Church History* (London: Lutterworth Press, 1970).

Williams, Glanmor (ed.), *Glamorgan County History, Vol. IV, Early Modern Glamorgan* (Cardiff: University of Wales Press, 1974).

Williams, Glanmor, *Grym Tafodau Tân: Ysgrifau Hanesyddol ar Grefydd a Diwylliant* (Llandysul: Gwasg Gomer, 1984).

Williams, Glanmor, *Recovery, Reorientation and Reformation: Wales, 1415–1642* (Oxford: Clarendon Press, 1987).

Williams, Glanmor, *The Welsh and their Religion: Historical Essays* (Cardiff: University of Wales Press, 1991).

Williams, Glanmor, *Wales and the Reformation* (Cardiff: University of Wales Press, 1997).

Williams, Glanmor, William Jacob, Nigel Yates and Frances Knight, *The Welsh Church from Reformation to Disestablishment, 1603–1920* (Cardiff: University of Wales Press, 2007).

Williams, Gruffydd Aled, *Ymryson Edmwnd Prys a Wiliam Cynwal* (Caerdydd: Gwasg Prifysgol Cymru, 1986).

Williams, T. Oswald, *Hanes Cynulleidfaoedd Undodaidd Sir Aberteifi* (Llandysul: Gwasg Gomer, n.d).

Williams, W. Moses, *Selections from the Welch Piety* (Cardiff: University of Wales Press, 1938).

Williams, W. Moses, *The Friends of Griffith Jones* (London: Hon. Soc. of Cymmrodorion, 1939).

Wynne, Ellis, *Rheol Buchedd Sanctaidd, yn dangos y Moddion a'r Arfeu i ynnill pob Gras ... ynghyd â Gweddïau, gan Jeremy Taylor DD* (1701) (Caerdydd: Gwasg Prifysgol Cymru, 1928).

Yardley, Edward, *Menevia Sacra*, ed. Francis Green (London: Cambrian Archaeological Assoc., 1927).

Individual chapters in composite works

Bowen, Lloyd, 'The Battle of Britain: History and Reformation in early modern Wales', in Tadhg Ó hAnnracháin and Robert Armstrong (eds), *Christianities in the Early Modern Celtic World* (Basingstoke: Palgrave Macmillan, 2014), pp. 135–50.

Dodd, A. H., 'Mr Myddleton, the merchant of Tower St', in S. T. Bindoff, J. Hurstfield and C. H. Williams (eds), *Elizabethan Government and Society: Essays Presented to Sir John Neale* (London: The Athlone Press, 1961), pp. 249–81.

James, E. Wyn, '"The New Birth of a New People": Welsh Language and Identity and the Welsh Methodists, *c.*1740–1820', in Robert Pope (ed.), *Religion and National Identity: Wales and Scotland, c.1700–2000* (Cardiff: University of Wales Press, 2001), pp. 14–42.

James, E. Wyn, 'Griffith Jones (1684–1761) of Llanddowror and his "Striking Experiment in Mass Religious Education" in Wales in the Eighteenth Century', in Reinhart Siegert (ed.), *Educating the People through Reading Material in the Eighteenth and Nineteenth Centuries* (Bremen: Edition Lumière, 2012), pp. 275–92.

Jenkins, Philip, 'The Anglican Church and the Unity of Britain: the Welsh Experience, 1560–1714', in Steven G. Ellis and Sarah Barber (eds), *Conquest and Union: Fashioning a British State, 1485–1725* (London: Longman, 1995), pp. 115–38.

Jenkins, Philip, 'Church, Nation and Language: the Welsh Church, 1660–1800', in Jeremy Gregory and Jeffrey S. Chamberlain (eds), *The National Church in Local Perspective: The Church of England and the Regions, 1660–1800* (Woodbridge: The Boydell Press, 2003).

Jones, David Ceri, 'A Glorious Morn? Methodism and the rise of Evangelicalism in Wales, 1735–62', in Mark Smith (ed.), *British Evangelical Identities Past and Present*, vol. 1 (Milton Keynes: Paternoster, 2008), pp. 97–113.

Jones, David Ceri, 'Calvinistic Methodism and the Reformed tradition in eighteenth century Wales', in Tadhg Ó hAnnracháin and Robert Armstrong (eds), *Christianities in the Early Modern Celtic World* (Basingstoke: Palgrave Macmillan, 2014), pp. 164–78.

Jones, J. Gwynfor, 'Robert Holland a *Basilikon Doron* y Brenin Iago', in J. E. Caerwyn Williams (ed.), *Ysgrifau Beirniadol*, 22 (Dinbych: Gwasg Gee, 1997), pp. 161–88.

Jones, J. Gwynfor, 'Wales and Hamburg: the problems of a younger son', in R. R. Davies and Geraint H. Jenkins (eds), *From Medieval to Modern Wales: Historical Essays in Honour of K. O. Morgan and Ralph A. Griffiths* (Cardiff: University of Wales Press, 2004), pp. 104–22.

Jones, R. Tudur, 'Yr Hen Ymneilltuwyr', in Gomer M. Roberts (ed.), *Hanes Methodistiaeth Galfinaidd Cymru*, vol. 1, *Y Deffroad Mawr* (Caernarfon: Llyfrfa'r Methodistiaid, 1974), pp. 13–42.

Jones, R. Tudur, 'Relations between Anglicans and Dissenters: the Promotion of Piety, 1670–1730', in David Walker (ed.), *A History of the Church in Wales* (Penarth: Church in Wales Publications, 1976), pp. 79–102.

Jones, R. Tudur, 'The sufferings of Vavasor', in Mansel John (ed.), *Welsh Baptist Studies* (Cardiff: South Wales Baptist College, 1976), pp. 76–91.

Jones, R. Tudur, 'The Healing Herb and the Rose of Love: the piety of two Welsh Puritans', in R. Buick Knox (ed.), *Reformation Conformity and Dissent: Essays in Honour of Geoffrey F. Nuttall* (London: Epworth Press, 1978), pp. 154–9.

Jones, R. Tudur, 'Athrawiaeth y Cyfamodau', in D. Densil Morgan (ed.), *Grym y Gair a Fflam y Ffydd: Ysgrifau ar Hanes Crefydd yng Nghymru* (Bangor: Canolfan Uwchefrydiau Crefydd yng Nghymru, 1998), pp. 9–16.

Morgan, D. Densil, 'Continuity, Novelty and Evangelicalism in Wales, c. 1640–1850', in Michael A. G. Haykin and Kenneth J. Stewart, *The Emergence of Evangelicalism: Exploring Historical Continuities* (Apollos: Nottingham, 2008), pp. 84–102.

Morgan, D. Densil, 'The Reformation and vernacular culture: Wales as a case study', in Jennifer Powell McNutt and David Lauber (eds), *The People's Book: the Reformation and the Bible* (Downer's Grove, IL: IVP Academic, 2017), pp. 69–88.

Morgan, Derec Llwyd, 'Dau Amddiffynnydd i'r Ffydd', in J. E. Caerwyn Williams (ed.), *Ysgrifau Beirniadol*, 5 (Dinbych: Gwasg Gee, 1970), pp. 99–111.

Morgan, Walter T., 'Yr Eglwys Sefydledig yng Nghymru, 1700–35', in Gomer M. Roberts (ed.), *Hanes Methodistiaeth Galfinaidd Cymru*, vol. 1, *Y Deffroad Mawr* (Caernarfon: Llyfrfa'r Methodistiaid Calfinaidd, 1973), pp. 43–80.

Nuttall, Geoffrey F., 'Another Baptist ejection (1662): the case of John Norcott', in William H. Brackney, Paul S. Fiddes and John H. Y. Briggs (eds), *Pilgrim Pathways: Essays in Baptist History in Honour of B. R. White* (Macon, GA: Mercer University Press, 1999).

Olson, Katherine K., '"Slow and cold in the true service of God": Popular beliefs and practice, conformity and reformation in Wales, c. 1530–c. 1600', in Tadhg Ó hAnnracháin and Robert Armstrong (eds), *Christianities in the Early Modern Celtic World* (Basingstoke: Palgrave Macmillan, 2014), pp. 92–110.

Owens, B. G., 'Rhydwilym Church, 1668–89: a study of West Wales Baptists', in Mansel John (ed.), *Welsh Baptist Studies* (Cardiff: South Wales Baptist College, 1976), pp. 92–107.

Roberts, Peter, 'Tudor Wales, national identity and the British inheritance', in *idem* and Brendan Bradshaw, *British Consciousness and Identity: The Making of Britain, 1533–1707* (Cambridge: Cambridge University Press, 1998), pp. 8–42.

Roberts, Stephen K., 'The sermon in early modern Wales: context and content', in P. McCulloch, H. Adlington and E. Rhatigan (eds), *The Oxford Handbook of the Early Modern Sermon* (Oxford: Oxford University Press, 2011), pp. 303–25.

Richards, Thomas, 'Nonconformity from 1620 to 1715', in J. E. Lloyd (ed.), *A History of Carmarthenshire*, vol. 2 (Cardiff: The London Carmarthenshire Society, 1939), pp. 133–84.

Thomas, Gwyn, 'Dau Lwyd o Gynfal', in J. E. Caerwyn Williams (ed.), *Ysgrifau Beirniadol*, 5 (Dinbych: Gwasg Gee, 1970), pp. 71–98.

Thomas, Gwyn, 'Rowland Vaughan', in Geraint Bowen (ed.), *Y Traddodiad Rhyddiaith* (Llandysul: Gwasg Gomer, 1970), pp. 231–46.

Thomas, M. Wynn, 'Seventeenth-century Puritan writers: Morgan Llwyd and Charles Edwards', in R. Geraint Gruffydd (ed.), *A Guide to Welsh Literature*, c.*1530–1700* (Cardiff: University of Wales Press, 1997), pp. 190–209.

Thomas, M. Wynn, 'Morgan Llwyd and the Foundations of the Nonconformist Nation', in Stewart Mottram and Sarah Prescott (eds), *Writing Wales, From the Renaissance to Romanticism* (Surrey: Ashgate, 2012), pp. 111–30.

Tudur, Geraint, '"Like a right arm and a pillar": the story of James Beaumont', in Robert Pope (ed.), *Honouring the Past and Shaping the Future: essays in honour of Gareth Lloyd Jones* (Leominster: Gracewing, 2003), pp. 133–58.

Walsh, John, 'Origins of the Evangelical Revival', in G. V. Bennett and J. Walsh (eds), *Essays in Modern English Church History* (London: Adam and Charles Black, 1966), pp. 132–62.

Ward, W. R., 'Evangelical awakenings in the North American world', in S. J. Brown and T. Ticketts (eds), *The Cambridge History of Christianity: Enlightenment, Reawakening and Revolution, 1660–1815* (Cambridge: Cambridge University Press, 2006), pp. 329–47.

White, B. R., 'John Miles and the structures of the Calvinistic Baptist mission to south Wales, 1649–60', in Mansel John (ed.), *Welsh Baptist Studies* (Cardiff: South Wales Baptist College, 1976), pp. 35–76.

White, Eryn M., 'Popular schooling and the Welsh language, 1650–1800', in Geraint H. Jenkins (ed.), *The Welsh Language before the Industrial Revolution* (Cardiff: University of Wales Press, 1997), pp. 318–41.

White, Eryn M., '"A Poor, Benighted Church"? Church and Society in mid-eighteenth century Wales', in R. R. Davies and Geraint H. Jenkins (eds), *From Medieval to Modern Wales: Historical Essays in Honour of K. O. Morgan and R. A. Griffiths* (Cardiff: University of Wales Press, 2004), pp. 123–41.

White, Eryn M., '"A Breach in God's House": The Division in Welsh Calvinistic Methodism, 1750–63', in Nigel Yates (ed.), *Bishop Burgess and his World* (Cardiff: University of Wales Press, 2007), pp. 85–102.

White, Eryn M., 'From Ejectment to Toleration in Wales, 1662–89', in Alan P. F. Sell (ed.), *The Great Ejectment of 1662: Its Antecedents, Aftermath and Ecumenical Significance* (Eugene, OR: Pickwick Publications, 2014), pp. 125–82.

Williams, Glanmor, 'Religion, Language and the Circulating Schools of Griffith Jones, Llanddowror (1683–1761)', in *idem, Religion, Language and Nationality in Wales: Historical Essays* (Cardiff: University of Wales Press, 1979).

Journal articles

'A breviat … against the clergie of the Diocese of Bangor … Julie 1623', *Archaelogia Cambrensis*, 3rd Series, 36 (1863), 283–5.

Barnard, E. A. B., 'Lewis Bayly, bishop of Bangor (d.1631) and Thomas Bayly (d.1657) his son', *THSC* (1928–9), 99–132.

Bowen, Lloyd, 'Representations of Wales and the Welsh during the Civil Wars and Interregnum', *Historical Research*, 77 (2004), 358–64.

Bowen, Lloyd, 'Wales and religious reform in the Long Parliament, 1640–2', *THSC*, N.S. 12 (2005), 36–59.

Brown, Roger L., '"Spiritual Nurseries": Griffith Jones and the Circulating Schools', *NLWJ*, 30 (1997), 27–49.

Clark, D. S. T. and Prys Morgan, 'Religion and magic in Elizabethan Wales', *JEH*, 27 (1976), 31–46.

Clement, Mary, 'John Vaughan (1663–1722), Cwrt Derllys, a'i waith', *THSC* (1942), 73–107.

Clement, Mary, 'Teulu'r Daltoniaid, Pembre, Sir Gaerfyrddin', *CCH*, 29 (1944), 1–12.

Clement, Mary, 'Pennod newydd o hanes Eglwys Loegr ym Morgannwg gyda chyfeiriad neilltuol at James Harris, Llantrisant (1663–1728)', *Seren Gomer*, N.S. 37 (1945), 35–8, 65–8, 77–85.

Davies, Ceri, 'The 1588 translation of the Bible and the world of Renaissance learning', *Ceredigion*, 11 (1988–9), 1–18.

Davies, J. H., 'A diary of a journey … by Revd Griffith Jones', *CCH*, 7 (1922), 10–14.

Davies, Pennar, 'Episodes in the History of Brecknockshire Dissent', *Brycheiniog*, 3 (1957), 11–65.

Davies, T. Eirug, 'Philip Pugh a'i lafur yn y Cilgwyn', *Y Cofiadur*, 14 (1937), 16–36.

Dodd, A. H., 'Wales and the parliaments of Charles I', *THSC* (1945), 16–49; (1946–7), 57–96.

Dodd, A. H., 'The pattern of politics in Stuart Wales', *THSC* (1948–9), 8–91.

Dodd, A. H., 'New England influences in early Welsh Puritanism', *BBCS*, 16 (1954), 30–7.

Dodd, A. H., 'Bishop Lewes [*sic*] Bayly, c.1575–1631', *TCHS*, 28 (1967), 13–36.

Dole, Emlyn, 'Trichanmlwyddiant geni Griffith Jones', *Y Traethodydd*, 139 (1984), 196–9.

Evans, A. O., 'Edmund Prys: Archdeacon of Merioneth, Priest, Preacher, Poet', *THSC* (1922–3), 112–68.

Evans, E. D., 'John Evans, bishop of Bangor, 1702–16', *THSC*, N.S. 7 (2000), 44–65.

Evans, E. D., 'A Providential Rescue? Griffith Jones and the Malabar Mission', *JWRH*, 8 (2000), 35–42.

Evans, Edward, 'Yr Ymraniad yn Hengoed', *Yr Ymofynnydd* (1847), 149–53.

Evans, Eifion, 'Thomas Jones Cwm-iou (1689–1772)', *CCH*, 8 (1984), 24–30.

Gibson, William, '"A Welsh Bishop for a Welsh See": John Wynne of St Asaph, 1714–27', *JWEH*, 1 (1984), 28–43.

Gregory, Brad S., '"The True and Zealous Seruice of God": Robert Parsons, Edmund Bunny and *The First Booke of the Christian Exercise*', *JEH*, 45 (1994), 238–68.

Griffiths, G. Milwyn (ed.), 'A Report of the Deanery of Penllyn and Edeirnion by the Revd John Wynne, 1730', *Merioneth Miscellany*, 1 (Dolgellau: Merioneth Historical and Record Society, 1955), pp. 5–29.

Griffiths, G. Milwyn, 'The Restoration in St Asaph: the Episcopate of Bishop George Griffith, 1660–66', *JHSCW*, 12 (1962), 9–27; 13 (1963), 27–40.

Griffiths, G. Milwyn, 'A Visitation to the Archdeaconry of Carmarthen, 1710', *NLWJ*, 18 (1974), 287–311.

Gruffydd, R. Geraint, 'Catechism y Deon Nowell yn Gymraeg', *JWBS*, 7 (1950–3), 114–15, 203–7.

Gruffydd, R. Geraint, 'Bishop Francis Godwin's injunctions for the diocese of Llandaff, 1603', *JHSCW*, 4 (1954), 14–22.

Gruffydd, R. Geraint, 'The Welsh Book of Common Prayer', *JHSCW*, 17 (1967), 43–55.

Hayden, Roger, 'The Particular Baptist Confession of 1689 and today', *BQ*, 32 (1988), 403–17.

Hughes, Garfield H., 'Emynyddiaeth gynnar yr Ymneilltuwyr', *Llên Cymru*, 2 (1953), 135–46.

James, Brian Ll., 'The evolution of a radical: the life and career of William Erbury (1604–59)', *JWEH*, 3 (1986), 31–48.

Jenkins, Geraint H., 'James Owen versus Benjamin Keach: a Controversy over Infant Baptism', *NLWJ*, 19 (1975), 57–66.

Jenkins, Geraint H., '"An old and much honoured soldier": Griffith Jones, Llanddowror', *WHR*, 11 (1983), 449–68.

Jenkins, Geraint H., 'Yr Eglwys "Wiwlwys Olau" a'i beirniaid', *Ceredigion*, 10 (1985), 131–46.

Jenkins, Geraint H., 'The Friends of Montgomeryshire in the Heroic Age', *Montgomeryshire Collections*, 76 (1988), 17–30.

Jenkins, Geraint H., 'Apostol Sir Gaerfyrddin: Stephen Hughes, c. 1622–88', *Y Cofiadur*, 54 (1989), 3–23.

Jenkins, Philip, '"The sufferings of the clergy": the Church in Glamorgan during the Interregnum', *JWEH*, 3 (1986), 1–17; 4 (1987), 9–41; 5 (1988), 73–80.

Jenkins, Philip, 'Welsh Anglicans and the Interregnum', *JHSCW*, 32 (1990), 51–9.

John, E. Stanley, 'Marmaduke Matthews a Richard Blinman: eu teuluoedd a'u cyfraniad', *Y Cofiadur*, 60 (1996), 3–25.

Jones, D. R. L., 'Fame and obscurity: Samuel Jones of Brynllywarch', *JWRH*, 1 (1993), 41–65.

Jones, E. D., 'A Letter Concerning Griffith Jones', *BBCS*, 10 (1939–41), 273–5.

Jones, E. D., 'The Ottley Papers', *NLWJ*, 4 (1945), 61–74.

Jones, E. D. (ed.), 'Llyfr Eglwys Mynydd Bach', *Y Cofiadur*, 17 (1947), 3–50.

Jones, E. D., 'Copi o Lyfr Pant-teg, Abergwili', *Y Cofiadur*, 23 (1953), 18–70.

Jones, E. D., 'Philip Pugh', *Diwinyddiaeth*, 15 (1964), 62–9.

Jones, Gwilym H., 'The Welsh Psalter of 1567', *JHSCW*, 17 (1967), 56–61.

Jones, J. Gwynfor, 'Henry Rowland, Bishop of Bangor', *JHSCW*, 26 (1979), 34–53.

Jones, J. Gwynfor, 'John Penry: government, order and the "perishing souls" of Wales', *THSC* (1993), 47–81.

Jones, J. Morgan (ed.), 'Llyfr Eglwys y Cilgwyn', *Y Cofiadur*, 1 (1923), 22–31.

Jones, J. T., 'John Morgan, Ficer Aberconwy', *Y Llenor*, 17 (1938), 16–30.

Jones, M. G., 'Two accounts of the Welsh Trust, 1675 and 1678', *BBCS*, 9 (1939), 71–80.

Jones, Owain, 'The Anabaptists of Llanafan-fawr and Llysdinam', *Brycheiniog*, 18 (1978–9), 71–7.

Jones, R. Tudur, 'Religion in Post-Restoration Brecknockshire, 1660–88', *Brycheiniog*, 8 (1962), 11–66.

Jones, R. Tudur and B. G. Owens, 'Anghydffurfwyr Cymru, 1660–62', *Y Cofiadur*, 31 (1962).

Knox, R. Buick, 'The Bible in Wales: The Life and Labours of Thomas Gouge', *CH*, 2 (1978), 38–43.

Lodwick, B. M., '"Poor Llandaff" during the episcopate of John Tyler, 1706–24', *Morgannwg*, 49 (2005), 34–61.

Lloyd, Nesta, 'Yr Ymarfer o Dduwioldeb a rhai o gerddi Rhys Prichard', *Y Traethodydd*, 150 (1995), 94–106.

Lloyd, Nesta, 'Rhys Prichard c. 1579–1644/5', *CA*, 34 (1998), 25–37.

McGrath, Alister E., 'The Emergence of the Anglican Tradition on Justification', *Churchman*, 98 (1984), 28–43.

Manning, Bernard Lord, 'Some characteristics of the Older Dissent',
 Congregational Quarterly, 5 (1927), 286–300.

Matthews, Hugh, 'David Rees, Limehouse (1683–1748): an eighteenth century
 London Welsh preacher', *THSC* (1983), 81–96.

Morgan, Adrian, 'Llenor anghofiedig: Trem ar fywyd a gwaith Robert
 Holland', *Llên Cymru*, 31 (2008), 139–64.

Morgan, D. Densil, '"Smoke, fire and light": Baptists and the revitalization of
 Welsh Dissent', *BQ*, 32 (1988), 224–32.

Morgan, D. Densil, 'Cefndir, Cymreigiad a Chynnwys Cyffes Ffydd 1689',
 TCHB (1990), 19–34.

Morgan, D. Densil, 'Welsh Baptist theology, c.1714–60', *JWEH*, 7 (1990),
 16–25.

Morgan, Gerald, 'Ieuan Fardd (1731–88): Traethawd yr Esgyb Eingl',
 Ceredigion, 11 (1990), 135–45.

Morgan, W. T., 'The Prosecution of Nonconformists in the Consistory Courts
 of St David's', *JHSCW*, 12 (1962), 28–54.

Nuttall, Geoffrey F., 'The correspondence of John Lewis Glasgrug with
 Richard Baxter and with Dr John Ellis, Dolgellau', *JMHRS*, 2 (1954),
 120–34.

Nuttall, Geoffrey F., 'Northamptonshire and *The Modern Question*: a
 turning-point in eighteenth century Dissent', *JTS*, 16 (1965), 101–23.

Nuttall, Geoffrey F., 'Welsh students at the Bristol Baptist College, 1720–97',
 THSC (1978–9), 171–99.

Nuttall, Geoffrey F., 'The Nurture of Nonconformity: Philip Henry's Diaries',
 THSC, N.S. 4 (1998), 5–27.

Owen, G. Dyfnallt, 'James Owen a'i Academi', *Y Cofiadur*, 22 (1952), 3–36.

Owen, J. Dyfnallt, 'Camre cyntaf Anghydffurfiaeth ac Annibyniaeth yn
 Sir Gaerfyrddin, 1660–1710', *Y Cofiadur*, 13 (1936), 3–56.

Parkinson, Elizabeth, 'Interpreting the Compton Census returns of 1676 for
 the Diocese of Llandaff', *Local Population Studies*, 60 (1998), 44–57.

Powell, Nia M. W., 'Dr William Morgan and his parishioners at Llanrhaeadr
 ym Mochnant', *TCHS*, 49 (1988), 87–108.

Pryce, W. T. R., 'The Diffusion of the "Welch" Circulating Schools in
 Eighteenth-Century Wales', *WHR*, 25 (2011), 486–519.

Roberts, Enid P., 'Gabriel Goodman and his native homeland', *THSC* (1989),
 77–104.

Richards, Gwynfryn, 'The Diocese of Bangor during the rise of Welsh
 Methodism', *NLWJ*, 21 (1979), 179–224.

Richards, Thomas, 'Bedyddwyr Cymru yng nghyfnod Lewis Thomas', *TCHB*
 (1916–19).

Richards, Thomas, 'The troubles of Dr William Lucy', *Y Cymmrodor*, 38
 (1927), 142–83.

Richards, Thomas, 'The Religious Census of 1676', *THSC* (1927), 1–110.

Roberts, Gomer M., 'Griffith Jones' opinion of the Methodists', *CCH*, 35 (1950), 53–6.

Roberts, Stephen K., 'Propagating the Gospel in Wales: the making of the 1650 act', *THSC*, N.S. 10 (2004), 57–75.

Shankland, Thomas, 'Anghydffurfwyr ac Ymneilltuwyr cyntaf Cymru', *Y Cofiadur*, 1 (1923), 33–44.

Sweet-Escott, Bickham, 'William Beaw: a Cavalier Bishop', *WHR*, 1 (1963), 397–411.

Thomas, Peter D. G., 'Jacobitism in Wales', *WHR*, 1 (1960), 279–300.

Trevett, Christine, 'William Erbury and his daughter Dorcas: Dissenter and Resurrected Radical', *JWRH*, 4 (1996), 23–50.

Tudur, Geraint, '"The king's daughter": a reassessment of Anne Harris of Trefeca', *JWRH*, 7 (1999), 55–76.

White, B. R., 'William Erbury and the Baptists', *BQ*, 23 (1969), 114–25.

White, Eryn M., '"The People called Methodists": Early Welsh Methodism and the Question of Identity', *JWRH*, 1 (2001), 7–20.

Williams, G. J., 'Stephen Hughes a'i gyfnod', *Y Cofiadur*, 4 (1926), 5–44.

Williams, Glanmor, 'William Morgan's Bible and the Cambridge connection', *WHR*, 14 (1989), 363–79.

Williams, Glanmor, 'Stephen Hughes (1622–88), "The Apostle of Carmarthenshire"', *CA*, 37 (2001), 21–30.

Williams, Gruffydd Aled, 'Edmwnd Prys (1543/4–1623): Dyneiddiwr Protestannaidd', *JMHRS*, 8 (1977–80), 349–68.

Williams, Gruffydd Aled, 'Mydryddu'r Salmau yn Gymraeg', *Llên Cymru*, 16 (1989), 114–32.

Williams, J. Gwynn, 'The Quakers of Merioneth during the seventeenth century', *JMHRS*, 8 (1978–9), 122–56, 312–39.

Wright, E. G., 'Humphrey Humphreys (1648–1712), Bishop of Bangor and Hereford', *JHSCW*, 2 (1950), 72–86.

Wood, Craig D., 'The Welsh response to the Glorious Revolution', *JWRH*, 1 (1989), 21–39.

Unpublished theses

John, E. Stanley, 'Bywyd, gwaith a chyfnod dau Biwritan Cymreig, Marmaduke Matthews a Richard Blinman' (PhD, University of Wales, Bangor, 1987).

Morgan, Derec Llwyd, 'A critical study of the works of Charles Edwards, 1628–?1691' (DPhil, Oxford University, 1967).

Thomas, Marian G., 'Astudiaeth o waith Jeremi Owen' (MA, University of Wales, Aberystwyth, 1975).

Thomas, Wynford, 'Matthias Maurice a'i Eglwysoleg' (PhD, University of Wales Trinity Saint David, 2011).

Index

Y

Z